MEASUREMENT AND TUNING OF COMPUTER SYSTEMS

MEASUREMENT AND TUNING OF COMPUTER SYSTEMS

Domenico Ferrari

Computer Science Division
Department of Electrical Engineering
and Computer Sciences
University of California, Berkeley

Giuseppe Serazzi

Istituto di Analisi Numerica del CNR
Istituto di Matematica
Universitá di Pavia, Italy

Alessandro Zeigner

Syntax-Olivetti
Milan, Italy

Prentice-Hall, Inc. *Englewood Cliffs, NJ 07632*

Library of Congress Cataloging in Publication Data

FERRARI, DOMENICO, (date)
Measurement and tuning of computer systems.

Rev. of: Le prestazioni degli elaboratori elettronici.
Includes bibliographies and index.
1. Electronic digital computers—Evaluation.
I. Serazzi, Giuseppe. II. Zeigner, Alessandro.
III. Title.
QA76.9.E94F4813 1983 001.64 82-20432
ISBN 0-13-568519-2

Editorial/production supervision
and interior design: **Kathryn Gollin Marshak**
Cover design: **Diane Saxe**
Manufacturing buyer: **Gordon Osbourne**

Printed in the United States of America

10 9 8 7 6 5 4 3 2 1

ISBN 0-13-568519-2

Prentice-Hall International, Inc., *London*
Prentice-Hall of Australia Pty. Limited, *Sydney*
Editora Prentice-Hall do Brasil, Ltda., *Rio de Janeiro*
Prentice-Hall Canada Inc., *Toronto*
Prentice-Hall of India Private Limited, *New Delhi*
Prentice-Hall of Japan, Inc., *Tokyo*
Prentice-Hall of Southeast Asia Pte. Ltd., *Singapore*
Whitehall Books Limited, *Wellington, New Zealand*

CONTENTS

PREFACE

Even though it can hardly be viewed as a settled discipline, system performance evaluation has made impressive progress during its relatively brief existence to date. A number of advances have been made in recent times in computer system modeling, especially in analytic techniques, as well as in workload characterization and forecasting, capacity planning, configuration design, and, to a lesser extent, in measurement techniques and tools, tuning procedures, and procurement techniques.

A number of books have appeared in the last few years covering performance analysis and evaluation topics. Most of these books, however, have been written for researchers and students rather than for the practitioners in the field or for their managers. Some other books, intended for the professionals, do not adequately cover some of the areas in which the most important advances have occurred, for instance that of analytic modeling.

Subjects that the informed practitioner could afford to ignore until a few years ago, as nothing really useful in coping with everyday problems could be extracted from them, have become important in practice, and their knowledge will soon be viewed as indispensable for technical survival in the world of performance evaluation. Like many other types of computer professionals, the successful evaluator can only remain successful by keeping abreast of the continuous developments not only of hardware and software technology, but also of performance measurement and modeling technology.

This book was motivated by the preceding considerations. It was felt that a simple, easily readable, practically oriented introduction to the performance evaluation field which would either cover or prepare the reader to understand even the most recent important advances in the area was still missing. It was also felt that students, perhaps even researchers, would benefit from a more pragmatic treatment of the subject, based on practical experience as well as on solid conceptual foundations. Such a book could not adequately deal with all the subjects that are now considered part of the discipline. We chose to emphasize measurement techniques (which we believe are the really fundamental ones: without measurement, system evaluation is impossible) and tuning projects. The context of most of the discussions and of the case studies is one in which the system whose performance is to be evaluated exists and is running; in this context, one of the main goals of evaluation activities is to improve the cost–performance ratio of the installation.

Chapter 1 introduces the basic concepts and problems, and presents a wide-ranging discussion of the fundamental performance indexes used in improvement studies. Our emphasis on measurement is reflected in the discussion of workload characterization in Chapter 2, most of which is oriented toward the construction and validation of executable workload models to be used in performance measurement experiments. The chapter also presents some recent results and research trends in the area.

The basic techniques for measuring computer systems or their simulators are studied in Chapter 3, while Chapter 4 discusses the most effective ways to represent measurement results for ease of interpretation, and Chapter 5 the predominant types of measurement tools and their characteristics. The application of techniques and tools to the problem of tuning an installation is described in general methodological terms in Chapter 6. A number of case studies encompassing a wide variety of systems, configurations, and application environments are presented in Chapter 7. Chapter 8 illustrates the particular methods and instruments that can be used to improve the performance of programs, an important problem for programmers as well as for system tuners; since systems go out of tune because of changes in their workload, workload improvement is often a very effective way of improving their performance.

Analytic models have an increasingly important role in tuning studies: they can provide substantial help in diagnosing certain performance problems and can predict the impact of an expensive or risky modification to the system before the change is actually implemented. Both operational analysis and queuing modeling techniques are discussed in Chapter 9, whose several case studies illustrate the various uses of models in performance improvement projects. Some of the cases show how a modeling approach can be taken in tackling problems that in Chapter 7 were dealt with only by empirical techniques.

The final chapter, Chapter 10, briefly addresses an important question, which is very seldom considered in technical discussions of performance evaluation: how beneficial is performance improvement? The question is a relevant one since tuning studies are not always advantageous. First, not all tuning efforts are successful. Second, even when such efforts are technically successful, their results may not be justified by their costs. A performance improvement study should be considered as an investment and evaluated on the basis of a cost–benefit analysis. Several case studies illustrating how this analysis can be performed accompany the discussion of the general principles and methods.

Each section of the book is identified by either two or three digits. The sections with two digits introduce a subject in an often qualitative form, and are oriented toward those readers who want to gain a general understanding of the problems and of their solutions. Three-digit sections provide more in-depth and more detailed treatment of the subject, or discuss specific real-world examples of the application of previously described techniques.

The authors are grateful to Dr. G. C. Baldovini, Chief Executive Officer of Syntax S.p.A., for his encouragement and support during the writing of the book and the preparation of the manuscript. The support of Professor F. Filippazzi of Honeywell Information Systems of Italy is also gratefully acknowledged. This book was conceived, and most of it was written, while D. Ferrari was Visiting Professor at the University of Pavia, with the support of the Regents of the University of California and of the National Science Foundation under Grants MCS78-24618 and MCS80-12900. Professors I. De Lotto of the Istituto di Informatica e Sistemistica of the University of Pavia and E. Magenes of the Istituto di Analisi Numerica of the same university made that visit possible and provided an appropriate habitat for the growth of this book. Two trips to Berkeley made by G. Serazzi to complete the first draft were supported by the Consiglio Nazionale delle Ricerche under Contracts 79.02332.62 and 80.02334.01, which provides funding for the joint Berkeley–Pavia NSF–CNR performance evaluation research project. For his financial and moral support, the authors are indebted to the contract's principal investigator, Professor M. Italiani.

This book is dedicated to the authors' wives and children in recognition of the countless hours of their husbands' and fathers' time it subtracted from them.

Domenico Ferrari
Giuseppe Serazzi
Alessandro Zeigner

MEASUREMENT AND TUNING OF COMPUTER SYSTEMS

1

PROBLEM DEFINITION

1.1 DEFINITIONS AND BASIC CONCEPTS

The term *performance* refers to services provided by people or machinery to whoever requires them. An *information-processing system* is a set of hardware and software components capable of processing data according to user-written programs. Thus the term *performance,* referred to an information-processing system, indicates all the facilities that the system is capable of providing for its users. These facilities include the programming languages that are used to communicate with the system, the tools that it offers for the design and development of the programs, the processing and fault recovery features, the level of data security provided, and so on.

However, the term performance will be used here with a more restricted meaning, the one that is used when considering other engineering systems, like automobiles. Although among car performance indexes one ought to consider a car's ease of use, comfort, and stability (and one usually does, even though the relative weights given to them depend on the buyer's requirements), the term usually refers to the car's maximum speed when fully loaded, to the time it takes to reach a given speed, to its fuel consumption, and to other quantities that somehow express the efficiency with which the car carries out its functions.

As for cars, the choice of a computer system depends on many factors, one of which is the performance required. The weight of this factor varies with the person and the type of application. Designers, buyers, installation managers, programmers, occasional users, and maintenance engineers usually consider differently the same system because they have different requirements and aims. This also applies to its performance, represented by indexes that are given different weights by different people or even by the same person in different circumstances. Each index is quantifiable and can therefore be an object of *evaluation*. A performance index can be evaluated in various ways: it can be measured, calculated, or estimated. These evaluations will always be quantitative. But it must be remembered that many of the factors considered when a system is to be selected are really of a qualitative nature and thus difficult to quantify.

This book covers the most common techniques for the quantitative evaluation of performance, which is an important component of a system's value (in the economic sense). Performance acquires great importance once a computer system has been chosen and installed. It is always convenient to keep the processing efficiency under control since the performance depends on both the type of load and the usage modes of the system, and can often be kept at acceptable levels with relatively simple types of intervention. If this results in performance values inferior to the ones required, or if the possibility of improving the system's performance seems to exist anyway, a careful analysis of the causes of inefficiency and of the best remedies to it must be carried out. This analysis will make use of the performance evaluation tools to be described in the sequel.

1.2 EVALUATION OBJECTIVES

The reasons that make performance evaluation worthwhile have already been briefly outlined. This section discusses them in more detail. All engineering systems are subject to performance evaluation. During the design, assembly, sale, and usage phases of a system, a system's performance is evaluated by various people with different aims and viewpoints to verify that the system satisfies given efficiency requirements and can be used for a certain purpose.

This rule also applies, or should apply, to computer systems. Clearly, verification that the requirements are satisfied becomes more important with expensive systems and with more critical performance requirements. Thus, the amount of resources to be invested in the evaluation of a minicomputer will be much smaller than the amount invested in a study for the performance improvement of a large machine or in the choice of a microprocessor that will be used in a certain product to be sold in large quantities.

The evaluation of a computer system's performance is necessary not only during the system's productive life but also during its design, when it is selected by a customer, and when it is installed. The applications of evaluation techniques can be classified in four main categories:

1. *Procurement:* All the evaluation problems concerning the choice of a system, or of system components, among various existing and available alternatives belong to this class, for example, installation design and hardware and software acquisition.
2. *Improvement:* This class includes all performance problems that arise in existing, running systems. They will be discussed in detail in this book.
3. *Capacity planning:* This is the class of the problems related to the prediction of when in the future the capacity of an existing system will become sufficient to process the installation's workload with a given level of performance.
4. *Design:* All problems that designers must face during the creation of a new system belong to this class.

Evaluation techniques can be used for problems in all these classes [FE78], [KO78]. Nevertheless, we shall almost exclusively refer to improvement studies in the sequel.

Thus, in the context of this book, the improvement of a system's efficiency will be the main object of evaluation studies. This improvement usually causes effects that are very important, but difficult to measure. For example, an increase of user happiness often entails an increase in programmer productivity, faster development of new applications, and an increased number of users. However, some consequences are easier to measure in economic terms, such as:

1. Reduction of the system's daily operating time, with the possibility of reducing the number or the work schedules of the operators.
2. Abolition or reduction of backlogs caused by peaks of load.
3. Decrease in the cost of the system's configuration (for example, due to the elimination of a superfluous channel or peripheral unit).
4. Postponement of the time at which workload increases will saturate the system, forcing its expansion or replacement.

Clearly, the real purpose of these studies is the improvement of the cost–performance ratio, rather than mere performance improvement. Cost reduction is a worthwhile result of a study as long as it is not accompanied by too large a decrease in performance. Economic aspects are always of primary importance, even if in what follows we shall almost exclusively deal with the technical aspects, that is, with the system's performance.

Together with the advantages to be derived from an evaluation study, one should always consider its cost. Before undertaking a study, both its benefits and its costs are unknown. It is therefore necessary to estimate these benefits and costs even if this is often difficult. The maximum gain that can be expected in terms of the cost–performance ratio depends on how far the system is from its optimal operating conditions. However, since the notion of optimum is vague in this case, and since this distance is very often unknown, the previous statement is not very useful. Thus, only partial estimates can usually be made, perhaps concerning the activity predicted for the near future.

The typical procedure for attacking the problem of improving the cost–performance ratio is, as shown in Fig. 1.1, an iterative procedure whose cycle contains a phase of *diagnosis* and one of *therapy*. The goal of the diagnostic phase is to establish the causes of the unsatisfactory cost–performance ratio. These causes are often identified with *bottlenecks*. In this case, a therapy will be effective if it is capable of eliminating or "widening" the bottlenecks that limit system performance. Obviously, if more than one therapy capable of ensuring the required improvements exists, the one with the lowest cost–improvement ratio will be chosen. As some therapies are very expensive (for example, those requiring an expansion of the configuration, or delicate operating system modifications, or workload changes), it is convenient to try to predict the effects of these therapies on the cost–performance ratio before applying them.

Some of the techniques that can be used in the diagnostic phase can also be used for performance prediction. The diagnosis–therapy cycle of the procedure outlined must sometimes be repeated because some bottlenecks show up once others have been eliminated. Nevertheless, the improvements obtained from these iterations are usually smaller and smaller, so it is often better to limit their number to only a few. By making use of

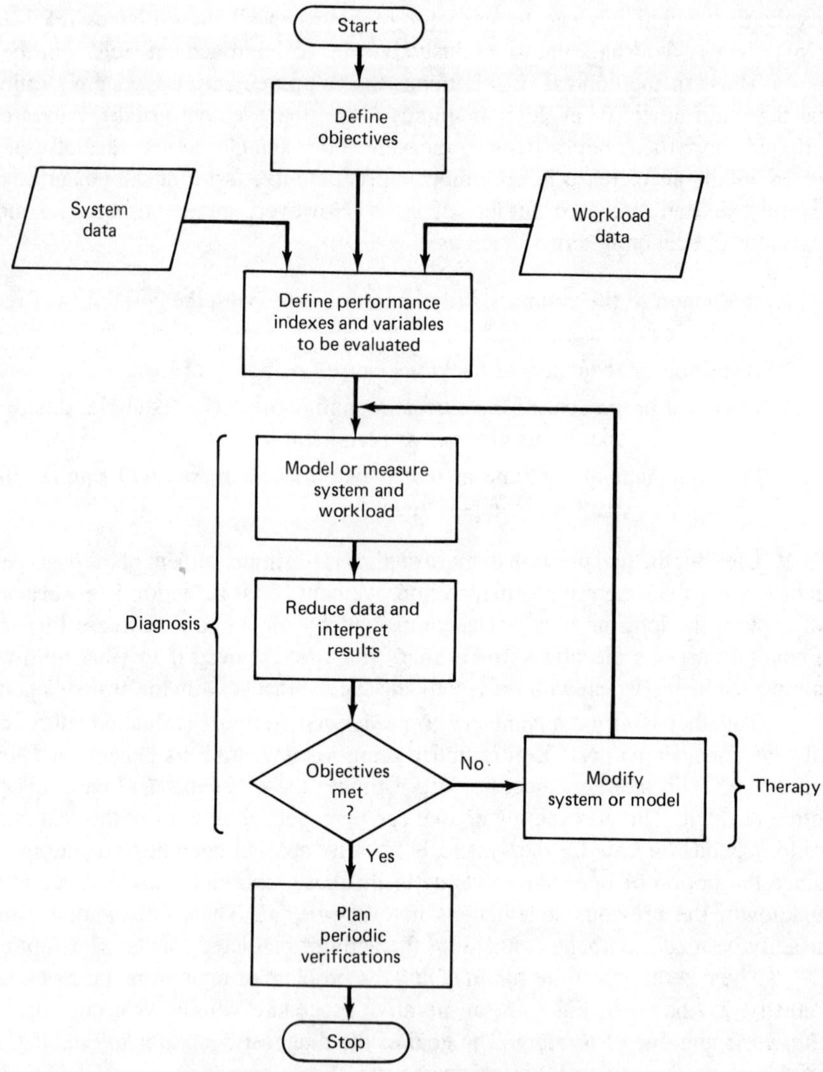

Figure 1.1 Scheme of a performance evaluation study.

evaluation techniques of the modeling type, it is also possible, although not always convenient, to postpone the application of the therapies suggested by all iterations to the end of the procedure.

1.3 THE REFERENCE SYSTEMS

The objects of the evaluation studies to be considered in this book have already been defined in Sec. 1.1; they are systems for the processing of information. To give the reader a more concrete definition, and a first approach to the viewpoint from which these systems are to be observed for performance evaluation purposes, we shall discuss some basic types of system configurations. They are systems whose configuration is variable within certain limits. For example, the number of their I/O or mass storage devices is not rigidly specified. Their distinguishing characteristics are mainly the usage modes and the types of resource management used by the operating system. Examples of all four types of systems that have been chosen as reference systems (RS for brevity) can be found in similar configurations among existing computer systems. They are presented here in ascending order of complexity.

1.3.1 Uniprogrammed Batch-processing Reference System (UBRS)

In this system, the batch-processing mode is used and the main resources of the computer are managed in uniprogramming mode. A possible system configuration is shown in Fig. 1.2. This configuration is characterized by two channels: one (C_0) for the system console C and the peripheral units (card reader CR, line printer LP), and the other (C_1) for the mass storage units (disks D and tapes T). Users gain access to the system by punching their programs, data, and commands to the operating system on cards, which are read by the card reader CR. Channel C_0 transfers the information punched on the cards to the memory M, where the central processing unit (CPU) processes it. Each *program* usually consists of several *program steps,* for example, compilation, object program loading, execution, and storing the program in the file system. The output from these steps is sent to C_0, which controls its printing, as soon as the program produces it. Even the reading of cards is carried out in steps: only when the first step has been completed are the cards for the second step read in, and so on.

Thus, in this system, all the memory space not used by the operating system is

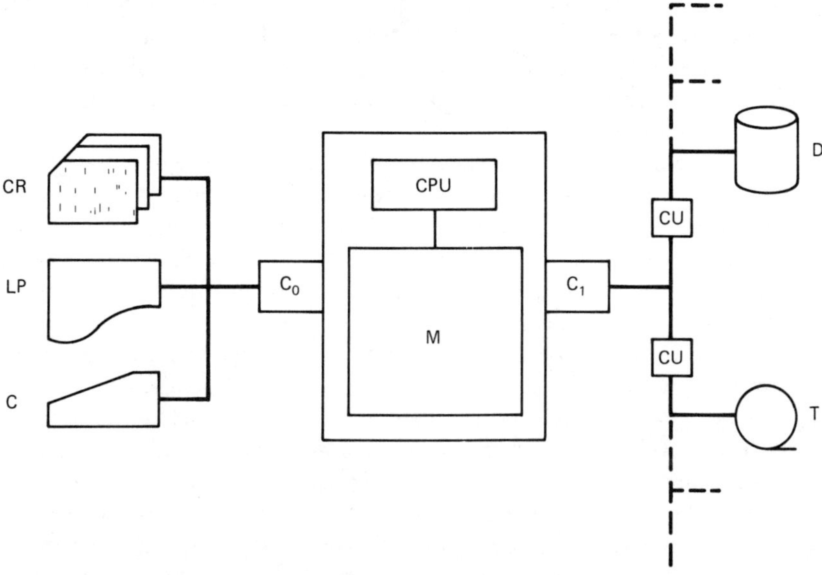

Figure 1.2 Typical UBRS configuration.

available to the job step being executed, and the CPU is not active during data transfers between the memory and the peripheral units or the mass storage devices. In Fig. 1.2 the abbreviation CU (control unit) indicates hardware components that control the activity of individual I/O devices, synchronizing them with the requests arriving through their channel.

1.3.2 Multiprogrammed Batch-processing Reference System (MBRS)

Historically, multiprogramming was first introduced in the rather limited form of *spooling* (SPOOL stands for Simultaneous Processing Operations On Line). This technique represents the simplest type of overlapping of activities. In a spooled system, the activities of the channels may overlap that of the CPU. Thus, a deck of cards can be read in, or the results of a program may be printed, while another is being executed. For this purpose, it is necessary to assign buffer areas in the memory M for the temporary storage of data arriving from the card reader or being produced by the program. These data will be accumulated on a mass storage device.

A spooled system could still be considered a uniprogramming system, as only one user program (or, rather, only one of its steps) resides in main memory at any given time. However, this type of system allows the overlapping of certain activities, while a pure uniprogramming system does not.

If, besides spooling, programs and data corresponding to job steps of various users may be present at the same time, we have a real multiprogramming system. The idea of multiprogramming derived from the desire to increase CPU usage and consequently the system's productivity. Each time a program step is suspended (for example, because it needs to access a peripheral or a mass storage device), the CPU stores the status of the suspended step and starts executing one of the programs ready for execution and loaded in memory. The CPU remains inactive only if none of the loaded programs can be immediately started or resumed. A possible MBRS configuration is shown in Fig. 1.3.

While C_0 and C_1 carry out the same functions as in UBRS, C_2 controls the transfer to and from some fixed-head disks (often called *drums* because their operation is similar to that of drums).

There are three different types of channels: *multiplexor, selector,* and *block multiplexor*. Multiplexor channels (sometimes called *byte multiplexor*) can transfer messages to and from I/O devices, intermixing them even at the single-character level. Since they connect slow devices to the memory, a character from the card reader may, for example, be followed by a character from a terminal or by one from the console. The channel C_0 of Figs. 1.2 and 1.3 is a typical multiplexor channel.

Selector channels are used with faster devices, whose messages are transmitted in records (for example, a disk record or a tape record). This is done because there is not enough time to switch channel control from one transfer to another or enough buffer space to do this without loss of information. Thus, a selector channel (or each of its independent subchannels if it has more than one subchannel) is entirely taken over by one of the devices it controls during a given transfer. However, the movements of the read–write heads or the rewind operations of a tape reel, and with some rotating devices even the latency time, may overlap the transfer to or from another unit controlled by the same channel.

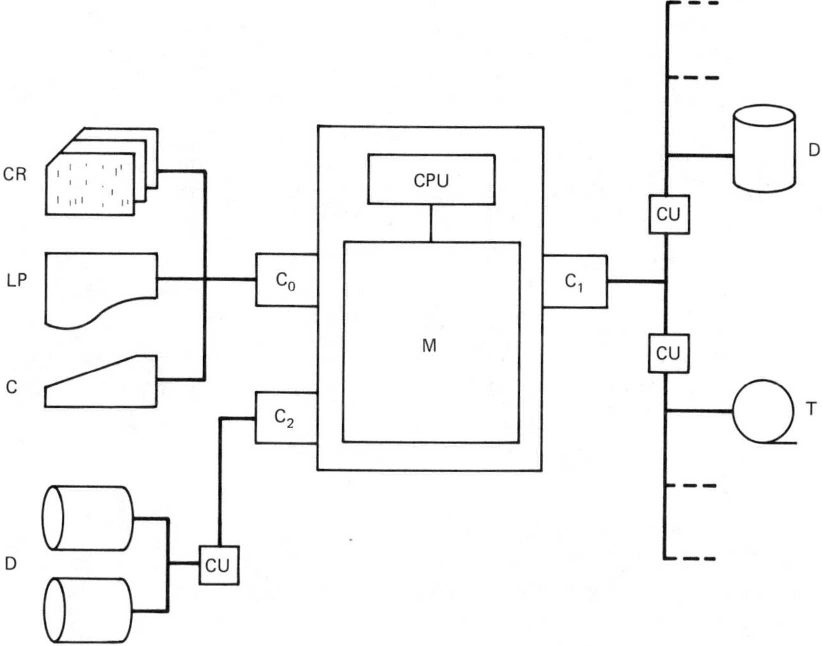

Figure 1.3 Typical MBRS configuration.

Block multiplexor channels are capable of mixing messages to and from a number of devices at the block level (a block consists of many characters) rather than at the single-character level. The devices these channels control are considerably faster than those usually connected to multiplexor channels. Both C_1 and C_2 in Figs. 1.2 and 1.3 may be of the selector or block multiplexor type.

1.3.3 Multiprogrammed Interactive Reference System (MIRS)

The usage mode of this system is mixed, since, along with the batch mode, it supports the interactive processing mode, characterized by the presence of interactive terminals through which users can converse with the system. An *interactive transaction* consists of a series of user–system interactions. An *interaction* is composed of a command or message sent to the system by the user through a terminal's input device (usually a keyboard) and of the reply given by the system to the same terminal.

In the configuration of Fig. 1.4, the terminals are connected to C_3, which is a multiplexor channel. For a dialogue to be feasible, the system must provide an immediate reply to *light* requests (for example, the deletion of a line of text, the replacement of a character, or the naming of a file). The *time-sharing* technique was introduced to reduce to a minimum the response time for light requests. This technique consists of limiting to a given maximum the time interval during which a request monopolizes a resource (in particular the CPU). If there are any awaiting requests, the one being currently served will be interrupted when its time quantum (that is, the time interval allotted to it, for example, 100 ms) expires. This method prevents *heavy* requests from seriously delaying

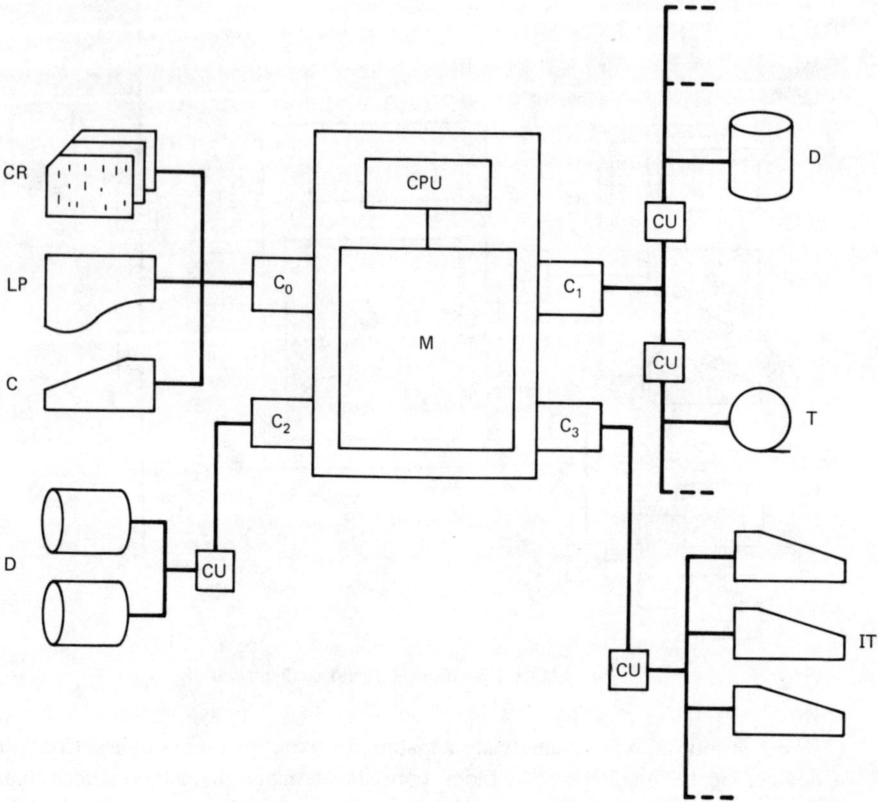

Figure 1.4 Typical MIRS and MVRS configurations.

lighter ones, many of which will be completed during their first time quantum. Time sharing is so commonly applied in interactive systems that these are often called *time-sharing systems*. This technique, however, is also found in noninteractive systems. For example, it can be used in batch systems to reduce turnaround time for the shorter programs.

1.3.4 Multiprogrammed Interactive Virtual-Memory Reference System (MIVRS)

Within this reference system, a configuration of which is shown in Fig. 1.4, the user can program, in an address space *(virtual-memory space)* distinct from that of the actual memory M, and generally much larger, without worrying about dividing a program that does not fit in the allotted memory space into segments *(overlays)* to be loaded into M when their turn comes.

In a virtual-memory machine, memory management is totally taken over by the system; in other words, it is totally automatic. The functions of the devices shown in Fig. 1.4 are the same as in MIRS, with the important exception of the disks connected to channel C_2; these will be used as *paging* devices, that is, as the second level in the memory hierarchy automatically managed by the system. Every program partially present in the memory M is stored completely in a paging device and is divided into equal parts called *pages*. When some instructions or data that the program requires are not in M, the page containing them is automatically transferred to M from the disk where the whole program is stored. The pages modified by the program in the real memory are rewritten on the disk by the operating system when there is no longer room for them in M.

1.4 PERFORMANCE INDEXES

The evaluation of a computer system's performance is of interest to many categories of people, each of which gives a particular meaning to the word "performance." The identification of performance with system efficiency made in Sec. 1.1 is only an initial and crude step toward a meaningful definition. We shall now proceed to describe these categories and their viewpoints in some detail, with the objective of refining our definition of performance.

A possible classification of the people who are confronted with evaluation problems is shown in Fig. 1.5. Although they have the same goal, that of making system operation efficient, the three categories in the figure consider the problem from quite different viewpoints.

Hardware and software designers must keep in mind the range of possible applications the system is to be used for, while installation managers must satisfy the requirements of a specific environment. Finally, users are only interested in the processing of their programs.

Going from designers to users, that is, from level 1 to level 3, the scope of the requirements to be satisfied becomes more and more restricted, and the possibility of influencing the performance (that is, the freedom to choose how the system will be used) becomes more limited. The three categories refer to specific variables to express their view of performance and, in some cases, they assign different weights to the same variables. A system designer is usually concerned with the utilization of system com-

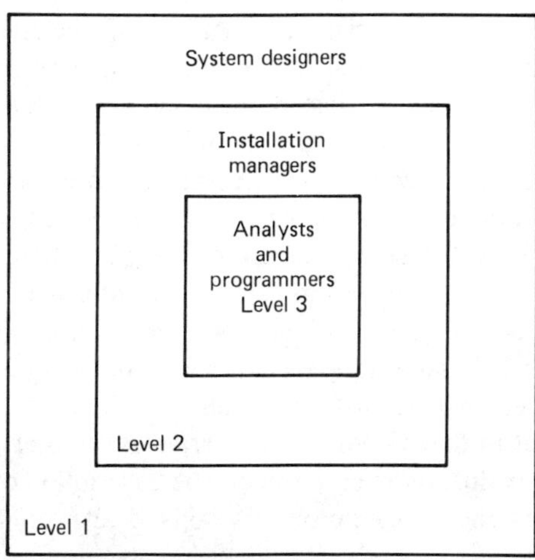

Figure 1.5 Levels of interest in performance evaluation.

ponents, which may be influenced by acting on such variables as memory access time, hardware speed, the organization of program libraries and data bases, memory allocation algorithms, and so on, while the values of other variables, such as the processing time of a program, are of lesser interest. An installation manager will mostly be concerned with a balanced and cost-effective use of the system's components, with providing satisfactory service to most users (or to the most important ones), and with fairness in charging for the use of the facilities. A single user influences performance by varying the load on the resources (CPU, peripherals, memory, channels) and evaluates processing efficiency in terms of execution time and cost, while variables that matter to other user categories are of little or no importance.

The differences in load on the various components of a system caused by user programs directly affect its global performance. One cannot evaluate a system without studying the characteristics of its workload. The *workload of a system* is made up of the programs, data, and commands that the users input to the system. The subjective viewpoints on performance that characterize the members of the various categories previously discussed can be made more objective by using unambiguously defined variables that objectively describe some specific aspects of the system's global performance.

Clearly, this does not eliminate subjectivity, but only separates it from objective evaluations. Subjectivity is still present in the choice of variables and in the weight given to each.

Many variables are not easily quantified or are not quantifiable at all (for example, the ease of use of a system or the power of an instruction set). However, in the sequel we shall only refer to variables that can be rigorously defined so that their quantitative evaluation is possible.

A performance evaluation study of an arbitrary system requires the values of the following variables:

1. The characteristics of the physical system being evaluated.
2. The operating conditions of the system at the time the evaluation is made.
3. The performance indexes of the system.

In the case of a computer system, class 1 variables will include data about both the hardware and software configuration of the system (for example, memory size, number of channels and disks, and the locations of system files) and the operation of the various components (CPU, channel types, disk access times, and so on). The latter data are vital when the performances of different systems are to be compared, whereas the configuration data are more important when the objective is the optimization of a single system.

Class 1 data may refer only to a subsystem, when the goal of the evaluation study only concerns those properties of the subsystem that are not influenced by other subsystems. For example, when determining the file placement that minimizes the movements of the heads for a disk pack, it is only necessary to study the subsystem composed of the channel, the disk controller, and the disk unit itself.

The operating conditions of the system (class 2 variables) consist of the description of the load present when the evaluation is performed. The description of a workload and its characterization are difficult and delicate problems, to be dealt with in Chapter 2. One of the most popular approaches is the probabilistic approach; it often represents the workload by random variables whose distributions are assumed to be statistically independent. For example, a very simple model of the workload, in which each program may be identified by a pair of values (its arrival time and its processing time), will consist of the distributions of interarrival and processing times.

A first classification of the indexes for class 3 variables distinguishes between *internal indexes,* which quantify the efficiency of usage of each system component, and *external indexes,* oriented toward an external evaluation of the system's processing efficiency.

Internal indexes are more often adopted by people belonging to levels 1 and 2 in Fig. 1.5, that is, by system designers and installation managers, whereas external indexes are usually chosen by users (level 3 in Fig. 1.5), who are concerned with them more directly. Table 1.1 gives some examples of internal and external performance indexes, which are briefly described next.

Turnaround time is defined as the time interval between the instant a program is submitted to a batch-processing system and the instant its execution ends. For an individual program, the value of turnaround time is given by $P - R$, where R is the moment at which the reading in the program begins and P that at which the printing of the results is completed. The mean turnaround time for n programs is given by

$$T_m = \frac{1}{n} \sum_{i=1}^{n} (P_i - R_i)$$

The mean turnaround time provides an indication of processing efficiency. However, the weighted turnaround time and the mean weighted turnaround time, which may be obtained from T_m, are often to be preferred. A more complete description can be found in Sec. 1.4.1.

Response time is defined as the time interval between the instant the inputting of a command to an interactive system terminates and the instant the corresponding reply begins to appear at the terminal. As for the turnaround time, neither the response time to a single command nor the mean response time usually provide enough information about the system's global performance. Thus, other statistical descriptions, like the standard deviation or the percentiles of the distribution of response times, are used (see Sec. 1.4.2).

Throughput (or *productivity*) can be informally defined as the amount of work performed by a system in a given unit of time. Its value may be expressed in many ways:

TABLE 1.1 EXAMPLES OF PERFORMANCE INDEXES

External indexes	*Internal indexes*
Turnaround time	CPU utilization
Response time	Overlap of activities
Throughput	Multiprogramming stretch factor
Capacity	Multiprogramming level
Availability	Paging rate
Reliability (e.g., MTBF)	Reaction time

as the number of programs processed per unit of time, the amount of data processed per unit of time, the number of transactions processed per unit of time, and so on.

The system's throughput is usually less than the theoretical value that the system is capable of providing (the *capacity*). This phenomenon is typical not only of computer systems, but of all complex systems. The value of throughput X must always be accompanied by a description of the workload with which it was evaluated. If, for example, we consider the ratio between the number N_p of programs executed and the total elapsed time t_{tot}, we have

$$X = \frac{N_p}{t_{tot}}$$

The value of X gives some indication of the speed of execution for the set of the N_p programs considered (the workload), but does not contribute any information about the efficiency with which each individual program is processed.

Throughput is influenced by many factors, among which are the characteristics of the workload with which it is evaluated, the system's hardware and software characteristics, the possibility of overlapping the use of some components, and the algorithms used for assigning system resources to the programs being executed. The importance of throughput as a performance index is primarily due to the fact that its value is strongly correlated with the system's usage cost. A more detailed discussion can be found in Sec. 1.4.3.

The *capacity* is defined as the maximum theoretical value that the throughput of a system can reach. In practice, given a certain workload, its value corresponds to the maximum amount of work that the system is capable of doing per unit of time. Usually, when the workload gradually increases, *saturation* phenomena occur that cause a reduction of throughput (see Fig. 1.6).

The *availability* is defined as the percentage of the total time during which the system is at the disposal of the users.

The *mean time between failures* is defined as the time interval between two consecutive system breakdowns.

The *CPU utilization* is defined as the percentage of system operating time during which the CPU is active. This utilization is normally subdivided into the contributions of the various types of CPU activity; for instance, into the percentage of time spent for

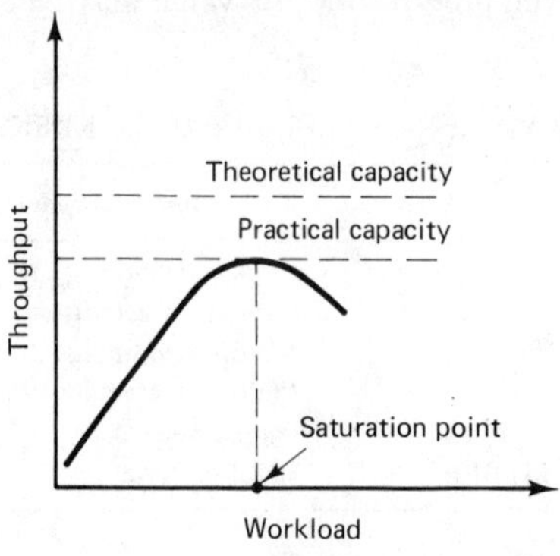

Figure 1.6 Throughput curve of a computer system.

user program execution and that spent for system overhead (supervisor command execution and operating system functions). The utilization of the CPU is also used as a system throughput index since throughput is often proportional to it.

The *overlap* is defined as the percentage of system operating time during which two or more resources are simultaneously busy. This index, clearly only meaningful for multiprogramming systems, is particularly important because it provides information about whether the overlap of the channels with each other and with the CPU is the maximum obtainable with the workload being considered. Usually, this index is broken down to show all the possible combinations of component activity (for example, channels 1 and 2 busy with the CPU busy, channels 1 and 2 busy with the CPU idle). These overlap indexes are often represented in a graph called a *utilization profile* (see Chapter 4).

The *multiprogramming stretch factor* is an index which can be used to evaluate the impact of multiprogramming on a program's turnaround time. It is expressed as the ratio between the turnaround time of a program in a multiprogramming environment (for example, in the reference system MBRS) and the turnaround of the same program when running on a dedicated system.

The *multiprogramming level* is defined as the number of programs in execution at the same time and, therefore, competing for the system's hardware and software resources.

The *paging rate* is an index that is typical of virtual memory systems (for example, MIVRS). It is generally defined as the frequency with which the programs constituting the workload generate references to information items not present in main memory. These references (called *page faults*) cause the transfer of the page from the paging device to the main memory, and sometimes also the transfer in the opposite direction of the replaced page.

The *reaction time* is the time the system requires to react to an external command, that is, the interval between the instant at which the system receives a command (from a terminal or in batch mode) and the moment at which the CPU starts executing it.

As may be seen from these examples, some indexes have the physical dimension of time, others are absolute numbers, and others are amounts of work performed per unit of time.

Considerable efforts have been (and are being) made to standardize the various aspects of performance measurement, which are characterized by an extreme variability both in the definitions and methods for the measurement of performance indexes and in the hardware–software configurations of the various systems to be evaluated.

An example of the developments in this direction is the introduction of the concepts of *software physics* [KO76]. On the assumption that the fundamental notions of the natural sciences can be applied to computer science, the concepts of software power, work, and energy have been rigorously defined. The general concept of a software unit encompasses all programs and sets of programs, starting from the shortest possible program, that consisting of only one instruction. A software unit is a set of executable instructions with the necessary operands or data. Examples of software units are individual instructions, modules or subprograms, procedures, the operating system, or the whole workload of an installation.

The concepts of software work and power are independent of the workload's characteristics, the multiprogramming level, the hardware–software configuration, and the technical characteristics of the system's components.

Further efforts have focused on the problem of obtaining a standard set of performance indexes independent of the configuration being evaluated and defined so as to eliminate or at least to reduce the amount of subjectivity present in system evaluations. The existence of this set would provide a simple and general solution to some of the crucial problems in the measurement area, since we would have (1) a set of rigorously defined indexes obtainable with standard methods, applicable to all configurations, and (2) a set of standard values to be compared with the measured values of the indexes for an immediate evaluation of current performance levels.

At the moment, such a set of indexes does not exist. However, in many evaluation studies some sets are used, which may be considered the results of the first attempts to define a standard set [SO75]. These indexes, displayed in Table 1.2, have been divided on the basis of the information they provide into four classes: efficiency, effectiveness, throughput, and reliability–availability.

Once the values of the performance indexes have been determined, their qualitative analysis, which consists of establishing whether these values are good or need to be improved, should be performed.

Let us consider, for example, the first index in Table 1.2, CPU utilization, which is among the most common performance indexes. In general we can say that a system

TABLE 1.2 A STANDARD SET OF PERFORMANCE INDEXES [SO75]

	Efficiency (internal evaluation)
CPU utilization	Ratio between total CPU busy time and total system operating time
Channel utilization	Ratio between total channel busy time and total system operating time
Memory utilization	Ratio between memory occupancy (possibly expressed as a number of fixed-size blocks) and available memory size during the given time interval
Multiprogramming level	Mean number of simultaneously active (i.e., memory resident) programs
	Effectiveness (attainment of objectives)
Fulfillment of plans	Function of programs or procedures executed according to the plans
Turnaround time	Mean turnaround time for programs being tested
Reruns	Total number of reruns during the interval being considered
	Productivity (ability to process the workload completely)
Programs executed per hour	Number of production programs processed in 1 hour
Program tests executed per hour	Maximum number of program tests feasible in 1 hour
	Reliability–Availability
Down time	Ratio between total system inactivity time due to failures and total theoretical operating time
Failure rate	Number of failures due to any cause per unit of time
Crash rate	Frequency of system crashes (failures that bring the system down completely)

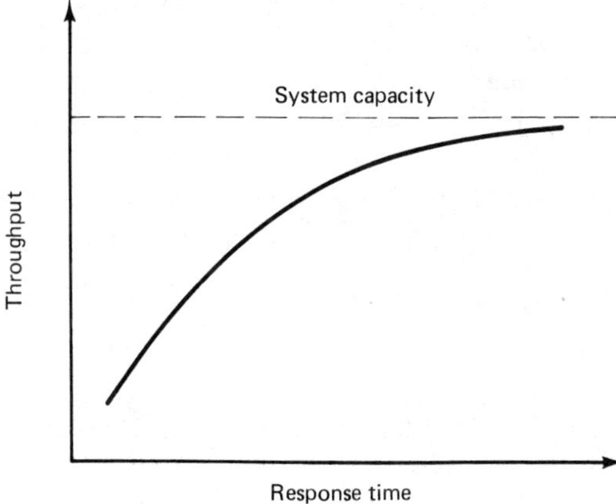

Figure 1.7 Relationship between throughput and response time for an interactive system (MIRS).

is oversized if the mean utilization of the CPU is less than 20 to 30 percent; also, it is likely that the CPU is the critical resource of the system if its mean utilization is above 80 to 90 percent.

However, these are extreme cases. In the vast majority of systems, the CPU is used between 30 and 80 percent of the time; can one draw quick conclusions about system performance from the value of CPU utilization in these cases? The question we really need to answer is what is a satisfactory level of CPU utilization for the installation we are dealing with.

If, for example, the mean response time is considered extremely important within the installation being evaluated, the utilization of the CPU cannot be treated with the same criteria that would be adequate in other cases, but will have to be viewed in the light of the main objective, which is to minimize the mean response time.

Sometimes the actions required to improve the values of some performance indexes cost so much with respect to the benefits they would produce that such improvement actions are not economically justified. In other cases, the improvement of some indexes corresponds to a worsening of other indexes. For example, to minimize the usage costs of an interactive system, one should maximize its throughput (to reduce the installation cost) and minimize its response time (to reduce programming costs). However, when throughput approaches the system's capacity, the responsiveness of the system is considerably degraded (see Fig. 1.7). Thus, a proper balance between the values of the performance indexes should be sought in order to minimize the system's usage cost, that is, to achieve the primary objective of the study.

1.4.1 Turnaround Time

Among the performance indexes described previously, turnaround time is the one each batch user is most sensitive to. The *external turnaround time* of the program is the time interval between the instant at which a user submits his program and the instant at which he receives the results. It is called "external" since it includes both the time required for manual input and output operations and the time required by the system to actually execute the program. The latter is called *internal turnaround time*.

Often the interval between when a program is handed in and when it is read into the system, added to the interval between when results are printed out and when they are delivered to the user, is much longer than the program's internal turnaround time. Thus, it is vital to keep these times at a minimum by a suitable organization of the work required for the manual input/output (I/O) operations.

The term *turnaround time* will be used in the sequel to indicate the internal turnaround time, whereas external turnaround time will always be designated explicitly as such.

The turnaround time T of a program is

$$T = P - R \tag{1.1}$$

where R is the moment at which the program's instructions start being read in and P that at which the printing of the results is completed.

The *stand-alone turnaround time* or *processing time* T_p of the program is defined as its turnaround time when it is the only program running on the system. Normally, the presence of many users makes the turnaround time greater than the processing time. Figure 1.8 represents pictorially the various times introduced so far.

The turnaround time T defined in Eq. (1.1) does not provide useful information for evaluating the efficiency with which a program has been processed by the system since its value depends on the program's processing time. Let us consider two programs, A and B, requiring respectively 1 and 30 min to be processed. Even if the turnaround times we obtain are 2 and 33 min, respectively, one cannot state that A has been processed more efficiently than B.

The *mean turnaround time* T_m, defined as,

$$T_m = \frac{\sum_{i=1}^{n} T_i}{n} \tag{1.2}$$

can lead to inaccurate conclusions about the processing efficiency, particularly if the value selected for n is small.

The *weighted turnaround time* T_w of a program is defined as the ratio between the turnaround time T and the program's processing time T_p:

$$T_w = \frac{T}{T_p} \tag{1.3}$$

Use of the weighted turnaround time, which is a pure number, makes the processing efficiencies of different programs more accurately comparable.

The *mean weighted turnaround time* T_{wm} is defined as

$$T_{wm} = \frac{\sum_{i=1}^{n} T_{wi}}{n} \tag{1.4}$$

The weighted turnaround time is affected by the resource management policies implemented by the system and by the characteristics of the workload.

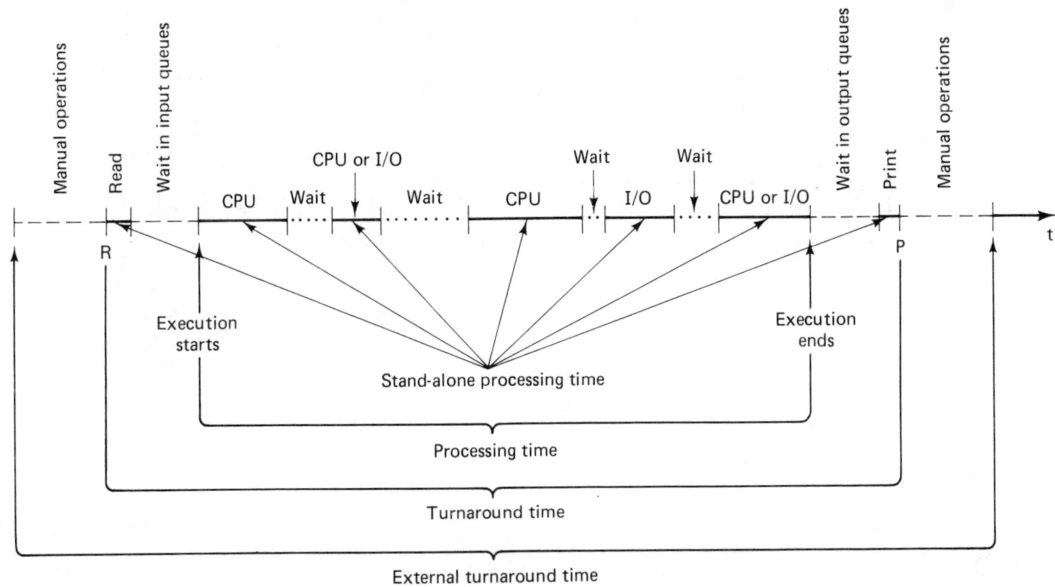

Figure 1.8 Times that characterize the processing of a program in an MBRS system.

Let us consider the processing of programs A, B, and C in a UBRS system. Table 1.3 shows their execution times and the sequence of their arrivals.

Figure 1.9 shows the values of T, T_m, T_w, and T_{wm} obtained with three different scheduling algorithms. The first algorithm (Fig. 1.9a) is first-come-first-served, the second (Fig. 1.9b) is shortest-job-first, and the third (Fig. 1.9c) is a future-knowledge type of algorithm. The last one is based on considerations derived from previous executions (for example, if it is very likely that at least one short program will arrive within the first 15 min after start-up, programs requiring more than 15 min are processed after this time has passed). Future-knowledge algorithms are not very popular since they are difficult to design properly.

While the values obtained for T_{wm} in the three cases considered are decreasing (6.15 in part a, 2.5 in part b, and 1.4 in part c), the value of T_m obtained in part b is less than the value found in part c. The user's *level of satisfaction* varies: for user A, algorithms a and b are better than algorithm c; for user B the converse is true. It is important to

TABLE 1.3 ARRIVAL AND PROCESSING TIMES OF PROGRAMS A, B, AND C

Program time	*Processing time (min)*	*Arrival sequence*
A	30	At time 0
B	55	After 5 min
C	5	After 10 min

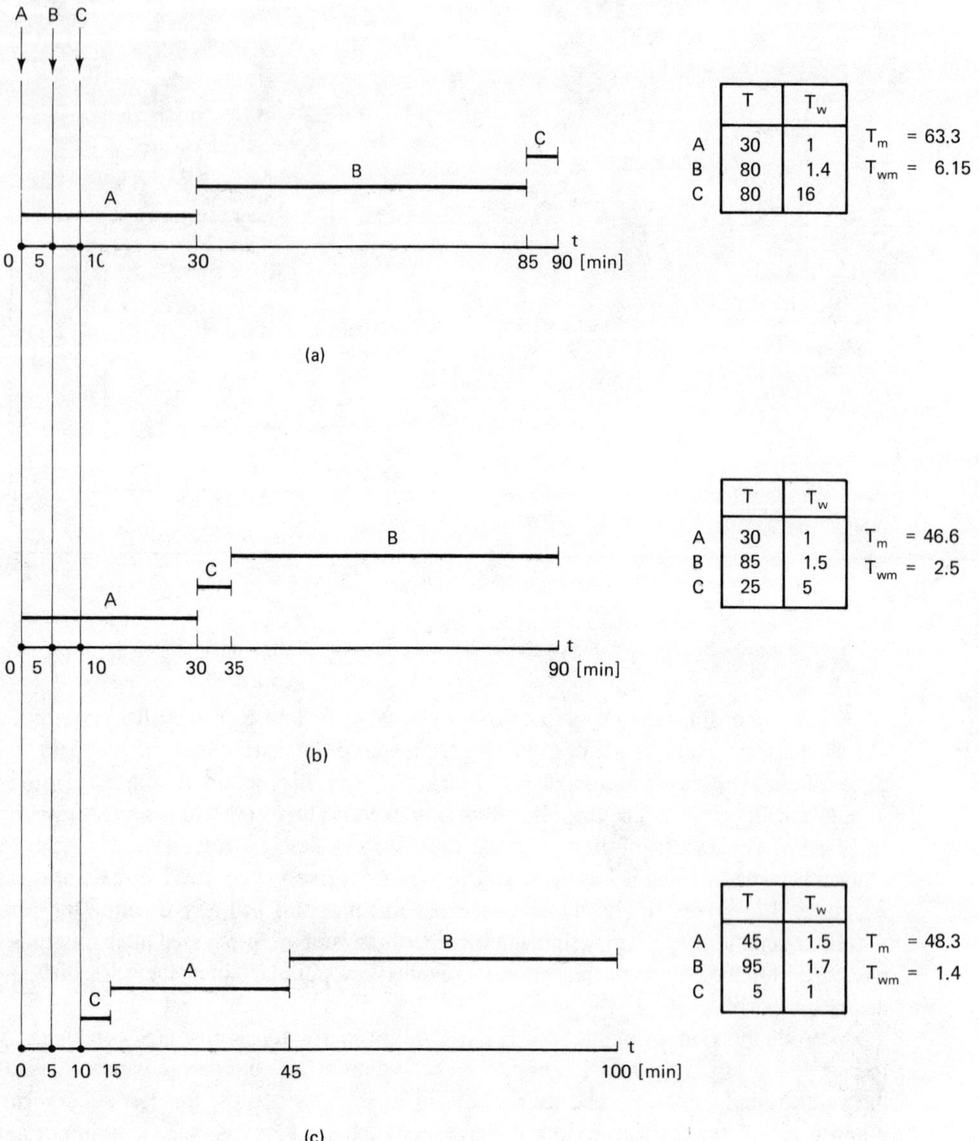

Figure 1.9 Turnaround times in a UBRS system under three different scheduling algorithms: (a) FCFS; (b) SJF; (c) a future-knowledge algorithm.

note that in case c the time required to process the three programs is 10 min longer than in the other two cases, even though case c corresponds to the minimum T_{wm}.

This example shows that minimizing T_{wm} does not mean minimizing all other turnaround times or, for that matter, necessarily improving other performance indexes.

Let us consider the scheduling algorithm of Fig. 1.9a again, but used in an MBRS system that allows the executions of A, B, and C to start exactly at the moment they arrive. Figure 1.10 shows the processing sequence of the programs and the values obtained for T, T_w, T_m, and T_{wm} in this case. In this example, the arrival sequence of the programs is the same as before, but the results obtained are better (T_{wm}, for instance, is reduced from 6.15 to 2.1). The values in parentheses in Fig. 1.10 are the times required to complete the execution of each program.

For simplicity we have assumed that the CPU is assigned in turn to the programs being executed for a fixed *time quantum* [SE72]. In Fig. 1.10 the CPU is assigned only to A for the first 5 min, and to both A and B in the time interval from 5 to 10; thus A and B will advance by 2.5 min each. In the time between 10 and 25, the CPU is shared by A, B, and C; thus each will advance by 5 min, and so on. Since these examples are intended to show the connections between scheduling algorithms and turnaround time, we have assumed that A, B, and C require only CPU service and no I/O operations. Our considerations are valid also for programs containing I/O operations, although the values in Figs. 1.9 and 1.10 will vary.

As stated previously, a reduction of T can be obtained by using system resources in a way that often contrasts with the objective of high component utilization. Let us consider the MBRS system for which curve 1 in Fig. 1.11 was obtained. Some modifications to increase system utilization are carried out. For example, the CPU scheduling policy or the disk file allocation policy is improved. Then, with the same test workload that produced curve 1 before the changes, we obtain curve 2. This means that more programs are processed without increasing the weighted turnaround time. A substantial improvement (curve 3) is obtained by changing the processing mode, that is, by going to an MIRS system. In this case, users can make use of interactive syntax analyzers that avoid unnecessary testing of programs, thereby decreasing the load on the CPU and increasing, for these programs, the possible number of daily runs.

In contrast with these improvements, the values of the performance indexes for the programs executed in batch mode become worse. This is primarily due to the memory restrictions caused by the presence of the program that manages interactive programs. Thus, their T_{wm} increases, and the possible number of their daily runs decreases.

Turnaround times depend on the existing workload. If, for example, we change the arrival times of the programs in Fig. 1.10, we can improve the values of T_m and T_{wm}.

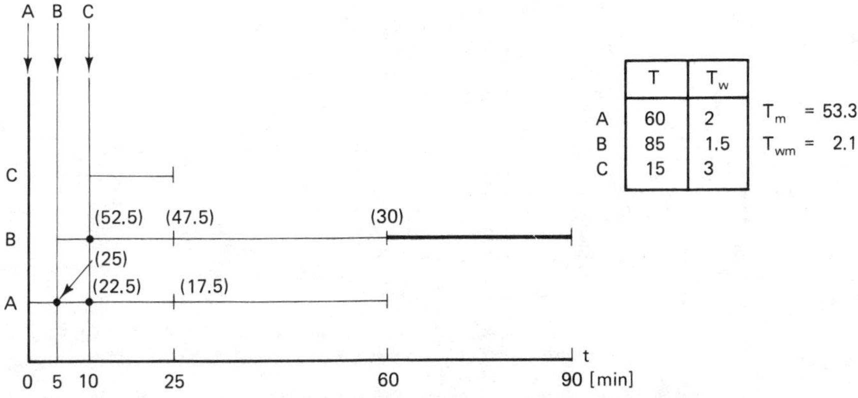

Figure 1.10 First-come-first-served scheduling in an MBRS system.

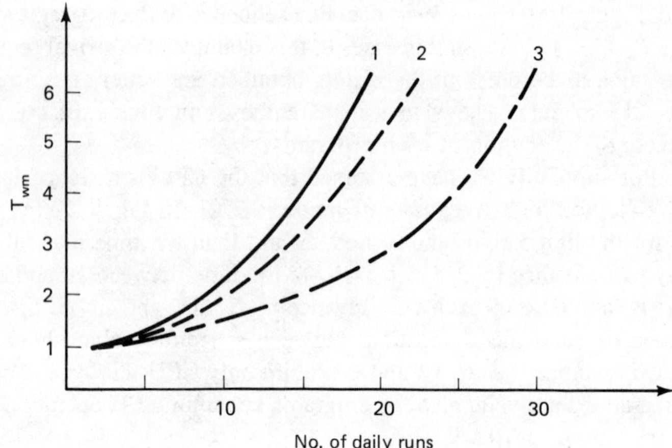

Figure 1.11 Mean weighted turnaround time versus the number of daily runs in a program testing environment for an MBRS (curves 1 and 2) and an MIRS system (curve 3).

Figure 1.12 shows the results that would be obtained if the order of arrival of our three programs were C, A, and B.

In many installations, users are allowed to select the order of magnitude of T_w for their programs. The smaller the value of T_w, the greater the processing charges. The number of programs in the night shift with a big T_w can usually be increased by reducing their processing charges. With similar policies, the workload characteristics of a system can be modified, causing a substantial alteration of all the performance indexes.

1.4.2 Response Time

The *response time* of an interactive system for a given command can be defined as the duration of the time interval between the instant at which the SEND key of the terminal being used is pressed and the instant at which the terminal starts to output the system's response (see Fig. 1.13). This time gap can be measured by a stopwatch if it is on the

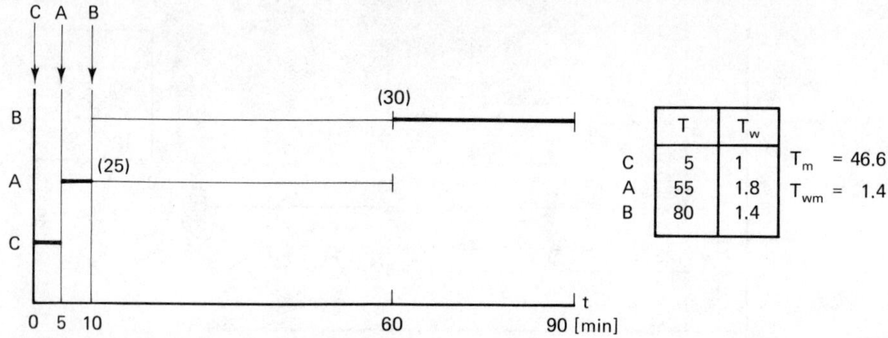

	T	T_w
C	5	1
A	55	1.8
B	80	1.4

Figure 1.12 Sensitivity of turnaround times to changes in the order of arrival of programs with FCFS scheduling (compare with Fig. 1.10).

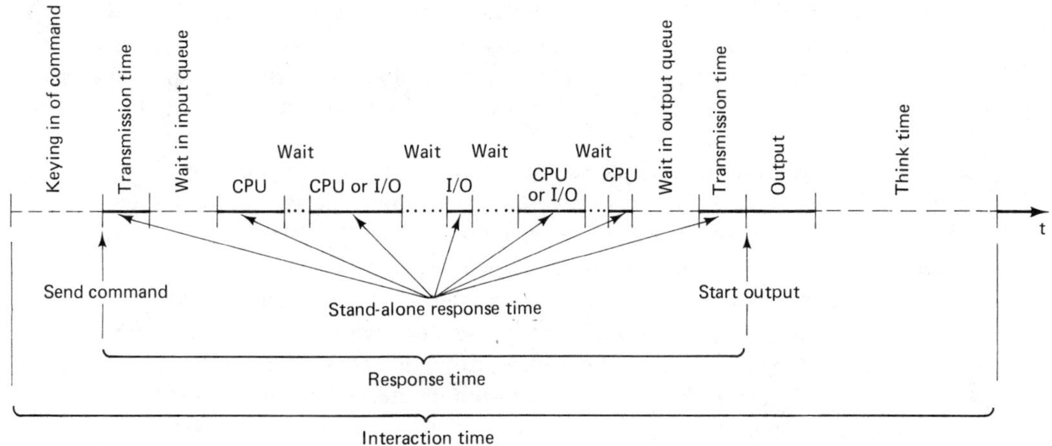

Figure 1.13 Components of response time (the command is assumed not to produce any output during its execution).

order of 1 second; for shorter times, hardware or software measurement tools should be used. The response time to a command depends also on the command. The rough distinction between *light* and *heavy* commands is usually made; a light command is often defined as one that requires a CPU time less than the time quantum allotted to it. Examples of light commands are editing commands (insertion, deletion, or modification of text), terminal output commands, log-on commands, and requests for such information as time and date.

A heavy request requires more than one time quantum to be executed. Among the heavy commands we usually have compilation, execution, assembly, sort, and merge commands.

Since the mean response time R_m does not provide complete information about an interactive system's performance [KL72] (for example, about the variability of that performance), we must consider as our index the distribution of response times. Some useful descriptors of this distribution, that is, the standard deviation, the median, the total deviation, the percentiles [SP72], and so on, will therefore have to supplement the value of R_m if a more complete and meaningful characterization of an interactive system's performance is desired.

The standard deviation σ of response times is given by

$$\sigma = \sqrt{\frac{1}{n}\sum_{i=1}^{n}(R_i - R_m)^2} \tag{1.5}$$

where R_i is the response time to the ith command. σ gives some indication of the variability of response times, that is, of their degree of dispersion around the mean value.

The total deviation of the values, that is, the difference between the extreme values, may also be used. For example, consider an MIRS system in which response times to light commands vary from 1 to 15 s (a total deviation of 14 s), with a mean value of 4 s and a standard deviation of 6 s. The high variability of response times in this installation lowers the user satisfaction level, and the system is likely to be used ineffectively. When the standard deviation appears too large with respect to the mean, a thorough analysis of the system's performance should be carried out, since the system is likely to be loaded in an anomalous way or to be inadequately sized.

During a working day, the response times often vary as shown in Fig. 1.14. The two peaks of the maximum response time curve immediately precede the lunch break and the end of the day. There is a tendency to overload the system just before leaving, thereby increasing substantially the corresponding response times.

Other distribution descriptors that are often worth using are the *percentiles*. Given a set of data in decreasing or increasing order, the value that divides the set equally in half is called the *median*. If the frequency distribution curve is unimodal and symmetric, as in Fig. 1.15, the median will coincide with the mean and with the mode (that is, the value corresponding to the peak). The values that divide the set into four equal parts are called *quartiles*. Below the first quartile, one-quarter of the values will be found, below the second (which coincides with the median) half of the values, and so on. The median is the 50th percentile, and the quartiles are the 25th, 50th, 75th, and 100th percentiles, respectively.

Thus, the percentiles are those values that divide an ordered set of data into 100 equal parts so that, for instance, 10 percent of the values are below the 10th percentile, and so on.

Saying that an observed response time is the pth percentile is equivalent to stating that p percent of all response times observed is below that value. Percentiles are particularly useful with asymmetric distributions.

It is often convenient to use the cumulative distribution of response times, that is, the curve that associates to each value of response time the percentage of the response

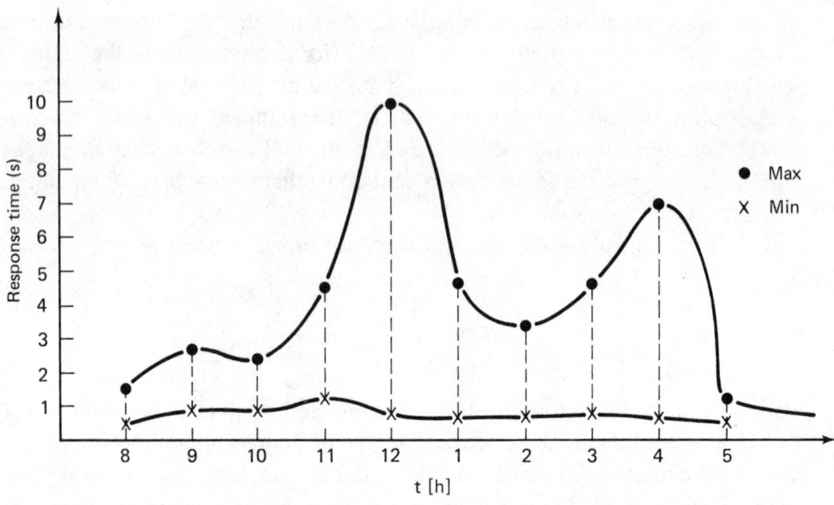

Figure 1.14 Variations of maximum and minimum response times during a working day.

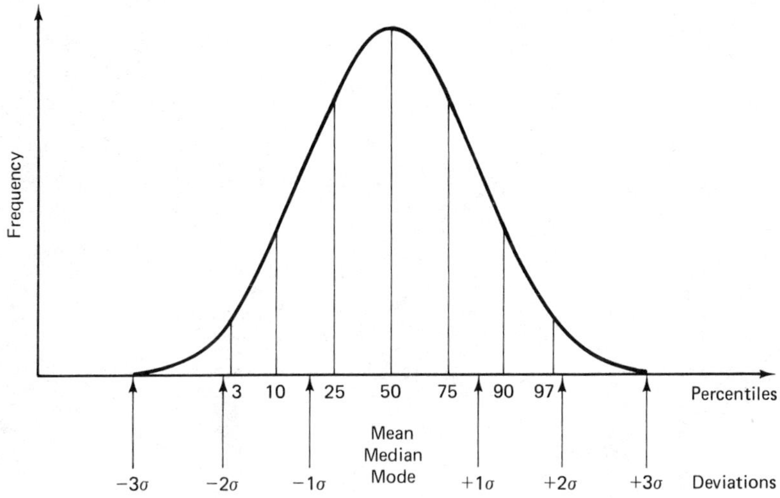

Figure 1.15 Percentiles and standard deviation for a unimodal and symmetric distribution.

times in the population less than or equal to that value. The curves in Fig. 1.16 [CA75] show two measured cumulative response time distributions. Curve 1 tells us that 50 percent of the observed response times are less than or equal to 23 percent of the maximum response time; for curve 2, the median is 27 percent of the maximum. The mean response times (indicated by a dot in Fig. 1.16) are respectively 40 and 35 percent of the maximum times.

In the same figure the small triangles indicate the mean response times as perceived by the users. It is interesting to note that they are above the 90th percentile. Figure 1.17

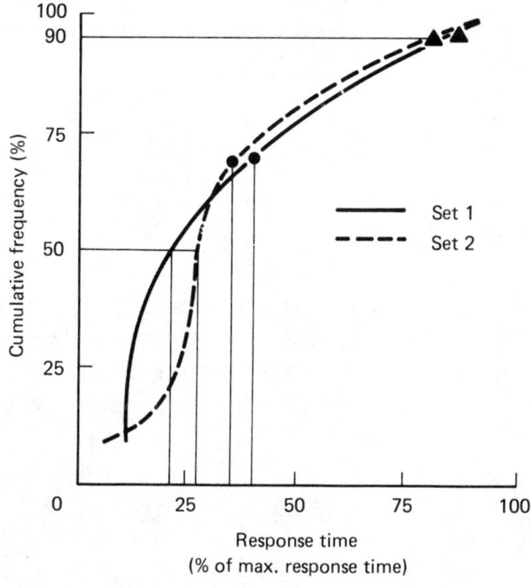

Figure 1.16 Two cumulative distributions of response times [CA75].

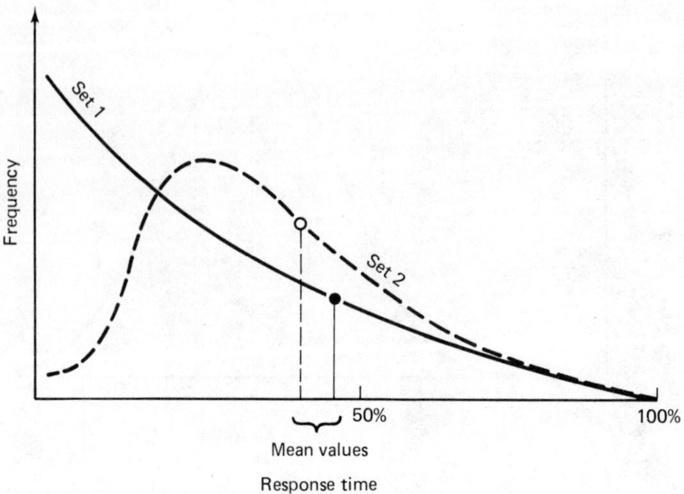

Figure 1.17 Two frequency distributions of response times.

shows the frequency distribution curves corresponding to the two cumulative distributions reported in Fig. 1.16.

Often users evaluate response times subjectively as they are more sensitive to maximum times, which only rarely occur, than to the much more common lower response times.

As far as the relationships existing between a system's response times and its other performance indexes are concerned, we could repeat the considerations made for turnaround times. Clearly, the value of the response time to a command depends also on the program that manages the terminals, on some of the terminal's characteristics, on the way in which the application programs were designed, on the number of interactive users logged on, and, finally, on the noninteractive load existing on the system during the processing of the command.

1.4.3 Throughput

The main objective of most evaluation studies is the improvement of a system's productivity or *throughput*. The importance of throughput is in its value as related to the cost of the system. Throughput may be defined in many ways, all of which express the concept of work performed during the unit of time. Since these definitions also apply to individual system components, one can speak of the throughput of an I/O channel or of a CPU.

Throughput can be expressed in terms of the number of programs executed, I/O operations performed, transactions processed, and so on, all with respect to the unit of time being considered.

A general definition of throughput is

$$X = \frac{N_p}{t_{\text{tot}}} \tag{1.6}$$

where N_p is the number of programs processed during t_{tot}, the measurement interval. When benchmarking techniques are used, N_p is the number of programs in the workload and t_{tot} is the time required for their execution.

The change from a serial processing system (UBRS) to those with parallel processing capabilities (MBRS), together with the technological evolution of I/O devices, has made it possible to obtain, with properly balanced configurations, high values of productivity.

In a UBRS system, or in an MBRS system that cannot execute the N_p programs in the workload in a multiprogramming mode since they all use the same nonsharable peripherals or the same data, the throughput is given by

$$X = \frac{N_p}{\sum_{i=1}^{N_p} T_i} \tag{1.7}$$

where T_i is the stand-alone turnaround time of the ith program.

When calculating the throughput of an MBRS system, the possibility of overlapped processing, that is, of the simultaneous operations of various system components, will have to be taken into account.

Theoretically, a given workload could be processed by the MBRS system shown in Fig. 1.3 (three channels and one CPU) with a productivity four times higher than by a UBRS system with a similar configuration. Indeed, in a UBRS system the processing time of a workload containing N_p programs, each requiring t_i seconds of service from each component, is

$$T_U = \sum_{i=1}^{N_p} \left(t_{i\text{CPU}} + \sum_{j=1}^{c} t_{i\text{ch}j} \right) \tag{1.8}$$

where c is the number of channels used. It is assumed that two or more components cannot be used at the same time.

In an MBRS system with a similar configuration, the execution time of the same workload is given by

$$T_M = \begin{cases} \sum_{i=1}^{N_p} t_{i\text{CPU}} & \text{if } \left(\max\limits_{j=1,c} \sum_{i=1}^{N_p} t_{i\text{ch}j} - \sum_{i=1}^{N_p} t_{i\text{CPU}} \right) \leqslant 0 \\ \max\limits_{j=1,c} \sum_{i=1}^{N_p} t_{i\text{ch}j} & \text{if } \left(\max\limits_{j=1,c} \sum_{i=1}^{N_p} t_{i\text{ch}j} - \sum_{i=1}^{N_p} t_{i\text{CPU}} \right) > 0 \end{cases} \tag{1.9}$$

In words, assuming that all the c channels can be simultaneously used by the N_p programs ($c < N_p$), if the maximum time for which a channel is busy is less than the total CPU time, then I/O activities and CPU activities will overlap completely. That is, the total time T_M will equal the CPU time (see Fig. 1.18a).

If, on the other hand, any one of the channels is busy for a time longer than the

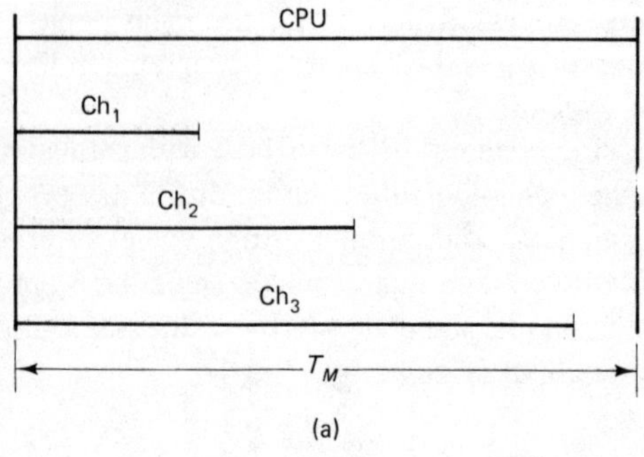

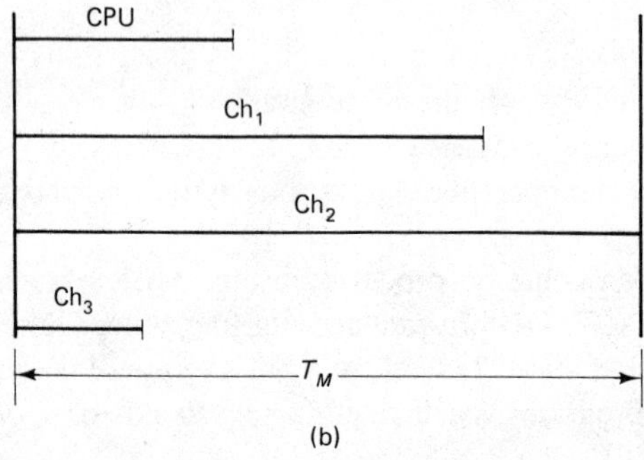

Figure 1.18 Timing diagrams of processing time in an MBRS system in the two conditions of Eq. (1.9).

total CPU time, the overlap of activities will only be partial. Thus, the value of T_M will equal the total time the busiest channel is active (see Fig. 1.18b).

The *throughput improvement factor F*, obtained by changing from uniprogramming to multiprogramming, can be defined as the ratio between T_U given by Eq. (1.8) and T_M expressed by Eq. (1.9).

F varies from 1, corresponding to no improvement when programs use only the CPU, to a maximum equal to the number of system components. This maximum is obtained when the service times required from each component are the same for all programs and all components:

$$F = \frac{T_U}{T_M} = 1 + \frac{N_p c t}{N_p t} = 1 + c \tag{1.10}$$

If the time required for I/O operations is, for all programs, much greater than the CPU time, F will be given by

$$F \cong \frac{\sum_{i=1}^{N_p} \sum_{j=1}^{c} t_{i\text{ch}j}}{\max_{j=1,c} \sum_{i=1}^{N_p} t_{i\text{ch}j}}$$

Assuming that all the service times required from the c channels are the same, we obtain

$$F \cong \frac{N_p ct}{N_p t} = c$$

Equation (1.10) expresses the maximum theoretical value of the improvement factor F, which equals the number of independent components used by the workload. This value is never reached in practice, since normally the workload does not satisfy the assumptions under which Eq. (1.10) is valid. Furthermore, the overlapping of operations would not be perfect anyway because of the various necessary interventions of the operating system.

Throughput, like other performance indexes, is influenced by the following factors:

- The characteristics of the load with which it is evaluated
- The configuration of the system
- The degree of multiprogramming allowed by the hardware
- The resource allocation algorithms used
- The speed of the hardware and software components

As throughput is an external performance index, it provides a global indication of a system's power but gives no useful information for the evaluation of a single program's performance. On the contrary, other indexes are sometimes made worse as a consequence of an improvement in throughput.

Let us consider, for example, the processing of a workload containing three programs, A (processing time 15 s), B (processing time 3 s), and C (processing time 8 s) on a UBRS system. These programs arrive at almost the same times in the order A, B, C. Using the FCFS scheduling algorithm for the CPU (see Fig. 1.19a), which assigns the CPU to each program until its execution is complete, the mean turnaround time and the mean weighted turnaround time are greater than the values that would be obtained with a round-robin algorithm (Fig. 1.19b), which assigns the CPU in turn to all programs for a given time quantum (in the example, for 2 s). As shown in Fig. 1.18, the values of T_m and T_{wm} are different in the two cases, although the throughput X is the same.

We shall now discuss two examples intended to show the influence of some of the factors mentioned on the throughput of the system. Figure 1.19 displays an example of the variation of the throughput in an MBRS system as a function of the workload. Figure 1.20a illustrates the characteristics (also in terms of CPU and I/O requirements) of the three programs A, B, and C that the workload consists of. For simplicity, we assume that all I/O operations use components connected to the same channel (for example C_1 in Fig. 1.3).

Thus, the I/O operations of the program may overlap the CPU activities of another, but I/O operations may not overlap other I/O operations. When a program is doing an I/O operation and another program issues an I/O request, the latter program must wait for the completion of the operation of the former; in the cases of Fig. 1.20b and d, these waiting times equal 5 and 7.5 time units, respectively. The CPU is cyclically assigned to the programs being executed for a time that is very short with respect to the scale used in the diagrams of Fig. 1.20.

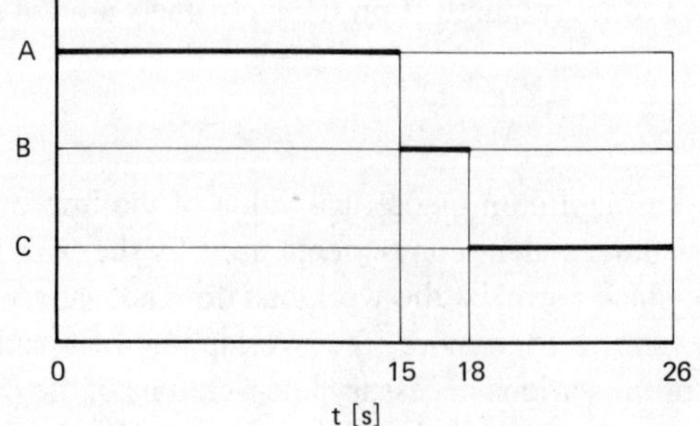

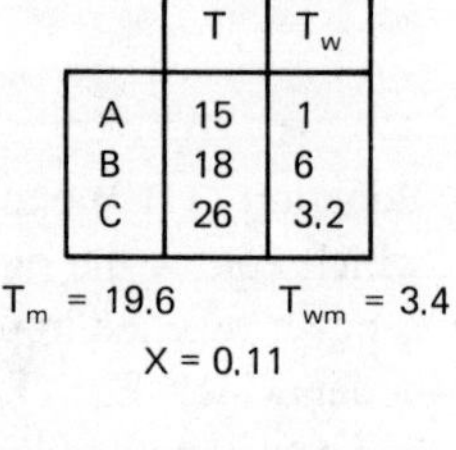

	T	T_w
A	15	1
B	18	6
C	26	3.2

T_m = 19.6 T_{wm} = 3.4
X = 0.11

(a) FCFS scheduling

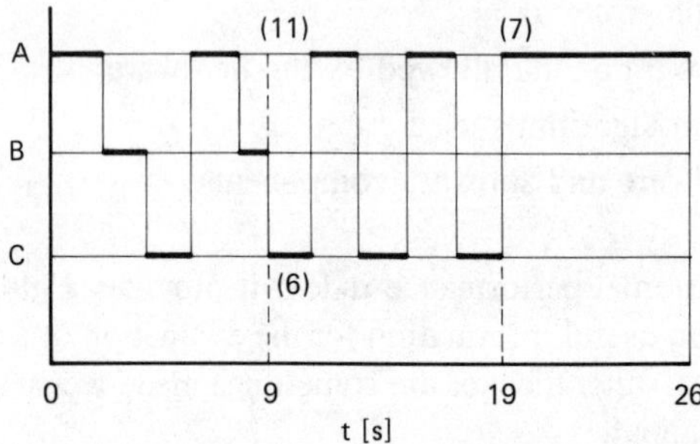

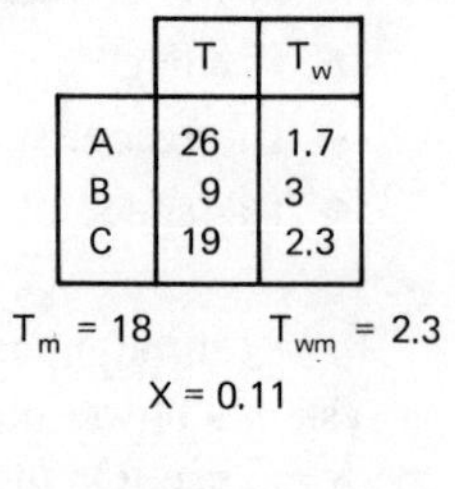

	T	T_w
A	26	1.7
B	9	3
C	19	2.3

T_m = 18 T_{wm} = 2.3
X = 0.11

(b) RR scheduling (time quantum: 2 s)

Figure 1.19 Independence between throughput *X* and turnaround time *T* (for a UBRS system).

One can see easily in Fig. 1.20 that the highest throughput (0.044) is obtained with the longest mean weighted turnaround time (1.65) and with a nonzero waiting time. This shows once again that the improvement of one performance index is often accompanied by a worsening of others. However, the maximum throughput is not to be reached at any cost in practice; there often are constraints to be satisfied. For example, it is normally unwise to go beyond a certain maximum value of weighted turnaround time.

In Fig. 1.21, the example of Fig. 1.20b is reconsidered, but the main memory size is assumed to be limited. The workload characteristics are those in Fig. 1.20a, and the available memory size M is 120 Kbytes. We assume the memory needed by A to be 80 Kbytes, that needed by B to be 60 Kbytes, and that needed by C 40 Kbytes.

B cannot start its execution when it arrives ($t = 5$), but will have to wait until $t = 32.5$, when 80 Kbytes of memory are released by A. The throughput obtained (0.034) is less than the throughput in the example in Fig. 1.20b (0.044), in which the memory size was considered to be unlimited but all other conditions were the same.

The factors previously discussed influence the throughput with different weights, each of which may be measured by the *sensitivity* of *X* to the factor's variation. The *sensitivity* of an index is usually defined as the ratio between the variation of the index and that of the factor being considered. However, when the factor is not quantitative, its

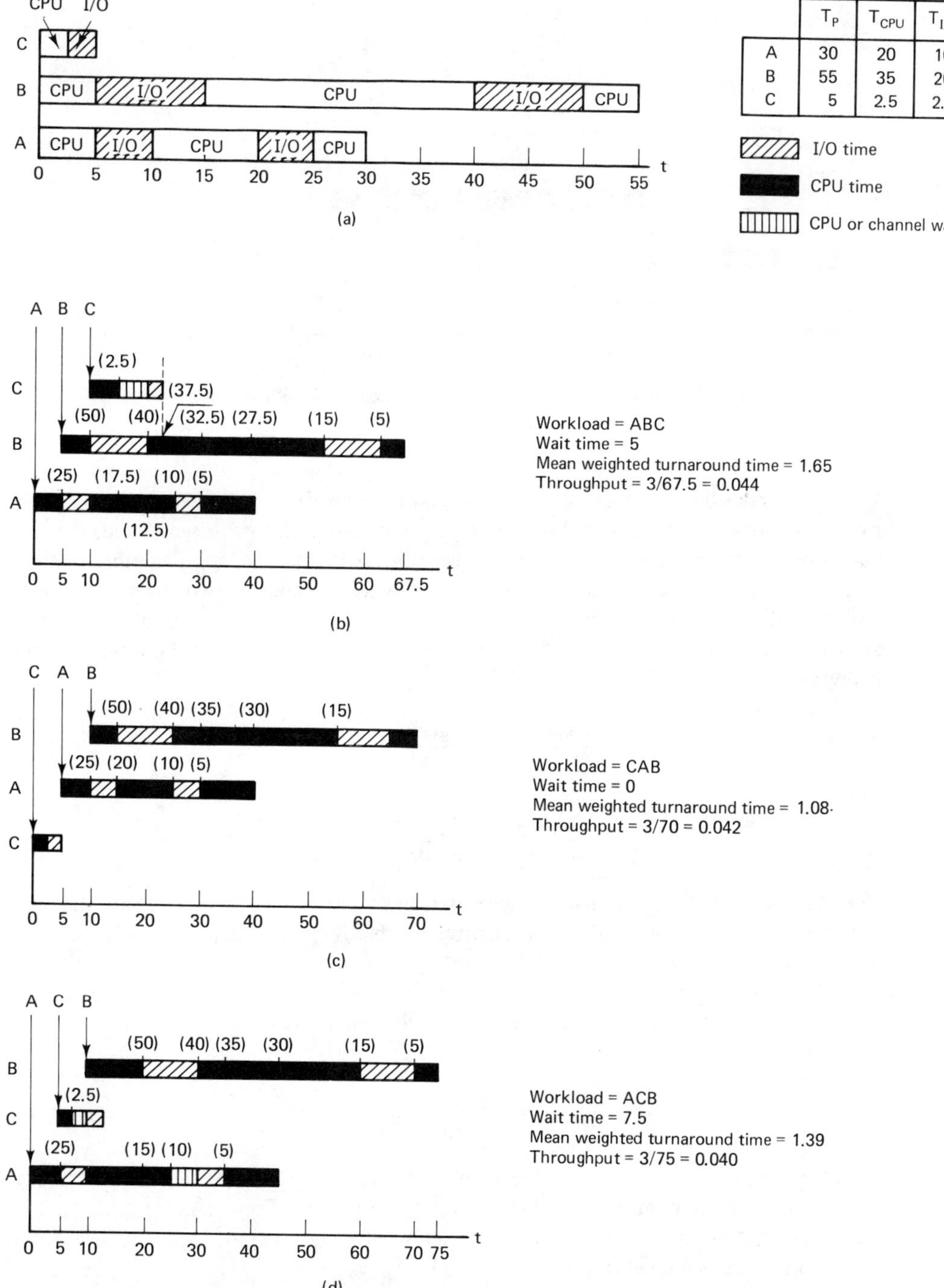

Figure 1.20 Throughput as a function of program ordering in an MBRS system.

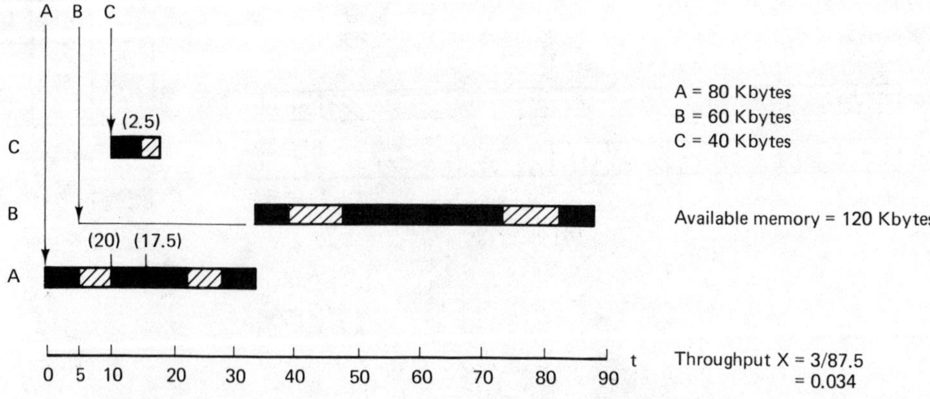

Figure 1.21 Throughput versus main memory size in an MBRS system (see also Fig. 1.19(b)).

variation cannot be expressed numerically, and the sensitivity will have to be measured by the variation in throughput. When two nonquantitative factors are involved, the four values of the index can be combined in various ways to obtain a single number that can still be considered as a sensitivity. For instance, when comparing two systems A and B with two different workloads W_1 and W_2, if we denote by $X_A(W_1)$ the throughput of system A measured with workload W_1, and so on, we may use one of the following two expressions [HE75]:

$$\frac{X_B(W_2)}{X_A(W_2)} - \frac{X_B(W_1)}{X_A(W_1)} \tag{1.11}$$

$$\frac{X_B(W_2) - X_A(W_2)}{X_B(W_1) - X_A(W_1)} \tag{1.12}$$

The value of Eq. (1.11) is usually less than the value of Eq. (1.12). Thus, the ratio between the two throughputs is less sensitive to (that is, more independent of) workload variations than their difference.

The throughput of a single component, for example, of an I/O subsystem (buffer area, channel, control unit, peripheral unit), if the program always uses only one file, is given by

$$X_{io} = \frac{b}{T_R + b/V_{io}} \text{ bits/s} \tag{1.13}$$

where b represents the mean number of bits in a record, T_R is the mean record access time, and V_{io} is the number of bits transmitted in a second. Equation (1.13) shows that the throughput of an I/O subsystem is a function of record length, hardware speed, file organization, and channel transmission speed.

Another definition of throughput, applicable to any component i (central processor as well as I/O subsystem), is [BU76a]

$$X(i) = \frac{U(i)}{t_s(i) \cdot N_{rp}(i)} \tag{1.14}$$

where $U(i)$ is the utilization of component i,

$$U(i) = \frac{\text{time during which } i \text{ is busy}}{\text{measurement interval } t_{\text{tot}}} \tag{1.15}$$

$t_s(i)$ is the service time of each request,

$$t_s(i) = \frac{\text{time during which } i \text{ is busy}}{\text{no. of requests serviced by } i \text{ in } t_{\text{tot}}} \tag{1.16}$$

and N_{rp} indicates the mean number of requests for component i made by each program,

$$N_{rp}(i) = \frac{\text{no. of requests serviced by } i \text{ in } t_{\text{tot}}}{\text{no. } N_p \text{ of programs executed}} \tag{1.17}$$

Substituting Eqs. (1.15), (1.16), and (1.17) into (1.14), we have

$$X(i) = \frac{N_p}{t_{\text{tot}}} \tag{1.18}$$

which coincides with the general definition of throughput given in Eq. (1.6).

Note that definition (1.18) is independent of the degree of multiprogramming, of the distributions of service times, and of the amount of overlap that is achievable.

For example, if in an MBRS system the mean CPU utilization is 70 percent, the mean processing time of each request is 15 ms, and the mean number of requests in each program is 10,000, the system's throughput will be

$$X = \frac{0.7}{15 \cdot 10{,}000} \text{ programs/ms}$$

$$= \frac{3{,}600{,}000 \cdot 0.7}{15 \cdot 10{,}000} = 16.8 \text{ programs/h}$$

The formalization of this and other fundamental relationships that can be used to describe the behavior of computer systems in a wide variety of situations has been recently performed by *operational analysis* [BU76b], [DE78] (see Section 9.3).

We shall now briefly present the result of an analysis carried out on an MIRS system [BE75] that shows the relationships among the size of a system and its throughput, response time, and workload. The workload mainly consisted of programs being tested (with many file accesses), programs to be executed, and programs requiring lengthy compilations in various languages (COBOL, ALGOL, FORTRAN).

In Fig. 1.22a, the mean response time for a given class of messages is plotted versus the number of interactive users. Figure 1.23 reports the utilizations of some resources in the same workload situation.

Under the given workload, the critical resource is the CPU: when the system is saturated (with about 16 users), increasing the number of users decreases their CPU usage,

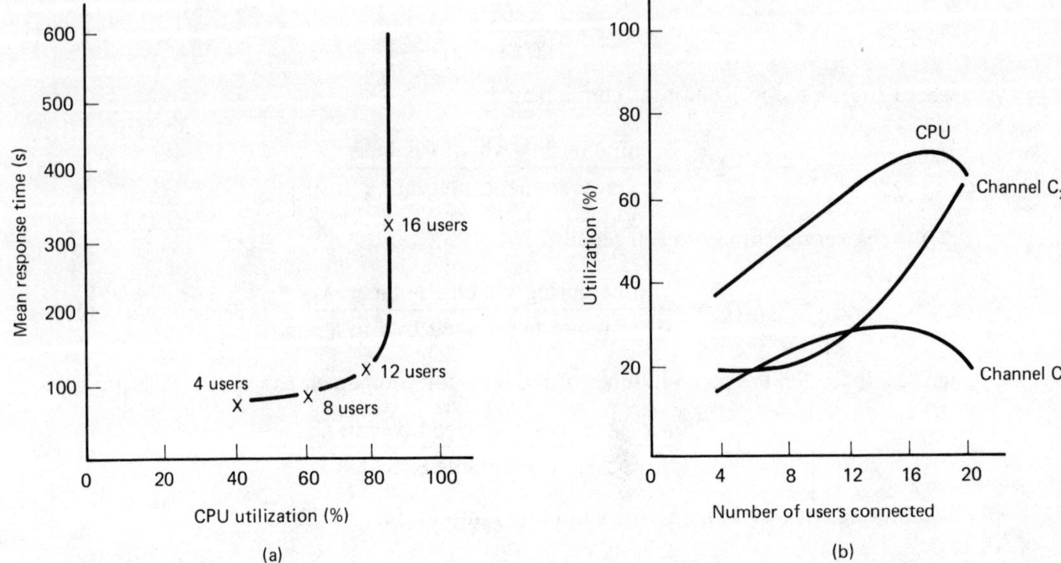

Figure 1.22 Throughput versus number of terminal users in an MIRS system.

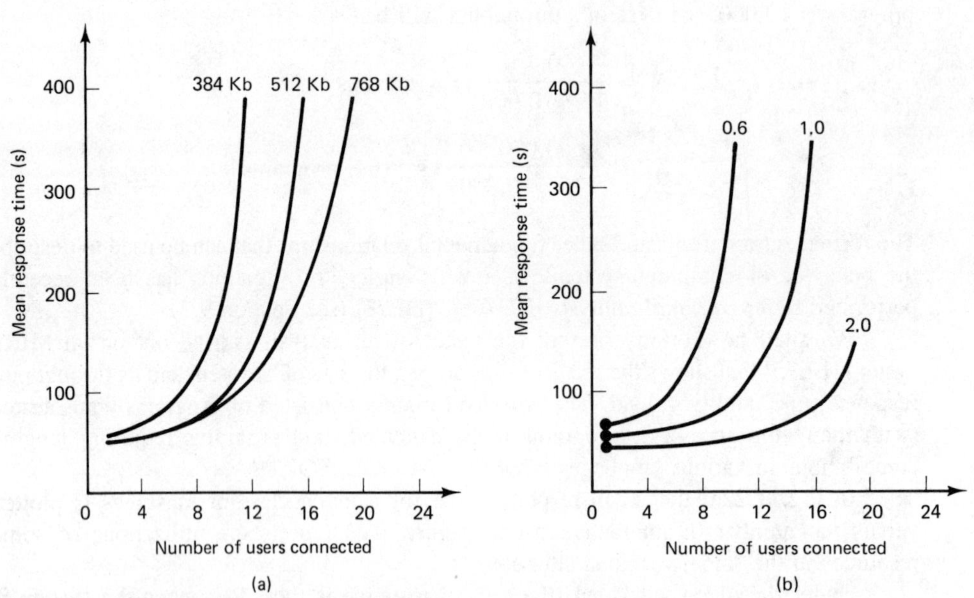

Figure 1.23 Sensitivity of the saturation curve of an MIRS system to (a) memory size M and (b) CPU power.

due to the corresponding increase of operating system overhead, which causes a reduction of productivity.

Figure 1.23a illustrates the effects on the mean response time of an increase in main memory size when all other conditions remain the same. Figure 1.23b shows the effects caused by variations of CPU power; two CPUs, one with a mean processing speed equal to about 60 percent of that of the original CPU, the other one twice as fast, were considered in this experiment.

We shall now examine the effects produced on the responsiveness of the system by two workloads different from the one used so far, which will be called workload 1. Workload 2 has less execution requests than workload 1 and uses more substantially the FORTRAN compiler, which requires less memory than the ALGOL compiler. Workload 3 only uses compilers of interactive languages like BASIC, which require only 36 Kbytes of main memory.

Figure 1.24 shows the *weighted response time* versus the number of users logged on. The weighted response time is the ratio between the actual and the stand-alone response time to a command, the latter being the time that would be obtained if the system were entirely dedicated to the processing of that command (see Fig. 1.13).

In this way, response times for different classes of commands can be compared. From Fig. 1.24b one concludes that the saturation curve is less dependent on memory size for workload 1 than for workload 2, and for workload 2 than for workload 3. This should not be surprising since, as appears in Fig. 1.22 for workload 1, the system is limited by the CPU, and thus an increase in M cannot cause great effects.

From the diagrams in Fig. 1.23, it is possible to determine the capacity of the system for a given response time. If a weighted response time not greater than 4 is required, one can see that the system allows for 13 users with workload 1, for 15 with

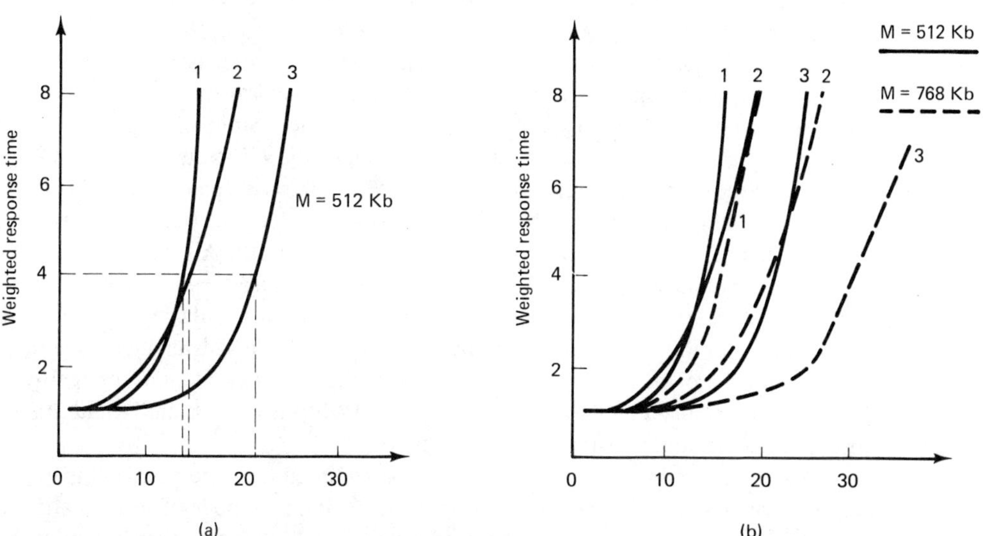

Figure 1.24 Sensitivity of the saturation curve of an MIRS system (a) to the workload and (b) to both workload and memory size M.

workload 2, and for 22 with workload 3. Other criteria that can also be used, based, for instance, on the value of CPU utilization, will be described in detail later.

1.5 EVALUATION TECHNIQUES

Section 1.2 discussed the main objectives of performance evaluation. After describing in Sec. 1.3 the reference systems to be used throughout this book, we introduced the performance indexes, that is, the primary quantities to be evaluated.

What techniques can we use to evaluate these quantities? Evaluation techniques, that is, methods by which the indexes may by obtained, can be subdivided into two main categories: (1) *measurement* (or *empirical*) techniques, and (2) *modeling* techniques.

Empirical techniques are based on direct measurements of the system to be evaluated, which therefore must exist and be available. When a system does not exist (for instance, during the design phase) or when it is not available (for instance, when the effect of an expensive system modification is to be determined before the change is made, or when the impact of workload that cannot be produced on the system under evaluation is to be predicted), other techniques must be used. An evaluator who wants to measure a system must use suitable tools, to be described in Chapter 5. The techniques on which the operation of most of these tools is based are illustrated in Chapter 3. It is important to note that the measurement of a system does not necessarily have to be performed while the system processes its natural workload (that is, the one actually produced by its users). As we will see in Chapters 2 and 3, it is possible and often convenient (especially for the reproducibility of the experiment) to load a system with a *test workload*.

Modeling techniques are of two types: *simulation* techniques and *analytic* techniques. Simulation can usefully be applied to the evaluation of a system's performance. As will be seen in Chapter 3, a simulation model reproduces in time certain aspects of the dynamic behavior of a system. It is thus possible to perform real measurements on a model using simulated tools. Performance indexes are obviously among the quantities that can be measured in this way, as long as the mechanisms that produce them in the real system have been suitably reproduced in the model. Simulation may therefore be considered as a measurement technique; for this reason it will be discussed in Chapter 3 together with the other measurement techniques. From this viewpoint, the main difference between simulation and other measurement techniques is in the fact that it does not require the existence and the availability of the system to be evaluated. All modeling techniques, compared to measurement techniques, exhibit this advantage, which makes them irreplaceable in certain studies (for example, those to be performed during the design phase of a system). On the other hand, they have a fundamental disadvantage: since they use models, which are inevitably partial and approximate representations of reality, they provide results whose credibility may always be doubtful, at least until valid arguments supporting the accuracy of the models are provided.

Analytic techniques differ from simulation techniques by the nature of the methods employed for studying the models. They use the analytic methods of mathematics rather than the principles of simulation. The need for the model to be mathematically solvable limits the modeler's freedom considerably and, as a consequence, also the accuracy of analytic models. Some deterministic models are probabilistic in nature. In particular,

TABLE 1.4 APPLICABILITY OF EVALUATION TECHNIQUES TO DIFFERENT TYPES OF STUDIES

		Evaluation technique		
			Modeling	
Type of study	*Object*	*Measurement*	*Simulation*	*Analytic*
Design	System	I	A	A
	Program	I	A	I
Procurement	System	A	A	I
	Program	A	A	I
Capacity planning	System	I	A	A
Improvement	System	A	A	A
	Program	A	A	A

A, adequate; I, inadequate.

those based on queuing theory are the most common and promising. Because of the importance of their use in performance evaluation in general and of their applications in system tuning in particular, these models will be introduced and discussed in Chapter 9, where a number of examples will be presented to illustrate their capabilities and limitations.

Table 1.4 shows the ratings of each major evaluation technique with respect to the main classes of evaluation studies (design, procurement, capacity planning, and improvement).

REFERENCES

Entries marked with an asterisk (*) are referenced in the text.

[AC71] *ACM SIGOPS Workshops on System Performance Evaluation at Harvard Univ.*, ACM, New York, 1971.

[AG75] Agajanian, A. H., A bibliography on system performance evaluation, *Computer*, vol. 8, n. 11, pp. 63–74, Nov. 1975.

[AG76] Agajanian, A. H., A bibliography on system performance evaluation, *ACM SIGMETRICS Perf. Evaluat. Review*, vol. 5, n. 1, pp. 53–64, Jan. 1976.

[AN72] Anderson, H. A., Sargent, R. G., Bibliography 31: modelling, evaluation and performance measurement of time sharing computer systems, *Comput. Rev.*, vol. 13, n. 12, pp. 603–608, Dec. 1972.

[BA73] Balke, K. G., et al., Performance evaluation bibliography, *ACM SIGMETRICS Perf. Evaluat. Review*, vol. 2, n. 2, pp. 37–49, June 1973.

[BE72] Bell, T. E., et al., Framework and initial phases for computer performance improvement, *AFIPS Conf. Proc., FJCC*, pp. 1141–1154, 1972.

*[BE75] Benwell, N., *Benchmarking—Computer Evaluation and Measurement*, Hemisphere Publ. Corp., Washington, D.C., 1975.

*[BU76a] Buzen, J. P., Fundamental laws of computer system performance, *Proc. ACM-IFIP Int. Symposium on Computer Performance Modeling, Measurement and Evaluation,* pp. 200–210, Cambridge, Mass., March 1976.

*[BU76b] Buzen, J. P., Operational analysis: the key to the generation of performance prediction tools, *Proc. COMPCON 76 IEEE,* pp. 166–171, Washington, D.C., Sept. 1976.

[BU78] Buzen, J. P., Operational analysis: An alternative to stochastic modeling, in: *Performance of Computer Installations, Proc. ICPCI,* D. Ferrari, ed., pp. 175–194, North-Holland, Amsterdam, June 1978.

*[CA75] Carlson, G., Measuring response time of interactive terminals, *EDP Performance Review,* Aug. 1975.

*[DE78] Denning, P. J., Buzen, J. P., The operational analysis of queuing network models, *ACM Computing Surveys,* vol. 10, n. 3, pp. 225–261, Sept. 1978.

[DR73] Drummond, M. E., *Evaluation and Measurement Techniques for Digital Computer Systems,* Prentice-Hall, Englewood Cliffs, N.J., 1973.

*[FE78] Ferrari, D., *Computer Systems Performance Evaluation,* Prentice-Hall, Englewood Cliffs, N.J., 1978.

[FU75] Fuller, S. H., *Performance Evaluation, Introduction to Computer Architecture,* H. Stone, ed., Science Research Associates, Chicago, Chapter 11, 1975.

[GI77] Gilb, T., *Software Metrics,* Winthrop Publ., Inc., Cambridge, Mass., 1977.

*[HE75] Hellerman, H., Conroy, T. F., *Computer System Performance,* McGraw-Hill, New York, 1975.

[KE72] Kerner, H., Kuemmerle, K., Performance measures, definitions and metric, *Proc. 6th Princeton Conference on Information Sciences and Systems,* pp. 213–217, March 1972.

*[KL72] Kleinrock, L., Muntz, R. R., Hsu, J., Tight bounds on the average response time for time shared computer systems, *Proc. IFIP Congress 71,* Feisman, C. V. ed., pp. 124–133, North-Holland, Amsterdam, 1972.

[KO71] Kolence, K. W., A software view of measurement tools, *Datamation,* pp. 32–38, Jan. 1971.

*[KO76] Kolence, K. W., *The Meaning of Computer Measurement: An Introduction to Software Physics,* Institute for Software Engineering, Inc., Palo Alto, Calif., 1976.

*[K078] Kolence, K. W., Applications of software physics to capacity planning, in *Performance of Computer Installations, Proc. ICPCI,* D. Ferrari, ed., North-Holland, Amsterdam, June 1978.

[LU71] Lucas, H. C., Jr., Performance evaluation and monitoring, *ACM Computing Surveys,* vol. 3, n. 3, pp. 79–91, Sept. 1971.

[MA74] Madnick, S. E., Donovan, J. J., *Operating Systems,* McGraw-Hill, New York, 1974.

[MO82] Morris, M. F., Roth, P. F., *Computer performance evaluation,* Van Nostrand Reinhold Co., New York, 1982.

[OT76] Otto, R. W., Auerbach, M., A computer performance prediction model, *AFIPS Conf. Proc., NCC* vol. 45, pp. 451–455, 1976.

[RO76] Rosen, S., *Lectures on the Measurement and Evaluation of the Performance of Computing Systems,* Society for Industrial and Applied Mathematics, Philadelphia, 1976.

*[SE72] Sekino, A., Performance evaluation of multiprogrammed time-shared computer systems, *MIT Project MAC Report TR-103,* Cambridge, Mass., Sept. 1972.

[SE75] Second thoughts on standard measures of performance, *EDP Performance Review,* vol. 3, n. 5, May 1975.

*[SO75] Some thoughts on standard measures of performance, *EDP Performance Review,* vol. 3, n. 1, Jan. 1975.

*[SP72] Spiegel, R. M., *Theory and Problems of Statistics,* Schaum's Outline Series, McGraw-Hill, New York, 1972.

[ST74] Stimler, S., *Data Processing Systems: Their Performance, Evaluation, Measurement and Improvement,* Motivational Learning Programs, Inc., Trenton, N.J., 1974.

[SV76] Svobodova, L., *Computer Performance Measurement and Evaluation Methods: Analysis and Applications,* Elsevier, New York, 1976.

2

THE WORKLOAD

2.1 THE PROBLEM OF WORKLOAD CHARACTERIZATION

A computer system can be viewed as a set of hardware and software resources that are utilized in a time-variant fashion by the processing requests generated by the user community. During any given time interval, the user community submits its processing requests to the system by inputing sets of programs, data, and commands. All this input information is usually designated by the collective term of *workload*.

Every time the value of a system performance index is given, the workload under which that value was obtained must be reported or, at any rate, known, since performance cannot be expressed by quantities independent of the system's workload. Thus, no evaluation problem can be adequately solved if the workloads to be processed by the system are not specified.

Furthermore, performance comparisons among systems or configurations, such as those needed in tuning or design activities, are only meaningful if the workloads processed by the various systems being compared are the same (see Fig. 2.1). Otherwise, the differences between the performance indexes will reflect those between the workloads, as well as those between the systems, and it will be difficult or impossible to separate the respective contributions of these two factors.

Even a small variation in the instantaneous composition of the workload may cause perturbations that propagate far in the future, and these perturbations may appreciably alter resource utilizations, and hence system performance.

A simple example is the one in Fig. 1.20, which shows the variations of the mean weighted turnaround time and of the throughput in an MBRS system due to different arrival sequences of three programs A, B, and C. Another example, illustrated in Fig.

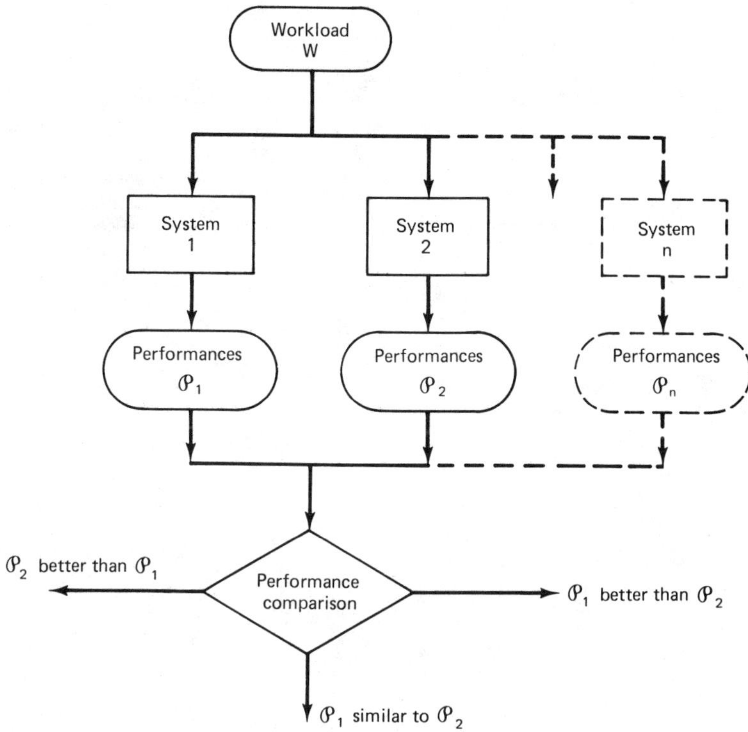

Figure 2.1 General scheme of performance comparisons among n systems. Depending on the context of the problem, systems 1, 2, . . . , n may represent different computer systems *(procurement),* the same system before and after various tuning interventions *(improvement)*, or versions of the same system corresponding to different technical solutions to a given problem *(design).*

2.2, presents the effects of a different factor, the processing mode (batch or interactive). In a batch environment, the arrival times of programs are not (or are only partially) influenced by the turnaround times of the programs just processed by the system, whereas in an interactive environment there is a very strict dependence of arrival times on response times. Thus, assuming that the commands A, B, C, D, E, F are input from two terminals (A, C, and E from terminal 1, and B, D, and F from terminal 2), and that all think times equal 0.5 time units, the timing diagrams in Fig. 2.2 show that the perturbations caused by a different order of execution (B before A) propagate up to time 4 in the batch case (Fig. 2.2b) and up to time 11 in the interactive case (Fig. 2.2d). We have assumed that programs A, B, C, D, E, F in the batch system and the corresponding commands in the interactive system require the same resources in the same amounts and have the same execution times. Thus, we conclude that the performance $\mathcal{P}$ of a system $\mathcal{S}$ can be evaluated only if the characteristics of the workload W processed by $\mathcal{S}$ are explicitly taken into account. Measurement and evaluation techniques for system component activities are discussed in later chapters. In this chapter, we cover the methods for describing a workload and for building workload models.

The relationships existing among $\mathcal{P}$, W, and $\mathcal{S}$ are quite complex. First, W is in

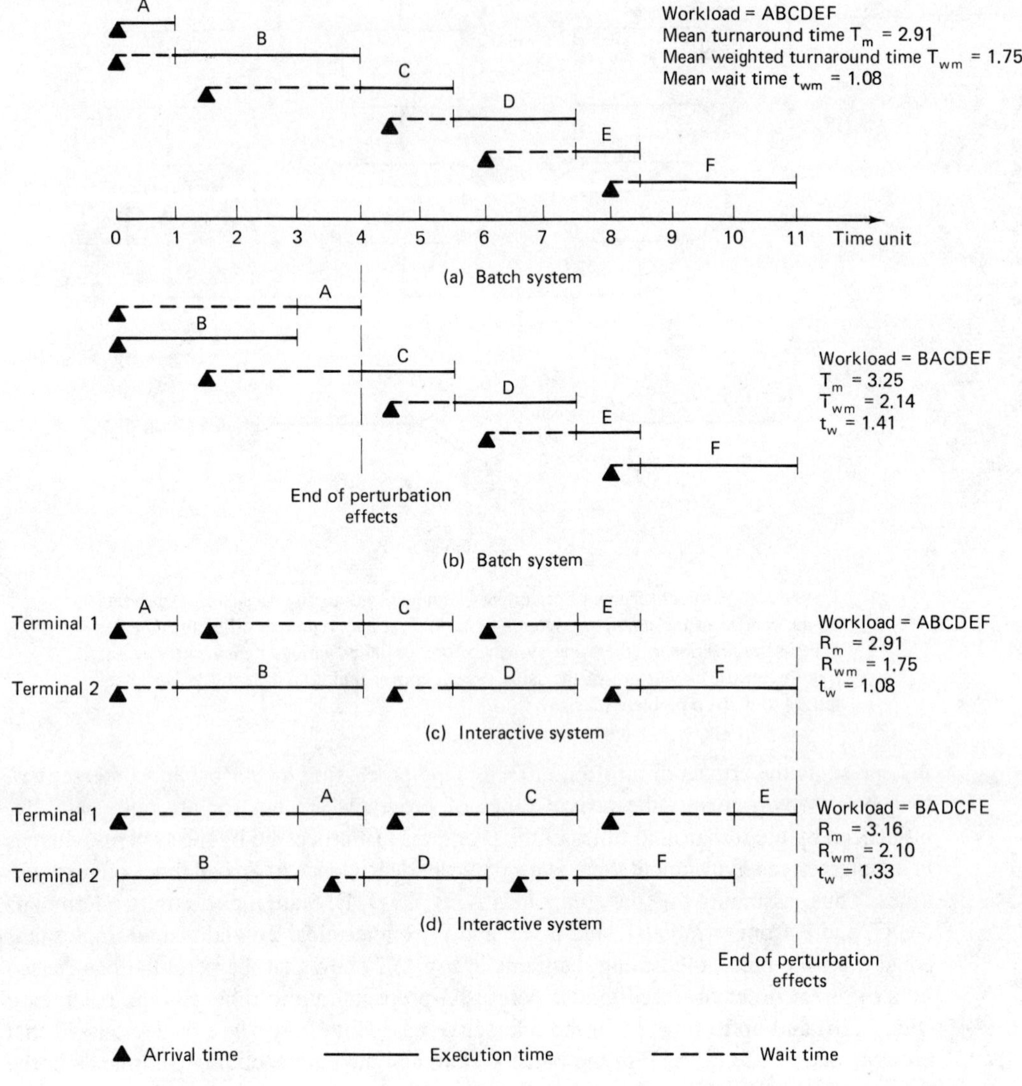

Figure 2.2 Effects of the perturbations caused in a uniprogramming system by the inversion of the order of execution of programs A and B in the batch-processing case (a and b) and in the interactive case (c and d).

general continuously fluctuating in time due to various causes. For instance, the execution time of a given program may vary considerably with the input data, with the allocation of its work files on secondary storage devices, with the position of a disk's arm when a new request arrives, with the angular position of the disk at that time, with the amount of contention existing for the various hardware and software components the program needs to access, and so on.

To these causes of variability, which may be considered as intrinsic to the programs in *W*, we must add those related to the organization of the installation and to the characteristics of the applications of the system being evaluated. Typical examples are the beginning or the termination of the testing phase of large software systems, or the periodic execution of payroll computations, inventory control packages, and other fixed-frequency applications.

Moreover, workloads are often influenced by feedback phenomena. Only the two more visible levels of feedback responsible for additional workload variations are shown in the block diagram in Fig. 2.3. The inner loop, called *level 2 feedback,* is the one implemented by the control algorithms of the operating system. For instance, the dynamic modification of priorities, the varying allocation of memory space to certain classes of programs, and the placement of work files on the devices with the smallest amount of contention are among the decisions that, because of their considerable influence on the efficiency of program execution, have a direct impact on the workload's composition.

The outer level of feedback in Fig. 2.3, designated as *level 1 feedback,* is that due to the influence of the system's performance and charging schemes on the behavior of the user community, and hence indirectly on the composition of the workload. For example, by establishing suitable charging policies, it is possible to persuade most users to have their heaviest programs processed during night shifts; also, by penalizing certain classes of batch programs with long turnaround times, some users may be lured into using interactive terminals.

The quantitative description of a workload's characteristics is commonly called *workload characterization.* A characterization is usually done in terms of workload parameters that can affect system behavior and are defined in a form suitable for a desired use. Thus, a workload is characterized correctly if, and only if, its result is a set of quantitative parameters selected according to the goals of the characterization operation.

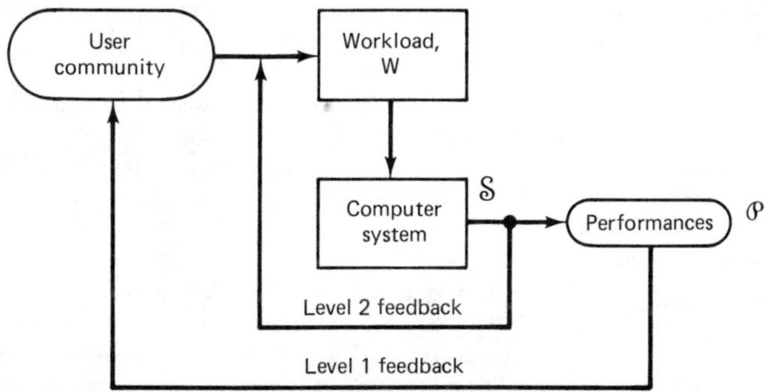

Figure 2.3 Mutual influences among the workload *W*, the system $\mathcal{S}$, and the performance $\mathcal{P}$. Two feedback levels are shown: the inner loop (level 2) and the outer loop (level 1).

The definition of these goals, that is, of the desired use of the characterization, is the first step of any performance evaluation study. Specifying the objectives will allow us to determine the parameters to be used and their representation. Thus, for instance, the analysis of resources that are overcommitted during short peak periods requires a characterization of the workload different from that appropriate for the prediction of the performance impact of adding a new application to the current workload.

Having established the objectives, the instruments to be used (analytic models, simulators, the real system, and so on) should be determined. At this point, it will be possible to specify the parameters needed and the form of their representation (single values, distributions, distribution descriptors, and so on).

As an example, Table 2.1 shows some of the parameters that may be used to characterize a workload. These parameters are subdivided into two groups depending on whether they refer to a basic component of a workload or to the whole workload.

No matter how it is implemented, a *test workload* is defined as the load processed by a system while a measurement experiment is being performed. In certain types of evaluation studies, the test workload can coincide with the workload actually processed by the system during the observation period being considered. However, as will be seen in more detail in Sec. 2.3, this type of test workload is not easily reproducible even if

TABLE 2.1 SOME PARAMETERS USED IN WORKLOAD CHARACTERIZATION

Parameter	*Description*
For Basic Workload Components	
CPU time	Total CPU time consumed by the program
I/O operations	Total number of I/O operations performed
Memory space	Memory space demanded by the program
Cards read	Total number of cards read in
Lines printed	Total number of lines printed out
External priority	Scheduling priority assigned by the user
Disk files	Total number of disk files (permanent and/or temporary) used
Tapes	Total number of tape units required
Instruction mix	Frequencies of execution of various instruction types
Mean CPU burst	Mean CPU time between two consecutive I/O operations
Mean I/O burst	Mean time required for the execution of an I/O operation
Branching probabilities	Probabilities of accessing the various devices at the end of a CPU burst
For The Whole Workload	
Arrival rate	Inverse of the mean time between the arrivals of two successive requests for the resource being considered
Interarrival time distribution	Distributions of the times between the arrivals of two consecutive requests for the resource being considered
For Interactive Workloads	
Number of users	Number of users simultaneously connected
User think time	Time between the arrival of a system message at a terminal and the beginning of the next command input by the user
Request intensity	Ratio between the mean response time and the mean think time
Traffic intensity	Ratio between the mean service time per interaction and the mean command interarrival time

the same set of programs is resubmitted to the same system. Note that the reproducibility of a component loading pattern is an essential condition for the valid comparison of results obtained in different experiments on various versions of a system. Furthermore, in many studies, among which are the predictive ones, the workload is known only *hypothetically,* and a test workload is obtained by extrapolating the parameters of the current workload and factoring in all available information about the installation's future.

As will be seen in the sequel, therefore, most test workloads are actually *workload models.* These models, besides being accurate representations of the workload to be modeled, will have to be, for practical and economical reasons, *compact;* that is, their resource demands will have to be much smaller than those of the workload to be modeled.

The duration of the time period during which the system or some of its components, the workload, and the performance indexes are to be observed varies with the characteristics of the workload and of the system and with the objectives of the study. We shall call *measurement session* the interval of minimum duration in which a measurement experiment will have to be performed. A measurement session need not be continuous, but may consist of two or more distinct subsessions. If, for example, a system is to be studied during the periods within a day when the mean response time to a certain class of commands is greater than 2.5 s, it may be convenient to collect measurements during two subsessions (see session 1 in Fig. 2.4). If, on the other hand, the system is to be observed when the mean response time exceeds 2 s, a single measurement session should be held (session 2 in Fig. 2.4).

An accurate analysis of the objectives of a study often allows adequate durations and start times to be defined for the measurement sessions required. Typical examples of interesting measurement sessions are the daily peak periods, the periods during which a program with special requirements (for example, minimum response time) is processed,

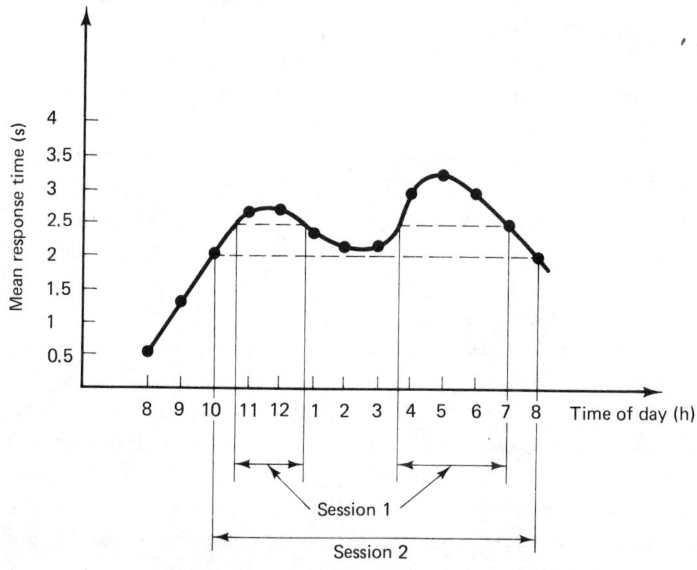

Figure 2.4 Measurement session composed of one or more measurement intervals.

one shift, weekly, monthly, yearly peak periods, periods of given duration needed to make meaningful predictions, and so on.

The minimum duration of a measurement session may even be established, after having specified the accuracy desired, by applying simple statistical techniques based on the central limit theorem if the observations to be collected are statistically independent (see Sec. 3.3.1). If a sampling monitor (see Sec. 5.2.1) is used, this condition is very often satisfied, whereas autocorrelations among observations are not usually negligible with event-driven monitors. Methods that can be applied in this case (for example, those of subsamples and of the sampling window) will be discussed later in this chapter.

2.2 THE REPRESENTATIVENESS OF A WORKLOAD MODEL

In the previous section, we have emphasized the need for supplementing every statement regarding the values of a system's performance indexes with a description of the system's workload. As a result, workload characterization is fundamentally important in all performance evaluation problems and is indispensable for designing useful workload models. The accuracy of a workload model is clearly an essential characteristic for the credibility, and hence for the practical usefulness, of any model. When a model is used to represent the real workload of a system, its accuracy is often referred to as the model's *representativeness*.

A workload may be modeled at various levels corresponding to the levels at which a computer system can be described. Thus, there is no single criterion for evaluating the representativeness of a model; depending on the modeling level adopted and on the objectives of the study, a suitable definition of representativeness and a consistent criterion for its evaluation will have to be selected.

Three of the most important modeling levels for a computer system, and hence for a workload, are the *physical,* the *virtual,* and the *functional* levels [FE79], [FE81b].

At the *physical level* (level 1), a workload model is based on the consumptions or consumption rates of the system's hardware and software resources. For example, each basic workload component may be characterized by the CPU time consumed or by the number of instructions executed, by the main memory and secondary storage space required, by the total I/O time consumed, by the number of work files used, by the I/O channel time and disk time consumed, and so on. This level of modeling, which is based on a resource-oriented characterization, is heavily system dependent and can therefore be meaningfully used in all performance studies that do not substantially alter the existing system's configuration. In particular, it is useful when the effectiveness of tuning actions is to be evaluated or when the residual capacity of a system is to be determined.

The majority of the parameters used at this modeling level are directly collected by the logging routines present in practically every operating system. Often, the values of the missing parameters can be devised from the measurements gathered by these routines. This is one of the main reasons why resource-oriented models are so popular.

At the *virtual level* (level 2), the logical resources of the system are considered. For instance, each basic component may be characterized by the number of higher-level language statements of each type, the number of accesses to each file or data base, the number and type of interactive commands, the virtual memory space required, and so on. Because of their parameter type, level 2 models are closer to the programmer's viewpoint and less system dependent than level 1 models. They are suitable for those evaluation studies in which modifications to the system's configuration would cause some of the level 1 parameters to become meaningless. This is, for example, the case of improvement studies in which the performance of a system after a new disk drive has been added or the main memory has been expanded is to be compared with the one the system produced before the modifications were made. Level 2 parameters are harder to obtain than those used at level 1, and special instruments are needed to measure some of them.

At the *functional level* (level 3), a workload is characterized by the applications it consists of. In the model there must appear programs that perform the same functions as in the original workload (for example, payroll computation, checking account updating, inventory control, sorting, compilation, and so on).

A workload's functions should be described in a system-independent fashion. Level 3 models are required in procurement studies, where different systems are to be compared or where the differences in the configurations being considered make some of the level 2 parameters meaningless.

Table 2.2 summarizes our discussion of the three modeling levels.

The accuracy (or representativeness) of a workload model is defined in different ways depending on the modeling level adopted. Given a workload W, some of the criteria that may be (and indeed have been) chosen to evaluate the representativeness of a model W' can be easily derived from the following definitions:

1. W' is a perfectly representative model of W if it demands the same physical resources in the same proportions as W.
2. W' is a perfectly representative model of W if it demands the same physical resources at the same rates as W.
3. W' is a perfectly representative model of W if it performs the same functions in the same proportions as W.

TABLE 2.2 WORKLOAD CHARACTERIZATION LEVELS

Level	*Main characteristics of model*	*Major model applications*
Physical	Physical-resource oriented System dependent Relatively easy to construct (measurement data usually available)	Tuning Capacity planning (determining the residual capacity of the system) Design
Virtual	Logical-resource oriented Less system dependent Closer to programmer's viewpoint	Upgrading Capacity planning Design
Functional	Application oriented System independent Difficult to design systematically	Competitive procurement Capacity planning Design

For instance, if the characterization of the workload is based on the total CPU time and the total number of I/O operations, criterion 1 states that the ratios between the values of these two parameters in W and in W' must be the same. Criterion 2, on the other hand, specifies that the mean durations of CPU *bursts* and I/O *bursts* in W must be equal to those in W'. According to criterion 3, if the workload to be modeled consists of 400 h of compilations, 250 h of test runs, 700 h of administrative data processing, and 300 h of scientific computations, W' will have to consist of, say, 20 min of compilations, 12.5 min of test runs, 35 min of administrative data processing, and 15 min of scientific computations. The validity of these criteria is directly related to the use to be made of the workload model W'.

Since a workload model is normally used for performance evaluation purposes, it seems obvious to use, for the characterization on which it is based, parameters whose relationships with performance are completely known. The models that satisfy one of the preceding criteria for representativeness may be based on parameters having unknown relationships with the performance indexes of interest.

If, for instance, we are interested in the turnaround times and in the throughput of a batch-processing system, the impact of such parameters as the mean program CPU time, the mean number of I/O operations, the mean number of cards read, and so on, on the values of these indexes is not known and quite difficult to determine.

Furthermore, the dynamic aspects of the workload are usually ignored. No attempt is made to reproduce the program mixes and their evolution in time. The workload is considered as an unordered set of programs. Criterion 2 permits the evaluation of certain dynamic aspects that are totally ignored by criterion 1. For instance, the calculation of the mean CPU burst duration requires that more dynamic information about a program's behavior be collected than that of the total CPU time consumed by the program.

A criterion for evaluating model representativeness that avoids some of the shortcomings we have just discussed is the following *performance-oriented criterion:*

4. W' is a perfectly representative model of W if it produces the same values of performance indexes $\mathcal{P}$ as W when running on the same system $\mathcal{S}$.

As for the preceding criteria, the distance between the criterion-related parameter values for W' and those for W may be taken as a measure of the model's accuracy. In Sec. 2.2.1 some examples of model representativeness evaluation will be discussed.

The use of criterion 4 allows one to evaluate the validity of a model based also on the effects it causes on the system (that is, the values of performance indexes) and not only on the possible causes (that is, the values of parameters not directly related to performance). Unfortunately, even this criterion produces system-dependent models. The values $\mathcal{P}_1$ of performance indexes that W produces in a system $\mathcal{S}_1$ must be very close to the values $\mathcal{P}'_1$ obtained by running W' on the same system $\mathcal{S}_1$. If W and W' are executed on a new system $\mathcal{S}_2$ (which may even be a different version or configuration of $\mathcal{S}_1$), there is no guarantee that they will still be acceptably close to each other.

The *compactness* of a workload model, that is, the factor by which a model's execution time is reduced with respect to that required by the original workload to be modeled, is evaluated according to the representativeness criterion adopted. The implementation of compact workload models satisfying a criterion like 1 or 2 is relatively straightforward, since it just consists of proportionally reducing the number of programs within each of the homogeneous groups into which the original workload has been partitioned, or of applying similar procedures to be described in the following sections.

Obtaining a compact model having the same functional characteristics as the original workload according to criterion 3 is not as simple. It is indeed generally unclear what "proportional representation of the various applications" really means. In some cases, this effect can be achieved by reducing the amount of the input data to be processed by an application program; in other cases, the size of the program is to be reduced; sometimes, the input data will have to be purposely chosen; at other times, an effective reduction will have to be obtained by applying all these methods in a suitable mixture. Furthermore, unwanted system dependencies may be introduced into the model when selecting a quantitative criterion for proportional representation, since functional characterizations are qualitative in nature, and it is natural to use resource-oriented quantities (for example, the CPU times consumed by the various applications) as common measures for the reduction factors.

A performance-oriented approach can generally produce models that satisfy reasonable compactness requirements. An advantage of these models is that program mixes and their effects on system performance are implicitly and automatically taken into account by the method used for their construction. However, the actual mixes present in the model and their dynamics certainly have a nonnegligible impact on the accuracy of the model when this is used to drive a modified system. Thus, even with a performance-oriented approach, realism in the reproduction of mixes and of mix dynamics is an important requirement.

In summary, there is no *absolute* and *unique criterion* for building and evaluating workload models: the characterization level and the characterizing parameters will have to be selected according to the objectives of the study for which the modeling effort is undertaken (see Fig. 2.5). It should be noted, however, that in general the criteria discussed, and others that may be similarly devised, are not mutually exclusive. The adoption of one criterion does not usually prevent a modeler from combining it with another criterion based on a different level of characterization. For example, criteria 1 and 3, or criteria 4 and 3, can be easily combined.

When a predictive study is to be performed, a particularly useful component for the construction of workload models is the *natural forecast unit* or *NFU* [KO76]. By analyzing the workload at the functional level, we identify the NFUs for each important application, that is, the application-oriented variables that are directly correlated to the amounts of resources consumed by each application. For instance, a convenient NFU for an inventory maintenance application is the number of inventory transactions, that for a payroll application is the number of employees on the payroll, and that for order processing is the number of orders to be processed. A forecast of the future workload will be obtained by determining the resource consumptions corresponding to each NFU of the application being considered and multiplying them by the predicted future number of NFUs in that application. Clearly, this procedure is based on the assumption that the amounts of resources consumed by an application are proportional to the number of NFUs.

Also, this type of characterization is system dependent, since the resources whose consumptions per NFU are to be determined are those of the current system. However, by applying the fundamentals of *software physics* [KO76], we can express the resource

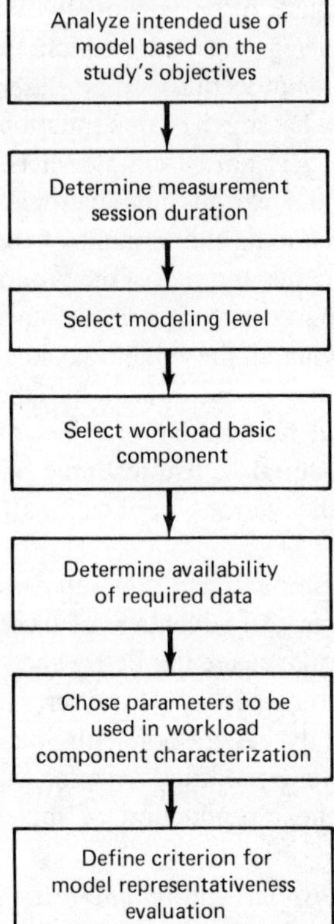
Analyze intended use of model based on the study's objectives
Determine measurement session duration
Select modeling level
Select workload basic component
Determine availability of required data
Chose parameters to be used in workload component characterization
Define criterion for model representativeness evaluation

Figure 2.5 Main steps of workload model formulation (the initial phase of workload model design procedures).

consumptions of an NFU in terms of *software work,* which is a more system-independent quantity.

In Sec. 2.6 we shall describe how this and other techniques can be used to forecast the workload in capacity planning problems. The purpose of the next section is to show by an example that the representativeness of a model varies with the objectives of the evaluation study.

2.2.1 Example of Model Representativeness Evaluation

An analysis of the objectives of the study to be performed has suggested the adoption of a resource-oriented characterization for the workload and the parameters to be selected for modeling each workload basic component, that is, each program step.

By applying one of the workload model design techniques described in the sequel of this chapter, three classes of program steps have been identified; these classes contain 94 percent of all program steps in the workload. The remaining 6 percent consist of heterogeneous program steps, whose characteristics differ substantially from those of the three classes. Since these program steps are a small fraction of the total, they have been ignored in the analysis. Using two different techniques, two models (W' and W'') have been obtained. Table 2.3 shows the mean values of the parameters for each class in the

TABLE 2.3 MEAN VALUES OF THE PARAMETERS CHARACTERIZING THE REAL WORKLOAD W AND THE TWO MODELS W' AND W''

Parameter			Class 1	Class 2	Class 3	Range
For W						
CPU time (s)	1	t_{CPU}	80	60	5	0–190
Disk I/O operations	2	$n_{I/O}$	150	1200	40	30–1650
Real memory used (Kbytes)	3	mem.	40	90	20	8–180
Disk files used	4	no. files	2.5	4.1	1.8	0–6
Lines printed	5	no. lines	300	1100	50	30–2250
For W'						
CPU time	1	t_{CPU}	75	62	4	
Disk I/O operations	2	$n_{I/O}$	144	1220	51	
Real memory used	3	mem.	38	89	18	
Disk files used	4	no. files	2.2	4.2	2.0	
Lines printed	5	no. lines	220	1250	65	
For W''						
CPU time	1	t_{CPU}	71	64	9	
Disk I/O operations	2	$n_{I/O}$	146	1190	48	
Real memory used	3	mem.	40	86	18	
Disk files used	4	no. files	2.4	4.1	2.1	
Lines printed	5	no. lines	320	1180	48	
Number of program steps per class (% of the entire workload W): q_j			27%	31%	36%	

real workload W and in the models W' and W''. The minimum and maximum values of each parameter over all classes are also reported in the table.

For our representativeness criteria to be applicable, workload parameters must be measured in the same types of units and their ranges of values must be about the same; in other words, parameter values must be *scaled*. Some existing scaling methods, which account for the presence of outliers and try to reduce the distortion the outliers introduce in the scaled parameter space, will be examined in Sec. 2.4.3. For the current application, a linear scaling technique that reduces all parameter ranges to the interval (0, 1) has been chosen. Let v_j be the value of the jth parameter for a generic program step. If v_{ij} is the mean value of the jth parameter for the ith class of steps, its rescaled value $v_{ij}^{(s)}$ is given by

$$v_{ij}^{(s)} = \frac{v_{ij} - v_j^{\min}}{v_j^{\max} - v_j^{\min}} \tag{2.1}$$

where

$$v_j^{\min} = \min_{\text{all prog. steps}} v_j \quad \text{and} \quad v_j^{\max} = \max_{\text{all prog. steps}} v_j$$

In Table 2.4 we report the scaled mean values of the parameters of W, W', and W''.

We shall now see how a resource-oriented criterion can be used to evaluate models

TABLE 2.4 SCALED MEAN VALUES OF THE PARAMETERS OF *W*, *W'*, AND *W''*

Parameter		*Workload W*			*Model W'*			*Model W''*		
		Class 1	*Class 2*	*Class 3*	*Class 1*	*Class 2*	*Class 3*	*Class 1*	*Class 2*	*Class 3*
1	t_{CPU}	0.4210	0.3157	0.0263	0.3947	0.3263	0.0210	0.3736	0.3368	0.0473
2	$n_{I/O}$	0.0740	0.7222	0.0061	0.0703	0.7345	0.0129	0.0716	0.7160	0.0111
3	mem.	0.1860	0.4767	0.0697	0.1744	0.4709	0.0581	0.1860	0.4534	0.0581
4	no. files	0.4166	0.6833	0.3000	0.3666	0.7000	0.3333	0.4000	0.6833	0.3500
5	no. lines	0.1216	0.4819	0.0090	0.0855	0.5495	0.0157	0.1306	0.5180	0.0081

W' and W'' in contexts characterized by different objectives. First, the distance between the mean values of each model's parameters and those of the workload's parameters are to be computed. We have chosen to define the distance as the absolute value of the difference between two corresponding parameter values. The distances computed according to this definition, $|v'_{ij} - v_{ij}|$ and $|v''_{ij} - v_{ij}|$, respectively, are displayed in Table 2.5. If we denote by q_i the percentage of program steps belonging to the ith class ($q_1 = 27\%$, $q_2 = 31\%$, $q_3 = 36\%$) and by w_j the weight associated to the jth parameter, for model W' we compute

$$D' = \sum_{i=1}^{3} \left(q_i \sum_{j=1}^{5} w_j \, |v'_{ij} - v_{ij}| \right) \tag{2.2}$$

and for model W'' the analogous expression of D''. The model with the smaller value of D will be the more representative.

Function D is the sum, weighted twice, of the distances between the parameters of the model and those of the workload to be modeled. Weight q_i accounts for the number of elements in the ith class, whereas the w_j's allow us to assign to each parameter the relative importance it has within the context of each study. We shall now consider three distinct objectives.

Objective 1. The study is to evaluate disk I/O activity, with the purpose of tuning the disk subsystem, while the activity of the line printer is of little interest. The most important parameters for this study are $n_{I/O}$ and the *number of files;* the *number of lines printed* is the least important. Weights w_j are selected as follows: $w_1 = 1$, $w_2 = 2$, $w_3 = 1$, $w_4 = 2$, $w_5 = 0.5$ (note that the standard value of the w_j's is 1). From Eq. (2.2) and the entries of Table 2.5, we obtain $D' = 0.1137$ and $D'' = 0.0989$. Thus, with respect to objective 1, W'' is more representative than W'.

Objective 2. The study is intended to evaluate the residual capacity of the CPU; the printer's activity is not very important since the capacity of this component substantially exceeds service demands. The main parameter in this study is t_{CPU}, the *number of lines printed* is the least important, and all the other parameters have an intermediate and equal importance. The parameter weights are chosen as follows: $w_1 = 2$, $w_2 = 1$, w_3

TABLE 2.5 DISTANCES BETWEEN THE PARAMETERS OF MODELS W' AND W'' AND THOSE OF THE REAL WORKLOAD W (SEE TABLE 2.4)

		$\lvert v'_{ij} - v_{ij}\rvert$			$\lvert v''_{ij} - v_{ij}\rvert$		
Parameters		*Class 1*	*Class 2*	*Class 3*	*Class 1*	*Class 2*	*Class 3*
1	t_{CPU}	0.0263	0.0106	0.0053	0.0474	0.0211	0.0210
2	$n_{I/O}$	0.0037	0.0123	0.0068	0.0024	0.0062	0.0050
3	mem.	0.0116	0.0058	0.0116	0.0000	0.0233	0.0116
4	no. files	0.0500	0.0167	0.0333	0.0166	0.0000	0.0500
5	no. lines	0.0361	0.0676	0.0067	0.0090	0.0361	0.0009

$= 1$, $w_4 = 1$, $w_5 = 0.5$. From Eq. (2.2) and Table 2.5, we have $D' = 0.0881$ and $D'' = 0.0989$, and W' is found to be more representative of W than W''.

Objective 3. A comparative study of the improvements due to tuning actions on various system components (memory, CPU, I/O subsystems) is to be performed. All parameters are equally important since their corresponding components are expected to be tuned. Thus, $w_1, w_2, w_3, w_4, w_5 = 1$. Expression (2.2) and Table 2.5 yield $D' = 0.0924$ and $D'' = 0.0791$, thereby showing that W'' is more representative than W' with respect to this objective.

2.3 TEST WORKLOADS

A test workload, that is, the workload processed by a system while measurement data are being collected, can always be viewed as a model of the real workload. The term "model" obviously can be applied to those sets of programs that are designed and implemented for the purpose of artificially loading a system during controlled experiments, as well as to the inputs of analytic and simulation models of a system. However, the same term can also be used to describe the workload that is processed by a system in normal operation during a measurement session. This is indeed the case, since the measurement interval (or intervals) should be selected so that the workload processed during that time (or those times) is representative of the much less compact workload under which the system's performance is to be evaluated.

For example, the choice of some short peak periods for collecting measurement data is conceptually equivalent to the construction of a compact model of a workload processed by the system during all the peak periods of, say, a whole year.

Some motivations for using models of the real workload instead of employing this workload directly in performance evaluation problems have already been discussed in Sec. 2.1. The most important of those motivations are:

1. To satisfy the requirement of *experiment reproducibility,* which makes the comparisons between the same performance indexes meaningful; these comparisons are essential in many types of studies, for instance when the effectiveness of several tuning actions is to be evaluated.
2. To *reduce* substantially the duration of each measurement session with respect to the one that would be required to run the whole real workload.
3. To obtain a representation of the load that is *consistent* with its use (for example, simulator input, analytic model input, and so on).
4. To avoid the *privacy* and *security* problems that sometimes limit the use of real programs and data in performance evaluation studies.

The implementation of a workload model can be performed by various methods. Depending on the technique used, test workloads can be classified in the following categories [FE72]:

- Real test workloads
- Synthetic test workloads
- Artificial test workloads

A *real test workload* consists of all the original programs and data processed during a given time interval. Thus, this is the workload that the system processes during a measurement session.

A *synthetic test workload* may consist either of a subset of the basic components (programs, interactive commands, and so on) of the real workload or of a mixture of real workload components and purposely constructed components (synthetic programs, kernels, synthetic scripts, and so on). The former may be called *natural synthetic workloads* or *benchmarks,* the latter *hybrid synthetic workloads.*

A test workload implemented without making use of any real workload components is said to be an *artificial test workload.* Artificial test workload can be subdivided into *executable artificial models* and *nonexecutable artificial models.* The latter consist of the inputs to a simulation or analytic model of a system.

We shall only examine the most popular types of test workloads in some detail, and shall study the techniques that can be used for their design and implementation. In Fig. 2.6 we summarize the classification of test workloads just described and list some artificial workload types to be discussed in Sec. 2.3.3. The characteristics of real and synthetic test workloads will be commented on in Secs. 2.3.1 and 2.3.2, respectively.

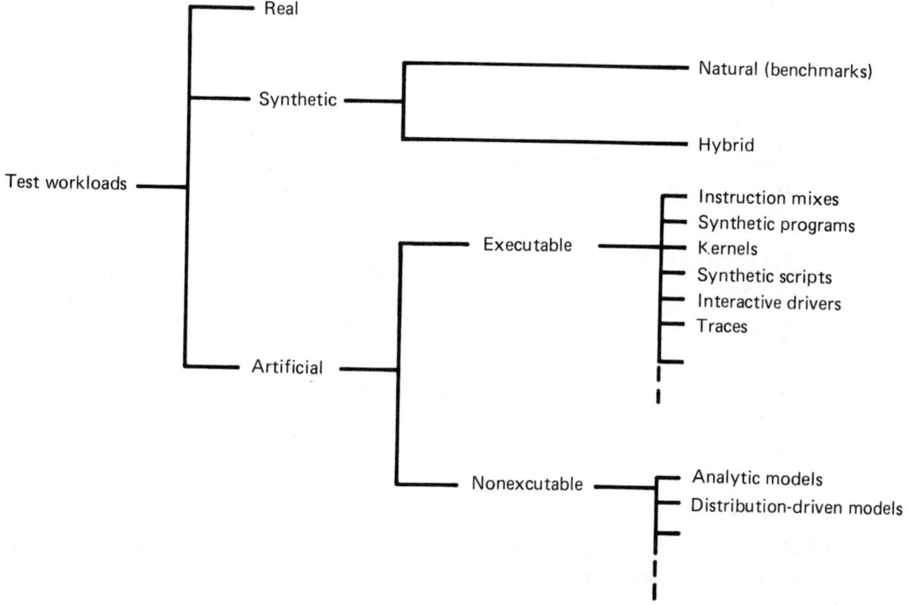

Figure 2.6 A classification of workload models.

2.3.1 Real Test Workloads

A test workload consisting of the load that is actually processed during a measurement session is, at least potentially, the most representative and the least expensive to implement. We have already recognized that such a load may be considered as a workload model in that its duration is usually much shorter than that of the workload to be represented. The only choice to be made by the modeler is that of the portion of real workload to be used in the measurement experiments, that is, of the instant at which a session is to start and of its duration.

A measurement session's duration is a function of the objectives of the experiment, of the nature of the applications, and of the processing mode (batch, interactive, real time). In some cases, the objectives of the study impose some implicit constraints on the starting instant and on the duration of a session. Thus, if the behavior of a system under a peak load condition on a given resource is to be analyzed, or if the performance impact of the activation of a teleprocessing network is to be determined, measurements will have to be collected only during the periods in which these phenomena are present. Assuming that peak loads occur most frequently between 10 A.M. and noon on working days, the test workload can be made to consist of only the loads processed in that time interval on some of the days during which measurements were collected.

On the other hand, when the study's objectives do not impose certain specific choices, the duration of a session can be chosen by resorting to statistical techniques. If the measured values (that is, the observations) are statistically independent, we can determine the minimum number of observations (the *sample size*) which guarantees that the estimate of, say, mean CPU or channel utilization can be affected by a given maximum error (the *confidence interval*) with a given minimum probability (the *confidence level*). This is the classical problem of determining the minimum sample size corresponding to a given accuracy of the results.

In practice, this problem can be easily solved by using diagrams like that shown in Fig. 3.10, which represents the maximum error we make when we replace the unknown mean with the known sample mean; this error is plotted as a function of the number of samples collected and of the confidence level selected.

The statistical independence assumption is almost always satisfied if sampling monitors are used to collect observations (see Sec. 3.3), provided that the observed variables are not synchronized in any way with the sampling process. The interested reader is urged to study Sec. 3.3.1, where this topic is discussed in detail and a practical example is examined.

A prerequisite assumption, which has not been explicitly mentioned so far, is that the sequence of observations of all variables be *stationary;* that is, their statistical distributions do not vary in time. This assumption is obviously not valid when we compare, for example, the frequency distribution of a workload or performance variable during one particular hour with that of the same variable over an entire day. It will be approximately valid, however, if we compare the former with the distributions observed during the same 1-hour period on the same day of the week in other weeks, or even on other days of the same week.

This assumption is often applied in tuning studies to verify, by means of real test workloads, the effectiveness of some system modifications without disrupting the normal

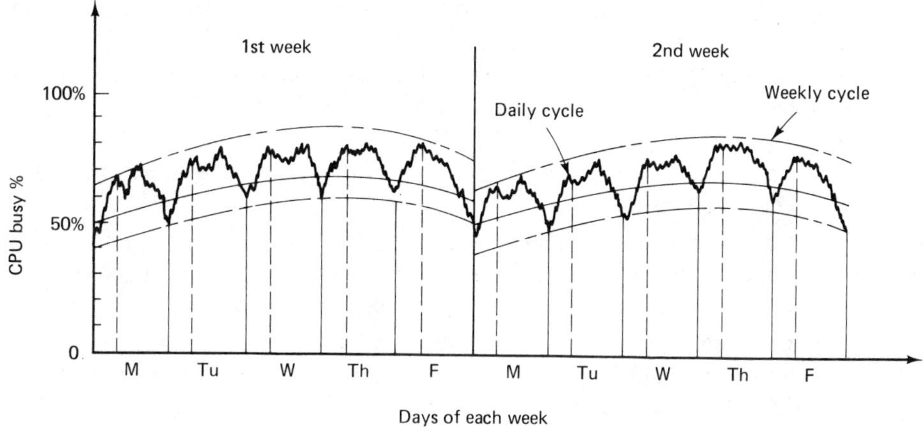

Figure 2.7 Mean hourly CPU utilization during the working days of two consecutive weeks versus time. The vertical broken lines correspond to the same hour of different days.

operation of the system. In any case, it is useful to verify with simple techniques the validity of this assumption, for instance, by estimating the variance of the variable's sample mean around the unknown true mean and calculating the confidence interval. Figure 2.7 shows a possible diagram of the mean hourly values of CPU utilization for a 2-week period. Two typical periods can be observed: a daily cycle and a weekly cycle. If we measure the system at the same times on consecutive days or, better yet, at the same times of the same days in consecutive weeks, the sequences of observations can be reasonably assumed to be much closer to being stationary. When several variables are to be observed, the condition of stationary behavior will have to be verified for each of them.

Table 2.6 displays the characteristics of the measurement sessions used to "imple-

TABLE 2.6 MAIN CHARACTERISTICS OF THE MEASUREMENT SESSIONS USED IN THE STUDIES BY HUNT ET AL. [HU71], MAMRAK AND AMER [MA77], AND SCHERR [SC67]

	[HU71]	*[MA77]*	*[SC67]*
Processing mode	Batch	Batch	Interactive
Measurement intervals			
Type	First shift	Weeks having the heaviest system usage during each academic quarter	Weekdays, 9 A.M. to 5 P.M.
Number	1	2	47
Range of duration	1 Shift	1 Week	1 h to 8 h
Average duration	1 Shift	1 Week	143 min
Measurement period	Various times during one year	Three academic quarters	More than one month
Workload size		50,800 programs	
Workload model size	1588 programs	750 programs	

ment" real test workloads in some published studies. The data missing in the table are those not explicitly given in the corresponding articles.

Among the main reasons that limit the use of real test workloads in experiments to be repeated with the same load conditions are:

1. *Lack of flexibility,* due to the nonmodifiability of the programs and of their resource consumptions.
2. Necessity of *reusing the original data* (files, data bases) when the real programs are to be reexecuted; all those data will therefore have to be copied to secondary memory, with considerable economic penalties and interference.
3. *Confidentiality* of certain programs and certain data, which may prohibit their duplication and force their replacement with programs or data having similar performance characteristics.
4. *Different hardware and software organizations* of different systems, or of different versions of the same system, which makes using a real test workload in procurement studies as well as in some tuning studies extremely difficult or impossible.

Table 2.13 in Sec. 2.3.3 contrasts the salient characteristics of real test workloads with those of artificial workload models.

2.3.2 Synthetic Test Workloads

A workload model consisting of programs extracted from the real workload to be modeled is said to be a *natural synthetic workload* or *benchmark*. Even though benchmarks can be used in all types of performance evaluation studies, their principal field of application is in upgrading and competitive procurement projects.

The techniques employed for the implementation of a benchmark are those that are used to build any other executable workload model (see Sec. 2.4). The objectives of the study heavily influence, even in this case, the choice of the most suitable techniques and criteria.

Some of the difficulties that the practical use of benchmarks often encounters have to do with certain conditions, external to the set of programs under consideration, that may have a remarkable impact on the performance measured on the various systems. For example:

1. *Execution priority:* each system deals with priorities in a different way; on certain systems, the priority assigned to a program by the scheduler is altered during execution, and this affects the sequence of execution, the job mix, and consequently the performance of the system.
2. *Maximum degree of multiprogramming:* this system parameter varies from system to system and influences quite substantially the performance indexes.
3. *Logging routines:* often these routines are the sources of the data used in evaluation studies; each system has its own routines, which sometimes assign similar names to variables with different meanings; before starting a study it would be advisable

to investigate the precise meanings of the variables measured by the logging routines and the errors by which they are affected.

4. *Parameters for operating system generation:* each operating system has several parameters whose values may be assigned during the generation phase; the values of these parameters affect the system's performance; this is the case also of other parameters that may be chosen by the installation or by the users, for example, the access methods, the channel–peripheral device connections, the options of a compiler, the locations in a storage hierarchy of operating system modules, files, and so on.

To reduce the difficulties that arise in designing benchmarking experiments, the prospective client usually specifies some rules to be followed by the vendor in running these experiments. The rules address those technical and organizational aspects that could impair the validity of the results. Thus, detailed descriptions of the client's objectives, of the operational rules for the execution of the benchmarks, of the printouts to be exhibited, and of the measurements to be collected during each run will accompany the benchmark.

An instructive example of a benchmark study is that described by Strauss [ST72]. The study was performed to determine, among five competing systems, the one having the lowest price–performance ratio for the desired applications. The benchmark consisted of 25 programs (6 COBOL, 13 FORTRAN, and 6 WATFIV programs) to be executed twice (run 1 and run 2) in different environmental conditions. The COBOL and FORTRAN programs consisted of compilations and executions. One COBOL program had been implemented to evaluate the diagnostic abilities of the compiler, and hence was never executed. The execution of one FORTRAN program had to be halted by the operator, since its function was to calculate the amount of CPU idle time.

The 25 programs in the benchmark were chosen from those of the real workload according to *proportionality* criteria (see Sec. 2.4.5), that is, trying to preserve the proportions in which resources were utilized by the various classes of programs in the real workload.

In Table 2.7 we show the utilizations of the CPU by the workload being considered (which consists of all program steps processed during one quarter and requiring more than 0.01 min of CPU time) and those by the benchmark. The value corresponding to FORTRAN executions in the benchmark column does not follow the proportionality criterion since, as stated, one FORTRAN program was an infinite loop. The languages were restricted to three for portability reasons. The operational rules are synthetically listed in Table 2.8. Similar tables prepared by the prospective client list in detail the types of results the client wants to have from each vendor.

Besides the standard accounting information and a description of the hardware and software configuration, the vendor must usually submit all output and console printouts, benchmark conversion information, and some data about the sensitivity of system performance to changes in the configuration or in some system variables like the degree of multiprogramming. From these data one may derive useful information about the efficiency of the compilers, both in terms of compilation times and in terms of the quality of the generated code, about the effectiveness of the resource management algorithms adopted by the operating system (priority assignment, queuing disciplines, resource al-

TABLE 2.7 CPU TIME DEMANDS BY THE VARIOUS CLASSES OF PROGRAM STEPS IN THE REAL WORKLOAD AND IN THE BENCHMARK [ST72]

	CPU time	
Classes of program steps	*Real work-load (min)*	*Benchmark (s)*
COBOL compilations	2,996	447.8
COBOL executions	657	92.8
FORTRAN compilations	1,459	82
FORTRAN executions	2,509	2,311.8
PL/1 compilations	1,406	
PL/1 executions	566	
Production programs (COBOL)	8,694	
Miscellaneous user programs	2,906	
Application packages	3,010	
Student compilers (WATFIV, PL/C)	1,563	210.9
Other (utilities, assembler, link editor, etc.)	3,000	
Total	28,766	3,063.3

location, management of the libraries, and so on), and about the stability of the proposed configuration (which can be assessed from sensitivity data).

If the evaluation study's objective is the selection of a software component, for example, the fastest sorting package, the same system should be used with the same load and the same input data. In this case, the benchmark may consist of various data files having different characteristics (that is, different key lengths, field lengths, initial orderings, and so on). Besides evaluating the performances and resource consumptions of the various packages, one will have to consider several other aspects, such as the reliability, documentation, and purchase and maintenance costs of the products.

Even in this case, as we already saw in Sec. 2.2.1 for the evaluation of a workload model's representativeness, in evaluating the results one will have to assign weights to the main characteristics of a package. These weights should express a subjective view

TABLE 2.8 SAMPLE OPERATIONAL RULES FOR TWO EXECUTIONS (RUN 1 AND RUN 2) OF A BENCHMARK [ST72]

1. Source code may not be optimized. All changes made to the source code must be documented.
2. Two basic runs (run 1 and run 2) are to be made.
3. In both runs 1 and 2:
   (a) All programs remain in given classes (if classes are defined).
   (b) The degree of multiprogramming is to be less than 5.
   (c) The given input ordering of programs cannot be modified.
   (d) All programs are to be assigned equal external priority.
4. Terminate benchmark run when all programs, except program 7, are complete.
5. For run 1, start execution after all programs have been read in; record read in, execution and print elapsed times.
6. For run 2, start execution as soon as possible; record total elapsed time.
7. Make other optimizing runs if desired, and report all differences with respect to the preceding rules.

of the relative importances of the various features of each package in the context in which the package will have to run. For instance, if a program for the management of source libraries is to be selected for a system with a relatively small secondary storage space, the compression algorithm for the source code is definitely more important than the ease of use of the commands or than the efficiency of the various levels of data protection.

When an interactive system is to be evaluated, an *interactive workload* model may be implemented starting from a set of scenarios. A *scenario* is a description, written in a natural language, of the functions performed by a user command stream. The description of an interactive workload at the functional level permits, to at least some extent, the implementation of a system-independent workload (see Sec. 2.2), which is an important property in those types of studies that, like procurement, involve several systems.

The criteria that may be used to identify the meaningful scenarios in an interactive workload are similar to those applied to batch workloads. However, since in the phase we are discussing only a description of the functions performed during a number of interactive sessions is needed, a considerable amount of help may come from the users, who are certainly more familiar with the functions than with the resource consumptions of their commands. Similar remarks apply also to functional models of batch workloads. The length of a scenario must be kept within reasonable bounds because of its direct influence on the cost of running the benchmark. Figure 2.8 displays a sample scenario described in a functional language.

Each system-independent scenario, in order to be executed, must be translated into a system-dependent stream of commands called *script*. A script is a sequence of commands sent from a terminal and of the think times that are to elapse between any two consecutive commands in the stream. Two descriptions of the same scenario at two different functional levels, and the corresponding script for a Honeywell Series DPS8 system, are shown in Figs. 2.9a, b, and c, respectively. The scenario can be divided into five parts. During the first, some editing operations are performed on program FIRST, which is stored in a preexisting file. These operations entail replacing the character strings A(12) and C(5)

---

1. Log onto the system.
2. Copy the resident file FORPROG (a source FORTRAN program) to file PROG1.
3. Edit file PROG1, adding a new subroutine (25 FORTRAN statements).
4. Renumber the statements of the program.
5. Compile the program in file PROG1.
6. Edit file PROG1, correcting a syntax error by replacing line 520 with: A(2) = B(3) * C(4) ** 4
7. Edit file PROG1, correcting a syntax error by replacing line 560 with: DO 28 J1 = 1,25
8. Compile the program in file PROG1 and store the object code in file PROG11.
9. Execute the program in file PROG11.
10. Permanently store the source program in file PROG1 under the name of the original version: FORPROG
11. Print out the text of program FORPROG.
12. Delete file PROG1.
13. Log out.

Think times for all user commands are 9s except that of command 10, which is 15s.

Figure 2.8 Sample functional scenario for the construction of an interactive benchmark.

	(a)	(b)	(c)
1	Edit program FIRST Write edited program to file PROV1A Execute PROV1A in batch mode	Read program file FIRST Replace A(12) with A(13) Replace C(5) with C1(5) Write to file PROV1A Append PROV1A to batch input queues	"OLD FIRST,R" "-RVS:/A(12)/;*:/A(13)/" "-RVS:/C(5)/;*:/C1(5)/" "SAVE PROV1A" "JRN PROV1A"
2	Edit program ONE Execute ONE interactively	Read program file ONE Replace END WORK with END PART1 Compile ONE and execute interactively	"OLD ONE,R" "-RVS:/END WORK/:/END PART 1/" "FRN *"
3	Append program SECOND to PROV1A Edit resulting program Write resulting program to file PROV2A Execute PROV2A in batch mode	Append program SECON to PROV1A Replace A(8) + B with A(8) − B Replace D(25) with D(28) Print statements containing the symbol $ Print statements 100 to 200 Print statements 1000 to 1100 Print last statement Delete statements 8370 to 8500 Delete statements 8990 to 12110 Write to file PROV2A Append PROV2A to batch input queues	"OLD PROV1A,R;SECON,R" "SEQU" "-RVS:/A(8)+B/;*:/A(8)-B/" "-RVS:/D(25)/;*:/D(28)/" "-PS:/$/;*" "LIST 100-200" "LIST 1000-1100" "LISTL" "DELE 8370-8500" "DELE 8990-12110" "SAVE PROV2A" "JRN PROV2A"
4	Execute ONE interactively	Read file ONE Compile ONE and execute interactively	"OLD ONE,R" "FRN *"
5	Delete work files PROV1A and PROV2A	Delete file PROV1A Delete file PROV2A	"PURGE PROV1A" "PURGE PROV2A"

Figure 2.9 (a) and (b) Description of a scenario at two different functional levels; (c) the corresponding script implemented for a Honeywell Series DPS8 system.

with A(13) and C1(5), respectively. Under its new name, PROV1A, the program is then submitted to the system for batch mode execution.

The second part consists of replacing string END WORK with END PAR1 in program ONE and interactively executing it. Some subroutines stored in file SECON are added in the third part to program PROV1A. Some substitutions are then made, some statements are printed out, and some groups of statements are deleted. The new program is called PROV2A and is submitted to the system for batch execution.

During the fourth part of the scenario, program ONE is executed interactively in its original version (that is, without the changes made in the second part). Finally, the two work files created in the previous parts are deleted in the fifth phase. Globally, the scenario specifies the execution of four programs, two in batch mode and two in interactive mode. All think times are assumed to equal 10 s.

A *natural synthetic workload* for an interactive system, that is, an *interactive benchmark,* is a test workload consisting of scripts extracted from a real workload. When there are reasons (for example, privacy, security, compatibility problems) that make using real programs in a test workload impossible, these programs can be replaced with *synthetic programs* or with *kernels*.

A synthetic program does not perform any useful work, but consumes amounts of system resources that are functions of the values of its *control parameters*. These parameter values are chosen by the user of the program; they usually determine such resource demands as the total CPU time, the number of I/O operations, the amount of memory space required, the number of cards to be read or punched, the number of lines to be printed, the number of files to be accessed, and so on.

One of the most important characteristics of synthetic programs is their flexibility, which allows them to simulate a wide spectrum of real programs from the viewpoint of resource consumptions. By means of nested loops, one can simulate the CPU–I/O cycles of a real program by specifying the number of instructions to be executed by the CPU and by controlling the number of I/O operations performed.

Synthetic programs with different structures can be built for the simulation of different types of applications. An example of a synthetic program for commercial applications is the one implemented by Buchholz in PL/1 [BU69] and later converted into FORTRAN [MA71]. As shown in Fig. 2.10, the program creates a master file and updates it with the records of a detail file. A report file, containing the documentation of the operations performed, is also created during the updating of the master file. The record to be updated is determined by a sequential search. All files are sequential, and the operations performed on the records to be updated require an amount of CPU time that can be modified by changing one of the program's parameters. There are three control parameters, which set the values of (1) the number of master file records to be read, (2) the number of detail records to be processed, and (3) the number of executions of the compute loop every time this loop is entered.

Synthetic programs have been used for a number of years in the implementation of both synthetic and artificial workload models (see for example [WO71], [KE73], [SR74]). In some cases they are purposely built for the particular problem at hand, whereas in other cases preexisting synthetic programs are utilized, possibly with some modifications. For instance, Sreenivasan and Kleinman [SR74] used Buchholz's synthetic pro-

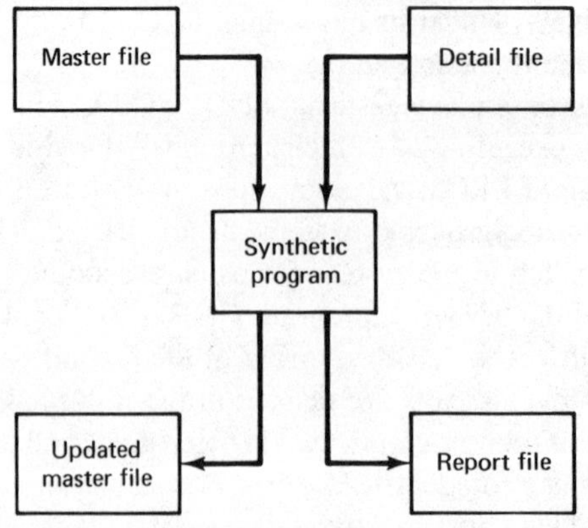

Figure 2.10 Files used by Buchholz's synthetic program.

gram after having added to it three more parameters to control the number of times the file updating process is repeated, the I/O buffer size, and the record size.

For evaluation studies concerned with virtual memory systems, some synthetic programs whose referencing behavior can be parametrically controlled have been proposed [BA81a], [BA81b], [FE81c].

Sometimes, a synthetic program may contain two additional types of parameters besides those used for control purposes: *correction parameters* and *calibration parameters*. The former can be used to eliminate or reduce the unwanted distortions of some resource consumptions due to changes in control parameters, which, ideally, should influence only other consumptions. For example, every time the number of I/O operations requested of a program is modified, even its CPU time demand changes; this time will therefore have to be corrected so as to obtain the value of CPU time specified by the corresponding control parameter.

Unlike correction parameters, which are built in and hence hard to modify, calibration parameters can be used for the fine tuning of a synthetic program during the *calibration phase*. This phase is necessary since a combination of control parameter values to which the desired resource consumptions will correspond can only rarely be found. After having determined the combination of input values corresponding to values of resource consumptions closest to the desired ones, the calibration parameters are modified to improve the accuracy of the synthetic program.

Kernels, unlike synthetic programs, are characterized by known, nonmodifiable resource consumptions. They may be either purposely built, *nonparametric programs* or programs extracted from some real workload in the past and preserved as building blocks for workload models. An example of a kernel is shown in Fig. 2.11. The two loops that determine the CPU time demand and the number of I/O operations, respectively, as well as the sizes of the three work files, can be easily modified. The resource consumptions corresponding to various combinations of the values of indexes J and I, which control the CPU and I/O loops, have been measured on a dedicated system and are reported in Table 2.9. By using this table it will be impossible to select the pair of values corresponding to consumptions closest to those desired. Kernels have a less general applicability than synthetic programs owing to their limited program modeling capabilities, but are immediately available since the calibration phase does not exist for them.

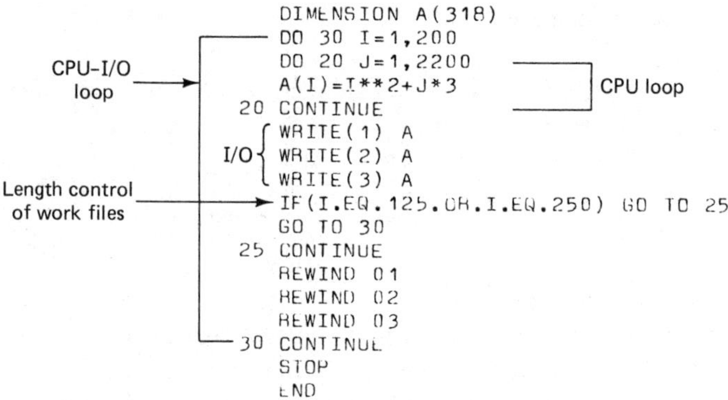

CPU–I/O loop
CPU loop
I/O
Length control of work files
DIMENSION A(318)
DO 30 I=1,200
DO 20 J=1,2200
A(I)=I**2+J*3
20 CONTINUE
WRITE(1) A
WRITE(2) A
WRITE(3) A
IF(I.EQ.125.OR.I.EQ.250) GO TO 25
GO TO 30
25 CONTINUE
REWIND 01
REWIND 02
REWIND 03
30 CONTINUE
STOP
END

Figure 2.11 A simple kernel. Index *I* modifies CPU time consumption and the number of I/O operations; index *J* influences the CPU time consumed before the execution of each I/O operation on a file; the IF statement controls the length of the work files.

In the realm of interactive systems, the equivalent of a synthetic program is a *synthetic script,* which is by no means easy to implement. Among the possible parameters for such a script, we shall mention the type-in rate, the think time, the number of times a certain sequence of commands is repeated in the script, and a few others.

A workload model consisting of a mix of programs drawn from the real workload and of synthetic programs or kernels is called *hybrid synthetic*. For an interactive system, a hybrid synthetic workload model consists of scripts from the real workload as well as of synthetic scripts.

TABLE 2.9 CPU TIMES VERSUS NUMBER OF I/O OPERATIONS FOR THE KERNEL IN FIG. 2.11

Number of CPU loops (index J) for each I/O operation	Number of I/O operations per file (index *I*)		
	100 *CPU time [s]*	*200* *CPU time [s]*	*300* *CPU time [s]*
10	0.8	1.3	1.7
100	0.9	1.5	2.1
200	1.0	1.7	2.4
1,000	2.0	3.7	5.4
1,600	2.7	5.1	7.5
2,000	3.2	6.0	8.9
2,600	3.9	7.5	10.9
3,000	4.4	8.5	12.6
4,000	5.6	11.0	16.3
5,000	6.9	13.4	19.9
6,000	8.1	15.8	23.5
9,000	11.7	23.0	34.4
10,000	12.9	25.4	37.9

2.3.3 Artificial Test Workloads

An artificial model of a given workload consists of basic components purposely devised to be used to load a real system or a model of it. Thus, no component of the workload to be modeled can be found in an artificial workload. This class of test loads has a large membership. In this section, only some of the most important types of artificial models will be examined.

Following the scheme in Fig. 2.6, we shall first describe some executable artificial test workloads, that is, loads in this class which may be directly executed on a real computer system. Later, we shall present some nonexecutable artificial workloads.

The analysis of the execution frequencies of the instructions in a workload provides useful information for its characterization. Any program having the same frequencies of instruction execution as another program (or set of programs) may be considered as an accurate model of that program with respect to the consumptions of CPU resources. A model of this type, an *instruction mix* model, may consist of a single program whose instruction execution frequencies coincide with those of the whole workload to be modeled.

Table 2.10 shows an example of instruction mix. The instructions in the machine's repertoire have been divided into eight classes. For each class, the table gives the frequency of execution f_i and the mean execution time $\bar{t}_i$. The mean execution time of the mix is

$$\bar{t} = \sum_{i=1}^{8} \bar{t}_i f_i \tag{2.3}$$

The value of $\bar{t}$ may be used to express the computational power of different CPUs processing the same mix. In some cases, depending on the objectives of the study and on the characteristics of the workload to be modeled, one may want to introduce some weights in Eq. (2.3) so as to obtain a mix representing more accurately some of the aspects of the problem at hand (see Table 2.10). For instance, in a scientific installation one may assign a higher weight to computational instructions than to I/O instructions, whereas the converse may be the case in a business data-processing center.

Instruction mixes were among the first test workloads used to evaluate the com-

TABLE 2.10 COMPUTING THE MEAN EXECUTION TIME OF AN INSTRUCTION MIX

Instructions	*Frequency of execution,* f_i	*Mean execution time per instruction,* t_i	*Weight*	*Mean weighted execution time*
1 Floating-point add/subtract	0.04	12	1	0.48
2 Floating-point multiply	0.08	8	1	0.64
3 Floating-point divide	0.05	8	1	0.40
4 Move (memory to memory)	0.10	3	1	0.30
5 Compare	0.14	3	1	0.42
6 Register to memory–memory to register	0.18	2	1	0.36
7 Conditional branch	0.20	2	1	0.40
8 Others	0.21	2	1	0.42
	1.00	Mean execution time		3.42

putational power of the CPU (see for example [RA64], [AR66], [WI74]). Of course, when two or more different CPU architectures are to be compared, instruction mixes are to be made as system independent as possible.

If it is not possible to derive directly an instruction mix from the actual workload, for example, when the system is still being designed or has not yet been installed (and there is no predecessor system that is being replaced), one may use mixes collected in installations supposed to have a workload similar in nature to that of the installation being considered. Among the various application-oriented mixes, the most widely known is the Gibson mix [GI70], which has been obtained from the workloads of a large number of scientific–technical installations.

The concept of instruction mix can be easily extended from the domain of machine languages to that of higher-level languages. In the latter case, it is more properly called a *statement mix*. Clearly, the load produced on a system by a statement mix depends not only on the architectural features of the CPU, but also on the language the mix refers to and on the characteristics of the compilers used.

Among the factors that influence the computational power of a CPU, some are memory related (cache memory size and management policies, cache and main memory bandwidth, access interferences, data path widths), others are related to instruction sequencing (instruction and operand prefetch, instruction buffers, CPU clock rate), and others yet have to do with address manipulation (effective address calculation, virtual-to-physical address translation). Since in an instruction mix all information related to the sequences of instructions that are executed is lost, mixes are inadequate load models for CPUs whose performance is heavily influenced by such sequences (for example, for pipelined CPUs).

A software instrument called CPCI-1 (CPU Power Calibration Instrument), developed by the Institute for Software Engineering [CP79] [FE81a] for the measurement of CPU power, makes use of instruction mixes. The power of a CPU is defined as the ratio between the number of bytes moved to or from the CPU and the time during which the CPU is executing instructions. Unlike instruction mixes, the CPCI-1 tool can measure the performance of a CPU taking into proper account some of the factors already listed (for example, cache hit ratios and concurrent I/O activity). The instrument incorporates three basic *kernels,* or sequences of machine instructions: a business-oriented arithmetic kernel, a sorting kernel, and a scientific kernel. By varying the kernel being executed, the experimenter can change the instruction mix. Since the number of kernel iterations within a given interval is measured by the tool, the value of CPU power can be easily computed. The instrument simulates concurrent I/O activities of various intensities by running another program that reads the data sets with a variety of block sizes. Figure 2.12 shows the listing in IBM assembler of the business-oriented arithmetic kernel, which includes branches, moves, compares, and packed decimal operations. The results obtained from the three instruction mixes produced by the three kernels for the computation of the basic powers (that is, those corresponding to zero I/O load) of various CPUs are displayed in Table 2.11.

Figure 2.13 shows the histogram of the instructions executed by the kernel in Fig. 2.12. The histogram has been obtained by using SAS, the Statistical Analysis System [SA79].

The instruction mixes we have dealt with so far are based on *dynamic frequencies,*

```
CPULOOP    EQU    *
           B      LOOPTEXT
LOOPID     DC     CL4'C001'
LOOPTEXT   EQU    *                          BEGIN LOOP
           XC     CAREA1,CAREA1
           MVC    CAREA1,CAREA2              MOVE
           CLC    CAREA1,CAREA2
           BNE    LOOPEND                    BRANCH IF NOT EQUAL
           LA     R6,1000
           CVD    R6,PACKAREA
           OI     PACKAREA+7,X'OF'
           AP     PACKAREA+4(4),PCON1        ADDITIONS
           AP     PACKAREA+4(4),PCON1
           AP     PACKAREA+4(4),PCON1
           LA     R6,1000                    CONVERT
           CVD    R6,PACKAREA
           OI     PACKAREA+7,X'OF'
           AP     PACKAREA+4(4),PCON1        ADDITIONS
           AP     PACKAREA+4(4),PCON1
           AP     PACKAREA+4(4),PCON1
           DP     PACKAREA,PCON2             DIVISION
           UNPK   UNPACK(16),PACKAREA(4)
           CLC    CAREA2,CAREA3
           BNE    LOOPEND                    BRANCH IF NOT EQUAL
CAREA1     DC     CL10' '
CAREA2     DC     CL10'*C001 TEST'
CAREA3     DC     CL10' '
PACKAREA   DS     1D
UNPACK     DS     CL16
PCON1      DC     PL4'10'
PCON2      DC     PL4'3'
LOOPEND    EQU    *                          END LOOP
```

Figure 2.12 Business-oriented kernel in IBM assembler [CP79].

TABLE 2.11 CPU POWERS (IN MBYTES TRANSFERRED TO OR FROM THE CPU PER SECOND) OBTAINED BY THE CPCI-1 INSTRUMENT WITH DIFFERENT INSTRUCTION MIXES AND ZERO I/O LOAD [CP79]

	CPU power		
CPU type	*Sorting kernel*	*Scientific kernel*	*Business arithmetic kernel*
AMDAHL V7	57.56	36.01	23.74
AMDAHL V6/2	46.27	29.56	18.34
AMDAHL V6/1	46.21	29.52	18.32
AMDAHL V5/2	26.17	23.89	13.71
AMDAHL V5/1	26.12	23.85	13.67
IBM 3033SE	54.46	30.23	16.25
IBM 3033	54.33	30.16	16.21
IBM 3032	25.24	13.94	10.57
IBM 3031	13.21	5.20	4.97

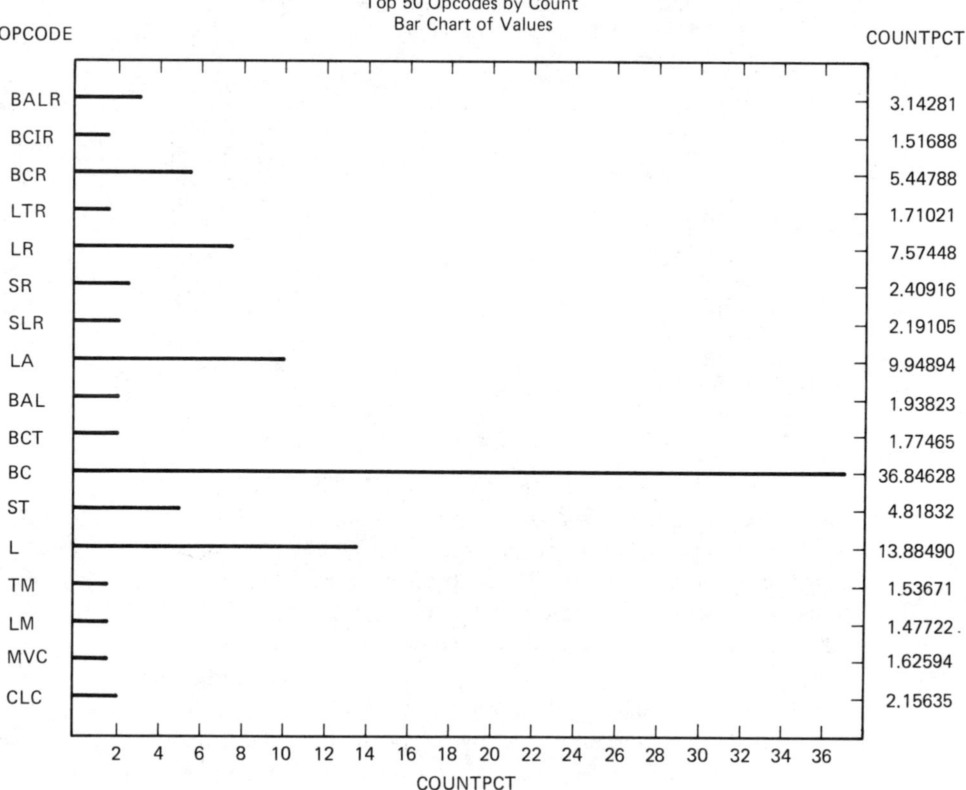

Figure 2.13 Histogram of instruction executions for the kernel in Fig. 2.12. The histogram has been obtained by SAS [SA79].

that is, on the frequencies of execution of the various instructions. One way in which these frequencies can be obtained is by adding counting instructions to the programs to be modeled. After running the modified programs, the frequencies of the various blocks of consecutively executed instructions are found in the memory locations which have been reserved for that purpose. These frequencies are generally quite different from those that can be derived from the listings of the programs, that is, from the *static frequencies*. *Static mixes* are used, for example, in compiler design. Table 2.12 displays the static and dynamic statement mixes obtained by Knuth [KN71] from 24 FORTRAN programs.

Executable artificial workload models, which, unlike instruction mixes, consist of a number of programs, are those that can be obtained by grouping together *synthetic programs* or *kernels*. Both types of programs have been defined in the preceding section; the techniques usable to construct sets of such programs that accurately represent the workload to be modeled will be described in the following sections. When these types of programs are used, additional problems arise, for instance, problems of design, implementation, and calibration. Similar considerations apply to *synthetic scripts* and to *kernel scripts* for an interactive system. To simulate the behavior of an interactive user, one often resorts to programs that generate "user commands" or "user messages." In general,

TABLE 2.12 DYNAMIC AND STATIC STATEMENT MIXES OBTAINED FROM 24 FORTRAN PROGRAMS BY KNUTH [KN71]

	Relative frequency f_i (%)	
Statements	*Dynamic*	*Static*
Assignment	67	51
IF	11	10
GO TO	9	9
CONTINUE	7	4
DO	3	9
CALL	3	5
RETURN	3	4
WRITE	1	5
READ	0	2
STOP	0	1

the alternative solution, that based on human users following synthetic scripts, is not practically viable owing to its high cost in terms of human and technical resources required and to the limited reproducibility of the experiments.

In principle, these programs intercept the messages directed to each user and submit the next message or command prescribed by the script they are following after an amount of time that accounts for the output, think, and type-in times also prescribed by the script.

If these programs run directly on the system being measured, they are called *internal drivers;* if they run on another system properly connected to the measured one, they are *external drivers*. It is important to observe that the latter do not appreciably influence with their presence the load they generate on the driven system, whereas the former perturb this load by superimposing on it the overhead they produce. Besides the problem of interference, the use of internal drivers also raises a representativeness problem mainly owing to their suppressing all terminal I/O operations. However, their cost is smaller than that of external drivers.

Both types of drivers have been employed in a large number of studies. Examples of internal driver usage can be found in [SA70] and [FO72]. An external driver consisting of a DEC PDP-8 minicomputer, which could simulate up to 12 interactive users and was connected to a GE 645 system running under the Multics operating system, is described in [GR69].

Another example of an external driver is the Communication User Emulation System for Traffic Analysis (CUESTA), implemented for Honeywell Systems. The CUESTA consists of a Honeywell Level 66 computer system controlling the communications with the driven system, which make use of 110- to 9600-baud asynchronous or synchronous lines. A schematic representation of the CUESTA and of the driven system is shown in Fig. 2.14. The scripts to be executed by the simulated terminals are predefined and stored into a "conversation map" by the external driver. The characteristics of the physical lines are defined in a module, and those of the terminals and of the network's topology are described in another module called GUIDE, which contains also the scripts to be executed. The CUESTA can store all logging data produced by an experiment on a dedicated disk for off-line data reduction.

The costs of designing and implementing complex workload models may be quite

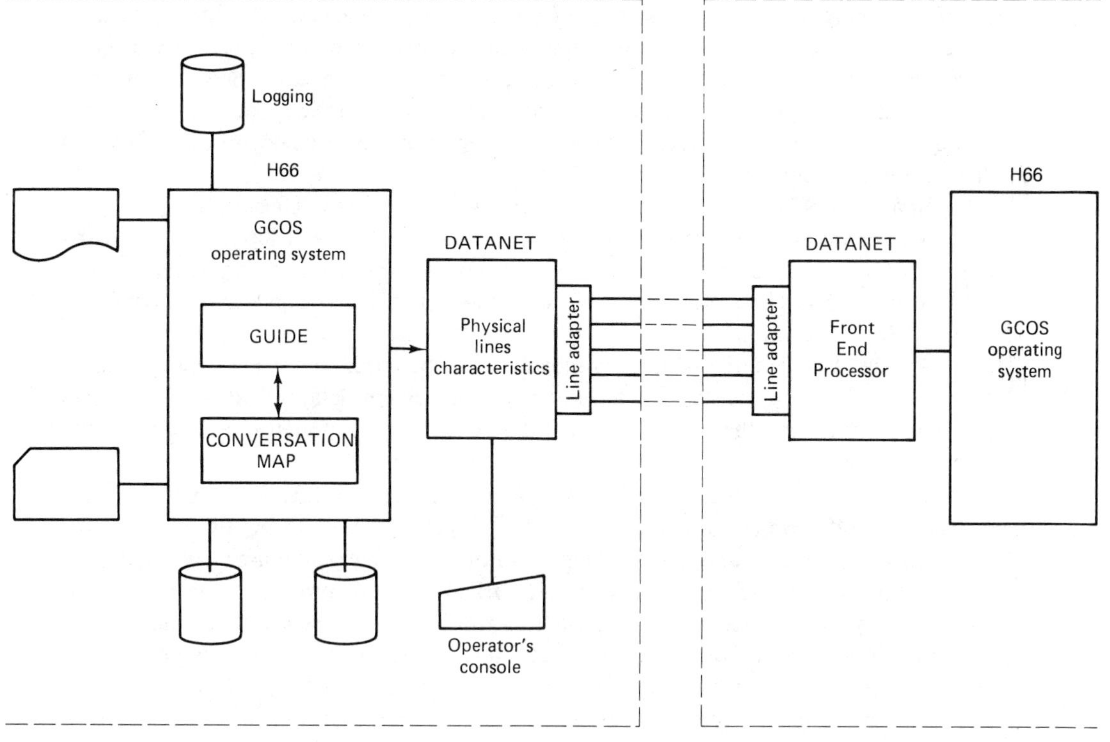

Figure 2.14 External driver consisting of a Honeywell Level 66 computer system that can drive series H66 or DPS systems.

high. In some studies, a simple measure of the magnitude of the load, such as that provided by the *terminal probe method,* may suffice. This method compares the magnitude of the current workload with that of an artificial workload composed of *n* copies of a command or a script called the *terminal probe*. The probe is sent from a terminal every time the load existing on the system is to be measured. Since the probe is always the same, the differences in the response times obtained in different applications of the probe will have to be attributed to the differences in the command and program mixes. To express the magnitude of the load, response times to the probe are also measured on the dedicated system while this is processing 1, 2, . . . , *n* copies of the probe itself. A load is equivalent to *x* probes if the probe response times with that load coincide with those obtained with *x* copies of the probe. The use of this method for load measurement is described by De Meis [DE69] and by Karush [KA69] [KA70], and an application of it to the comparative analysis of several systems is illustrated in [CA81].

When a modeling technique is to be adopted in an evaluation study, the test workload will have to be made compatible with that technique. Thus, for instance, if the system is modeled as a queuing network, the workload is to be described by such parameters as the distribution of program interarrival times, the number of visits of each program to each resource, the distribution of service times for each resource, and so on.

In these cases, the construction of a workload model seems simple, since it only entails assigning numerical values to the characteristic parameters. In reality, estimating these values correctly, without introducing serious errors in the results, is a very difficult endeavor. The representativeness of the workload models for queuing networks is often quite limited, mostly because of the assumptions that must be introduced in the model in order to make it mathematically tractable. Examples of analytic models of the workload can be found in Chapter 9.

In a *probabilistic* test workload, the parameters are usually considered as independent random variables whose distributions may be estimated from the frequency distributions measured in the real workload, when they are available, or approximated with analytic functions. The simulators using these models of the workload are called *distribution-driven simulators*.

Another type of artificial test workload that is often used to drive system simulators is the *trace*. A trace consists of a chronological sequence of data, recorded on a suitable medium, representing the events of certain types that have occurred in a system during a measurement session.

An *event* is a change of state in some component of a system. Examples of events include the initiation and the completion of a program, the allocation of a device, the execution of an instruction, and the logging in of a new interactive user. For models of batch workloads, interesting events are the arrival times of programs, the times their executions began, the CPU context switching times, the I/O request times, and so on. When modeling interactive workloads, traces have to include data concerning each command (for example, the CPU time and the number of I/O operations it demands) and terminal user behavior (typing-in time, think time). A simple example of a trace is shown in Fig. 3.7.

The representativeness of a trace is quite high. However, collecting a trace often causes so much overhead that the times and even the sequence of events recorded may be substantially perturbed by the presence of the tracing tool. A trace is generally expensive to collect and to use, since storing it requires a large amount of secondary memory space, and is quite inflexible. There is abundant literature on the applications of traces. For instance, traces have been utilized in [SH72] to identify an optimum scheduling policy for a CPU, and in [SM78] trace data taken from an operational data base system are used for the study of prefetching policies and the determination of optimal block sizes.

In Table 2.13 we present a synthetic comparison of the main characteristics of artificial workload models with those of real workload models.

2.4 WORKLOAD MODEL IMPLEMENTATION TECHNIQUES

As for the implementation of any model, the operations for implementing workload models can be grouped into three phases: *formulation, construction,* and *validation*. Workload models may consist of a *set of components* (programs, program steps, and so on) or they may be *monolithic* (instruction mixes, traces). The models of the first type are more popular and have been applied in most of the performance studies in the literature; those of the second type have limited application in some design or CPU selection studies. Because of the objectives of this book, in the sequel we shall analyze only techniques

TABLE 2.13 COMPARISON OF THE MAIN CHARACTERISTICS OF ARTIFICIAL WORKLOAD MODELS WITH THOSE OF REAL WORKLOAD MODELS

	Real workload models	*Artificial workload models*
Representativeness	Potentially high	Usually lower
Implementation cost	Low	Higher
Usage cost	Low (no disruption of service)	Higher
Flexibility	Low	High
Reproducibility	Low	High
Compactness	Low	High
System independence	Low	Usually higher
Experimental conditions	Uncontrolled	Controlled
Data collection and reduction costs	High	Lower
Studies for which suitable	Tuning	Design, tuning, procurement

for constructing workload models of the first type. It should be noted, however, that some of these techniques can be applied also to the implementation of models of the second type.

The main operations that are to be performed in implementing workload models are shown in Fig. 2.15. In that figure we may distinguish the decision-making path from the operational path. The *formulation phase* consists of decision-making paths only. The decisions that are to be made are influenced by the objectives of the study. The definition of the workload basic components, that is, the identification of the smallest level of detail that is to be modeled and of the set of parameters to be used for their description, is among the first operations to be performed. The *workload basic component* is the smallest unit of work that will be considered. As basic components, one may select the applications, programs, program steps, scripts, commands, source level instructions, machine instructions, and so on. Obviously, the higher the level of the basic component, the lower the amount of detail with which the workload is described. For example, if the program is selected as the basic component, users will be characterized only in terms of their global consumption of resources at the level of the programs, and the differences existing among programs in terms of the resource demands of individual program steps will not be taken into consideration. The *analysis of the intended use* of a model will allow us to define the basic component and therefore influence the selection of parameters to be used in its quantitative description.

Another factor that influences the choice of parameters is their *availability*. Very often in the implementation of workload models one uses the values of parameters recorded by the accounting routines of the system. These values are sometimes not available for the desired period; at other times they are incomplete or incorrect. For example, whereas in some types of systems one can easily obtain the number of I/O operations performed for each program step, in other types of systems this information is not recorded, but in its stead one may find the total I/O time, which includes also the I/O waiting time.

The parameters to be used to characterize the basic components are selected on the basis of the modeling level of detail, determined after studying the objectives and verifying their availability. If the model is constructed at the physical resource level, one can use such parameters as CPU time, memory space demand, number of I/O operations, number

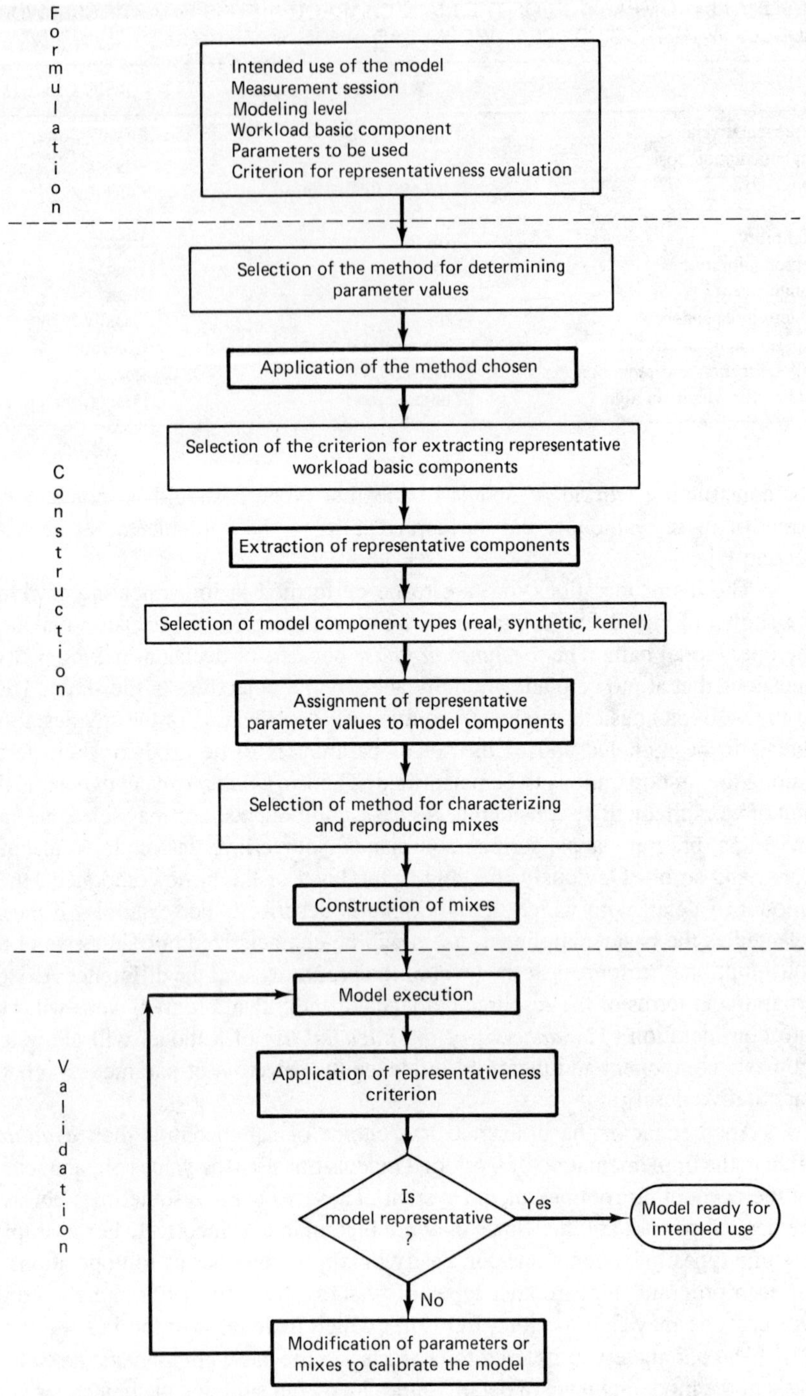

Figure 2.15 Design and implementation of an executable workload model. Operations are represented by heavy boxes, decisions by the others.

of work files, number of tapes, and so on; if, on the contrary, the model is to be implemented at the functional level, its parameters will be, for instance, the number of compilations and the number of executions of FORTRAN programs, the number of executions of certain systems programs, the number of compilations and the number of executions of COBOL programs, the number of SORT routine executions, the number of payrolls produced, and so on. Since these values will be analyzed with the objective of identifying the affinities and of clustering similar components, it is necessary to pay particular attention to the choice of the *number of parameters* to be used and to the homogeneity of their values. If the number of parameters is too low, it may be difficult to identify distinct classes of components, whereas if their number is too high, the opposite problem may arise. It may seem obvious that the types of parameters selected should be homogeneous. However, sometimes their lack of homogeneity is not evident and may cause undesirable mistakes. For example, in a resource-oriented approach, if the number of I/O operations performed by each component is not available, this parameter may be replaced with the value of the global I/O time, which includes also the waiting time spent in the I/O queues for each device. Waiting times are mix dependent. Thus, a certain component may have values of its parameters that vary according to the time at which they have been executed, and this will very likely cause classification errors. Some types of parameters and basic components that have been used in the literature, as well as in the study to be discussed in Sec. 2.5.1, are collected in Table 2.14.

The model *construction phase* consists of four fundamental operations (see Fig. 2.15): the analysis of parameters, the extraction of representative values, their assignment to the components of the model, and the reconstruction of the mixes of significant components. Having established, based on the previous considerations, the set of parameters to be used to characterize the workload basic components, the first operation to be performed consists of identifying the most convenient method to derive the values of parameters for the representative components. To do so, it may be useful to consider the parameters as belonging to two classes depending on whether they represent global values or sequences of values for each basic component. Among the parameters in the first class, which are more popular, we have the CPU time, the number of I/O operations on disk and on tape, the memory space demand, and so on. Parameters in the second class reflect, even though incompletely, the dynamics of the components' executions; in this class, we find for example the sequences of CPU bursts (that is, of uninterrupted CPU times), those of I/O bursts, the lengths of the blocks transferred between two levels of the memory hierarchy, and so on. Parameters in the first class will be called *single-value parameters,* those in the second class *sequence-type parameters*.

The workload may be considered as a set of vectors in a space with a number of dimensions equal to the number of the workload parameters. Since the amount of resulting data is generally considerable, their analysis for the purpose of identifying groups of components with similar characteristics will have to be performed by statistical techniques that can handle multidimensional samples, that is, techniques that deal with multiple factors. When the number of parameters is less than or equal to two, classical data analysis techniques such as goodness-of-fit tests for distributions, correlation analysis, and regression analysis may be applied. In all other cases, one can use various techniques that differ among themselves in the way multidimensional data sets are represented. Among these techniques are description methods by *clustering,* which partition the data set,

TABLE 2.14 WORKLOAD BASIC COMPONENTS AND PARAMETERS SETS USED IN SOME WORKLOAD CHARACTERIZATION STUDIES

System	*UNIVAC 1108*	*CDC 6400*	*IBM 370/168*	*Honeywell DPS8/44*	*IBM 370/168*
Study	*[AG76]*	*[HU71]*	*[MA77]*	*Sec. 2.5.1, Case 2.1*	*[AR78]*
Workload basic component	Application (a set of programs)	Program	Program	Program step	Data base transaction
Parameters	CPU time	CPU time	CPU time	CPU time	CPU time
	CPU time for I/O instructions	Number of lines printed	Number of lines printed	Number of lines printed	Number of data base calls
	Average memory used	Number of cards read	Number of cards read	Memory used	Number of message queue requests
	Number of steps	Peripheral processor time	Memory used	Number of tapes	Number of lock requests (request or release a serial resource)
	Elapsed time	Memory space	Number of disk I/O operations	Number of work files	
	I/O time (disks)	Number of tape drives	Number of tape I/O operations	I/O time (disks)	
	I/O time (tapes)	Cost to user	Number of data and device specification cards		
	I/O time (drums)				

description methods by *graphs* in which nodes, edges and paths are used to interpret the data structure, and description methods by *geometric* plane representations in which the properties of the data set are illustrated by projection. The application of these methods requires the definition of suitable criteria to evaluate the similarity and dissimilarity between vectors. Some of their possible applications to the solution of problems arising in computer systems analysis may be found in [SC78]. Among the available statistical methods, those that are applied to problems of workload characterization are:

1. Sampling of single parameter distributions
2. Sampling of workload components
3. Clustering algorithms
4. Reduction of the joint probability distribution of the parameters
5. Markov models
6. Principal component analysis

A brief description of these methods is reported in this section. Some applications of these techniques will be described in detail in Secs. 2.4.1 through 2.4.5.

Method 1 consists of deriving the values of model parameters by sampling their distributions separately. The probability distributions of workload parameters are assumed to be known, either by direct measurement or by estimation. In method 2, to each component of the model are assigned parameter values corresponding to those of components extracted by direct sampling from the actual workload. The workload is subdivided in method 3 into classes of components that are similar to each other based on some predefined criteria; from each class, representative components will then be extracted, and their single-value parameters will be assigned to the components of the model.

To apply method 4, we must construct the joint probability distribution of all single-value parameters of the actual workload. We will then extract from this distribution the components of the model so as to preserve the joint probability distribution of the parameters. After having defined the state for each component in terms of ranges of values for the parameters, method 5 requires the construction of the state-transition probability matrixes for the components of the actual workload and their use to obtain the sequence-type parameter values for each component of the model [LA73], [LI75].

By analyzing the correlations existing among the workload parameters, method 6 tries to find a subspace of lower dimensionality than the parameter space such that the projection of the data on this subspace accounts for a significant proportion of the total variance of the original set of data.

Examinations of the values of the actual workload's parameters should allow us to define the values that belong to the representative components of the workload. Depending on the method used for the analysis, various criteria will be applied to extract from the workload the representative components. The number of components that will constitute the model is an important decision to be made since it influences directly the model's representativeness and inversely its compactness. For example, by using the workload sampling method, we can extract the components that are in execution at the sampling instants, or we may extract one component every n whose execution has started; if, on the other hand, we have obtained by a clustering algorithm groups of components with similar characteristics, the components that are closest to the center of mass of their group may be considered as representatives of that group, and so on. Some of the most popular extraction techniques will be discussed in the following sections, which cover in detail various statistical analysis methods used in workload characterization.

The transformation of representative values into executable components is the objective of the third fundamental operation of workload model construction. If components of the actual workload or kernels are to be employed, we will have to search for those whose parameter values are closest to the values of the representative components. If, on the other hand, synthetic components are to be used, we will assign to their control parameters the parameter values of the representative components, and we will have to calibrate the model by modifying the appropriate calibration parameters of the synthetic programs.

The last operation in workload model construction consists of *reproducing the mixes* of the significant components in the actual workload. The purpose of this operation is to reconstruct within the model situations similar to those produced by the actual workload. For example, it is likely that, during workload peak intervals, which occur at about the same times everyday, similar mixes of components will be in execution. Therefore, if the objective is to implement a model that represents the peak workload, it will be desirable to reproduce in the model a sequence of representative components similar to those that we found in the actual workload. This will increase the likelihood that the same situations of contention for the critical resources will occur in the system under the workload model.

To reproduce mixes, we will have to analyze the strings of workload components as time series and to study the sequences of values that they contain. A possible method consists of classifying components into groups with similar characteristics and determining the groups to which components in execution at certain sampling times belong. In this way, *n*-tuples of values can be obtained whose analysis will allow us to identify the most frequently executed mixes [AR78]. Another method groups components with similar characteristics and examines the sequences of their lower-level components. The probabilities with which these lower-level components follow each other within higher-level components in each group can be determined. For example, one can compute the probability of each sequence of the various types of the program steps within applications in the various groups [AG78a]. In Sec. 2.5.2, we shall describe a workload model for an interactive system in which the mixes of subcomponents, that is, the interactive commands in execution, are reproduced by selecting sequences of commands found in representative components. The basic components in that model are the *intervals,* and each interval consists of an equal number of executions of interactive commands. Intervals are grouped based on the values of some performance indexes, and the model consists of those intervals whose performances are closest to the center of mass of the various groups.

The implementation of executable workload models for interactive systems and of repeatable experiments requires a greater amount of information than that needed for batch systems (see Sec. 2.4.6). The problem of analyzing the mixes of a workload's components and of reproducing them in a model will also be considered in Sec. 2.4.6.

The evaluation criteria for the representativeness of a model, based on the objectives of the study in the formulation phase, must be applied in the *validation phase* to establish the validity of the implemented model. In this phase we shall not only evaluate the representativeness of the model with the particular set of parameters being considered, but we will have to perform tests to determine the *model's domain of validity* (the shaded area in Fig. 2.16). Assuming that the criterion for evaluating the model's representativeness, and hence its validity, is expressed by the inequality

$$\sum_{i=1}^{n} (P_i - P_i')^2 \leq \varepsilon \qquad (2.4)$$

where the P_i are the values of the performance indexes obtained under the actual workload, the P_i' are the values of the indexes given by the model, and ε is the maximum acceptable error, the model's domain of validity will be defined as the set of points in which inequality (2.4) is satisfied.

We normally know the values of the P_i only in a few points, those corresponding to our measurements of the workload to be modeled. In those points, or in most of them, we will have to calibrate the model. Determining the width of the domain of validity of a model is generally extremely difficult. We only know that a structurally correct, carefully designed model tends to be more valid than one that is not. Also, calibrating a model with a criterion based on more performance indexes than strictly required by the objectives of the study will generally make the model's domain of validity wider.

A model can be calibrated by modifying some of the values of the parameters that influence its performance. The *calibration phase* (see Fig. 2.17) consists of an iterative procedure during which the values of the performance indexes produced by the model W' are compared with those produced by the workload W to be modeled, using in both cases the same system $\mathcal{S}$. The performance indexes to be compared are those that the representativeness criterion being considered refers to, and the calibration parameters are determined by the techniques employed for constructing the model. For instance, one can modify the criterion for extracting the representative components, the number of basic components that constitute the model, some of the arguments of the synthetic

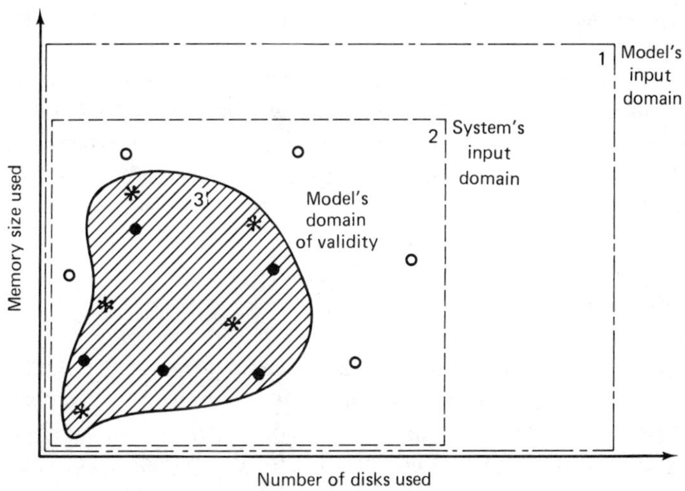

Figure 2.16 Domain of validity of a model in the (memory size, number of disks) plane. Stars denote calibration points; circles are points in which the model is not valid.

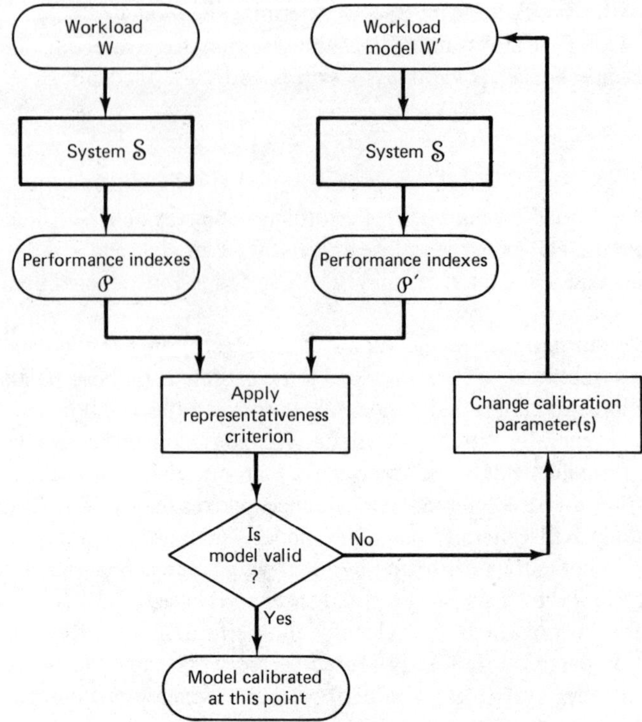

Figure 2.17 Calibration of a workload model.

components, the size of the sample processed by the clustering algorithm, or some of the parameters that are typical of the particular technique employed to construct the model.

In the following sections, we shall describe some techniques for implementing executable workload models. For each, we shall emphasize not so much the theoretical aspects as the practical difficulties that are encountered when applying it. Section 2.4.6 is devoted to the implementation problems that arise after applying any of the techniques described in the preceding sections.

2.4.1 Distribution Sampling

When the parameter values for all the components of the workload to be modeled are known or can be estimated, we can derive from them their probability distribution functions $F(x)$. Simple sorting programs or some statistical software packages such as BMDP and SPSS [DI79], [NI75] can be used for this purpose. For example, Fig. 2.18 shows the probability distribution function of the parameter "memory used" for 1105 program steps. This function has been obtained by using BMDP5D and is presented in both

```
CUMULATIVE HISTOGRAM OF VARIABLE    4CORE
                        SYMBOL   COUNT      MEAN      ST.DEV.
                          X      1105      14.770      18.911
```

Axis scale (top and bottom): 75 150 225 300 375 450 525 600 675 750 825 900 975 1050 1125 1200

INTERVAL NAME	FREQUENCY INT.	FREQUENCY CUM.	PERCENTAGE INT.	PERCENTAGE CUM.
0.0000	0	0	.0	.0
2.0000	106	106	9.6	9.6
4.0000	70	176	6.3	15.9
6.0000	9	185	.8	16.7
8.0000	145	330	13.1	29.9
10.000	160	490	14.5	44.3
12.000	200	690	18.1	62.4
14.000	51	741	4.6	67.1
16.000	22	763	2.0	69.0
18.000	64	827	5.8	74.8
20.000	67	894	6.1	80.9
22.000	13	907	1.2	82.1
24.000	18	925	1.6	83.7
26.000	15	940	1.4	85.1
28.000	12	952	1.1	86.2
30.000	8	960	.7	86.9
32.000	4	964	.4	87.2
34.000	7	971	.6	87.9
36.000	55	1026	5.0	92.9
38.000	45	1071	4.1	96.9
40.000	1	1072	.1	97.0
42.000	1	1073	.1	97.1
44.000	3	1076	.3	97.4
46.000	1	1077	.1	97.5
48.000	1	1078	.1	97.6
50.000	1	1079	.1	97.6
52.000	1	1080	.1	97.7
54.000	1	1081	.1	97.8
56.000	7	1088	.6	98.5
58.000	1	1089	.1	98.6
60.000	5	1094	.5	99.0
62.000	0	1094	.0	99.0
64.000	1	1095	.1	99.1
66.000	1	1096	.1	99.2
68.000	1	1097	.1	99.3
70.000	2	1099	.2	99.5
72.000	0	1099	.0	99.5
74.000	0	1099	.0	99.5
76.000	0	1099	.0	99.5
78.000	2	1101	.2	99.6
80.000	2	1103	.2	99.8
82.000	0	1103	.0	99.8
84.000	0	1103	.0	99.8
86.000	0	1103	.0	99.8
88.000	0	1103	.0	99.8
90.000	0	1103	.0	99.8
92.000	0	1103	.0	99.8
94.000	1	1104	.1	99.9
96.000	0	1104	.0	99.9
98.000	0	1104	.0	99.9
100.00	0	1104	.0	99.9
LAST	1	1105	.1	100.0

Figure 2.18 Probability distribution function of parameter "memory used" for 1105 program steps.

graphical and table form. The method described in this section derives, from the probability distribution functions of the workload parameters, sets of parameter values that have the same distributions as the measured ones. To obtain these values, it will be sufficient to use a pseudorandom number generator, that is, an algorithm capable of producing sequences of numbers characterized by a quasi-uniform distribution within a certain interval (for example, the interval (0, 1)) and by very small autocorrelation coefficients. It is easy to prove that, given a random variable Y uniformly distributed between 0 and 1 and a probability distribution function $F_X(x)$, the random variable x^* (0

$\leqslant x^* < +\infty$), which is obtained by the method graphically illustrated in Fig. 2.19, has a probability distribution function equal to $F_X(x)$. The procedure consists of the following steps:

1. The pseudorandom number generator produces a value, say y^*.
2. y^* is used to determine by intersection or by interpolation the value of $F_X(x^*)$ [if $F_X(x)$ is known analytically, it will be sufficient to derive its inverse function and to substitute in it the random number y^* generated].
3. The value determined by intersection or interpolation is projected on the horizontal axis to determine the value of x^*; thus, $F_X(x^*) = y^*$.

Since in most cases the workload to be modeled consists of several thousand components, the probability distribution functions are usually presented in table form; in each row of the table we find the pair $(x, F_X(x))$; the x^* values will therefore be obtained by simple interpolation.

Having established the number N of components for the model, each distribution will have to be sampled to obtain for each workload parameter N values, which are distributed according to the same function as that measured in the real workload. Each value will be assigned to a different component in the model. The number N of components in the model is chosen based on statistical considerations and must be large enough to allow the distributions of its parameters to be considered as good approximations of those in the original workload.

Since the distributions of parameters are sampled separately, this method *does not take into consideration the correlations* that usually exist among the parameters. In other words, the method assumes that the performance of the system does not depend on the correlations among the parameters for the components being considered. This assumption is usually not valid and may result in models whose performance is quite far from that produced by the original workload. Some correlations that are often found in practice are those among I/O time, CPU time, and memory space. It is evident that, if these correlations are not considered, the model obtained by this method might reproduce the global utilization of resources but will be likely to result in different performance index

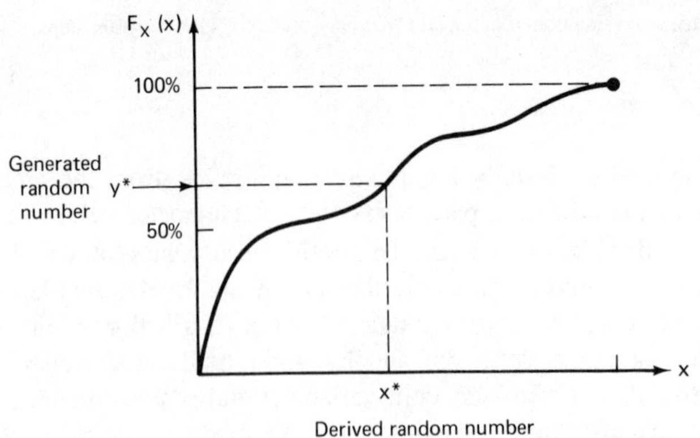

Figure 2.19 Graphical representation of the procedure to generate random variables with a given probability distribution function $F_x(x)$.

values, since program mixes will tend to be quite different from those that could be found in the workload to be modeled.

Another practical difficulty arises when the values obtained by sampling parameter distributions are assigned to the model's components. There are relationships that must be satisfied among the parameter values of a given component. For example, the number of I/O operations imposes a minimum value for the CPU time, corresponding to that required for the preparation and management of those operations.

The main advantage of this method, one of whose applications is described in [SC72], is its immediacy. Constructing probability distribution functions is quite simple, and generating parameter values by sampling those distributions is fast and inexpensive. Note that both types of parameters, single value and sequence type, can be dealt with by the method.

2.4.2 Real Workload Sampling

Sampling the real workload directly eliminates most of the problems that plague the distribution sampling method described in the previous section. This method consists of sampling the actual workload and assigning to each component of the model the n-tuple of values of the parameters of each component extracted. In this way the correlations existing among the parameters in the actual workload are automatically considered. Another interesting characteristic of this method is the ease with which artificial components can be constructed. When the extracted components cannot be directly used in the model, it is relatively easy to implement synthetic programs or to find kernels that have the same parameters as those of the extracted components, since these components are real. The critical aspects of this method are those concerned with the sampling procedure and with the sample size.

The *time-sampling* criterion consists of extracting from the actual workload those components that are in execution at the sampling instants. In this case, the probability of extracting a component is proportional to its execution time.

The *one-out-of-n sampling* criterion consists of extracting from the actual workload one out of every n components executed on the system. Each component has in this case an equal probability of being extracted, no matter what its characteristics are.

The time-sampling criterion tends to attribute excessive weight in the model to components with long execution times. The latter criterion, on the other hand, gives these components too little attention. To verify the validity of the sample, one may apply statistical techniques ranging from simple calculations of the mean, standard deviation, and skewness of each parameter to goodness-of-fit tests.

The problem of the model's representativeness is clearly related to the number of components extracted. This number cannot be too small since the workload to be modeled is usually composed of thousands or tens of thousands of components. The size of the initial population and the variances of its parameters impose a lower bound on the size of the sample. To implement a compact model, one will tend to choose relatively long sampling intervals or relatively large values of n, thereby making the model's representativeness critical. It is therefore possible to exert only a limited amount of control on the representativeness and compactness of the model. Note that no attempt is usually made, when employing this method, to reproduce the mixes of components found in the actual workload.

2.4.3 Clustering

The goal of cluster analysis is to subdivide a set of points into groups, to be called *classes* or *clusters* in the sequel, so as to make the differences among the members of a group smaller, according to a certain criterion, than those among members of different groups. The method tries to represent the affinity among points in terms of standard similarity structures like *partitions* or *trees*.

The objective is thus the one of recognizing and interpreting a structure that already exists in the set considered. In our case, the set of points is the set of workload basic components. Each component can be seen as a point in an n-dimensional space, n being the number of parameters used to describe each component. The need to utilize a clustering algorithm is due to the fact that in most cases the number of parameters is large, and hence the space has many more than two dimensions. Furthermore, the classes of components are often structured in such a way that, when going from one class to the next, the values of the parameters do not exhibit discontinuities. In other words, class boundaries are generally rather fuzzy.

Situations like that represented in Fig. 2.20, in which components can be grouped into three sharply distinguishable classes, are seldom encountered in practice. In the specialized literature, one can find dozens of clustering algorithms. These algorithms differ from one another in the clustering criterion that they use, in the method they exploit to satisfy that criterion, or in both.

A possible classification is one that distinguishes *nonhierarchical* methods from *hierarchical* methods. Among the nonhierarchical methods that have been most frequently applied in workload characterization problems we find the *iterative methods*. In these methods the initial subdivision into K classes is iteratively improved by shifting, based on the selected criterion, the elements of a cluster to another and computing after each assignment the new center of mass of the clusters. The optimum configuration is obtained

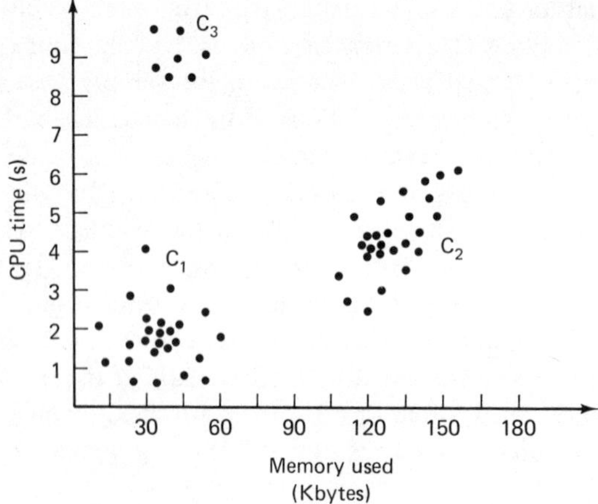

Figure 2.20 Ideal case for the application of a clustering algorithm.

when points can no longer be reassigned. Since the number of iterations needed to reach this condition may be too high, in practice one often limits oneself to applying a local optimality criterion. The number of clusters may be specified a priori or computed by the algorithm itself.

Hierarchical methods construct a tree by grouping the "closest" points initially, then the points closest to the clusters so generated, and so on, until all points have been grouped in a single class. The segments that connect pairs of contiguous points create a tree structure in which each level of aggregation represents a partition of the given set of points.

Among the most popular iterative nonhierarchical algorithms, the *nearest centroid methods,* also called *K-means methods,* are well known [AN73], [HA75]. In this case, the problem is that of determining a partition of the given set that minimizes the sum of squares of the (Euclidean or non-Euclidean) distances between each point and the center of mass of its class. The *center of mass,* or *centroid,* of a class is the point whose coordinates are the means of the parameter values of all points in the class. A K-means algorithm constructs a number of clusters increasing from 1 to K, where K is a preassigned integer. If we denote by a_i $[a_{ij}]$ the matrix of the coordinates of the given points and by b_r the vector whose elements are the coordinates of the centroid of class P_r, the problem may be formulated as follows: determine the partition $P = (P_1, P_2, \ldots, P_k)$ so that

$$\min \sum_{r=1}^{k} \sum_{i=1}^{m} \sum_{j=1}^{n} (a_{ij} - b_{rj})^2 x_{ir}, \tag{2.5}$$

where n is the number of parameters, m the number of points to be partitioned, k the number of classes, and x_{ir} is a Boolean variable defined as

$$x_{ir} = \begin{cases} 1, \text{ if } a_i \in P_r \\ 0, \text{ otherwise} \end{cases}$$

Initially, a single cluster is built, which contains all points, and the position of its centroid is determined. To obtain two clusters, two new centroids are determined by separately considering the contributions of the parameters whose values are greater and, respectively, smaller than those of the single centroid. All points are reconsidered and assigned to that cluster whose centroid is closer. The position of the centroid of each cluster is adjusted after the assignment of each new point to the cluster. Points are reassigned to the two clusters several times until no point will switch from one cluster to the other during a complete iteration or until a given maximum number of iterations is performed.

To increase the number of clusters, the cluster in which the variance of any one of the parameters is maximum is determined, and its centroid is replaced by the two centroids resulting from considering greater and smaller parameter values, respectively, for all the points in the cluster. A new assignment of all points is then performed, again based on the principle of minimum distance from the centroids, and the procedure terminates when the desired number of clusters is reached.

The *minimal spanning tree* (MST) method is a hierarchical clustering algorithm based on constructing the minimum tree that connects all points of the given set [ZA71].

The weight associated with each branch of the tree is in this application a numerical value proportional to the Euclidean distance between the nodes. If we define as the *weight* of a tree the sum of all weights of its branches, for a given graph an MST is a *spanning tree of minimum weight*. After having constructed an MST, one can use various methods to reduce the number of nodes and the number of edges by aggregation. These methods differ in the representation of the already aggregated points and in the definition of the distance between a set of aggregated points and all the other points.

For instance, for the tree shown in Fig. 2.21 the sets of clusters that can be obtained are listed in Table 2.15. If we cut the tree at level A, Fig. 2.21 shows that we obtain three clusters whose distances between any pair of points within the clusters themselves are less than A. Varying A results in different partitions of the given set.

The choice of the clustering algorithm best suited to a given problem is not straightforward, since it depends on the objectives of the study and the characteristics of the data. Some algorithms can identify and isolate ellipsoidal clusters, whereas others (for example, the hierarchical "single linkage" method) can outline nonellipsoidal clusters quite well. Furthermore, the costs of the various techniques in terms of resource consumptions are quite different, and sometimes the choice of the algorithm is constrained by the available resources (for example, by the system's configuration). For instance, several hierarchical algorithms require a high number of comparisons between distances and need to store the distance matrix. It is often convenient to apply various methods to small samples of the given data and to select the most promising algorithm based on the results of these tests.

All clustering algorithms require the *distance* between two points to be defined in order for the criterion of similarity among points to be established. The most popular definition is that of Euclidean distance, but sometimes distances derived from it (for example, by assigning weights to the parameters) or based on the profiles of the data (for example, the chi-square distance) are used.

It is important to observe that usually the parameters are expressed in nonhomogeneous units. To make them comparable, a *scale change* must be performed. For instance, CPU time in seconds may have a 1 to 10^4 range, while the number of tapes used by a program may vary between 0 and 10 or slightly more. Similar situations arise

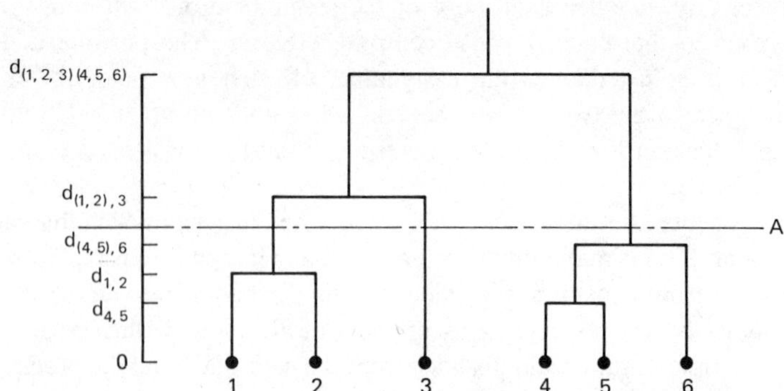

Figure 2.21 Tree constructed by a hierarchical clustering algorithm; d_{ij} represents the distance between point i and point j.

TABLE 2.15 CLUSTERS THAT MAY BE OBTAINED FROM THE TREE IN FIG. 2.21

Number of clusters	*Clusters*
1	(1, 2, 3, 4, 5, 6)
2	(1, 2, 3), (4, 5, 6)
3	(1, 2), (3), (4, 5, 6)
4	(1, 2), (3), (4, 5), (6)
5	(1), (2), (3), (4, 5), (6)
6	(1), (2), (3), (4), (5), (6)

with the number of I/O operations and the memory occupancy, and with other parameters as well.

A widely used *normalization formula* is

$$x'_{ij} = \frac{x_{ij} - \bar{x}_j}{\sigma_j} \qquad (j = 1, n;\ i = 1, m) \tag{2.6}$$

where x'_{ij} is the normalized value of the jth parameter for the ith component, $\bar{x}_j$ is the mean value of the jth parameter, and σ_j is its standard deviation. This transformation yields a zero mean and a standard deviation equal to 1 for the data (see Sec. 3.3.1) and is recommended when the clustering algorithm to be used adopts the Euclidean definition of distance. When the parameters have very different standard deviations, transformation (2.6) may give rise to some problems.

Another normalization technique consists of assigning a *different weight* to each parameter. The value x_{ij} is replaced by

$$x'_{ij} = w_j x_{ij} \qquad (j = 1, n;\ i = 1, m;\ w_j \in \mathbf{R}^+) \tag{2.7}$$

Two criteria that may be adopted for selecting w_j are:

1. The weight of a parameter is based on model representativeness considerations, and hence on aspects *external* to the data to be analyzed.
2. The weight of a parameter is inversely proportional to its *variance* so as to obtain contributions to the computation of the similarities among the points in each cluster having the same order of magnitude for each component.

Yet another normalization method is based on the following transformation:

$$x'_{ij} = \frac{x_{ij} - \min_i x_{ij}}{\max_i x_{ij} - \min_i x_{ij}} \qquad (j = 1, n;\ i = 1, m) \tag{2.8}$$

Here, the minimum value of each parameter becomes 0 and the maximum is set equal to 1.

In many cases the most suitable approach is not known a priori. Thus, various transformations must be tested to determine the one that, because of the characteristics of the data, results in the most reasonable partitioning [SP80].

Before applying scaling techniques, and especially those like the one in Eq. (2.8), one should eliminate the *outliers,* that is, those points some of whose parameters have values too distant from the corresponding parameter values of the other points. Outliers may indeed distort the transformation by causing the other points to be assigned too much or too little weight.

An analysis of the cumulative distributions of parameters may be useful to identify the outliers and therefore to determine which points will not have to be considered in the scaling and clustering procedure. For example, in [AR78] the original data distributions were trimmed by removing 5 percent of the values (those at the two tails). On the remaining data, the scaling formula (2.6) was applied. In [AG76], a scaling technique similar to that summarized in Eq. (2.8) was used, and 98 percent of the values of each parameter fell within the 0 to 10 range.

The statistical analysis of the original data, especially of the histograms of their parameters, allows us also to determine when it would be useful to apply to them a *logarithmic* or *another transformation.* By logarithmically transforming highly skewed parameter distributions (see for example Fig. 2.22a), it is possible to avoid or to reduce correlations among means and variances of the clusters. Figure 2.22 shows the histograms of the CPU times of 14,942 program steps before (Fig. 2.22a) and after (Fig. 2.22b) a logarithmic transformation. The histogram in Fig. 2.22b provides us with much more information on the structure of the distribution than the one in Fig. 2.22a.

Because of the long processing times and large amounts of memory required, the number of points to be clustered should be kept at reasonably small values. Thus, only a *sample* drawn from the original set of data is often submitted as input to the clustering algorithm (or algorithms). Among the possible *extraction criteria,* a random sampling procedure will guarantee to the various classes of components a representation proportional to their sizes in the original set. The sample should be subjected to statistical significance tests.

The representativeness of the sample and the adequacy of the clusters obtained from the procedure may be verified a posteriori by assigning the points outside the sample to the clusters produced by considering the points inside. The fraction of points that cannot be assigned to the existing clusters (those points some of whose parameter values lie outside the parameter ranges of the various clusters) can be used as a measure of the procedure's validity.

Artis describes in [AR78] some applications of clustering techniques to workload characterization and states that, by the use of a sample as small as 2 percent of the entire population, one can usually obtain clusters to which only 1 percent or less of the remaining points cannot be assigned. In Table 2.16 we report the values of the parameters for 4 out of the 17 clusters obtained in [AR78] from a sample of 2,000 out of 10,000 program steps and TSO session. That study used the ISODATA clustering algorithm [BA65], which is nonhierarchical and is characterized by efficient heuristics to minimize the processing time for large sets of data.

Another particularly important aspect of the application of clustering algorithms is the *choice of the parameters* used to characterize the workload components. First, it should be noted that the number of parameters is the dominant factor of the processing

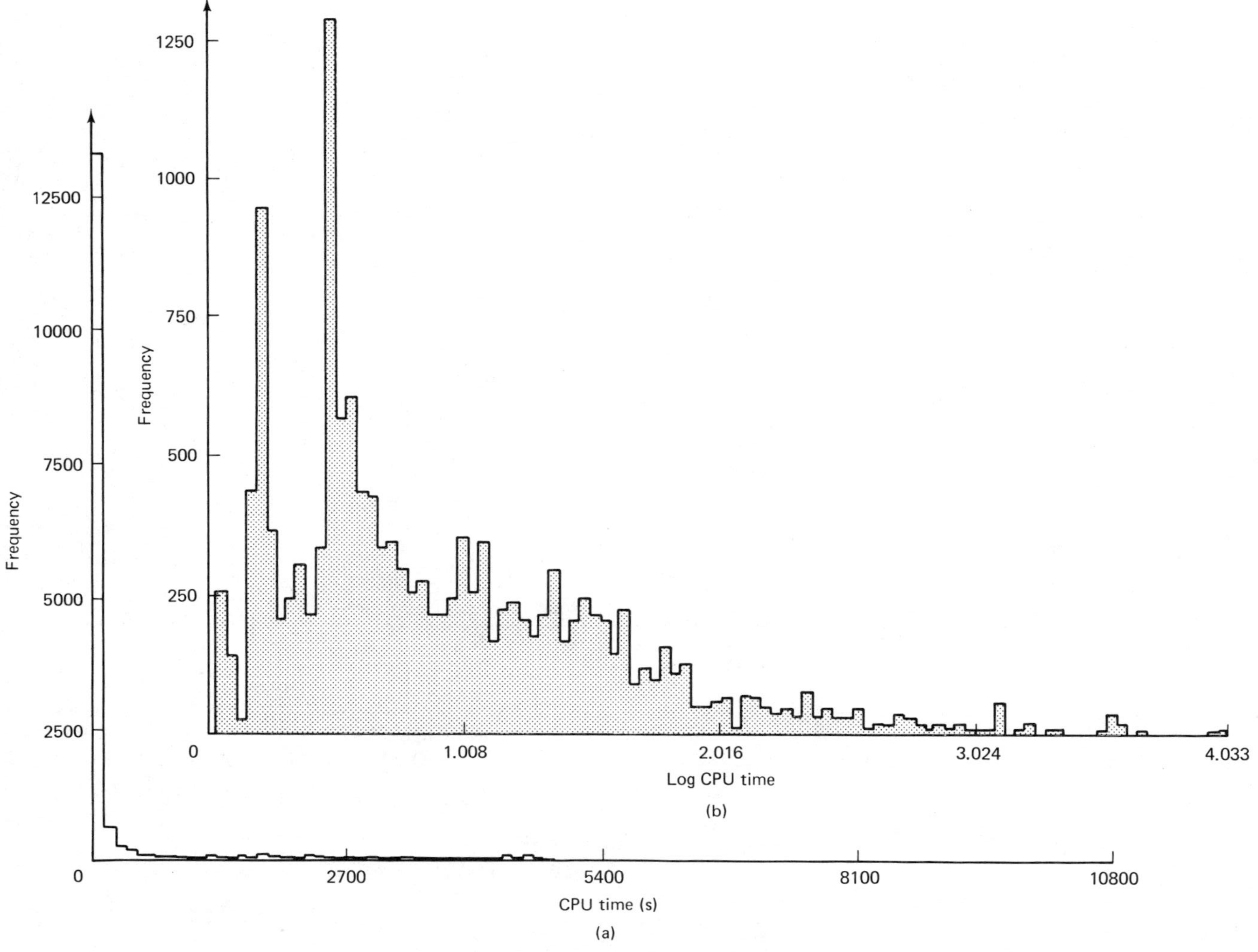

Figure 2.22 Histograms of CPU time (a) before; (b) after a logarithmic transformation.

TABLE 2.16 PARAMETER VALUES FOR 4 OUT OF THE 17 CLUSTERS OBTAINED BY ANALYZING 2000 PROGRAM STEPS THROUGH THE ISODATA CLUSTERING PROGRAM [AR78]

	Cluster 1			*Cluster 2*			*Cluster 3*			*Cluster 4*		
Parameters	*Mean*	*Min.*	*Max.*	*Mean*	*Min.*	*Max.*	*Mean*	*Min.*	*Max.*	*Mean*	*Min.*	*Max.*
I/O rate (number of I/O op./CPU time)	78.6	0	366.8	932	629.8	1356.8	139.1	0.1	346.5	44	5.2	207.2
Memory used (Kbytes)	113.3	4	343.9	264.7	32	511.9	73.3	8	271.9	436	243.9	931.9
Number of tapes allocated	0	0	0	0.1	0	1	1	1	1	1	1	1
Number of disks (3330) allocated	1.8	0	4	4.6	2	12	0.7	0	4	2.7	0	5
% of the sample		43.29			0.94			4.14			14.59	

cost required by clustering algorithm. For reasons of computational complexity, several methods can only be applied to problems of limited size both in terms of data and of parameters.

Furthermore, the presence of a large number of parameters may make the partitioning of the components difficult if not impossible. If some of the parameters are not pertinent to a particular objective of the study, a deterioration in the apparent separation between clusters may result. The fundamental task is to pick out the individual parameters that provide the greatest amount of information with respect to the partitioning problem. Thus, a set of workload parameters that are best from this viewpoint should be selected or determined.

Mamrak and Amer [MA77] describe the application of a technique for the selection of the subset of parameters that are most effective in characterizing class membership for a given classification. They obtain six clusters by applying a nonhierarchical clustering algorithm to a sample of 750 workload components described by seven parameters. The parameter selection technique identifies and eliminates the parameter that is the least effective in predicting the class membership of each component when considering the classification produced by clustering components based on all the parameters. This procedure may be iterated to eliminate various parameters successively. Table 2.17 displays the seven parameters and their rank of importance (increasing from 1 to 7) and the coordinates of the centroids for the six clusters obtained by considering seven and five parameters. In the five-parameter case, the two missing parameters are the least significant ones (CPU time and number of cards read). As one can see in Table 2.17, the new subdivision based on five parameters is substantially different from the previous one only in cluster 1, which, however, accounts for 1 percent of the components in the sample, and in the number of disk I/O operations of cluster 2. Thus, the two classifications obtained with different numbers of parameters are very similar to each other, and, if the objectives of the study are not mainly concerned with the characteristics of cluster 1 or with disk I/O operations, the workload analyzed in [MA77] may be characterized by five parameters instead of by seven.

Another method utilized to reduce the number of parameters is the principal-component analysis technique to be described in Section 2.4.5.

In summary, among all the problems encountered when applying cluster analysis in practice, the most important are:

- Definition of the number of workload components to be considered
- Selection of the parameters and of their weights
- Selection of the clustering algorithm and acquisition or implementation of a program that realizes it
- Definition of the strategy for applying the clustering algorithm
- Treatment of outliers and choice of a scaling technique
- Interpretation of the results

A systematic treatment of these subjects can be found in Chapters 9 and 10 of [AN73].

After partitioning the workload components into homogeneous clusters, the *re-*

TABLE 2.17 COORDINATES OF THE CENTROIDS OF THE CLUSTERS OBTAINED BY CONSIDERING SEVEN AND FIVE PARAMETERS, RESPECTIVELY [MA77]

Parameters	Rank of importance	*Clusters*											
		1		2		*3*		*4*		5		6	
		No. of param.		*No. of param.*		*No. of param.*		*No. of param.*		*No. of param.*		*No. of param.*	
		7	5	7	5	7	5	7	5	7	5	7	5
CPU time (s)	1	15.1	—	45.3	—	15.1	—	25.2	—	5.0	—	5.0	—
Number of cards read	2	652	—	93	—	280	—	932	—	93	—	186	—
Number of disk I/O	3	5987	1996	1996	2993	499	333	665	831	166	166	499	499
Number of tape I/O	4	434	145	4125	4125	72	72	0	0	0	0	0	0
Number of lines printed	5	3585	1103	1655	1655	827	965	4412	4688	417	417	689	689
Number of data and device specification cards	6	47	42	16	17	7	7	9	10	4	4	20	16
Memory used (Kbytes)	7	164	164	170	164	248	252	195	170	101	101	120	120
% of the workload		1	3	2	2	18	18	7	6	49	44	23	27

presentatives of each cluster must be selected. Some of the criteria that may be adopted to choose the number of representatives are to make this number:

1. Proportional to the *number* of components in the cluster.
2. A function of the *number* and *weight* of the components in the cluster.
3. Proportional to the *influence* of the cluster on *performance*.

Each of these criteria has positive and negative aspects, and is more or less suitable for the implementation of a workload model depending on the objectives of the study in which the model will have to be used.

Criterion 1 is clearly the simplest, but it may eliminate the outliers present in the sample, thereby possibly yielding an insufficiently representative model. Criterion 2 seems more reasonable, but raises the problem of assigning a proper weight to each cluster. This weight should be chosen so as to be compatible with the representativeness criterion adopted for the model. If, for instance, a resource-oriented characterization level (see Sec. 2.2) is selected, a consistent definition of a cluster's weight may coincide with the vector of the resource-oriented parameters evaluated in the center of the cluster. In this case, the cluster containing relatively light components may turn out to be underrepresented. In general, with this criterion, one has less control over the execution time of the model.

Criterion 3 seems to be the most convenient when the model is based on a performance-oriented characterization. The influence of a cluster on performance may be defined in various ways, depending on the objectives of the study. If, for instance, the evaluation of the representativeness of the model is based on turnaround times, the influence of a cluster may also be defined as being proportional to the mean turnaround times of its components.

A problem to be subsequently solved, after deciding how many representatives each cluster will have, is the choice of representative components within each cluster. These may be the closest ones to the cluster's centroid, or they may be extracted at random; another alternative is to implement an artificial component (for example, a synthetic program) whose parameters coincide with those of the cluster's centroid.

Case 2.1, described in Sec. 2.5.1, is devoted to the application of a nonhierarchical clustering algorithm to a workload characterization problem (see also [SE81], [BO82], [HA82]).

2.4.4 Joint Probability Distribution Sampling

The method described in this section allows us to eliminate a drawback of the distribution sampling method (Sec. 2.4.1), that is, the separate sampling of parameter distributions. In this method, it is the joint probability distribution of all the parameters of the workload to be modeled that is sampled. The method consists of the following steps:

1. Construct the joint probability distribution of all workload parameters.
2. Derive from this distribution a set of components whose parameter values have approximately the same joint distribution.

3. Use the parameter values of these components to characterize the components of the workload model.

The operations to be performed in each step will now be described; to simplify our treatment, a two-parameter characterization will be considered.

Let the two parameters be x and y. In *step 1* the two-dimensional space, in which each component is represented by one point, is subdivided into a finite number of rectangular cells. If the range spanned by these points on each axis is subdivided into h parts, there will be h^2 cells. Denoting by N_{ij} the number of workload components in the cell whose center has coordinates (i, j), the probability of finding a component in this rectangle may be estimated as

$$p_{ij} = \frac{N_{ij}}{N} \qquad (i, j = 1, 2, \ldots, h) \tag{2.9}$$

where N is the global number of components in the workload to be modeled. The p_{ij} approximate the joint probability distribution of the two parameters x and y.

Step 2 consists of determining from the p_{ij} the numbers N'_{ij} of the model components in cell (i, j). If N' is the total number of components in the model, we have

$$N'_{ij} = p_{ij} N' \tag{2.10}$$

N' may be selected according to the objectives of the study. In certain cases, for instance, the value of N' will be given; in others it might be derived from some of the design constraints of the model. The latter is the case when the global value of a parameter, say x, must be less than or equal to a preassigned value; that is,

$$\sum_i (x_i \sum_j N'_{ij}) \leq K \tag{2.11}$$

Using Eq. (2.11), N' can be determined by successive approximations. An initial value of N' is to be chosen. The N'_{ij} values are computed from Eq. (2.10) and are plugged into Eq. (2.11) to see whether this inequality holds. If it does not, the value of N' is modified and the procedure is repeated until Eq. (2.11) is satisfied.

Sreenivasan and Kleinman [SR74] describe an application of this method in which the workload to be modeled consisted of 6126 programs, and the model could not require more than 1800 s of CPU time. The value of N' derived as just illustrated was 88.

With certain joint probability distributions, this method may produce models that are not very representative. Computing the N'_{ij} with Eq. (2.10) is equivalent to reducing the number of workload components in each cell by the same factor. Thus, all components are implicitly given the same weight. This is clearly in contrast with the fact that the more demanding components (in terms of system resources) are also those whose influence on processing efficiency is greater.

Consider, for instance, the workload whose joint probability distribution for the two parameters t_{CPU} (CPU time) and $n_{I/O}$ (number of I/O operations) is shown in Fig. 2.23a. Assuming a reduction factor equal to 3, in the scaled-down joint probability distribution shown in Fig. 2.23b the components characterized by high values of t_{CPU} and $n_{I/O}$, for example, those in cells (5, 3), (5, 4), (6, 3), (6, 4), are not represented.

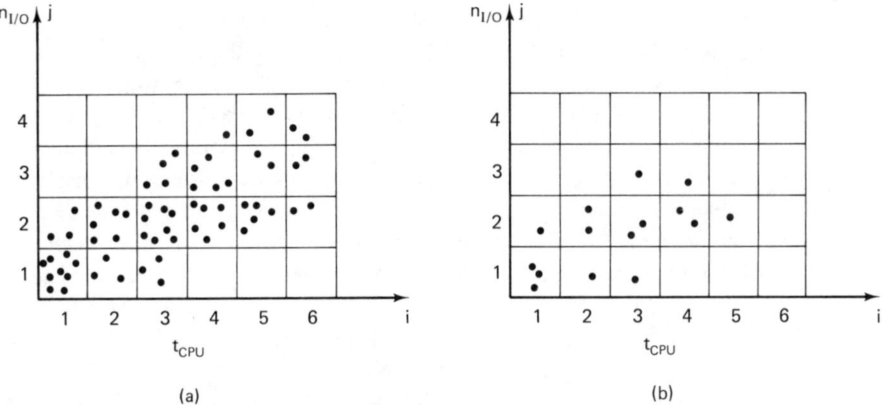

Figure 2.23 Applying the joint probability distribution sampling method. The reduction factor is 3. The workload model obtained consists of 15 components. The heavy consumers of resources are underrepresented.

This proportional reduction criterion may considerably affect the model's representativeness.

To select the representative components for each cell, we may apply the same techniques described in Sec. 2.4.3 for the case of clusters, if each cell is treated as if it were a cluster.

The representativeness problems discussed here can be reduced or eliminated by selecting a different reduction factor for each cell, or, what is in some sense equivalent, by varying the weights of the parameters and/or the sizes of the cells. These modifications to the method allow us to adapt it to the representativeness criterion selected and to the objectives of the study.

The method described in this section is preferable to the clustering approach when the latter would yield unsatisfactory results due to the lack of sharply defined clusters in the data. The two methods may also be jointly applied to the same set of points: initially, some clusters are identified; then the joint probability distribution sampling technique is employed for those sets of points that cannot be adequately subdivided by a clustering algorithm. This hybrid approach allows one to adapt optimally the model design technique to the characteristics of the original data.

2.4.5 Principal Component Analysis

The term *factor analysis* usually refers to those statistical techniques that describe multidimensional sets of data by means of *geometric* representations. A subspace of the variable space has to be chosen so that the projection of the set of data on this subspace will preserve as much information of the original set as possible. Thus, the most important property of factor analysis techniques is their size reduction capability.

Among factor analysis methods, *principal component analysis* is a technique that transforms a set of variables into another set (the set of *principal components*) characterized by linear dependence on the variables in the original set and by orthogonality among its own variables. The criterion for choosing the first principal component is that of maximizing the variance of the linear function expressing the dependence of the transformed variables on the original variables. The second is then chosen to maximize the remaining variance under the constraint that it must be orthogonal to the first, and so on.

In practice, this technique consists of finding the eigenvalues (in order of decreasing magnitude) and the corresponding eigenvectors of the correlation matrix of a given set of variables based on a given set of their values. The relative size of each eigenvalue gives the variance of the principal component (that is, the eigenvector). A complete description of the principal component analysis technique may be found in most statistics textbooks (see for instance [HA67], [RU70]). Since several software packages that apply this technique are available, in the rest of this section we shall discuss the interpretation of the results in more detail than the theory on which it is based.

Assuming that most of the points are distributed in the variable space as a hyperellipse (this may often be approximately obtained by suitable transformations, for example by logarithmically transforming variables with highly skewed distributions), the *factors* or *principal components* may be viewed as corresponding to its axes. In particular, the first factor corresponds to the longest axis, the second to the next longest, and so on. The importance of a factor may be expressed in terms of the amount of total variance in the data it accounts for. The variance accounted for by each factor is the variance of the distances between the projections of the data on the axis corresponding to the factor and the centroid of the hyperellipse. Since each factor has been chosen so as to minimize the variance remaining in the data after the extraction of the previous factors, the first few factors usually *explain* most of the total variance in the data. Hence, it is very important to determine the fraction of the variance accounted for by each factor both to make a proper decision about the number of factors that are to be considered and to evaluate the error due to the reduction in the number of factors.

The *loading* of a variable on a factor related to the fraction of variance of the variable that can be accounted for by the factor. If we denote by a_{ji} the factor loading of variable j on factor i, the variance of variable j accounted for by factor i is given by a_{ji}^2, and the fraction of the total variance accounted for by the same factor is

$$\sum_{j=1}^{n} \frac{a_{ji}^2}{n} \qquad (i = 1, 2, \ldots, n) \tag{2.12}$$

It should be noted that the variance of each variable is 1 since all parameter values are normalized; thus, the total variance coincides with the number n of variables considered.

The main steps required by the application of this technique are:

1. Computation of the correlations between the variables, that is, between the parameters of the workload components.
2. Computation of the initial loadings of the variables on each factor.
3. Rotation (orthogonal or oblique) of the initial factors to obtain the terminal factors.

Step 3 is intended to produce larger differences among factor loadings so that it will be easier to interpret the meaning of the various factors (see Fig. 2.24c).

Usually, the operations in the three steps can be performed by any of the several

P.C.ANALYSIS-1448 WORKLOAD COMPONENTS-FEBRUARY 1981 03/02/81

FILE NONAME (CREATION DATE = 03/02/81)

CORRELATION COEFFICIENTS..

(a)

	IODISK	SYSOUT	KWORDS	CPUTIME	NBWFILE	NMBTAPE
IODISK	1.00000	0.35682	0.27730	0.79285	0.37040	0.08584
SYSOUT	0.	1.00000	0.24010	0.48249	0.01150	0.03330
KWORDS	0.	0.	1.00000	0.37470	0.21992	-0.03316
CPUTIME	0.	0.	0.	1.00000	0.24750	0.18151
NBWFILE	0.	0.	0.	0.	1.00000	0.00054
NMBTAPE	0.	0.	0.	0.	0.	1.00000

(b)

VARIABLE	EST COMMUNALITY	FACTOR	EIGENVALUE	PCT OF VAR	CUM PCT
IODISK	1.00000	1	2.47006	41.2	41.2
SYSOUT	1.00000	2	1.06104	17.7	58.9
KWORDS	1.00000	3	0.98432	16.4	75.3
CPUTIME	1.00000	4	0.75768	12.6	87.9
NBWFILE	1.00000	5	0.55334	9.2	97.1
NMBTAPE	1.00000	6	0.17356	2.9	100.0

QUARTIMAX ROTATED FACTOR MATRIX

(c)

	FACTOR 1	FACTOR 2	FACTOR 3	FACTOR 4	FACTOR 5	FACTOR 6
IODISK	0.94098	0.00930	0.06533	0.17759	0.09323	-0.26452
SYSOUT	0.28458	0.00572	0.09871	-0.03027	0.95305	0.00359
KWORDS	0.20171	-0.02671	0.97001	0.09356	0.09434	0.00395
CPUTIME	0.89068	0.10859	0.17572	0.05591	0.22197	0.33411
NBWFILE	0.20639	-0.00763	0.09241	0.97366	-0.02817	0.00024
NMBTAPE	0.08481	0.99605	-0.02429	-0.00715	0.00591	0.00349

Figure 2.24 (a) Correlation matrix for the six parameters characterizing 1448 program steps; (b) eigenvalues and percentages of the total variance accounted for by each factor; (c) rotated factor matrix.

commercial packages. The user has only to prepare the data in the format prescribed by the package at hand.

Hunt and others [HU71] applied this technique to the study of a workload composed of 1588 programs, each characterized by seven parameters. The factor loadings obtained from the first two steps are shown in Table 2.18. The fraction of the total variance accounted for by the first three factors is 77 percent. Factor 1 is characterized by high loadings of CPU time, number of lines printed, number of cards read, peripheral processor time, and cost. Factor 1 accounts for more than 50 percent of the variance of these variables (the square of the factor loadings), and the fraction of the total variance explained by it is 50 percent [see Eq. (2.12)]. This factor represents the characteristics of most of the programs in the workload. Note that the variance of memory requirements is quite low for all three factors.

TABLE 2.18 INITIAL LOADINGS OF SEVEN PROGRAM PARAMETERS ON THE FIRST THREE FACTORS [HU71]

Parameters	*Factor 1*	*Factor 2*	*Factor 3*
CPU time (log)	0.84	0.13	−0.07
Number of lines printed (log)	0.65	0.14	0.45
Number of cards read (log)	0.72	0.35	0.12
Peripheral processor time (log)	0.76	−0.40	0.18
Memory space	0.55	0.34	−0.71
Number of tape drives charged	0.35	−0.83	−0.26
Cost to user (log)	0.92	−0.05	0.02
% of variance (cumulative)	50	66	77

The second and the third factor have high loadings on the number of tape drives and, respectively, the amount of memory used. They represent the differences between programs that require tapes and a relatively large amount of memory space and those that do not.

We shall now describe another example of application of principal component analysis to a set of 1448 program steps characterized by six parameters. For this analysis the FACTOR subprogram of the SPSS statistical package has been used. In Fig. 2.24a we present the matrix of the correlations between the six parameters that is to be input into FACTOR. The six parameters are the I/O time for disk operations (IODISK), the number of lines printed (SYSOUT), the amount of memory used (KWORDS), the CPU time consumed (CPUTIME), the number of work files (NBWFILE), and the number of tape drives (NMBTAPE). Figure 2.24b provides us with the percentage of the total variance accounted for by the first three factors: 75.3 percent.

Factor 1 has a high loading of IODISK and CPUTIME. The variances of these two parameters accounted for by the variation in factor 1 are given by $(0.94098)^2 = 0.88544$ and $(0.89068)^2 = 0.79331$, respectively. Thus, 88 percent of the total variance of IODISK and 79 percent of the total variance of CPUTIME are accounted for by factor 1. These results, together with the observation that the total amount of variance accounted for by factor 1 is quite high (41.2 percent from Fig. 2.24b), suggest that in most workload components the parameters IODISK and CPUTIME have large variations and are also strongly correlated, whereas the variations of the other parameters are quite small.

The heaviest loading of factor 2 is on the parameter NMBTAPE, and the factor loadings on all the other parameters are very low. This factor is generated by the variations between the parameter values of the components using tapes and those of the components not using tapes. The variance of NMBTAPE accounted for by factor 2 is $(0.99605)^2 = 0.99211$, that is, almost its entire variance.

The variation in memory use by particular program steps having values of KWORDS outside the range described by factor 1 is reflected in factor 3. Indeed, the loading of KWORDS on factor 3 is 0.97001, and the fraction of its variance explained by factor 3 is $(0.97001)^2 = 0.94091$. This high variability of memory demand, accompanied by a uniform request of other resources, can be attributed in part to the effect of runs aborted due to control card errors (minimum memory usage), and in part to some scientific programs that require large amounts of memory and relatively small amounts of the other resources (among these we also find programs being tested that are terminated during the initial phases of their execution).

The package that was used also provides a graphical presentation of the rotated orthogonal factors. A set of plots, one for each pair of factors, can be generated. Figure 2.25 shows the diagram for factors 1 and 2. By analyzing the relative positions of the parameters we can identify those that may be grouped together. For example, in Fig. 2.25 we see that the loadings of parameters 4 and 1 on both factors 1 and 2 are similar (both high on factor 1 and low on factor 2), whereas those of parameter 6 are totally different (high on factor 2 and low on factor 1). Parameters 2 and 5 have similar (low) loadings on factor 1, and almost zero loadings on factor 2. Since the elements of the pairs (4, 1) and (2, 5) are in close proximity even in the diagram for factors 1 and 3 and

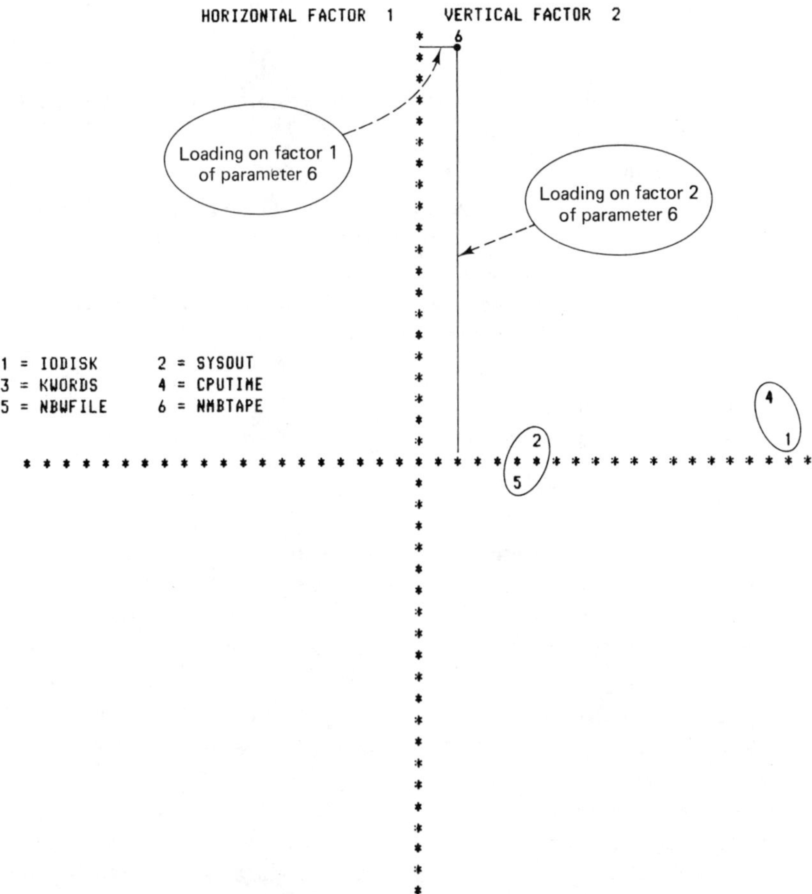

Figure 2.25 Diagram showing the loadings on factor 1 and factor 2 of the parameters considered.

in that for factors 2 and 3, we can conclude that the parameters of each pair turn out to be highly correlated when only factors 1, 2, and 3 are taken into account. Thus, if only the first three factors are considered, 75.3 percent of the total variance of the original resources (among these we also find programs being tested that are terminated during the initial phases of their execution).

Principal component analysis is particularly useful in the validation of the results obtained by other statistical techniques (for example, clustering algorithms) and in the study of the main aspects of variability in each workload component's demands (see [SE81]).

2.4.6 Implementation of a Workload Model

After obtaining, by means of the statistical techniques described in the preceding sections, the parameter values of the workload's representative components, the following operations will have to be performed in order to implement a model of the workload (see Fig. 2.15):

1. Transformation of the parameter values of each model component into an *executable component* of the model.
2. Reproduction in the model of the mixes of components found in the modeled workload (when this is required by the objectives of the study).

The careful examination of the objectives will allow one to select the type of test workload to be implemented and the type of component to be utilized. The executable components of a workload model may be:

- Real components
- Kernels or nonparametric components
- Synthetic or parametric components

Real components are to be extracted from the workload to be modeled so that their parameter values will be as close as possible to those identified as representative. Clearly, the components extracted will have to be accompanied by all the files and utility programs they need to run. A model composed of real components is usually called a *benchmark*.

The *kernels* will have to be chosen with the same closeness criterion. Since a model consisting of kernels is not parametrically modifiable, the accuracy with which the representative components can be reproduced in the model depends on the number and variety of the available kernels.

Using *synthetic components* allows us to implement a relatively wide spectrum of representative components with reasonable accuracy. In practice, a *calibration phase* will usually be needed, in which the parameter values of the synthetic components will be adjusted so as to make their behavior closer to that of the representatives. The characteristics of kernels and synthetic components have been discussed in Sec. 2.3.2.

An executable model of an interactive workload consists of a set of *scripts,* obtained from a set of representative *scenarios,* that are executed under the control of *drivers.* A detailed description of these components may be found in Secs. 2.3.2 and 2.3.3. Depending on the level of characterization adopted for the interactive workload, there are various procedures for a model's implementation. Table 2.19 summarizes the most popular model-building procedures and the corresponding basic workload components. The descriptions of the procedures in the table may be easily adapted to the construction of models for batch workloads.

In Sec. 2.4 we have already stated that accurately reproducing in the model the *mixes of components* of the workload to be modeled is not always necessary in order to obtain a representative model. The objectives of the study may indeed not require the evaluation of performance indexes that are mix dependent. This is, for instance, the case in certain workload forecasting studies (see Sec. 2.6). Then, the workload basic components may be analyzed by an unordered-set philosophy. The workload's dynamics are ignored, and workload components are dealt with as if no temporal relationships existed among them.

When, on the other hand, the indexes are mix dependent, such as for instance the turnaround time, or when it is necessary to reproduce the same load situations and load sequences that have been found on the system's resources during certain periods of time, a mechanism for reproducing mixes is needed.

The characterization of mixes may be performed by techniques to be applied to the workload data after analyzing them with some of the methods illustrated in the preceding sections. The study of the workload components and of their temporal clusters tries to determine the salient dynamic properties of the time series describing the behavior of their parameters. Even in this case, the intended use of the model will influence the approach to be adopted.

TABLE 2.19 PROCEDURES FOR BUILDING EXECUTABLE MODELS OF INTERACTIVE WORKLOADS.

Workload characterization levels	*Basic workload component*	*Model-building procedures*
Physical	Total resource demand {Total resource demand rate}*	Measure resource consumptions {Measure resource consumptions rates}* Scale them down Translate into scripts
Physical–virtual	Command (resource demand)	Measure command resource consumptions Cluster commands according to their consumptions Select representatives of each cluster
Virtual	Command (type)	Measure command frequencies Build set of scripts with same frequencies
Functional	Function of script	Prepare scenarios from measurement data Select representatives of scenarios Translate the representative scenarios into a set of scripts

*Braces enclose alternative components or steps.

Sometimes, we shall have to identify the mixes executed during peculiar load situations, for example, during periods of high utilization of a single resource or of the whole system, during intervals of assigned length, and so on. At other times, the model's execution will have to reproduce the same mixes, or at least the most frequent or important ones, that are present in the system while the actual workload is processed.

Denoting the workload components in execution by the identifiers of the classes to which they have been assigned based on the values of their parameters, mixes can be represented by vectors **V** having as many elements as there are classes in the workload. For example, if there are five classes, the mix in execution at some time t may be identified by vector $\mathbf{V}_t = \{1, 0, 2, 0, 3\}$. This means that at time t the set of executing components consists of one component of class 1, two components of class 3, and three components of class 5. If we sample the executing mixes at various instants of the measurement interval, for example at equidistant times or whenever the value of an element of the mix changes, we obtain a set of vectors $\mathbf{V}_i$ whose analysis will yield the execution frequencies of the various mixes.

An approach similar to the one just described has been used in [AR78], where, to reduce to a minimum the number of distinct mixes to be considered, the *generating mix* was introduced. A generating mix represents all mixes that differ from it in the (higher) value of one of its elements. Thus, for instance, the vector $\mathbf{V}_t$ just defined is a generating mix for the mixes {1, 1, 2, 0, 3} and {1, 0, 2, 0, 5}. The analysis of all mixes in the workload at hand in [AR78] shows that a large fraction of them (about 78 percent) can be generated by only four mixes. Each generating mix is characterized not only by the values of its elements, but also by the maximum of such values. By executing the generating mixes separately and varying in each run the value of one element until it reaches its maximum value, one can produce with a limited number of experiments a large portion of all mixes present in the workload to be modeled.

Another approach consists of replacing the temporal sequence of the executions of workload components by a much shorter sequence having the same dynamic properties. From the string of the numbers that identify the classes of the various components listed in chronological order according to the beginning of their execution, one can derive the component from one class that starts executing immediately following a component from another class.

Under suitable assumptions, this string may be seen as produced by an irreducible discrete-time *Markov chain* whose number of states K is equal to the number of classes. When a component of class i starts executing, we shall say that the chain is in state i. State transition probabilities correspond to the probabilities of finding the corresponding pair of states in adjacent locations in the string.

The problem is therefore the one of constructing a new string having approximately the same transition probability matrix as the original string, but a substantially smaller number of components. Let p_{ij} be the probability that the execution of a component of class j is started immediately after the execution of a class i component has begun. The transition probability matrix **P** is a $(k \times k)$ matrix whose entries are such that

$$0 \leq p_{ij} \leq 1, \qquad \sum_{j=1}^{k} p_{ij}\ 1 \qquad (1 \leq i, j \leq k), (i = 1, 2, \ldots k) \tag{2.13}$$

The p_{ij}'s can be easily estimated from the original string by counting the total number of transitions from state i to state j and dividing it by the total number of transitions whose initial state is i.

From **P** we may derive **C,** the matrix of cumulative distributions of the p_{ij}'s over the range of state j. The entry c_{ij} of **C** is given by

$$c_{ij} = \sum_{h=1}^{j} p_{ih} \qquad (1 \leq i, j \leq k) \tag{2.14}$$

Obviously,

$$c_{ik} = 1 \qquad (1 \leq i \leq k) \tag{2.15}$$

Each row of **C** contains a discrete probability distribution function. By sampling the k cumulative distributions in **C** separately with a technique similar to the one illustrated in Fig. 2.19, a string shorter than the original one and with a transition probability matrix **P′** similar to **P** can be constructed. The sampling of the row corresponding to the initial state of a transition will yield the final state, which will then be treated as the initial state for the next transition, and so on. The reduced string obtained in this way provides the sequence of initiations of the model's components. To reproduce, even approximately, the mixes of the workload to be modeled, information about the duration of each state may be needed. In this case, the distributions of the times spent in each state may fulfill such a need, but the string will have to be modeled as a semi-Markov process.

Agrawala and Mohr [AG78a] describe the implementation of Markov models of programs that may be employed to represent each of the clusters into which a given workload has been partitioned. The workload component they consider is the program, characterized by eight resource-oriented parameters. Applying a clustering algorithm to a set of 22,058 programs resulted in the identification of 11 clusters.

For the programs in each cluster the sequence of program steps was treated as a Markovian sequence. This allowed the differences among the Markov processes corresponding to the various clusters to be interpreted as differences among program behaviors of the clusters themselves.

Another technique for reproducing mixes consists of using workload components containing sequences of lower-level components. Thus, for example, if in an interactive system we take as workload components the *intervals,* which are subworkloads consisting of the commands input into the system during n interactions, we can apply to them the techniques previously described and obtain representative intervals. An advantage of this approach is that each representative component also contributes to the reproduction of some aspects of the workload's dynamic behavior, that is, of the execution sequence of its lower-level components. An application of this technique is discussed in Case 2.2, Sec. 2.5.2.

The method for the reproduction of mixes will have to be selected according to the intended use of the model. Thus, for instance, the choice of the heaviest mixes will be useful to determine the capacity of the system; also, the mixes that impose a bigger load on a critical resource will be suitable for the evaluation of the impact of a new system component which provides that resource or of possible workload modifications. Reproducing the execution sequence of workload components is useful in the study of the effects of tuning actions and in the evaluation of new systems.

After identifying the mixes to be reproduced, one faces the problem of their actual implementation in the system. In an interactive system, command sequences (that is, scripts) are reproduced by an internal or external driver. Drivers can simulate the arrival of a command at a given instant of time; hence, they can generally achieve the desired load situations. In a batch system, a driver (usually internal) that is capable of initiating the execution of a workload component at a preassigned instant must be built. This component will have to be stored in a mass storage device together with the data required for its execution before it is initiated.

2.5 WORKLOAD MODEL IMPLEMENTATIONS

Having examined in the previous sections the phases of workload model implementation projects and the various techniques that may be utilized, we shall now discuss two sample implementations. The two case studies to be dealt with have been selected so that their objectives would be similar to those of many practical evaluation studies. Case 2.1 is concerned with the implementation of a workload model for batch systems and adopts a hybrid (resource-oriented and functional) approach, as well as clustering techniques.

Case 2.2 deals with an interactive workload, which is modeled following a performance-oriented approach. In both cases, the methodology and the problems encountered in the application of each approach will be emphasized at the expense of the minute details of the approaches themselves.

2.5.1 Case 2.1: A Resource and Functional Model of a Batch Workload

The objectives of the study are:

1. To characterize the workoad of a batch system according to a resource-oriented approach.
2. To determine whether and to what extent the characterization obtained in objective 1 can be interpreted in functional terms.

The basic component of the workload being considered is the program step. The workload to be modeled consists of the 14,942 program steps processed by an MBRS system (see Fig. 1.3) all working days in a month between 8 A.M. and 9 P.M. To reach objective 1, the resource-oriented parameters that describe the program steps in the workload have been classified by the use of clustering techniques. Objective 2 has been attained by analyzing the resource-oriented groups identified in objective 1 and evaluating their correspondence to some given functional categories.

The six resource-oriented workload parameters to characterize each program step are:

IODISK:	the time required for the execution of disk I/O operations by the program step, in seconds
SYSOUT:	the number of lines printed by the program step
KWORDS:	the size of memory required by the program step, in Kwords (note that the system we are considering does not have virtual memory)
CPUTIME:	the CPU time consumed by the program step, in seconds
WFILES:	the number of work files required by the program step
NTAPE:	the number of tapes used by the program step

The distribution descriptors of these parameters for the 14,942 program steps in the workload to be modeled are displayed in Table 2.20. Since the distributions of IODISK, SYSOUT, and CPUTIME are highly positively skewed, logarithmic transformations have been applied to them. The histograms of CPUTIME before and after the logarithmic transformation are shown in Fig. 2.22. Those of the other two parameters transformed have similar shapes.

To eliminate the most obvious outliers, the program steps with at least one parameter value beyond the 99th percentile of that parameter's distribution were discarded. This operation reduced the population by only 4 percent.

Then a random sample of 729 program steps was extracted from the population without the outliers. This was done by selecting those program steps whose records in the log file are identified by numbers equal to those produced by a pseudorandom number generator invoked 729 times. By applying the chi-square test to the parameters of the sample, we saw that the sample was not significantly different from the population without outliers.

The statistics for the 729 program steps in the sample have been collected in Table 2.21. To facilitate the interpretation of this and the following tables, the parameters that have been logarithmically transformed or scaled are also reported with their original values.

Before applying the clustering algorithm, the values of the parameters of the sample were linearly rescaled by the transformation in Eq. (2.8), restricting all of them to the 0 to 1 range.

The *K*-means clustering algorithm, whose listing is reported by Hartigan [HA75,

TABLE 2.20 DESCRIPTIVE STATISTICS FOR THE 14,942 PROGRAM STEPS IN THE WORKLOAD TO BE MODELED

Parameters	*Mean*	*Standard deviation*	*Minimum*	*Maximum*	*Skewness*	*Kurtosis*
IODISK (s)	15.98	95.82	0.18	7092.67	35.91	2184.53
SYSOUT	631.14	1986.54	0	51340.00	10.07	158.45
KWORDS	24.74	11.19	1.00	120.00	1.03	3.51
CPUTIME (s)	63.97	358.54	0.06	10800.18	12.79	238.89
WFILES	3.25	1.21	0	7.00	−0.06	−0.82
NTAPE	0.10	0.35	0	3.00	3.66	13.66

TABLE 2.21 DESCRIPTIVE STATISTICS FOR THE 729 PROGRAM STEPS IN THE SAMPLE AFTER THE ELIMINATION OF THE OUTLIERS

Parameters	*Mean*	*Standard deviation*	*Minimum*	*Maximum*
IODISK (s)	9.78	26.64	0.51	311.48
SYSOUT	441.37	1027.90	0	10731
KWORDS	23.87	10.25	8.00	61
CPUTIME (s)	33.91	164.03	0.11	2392.01
WFILES	3.24	1.20	0	5
NTAPE	0.10	0.35	0	2

pp. 108–111], was used. Since this algorithm produces a number of clusters ranging from 1 to K, where K is selected by the user, the first problem was the one of establishing the best value of K based on the available sample. The indexes employed to evaluate the significance of a partition were the overall mean square ratio and, for each parameter, the ratio between the intercluster variance and the within-clusters variance. The overall ratio can be used to determine by how much the variance of the parameters decreases when going from K to $K + 1$ clusters. Large values (for example, greater than 10) of this ratio generally justify adding one more cluster. The best partition should also be characterized by values greater than 1 of all the ratios between intercluster and intracluster variance for each parameter. These conditions are reached with an eight-cluster partition of the sample. The mean values of the parameters for the eight clusters are shown in Table 2.22.

Since the algorithm produces the results for all partitions from 1 to K clusters, one can study the dynamics of the successive subdivisions in terms of the characteristics of program steps in each cluster. With *two clusters*, program steps are partitioned according to the value of NTAPE. The first cluster consists of the program steps not using tapes, which amount to 91.3 percent of the program steps in the sample. When going from two to *three clusters*, the first cluster is partitioned according to the values of WFILES. The first of the three clusters thus obtained (58.16 percent of the sample) consists of program

TABLE 2.22 MEAN VALUES OF THE PARAMETERS FOR THE EIGHT-CLUSTER PARTITION PRODUCED BY A *K*-MEANS ALGORITHM

	Clusters							
Parameters	*1*	*2*	*3*	*4*	*5*	*6*	*7*	*8*
IODISK (s)	17.27	3.06	10.11	5.13	11.67	6.39	238.17	125.62
SYSOUT	743.42	283.73	363.05	496.17	374.81	113.5	249.60	2682.59
KWORDS	35.26	11.42	23.05	26.65	18.78	17.85	26.25	39.59
CPUTIME (s)	39.92	10.32	32.3	14.74	66.29	9.85	387.34	1786.28
WFILES	4.59	1.97	2.32	2.65	3.07	4.45	3.75	4.8
NTAPE	0.02	0	1	0	2	0.02	0.25	0
% of the sample	18.8	16.6	5.07	38.13	1.92	18.38	0.5	0.6

steps requiring 2 to 5 files and no tapes, the second (34.84 percent) contains program steps needing 0 or 1 tapes and 0 to 3 files, and the third (7 percent) requires 1 or 2 tapes.

The characteristics of the first two clusters (54.3 and 37.7 percent of the sample, respectively) in the case of *four clusters* remain similar to those of the corresponding clusters in the previous partition, with the only exception of the number of tapes required, which is 0 for all the program steps in both clusters. The program steps in the third cluster (4.1 percent) require 22 s of CPU time on the average and 0 to 3 files. Those in the fourth (3.9 percent) are characterized by higher CPU time demand (54 s) and more files (3 to 5).

The move from four to *five clusters* alters only the last two clusters of the preceding subdivision. In the third cluster (3.3 percent), program steps require 0 to 2 files, 1 to 2 tapes, and a low mean I/O time (3.8 s), whereas in the fourth cluster (3.1 percent) they need more files (3 to 5), 1 tape, and larger I/O and CPU times. The fifth cluster (1.6 percent) groups together all program steps that require 2 tapes.

The first two clusters (27 and 25.6 percent of the sample, respectively) of the partition into *six clusters* are characterized by no tape usage. However, the first utilizes all the resources considerably, while the second contains low-consumption program steps. The third cluster (3.6 percent) is similar to the fourth in the $K = 5$ case. In the fourth cluster (38.6 percent), memory space, number of files, and disk I/O time demands are larger than in the second, whereas the converse is true for CPU time demand. The fifth (1.92 percent) contains program steps requiring two tapes, while the sixth (3.3 percent) groups those that require 3 to 5 files, 0 to 1 tape, and have the other parameter values spread over a relatively wide range.

In the subdivision into *seven clusters,* the first (21.8 percent) contains program steps that make heavy use of the resources (especially of memory space and number of lines printed), whereas only light program steps are included in the second (20.9 percent). The third cluster (5 percent) is characterized by 1 tape and average resource consumptions, the fourth (30.7 percent) by a large mean memory space, 26.65 Kwords. The fifth cluster (1.9 percent) groups the program steps requiring 2 tapes; the sixth (18.9 percent) uses a large number of files (from 3 to 5) but does not consume substantial amounts of the other resources. Finally, the seventh cluster (0.8 percent) contains those program steps whose heterogeneous characteristics prevented them from being classified in one of the previously constructed clusters.

We shall now briefly describe the characteristics of the *eight clusters* whose centroids are reported in Table 2.22. Due to the way the algorithm has been implemented, the program steps in clusters 7 and 8 (0.5 and 0.6 percent of the sample) have quite peculiar characteristics. These program steps can actually be considered as the outliers in the sample, as they include those having maximum CPU time, disk I/O time, number of lines printed, number of files allocated, and memory space. Therefore, the characteristics of these two clusters, which represent only 1.1 percent of the sample, will not be considered in the following comparison among clusters.

Cluster 1 contains program steps that make substantial use of all resources except tapes. Cluster 2, on the contrary, is characterized by a light use of all resources, while in cluster 3 all program steps require one tape and consume more resources than those in cluster 2.

In cluster 4 no tapes are used, and the memory space demand is uniform (that is, has low variability): the mean is 26.65 Kwords, and the standard deviation is very small. The other resources are lightly used, although a little more than in cluster 2. The program steps in cluster 5 require 2 tapes and large CPU times. Cluster 6 is characterized by a large number of files and a low CPU time demand.

The validity of this partition was evaluated by forcibly assigning the program steps in the population, except those in the sample, to the eight clusters obtained from the sample. The parameter values of each program step were checked against the parameter ranges of the eight clusters to determine whether they were compatible with the range of at least one of the clusters. Where this compatibility was found to exist with more than one cluster, the program step was assigned to the cluster with the closest centroid. A program step with one or more parameter values outside the corresponding range of a cluster was not assigned to that cluster.

Only 1.66 percent of the program steps in the population (those in the sample having been excluded) could not be assigned to any cluster. The percentages of those assigned to clusters 1 through 8 were 19.8, 18.4, 4.9, 32.8, 2.5, 12.6, 0.9, and 1.3, respectively. These percentages are quite close to those in the sample. Furthermore, the fraction of the population that could not be assigned to any cluster is negligible. Thus, the partition based on the sample may be viewed as significant also for the entire population.

The second objective of the study was to verify the existence of a resource-oriented characterization corresponding to a functional characterization of program steps based on the source language (FORTRAN, COBOL, Assembler) used and on the distinction between compilations and executions.

The program steps in the population were subdivided into the following eight categories:

COMPFOR:	FORTRAN compilations
COMPCOB:	COBOL compilations
COMPASS:	Assembler translations
EXECFOR:	Executions of program steps originally written in FORTRAN
EXECCOB:	Executions of COBOL program steps
EXECASS:	Executions of Assembler program steps
EXECSYS:	Execution of systems programs
EXECOTH:	Executions of program steps included in a user object program library and obtained from the translation of a program written in an unknown source language

To assign the program steps in the sample to the various categories, a program was implemented to analyze the log file. For each execution, the program tried to identify the corresponding compilation and hence the source language that had been used. The functional categories were found to exist in the following percentages in the sample: COMPFOR, 20.2; COMPCOB, 6.8; COMPASS, 4.9; EXECFOR, 13.7; EXECCOB, 3.1; EXECASS, 4.5; EXECSYS, 16.2; EXECOTH, 30.6.

The identification code of the category was added to the record of each program step to make the automatic analysis of the relationships between categories and clusters possible. A new characterization of the groups based on the resource-oriented parameters (see Table 2.22) was then made in terms of the functional categories to which their program steps belong. Table 2.23 shows the breakdowns of the eight categories over the eight clusters. Two values correspond in the table to each category and each cluster: the value in row *a* is the percentage of the program steps in the cluster that belong to the category being considered (the sum of the row *a* values in each column is 100); the value in row *b* is the percentage of the program steps in the category that belong to the cluster (the sum of the row *b* values in each row is 100).

In Table 2.23 we can see that all COBOL compilations fall into cluster 1, almost all FORTRAN compilations (93.3 percent of them) are in cluster 4, and Assembler translations are found in either cluster 4 or 6. The overlap between the FORTRAN compilations and part of the Assembler translations (those with a small number of statements) in cluster 4 is explained by the low consumption of resources that characterizes both. When a relatively long Assembler program is translated, a large number of files (4 or 5) is required and the corresponding program step falls into cluster 6.

The relationships between clusters and categories are less simple for executions. Approximately one COBOL execution out of four joins COBOL compilations in cluster 1. The other three fall into one of clusters 3, 4, or 6 depending on the amounts of resources they consume. Assembler executions can be found in cluster 6 (57.7 percent) together with Assembler translations, as well as in cluster 1 (21.2 percent) with COBOL compilations. Half of the FORTRAN executions are in cluster 4 with almost all the FORTRAN compilations, 26.1 percent of them are in cluster 2, which is characterized by minimum consumptions, and 10.4 and 10.5 percent are in clusters 1 and 6.

Many systems programs (58.8 percent), which do not require tapes, can be found in cluster 2, while the others are in clusters 3 or 6. The executions of programs whose

TABLE 2.23 DISTRIBUTIONS OF PROGRAM STEPS OVER THE EIGHT FUNCTIONAL CATEGORIES AND THE EIGHT RESOURCE-ORIENTED CLUSTERS IN TABLE 2.22

		Clusters							
Functional categories		*1*	*2*	*3*	*4*	*5*	*6*	*7*	*8*
FORTRAN compilations	a*	2.9	0.8	//	49.6	//	3.7	//	//
	b	2.7	0.6		93.3		3.4		
COBOL compilations	a	36.7	//	//	//	//	//	//	//
	b	100							
Assembler translations	a	//	//	//	6.8	//	12.7	//	//
	b				52.8		47.2		
FORTRAN executions	a	8	20.6	8.1	17.7	7.2	8.2	//	//
	b	10.4	26.1	2.1	49.9	1	10.5		
COBOL executions	a	4.3	0.8	10.8	2.1	7.2	3.7	//	//
	b	26.1	4.3	17.4	26.2	4.2	21.8		
Assembler executions	a	5.1	//	5.4	1.1	14.2	14.1	//	//
	b	21.2		6	9.1	6	57.7		
Systems programs executions	a	0.7	58.8	59.5	3.6	28.5	6.7	25	//
	b	0.9	60.3	18.6	8.5	3.3	7.6	0.8	
Other programs executions	a	42.3	19	16.2	19.1	42.9	50.9	75	100
	b	26.2	10.3	2.7	23.9	2.7	30.6	1.3	2.3

*Row *a* values refer to the cluster, row *b* values to the category of the program steps

original language is unknown are distributed over clusters 1, 4, and 6. Based on the amounts of resources consumed within these clusters, we may conjecture that most of those falling into cluster 1 are COBOL executions, most of those into cluster 4 are FORTRAN executions, and most of those in cluster 6 are Assembler executions.

The main characteristics of the clusters in terms of the functional categories can be summarized as follows:

Cluster 1: COBOL compilations, heavy COBOL executions
Cluster 2: Systems programs executions, light FORTRAN executions
Cluster 3: Systems programs, FORTRAN, and COBOL executions using one tape
Cluster 4: FORTRAN compilations, Assembler translations (short and medium programs), medium FORTRAN executions
Cluster 5: Various executions using 2 tapes
Cluster 6: Assembler translations (long programs), FORTRAN, COBOL, and Assembler executions requiring a large number of files (4 or 5)
Clusters 7 and 8: Outliers

The greater spread of executions over the clusters is essentially due to their resource usages being much more variable than those of the language processors. Note also that compilations and assemblies represent 31.9 percent of the program steps in the sample.

We can therefore conclude that objective b of the study has been achieved, since to the proposed functional characterization there corresponds a reasonably simple resource-oriented characterization. The former is practically appealing since it is much simpler than the latter to derive from a log file; it only entails easy calculations such as those of means and standard deviations, whereas a resource-oriented approach may require the use of more sophisticated and expensive techniques like clustering algorithms. The viability of a functional approach will obviously have to be verified against the objectives of the study to be undertaken and against the intended use of the workload model.

2.5.2 Case 2.2: An Interactive Workload Model Based on a Performance-oriented Criterion

This case describes an approach to the design and implementation of a workload model for an MIRS system based on the performance-oriented criterion introduced in Sec. 2.2. A complete discussion of the design procedure can be found in [FE81b]. This approach eliminates or reduces two of the drawbacks of the workload models based on other criteria, since it (1) uses the performance indexes as the workload-characterizing parameters, and (2) accounts for the dynamic behavior of the real workload by trying to reproduce some of the *command mixes* in it.

An executable model of an interactive workload consists of a set of *scripts,* each script being a sequence of commands from a terminal and of the think times that are to elapse between any two consecutive commands (see Sec. 2.3.2). The set of activities that take place between two consecutive returns of the user–system complex to the same state (for instance, two consecutive instants when the user begins to type in a command) is an *interaction*. The duration of an interaction, in our simple model of the user–system

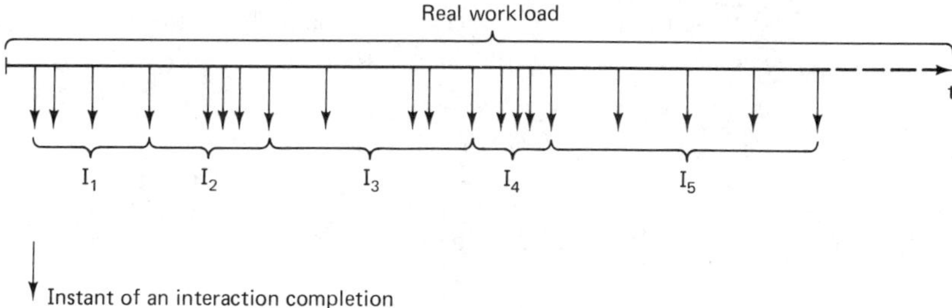

Figure 2.26 Intervals I_1, I_2, . . . into which a real workload has been subdivided as seen on the time axis. Each interval contains four interaction completions.

dialogue, is the sum of the four intervals into which it may be subdivided: the input, response, output, and think times.

The basic workload component chosen by the approach to be adopted is the *interval*. An interval is a set of scripts that are executed concurrently in the workload to be modeled. More precisely, the beginning and the end of an interval may be chosen to correspond to the completion of two interactions. A completion is defined as the return of the user–system complex to a given state (for example, the beginning of the input time). The interval delimited by these two completions consists of all the command sequences input from all terminals during the corresponding period. In our case, we will select the interaction completions that will mark the end of an interval and the beginning of the next one so that the number of such completions within each interval is constant (see Fig. 2.26). Note that interval durations are generally different from each other. The use of intervals as workload model components guarantees that some attention is paid to the command mixes in the real workload and that some of them will be reproduced in the model. Also, the commands corresponding to the interactions that are incomplete at the beginning or at the end of an interval (more precisely, that part of their execution which takes place after the beginning or before the end of an interval) will have to be included in that interval.

Each interval is characterized by the values of the performance indexes $\mathcal{P}_i$ ($i = 1, \ldots, l$) it has produced, and may be considered as a point in the l-dimensional space of these indexes, which have been selected according to the objectives of the study. By one of the classification techniques described in the previous sections (in our case a clustering algorithm has been used), the intervals of the real workload are partitioned into g *groups*. Each group contains intervals whose performance indexes are substantially closer to each other than to those of the intervals in other groups. Group $\mathcal{G}_k$ ($k = 1, \ldots, g$) consists of m_k intervals I_j^k ($j = 1, \ldots, m_k$). Let $\mathcal{P} = \{\mathcal{P}_1, \ldots, \mathcal{P}_l\}$ denote the vector of performance index values produced by the real workload W, and $\mathcal{P}' = \{\mathcal{P}'_1, \ldots, \mathcal{P}'_l\}$ the vector of performance index values produced by the workload model W'.

Each interval gives its contribution to the global value of each performance index. If the index values for the whole workload can be obtained by a simple averaging of the corresponding values produced by each basic component, then we have

$$\mathcal{P}_i = \frac{1}{m} \sum_{k=1}^{g} \sum_{j=1}^{m_k} \mathcal{P}_{i,j}^k \tag{2.16}$$

where m is the total number of intervals in W and $\mathcal{P}^k_{i,j}$ is the value of the ith index for interval I^k_j. The value of the ith index for group $\mathcal{G}_k$ is

$$\mathcal{P}^k_i = \frac{1}{m_k} \sum_{j=1}^{m_k} \mathcal{P}^k_{ij} \tag{2.17}$$

and therefore Eq. (2.16) can be written as

$$\mathcal{P}_i = \frac{1}{m} \sum_{k=1}^{g} m_k \mathcal{P}^k_i \tag{2.18}$$

We now choose as the representative of each group the interval closest to the group's center of mass (according to Euclidean distances in the l-dimensional space of performance indexes), and we take the set of these intervals as our workload model. The intervals in the model are to be run independently of each other. While they run, we measure the $\mathcal{P}'^k_{i,j}$. Then we compute the value of $\mathcal{P}'_i$ as

$$\mathcal{P}'_i = \frac{1}{m} \sum_{k=1}^{g} m_k \mathcal{P}'^k_{ij} \tag{2.19}$$

Since, because of the criterion according to which the representative intervals of each group were chosen, we have $\mathcal{P}'^k_{i,j} \cong \mathcal{P}^k_i$, then from Eqs. (2.18) and (2.19) we also have $\mathcal{P}_i \cong \mathcal{P}'_i$. Since this approximate equality holds for all i, the performance-oriented criterion is satisfied. Expression (2.19) shows that the value of $\mathcal{P}'_i$ is given by a weighted sum of interval contributions with weights equal to m_k/m, i.e., to the proportions of group representations in W.

With some modifications and approximations, this approach can be applied also when some of the indexes do not satisfy condition (2.16); this is for instance the case of the variance of response times (see [FE81b]).

The fundamental steps of the model-building procedure will now be summarized:

Step 1. Measure the performance indexes we are interested in and all the other necessary information in the workload to be modeled.

Step 2. Choose the number n of interaction completions per interval, and compute the indexes for each of the m intervals thus defined.

Step 3. Cluster the m intervals into g groups (depending on the clustering algorithm, g may be determined by the clustering algorithm itself or may have to be selected by the modeler).

Step 4. Select the g intervals whose indexes are closest to the center of mass of each group (note that having only one representative interval per group makes the resulting model extremely compact; model accuracy considerations may make an increase in the number of these representatives or in the number of groups desirable).

Step 5. Run each of the g intervals independently, measure the values of the performance indexes they produce, and compute the performance of the model by Eq. (2.19).

Some of the practical problems that arise in applying this procedure have already been discussed in previous sections, since they are encountered also in other model-building methods. For instance, the problems of selecting performance indexes, the number of interaction completions per interval, and the number of groups are to be solved by considering the objectives of the study, the size of the workload to be modeled, the size desired for the model, the accuracy needed, and so on.

Since recording all the system's input would generally be too expensive, this operation could be limited to a fraction of the intervals in the original workload. This approach works if the sample intervals recorded fall into all groups and at least one of them per group is not too far from that group's center of mass. The value of the performance indexes must be continuously collected also for those intervals that are *not* recorded. Another solution of this problem would be to use synthetic scripts to assemble *synthetic intervals,* that is, intervals whose performance index values may be modified by properly changing the values of suitable parameters.

A peculiar problem of the model-building procedure described is that of reconstructing the initial state of the system for the execution of each representative interval. An accurate reconstruction is necessary since the values of performance indexes are usually quite sensitive to the initial state. To determine how accurate the reconstruction should be, and to study the validity of a model resulting from the application of the procedure, a simulator of a simple interactive system was constructed and used as if it were the real system whose workload had to be modeled. The simulated environment allowed several changes to the system's configuration to be made quite inexpensively and comparisons between workload and model performance indexes to be performed.

The simulated MIRS system (see Fig. 1.4) has one CPU, one disk drive, and 16 terminals. The CPU, disk, and memory queues, as well as the CPU and memory quanta, are represented in the simulator.

The workload consists of 16 command streams entered from the terminals. Each command in a stream is of one of four types. Two of these types have the resource request patterns reported in Tables 2.24 and 2.25. At the end of each interaction a terminal may issue the next command in its stream or disconnect itself for a certain amount of time. Two examples of command sequences are shown in Fig. 2.27, which also indicates that command streams are cyclically input by the terminal to which they have been assigned.

TABLE 2.24 RESOURCE REQUEST PATTERN CORRESPONDING TO COMMAND C1

Command C1	
Resource	*Time (ms)*
THINK	14,000
CPU	100
DISK	50
CPU	30
DISK	70
CPU	150
DISK	30
CPU	20
OUT	40

TABLE 2.25 RESOURCE REQUEST PATTERN CORRESPONDING TO COMMAND C2

	Command C2
Resource	*Time (ms)*
THINK	5,000
CPU	200
DISK	80
CPU	100
OUT	20

Both the resource patterns of the commands and the 16 different command streams have been constructed after having analyzed a real interactive workload.

The main features of the workload to be modeled and the values of some model and procedure parameters are displayed in Table 2.26. For the system model in this study and with the parameter values in Table 2.26, it was found that, for the model's representativeness to be acceptable, the initial state of each interval in the workload model must be reconstructed by using the following data (which have therefore to be collected at the beginning of each interval being recorded when monitoring the real workload):

- The command being executed by each terminal
- The contents of each queue
- The time (if known) each process is scheduled to leave the resource (or resources) it is using
- The activities that each process has to perform before completing the execution of the current command
- The remaining time before memory quantum expiration for each process in memory
- The remaining time before CPU quantum expiration for the process (if any) that is using the CPU

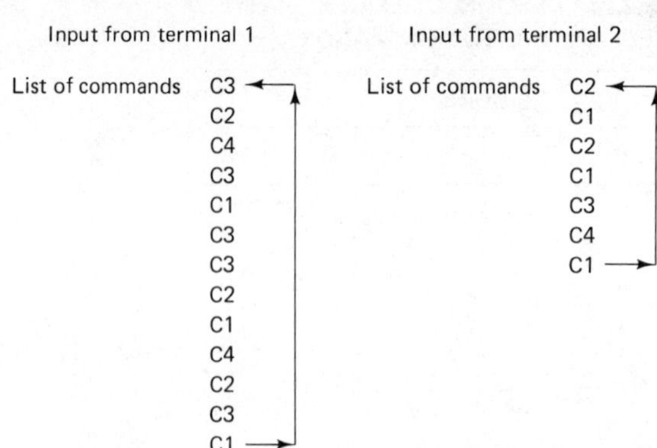

Figure 2.27 Sample scripts executed by terminals in the MIRS simulator. Each script is cyclically input by a different terminal until the end of the simulation, with some possible pauses during which the terminal is not connected to the system. Execution of the script may be started at any point in the cycle. The scripts actually used were substantially longer.

TABLE 2.26 MAIN CHARACTERISTICS OF THE WORKLOAD TO BE MODELED AND OF THE MODEL TO BE CONSTRUCTED (INITIAL STATE RECONSTRUCTION EXPERIMENTS)

Total execution time of the workload: 20,000 s (5 h, 33 min)	
Number of interaction completions per interval: $n = 100$	
Number of intervals: $m = 246$	
Mean interval duration: 81 s	
Number of interval groups: $g = 19$	
Performance indexes considered:	Mean response time
	Standard deviation of response times

Having clustered the 246 intervals into 19 groups, the 19 representative intervals were identified. The model's performance computed by Eq. (2.19) was found to be very close to that produced by the full workload, since the only errors introduced by the procedure are those due to the nonzero distance between each representative interval and its group's center of mass, and to the approximations made in the treatment of standard deviations. Even though no efforts whatsoever were made to obtain a distribution of response times in the model as close as possible to that measured on the full workload, the two distributions turned out to be almost identical.

Note that it is possible by using Eq. (2.19) to check whether the representative intervals have been properly chosen before assembling the model, designing the experiments, and running them.

The model consisting of 19 intervals was run many times, both to determine the amount of accuracy needed in the reconstruction of each interval's initial state and to study the sensitivity of the model's accuracy to system configuration changes. The conclusion of the former set of experiments was that all the information listed previously must be taken into account when initializing the system for execution of a representative interval. Thus, the system's driver will have to be capable of setting the system in the initial state specified by the experimenter, and this requires that a quite sophisticated driver be available. The latter set of experiments was supplemented with a corresponding set of simulations under the workload to be modeled so that the model's performance could be compared with that produced by the modeled workload in each different system configuration. For economical reasons, the size of the full workload was roughly halved in this second set of experiments, as shown in Table 2.27.

TABLE 2.27 MAIN CHARACTERISTICS OF THE WORKLOAD TO BE MODELED AND OF THE MODEL TO BE CONSTRUCTED (MODEL VALIDITY EXPERIMENTS)

Total execution time: 10,000 (about 2 h, 46 min)	
Number of interaction completions per interval: $n = 100$	
Number of intervals: $m = 118$	
Mean interval duration: ~84 s	
Number of interval groups: 11	
Performance indexes considered:	Mean response time
	Standard deviation of response times

In Fig. 2.28a we show a plot of the workload W to be modeled for model validity studies in the plane of the two performance indexes being considered. Each of the 118 intervals in W is represented by a point, and the 11 groups produced by the clustering algorithm with their respective weights are also shown. In Fig. 2.28b we report a representation of the model W' in the same plane. Each group in W' consists of a single point, which represents the interval closest to the group's center of mass.

The configuration parameters that were modified, that is, the factors of these experiments, were the memory size (MSZ), the memory quantum length (MQU), the CPU quantum length (CQU), the speed of the CPU (CSP), and the speed of the disk (DSP). Eight one-factor experiments, five two-factor experiments, and one three-factor experiment were performed. Their results are reported in Table 2.28. The errors shown in this table are in most cases acceptable. It should be noted that the larger errors correspond to substantial variations in system parameter values; for instance, the speed of the CPU has been doubled in test 6, the speeds of both the CPU and the disk have been doubled in test 13, and in test 14 also the size of the memory has been increased by 25 percent.

Figures 2.29a, b, and c compare some of the histograms of response times computed from measurements taken on W' with the corresponding histograms derived from mea-

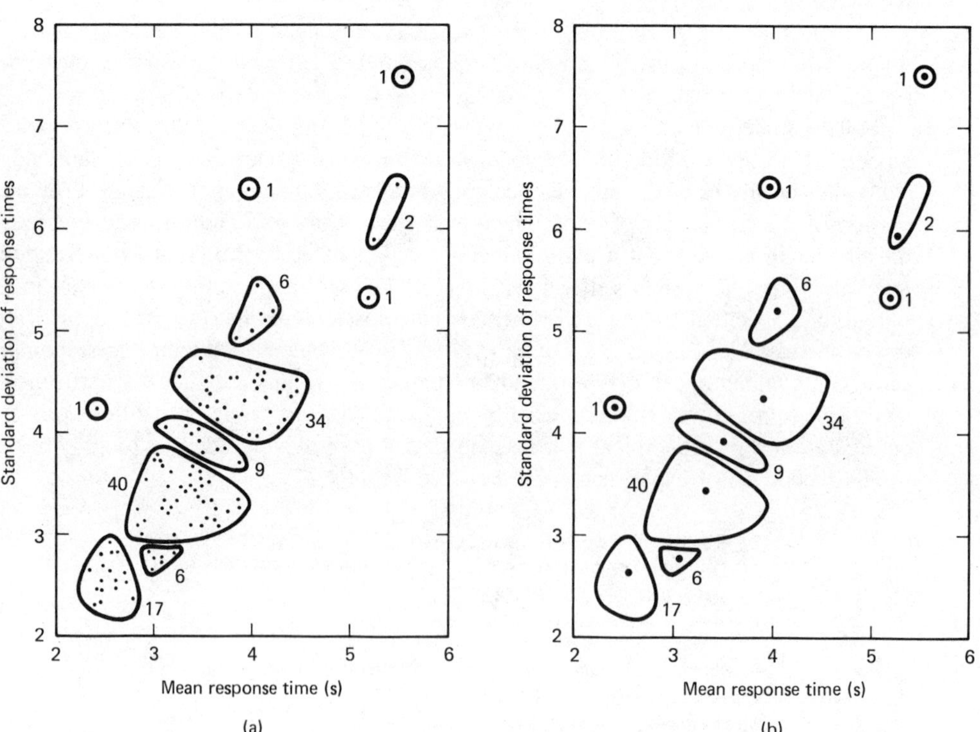

Figure 2.28 Intervals and groups (a) in the workload W to be modeled; (b) in the model W' constructed for validity experiments. Five of the 11 groups contain outliers.

TABLE 2.28 RESULTS OF MODEL VALIDITY TESTS OBTAINED BY SIMULATION

	Test no.	Factors modified	Amount of change (%)	Mean response time W (s)	Mean response time W′ (s)	Mean response time Error (%)	St. dev. of response time W (s)	St. dev. of response time W′ (s)	St. dev. of response time Error (%)
One-factor experiments	1	MSZ	−25	3.13	3.24	+3.5	3.42	3.69	+7.8
	2	MSZ	+25	3.52	3.64	+3.4	3.75	3.92	+4.5
	3	MQU	−40	3.38	3.45	+2.0	3.65	3.73	+2.1
	4	MQU	+40	3.54	3.74	+5.6	3.78	3.99	+5.5
	5	CSP	−50	10.77	10.66	−1.0	10.56	9.79	−7.2
	6	CSP	+100	1.06	1.22	+15.0	1.20	1.45	+20.8
	7	DSP	−50	3.59	3.72	+3.6	3.65	3.77	+3.2
	8	DSP	+100	3.42	3.52	+3.6	3.81	3.85	+1.0
Two-factor experiments	9	CQU MQU	−50 +40	3.46	3.74	+8.0	3.63	3.97	+9.3
	10	CQU MQU	+50 +40	3.50	3.75	+7.1	3.77	4.02	+6.6
	11	CSP MSZ	−50 −25	10.24	10.48	+2.3	10.68	10.54	−1.3
	12	CSP MSZ	−50 +25	10.99	10.94	−0.4	10.34	10.83	+4.7
	13	CSP DSP	+100 +100	0.97	1.09	+12.3	1.17	1.41	+20.5
Three-factor experiment	14	CSP DSP MSZ	+100 +100 +25	0.98	1.13	+15.3	1.19	1.48	+24.3

surements of W. The cases shown in these figures were those in which the largest differences between workload and model histograms were observed.

The validity of these results allows us to conclude that, if the problems outlined can all be satisfactorily solved, this procedure, or similar ones, will be practically usable to construct representative models of interactive workloads.

2.6 WORKLOAD FORECASTING FOR CAPACITY PLANNING

A main goal of system capacity planning, and perhaps the most important one, is determining the fraction of the system's total capacity utilized by the current workload. The purpose of this investigation is to predict the amounts of capacity that will be needed in the future to process the expected workloads with the required levels of service. Our first task, however, is to define the concepts of *capacity of a resource* and *capacity of a system*. In Sec. 1.4 the capacity of a system was defined as the maximum amount of work the system is capable of doing per unit time given a certain workload. Thus, the capacity of a system is a function of the characteristics of the individual resources, their interconnections (that is, the system's configuration), and the way they are used (that is, the patterns of resource requests made by the workload). According to another definition

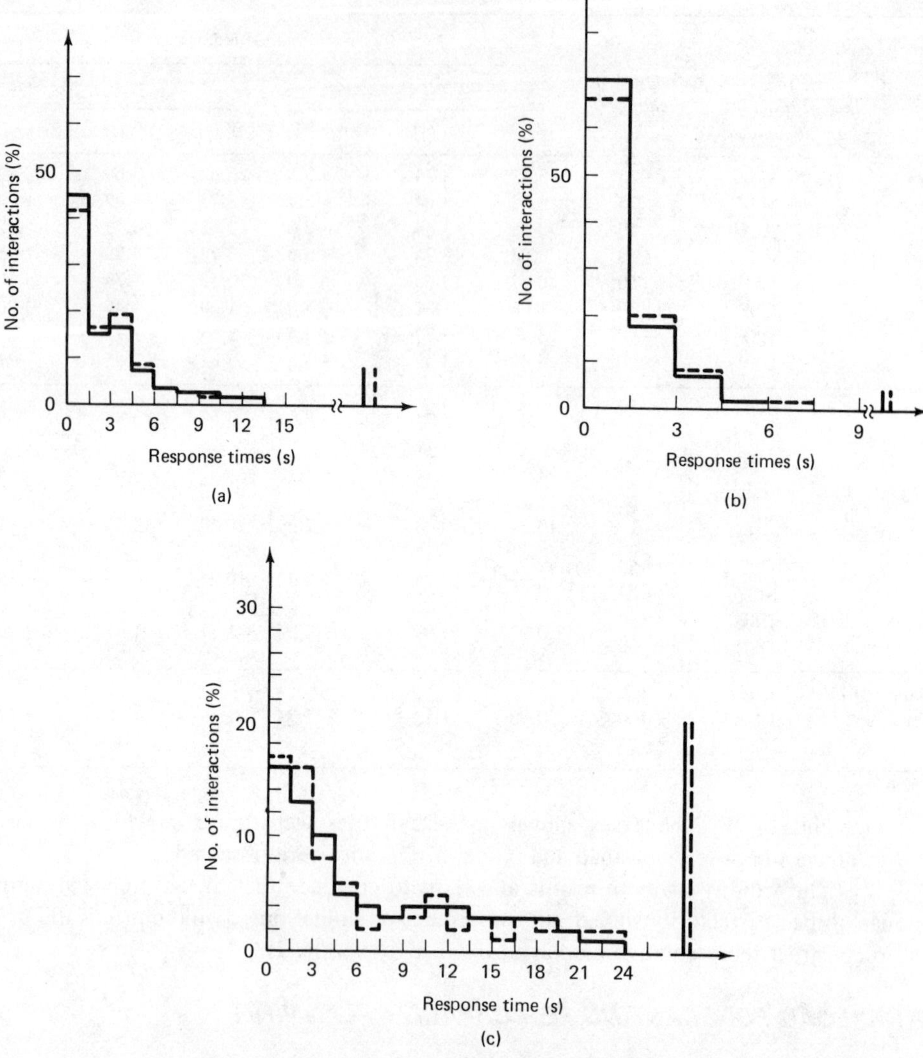

Figure 2.29 Histograms of response times obtained with W (solid line) and W' (broken line) for the following system parameters changes: (a) memory size: −25%; (b) CPU speed: +100%; (c) CPU speed: −50%; memory size: +25%.

[K076], the capacity of a system is identified with a theoretical value that represents the maximum amount of work obtainable from a system. The capacity of a resource may be defined as the maximum rate at which the resource may process the requests.

Bronner [BR80] includes the *user service objective* among the parameters that contribute to the capacity of a resource. In general, this capacity cannot be expressed by a single quantity, since the conditions under which it has been measured must also be specified. A resource, when considered in isolation, has an actual capacity equal to 100 percent of its theoretical capacity. However, if one takes into account the constraints to its operation imposed by the workload's characteristics (for example, different block sizes in disk I/O operations) and by the system's configuration (for example, the number of spindles and the types of disk drives connected to a channel), one often concludes that a resource's actual capacity will not be allowed to grow beyond a fraction (sometimes quite small) of its theoretical capacity. These maximum values of capacity can be further decreased by the *installation service objectives*. For instance, the maximum actual capacity of a disk channel may be lower than that computed according to the characteristics of the configuration and of the workload if the interactive response times corresponding to the computed value are longer than those required by the service objectives.

We can summarize this discussion by saying that there are various levels at which the capacity of a system can be defined. In general, one can make a distinction among *theoretical capacity, available capacity,* and *utilizable capacity*. The first is computed considering the characteristics of the resources *in isolation,* the second takes into account the constraints imposed by their interconnections, and the third factors in all the installation's constraints, including the workload's characteristics and the service objectives. In the sequel, the term *capacity* will always refer to the utilizable capacity.

The main activities capacity planning consists of may be grouped under the following headings:

1. *Measurement and analysis* of data concerning the current and past workloads and the system's configuration.
2. *Definition of the installation's service objectives* based on user requirements, and computation of the corresponding capacities required of the various resources.
3. *Planning* of resource capacities to satisfy future requirements; this activity is based on the information acquired in the previous activities and on that gathered by forecasting user requirements in terms of service levels and amounts of work to be performed.
4. *Reporting* in suitable form the results to the various categories of persons involved (management, administrative staff, technical staff) so that the most appropriate decisions can be made at the various levels within the organization.

Clearly, two activities that are indispensable in performing *all* the functions described are *workload characterization* and *workload forecasting*. The techniques that may be used to characterize a workload have been presented and discussed in the preceding sections. This section will examine some workload forecasting methods.

First, we must note that characterization and forecasting can in reality be considered as a single function. Their interactions are so strong that the approach to the characterization of the workload will be influenced by the workload variables whose future values are to be predicted. The difficulties of forecasting, which supplement those of the characterization itself, can be seen in diagrams like that in Fig. 2.30, which often appear in the relevant literature. These diagrams usually have a *qualitative* purpose: they show the possible trends of a workload's evolution but are not very reliable as quantitative predictors, since the quantitative aspects are influenced by the characteristics of each indi-

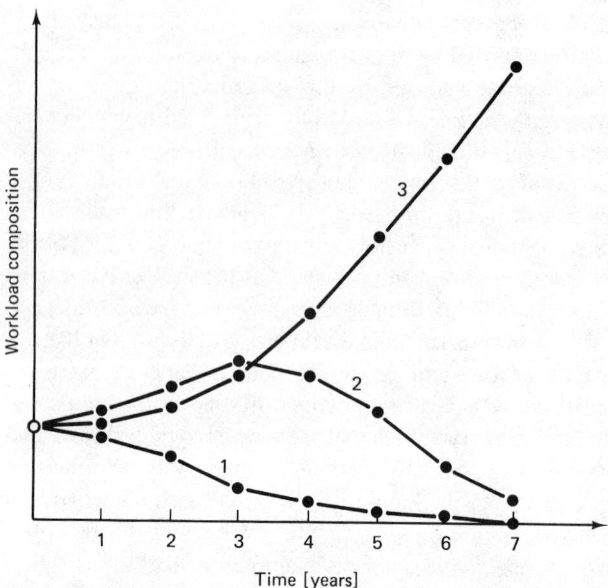

Figure 2.30 Qualitative plot of a workload's composition versus time. Curve 1 refers to programs that have been in production for some time, curve 2 to new production programs, and curve 3 to programs being developed or debugged. Uncertainty grows as one moves from curve 1 to curve 3.

vidual installation and by the lifetimes of the programs executed. Curve 1 describes a workload composed of old production programs, which tend to be less utilized as time progresses. Curve 2 refers to a workload consisting of programs that have just entered the production state. A workload produced by new applications being implemented or tested has the time behavior represented by curve 3.

Our knowledge of workload characteristics decreases when going from type 1 workloads to type 3 workloads. Based on the shapes of the diagrams, we can say that the uncertainty about workload characteristics grows almost exponentially with time.

An examination of curves 2 and 3 suggests that, for forecasting purposes, it is useful to distinguish *current applications* from *new applications*. The load produced by current applications tends to grow according to trends that can be predicted from historical data, while the load due to new applications is predictable with less accuracy. New applications may in turn be subdivided into two groups: those that may be considered as being similar to existing applications, and hence that produce a somewhat familiar load, and those that, performing completely new functions, produce a load of unknown characteristics.

A technique that may be used to predict the loads produced by the latter will be described in Section 2.6.1. In the remainder of this section, we shall discuss methods for predicting workloads due to current applications and to new applications that may be approximately estimated in terms of existing applications.

The initial step of a workload forecasting project is the *definition of objectives,* which is needed to select among all the data in the log file those to be considered for extrapolation. The approaches to log data analysis may be classified into two categories: (1) window analysis, and (2) functional analysis.

A *window* is a time interval during which the events the study is concerned with occur, for instance, the daily periods when the mean response time is greater than a given threshold or the periods during which certain classes of programs are executed. Window analysis restricts the data to be considered for forecasting to data measured during those intervals, which are sometimes called *observation periods*. A useful way to show the windows in a daily workload is depicted in Fig. 2.31. If, for instance, we want to predict the variations of the load referred to in Fig. 2.31 with the volume of teleprocessing applications, we have to make use of the daily historical data observed within the windows identified by the shaded areas in the figure. Some applications of this technique are described in [K076] and [AR80].

The partitioning of the workload based on the *functions* performed by the applications allows us in some cases to forecast future workloads by the composition of the loads each application will produce with estimated variations of the volume of data to be processed. These variations will have to be derived from corporate plans, and their expected effects on the installation's workload will have to be determined.

For example, if corporate management expects the number of employees to grow by 500 within one year, the payroll processing application should be expected to have to compute 500 more paychecks per month within one year. If the load produced by the computation of a paycheck (which is the *unit of load* in this case) is known, it will be easy to predict by linear extrapolation the load due to 500 more paychecks.

The unit of load obviously varies with the application. For instance, in banking applications one unit of load is the updating of one checking account. Various terms are used in the literature to designate the units of load, for example, *natural forecast units* [KO76], *natural business units* [BR80], and *key volume indicators* [AR80]. Functional analysis is also called *application profiling*.

The second step in a workload forecasting project is the computation of the load produced by each category of programs involved. Considering again the example in Fig. 2.31, the fraction of the utilization of each resource to be attributed to the teleprocessing

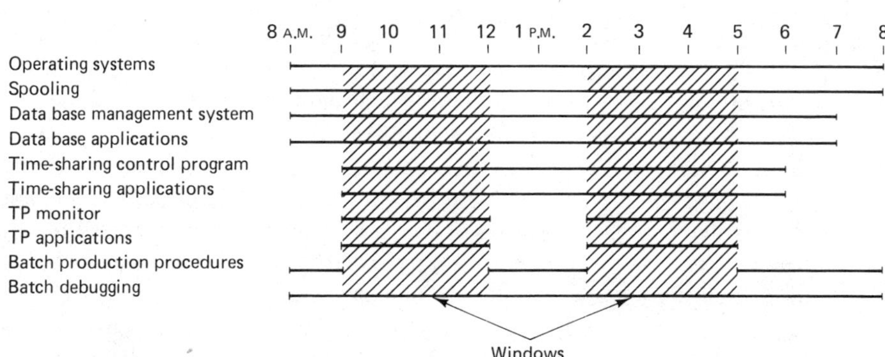

Figure 2.31 Identification of the windows to be considered in the study of the load produced by teleprocessing applications. Horizontal segments show the periods of execution of the corresponding classes of programs.

applications must be estimated. The most delicate problems encountered in this phase have to do with:

- *Accuracy* of the data recorded in the log file
- *Availability* of the data needed for forecasting
- *Significance* of the windows

If the problem of the accuracy of the data is ignored, large errors in the projections may result. For instance, the fraction of total CPU time reported by SMF, a software tool incorporated into the IBM OS operating system and all of its versions and descendants, may vary between 36 percent for trivial TSO commands to 97 percent for heavily CPU-bound programs [CO80].

The *availability* of the data may influence the selection of the approach to be adopted. To reduce the measurement overhead, several types of resource usage data are not usually recorded in the log file.

For some of the data, only global values are recorded and not breakdowns by applications. Thus, before selecting the applications for the functional projection approach, one should check whether the necessary data have been recorded or can be derived from those actually recorded in the log file.

The *significance* of the windows must also be verified, since historical data might be affected by errors due to observation periods where abnormal events have occurred. Among these periods are those during which the system (or some of its components) has been down or its workload has been atypical (for example, the summer quarter in a university, a holiday, a strike period), or some of the data have been lost.

The choice of applications for forecasting purposes will depend on the objectives of the study, on the type of system, and on the organization and other characteristics of the corporation or institution under consideration. Thus, for example, one may decide to project applications that are particularly important, such as payroll, inventory control, checking account updating, and so on; or groups of applications related to the company's divisions, such as research and development, production, sales, personnel, and so on; or, again, one may compute the capacity required by all applications belonging to such classes within the workload as time sharing, teleprocessing, batch, and so on.

Among the possible subdivisions of the workload that are suitable for forecasting purposes, one can also include clusters of applications having similar resource usage characteristics. Since these clusters may also correspond to reasonably well defined functions, for example, FORTRAN compilations, COBOL compilations, FORTRAN executions, and so on (see Case 2.1 in section 2.5.1), it will be sufficient to apply to single clusters the respective fractions of the total variation expected for each of the functions they represent. In this case, the load produced by the program step closest to the centroid of each cluster may be taken as the *unit of load*.

To evaluate the load produced by an application, in particular by a unit of load, various techniques are available. The most expensive but most reliable consists of executing the application several times on a dedicated machine, varying each time the number of units of load being processed. For each resource one can obtain by this approach, filtering the results with such approximation techniques as the least squares method and extrapolating, the utilization due to a single unit of load. Furthermore, since the system is dedicated to the application under study, the *indirect load* (that is, the overhead due to the processing of a unit of load) can be evaluated. This load must be considered in extrapolations in order for reliable results to be obtained.

All common forecasting techniques can be applied also to the workload forecasting problem. Depending on the length of the period over which forecasts are to be made, we have *short-term forecasts* (those based on units of days or months), *medium-term forecasts* (months or quarters), and *long-term forecasts* (years). The choice of the forecasting technique will be made considering the *planning horizon* (the duration of the prediction period) and the *dynamic characteristics* of the load (for instance, seasonal productions, weekly peaks for data base updatings, cyclic applications, and so on). Some of the forecasting techniques most frequently applied to the forecasting of workloads are the moving average, exponential smoothing, and regression methods (see for example [GI77]).

To achieve meaningful results by using prediction techniques, it is essential:

1. To consider the workload's trends with respect to all the system's resources, not only those related to the resources directly concerned with the objectives of the study.
2. To evaluate future utilizations of the resources both for the whole workload and for each individual class of programs or application into which the workload has been partitioned for the purpose of the study.

If these operations are not performed, the results may be affected by errors so large as to make them meaningless.

As an example, Fig. 2.32 reports for the system referred to in Fig. 2.31 the trends of CPU and channel 1 utilizations both for the whole workload and for the subworkload produced by teleprocessing applications. If we consider only the CPU capacity needed by the whole workload, we may derive from Fig. 2.32a the conclusion that a new CPU will have to be installed within 10 months; however, if we also take into account the capacity of channel 1 required by the entire workload, Fig. 2.32b tells us that an upgrade of that resource will have to be made within $6^1/_2$ months.

The objective of the study is to determine whether the current capacities of the resources are sufficient to support the new teleprocessing load, which corresponds to an increase in the transaction rate and to a new application whose load has been estimated and that should become operational in production mode in about 4 months. For this reason, the data concerning teleprocessing applications have been extracted from those describing the whole workload. As can be seen in Fig. 2.32a, to keep the current *teleprocessing service levels* it is necessary to increase the capacity of the CPU within 5 months (and not 10 months as previously predicted). The upgrading of channel 1 can on the other hand take place at the same time as previously expected, that is, in about $6^1/_2$ months. The increase in CPU demand shown for the entire workload in Fig. 2.32a is due in part to the new teleprocessing load and in part to the overhead produced by this new load.

Extrapolations like those shown in Fig. 2.32 must be recomputed after each modification, since changing the capacity of a resource may alter the distribution of the load

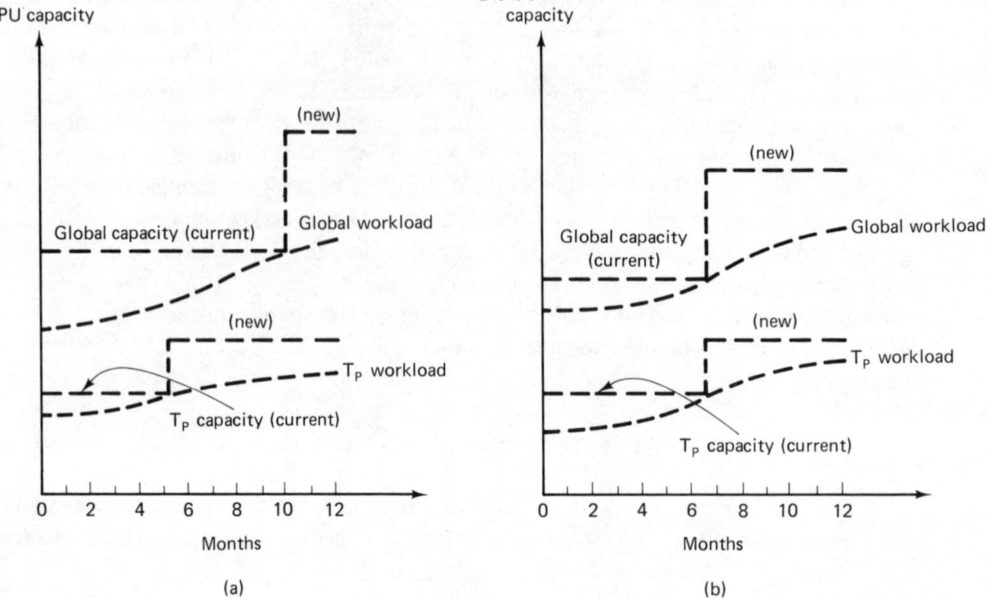

Figure 2.32 Identification of the times at which the capacities of the CPU and of channel 1 are to be upgraded. Also, the load increases due to teleprocessing applications are shown.

on the other resources so as to make the previous assumptions meaningless. These alterations are essentially due to the following phenomena:

1. The migration of contention situations from one resource to another (*bottleneck migration* or *bottleneck switching*).
2. Unpredictable modifications in the workload's composition due to the *latent workload,* to be defined later.

When we extrapolate, we implicitly assume that the loads of the various resources can be modified *only* by changes in the number of units of load processed by the application involved. In other words, the assumption is made that in the system no other phenomena occur induced by the new load corresponding to the application and capable of modifying the patterns of requests for the various resources. This assumption may be deemed valid, within certain bounds, when all resources have substantial amounts of unused capacity. In other situations, the assumption's validity is questionable. For example, an increase in the I/O activity due to the application being considered may cause an increase in the mean page transport time, thereby altering the loads caused by all other applications. Another case in point is that of the saturation of a resource: when, say, the CPU reaches its maximum utilization, all processes are slowed down, and the loads on the other resources decrease.

The use of simulation or analytic *models* allows the performance effects of a workload increase to be studied, accounting for the interactions among the resources and among their individual loads. These techniques potentially produce reliable forecasts.

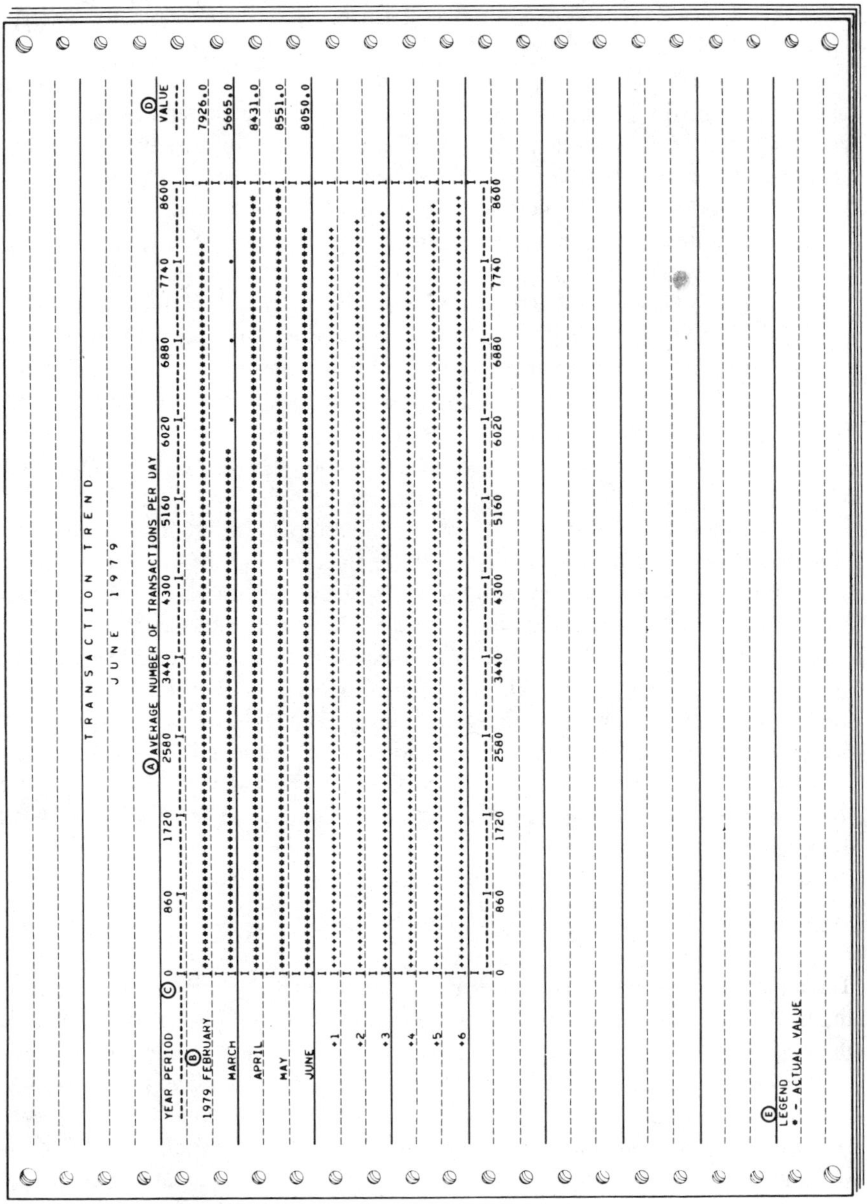

Figure 2.33 Forecast of the number of transactions executed per day for the next 6 months. The forecast has been obtained by the MANAGE IMS package [MA79] using the exponential smoothing technique.

Since the input data for the models are in any case to be computed with the methods based on windows or application profiles, in practice the best approach to workload forecasting is one that integrates in a single methodology the techniques described previously.

It is quite hard to predict the modifications induced by variations in the capacity of the resources on the composition of the workload. This entails evaluating the *latent workload,* that is, the portion of a workload that, due to various constraints, is not submitted to the system. For instance, one should determine how (following what law) the on-line workload would increase with the number of terminals, or how the degree of multiprogramming increases with the memory size (and how the mean size of a program varies with memory size).

The constraints just mentioned (the number of terminals and the memory size) may be seen as *direct constraints*. There are also *indirect constraints* imposed on the user community by the system's performance and by the charging policy. For instance, when the turnaround time of batch programs goes beyond a certain threshold, users tend to exploit more often the on-line facilities of the system. Also, depending on a user's economic situation, high-priority daytime execution or low-priority nighttime execution will tend to be selected for that user's programs.

Even though the reliability of these predictions is uncertain, it is useful to try to formulate reasonable hypotheses by carefully interviewing the various people involved (for example, programmers, systems analysts, managers, and corporate planners).

The study of the temporal trends of some global performance indexes (for example, response time, turnaround time, transaction execution rate, program execution rate) will in most cases provide useful indications for the analysis of workload and resource usage dynamics. Several commercial software tools are available for the statistical analysis of historical data. Some of these tools are also capable of making projections. In Fig. 2.33 we show a report produced by the MANAGE: IMS package [MA79], which presents a forecast (based on the exponential smoothing technique) of the number of transactions executed per day.

2.6.1 Estimation of the Load of a New Application

The techniques described in the previous section cannot be applied to the forecasting of the load produced by new applications. Since there are no historical data to refer to for these applications, their presumed similarity with other applications from the viewpoint of the load they produce cannot be verified, nor can extrapolations be based on values of workload variables measured in the recent past. On the other hand, this category of programs, which curve 3 in Fig. 2.30 refers to, will in most installations be the dominant portion of the system's future load. Thus, no capacity planning study can be performed without the knowledge, although approximate, of the load that will be produced by new applications.

The only installations for which this problem does not exist are those dedicated to a particular application (for instance, reservations, process control, on-line inventory control), whose future load only differs from the current one in the number of units of load to be processed and not in its nature or type.

In general, the forecasting of the load due to new applications is performed by applying empirical rules essentially based on the experience of the forecaster. The new application is subdivided into parts, or modules, that perform complete functions, for example, the printing of a report having a given length or the search for data in tables of known size. For each module, a similar part of an existing application is sought; the load that will be caused by the module is then estimated from the load due to its corresponding part of the current load, if one can be found. Evidently, this method is not very precise.

In other cases, the workload measurements on which extrapolation will be based are taken when the new application is still being debugged and tested. However, even this method may introduce errors that will make predictions meaningless. These errors are due to particular workload conditions that may exist during the debugging phase: the processing of the application may be incomplete because of the missing portions of the application, or the coded portions may contain bugs that have not yet been detected.

It should also be observed that the load produced by an application need not be proportional to the number of units of load processed, and that this proportionality is particularly questionable for low numbers of units of load. Thus, even with dedicated systems, extrapolations must be performed with great caution.

A more rigorous approach to the problem consists of building a probabilistic model of the new application; this model is a *graph* that can be reduced by suitable techniques. The principles of this approach, which have been described by Beizer [BE70], [BE74], [BE78], will now be outlined.

Those points in a flow chart where flow lines converge or diverge, that is, the *junctions* and the *decisions,* may be seen as the *nodes* of a graph whose *links* are the flow lines connecting the nodes (see Fig. 2.34). The operations within the boxes of the flow chart are replaced by the values of the *parameters* or *weights*, selected according to the objectives of the study, which are associated to the corresponding links. For instance, if the goal is to predict the execution time of the application, the weights of the links will be the mean execution times of the instructions they represent; if, on the other hand, the request rates to the various resources are to be predicted, the weights will be the mean numbers of operations to be performed by the CPU, the disk, the tapes, and so on. In other cases, the weights may consist of the types of machine instructions and their mean numbers, the mean block lengths, the mean values of the software work requested by the instructions associated to the links, or may be expressed as functions of the characteristics of the data. In more complete studies, the variances σ^2 of the link parameters will be considered along with their means μ.

For each decision node, probabilities of execution of the various outcoming links are to be assigned. This is undoubtedly the most delicate aspect of this technique. Depending on how their values are determined, there are three types of branching probabilities:

1. Probabilities that can be estimated based on conditions *external* with respect to the application.
2. Probabilities whose values depend on the *structure* of the application.
3. Probabilities whose values are functions of the *input data*.

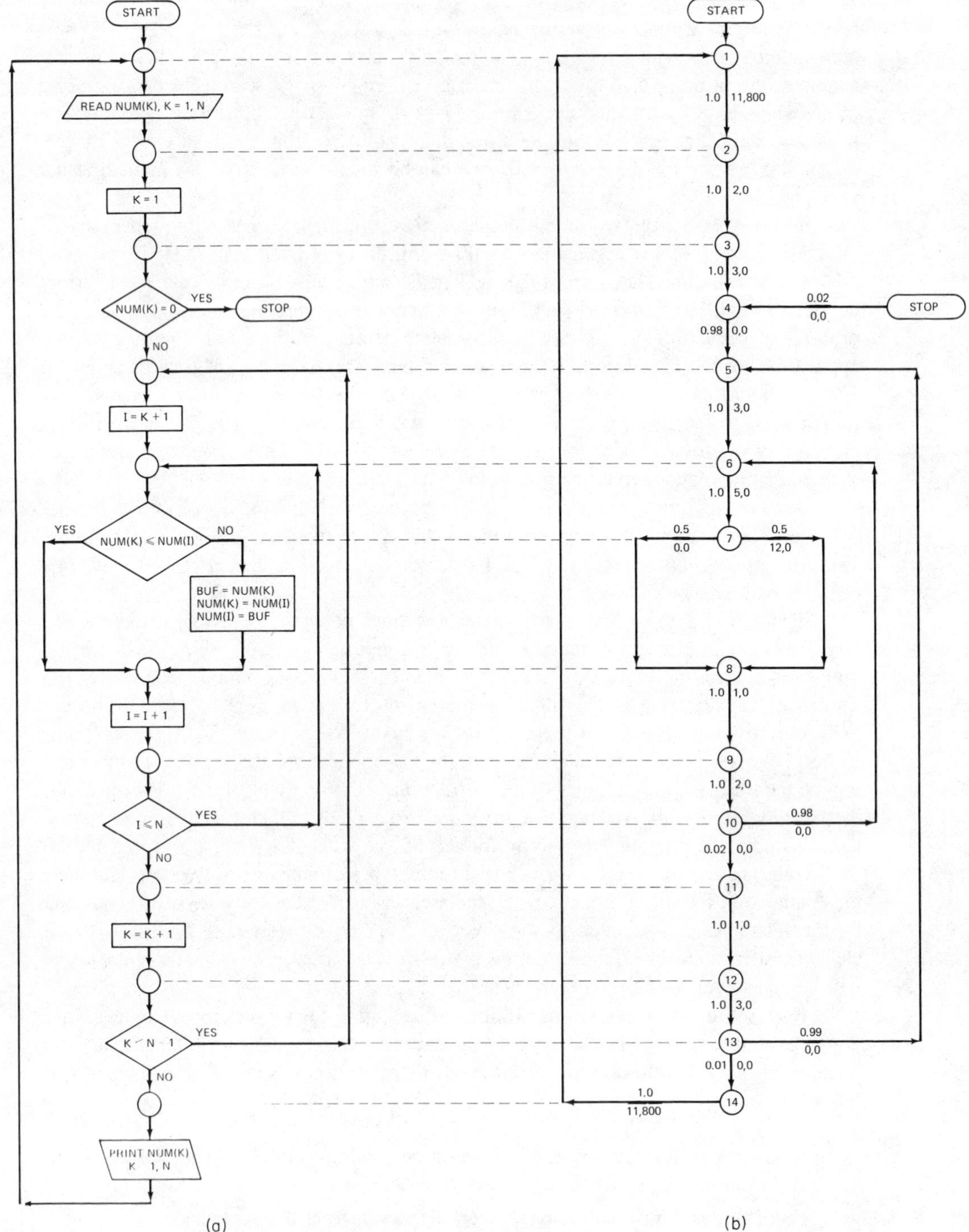

Figure 2.34 (a) Flow chart of a program for printing the N components of a variable number of vectors NUM (K); (b) its graph model. Each link has two weights, corresponding to mean CPU and I/O times required by the instructions it represents.

Probabilities of type 1 are assigned after examining the functional characteristics of the application. Often, if the function requested among those performed by the application is known, one can assign a priori the values of the branching probabilities for all tests concerned with that function. When all probabilities are of type 1, or are known a priori anyway, the mean and the higher-order moments of the weights for the entire application can be computed.

An analysis of the structure of the application allows us to estimate, usually with good precision, the probabilities of type 2. For instance, this is the case of tests needed to determine whether a given record is the last one in the file, of tests that check the validity of the input data, of tests on binary variables having a certain value on the first traversal and the other value on all the successive traversals, and so on. In general, this class of branches includes those that test for the occurrence of peculiar and rather infrequent conditions, like that corresponding to node 4 in Fig. 2.34b, which is to determine when the vectors to be sorted have been completely scanned.

The probabilities of type 3, which depend on the input data and/or on the history of the execution, can be subdivided into two groups: (1) those whose values can be expressed as simple functions of some input parameters, and (2) those for which no relationships with the data can be found. With probabilities in the first group only, the graph can be reduced until the mean values of the application's weights, as well as their higher-order moments, are determined as functions of the input parameters. Probabilities of this type are often associated with loop control tests and tests on variables for subroutine calls. Examples can be found at nodes 10 and 13 in Fig. 2.34b.

Even when the graph includes probabilities in the second group, applying this method is convenient since it reduces the model of an application to a simpler one, containing only the unknown probabilities in explicit form. Sensitivity studies can thus be performed on the reduced model, which can also be simulated more easily and rapidly than the original model. For instance, the probabilities associated to node 7 in Fig. 2.34b are data dependent. It should also be noted that the values of some probabilities are unimportant since they discriminate among branches whose corresponding links have similar weights.

The original graph, whose nodes correspond one to one with the junctions and the decisions of the application's flow chart, can be reduced by iterative node eliminations of the star-mesh transformation type. Nodes may be connected in *series,* in *parallel,* or may be the places of *loops*. Since the operations required for their elimination can be obtained by simple probabilistic considerations, only the final formulas and not their derivations, will be reported. For the sake of simplicity, only the mean values of the weights have been associated to the links; the computations of their variances, which can be easily performed (see [BE78, p. 128]), have been omitted.

The elimination of a node k connected *in series* to nodes h, i, j, and m is illustrated in Fig. 2.35. Denoting by p_{hk} the probability that the link between nodes h and k be taken and by μ_{hk} its mean weight, the values p_{hm} and μ_{hm} associated to the link between nodes h and m, obtained from the elimination of node k, are given by

$$p_{hm} = p_{hk}\, p_{km}, \qquad \mu_{hm} = \mu_{hk} + \mu_{km} \tag{2.20}$$

Similar relationships yield p_{jm}, μ_{jm} and p_{im}, μ_{im}.

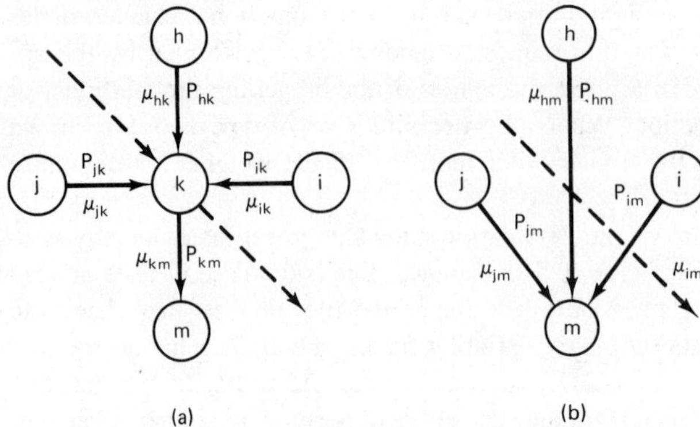

Figure 2.35 Elimination of node k connected in series to nodes h, i, j, and m.

In the Fig. 2.36, the two nodes h and k are connected *in parallel* by two links, which can be reduced to a single link. If there were more than two links in parallel, they could be reduced to one link by applying iteratively transformation (2.21).

The values of p_{hk} and μ_{hk} for the resulting link in Fig. 2.36b are

$$p_{hk} = p'_{hk} + p''_{hk}, \qquad \mu_{hk} = \frac{p'_{hk}\mu'_{hk} + p''_{hk}\mu''_{hk}}{p'_{hk} + p''_{hk}} \tag{2.21}$$

Figure 2.37 shows a node h where, due to previous reductions of the original graph, a *loop* has appeared, and its transformation into a loopless node. The values of p_{hk} and μ_{hk} for the link outcoming from the loop node can be computed as

$$p_{hk} = \frac{p'_{hk}}{1 - p_{hh}}, \qquad \mu_{hk} = \mu'_{hk} + \frac{p_{hh}\mu_{hh}}{1 - p_{hh}} \tag{2.22}$$

By applying iteratively the elementary transformations described, the original graph in Fig. 2.34b can be reduced to a single-link graph, whose link connects the START and STOP nodes (Fig. 2.38k). In the flow chart in Fig. 2.34a the vector NUM is read in at the beginning of each cycle and is printed out at the end of each cycle with its components sorted in increasing order. The number of vectors to be sorted is not preassigned, and the program terminates when a vector is read in whose first component is zero.

To assign numerical values to all probabilities, we have assumed that the mean number N of components per vector equals 100 and that the mean number M of vectors to be sorted is 50. As a result, the YES branch coming from node 4 is taken on the

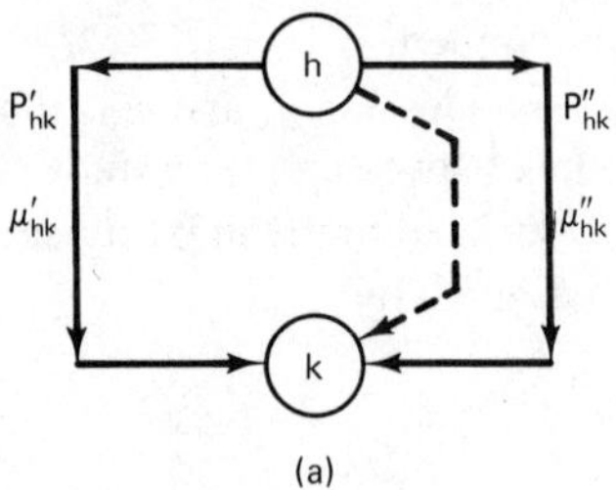

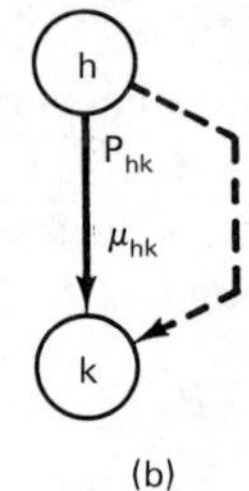

Figure 2.36 Reduction of two parallel links to a single equivalent link.

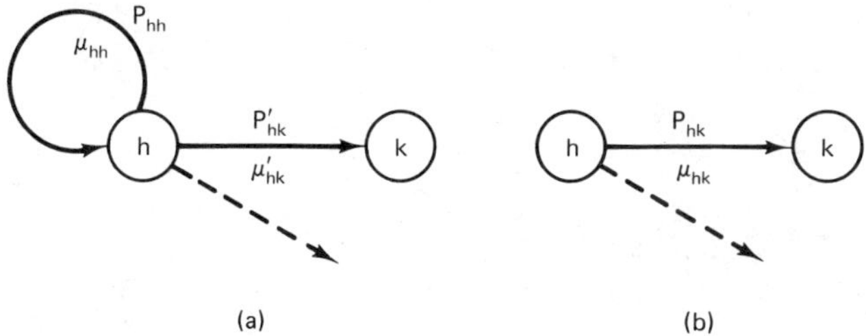

Figure 2.37 Elimination of the loop at node *h*.

average once every 50 times that the NO branch is taken. A simple analysis of the program's structure shows that, for each vector, the YES branch out of node 10 is taken $(N - 1)\,[(N/2) - 1]$ times while the NO branch is executed $(N - 1)$ times; also, the YES branch out of node 13 is taken $(N - 2)$ times for every time the NO branch is gone through. We cannot make any a priori assumptions on the probabilities associated with the outcoming branches of node 7, since their values depend on the initial ordering of the components of NUM. Thus, as a first approximation, equal values have been taken for them.

By convention, the weight corresponding to the execution of a test has been accounted for in the link preceding the decision node representing the test. The links outcoming from that node will have zero weights but significant probabilities. Since in our example we had to evaluate the mean execution time of the program as the sum of the mean CPU and I/O times, two values have been associated to each link, those of the CPU and I/O times required by the instructions in the link. Note that these times are expressed in the same conventional unit of time.

Figure 2.38 illustrates the reduction procedure for the graph in Fig. 2.34b. The elementary transformations have been applied in the following order:

1. Elimination of nodes 2 and 3, 9, 11 and 12, 14 connected in series to other nodes, and transformation of the parallel connection of nodes 7 and 8 into a series connection (Fig. 2.38a);
2. Elimination of nodes 7 and 8 connected in series to nodes 6 and 10 (Fig. 2.38b);
3. Elimination of node 10 connected in series to 6 and 13; this operation generates a loop around node 6 (Fig. 2.38c);
4. Elimination of the loop around 6 (Fig. 2.38d) and elimination of node 6, which is now connected in series to nodes 5 and 13 (Fig. 2.38e);
5. Elimination of 13, connected in series to 5 and 1; this elimination generates a loop around node 5 (Fig. 2.38f);
6. Elimination of the loop around 5 (Fig. 2.38g) and of node 5 owing to its being connected in series to nodes 4 and 1 (Fig. 2.38h);
7. Elimination of node 4 connected in series to 1; a loop is generated around 1 (Fig. 2.38i);
8. Elimination of the loop around 1 and calculation of the total mean CPU and I/O times demanded by the program.

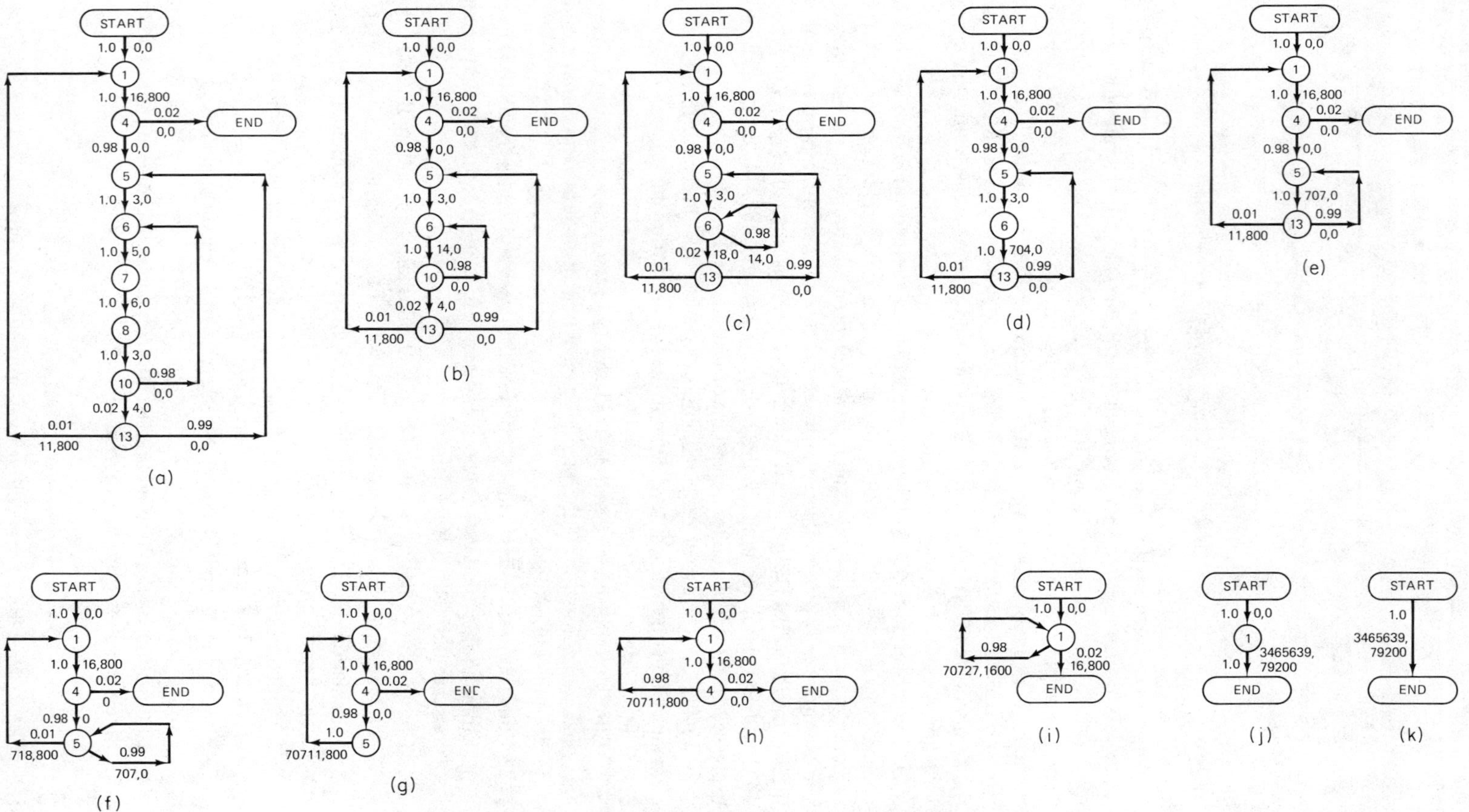

Figure 2.38 Iterative reduction of the graph in Fig. 2.34b to a single link.

When the mean values of M and N cannot be estimated, or when maximum accuracy predictions are required, the probabilities of the branches outcoming from nodes 4, 10, and 13 can be expressed as functions of M and N. Thus, the probability of a NO outcome from node 4 is $M/(M + 1)$, the one from node 10 is $(N - 1)/(N - 1)\left(\frac{N}{2} - 1\right) + (N - 1))$, and the one from node 13 is $1/(N - 1)$. The final values of the weights will then be functions of M and N, and their sensitivities to variations of N and M will become easy to derive. If the probabilities at the exits of node 7 are varied, we can also evaluate the ranges of global weights corresponding to the *best case* (that is, the case when the input vector is sorted in increasing order) and those corresponding to the *worst case* (that is, the case when the input vector is sorted in decreasing order).

Similar considerations can be made also for the weights of some links, which can be expressed as functions of some parameters to appear in symbolic form in the expression of the global weights. The graph associated to a *routine* can be reduced separately with respect to the graph of the program; the probabilities and the weights of its links can be expressed as functions of the values of the routine's arguments. Thus, the routine will appear in the program's graph as a single link whose weights are functions of the arguments.

Clearly, not all the programs or routines have a single-entry, single-exit flow chart such as the one shown in Fig. 2.34a. A trivial example of a graph with two entry points and one exit point is reported in Fig. 2.39. The weights in the graph are the mean execution times of the instructions corresponding to each link. Assuming, for instance, that the graph represents a subroutine that may be called at ENTRY 1 and ENTRY 2, and that the probabilities of ENTRY 1 calls and of ENTRY 2 calls are known (for example, 0.8 and 0.2, respectively), the mean execution time of the subroutine can be computed by suitably modifying the probabilities of the links in Fig. 2.39f and reducing the corresponding graph to a single link. The weight of this link will be $0.8 \times 13.2 + 0.2 \times 7.49 = 12.058$. Even in this case the probabilities of taking ENTRY 1 or ENTRY 2 (hence the mean execution time of the whole subroutine) could be expressed as functions of some parameters. The variations of the mean execution time with the entry probabilities or with these parameters will be easily derivable.

The degree of detail of a graph model depends on the objectives of the study. For example, if a procedure consists of several programs, one may reduce the graphs of each individual program first, and then the graph whose links correspond to the various programs. It is important to consider, when computing the weights of the links, the *indirect load* due to the actions corresponding to those weights. For instance, if the weights represent the CPU and I/O times required by the execution of each link, the calculation of CPU times will have to include the overhead caused by the I/O operations. The value of this overhead can in general be derived, for existing applications, from suitable experiments (for example, by executing the application repeatedly with increasing numbers of I/O instructions). If the flow charts of the system's routines invoked to perform a given function are known, one can build graph models for these routines and reduce the models by using the techniques described. A case study dealing with the forecasting of the load created by an application, in which the overhead is explicitly considered, is reported in Sec. 2.6.2.

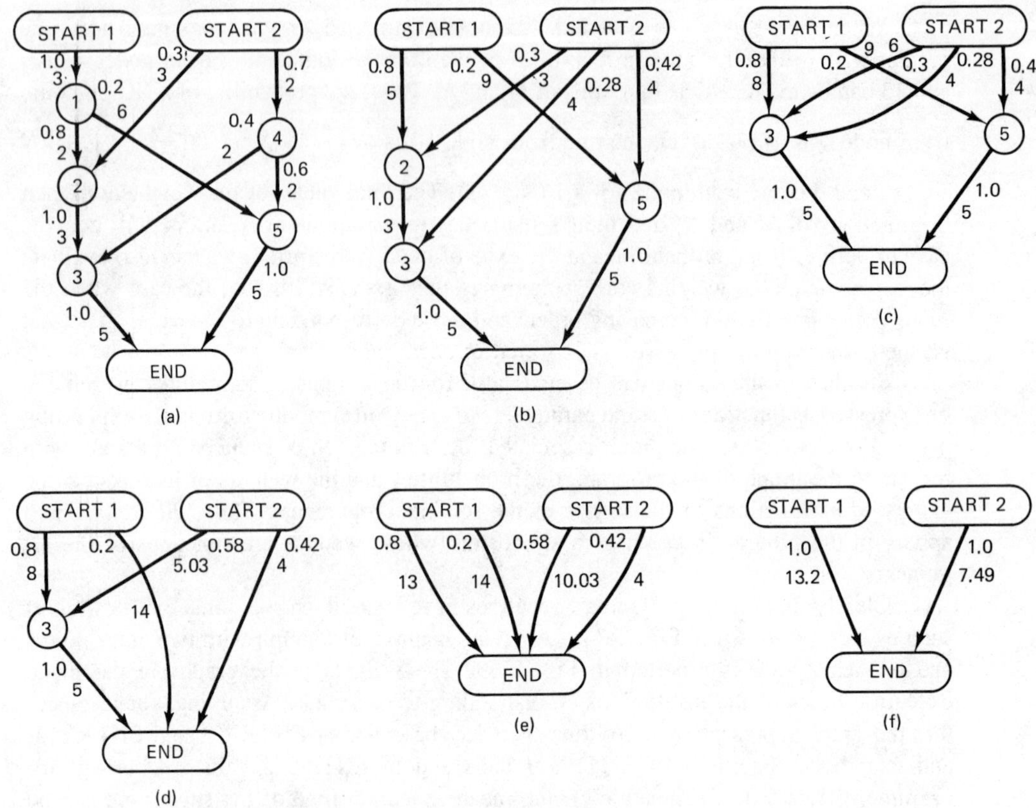

Figure 2.39 Reduction of a graph with two entry points and one exit point.

2.6.2 Case 2.3: Forecasting the Load of a Real-time Application

The load due to an application to be processed in real time on a minicomputer is to be predicted. The minicomputer is connected to a large remote computer, henceforth to be called the *Host*. The main components of the minicomputer, shown in Fig. 2.40, are the CPU, one disk drive, the *Terminal Control Units,* which control three video display terminals, the interface to the host, and a local printer. Because of the high traffic between the system and the terminals and because of the performance requirements of the application, a star connection of the lines that link the terminals to the system has been selected.

The main function of the application is the real-time reservation of seats. Depending on the request, data are found either in a local data base DB1, which is stored in the local disk, or in a remote data base DB2, stored in the host's disks. For the purposes of their future use (see Sec. 9.4.5, Case 9.7), the mean values of the following variables or the following events will have to be estimated both for the application and for the systems routines it will need:

1. CPU time, in milliseconds, required to execute the application and the relevant systems routines.
2. Numbers of requests to the local disk (DISK), to the remote computer (HOST), and to the terminals (TCU).
3. Number of times a process is sent to the CPU queue either at the end of an I/O transfer or at the end of a waiting period for an event (in other words, the number of times the scheduler is called on behalf of the process).

In what follows, we report the flow charts of the application and of the relevant systems routines. Beside the description of each operation, we show the values of the variables associated with it. For the sake of brevity, we shall deal with intermediate-level flow charts.

At the beginning of the application (see Fig. 2.41), we find typical initialization operations like the resetting of memory areas to zero, the assignment of initial values to variables, the allocation of buffers, and so on. After these operations, a command is sent to the terminal selected to display the first line on the screen, that is, of the heading. In

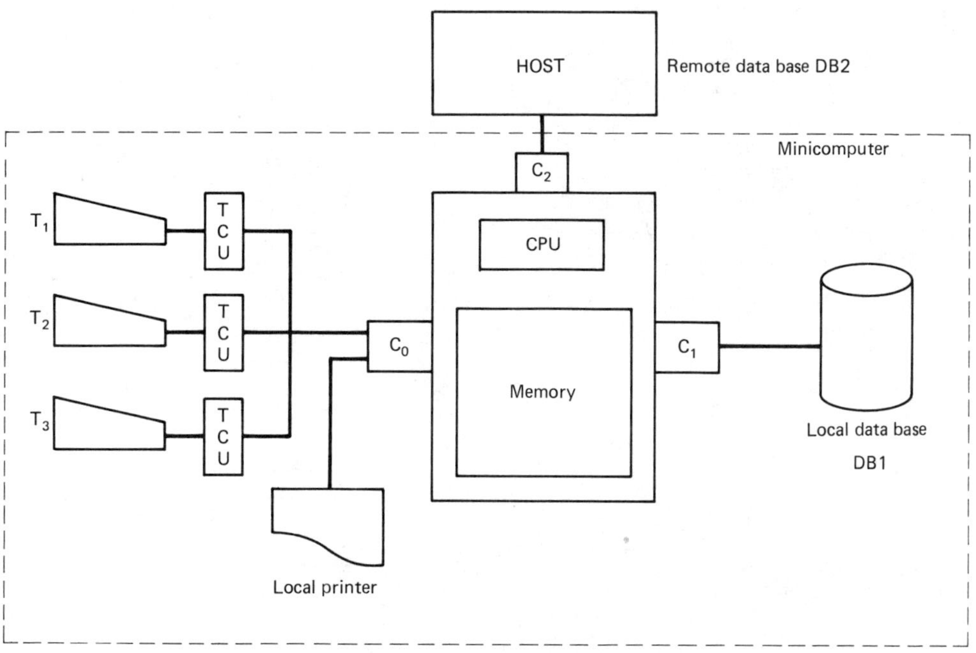

Figure 2.40 Configuration of the minicomputer for the seat reservation application.

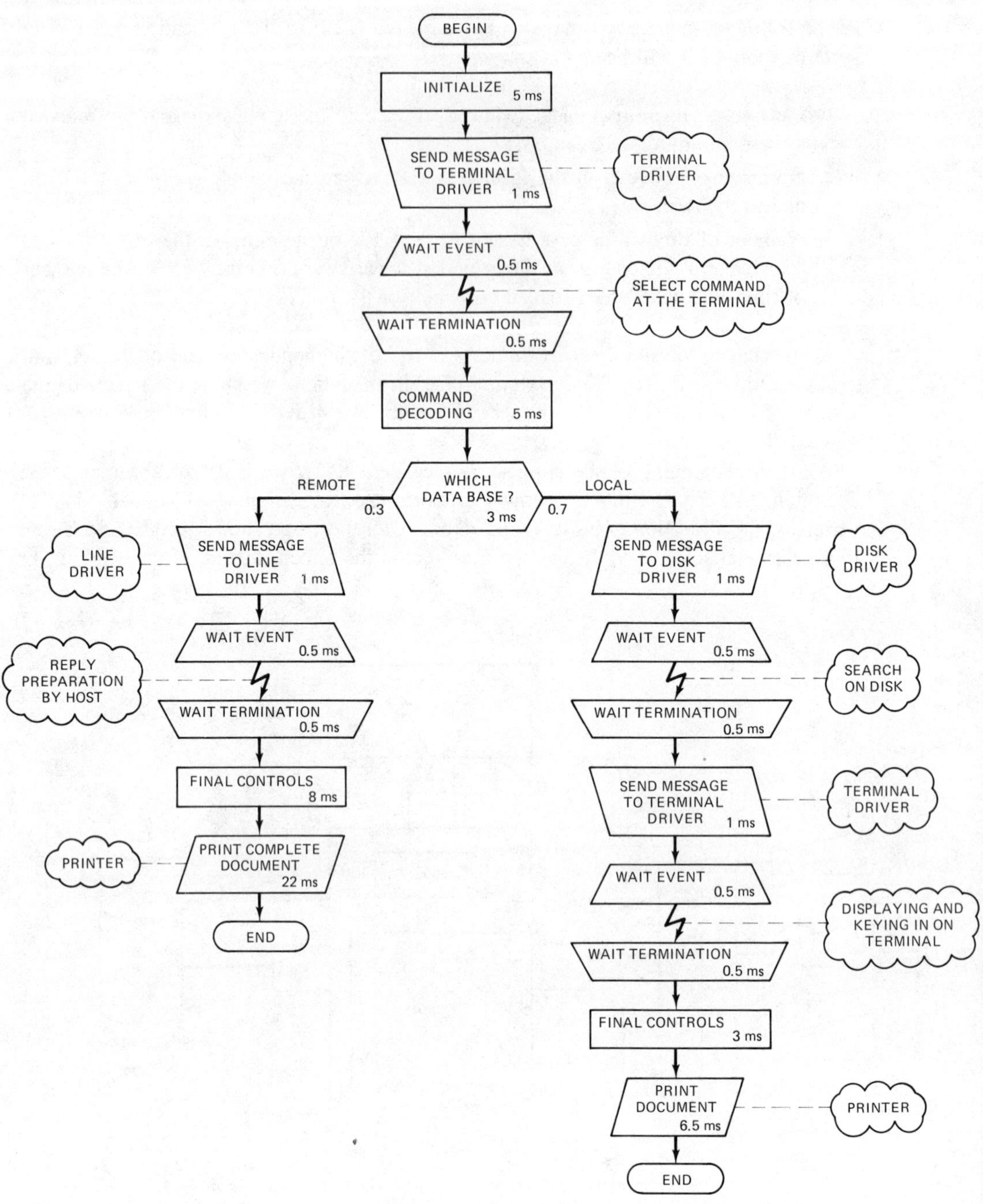

Figure 2.41 Flow chart of the application, showing the calls to the drivers.

this and subsequent flow charts, the shipment of a message to a peripheral unit (which is performed by invoking a *driver*) is always followed by a sequence of two operations, *Wait Event* and *Wait Termination*. These two operations handle the communications with the driver to be invoked. The former takes care of the operations required to activate the driver, for instance, accessing the queue for communicating with the routine called by the application, allocating a buffer for input data, and testing for the occurrence of the event we are waiting for.

The operations denoted by *Wait Termination* are performed when the event we were waiting for has occurred. In our particular case, this event consists of the arrival from a terminal of a command to select the desired function (for example, reserving a seat or canceling a reservation). These operations update the queue for communicating with the called routine and trigger, when necessary, the appropriate system activities to bring that routine to the running state.

After decoding the command from the terminal, the data base to be accessed is selected. Based on a statistical analysis of the traffic of requests and of the data in the data bases, the two probabilities of accessing DB1 and DB2 have been estimated to be 0.7 and 0.3, respectively. If the local data base DB1 is to be accessed, a message is sent to the disk driver, containing the key of the record to be accessed. The *Wait Event* operation described previously is then executed, and when the search for the record has been completed, we perform the *Wait Termination* operation. At this point, the data requested are in the memory buffer used for communicating with the disk. A message is therefore sent to the terminal driver so that the data are displayed with the desired format. Some final controls are then performed, for example, that the keys of the various sections of the data base have kept their correct values, that all pending operations have been completed, that the mutual exclusion requirement for access to the record has not been violated, and so on. At the end, a brief report on what has been done is printed out on the printer.

If the access is to be made to the remote data base DB2, the line driver that manages the communications with the host is invoked. When the data requested have been stored in the line buffer, final controls are performed and a full report is printed out. A flow chart of the *terminal driver* is shown in Fig. 2.42. The initial dequeuing operations on the queue for the communications between the calling process and the called driver are followed by the decoding of the command to be executed and by the shipment of the command to the TCU, which will trigger the transmission of the characters on the channel.

At the same time, the operating system starts waiting for the end of this event. The end of transmission of all characters in a message is signaled by the channel via an interrupt, which will be inserted in the interrupt vector. The scheduler, which is then called, appends the process suspended at the *Wait Event* to the ready queue, that is, to the queue of the processes waiting for the CPU. When the turn of this process comes, the dispatcher reconstructs its context and gives it control of the CPU.

Since the terminal operation is a *Write with Reply,* the buffer for the reply is now initialized. Then, the command for inputing the reply data is emitted. When the terminal that is to send the reply is polled successfully, a sequence of scheduling operations identical

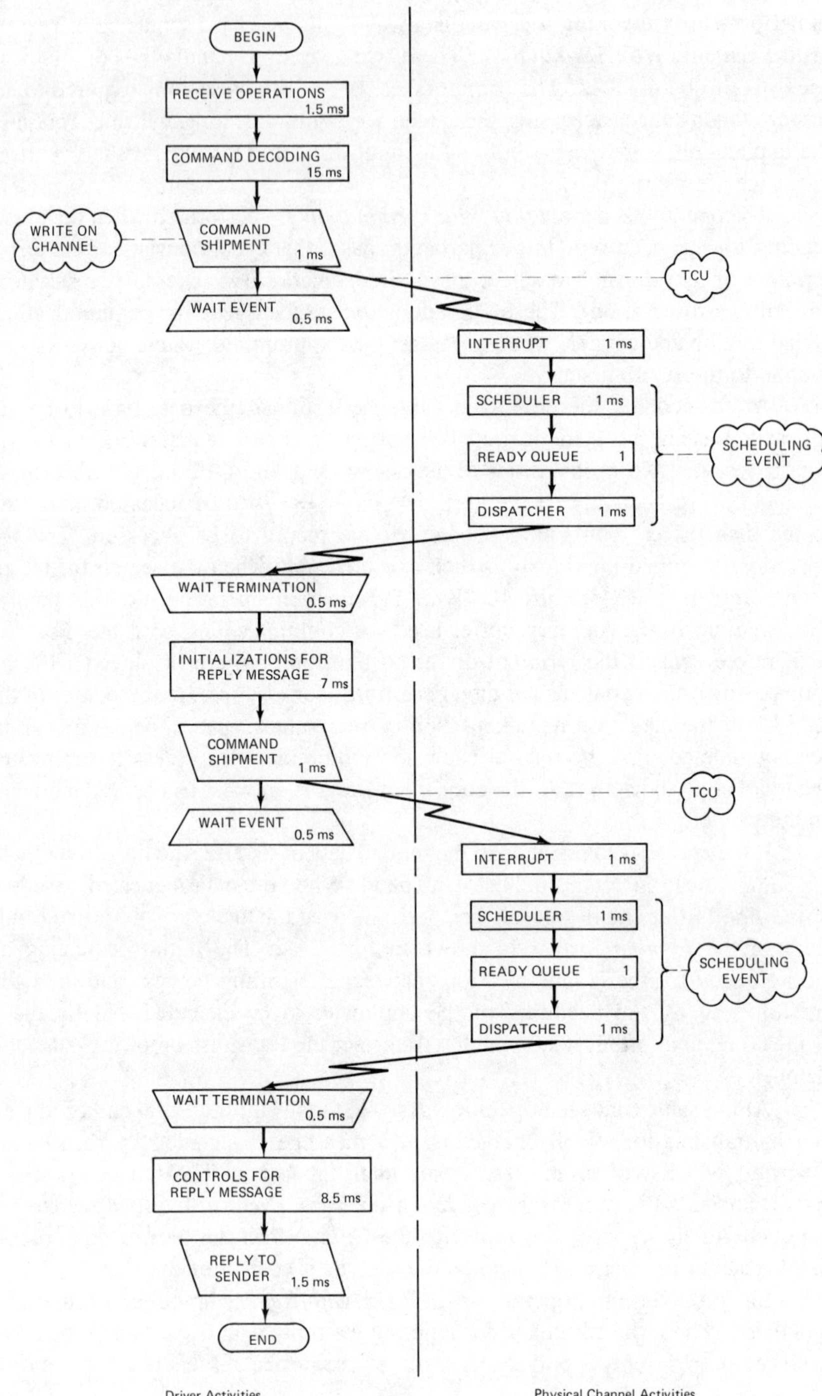

Figure 2.42 Flow chart of the terminal driver.

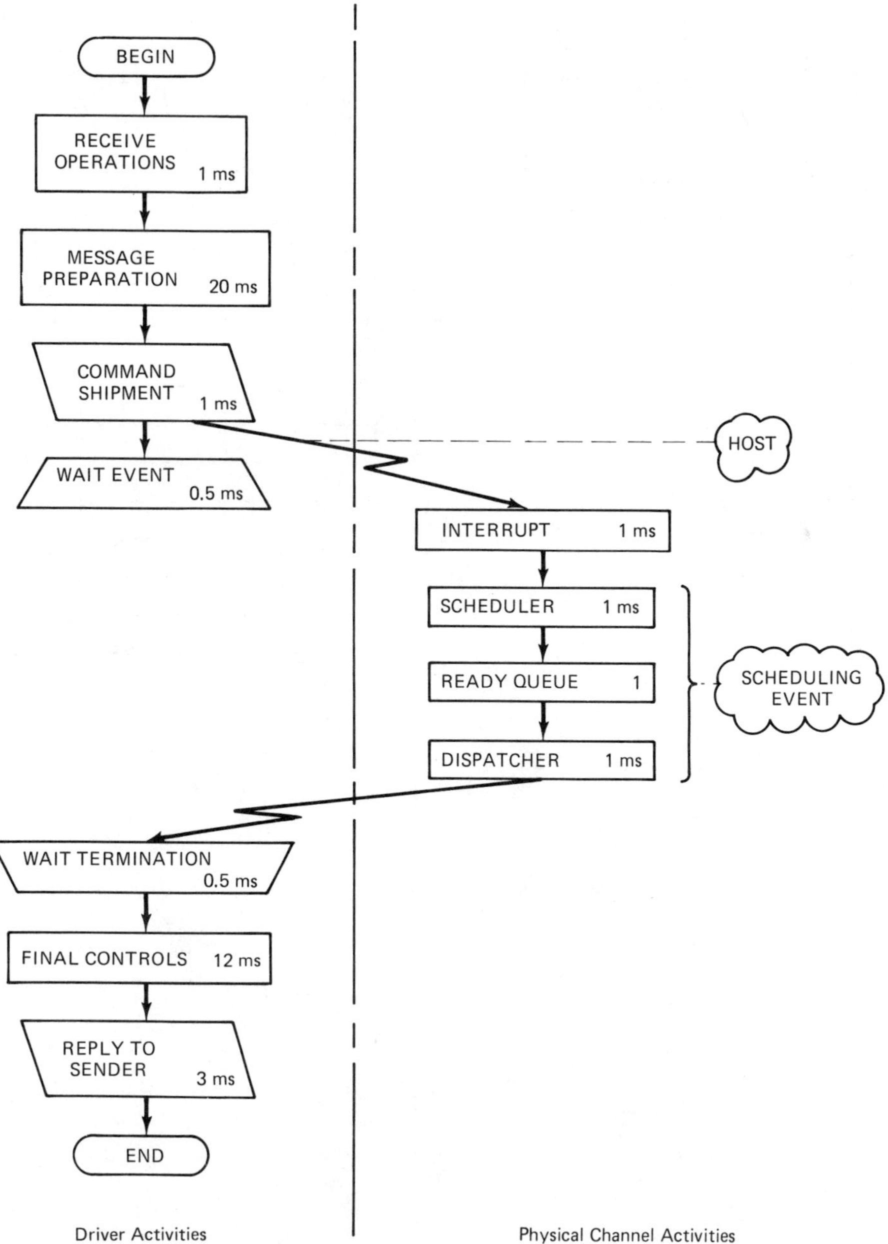

Figure 2.43 Flow chart of the host driver.

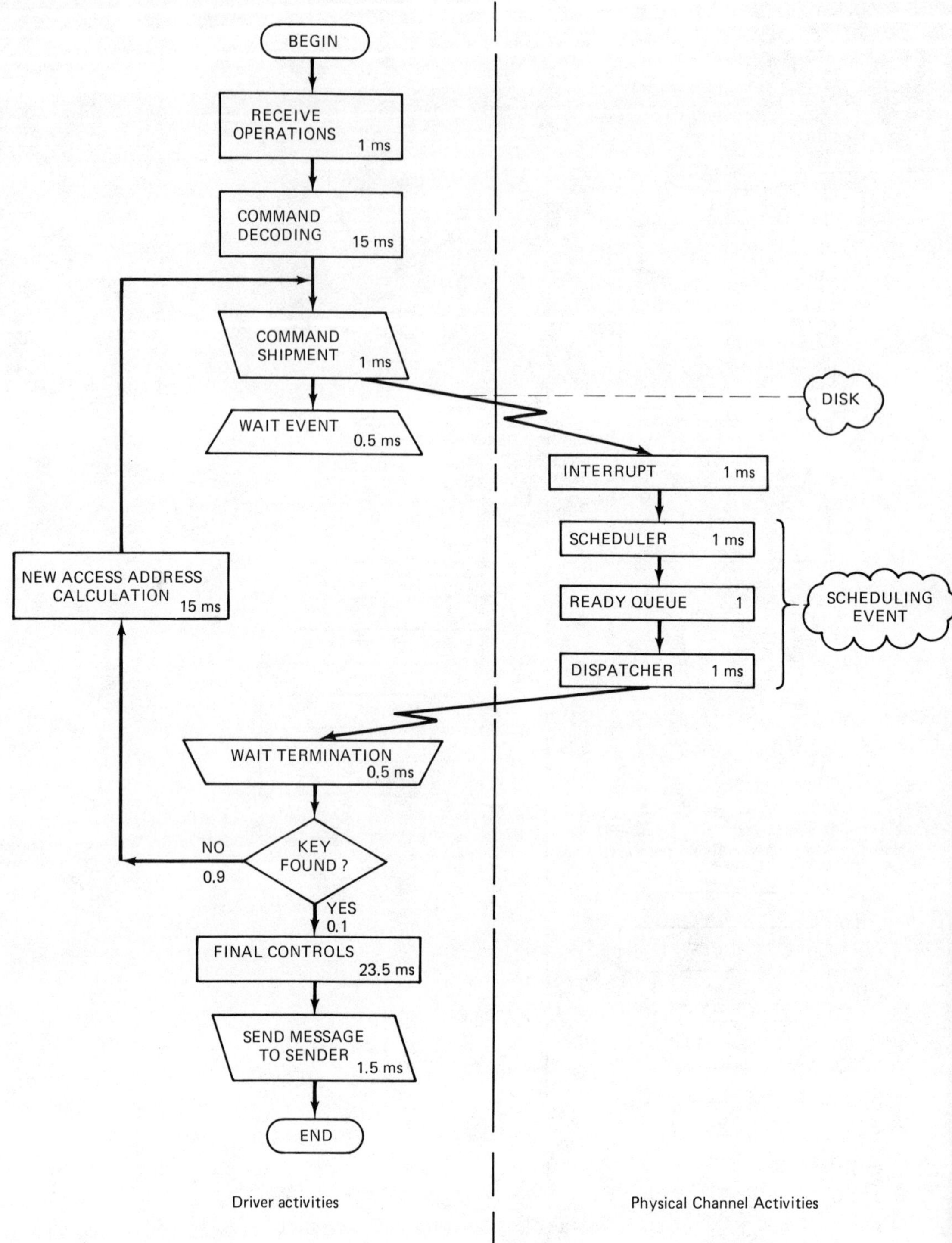

Figure 2.44 Flow chart of the disk driver.

to the one just described is started, and when the terminal driver resumes its execution, the reply message is analyzed and then sent to the application process.

The *host driver* is schematically represented in Fig. 2.43. The initial receive operations are followed by those needed to prepare the message to be sent to the host. For instance, a header and a trailer are added to the text of the message as required by the transmission protocol. As soon as the message has been sent, the driver starts waiting for the reply, which is then shipped, after the same final controls described previously, to the application process.

The flow chart of the *local disk driver*, illustrated in Fig. 2.44, consists of operations already described for the preceding drivers. The only difference is due to the loop for determining the new record to be accessed until the one with the desired key is found.

The graph associated with the terminal driver and the corresponding reduced graph

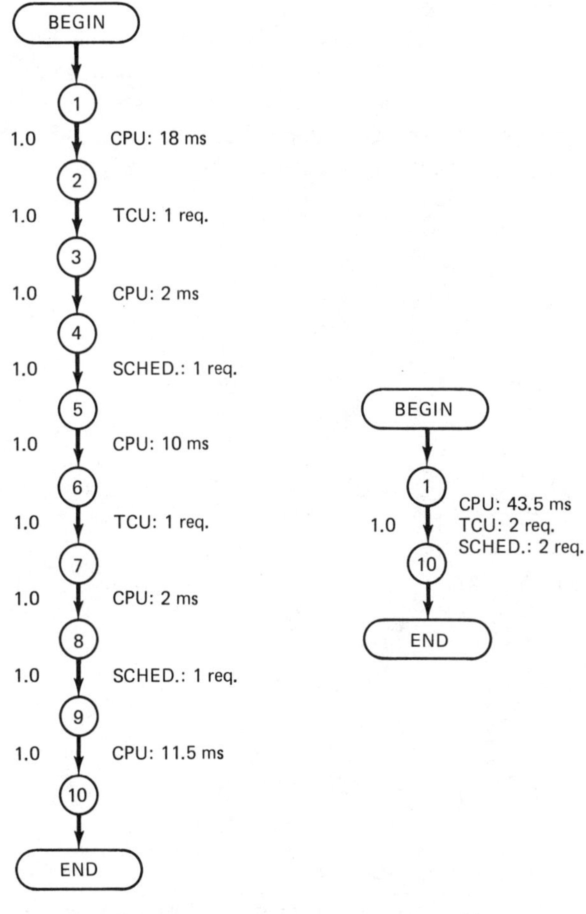

Figure 2.45 Graph associated with the terminal driver (see Fig. 2.42) and reduced graph.

are presented in Fig. 2.45. Each branch is labeled with the mean values of its probability of execution and of its variables (that is, CPU time, numbers of disk, host, and TCU requests, and number of dispatchings). For the sake of conciseness, all elementary sequential operations for a given type of event in this and the subsequent graphs have been collapsed into a single branch. Reducing the graph in Fig. 2.45a to the one in Fig. 2.45b is very easy since all branches are in series.

The graph associated with the host driver and its reduced graph are reported in Fig. 2.46. All branches are connected in series even in this case. Figure 2.47 shows the graph model of the disk driver and its successive reductions. The reduction procedure is in this case less trivial because of the presence of a loop.

The knowledge of the reduced graphs corresponding to the drivers involved allows us to construct the graph of the application, which will then be reduced in turn. For each call to a driver, the number of scheduling requests has been increased by two to account for those needed for entry and exit into and from the driver.

Figure 2.48 shows the graph associated with the application and the steps required for its reduction. The mean parameter values of the load produced by the application on the minicomputer are presented in Fig. 2.48c. In Case 9.7, these values will be used as inputs to a model of the minicomputer. It should be noted that both the *direct* load produced by the application and the *indirect* load due to the operating system's routines called during its execution have been evaluated by using the method described.

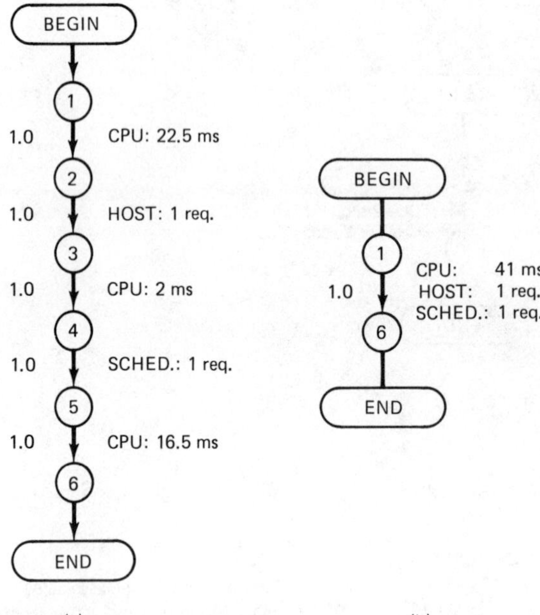

Figure 2.46 Graph associated with the host driver (see Fig. 2.43) and reduced graph.

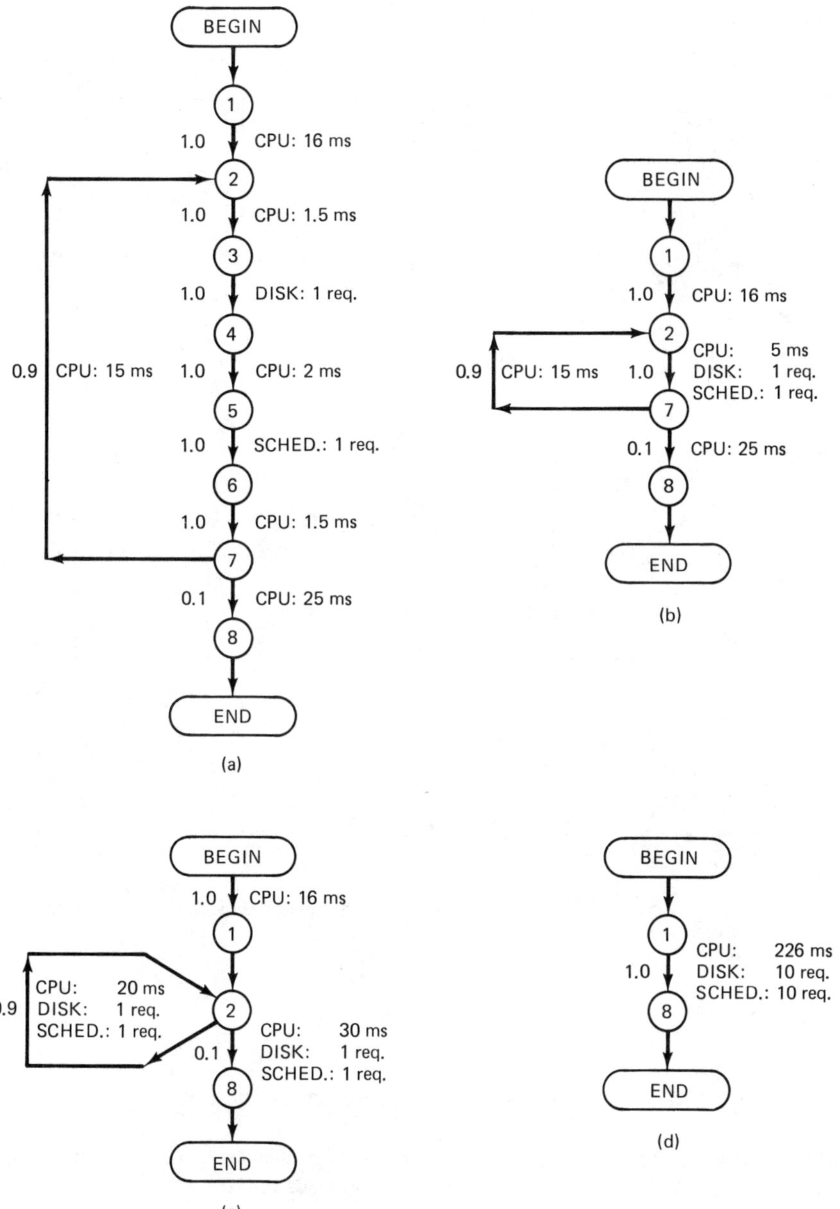

Figure 2.47 Graph associated with the disk driver (see Fig. 2.44) and reduced graph.

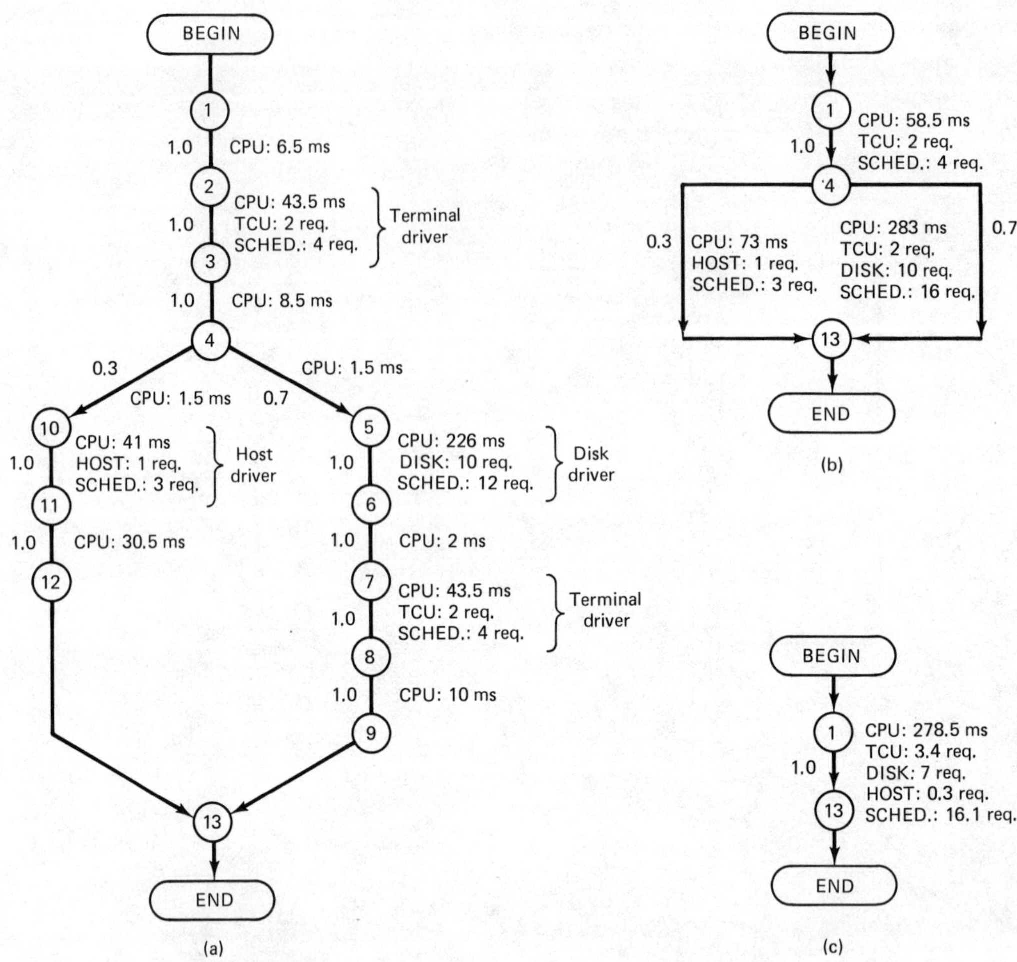

Figure 2.48 Graph associated with the application and its reduced graph.

REFERENCES

Entries marked with an asterisk (*) are referenced in the text.

[AB77] Abrams, M. D., Treu, S., A methodology for interactive computer service measurement, *CACM,* vol. 20, n. 12, pp. 936–944, Dec. 1977.

*[AG76] Agrawala, A. K., Mohr, J. M., Bryant, R. M., An approach to the workload characterization problem, *Computer,* pp. 18–32, June 1976.

*[AG78a] Agrawala, A. K., Mohr, J. M., A markovian model of a job, *Proc. CPEUG,* pp. 119–126, Oct. 1978.

[AG78b] Agrawala, A. K., Mohr, J. M., A comparison of the workload on several computer systems, *Proc. CMG IX,* pp. 177–183, Nov. 1978.

*[AN73] Anderberg, M. R., *Cluster Analysis for Applications,* Academic Press, New York, 1973.

*[AR66] Arbuckle, R. A., Computer analysis and thruput evaluation, *Computers and Automation,* vol. 15, n. 1, pp. 12–15, Jan. 1966.

*[AR78] Artis, H. P., Capacity planning for MVS computer systems, in: Ferrari, D. (ed.), *Performance of Computer Installations,* North-Holland, Amsterdam, pp. 25–35, 1978.

*[AR80] Artis, H. P., Forecasting computer requirements: an analyst's dilemma, *EDP Perf. Review,* vol. 8, n. 2, pp. 1–5, Feb. 1980.

*[BA65] Ball, G., Hall, D., *ISODATA, A Novel Method of Data Analysis and Pattern Classification,* AD 699616, Stanford Research Institute, Menlo Park, Calif., 1965.

*[BA81a] Babaoglu, Ö., On constructing synthetic programs for virtual memory environments, in: Ferrari, D., Spadoni M. (eds.), *Experimental Computer Performance Evaluation,* North-Holland, Amsterdam, pp. 195–204, 1981.

*[BA81b] Babaoglu, Ö., Efficient generation of memory reference strings based on the LRU stack model of program behaviour, *Proc. of the 8th Int. Symp. PERFORMANCE 81,* North-Holland, Amsterdam, pp. 373–383, 1981.

*[BE70] Beizer, B., Analytical techniques for the statistical evaluation of program running time, *AFIPS Conf. Proc. FJCC,* vol. 37, pp. 519–524, 1970.

*[BE74] Beizer, B., Analytical preconditions to simulation, in: *Computer Systems Measurement, Infotech State of the Art Report 18,* pp. 477–499, 1974.

*[BE78] Beizer, B., *Micro-Analysis of Computer System Performance,* Van Nostrand Reinhold Co., New York, 1978.

[BE75] Benwell, N. (ed.), *Benchmarking: Computer Evaluation and Measurement,* Hemisphere Publishing Corp., Washington, D.C., 1975.

*[BO82] Bolzoni, M. L., Calzarossa, M., Mapelli, P., Serazzi, G., A package for the implementation of static workload models, *ACM SIGMETRICS, Perf. Evaluat. Review,* vol. 11, n. 4, pp. 58–67, 1982.

*[BR80] Bronner, L., Overview of the capacity planning process for production data processing, *IBM Syst. J.,* vol. 19, n. 1, pp. 4–27, 1980.

*[BU69] Buchholz, W., A synthetic job for measuring system performance, *IBM Syst. J.,* vol. 8, n. 4, pp. 309–318, 1969.

*[CA81] Cabrera, L. F., Benchmarking UNIX: A comparative study, in: Ferrari, D., Spadoni, M. (eds.), *Experimental Computer Performance Evaluation,* North-Holland, Amsterdam, pp. 205–216, 1981.

*[CO80] Cooper, J. C., A capacity planning methodology, *IBM Syst. J.,* vol. 19, n. 1., pp. 28–45, 1980.

*[CP79] *CPU Power Analysis Report,* Institute for Software Engineering, Menlo Park, Calif., 1979.

*[DE69] De Meis, W. M., Weizer, N., Measurement and analysis of a demand paging time sharing system, *Proc. 24-th ACM Nat. Conf.,* pp. 201–216, 1969.

*[DI79] Dixon, W. J., ed., *BMDP—Biomedical Computer Programs,* University of California Press, Berkeley, 1979.

*[FE81a] Febish, G. J., Experimental software physics, in: Ferrari, D., Spadoni, M. (eds.), *Experimental Computer Performance Evaluation,* North-Holland, Amsterdam, pp. 33–55, 1981.

*[FE72] Ferrari, D., Workload characterization and selection in computer performance measurement, *Computer,* vol. 5, n. 4, pp. 18–24, July–Aug. 1972.

[FE78] Ferrari, D., *Computer Systems Performance Evaluation,* Prentice-Hall, Englewood Cliffs, N.J., 1978.

*[FE79] Ferrari, D., Characterizing a workload for the comparison of interactive services, *AFIPS Conf. Proc. NCC,* vol. 48, pp. 789–796, 1979.

*[FE81b] Ferrari, D., A performance-oriented procedure for modeling interactive workloads, in: Ferrari, D., Spadoni, M. (eds.), *Experimental Computer Performance Evaluation,* North-Holland, Amsterdam, pp. 57–78, 1981.

*[FE81c] Ferrari, D., Characterization and reproduction of the referencing dynamics of programs, *Proc. 8th Int. Symp. PERFORMANCE 81,* North-Holland, Amsterdam, pp. 363–372, 1981.

[FL74] Flynn, M. J., Trends and problems in computer organizations, *Information Processing 74, Proc. IFIP Congress 74,* North-Holland, Amsterdam, pp. 3–10, 1974.

*[FO72] Fogel, M., Winograd, J., EINSTEIN: An internal driver in a time-sharing environment, *Operating Systems Rev.,* vol. 6, n. 3, pp. 6–14, Oct. 1972.

[FR81] Friedman, H. P., Statistical methods in computer performance evaluation, in: Ferrari, D., Spadoni, M. (eds.), *Experimental Computer Performance Evaluation,* North-Holland, Amsterdam, pp. 79–103, 1981.

*[GI70] Gibson, J. C., The Gibson mix, *IBM T.R. 002043,* June, 1970.

*[GI77] Gilchrist, W., *Statistical Forecasting,* Wiley-Interscience, New York, 1977.

*[GR69] Greenbaum, H. J., A simulator of multiple interactive users to drive a time-shared computer system, *Project MAC TR-58,* MIT, Cambridge, Mass., Jan. 1969.

*[HA67] Harman, H. H., *Modern Factor Analysis,* University of Chicago Press, Chicago, 1967.

*[HA75] Hartigan, J. A., *Clustering Algorithms,* Wiley, New York, 1975.

*[HA82] Haring, G., On state-dependent workload characterization by software resources, *ACM SIGMETRICS, Perf. Evaluat. Review,* vol. 11, n. 4, pp. 51–57, 1982.

[HU74] Hughes, P. H., Towards precise benchmarks, in: *Infotech State of the Art Report on Computer System Measurement,* Infotech Ltd., England, 1974.

*[HU71] Hunt, E., Diehr, G., Garnatz, D., Who are the users? An analysis of computer use in a university computer center, *AFIPS Conf. Proc. SJCC,* vol. 38, pp. 231–238, May 1971.

*[KA69] Karush, A. D., The benchmark method applied to time-sharing systems, *Rept. SP. 3347,* System Development Corp., Santa Monica, Calif., Aug. 1969.

*[KA70] Karush, A. D., Two approaches for measuring the performance of time-sharing systems, *Software Age,* Mar., Apr., May 1970.

*[KE73] Kernighan, B. W., Hamilton, P. A., Synthetically generated performance test loads for operating systems, *Proc. 1st ACM-SIGME Symp. on Measurement and Evaluation,* pp. 121–126, Feb. 1973.

*[KN71] Knuth, D. E., An empirical study of FORTRAN programs, *Software—Practice and Experience,* vol. 1, pp. 105–133, 1971.

*[KO76] Kolence, K. W., *The Meaning of Computer Measurement: An Introduction to Software Physics,* Institute for Software Engineering, Inc., Menlo Park, Calif., 1976.

*[LA73] Lasseter, G. L., and others, Statistical and pattern based models for CPU burst prediction, *Proc. Computer Science and Statistics: 7th Annual Symp. on the Interface,* pp. 123–129, Oct. 1973.

*[LI75] Lindsay, D. S., *A Study in Operating System Performance Measurement and Modeling*, Ph.D. thesis, University of California, Berkeley, June 1975.

[LU72] Lucas, H. C., Synthetic program specifications for performance evaluation, *Proc. ACM Nat. Conf.*, vol. 2, pp. 1041–1058, Aug. 1972.

*[MA77] Mamrak, S. A., Amer, P. D., A feature selection tool for workload characterization, *CMG VIII Sigmetrics*, pp. 113–120, 1977.

*[MA79] *MANAGE:IMS-User Guide*, Capex, P.O. Box 13529, Phoenix, Ariz., 1979.

*[MA71] Maranzano, J., Bell, T. E., Fortran version of Buchholz's synthetic program, *Proc. 3rd. Meeting Comput. Perf. Evaluation User Committee*, Washington, D.C., July 1971.

[ME78] Mead, R. L., Schwetman, H. D., Job scripts—A workload description based on system event data, *AFIPS Conf. Proc. NCC*, vol. 47, pp. 457–464, 1978.

*[NI75] Nie, N. H., and others, *SPSS-Statistical Package for the Social Sciences*, McGraw-Hill, New York, 1975.

[NO74] Nolan, L. E., Strauss, J. C., Workload characterization for time sharing system selection, *Software Practice and Experience*, vol. 4, n. 1, pp. 25–39, Jan.–Mar. 1974.

[OL74] Oliver, P., and others, An experiment in the use of synthetic programs for system benchmarks, *AFIPS Conf. Proc. NCC*, vol. 43, pp. 431–438, 1974.

*[RA64] Raichelson, E., Collins, G., A method for comparing the internal operating speeds of computers, *CACM*, vol. 7, n. 5, May 1964.

*[RU70] Rummel, R. J., *Applied Factor Analysis*, Northwestern University Press, Evanston, Ill., 1970.

*[SA70] Saltzer, J. H., Gintell, J. W., The instrumentation of Multics, *CACM*, vol. 13, n. 8, pp. 495–500, Aug. 1970.

*[SA79] *SAS—Statistical Analysis System—User's Guide*, SAS Institute, Inc., Box 8000, Cary, N.C., 1979.

*[SC67] Scherr, A. L., *An Analysis of Time-Shared Computer Systems*, MIT Press, Cambridge, Mass., 1967.

*[SC78] Schroeder, A., How multidimensional data analysis techniques can be of help in the study of computer systems, *Proc. CPEUG 14th Meeting*, pp. 149–165, 1978.

*[SC72] Schwetman, H. D., Browne, J. C., An experimental study of computer system performance, *Proc. ACM Nat. Conf.*, pp. 693–703, 1972.

*[SE81] Serazzi, G., A functional and resource-oriented procedure for workload modeling, *Proc. 8th Int. Symp. PERFORMANCE 81*, North-Holland, Amsterdam, pp. 345–361, 1981.

*[SH72] Sherman, S., Baskett, III, F., Browne, J. C., Trace driven modeling and analysis of CPU scheduling in a multiprogramming system, *CACM*, vol. 15, n. 12, pp. 1063–1069, Dec. 1972.

*[SM78] Smith, A. J., Sequentiality and prefetching in data-base systems, *ACM Trans. Data-base Systems*, vol. 3, n. 3, pp. 223–247, Sept. 1978.

*[SP80] Spath, H., *Cluster Analysis Algorithms for Data Reduction and Classification of Objects*, Ellis Horwood Ltd., Chichester, England, 1980.

*[SR74] Sreenivasan, K., Kleinman, A. J., On the construction of a representative synthetic workload, *CACM*, vol. 17, n. 3, pp. 127–133, March 1974.

*[ST72] Strauss, J. C., A benchmark study, *AFIPS Conf. Proc. FJCC*, vol. 41, pp. 1225–1233, 1972.

[WA77] Watkins, S. W., Abrams, M. D., Remote terminal emulation in the procurement of teleprocessing systems, *AFIPS Conf. Proc. NCC,* vol. 46, Dallas, Tex., pp. 723–727, June 1977.

*[WI74] Wichmann, B. A., The design of synthetic programs—1, *Proc. Conf. Benchmarking/4,* Churchill College, Cambridge, U.K., Oct. 1974.

*[WO71] Wood, D. C., Forman, E. H., Throughput measurement using a synthetic job stream, *AFIPS Conf. Proc. FJCC,* vol. 39, pp. 51–56, 1971.

*[ZA71] Zahn, C. T., Graph theoretical methods for determining and describing gestalt clusters, *IEEE Trans. Computers,* vol. C-20, n. 1, pp. 68–86, 1971.

3

MEASUREMENT PRINCIPLES

3.1 GENERALITIES

When facing phenomena of a complex nature, which result from the coexistence and interaction of many factors, we need to describe as precisely as possible what we observe, since we have to explore the connections among events in order to be able to explain and to predict them. A vital method for reaching this objective is that of *measurement*. Measurement allows phenomena to be treated quantitatively; that is, it allows us to suggest, verify, and establish the relationships among the quantities that characterize a phenomenon.

The study of a computer system, both when it is being designed and when it is running, requires the use of measurement techniques, which are particularly useful for determining the system's performance. What does it mean *to measure a system?* Generally, it means collecting information on the system's activity while it serves the users, who may be real or simulated users (in the latter case, the system is measured when executing an artificial workload). In some cases, information is collected by observing a model of the system (a simulator) that can predict the behavior the real system will exhibit when it will serve its users.

We have seen in Chapter 1 what reasons may be behind the desire to evaluate a computer system's performance and we have already said *why* we should measure. In this chapter we will try to give a reply to the question of *how* a system can be measured by studying the principles of measurement and the available techniques.

Measurements can be classified into two major categories: the measurements requested by a system's users and those requested by the system itself. All measurements concerning the utilization of the system's resources carried out to evaluate its performance, control its use, and plan the addition of new resources belong to the first category. Measurements used by the system to govern itself, which allow it to adapt dynamically to the factors conditioning its activity (mainly the workload), belong to the second category. They allow the system to maintain a sufficient level of external performance (for example, the periodic review of program priorities on the basis of the program's CPU utilization, the analysis of page usage so that the most used pages can replace the least used ones, and the swapping out of programs causing excessive paging).

In general, neither the hardware nor the software of a computer system is purposely designed to be measured. This often restricts the measurements that can be performed on a system, and requires some of its functions to be modified or expensive instrumentation to be added to it if these restrictions are to be overcome.

The *measurability* of a computer system [SV76] is defined as a function of the information obtainable with a monitor and of the cost of the measurements. Thus, a system's measurability may vary between two extremes, corresponding to the possibility of measuring each individual system component at the desired level of detail and to a total inaccessibility to the system, respectively. In the latter case, only the system's response time to various stimuli can be observed.

The difficulties encountered in measuring a system are inversely related to its degree of measurability. To reach the objectives of a performance evaluation study, it is sometimes necessary to determine global indexes such as the mean turnaround time, the mean response time, the utilization of peripheral devices, and so on. In this case we have a *macroscopic* analysis. When a higher degree of detail is required, as when the contribution of each instruction type to CPU usage must be determined or the number of pages loaded during a given time interval needs to be measured, the analysis will be *microscopic* [NU75]. The distinguishing factors for these two types of analysis are the duration of the observed phenomena and the frequency with which they occur in time.

There are many techniques for measuring a computer system. The choice depends on the desired type of analysis and on the level at which it is to be performed. Since an *event* is a change of the system's state, a way of collecting data about certain system activities is to capture all associated events and to record them in the same order in which they occur. In this case, the measurement is done by *event detection*. At a later stage these data will be analyzed or used to drive a model.

A technique that is often preferred to the one just described, because it does not interfere with the system as much, is that of *sampling*. At regular time intervals the system is interrupted to detect the state of some of its components. If the number of samples collected is sufficiently large, this type of measurement may be made sufficiently accurate.

Each performance measurement experiment requires a choice of the workload to be processed during the collection of the data. To perform comparative evaluations, it is necessary that the experiment be repeatable; this is easier to achieve if a set of programs or interactive scripts faithfully representing the workload of the system to be measured is used. This artificial workload is usually called a *benchmark*. Note that the type of workload (natural or artificial) used during an experiment is independent of, and does not influence, the measurement techniques adopted to collect the data.

Finally, in certain cases, it may be useful (or necessary) to analyze the behavior of a model built especially to investigate specific phenomena, rather than that of the real system. This technique gives the user the possibility of dealing with and observing only those variables and parameters that are characteristic of the problem to be investigated.

If the model is a *simulator,* that is, if it contains a mechanism that simulates the behavior in time of the system under a given workload, the measurements that should be performed on the real system may be carried out on the model.

3.2 EVENT DETECTION

In the previous section we defined an event in a computer system to be any change of the system's state. Events are, for example, the beginning of an I/O operation, its completion, the transition of the CPU from the busy to the idle state, or vice versa. Also, the recognition of a page fault, the initiation and the termination of a program, and the beginning of a disk may be events of interest.

When an event is associated with a program's function, it is said to be software correlated or a *software event* [SV76]. An event of this kind occurs when a program reaches a certain stage of its execution (for example, when an I/O operation starts). Similarly, a hardware-related event or *hardware event* consists of the appearance of one or more signals in the circuits of a system component. A hardware event is independent of the logical content of the program being executed at that moment (consider, for example, the movements of a disk arm).

Many hardware events can be recognized via software because they are accompanied by a modification of some memory locations (that is, by a software event). When measurements by event detection are discussed, software-recognizable events are usually implied. Therefore, this technique will be illustrated referring to software events. But it is conceptually applicable to, and in practice often used in, hardware measurements.

The principle of software event detection is that of inserting a special code *(trap code, hook)* in specific places of the operating system. When an event to be intercepted occurs, this code will cause control to be transferred to an appropriate routine. The routine records the occurrence of the event and stores in a buffer area relevant data to be later written on tape or disk; then it returns control to the operating system. The set of instructions and data used for this purpose constitutes a *monitor,* that is, a mechanism for collecting information on the system's activity. In particular, this type of monitor is said to be *event-driven* since it is activated by the occurrence of an event. An event-driven monitor may be said to collect an *event trace*. The data stored on tape will be processed at the end of the tracing period by an analysis program that performs a *data reduction* in order to make the data more easily interpretable. Given a group of events to be detected, the choice of *full trace monitoring* may lead to the collection of an exorbitant mass of data, which will require a considerable amount of CPU time for their reduction. On the other hand, the tracing technique has the advantage of providing more information than any other on certain aspects of a system's behavior.

It should be noted that the use of tracing in software measurements must be selective, since intercepting too many events would slow down the normal operation of the system unacceptably. The overhead caused by the monitor is in fact directly proportional to the number of event types to be intercepted and to their frequencies.

Another critical factor is buffer space. Since this space must be kept within certain limits, buffer contents must be written to mass storage with a frequency only a few orders of magnitude lower than that with which events occur. Event frequency may be very high if, for example, we are investigating some aspects of the microscopic behavior of the operating system. When an event (or group of events) occurs and the buffer (or buffers, if double buffering is used) is full but the transfer of its contents has not been completed, either (1) the system waits for the completion of the transfer [DE69], or (2) the system continues normally.

In the first case the system's activity might be appreciably slowed down due to the frequent waits. In the second, all data concerning events that occur before the buffer is available again are lost [GT72].

In interrupt driven systems, one can adopt a slightly different technique to detect the occurrence of certain events. In this case, the address of the routine handling a given interrupt may be replaced by the measurement routine's starting address [KE68]. This allows the monitor to intercept each interrupt of that kind and to read, when the interrupt occurs, the contents of certain memory locations or tables. These data will be recorded on tape before "returning" the interrupt to the operating system for its processing.

Using the interrupt intercept method, it is fairly easy to trace a system's activity. An application to the GECOS system is described in [CA68]. However, even with this method the interference with the system is often considerable.

Some systems are equipped with hardware that makes event tracing less cumbersome. In general, however, this hardware has not been designed to help evaluate a system's performance but as an aid in hardware or software debugging [IB70].

In most cases, event detection by software is difficult to implement, since it requires the operating system to be modified, and expensive in terms of the system resources required. Although it can provide more data than any other method, it cannot be adopted as the basic technique for tools that can be added to an existing operating system.

The problem of implementing an event-driven software tool that gives the user the ability to change the event types to be detected has been considered in the SMT project [FE74]. The SMT is a tool that allows its user to insert interactively software probes into a program to be instrumented, and, always interactively, delete them, and turn them on or off. This gives event-driven monitoring the desired flexibility and ease of use by shifting the burden of program modification from the evaluator to the machine itself. The various probes inserted by the SMT can be connected to different measurement routines that will have to collect the data when the corresponding event is detected.

3.3 SAMPLING

The event detection technique discussed in Sec. 3.2 is based on the interception and recording of all the events of a given kind. It is therefore a technique to be used only when it is necessary to know the sequence of these events or the exact number of their occurrences in a given time interval. When the knowledge of these items is not essential for the study of a problem, the *sampling method* may be adopted.

Sampling is a statistical technique usable whenever the measurement of all the data that characterize a set of people, objects, or events is impossible, impractical, or too expensive. Instead of examining the whole set or population, the method analyzes only a part of it, called a *sample*. From this sample it is then possible to estimate, often with a high degree of accuracy, some parameters that are characteristic of the population.

In measuring the performance of a computer system, this technique presents the advantage of producing a much smaller amount of data, thus shortening and simplifying its analysis. The process of data collection by sampling causes less disturbance to the system than event detection by software. The reduction of interference makes the alteration of system performance due to the measurement tool often irrelevant and always more easily controllable.

Sampling may be used for two different purposes:

1. To measure the fractions of a given time interval each system component spent in its various states. The data collected during the measurement interval are subjected to an a posteriori analysis to determine what happened during the interval, in what ratios the various events occurred, and how different types of activity were related to each other.
2. To follow the evolution of the system and to predict its future behavior so that decisions that will have a positive influence on its performance can be made.

The first goal is reached with specific measurement tools, normally employed by the users of a system to evaluate the efficiency of resource usage. The accuracy of the results is determined by the size of the sample (see Sec. 3.3.1). It should be noted that, since the sampled quantities are functions of time, it would be necessary to assume that the workload is stationary to guarantee the validity of the results. In practice, it is rare for the workload to be stationary during long periods of time.

However, fairly stationary situations can usually be obtained by subdividing the measurement interval into relatively short periods (from fractions of a minute to several minutes) and by grouping homogeneous blocks of data together. Logical recordings of the data extracted are made to correspond to these shorter periods.

The second goal is reached when the measurement is an integral part of the process of controlling an operating system's activity. Many of the functions an operating system provides must adapt dynamically to workload variations or, more generally, to variations of the system's operating conditions. The estimates of the parameters on which certain decisions are based take into proper account the recent history of their values. Since the evolution of the system cannot be deterministically predicted, it is necessary to create a model based on an assumed underlying stochastic process. In particular, in a computer system, the variables representing the states of system components at time t are piecewise constant with jumps at random instants; thus, they are discrete random variables.

A model that represents a wide class of problems connected with performance measurements for control purposes is described at length in [DE71]. That study discusses the problem of choosing an efficient estimator of an unknown parameter, given a limited number of observed events. The study also examines the sensitivity of a given decision rule to the degree of uncertainty implicit in the estimate of the parameter being considered.

These problems, although important, since many resource allocation procedures base (or should base) their decisions on estimates obtained using a sample of recent events, will not be discussed here because of their much higher relevance to the design phase of a system than to its evaluation and improvement.

3.3.1 Sample Selection and Accuracy

A necessary condition for a correct estimate of a population's descriptors (mean, variance, proportions, and so on) is that the sample taken be representative. If the sample were perfectly representative of the population from which it has been extracted with respect to the variables being considered, it would lead to exact estimates of the population's descriptors. Sometimes, to obtain a sufficiently representative sample, it is necessary to make use of any information that may be known about the variables being observed. When we have no knowledge of their distribution, we use the *random sampling* technique. This technique ensures the representativeness of a sample for a sufficiently large number N of elements extracted (N is said to be the *size of the sample*), since with this method each population element has the same probability of being selected as part of the sample. Therefore, when using this method, an aspect to be carefully considered is the choice of the sample size.

Let us consider a sample of size N from a given population, and let D be the population descriptor to be estimated on the basis of a similar descriptor, or statistic, d of the sample. Usually, the estimate of D is accompanied by an indication of its degree of accuracy, that is, by a *confidence interval,* within which the value of D lies with a certain degree of certainty. Interval estimates are usually preferred to point estimates, where only the estimate of the descriptor is given without specifying the probability that it differs from the true unknown value by less than a given error bound.

To obtain the confidence intervals of an estimate, we must know the probability distribution of the statistic d. The distribution of d could be obtained by extracting all the possible samples of size N from the population being considered and by calculating the statistic d for each sample. This distribution is called the *sampling distribution* of d.

For a sufficiently large N (often $N \geqslant 30$ is enough), the sampling distribution of several statistics (mean, variance, sums and differences of descriptors, proportions, and so on) are approximated by the normal or Gaussian distribution for any type of population distribution. This is true as long as the size of the population is sufficiently large, at least twice the sample size. This result is reached by applying the fundamental theorem of stochastic convergence (the *central limit theorem*) and the *law of large numbers,* which state that, under very general assumptions, the distribution of the sum of many random variables, either independent or slightly correlated with each other, tends to a normal Gaussian distribution for $N \rightarrow \infty$ [CR47].

If one value of the statistic d is taken as an estimate of the value of the population descriptor D, an error is made due to the differences among samples and to those between any d and D. The mean square deviation of the sampling distribution is called the *standard error*.

The equation describing the probability density function of the normal distribution is

$$y = \left(\frac{1}{\sigma\sqrt{2\pi}}\right) \exp\left[\frac{-(x-\mu)^2}{2\sigma^2}\right] \tag{3.1}$$

where y is the probability density corresponding to each value of the random variable x, and μ and σ are, respectively, the mean and the standard deviation of the distribution of x. Figure 3.1 is a plot of this probability density function.

An important property of this curve is its symmetry with respect to the point $x = \mu$. Also, the areas below the curve delimited by the ordinates corresponding to the points $\mu - \sigma$ and $\mu + \sigma$, $\mu - 2\sigma$ and $\mu + 2\sigma$, and $\mu - 3\sigma$ and $\mu + 3\sigma$ are, respectively, 68.27, 95.45, and 99.73 percent of the total area below the curve and do not depend on μ and σ (see Fig. 3.1).

If x is a random variable whose density is given by Eq. (3.1), the area below the curve delimited by the x axis and by the ordinates corresponding to two values of x represents the probability of x being between these two values. We can apply to x a transformation that will produce a new variable z normally distributed with zero mean and a standard deviation equal to 1. The curve obtained in this way is called the *standardized normal curve*. The main advantage of this transformation lies in the fact that the values of the areas below the standardized normal curve can easily be derived from simple tables (see for example [SP72]). The transformation which is used,

$$z = \frac{x - \mu}{\sigma}$$

modifies the position and shape of the normal curve, making it symmetric with respect to the vertical axis and its standard deviation coincident with the abscissa $z = 1$ (see Fig. 3.2).

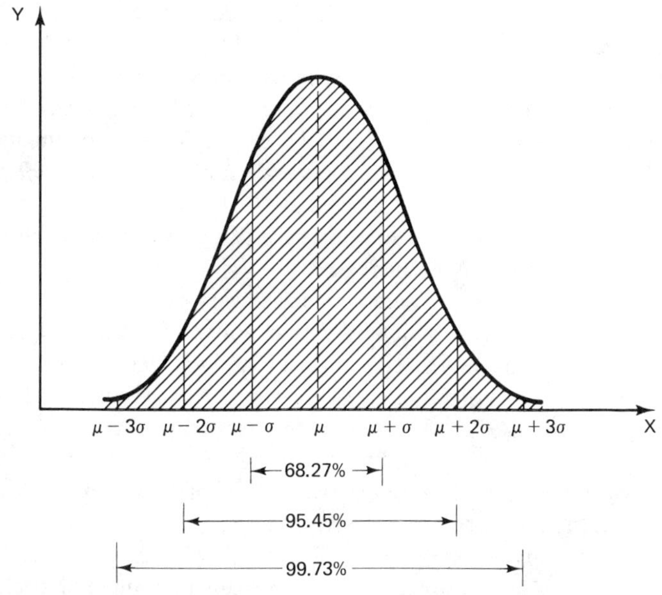

Figure 3.1 Normal probability density curve. The areas are expressed as percentages of the total area.

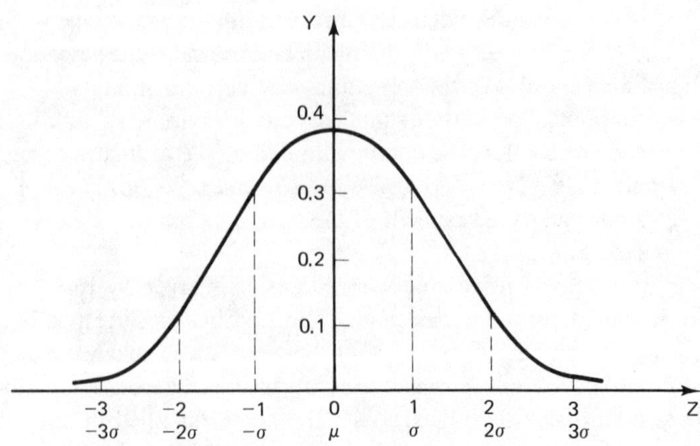

Figure 3.2 Standardized normal probability density curve.

Let us assume that μ_d and σ_d are the mean and the standard deviation of the sampling distribution of statistic d. Then, if this distribution is approximately normal, for a given sample of size N the value of d will fall between $\mu_d - 2\sigma_d$ and $\mu_d + 2\sigma_d$ 95.45 percent of the time or between $\mu_d - 3\sigma_d$ and $\mu_d + 3\sigma_d$ 99.73 percent of the time. Thus, we are 95.45 percent *confident* that d lies between $\mu_d - 2\sigma_d$ and $\mu_d + 2\sigma_d$, while we are 99.73 percent confident that it lies between $\mu_d - 3\sigma_d$ and $\mu_d + 3\sigma_d$.

These probabilities are called *confidence levels,* the intervals, *confidence intervals,* and some coefficients used to calculate confidence intervals, *confidence coefficients*. The confidence interval represents probabilistically the limits of the error made by considering d rather than μ_d (for the mean and the proportions, we have $\mu_d = D$; in general, when this is true, the statistic d is said to be an *unbiased estimator* of the population descriptor D). The confidence level represents the probability that the unknown error will respect these limits. The most common confidence levels are 95 and 99 percent, for which the corresponding confidence coefficients are 1.96 and 2.58. Using multiples of the standard error, it is therefore possible to reduce the risk of errors to the desired level. As we shall see, this requires that N be increased.

It has been stated that sampling can be very useful for measuring a computer system. For this purpose, a tool, be it hardware or software, must be available that extracts from the system an adequately sized sample of the variables of interest. We shall thus be able to estimate the relative durations of certain system activities and the relative frequencies of given events [KO71]. A technique that is used to obtain representative samples of the state transitions occurring in the system will be discussed in Sec. 5.2.

As an example of sampling, and to complete with a practical case what has been said about the estimation of a descriptor, we shall evaluate the utilization of a system's CPU during a given time interval. The CPU may be either *busy* or *idle*. By observing its state N times at N distinct instants, we extract a sample of size N from the population of the CPU's states during the measurement period. We have to determine the proportion P of busy states in the set of states constituting the sample. Also, we have to determine the confidence level, that is, the probability that the error made by considering d as the utilization of the CPU will remain within a certain interval (the confidence interval).

We shall use the following notation:

P_a: proportion of CPU busy states in the population

P_i: proportion of CPU idle states in the population

p_a: proportion of CPU busy states in the sample

p_i: proportion of CPU idle states in the sample

μ_{pa}: mean of the sampling distribution of the proportions of CPU busy states

σ_{pa}: standard deviation of the sampling distribution of the proportions of CPU busy states

In general, the mean μ and the standard deviation σ of the sampling distribution of proportions are given by

$$\mu = P, \qquad \sigma = \sqrt{\frac{PQ}{N}}$$

where P is the proportion of cases in which a certain event occurs in the population and Q is the proportion of cases in which it does not occur ($Q = 1 - P$).

Thus, for the current problem we have

$$\mu_{pa} = P_a, \qquad \sigma_{pa} = \sqrt{\frac{P_a(1 - P_a)}{N}}$$

If we choose a 95 percent confidence level, the confidence interval is given by

$$P_a \pm 1.96 \sqrt{\frac{P_a(1 - P_a)}{N}}$$

The standard error, which is given by $\sqrt{P_a(1 - P_a)/N}$, cannot be calculated, since both P_a and P_i are unknown; in fact, these are exactly the values to be determined. Thus, the standard error must be estimated. There are two fairly simple procedures to do this.

The first, which is less reliable in that it adds an extra error to the standard error's estimate, consists of taking p_a as an estimate of P_a and p_i as an estimate of P_i. In this way a confidence interval is obtained that is close to the correct one if the sample size is large.

The second procedure, which is considered more conservative and is more commonly used, is based on the observation that the standard error is greatest when the product $P_a(1 - P_a)$ reaches its maximum value, that is, when $P_a = 0.5$. Consequently, the confidence interval will be maximum when the proportion of states considered (in this case, CPU busy states) is 50 percent. Since we want the interval to be as small as possible, using the largest interval amounts to considering the worst case. With this method, the limits of the interval are given by

$$p_a \pm 1.96 \sqrt{\frac{(0.5)^2}{N}} = p_a \pm 1.96\sigma_N$$

where σ_N is the maximum value of σ_{pa} for a sample of size N. The product $E_N = 1.96\sigma_N$ represents the maximum error possible at the 95 percent confidence level for a sample of size N when p_a is taken as an approximation to P_a.

If the proportion of CPU busy states found by sampling is, for example, 68 percent (that is, $p_a = 0.68$), and a sample of 10,000 CPU state observations has been taken, we can assume that the CPU was busy 68 percent of the time with an error smaller than

$$1.96 \sqrt{\frac{(0.5)^2}{(100)^2}} \cong 0.01$$

This means that, if the measurement could be repeated 100 times, each time for a period of the same duration, always taking a sample of 10,000 observations and *under the same workload,* at least 95 times the measured CPU utilization would be between 67 and 69 percent.

In practice, the procedure that is actually followed is more often the inverse of the one described. That is, the accuracy level to be achieved in a measurement is given, and the problem consists of determining the sample size. First, the desired confidence level and the precision with which the measured descriptor is to be estimated must be decided. If the descriptor is the proportion of specific states in a given set of observed states (this is perhaps the most frequently measured type of descriptor when evaluating a system's performance), the size of the sample may be derived from the confidence curves in Fig. 3.3. These represent the maximum error for the three confidence levels of 90, 95, and 99 percent as a function of the sample size N according to the relationship

$$E_{NC} = K_C \sqrt{\frac{(0.5)^2}{N}} = K_C\sigma_N$$

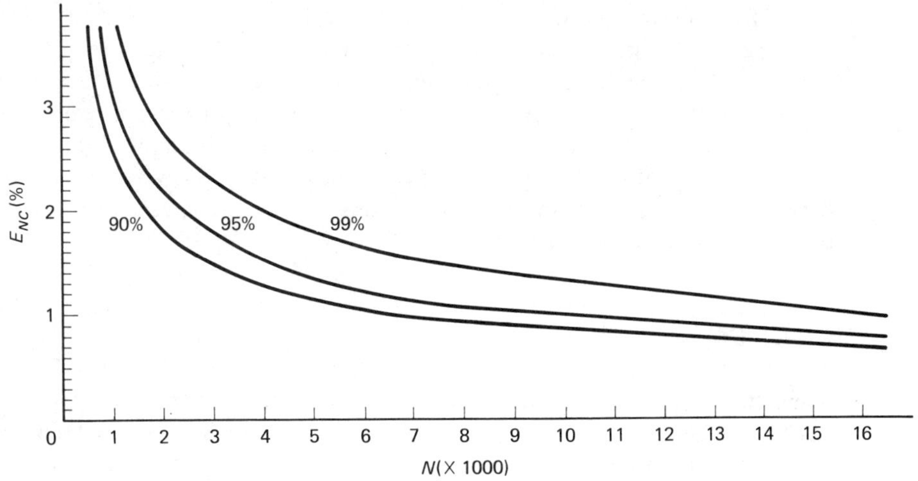

Figure 3.3 Confidence curves at the 90, 95, and 99 percent confidence level.

where K_C is the confidence coefficient corresponding to confidence level C. For the three levels of 90, 95, and 99 percent, K_C equals 1.65, 1.96, and 2.58, respectively.

Table 3.1 shows the confidence coefficients corresponding to different confidence levels. It also shows the confidence levels corresponding to integer confidence coefficients, that is, the areas below the normal distribution curve between points that correspond to integer multiples of the standard deviation (see Fig. 3.2).

Finally, we must point out that the calculation of statistical accuracy, as we have discussed it, is based on the assumption that the observed phenomena (that is, the operating states of the various system components) are independent of the time instants at which the sample elements are collected. The technique according to which these elements are taken consists of interrupting the system's operation when these instants occur (see Section 5.2).

TABLE 3.1 CONFIDENCE COEFFICIENTS

Confidence level (%)	*Confidence coefficient*
50.00	0.6745
68.27	1.0
75.00	1.150
80.00	1.281
90.00	1.65
95.00	1.96
95.45	2.0
99.00	2.58
99.73	3.0
99.90	3.29
99.999	4.0

There are two circumstances in which independence is not satisfied and which may therefore cause systematic sampling errors. One occurs when the observed phenomenon is somehow *synchronized* with the sampling interrupts; the other occurs when, at the instant at which the interrupt should occur, the operating system is executing an *uninterruptable* function. In the latter case the interrupt will be postponed, and thus the state detected will be different from the one in which the system was when the interrupt should have occurred. As these are systematic errors and thus relatively easily detected, it is often possible to account for them.

3.4 SIMULATION

Simulation is a technique that differs from the ones dealt with in the previous sections since it measures a *model* of a system rather than the system itself. A model is a representation of some aspects of a system's behavior built in order to study them. Thus, for every system many models may be built. Simulation models represent the dynamic behavior of a system by reproducing its states and following the state transitions caused by an appropriate sequence of external stimuli (that is, in our context, by a suitable model of the workload).

The measurements required for system evaluation can be carried out on a model using the techniques examined in this chapter. This leads to simulated experiments during which the quantities to be evaluated are measured by event detection or by sampling or by both. It is important to realize that, once a model is built, it may be dealt with *exactly as if it were* the real system. Clearly, this applies within the limits of its degree of detail. With respect to direct measurements, those made on a *simulation model* (or *simulator*) have the advantage of not requiring the system's existence nor its availability. If the system (or a new version of it) does not yet exist, simulation models, like all other models, allow us to *project* performance, and this is particularly useful in improvement studies, capacity planning, system design, and configuration design.

The main disadvantage of modeling techniques is the difficulty of establishing whether the results obtained are sufficiently accurate. There are many sources of errors in direct measurements, to which we have to add, in the case of simulation, those stemming from the inevitable differences between the behavior of the model and that of the system. There are statistical methods for increasing the credibility of these results [FI73], but the best methods are an accurate reproduction of system functions and, whenever possible, a careful comparison of the results obtained with those found by direct measurements.

The accuracy of a model depends first on the system description, in terms of states and transitions, that has been adopted in designing the model. The identification of a system's states is not unique, and this type of characterization will have to be made based on the objectives of the study. To build a model that can be used in practice, all the system aspects to be studied and that can influence simulation results should be reproduced with the minimum degree of detail compatible with the accuracy required. The other aspects should be either ignored or very concisely represented.

However, this distinction is difficult to make, and the simulators that result are often either so coarse and inaccurate that they can only be used in some rough, preliminary studies, or too massive and hence too expensive to build and to use. As there are no systematic methods to choose the optimum degree of detail, the choice is left to the modeler's ability and experience, and is limited by the amount of known information about the system and its workload. Some descriptions at different levels of detail of the simple UBRS system whose configuration is shown in Fig. 3.4 are reported in Fig. 3.5.

The identification of a system's states implies that of the state transitions and is in fact influenced by it. The modeler determines which of the transformations occurring in a system are important, that is, are likely to influence appreciably the results of the measurements performed on the model. These transformations, which have already been called *events* in the previous sections, must appear as state transitions in the model; otherwise they cannot be detected. For example, in the state diagrams in Fig. 3.5a and b, the operating system calls made by user procedures are not represented, while in Fig. 3.5c they are.

A simulator is a dynamic model since it follows the evolution in time of the system it represents. Thus, there is a time, called *simulated time,* within which a simulator operates. The interrelations between system time and simulated time are not simple: while the first flows continuously with perfect regularity, the second can proceed intermittently by intervals of different lengths. Since in a model nothing happens between the occurrences of two consecutive events, all simulated time intervals without events can be ignored; this is the principle of the *next event technique*. When considering the running cost of a simulator (which is usually a program), an important index is the ratio between simulated time and the simulator's execution time. If, for example, to simulate 1 min of the system being represented 10 s of a given (dedicated) system's time are needed, the value of this ratio is 6. If everything else remains constant, the ratio increases (and the execution time decreases) as the simulator's accuracy decreases.

There are two types of simulators: commercial simulators and programs built by modelers for specific evaluation studies. To run commercial simulators developed and distributed by specialized companies, a description of the system and of its workload must be provided. The other simulators are designed and built for purposes much more specific than those of the commercial simulators, which must be adaptable to a large range of systems, configurations, and applications. When building a simulator, a fundamental choice is that of the language to be used.

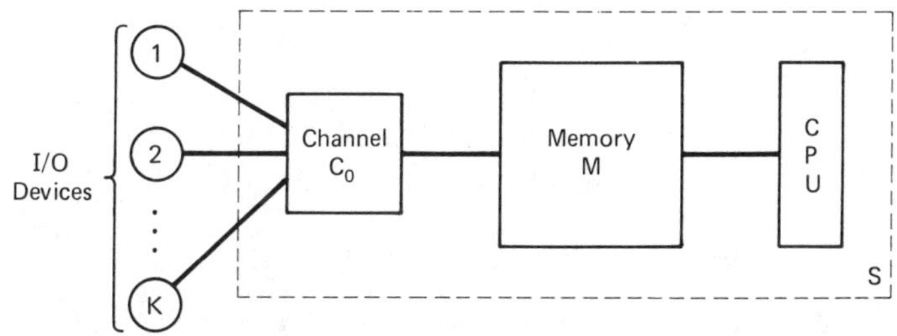

Figure 3.4 Configuration of a single-channel UBRS or MBRS system.

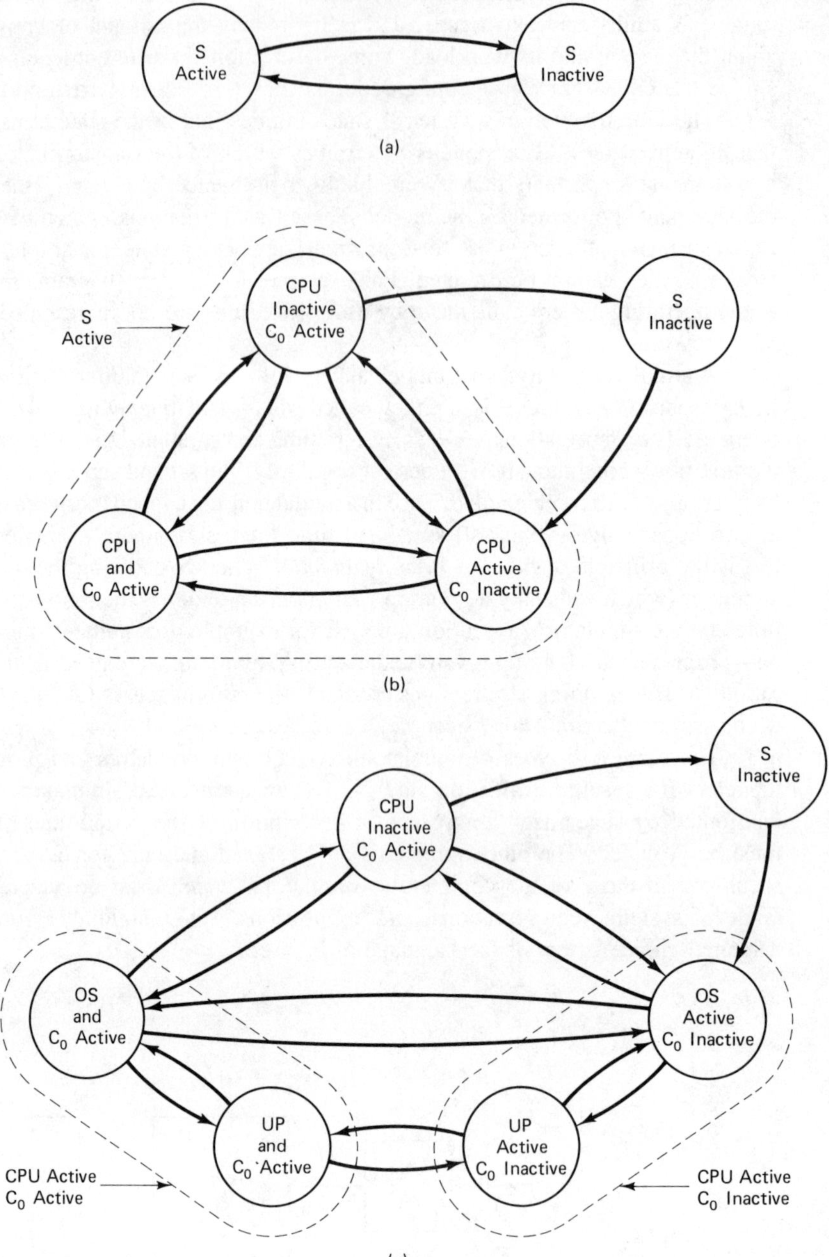

Figure 3.5 Three state diagrams for a single channel UBRS system, with three levels of detail (OS: operating system; UP: user process).

The available languages can be classified into the following categories:

- General languages
- Extensions of general languages for simulation purposes
- Simulation languages

In the first category we find languages such as FORTRAN, ALGOL, PASCAL, and PL/1, which do not have any of the structures and functions that are so helpful in the implementation and verification of a simulator. Thus, their use requires the programmer to create the necessary mechanisms (such as that for advancing simulated time) and data structures. On the other hand, these languages are usually very well known, widely available, and very well tested and documented.

The typical functions of simulation may be added to a general language in the form of a library of subprograms or procedures that can be called by the simulators written in that language. With this extension one of the main disadvantages of the general languages either disappears or is drastically reduced. In the second category of languages we find GASP [PR69], an extension of FORTRAN.

A simulation language, on the other hand, provides its users with (but also forces them to adopt) its "world view." The use of such a language simplifies model construction, that is, the description of a system's operation. For this reason, a simulation language is an excellent means of communication and documentation. The models it allows to be built follow given rules and use certain conceptual schemes, which form its "world view" and which simplify a modeler's task considerably.

Sometimes, however, the most natural representations of some aspects of a system's behavior cannot easily be fitted into the conceptual framework on which a simulation language is based. Even though, with respect to the general languages, simulation languages offer advantages of clarity and ease of use, often the simulators produced by using them will be less efficient. Among the most common simulation languages are SIMULA 67 [DA68], SIMSCRIPT [KI69], and GPSS [GO75]. When a computer system's simulator is to be constructed, the workload of the system to be modeled must also be represented, and its model must be compatible with that of the system. There are two main types of representation of a workload, the probabilistic type and the deterministic type.

A *probabilistic model* characterizes each of the workload's elements (each process) with a finite number of parameters (for example, CPU time, number of I/O operations, and memory space used). The probabilistic distributions of these parameters, generally considered statistically independent of each other, are used by the simulator to generate descriptions of processes whose parameters follow the given distributions. Also, the arrival time of each process can be considered as a workload parameter. To determine its value, we may assign to the simulator the distribution of the interval lengths between consecutive arrivals, from which at each arrival the simulator will derive the simulated time of the next arrival. This mechanism is systematically applied to all types of events; when an event relative to a process occurs, the instant at which the future event (for example, for the same process) occurs is computed, or else the conditions for the occurrence of a future event are established. This allows the simulation, which reproduces event occurrences in chronological order, thereby following many activities at the same time, to sustain itself.

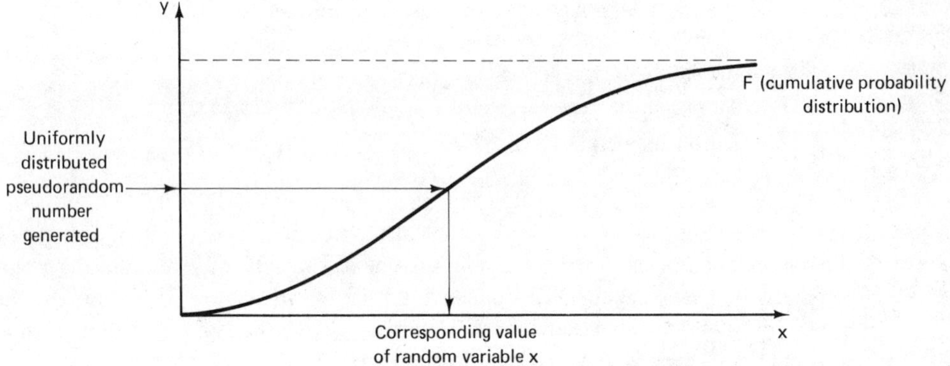

Figure 3.6 Generation of values of a random variable x whose cummulative probability distribution is to coincide with function F.

In a probabilistic model of the workload, a pseudorandom number generator is used to obtain parameter distributions approximating the given ones. As shown in Fig. 3.6, the value of each parameter is derived by projecting, according to the distribution given for that parameter, a uniformly distributed pseudorandom number on to the x axis. This method can easily be extended to discrete distributions (those of parameters that can only take on a finite number of distinct values) and is sometimes used also in other parts of the simulator when, for convenience, we choose to model an aspect of the system in a probabilistic way rather than deterministically.

In a *deterministic model* each process is represented by a set of parameter values that cannot be generated during the simulation, as for probabilistic models, but are specified one by one from the beginning.

When the *history* of each process (that is, the sequence and durations of the states in which each process would be if it were alone in the system) is assigned, the simulator is *trace driven*.

The traces used to drive a simulator are usually the result of real workload measurements by chronological recording of events, usually reprocessed to adapt them to the requirements of the simulator of which they are to be the inputs. A deterministic model is a potentially more accurate representation of the real load, since it automatically accounts for correlations between the parameters of a process. However, it requires much more secondary memory space and, if consisting of traces, is much less easily modifiable than a probabilistic model. By keeping the workload model separate from that of the system when designing a simulator, it is possible to make the simulator independent of the workload model type, that is, to make inputs generated by probabilistic as well as by deterministic models acceptable to it.

3.4.1 Construction of a Simple Simulator

The states and the events represented in Fig. 3.5 are inadequate for a system simulator whose workload consists of a set of single process models. A much more adequate characterization, shown in Fig. 3.7, is based on the states of a process during its life-

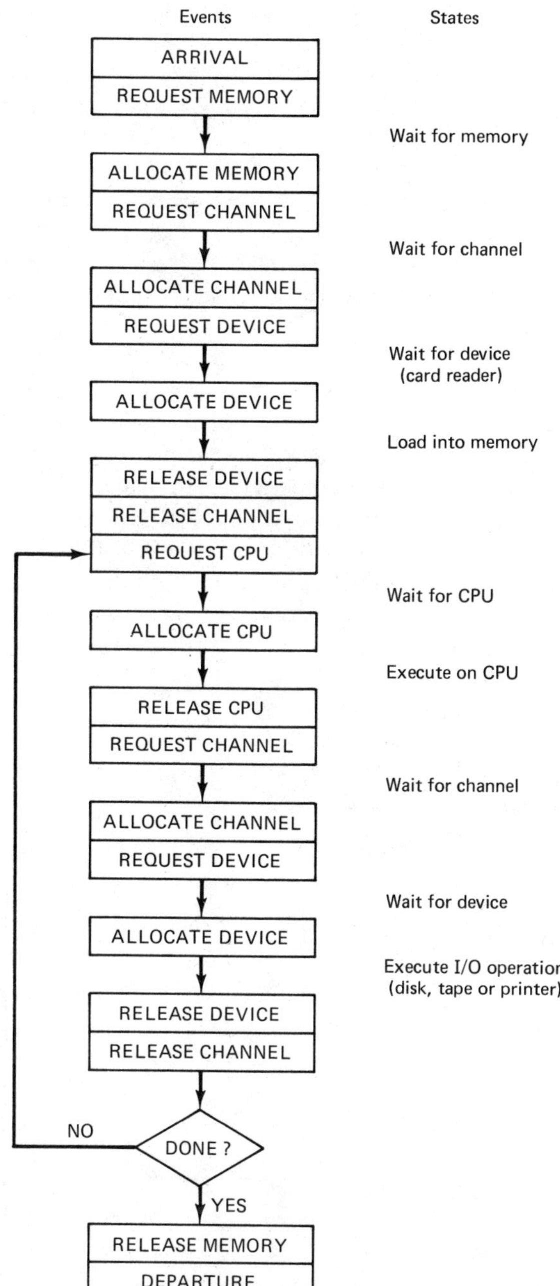

Figure 3.7 States and event diagram of a process in the MBRS system of Fig. 3.4.

time in the system and on the events corresponding to the transitions between these states. Note that the system in Fig. 3.4 is now assumed to be of the MBRS type. The figure suggests a simple way of structuring a simulator. If, for each type of event appearing in the state diagram, a subprogram is created, a mechanism operating like the one described in Sec. 3.4 can be obtained. Each subprogram must have as an argument the name of the process referred to by the event and, among other tasks, must determine when the next event concerning that process will occur. The structure of this type of simulator may be represented as in Fig. 3.8.

In the event diagram in Fig. 3.7 we can identify three event types: request events, allocate events, and release events. Note that arrival and departure coincide in time with the only instances of the request memory and release memory events, respectively. Hence, there is no need for separate subprograms to implement arrivals and departures. The schematic flow charts of the request, allocate, and release subprograms are shown in Figs. 3.9, 3.10, and 3.11, respectively.

The characterization of each process consists of the parameters listed in Table 3.2. They may be assigned to the simulator either in deterministic form (as in Table 3.2) or in probabilistic form. In the latter case, the user may specify the distributions of t, n, m, l, i, d, and x or of some equivalent random variables (for example, the probability of having completed execution when the I/O subsystem is released), and let the simulator determine the actual values of a process's parameters at run time. This is the solution we shall adopt in our implementation of the simulator. A function SAMPLE (DISTRIBUTION) will sample the given DISTRIBUTION and return the value of the corresponding variable.

The resources the system to be simulated consists of are represented in Fig. 3.4

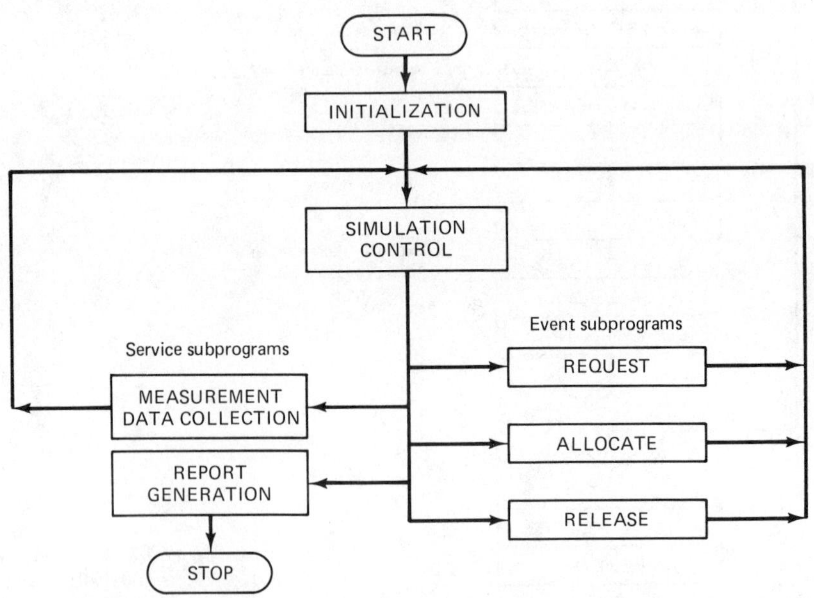

Figure 3.8 Structure of a simulator based on the next event approach.

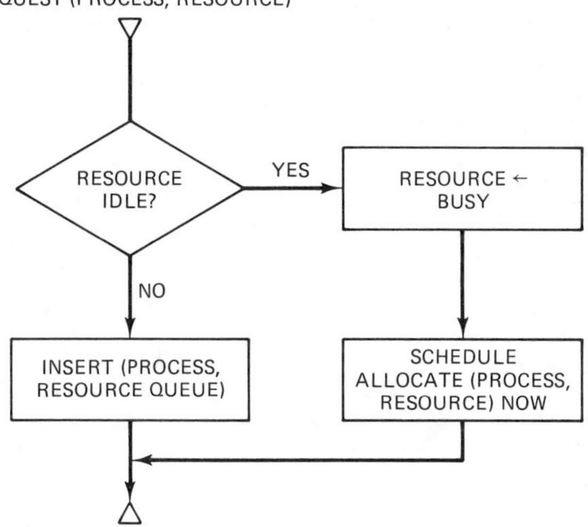

Figure 3.9 Flow chart of the request subprogram.

and listed in Fig. 3.12, which also shows the names of the queues to the various resources, the *event list,* where the simulation control program always finds the next event, and which therefore is to be kept in chronological order. An extract of the event list is shown in Fig. 3.13. The event routines insert records of future events into the event list, which is "popped" by the simulation control program. The two primitive operations that can be performed on any queue are:

1. POP (ELEMENT,QUEUE): extracts the first eligible element from the queue QUEUE, deletes it from the queue, and returns it as the value of ELEMENT; the condition of eligibility is tested by comparing the contents of the third component of the element with a given value; all elements will be eligible in our queues except those of the memory queue, where the size of each process will be compared with the amount of free memory space to determine the loadability of each process; if there are no eligible elements, ELEMENT is set equal to 0.
2. INSERT (ELEMENT,QUEUE): inserts the element pointed to by ELEMENT into the queue QUEUE in the proper position; the position is determined by the value

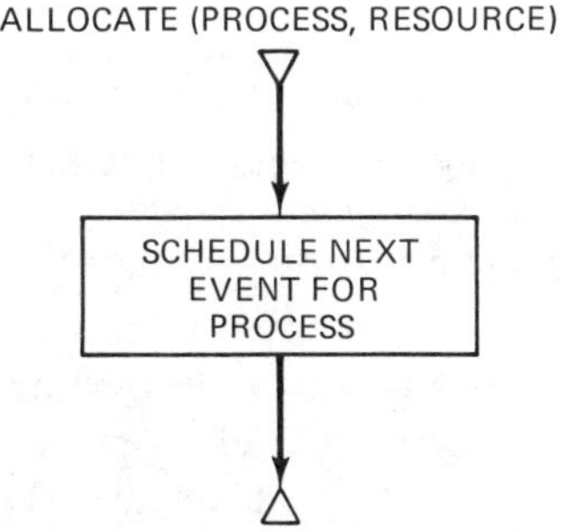

Figure 3.10 Flow chart of the ALLOCATE subprogram.

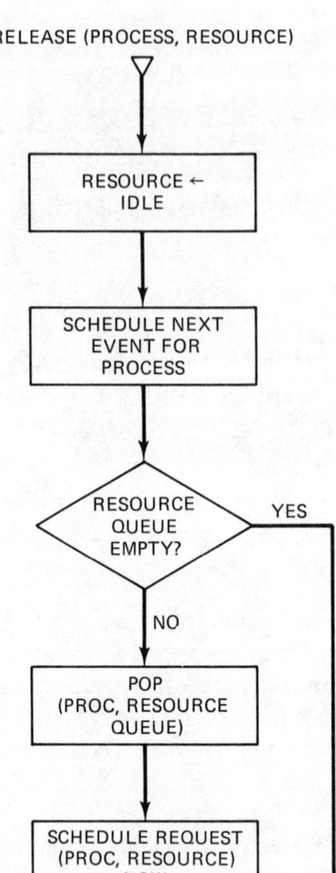

Figure 3.11 Flow chart of the RELEASE subprogram.

of the second component of the element, since the values of these components are kept in ascending order in all queues; when two priority values are the same, the chronological order is adopted.

The partial listing of a FORTRAN implementation of our simulator is presented in Fig. 3.14. All declaration statements, all FORMAT statements, some parts of the initialization portion of the main program, some subprograms, and all measurement statements have been omitted. The type of all variables is integer. Each process has an associated vector called DESCRIPTION (PROCESS, J), where PROCESS is the number that identifies the process. Note that, in order not to waste too much memory, process numbers can be recycled when they are no longer used by processes that have departed. DESCRIPTION contains various parameters of the process, including its memory space demand (called MEMORY DEMAND in subroutine REQUEST), its total number of

TABLE 3.2 PROCESS CHARACTERIZATION FOR THE SIMULATOR IN FIGS. 3.7 AND 3.14

t	=	arrival time (since the last arrival)
n	=	number of CPU–I/O cycles
m	=	memory space demand
l	=	program length (number of bytes)
i_1	=	number of CPU instructions to be executed (first visit to CPU)
(d_1, x_1)	=	number x_1 of bytes to be transferred to or from device d_1 (first visit to I/O)
		⋮
i_n	=	number of CPU instructions to be executed (nth visit to CPU)
(d_n, x_n)	=	number x_n of bytes to be transferred to or from device d_n (nth visit to I/O)

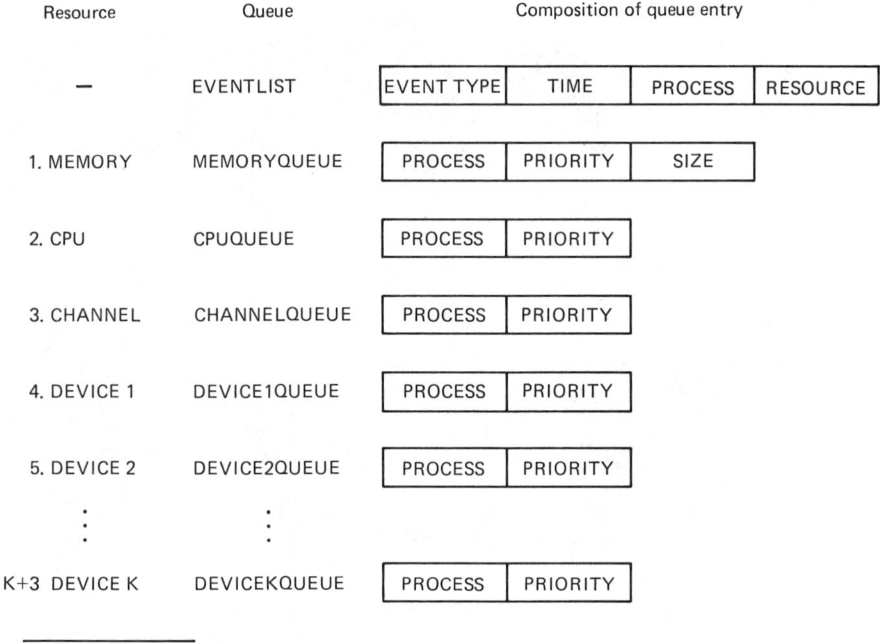

Event types

1. REQUEST
2. ALLOCATE
3. RELEASE
4. COLLECT DATA
5. REPORT

Figure 3.12 Queues and their composition for the simulator in Fig. 3.4 and 3.7 through 3.11.

EVENT TYPE	TIME	PROCESS	RESOURCE
RELEASE	102847	41	D2
REQUEST	102849	53	MEMORY
RELEASE	102856	44	CPU
COLLECTDATA	120000	–	–
REPORT	200000	–	–

Figure 3.13 Extract of the contents of the event list.

visits to the CPU (called CYCLES in RELEASE), the number of visits already paid to the CPU (called VISITS in RELEASE), its arrival time, the times of important events that have already occurred (to be kept for measurement purposes), and so on. Most of the entries in this vector are derived and stored there by subroutine CREATE (PROCESS) called by REQUEST when a new process arrives. The contents of the vector are erased, after they have been used for reporting purposes, by subroutine DELETE (PROCESS), which is called by RELEASE when a process leaves the system. The listings of both CREATE and DELETE have been omitted in Fig. 3.14.

The only variable aspect of the modeled system's configuration is the number of

```
C          MAIN PROGRAM
C          --------------
C          INITIALIZATION
              (OMITTED)
C          --------------
C          READ REPORT AND TERMINATION CONDITIONS
       READ(5,..) (EVENT(I),I=1,4)
       CALL INSERT (EVENT,EVENTLIST)
       READ(5,..) (EVENT(I),I=1,4)
       CALL INSERT (EVENT,EVENTLIST)
C          ----------------
C          READ DISTRIBUTIONS
                (OMITTED)
C          ----------------
C          READ CHARACTERISTICS OF RESOURCES
C          SET RESOURCE STATES TO IDLE
       READ(5,..) K,(RESCHAR(I),I=1,K+3)
       DO 1 I=1,K+3
       STATE(I)=0
     1 CONTINUE
C          -------------------------------------
C          READ DETAILED DESCRIPTIONS OF DEVICES
                      (OMITTED)
C          -------------------------------------
C          CREATE FIRST ARRIVAL
       EVENT(1)=1
       EVENT(2)=0
```

Figure 3.14 FORTRAN implementation (Partial listing) of a simulator of the system in Fig. 3.4.

```
      EVENT(3)=1
      EVENT(4)=1
      CALL INSERT(EVENT,EVENTLIST)
      ---------------------------------
C        SIMULATION CONTROL
    5 CALL POP(EVENT,EVENTLIST)
      TYPE=EVENT(1)
      TIME=EVENT(2)
      PROCESS=EVENT(3)
      RESOURCE=EVENT(4)
      GO TO (10,20,30,40,50),TYPE
   10 CALL REQUEST(PROCESS,RESOURCE)
      GO TO 5
   20 CALL ALLOCATE(PROCESS,RESOURCE)
      GO TO 5
   30 CALL RELEASE(PROCESS,RESOURCE)
      GO TO 5
   40 CALL COLLECTDATA
      GO TO 5
   50 CALL REPORT
      STOP
      END


      SUBROUTINE REQUEST(PROCESS,RESOURCE)
      ............................
      IF(RESOURCE.GT.1) GO TO 10
      CALL CREATE(PROCESS)
      MEMORYDEMAND=DESCRIPTION(PROCESS,1)
      IF((RESCHAR(1)-STATE(1)).LT.MEMORYDEMAND) GO TO 30
      STATE(1)=STATE(1)+MEMORYDEMAND
      EVENT(1)=1
      EVENT(2)=SAMPLE(ARRDISTRIBUTION)+TIME
      EVENT(3)=PROCESS+1
      EVENT(4)=1
      CALL INSERT(EVENT,EVENTLIST)
      GO TO 20
   10 IF(STATE(RESOURCE).NE.0) GO TO 30
      STATE(RESOURCE)=1
   20 EVENT(1)=2
      EVENT(2)=TIME
      EVENT(3)=PROCESS
      EVENT(4)=RESOURCE
      CALL INSERT(EVENT,EVENTLIST)
      RETURN
   30 CALL INSERT(PROCESS,RESOURCE)
      RETURN
      END


      SUBROUTINE ALLOCATE(PROCESS,RESOURCE)
      ......................
      EVENT(3)=PROCESS
      IF(RESOURCE.NE.1) GO TO 10
      EVENT(1)=1
      EVENT(2)=TIME
      EVENT(4)=3
      GO TO 40
```

Figure 3.14 *(continued)*

```
10 IF(RESOURCE.NE.2) GO TO 20
   EVENT(1)=3
   EVENT(2)=SAMPLE(CPUDISTRIBUTION)*RESCHAR(2)+TIME
   EVENT(4)=2
   GO TO 40
20 IF(RESOURCE.NE.3) GO TO 30
   EVENT(1)=1
   EVENT(2)=TIME
   EVENT(4)=SAMPLE(DEVICEDISTRIBUTION)
   GO TO 40
30 EVENT(1)=3
   CALL DEVICE(RESOURCE,DEVTIME)
   EVENT(2)=DEVTIME+TIME
   EVENT(4)=RESOURCE
40 CALL INSERT(EVENT,EVENTLIST)
   RETURN
   END


   SUBROUTINE RELEASE(PROCESS,RESOURCE)
   ...........................
   IF(RESOURCE.GT.1) GO TO 10
   STATE(1)=STATE(1)-MEMORYDEMAND(PROCESS)
   CALL DELETE(PROCESS)
   GO TO 50
10 IF(RESOURCE.GT.2) GO TO 20
   EVENT(1)=1
   EVENT(2)=TIME
   EVENT(3)=PROCESS
   EVENT(4)=3
   CALL INSERT(EVENT,EVENTLIST)
   GO TO 50
20 IF(RESOURCE.GT.3) GO TO 40
   IF(CYCLES(PROCESS).GT.VISITS(PROCESS)) GO TO 30
   EVENT(1)=3
   EVENT(2)=TIME
   EVENT(3)=PROCESS
   EVENT(4)=1
   GO TO 50
30 VISITS(PROCESS)=VISITS(PROCESS)+1
   EVENT(1)=1
   EVENT(2)=TIME
   EVENT(3)=PROCESS
   EVENT(4)=2
   GO TO 50
40 EVENT(1)=3
   EVENT(2)=TIME
   EVENT(3)=PROCESS
   EVENT(4)=3
50 CALL POP(PROC,RESOURCE)
   IF(PROC.EQ.0) RETURN
   EVENT(1)=1
   EVENT(2)=TIME
   EVENT(3)=PROC
   EVENT(4)=RESOURCE
   CALL INSERT(EVENT,EVENTLIST)
   RETURN
   END
```

Figure 3.14 *(continued)*

the I/O devices (see Fig. 3.4), besides, of course, the types of these devices, their technical characteristics, the speed of the CPU, and the size of the main memory. These parameters are read in at the beginning by the main program and stored into vector RESCHAR. Devices that need more than one parameter for their description (for example, disks, for which, besides their transfer rate, we must specify at least one parameter, their access time) will have their own vector of parameters, also to be filled with data read from cards at the beginning of the simulation. Note that these parameters could be permanently stored in a file so that only the type of each device (for example, IBM 3350 disk drive) would need to be specified by the user.

When the resource to be allocated is the channel, the ALLOCATE subroutine samples the discrete probability distribution called DEVICE DISTRIBUTION to determine which I/O device is to be requested by the process. When this device is then allocated to the process, the same subroutine calls the subroutine DEVICE (RESOURCE, DEVTIME), which, based on the type of device RESOURCE, computes the service time of the request and returns it as the value of variable DEVTIME. Even the listing of DEVICE, as well as those of COLLECTDATA, REPORT, INSERT, POP, and SAMPLE, has been omitted in Fig. 3.14.

A simulator can compute the distributions of each state's duration (thus, also their means, variances, maxima, and minima) and the frequency of each transition. Simulation makes the measurement of all variables represented in the model easy. Also, these measurements can be carried out without interfering with the operation of the model, even when they are event-driven. Although real resources must be used, it is possible to avoid consumption of simulated resources. Hence the results will not be affected by errors due to the presence of measurement tools, as is the case of the measurement techniques described in the previous sections. Of course, the sampling technique may also be applied, for example, by having a subroutine like COLLECTDATA reschedule its next wake-up time whenever it is called.

REFERENCES

Entries marked with an asterisk (*) are referenced in the text.

[AG75] Agrawala, A. K., Mohr, J. M., A model for workload characterization, *Proc. ACM-SIGSIM Symposium on the Simulation of Computer Systems,* Aug. 1975.

[BE72a] Beilner, H., Waldbaum, G., Statistical methodology for calibrating a trace-driven simulator of a batch computer system, in: Freiberger, W., ed., *Statistical Computer Performance Evaluation,* pp. 423–459, Academic Press, New York, 1972.

[BE81] Beilner, H., On the construction of computing system simulators, in: Ferrari, D., and Spaolini, M., eds., *Experimental Computer Performance Evaluation,* pp. 1–31, North-Holland, Amsterdam, 1981.

[BE72b] Bell, T. E., Objectives and problems in simulating computers, *AFIPS Conf. Proc., FJCC,* vol. 41, pp. 287–297, 1972.

[BE73] Beretvas, T., System-independent tracing for prediction of system performance, *Proc. ACM-SIGSIM Symposium on Simulation of Computer Systems,* pp. 209–213, 1973.

[BO73] Bowdon, E. K., Mamrak, S. A., Salz, F. R., Simulation: a tool for performance evaluation in network computers, *AFIPS Conf. Proc., NCC,* pp. 121–131, 1973.

*[CA68] Cantrell, H. N., Ellison, A. L., Multiprogramming system performance measurement and analysis, *AFIPS Conf. Proc., SJCC,* vol. 32, 1968.

[CH77] Chandy, K. M., Hogart, J., Sauer, C. H., Selecting capacities in computer communication systems, *IEEE Trans. Software Engineering SE-3,* n. 4, pp. 290–295, July 1977.

[CH69] Cheng, P. S., Trace-driven system modeling, *IBM Systems J.,* vol. 8, n. 4, pp. 280–289, 1969.

[CO76] Coffman, E. G., Jr., *Computer and Job-shop Scheduling Theory,* Wiley, New York, 1976.

[CR74] Crane, M. A., Iglehart, D. L., Simulating stable stochastic systems 1. General multiserver queues, *J. ACM,* vol. 21, pp. 103–113, 1974.

*[CR47] Cramer, H., *Mathematical Methods of Statistics,* Princeton University Press, Princeton, N.J., 1947.

*[DA68] Dahl, O. J., Myhrhang, D., Nygaard, K., The SIMULA 67 Common base language, *Norwegian Computing Centre,* Oslo, 1968.

*[DE69] Deniston, W. R., SIPE: AITSS 360 software measurement technique, *Proc. ACM Nat. Conf.,* 1969.

*[DE71] Denning, P. J., Eisenstein, B. A., Statistical methods in performance evaluation, *Proc. ACM-SIGOPS Workshop on System Performance Evaluation,* Harvard University, Cambridge, Mass., Apr. 1971.

[DR73] Drummond, M. E., *Evaluation and Measurement Techniques for Digital Computer Systems,* Prentice-Hall, Englewood Cliffs, N.J., 1973.

*[FE74] Ferrari, D., Liu, M., A general-purpose software measurement tool, *Proc. 2nd ACM-SIGME Symposium on Measurement and Evaluation,* pp. 94–103, Sept. 1974.

*[FI73] Fishman, G. S., *Concepts and Methods in Discrete Event Digital Simulation,* Wiley, New York, 1973.

[GO69] Gordon, G., *System Simulation,* Prentice-Hall, Englewood Cliffs, N.J., 1969.

*[GO75] Gordon, G., *The Application of GPSS V to Discrete System Simulation,* Prentice-Hall, Englewood Cliffs, N.J., 1975.

[GR72] Grenander, U., Tsao, R. F., Quantitative methods for evaluating computer system performance: a review and proposals, in: Freiberger, W., ed., *Statistical Computer Performance Evaluation,* pp. 73–98, Academic Press, New York, 1972.

*[GT72] *GTF (Generalized Trace Facility),* IBM System 360 Operating System Service Aids, S360-31, GC 28-6719-2, 1972.

[HA71] Hanssmann, F., Kistler, W., Schultz, H., Modelling for computing center planning, *IBM Systems J.,* vol. 10, n. 4, 1971.

[HU67] Huesmann, L. R., Goldberg, R. P., Evaluating computer systems through simulation, *Comput. J.,* vol. 10, pp. 150–156, 1967.

*[IB70] *IBM System 370 Model 145 Operating Procedure,* IBM SRL GA 24-3554-0, 1970.

*[KE68] Keefe, D. D., Hierarchical control programs for system evaluation, *IBM Systems J.,* vol. 7, n. 2, 1968.

*[KI69] Kiviat, P. J., Villanueva, R., Markowitz, H., *The SIMSCRIPT II Programming Language,* Prentice-Hall, Englewood Cliffs, N.J., 1969.

*[KO71] Kolence, K., A software view of measurement tools, *Datamation,* pp. 32–38, Jan. 1971.

[MA70] MacDougall, M. H., Computer system simulation: an introduction, *Computing Surveys,* vol. 2, n. 3, pp. 191–209, Sept. 1970.

[NO72] Noe, J. D., Nutt, G. J., Validation of a trace-driven CDC 6400 simulation, *AFIPS Conf. Proc., SJCC,* vol. 40, pp. 749–757, 1972.

[NU73] Nutt, G. J., The computer system representation problem, *Proc. ACM-SIGSIM Symposium on the Simulation of Computer Systems,* pp. 145–149, June 1973.

*[NU75] Nutt, G. J., Tutorial: computer system monitors, *Computer,* vol. 8, n. 11, pp. 51–61, Nov. 1975.

*[PR69] Pritsker, A. A., Kiviat, P. J., *Simulation with GASP II,* Prentice-Hall, Englewood Cliffs, N.J., 1969.

[RO69] Roek, D. J., Emerson, W. C., A hardware instrumentation approach to evaluation of a large scale system, *Proc. ACM Nat. Conf.,* pp. 351–367, 1969.

[RO75] Roth, P. F., Simulation of computers: a tutorial introduction, *Proc. ACM-SIGSIM Symposium on the Simulation of Computer Systems,* Aug. 1975.

[SH73] Sherman, S. W., Browne, J. C., Trace driven modeling: review and overview, *Proc. ACM-SIGSIM Symposium on the Simulation of Computer Systems,* pp. 201–207, June 1973.

*[SP72] Spiegel, M. R., *Statistics,* McGraw-Hill, New York, 1972.

*[SV76] Svobodova, L., *Computer Performance Measurement and Evaluation Methods: Analysis and Applications,* Elsevier, New York, 1976.

[TE66] Teichorew, D., Lubin, J. F., Computer simulation—Discussion of the technique and comparison of languages, *CACM,* n. 9, pp. 723–741, 1966.

4

THE REPRESENTATION OF MEASUREMENT DATA

4.1 INTRODUCTION

All measurement techniques described in Chapter 3 collect data that allow component activity to be evaluated and therefore system inefficiencies to be identified. The amount of data to be collected varies considerably as a function of the measurement technique and of the objectives of the investigation. For example, a study for the improvement of disk file allocation only requires data about disk activity, whereas a study for global system tuning will usually involve data collected from all system components.

In any case, since the amount of data recorded is considerable, a manual analysis is cumbersome and sometimes impossible. The analysis is made even more complex by the large number of quantities that are normally measured. Thus, detecting logical relationships among the collected data is only possible if the data are properly summarized and presented.

Diagrams and tables may be prepared by an installation's staff from data collected by accounting and logging routines. These data, stored in a log file, may be processed to extract the interesting information about the system's behavior, for such purposes as computing charges for machine use, analyzing periodically workload parameters, identifying critical programs, and examining the variation of performance indexes. When hardware or software monitors are used, data presentation is directly taken care of by the tool during the data reduction phase. The more complete and synthetic the reports produced, the more effective the use of the tool.

The purpose of this chapter is to describe the most common methods and types of reports that can be obtained by processing the data collected by the most frequently used measurement tools. The types of representation to be shown are only some of those that have been used in performance evaluation studies. The evaluator will certainly be able to introduce and use diagrams of different kinds whenever necessary. For each measurement area, we shall provide suggestions on how typical quantities can be represented so as to make the results easy to interpret and compare. The evaluator, having measured the variables of interest, chooses among the possible representations at his disposal, the one (or the ones) that more clearly presents the interesting data and their interrelationships.

The presentation of measured data is useful for identifying areas and components that require attention, but does not usually suggest the action or actions to be taken. The diagrams to be shown are only diagnostic tools and do not provide operational directives.

4.2 TABLES AND DIAGRAMS

The large number of variables and the different objectives that may be considered make it impossible to define a standard method for data presentation. Each quantity may be represented in various ways, all of which should satisfy the requirements of clarity and conciseness while shedding light on different aspects of the phenomena being observed.

Thus, the most important problem is not so much that of determining the number and type of the graphs to be produced, but that of how to group the various quantities in the tables and diagrams. Among the possible types of representation of a single variable, histograms are the most popular since they allow the spectrum of the values taken on by the variable to be evaluated at a glance.

The diagrams considered in this chapter will be subdivided on the basis of the type of data they represent into three categories: *hardware, system software,* and *workload.*

1. Hardware

The CPU. Every performance evaluation study includes an analysis of CPU activity. Usually, besides global utilization, one must also show the fractions of CPU time consumed by the operating system and by the user programs.

The global CPU usage may be represented by diagrams like those in Fig. 4.1. The percentages on the vertical axis represent the values of CPU utilization during the interval considered. Figure 4.1a represents the distribution of CPU utilization in time (percentage values of the interval considered). From it we learn that the CPU was 100 percent utilized 10 percent of the session, 90 percent utilized 20 percent of the session, 80 percent utilized 10 percent and so on. The diagram in Fig. 4.1b provides us with a more complete description of the phenomenon observed: it displays the time behavior of CPU utilization during the session. The length of the intervals on the horizontal axis can be days, hours, minutes, or seconds, depending on the level of detail required.

Sometimes diagrams of the latter type become very large. Once the interval length is established, the length of the diagram is proportional to the session's duration. It is thus important to analyze before the measurement the phenomenon to be measured in order to establish, while preserving the significance of the diagram, the largest value to be adopted for the scale. Obviously, the diagrams in Fig. 4.1a are more compact, but they also contain less data.

Figure 4.2 shows, by continuous curves, the utilization of the CPU by the operating

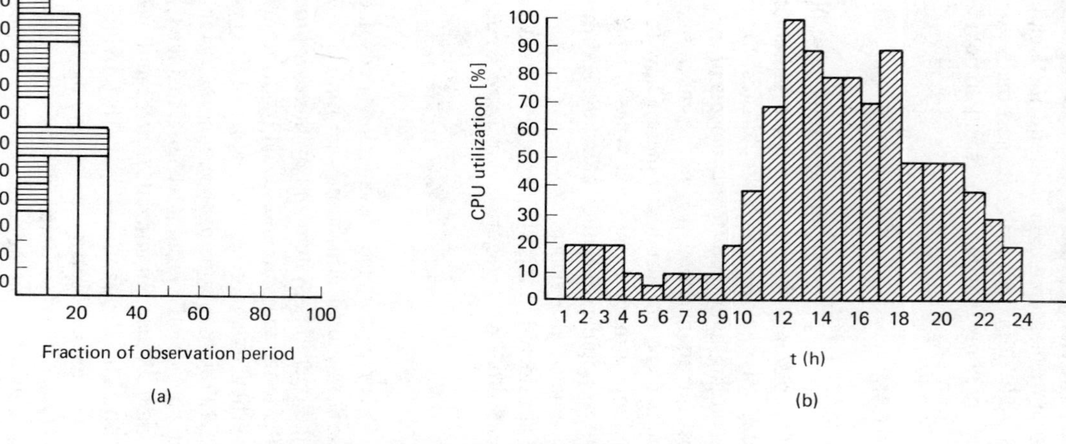

Figure 4.1 Representation of global CPU utilization.

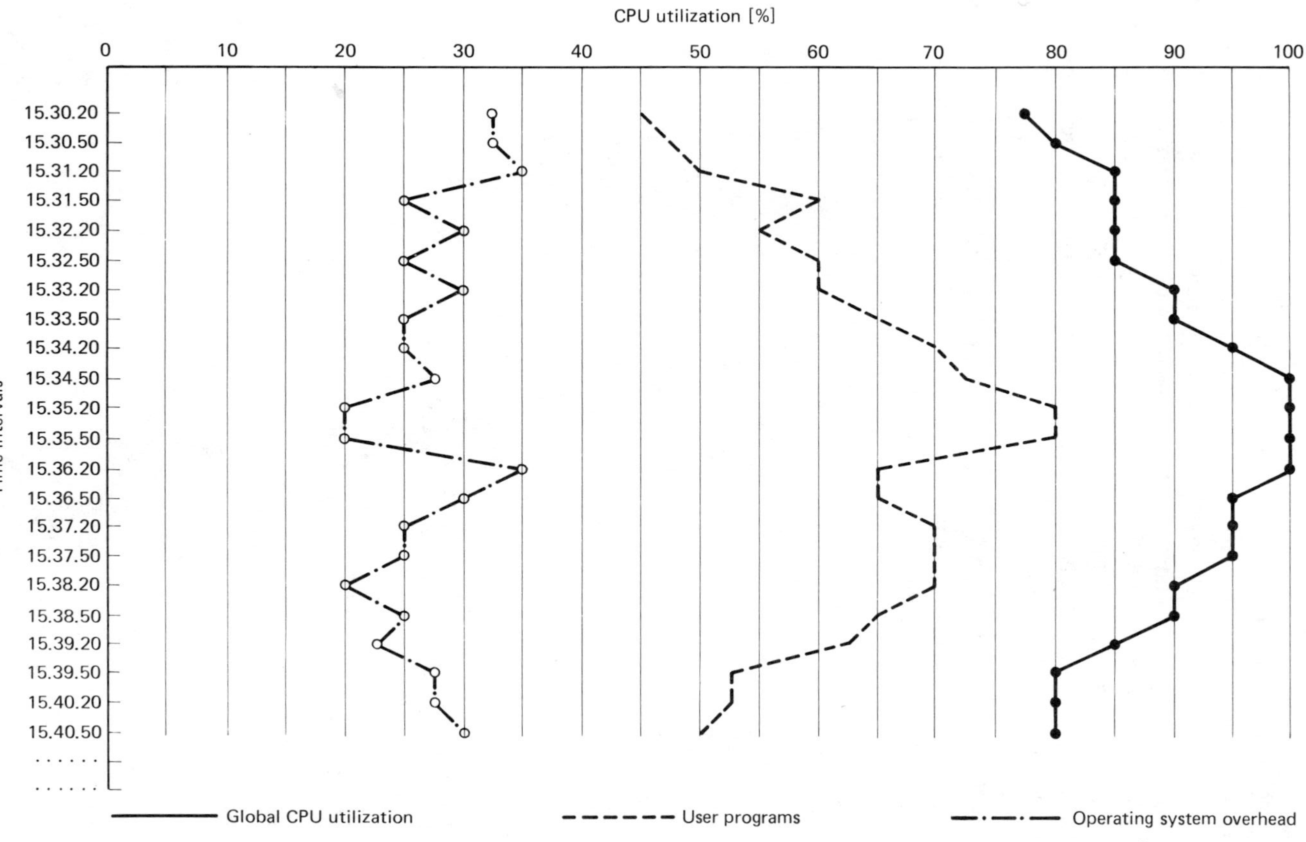

Figure 4.2 CPU utilization and its components versus time.

system and by user programs during a given time interval. Another example of useful continuous curves, produced by a commercial hardware monitor [TE80], is given in Fig. 4.3.

Histograms are often used to describe in more detail the causes of CPU activity. In these histograms, total usage is broken down into the contributions of each type of user and, sometimes, of each single program. For example, Fig. 4.4 shows CPU utilization during one day by the operating system, by the batch users, and by the interactive users. Diagrams of this type may be useful for workload analyses aiming at the establishment of adequate scheduling policies and for the correct sizing of a system. Histograms similar to that in Fig. 4.4 may also be used when we want to emphasize the relationships among the CPU times used by various classes of programs.

Channels. The global activity of channels may be represented by diagrams similar to those in Fig. 4.1. Figure 4.5 shows the utilizations of three channels during a working day. In this figure we can easily see the behavior of channel activity in time, the imbalances of the loads on the different channels, and (within the accuracy limits of the diagrams) the amount of interchannel overlap.

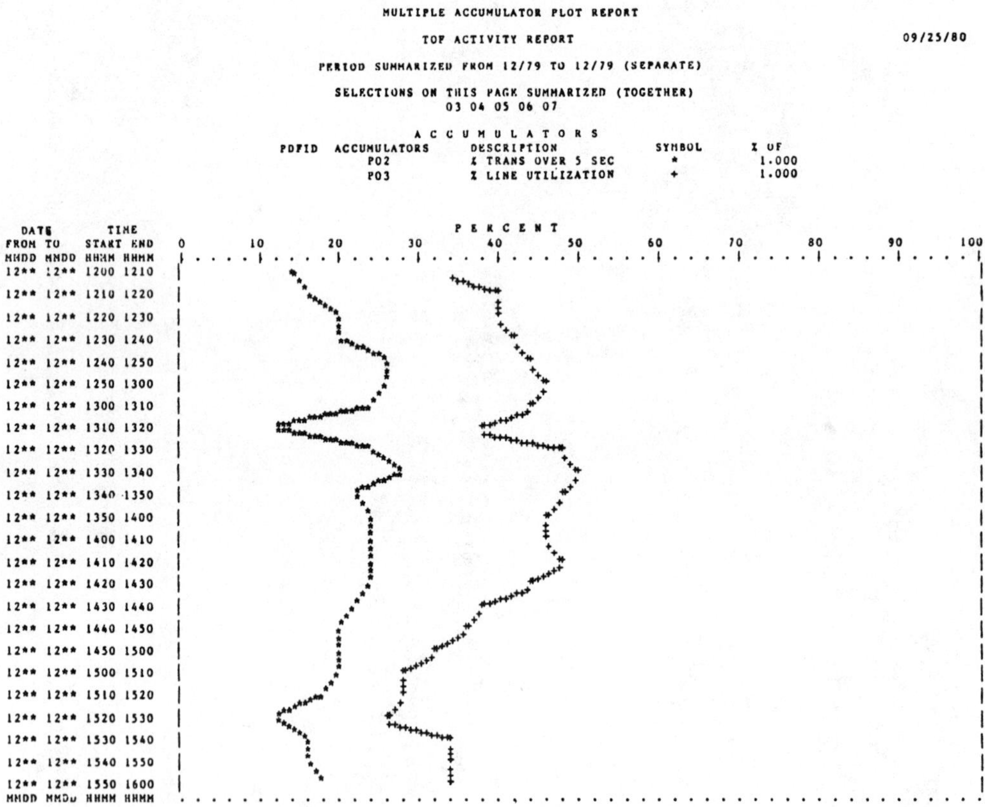

Figure 4.3 Transaction traffic and line utilization versus time [TE80].

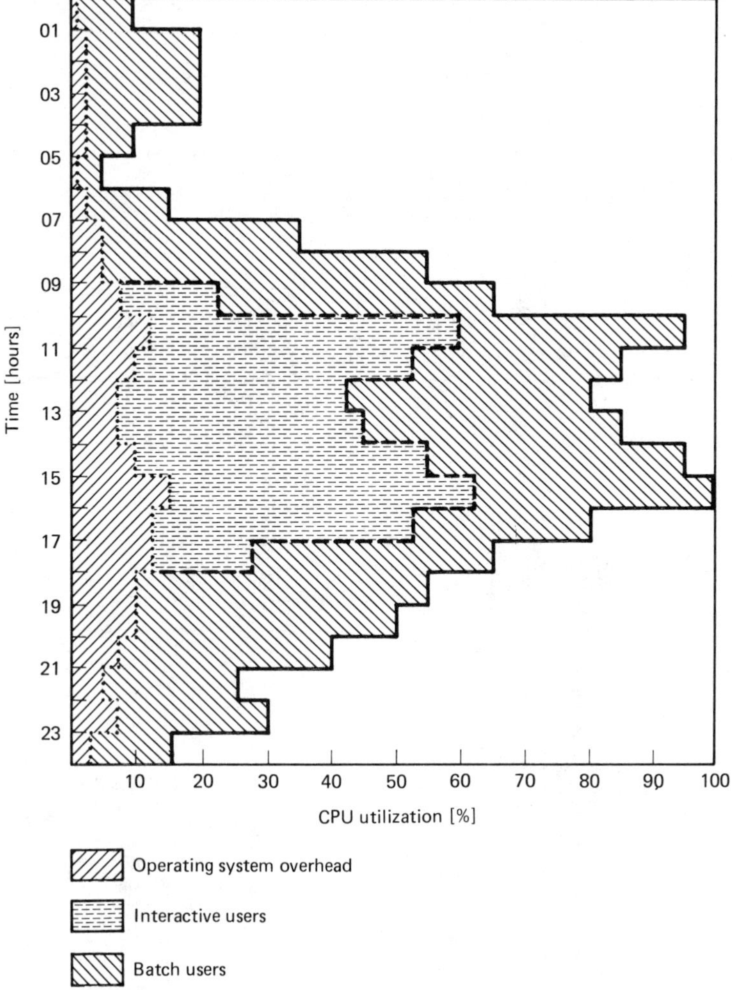

Figure 4.4 Histograms of CPU utilization by user types (operating system, batch users, and interactive users).

To evaluate visually the overlap of channel activities, both with each other and with the CPU, other types of diagrams are normally used, such as utilization profiles and Kiviat graphs (see Fig. 4.6), which are more compact than the diagram in Fig. 4.5. Utilization profiles, or Gantt diagrams, and Kiviat graphs are described in Sec. 4.2.1 and 4.2.2, respectively.

When the channel activity of a system must be described in detail, including the service time, the usage level and the number of I/O operations executed in a given period by each channel, it is useful to present these data in a summary containing the histograms of the most significant variables (see Fig. 4.7). Diagrams of this type can also be obtained on the screen of display terminals in real time by using suitable on-line measurement

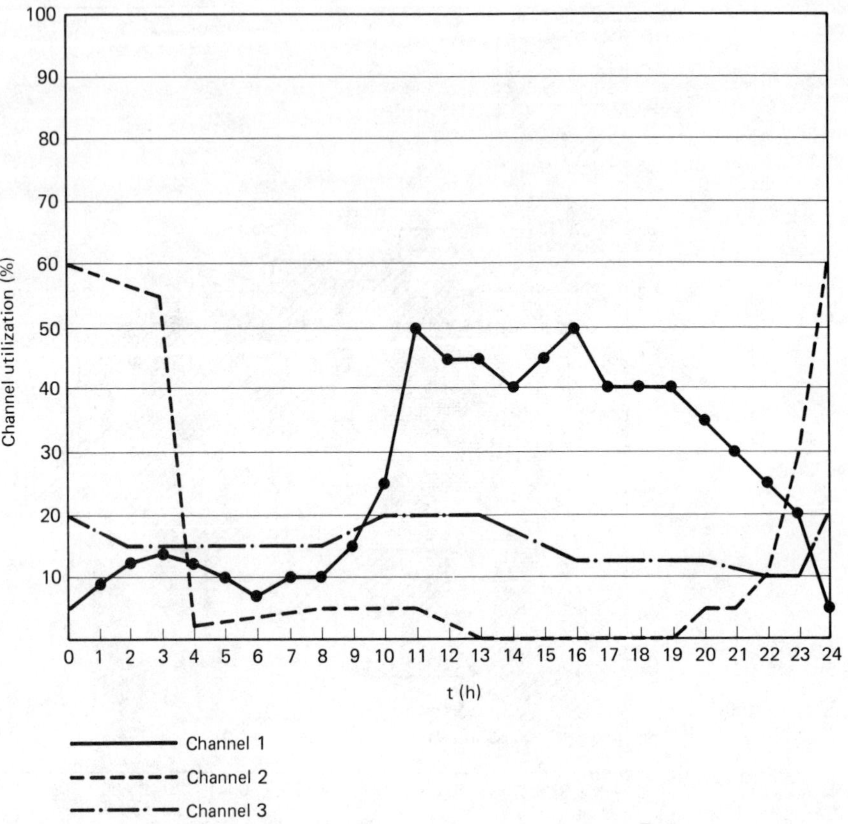

Figure 4.5 Channel activity during a working day.

tools. For instance, the one in Fig. 4.7 has been produced by a commercial software monitor [CM77]. The system being evaluated includes two CPU's, each with six channels, and the histograms in Fig. 4.7 are those of the mean service time (STCHNO1) and the utilization (BPCHNO1) of channel 01.

To perform a more detailed analysis of CPU-channel overlap, evaluators often use tables containing the logical combinations (of the AND-OR-NOT type) of CPU and channel activities. Table 4.1, which has been obtained by measuring a one-CPU, two-channel system, shows that the activities of the two channels are unbalanced (channel 1 is 19 percent utilized; channel 2, 83 percent), and their overlap with CPU activity is small. This is one of the several possible representations of the same quantities, and each user will choose the one (or the ones) that seems most convenient for the study at hand.

It is normally useful to supplement the table with data about the CPU and channel queues. The data will generally include the percentage of time each queue existed (that is, was not empty), its mean length, and its maximum length.

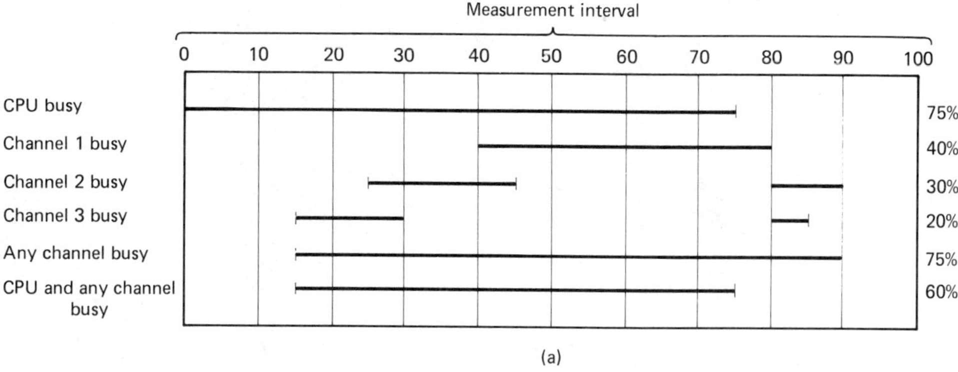

(a)

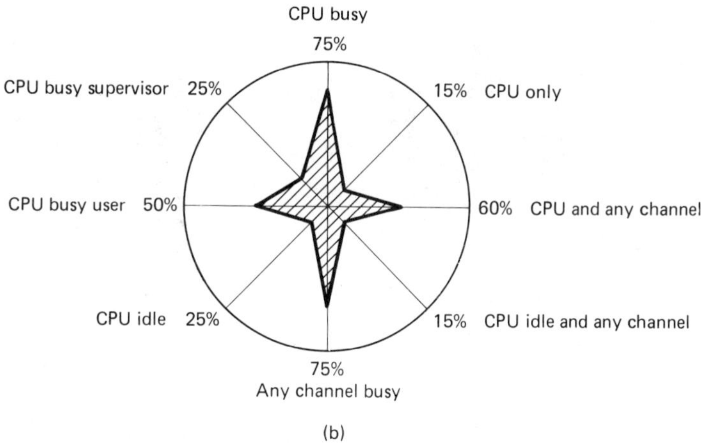

(b)

Figure 4.6 Examples of (a) a utilization profile; (b) a Kiviat graph.

Secondary memories and peripherals. When the activity of secondary memories and peripherals is to be analyzed, it is useful to subdivide the data according to the device type (for example, direct or sequential access) so that the reports can display the characteristic data of each class of I/O devices that we are interested in.

Initially, the data about the various devices may be grouped on the basis of the channel to which the devices are connected. This allows us to obtain tables and graphs that provide a breakdown of channel usage summarized in the diagrams described previously.

If disk units are connected to the channel being examined, the data of the various units may be organized in tables (see for example Table 4.2), which list the reasons for the unit's activity (positioning of the read–write heads, data recovery attempts due to I/O errors, transfers). These tables may also contain information about the queues of each

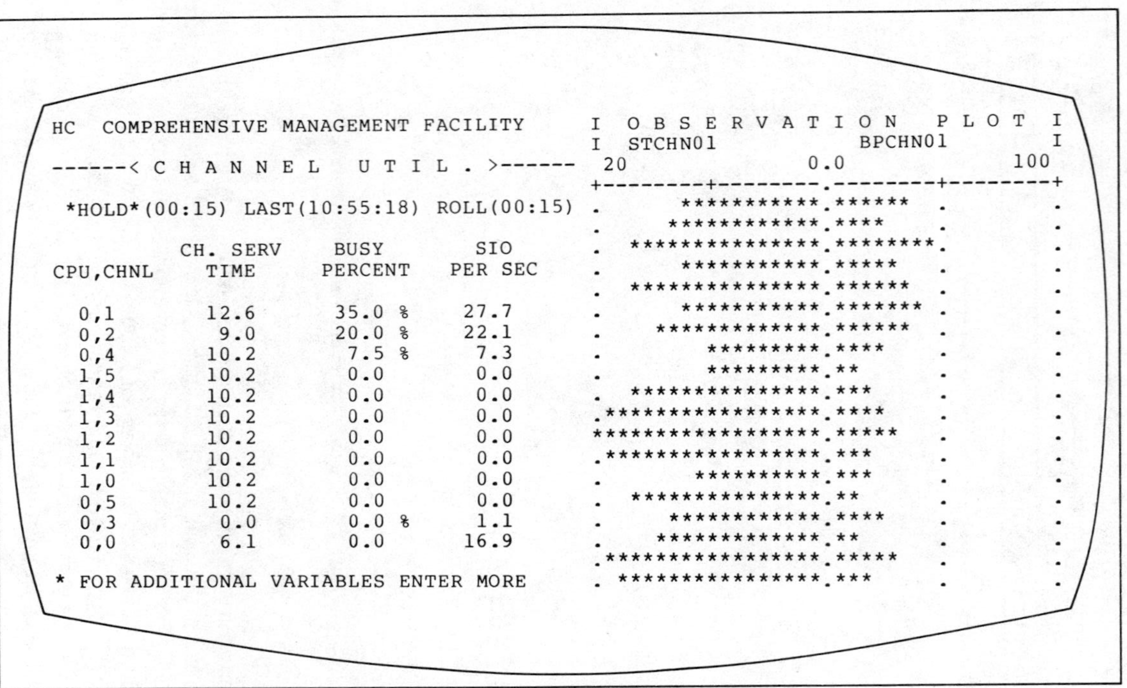

HC COMPREHENSIVE MANAGEMENT FACILITY
------< C H A N N E L U T I L . >------
HOLD(00:15) LAST(10:55:18) ROLL(00:15)
CPU,CHNL | CH. SERV TIME | BUSY PERCENT | SIO PER SEC
0,1 12.6 35.0 % 27.7
0,2 9.0 20.0 % 22.1
0,4 10.2 7.5 % 7.3
1,5 10.2 0.0 0.0
1,4 10.2 0.0 0.0
1,3 10.2 0.0 0.0
1,2 10.2 0.0 0.0
1,1 10.2 0.0 0.0
1,0 10.2 0.0 0.0
0,5 10.2 0.0 0.0
0,3 0.0 0.0 % 1.1
0,0 6.1 0.0 16.9
* FOR ADDITIONAL VARIABLES ENTER MORE
I O B S E R V A T I O N P L O T I
I STCHN01 BPCHN01 I
20 0.0 100

Figure 4.7 Summary of channel activity produced by an on-line software monitor [CM77].

TABLE 4.1 TABLE REPRESENTATION OF CPU–CHANNEL OVERLAP

		CPU busy (46%) and:	*CPU idle (54%) and:*
No channel busy		3%	13%
Channel 1 busy		8%	11%
Channel 2 busy		42%	41%
Channels 1 or 2 busy		43%	41%
Channels 1 and 2 busy		7%	11%
Any channel busy	84%	43%	41%

unit (percentage of time during which they exist, average and maximum number of requests waiting), and any other data considered useful. Tables like these may also be used for the representation of data about channels serving sequential access units, although obviously headings like "arm positioning time" will not be there. In Table 4.2, the most heavily used devices can be easily identified, and it is these devices that are the most likely causes of channel contention (that is, of long channel queues). It is also possible to identify partially damaged disks and tapes since these spend a relatively large time trying to read–write in consequence of I/O errors.

After examining the global activity of secondary storage and peripheral devices, it is often useful to identify the files that cause the heaviest traffic in each device, and in particular those causing most of the arm movements. The improvement of the disk's access time requires minimizing seek by analyzing and modifying file placement on the unit being considered. To perform this optimization, we should examine the data con-

TABLE 4.2 ACTIVITIES OF DIRECT-ACCESS DEVICES

				Utilization				*Device queue*			*Control unit*
	Device address	*Device model*	*Availability [%]*	*Head positioning*	*Read–write*	*Retries due to I/O errors*	*Total*	*Time of existence [%]*	*Mean length*	*Max length*	*queue (mean length)*
Channel 1	123	A	100.00	12.50	1.84	0.00	14.34	10.20	1.54	4	0.25
	124	A	100.00	15.21	3.52	0.00	18.73	28.45	2.30	3	1.72
	125	A	69.05	18.14	0.58	0.85	19.57	1.12	1.16	2	0.68
	126	A	0.00	0.00	0.00	0.00	0.00	0.00	0.00	0	0.00
	127	A/D	100.00	21.41	0.62	0.46	22.59	0.08	0.55	2	0.11
	128	A/D	100.00	24.13	3.12	0.00	27.25	2.11	1.33	3	0.00
Channel totals							. . .	. . .	. . .	. . .	
Channel 2	. . .	. . .	. . .	. . .	. . .	. . .	. . .	. . .	. . .	. . .	. . .
	. . .	. . .	. . .	. . .	. . .	. . .	. . .	. . .	. . .	. . .	. . .
	. . .	. . .	. . .	. . .	. . .	. . .	. . .	. . .	. . .	. . .	. . .
Channel totals							. . .	. . .	. . .	. . .	
Channel *n*	. . .	A	. . .	. . .	. . .	. . .	. . .	. . .	. . .	. . .	. . .
	. . .	A/D	. . .	. . .	. . .	. . .	. . .	. . .	. . .	. . .	. . .
	. . .	A	. . .	. . .	. . .	. . .	. . .	. . .	. . .	. . .	. . .
Channel totals							. . .	. . .	. . .	. . .	

TABLE 4.3 TABLE FOR STUDYING THE PLACEMENT OF FILES A, B, AND C ON A DIRECT-ACCESS DEVICE

	File name	*Total no. of seeks within pair*	*Total seek time (ms)*	*Mean seek time (ms)*	*I/O error time (ms)*	*Total seek time (% of total time)*
Device 1	A–B	3431	81321	23.7	43.0	33.0
	A–C	2436	93432	38.3	0.0	37.9
	B–C	. . .	. . .	. . .	. . .	. . .
	A–A	. . .	. . .	. . .	. . .	. . .
	B–B	. . .	. . .	. . .	. . .	. . .
	C–C	. . .	. . .	. . .	. . .	. . .
Device 2	. . .	. . .	. . .	. . .	. . .	. . .
	. . .	. . .	. . .	. . .	. . .	. . .
	. . .	. . .	. . .	. . .	. . .	. . .

cerning seeks, in particular the initial and final addresses of each arm movement and the percentage of time spent between each pair of cylinders with respect to the total arm movement time.

These data can be arranged in tables (see for example, Table 4.3) and diagrams (see Fig. 4.8). The diagrams in Fig. 4.8 provide a concise and easy to read representation of all the arm movements observed. Note that the information they contain is complementary to that in Table 4.3.

Using utilization profiles showing the utilizations of the channels and of the devices

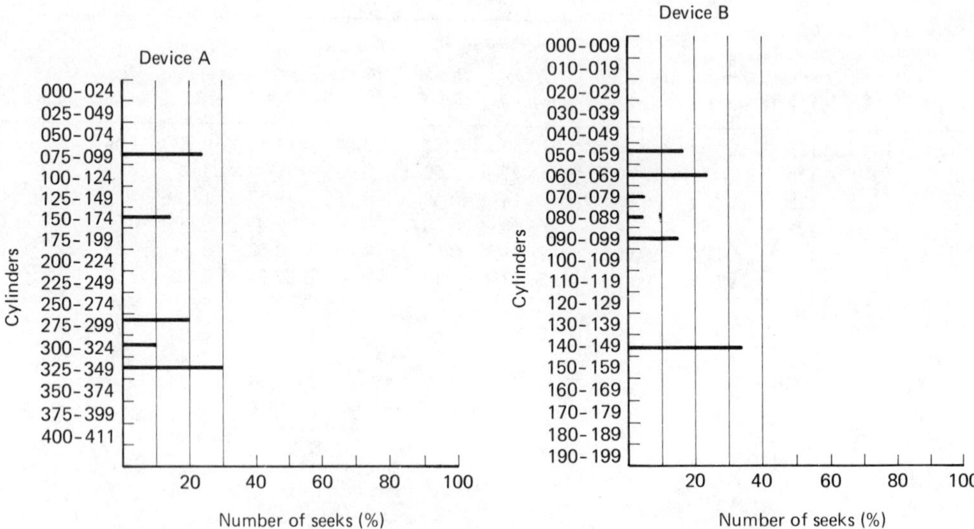

Figure 4.8 Histograms of cylinder addresses where head movements were observed.

connected to them, it is possible to represent the total seek time of each unit (see Fig. 4.16).

The activities of the slow I/O peripherals (line printers, card readers, card punches, and so on) can be represented by a single scalar, for example the number of cards read or the number of lines printed during a certain time interval, or by diagrams describing the variation of these quantities in time.

2. System Software

The analysis of resource usage by operating system modules is an important part of improvement studies. A tabular presentation is particularly useful (see for instance Table 4.4). Once the period of observation has been selected, the utilization of resources (in the example in Table 4.4, CPU utilization) by each module being considered is reported for each program that called the module during that time. The various executions of a single program are grouped together, and for each run the start and end times are reported together with the amounts of resources consumed.

The activity of the operating system's work files may be represented by tables and graphs similar to those shown previously for user files.

A histogram is useful when analyzing calls to supervisor modules that are not permanently resident in main memory. In this case, showing the absolute and relative number of calls to each module will greatly facilitate intermodule activity comparisons. The load generated by frequently used modules and system programs can be represented by continuous graphs as in Fig. 4.9, which refers to an MIVRS system. These modules include sorting programs, copy and dump-restore modules, teleprocessing managers, and others. For these purposes, we can make use of the same graphs and tables by which we describe the load generated by user programs.

TABLE 4.4 LOAD GENERATED BY OPERATING SYSTEM MODULES (MARCH 6 THROUGH 10, 1978)

	CPU time demand			*Dates of run*			
Module name	*By the module*	*Cumulative*	*Programs*	*Initial*		*Final*	
AAAA1	0.18	0.18	FER12	Mar. 9 78	15.21.53	Mar. 9 78	15.34.20
	0.20	0.38		Mar. 10 78	12.20.25	Mar. 10 78	12.32.51
	0.19	0.57		Mar. 10 78	18.05.42	Mar. 10 78	18.17.54
	5.23	6.20	SER12	Mar. 6 78	09.02.58	Mar. 6 78	09.24.32
	0.04	6.24		Mar. 8 78	09.08.22	Mar. 8 78	09.08.54
	5.56	12.20		Mar. 8 78	14.23.46	Mar. 8 78	14.54.23
	...	...		...	...	...	...
	...	...	ZEI42	...	...	...	...
BBBB5	0.19	0.19	PIP23	Mar. 6 78	08.23.55	Mar. 6 78	08.38.22
	0.21	0.40		Mar. 7 78	09.15.07	Mar. 7 78	09.29.06
	...	...		...	...	...	...
	...	...	SEI45	...	...	...	...
...	...	...	...	...	...	...	...

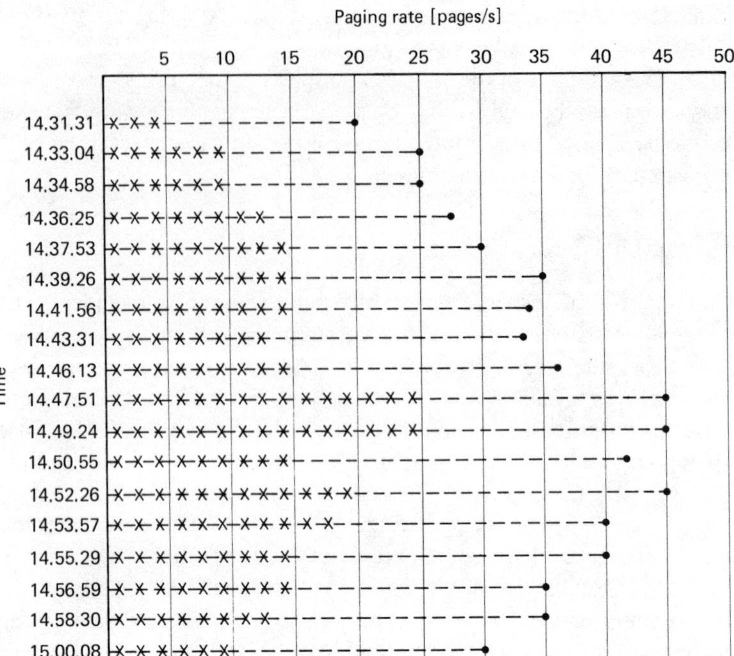

Figure 4.9 Paging activity of a TP manager.

3. The Workload

Some of the reports in this area refer to the global workload, that is, to the set of programs processed by the system, and display the values of the characteristic variables for this set of programs. Other reports are concerned with the individual programs in the workload and contain the values of each program's characteristic variables.

The diagrams and other representations of workload variables cannot be discussed in general terms since the requirements by which they are generated vary from one installation to another. Only some examples of representations will be given here. The most significant data about system usage can be organized in tables, which are usually produced monthly. From these tables, evaluators can derive general information on the installation's operation during the last time period.

If data on system use are grouped on a working day basis, and possibly divided into shifts, we obtain more detailed indications about the workload's characteristics in different periods (see Table 4.5). In some cases, plotting a more detailed diagram covering a shorter period (see Fig. 4.10) may be quite useful.

The need to acquire information for the classification of the programs in a workload suggests the use of tables or histograms showing the distributions of the values of each

TABLE 4.5 DAILY ACTIVITY DATA

Shifts	*No. of runs*		*No. of interactive users connected*		*CPU busy for user programs*		*Disk I/O operations*		*Tape I/O operations*		*Lines printed*		*Cards read*		*Pages transferred*		*Suspended runs due to program errors*		*No. of system crashes*	
	Value	*%*	*Value*	*%*	*Value*	*%*	*Value*	*%*	*Value*	*%*	*Value*	*%*	*Value*	*%*	*Value*	*%*	*Value*	*%*	*Value*	*%*
0–8 A.M.	58	14.4	0	0	. . .		. . .		. . .		. . .		. . .		. . .		2	6.3	0	0
8 A.M.–4 P.M.	230	57.1	21	58.4	. . .		. . .		. . .		. . .		. . .		. . .		16	50.0	2	66.7
4 P.M.–12 P.M.	115	28.5	15	41.6	. . .		. . .		. . .		. . .		. . .		. . .		14	43.7	1	33.3
	403		36		. . .		. . .		. . .		. . .		. . .		. . .		32		3	

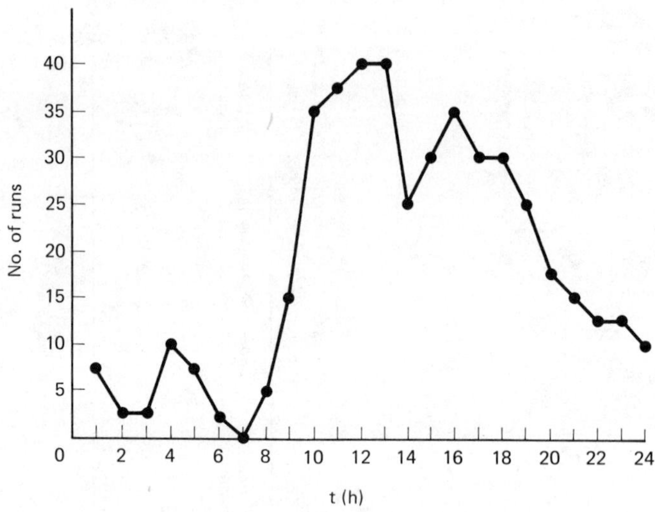

Figure 4.10 Mean hourly number of programs executed versus time.

program's characteristics. Figure 4.11a contains a table with the turnaround time distribution of the 1400 programs executed during a day; the turnaround time intervals considered are those from 0 to 5 min, from 5 to 10 min, and so on. The shape of this distribution can be easily visualized by plotting the corresponding histogram (see Fig. 4.11b). When the variations of the most significant variables are to be examined, it is useful to collect into a single table the current mean value of each variable and those for

Turnaround time [min]	No. of programs			Turnaround time	
	No.	%	cumul.	%	cumul.
0-5	140	10	10	0.89	0.89
5-10	266	19	29	5.92	6.81
10-20	336	24	53	14.96	21.77
20-40	210	15	68	16.70	38.47
40-60	84	6	74	0.85	39.32
60-120	168	12	86	42.76	82.08
120-240	84	6	92	3.24	85.32
240-600	70	5	97	5.72	91.04
600-900	28	2	99	5.1	96.14
900-1440	14	1	100	3.86	100.00
> 1440	0	0		0.00	

(a)

No. of programs [%]

(b)

Figure 4.11 Distribution of turnaround times of the programs executed during a working day.

TABLE 4.6 TRENDS OF SOME SIGNIFICANT VARIABLES REPRESENTING A MONTHLY WORKLOAD

Variables	*Month X (current month)*	*Month X − 1*	*Month X − 2*	*Month X − 3*	*Variation between X and X − 1 (%)*	*Variation between X − 1 and X − 2 (%)*	*Variation between X − 2 and X − 3 (%)*
System							
System busy (%)	85	82	80	75	3.65	2.5	6.66
System idle (%)	. . .	. . .	. . .	. . .	. . .	. . .	. . .
System busy for user prog. (%)	. . .	. . .	. . .	. . .	. . .	. . .	. . .
Multiprogramming level	. . .	. . .	. . .	. . .	. . .	. . .	. . .
Mean no. of runs/hour	21	18	20	16	16.6	−10	25
Disk I/O operations	. . .	. . .	. . .	. . .	. . .	. . .	. . .
Tape I/O operations	. . .	. . .	. . .	. . .	. . .	. . .	. . .
Paging rate (pages/s)	. . .	. . .	. . .	. . .	. . .	. . .	. . .
Batch workload							
No. of jobs executed	12,409	12,851	12,306	11,950	−3.43	4.42	2.97
Mean turnaround time	. . .	. . .	. . .	. . .	. . .	. . .	. . .
No. of aborted runs	1,012	1,021	1,062	970	−0.88	−3.86	7.59
Mean memory occupancy	. . .	. . .	. . .	. . .	. . .	. . .	. . .
No. of FORTRAN compilations	. . .	. . .	. . .	. . .	. . .	. . .	. . .
No. of COBOL compilations	. . .	. . .	. . .	. . .	. . .	. . .	. . .
No. of Assembler translations	. . .	. . .	. . .	. . .	. . .	. . .	. . .
. . .							
. . .							

TABLE 4.6 (Continued)

Variables	*Month X (current month)*	*Month X − 1*	*Month X − 2*	*Month X − 3*	*Variation between X and X − 1 (%)*	*Variation between X − 1 and X − 2 (%)*	*Variation between X − 2 and X − 3 (%)*
Interactive workload							
Mean no. of active terminals	6.2	5.8	5.1	4.5	6.89	13.72	13.33
Mean CPU time per session	. . .	. . .	. . .	. . .	. . .	. . .	. . .
Mean no. of interactions/hr	. . .	. . .	. . .	. . .	. . .	. . .	. . .
Mean connect time	26.12	21.05	19.02	19.45	24.26	10.77	−3.62
CPU utilization by interactive programs	. . .	. . .	. . .	. . .	. . .	. . .	. . .
Disk utilization by interactive programs	. . .	. . .	. . .	. . .	. . .	. . .	. . .
Tape utilization by interactive programs	. . .	. . .	. . .	. . .	. . .	. . .	. . .

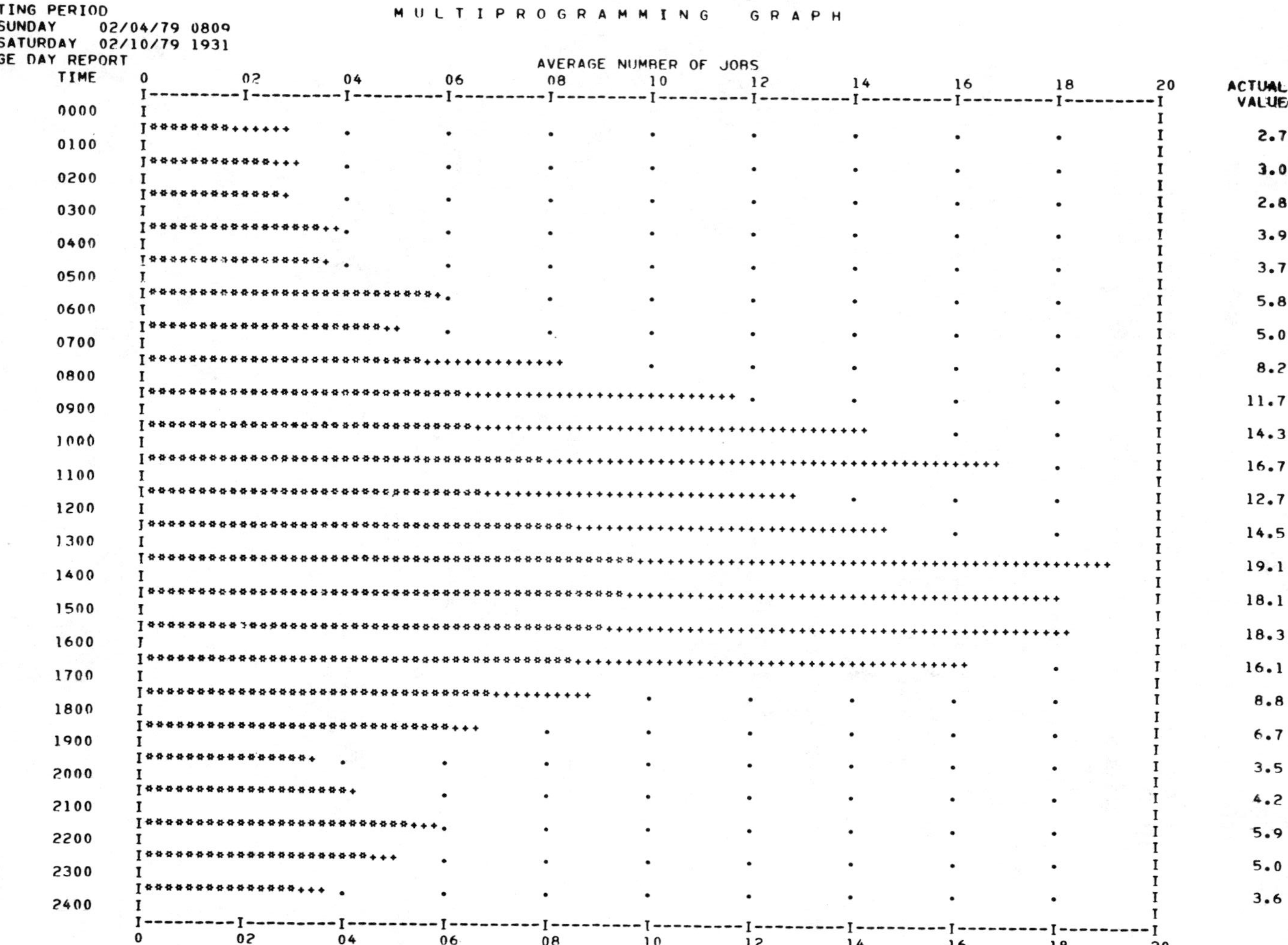

Figure 4.12 Variations of the multiprogramming level during a working day [PL77].

the previous months, as well as, for each variable, its percent of variation with respect to the previous month. The variables considered in Table 4.6 are only given as examples.

The time behavior of certain variables characterizing the workload or the individual programs, or both, may be represented by their mean hourly values plotted in diagrams that encompass one day. Figure 4.12 shows the diagram, obtained with a commercial tool [PL77], of a system's degree of multiprogramming during a day.

The characteristics of the individual programs in the workload are often collected in tables where the programs are ordered by decreasing values of the utilization of a given resource. Thus, for example, tables indicating which programs were executed in a given period, ordered by decreasing CPU, memory, or I/O usage, may be quite useful. When determining a program's consumption of resources, it is necessary to distinguish between the amount of resources consumed by a single run of the program and those consumed by all runs (see, for example, Fig. 8.2). The latter values of consumption allow us to evaluate a program's share of the global consumption due to the whole workload.

4.2.1 Utilization (or Gantt) Profiles

The need to represent simultaneously in a single diagram the most significant variables of a system's activity may be satisfied with *utilization profiles* (or *system profiles*). These diagrams, which are Gantt charts, provide a comprehensive, although approximate, picture of the loading of the system's components.

In the graphical representation of a utilization profile (Fig. 4.13), each horizontal segment has a length proportional to the percentage of time during which the corresponding component is active or, more generally, during which the corresponding Boolean variable is true. The reciprocal positions of these segments represent the degree of simultaneity of the respective activities and provide indications of the overlaps between these activities.

The diagram in Fig. 4.13 refers to a system that was idle during the measurement session (CPU idle and no channel busy) 10 percent of the total time, and that had a CPU activity overlapped with that of at least one channel 22 percent of the total time. Often a utilization profile also displays logical combinations of the activities of single components. Thus, as shown in Fig. 4.14, Boolean variables like *CPU busy and channels idle, CPU and channels busy, CPU idle and channels busy, CPU and channels idle* may be displayed.

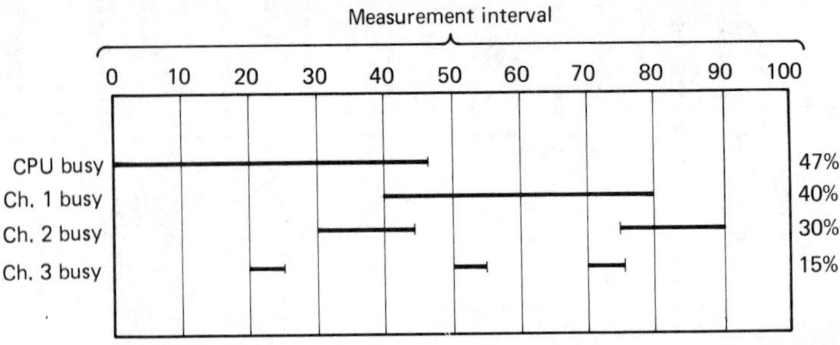

Figure 4.13 Utilization profile (Gantt chart).

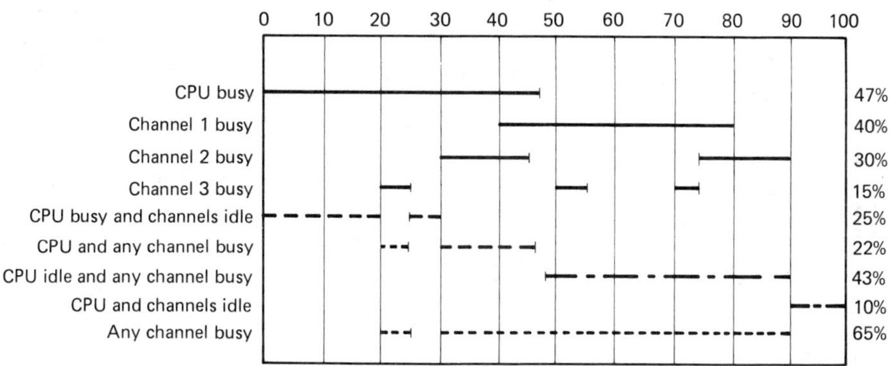

Figure 4.14 Utilization profile with logical combinations of variables.

The indications that can be derived from a utilization profile provide an initial picture of the situation, which can be used as a basis for successive analyses. For example, if there is little overlap, the composition of the workload should be analyzed, whereas if the CPU is busy most of the time, one should determine how this time is spent (for example, for user programs versus system activities). This topic is discussed in detail in Chapter 6.

Utilization profiles can be effectively used for quick consultation when evaluating the results of periodic measurements by which, according to a preordered plan, we intend to monitor system utilization as the workload varies. The data concerning channel utilization do not completely describe the I/O activities performed by a system. An I/O subsystem (controller and devices) may be thought of as being active when any of the devices connected to it is working, and not only when the corresponding channel is busy.

In a disk system, for example, the channel may often be idle when a control unit, or at least a disk arm, is active. Thus, in a utilization profile (see Fig. 4.14) the variable *any channel busy* does not provide a complete picture of the real I/O subsystem utilization. Similarly, the variable *CPU and channels idle* does not represent the percentage of time the whole system is idle. The system is usually considered idle when not only the CPU and the channels, but also all devices and peripherals are idle.

Figure 4.15 shows a profile of an MBRS system with 4 channels and a CPU, measured with a commercial tool [CU77]. The profiles in Figs. 4.13 and 4.15 could be completed with segments representing the utilization of individual devices.

The applications of utilization profiles are not restricted to the variables considered in the example of Fig. 4.14, but extend to all those variables that represent utilizations or overlaps to be evaluated. For example, the profile in Fig. 4.16 includes the seek time for a disk unit connected to channel 1.

The data in Fig. 4.13 can also be represented in a matrix called *overlap matrix* (see Table 4.7). The rows and columns of this matrix represent the variables being considered (CPU busy, channel 1 busy, and so on). The values on the main diagonal represent nonoverlapped utilizations, that is, the fractions of time when no overlap exists between the activity of the corresponding unit and that of the CPU. The other values represent the overlaps of the activities of the corresponding components.

```
PRODUCED BY                         CONFIGURATION USAGE REPORT (CONTINUED)                          PAGE   2
BOOLE AND BABBAGE, INC.                                                              ANALYSIS RUN NUMBER-0001

                                              STUDY REPORT 1

B. CPU / PHYSICAL CHANNEL ACTIVITY CHART

                  PERCENT OF                           GRAPHIC DISPLAY OF TOTAL TIME
                  TOTAL TIME  0        10        20        30        40        50        60        70        80        90       100
                              +---------+---------+---------+---------+---------+---------+---------+---------+---------+---------+
                              .         .         .         .         .         .         .         .         .         .         .
   CPU BUSY          47.17    .BBBBBBBBBBBBBBBBBBBBBBBBBBBBBBBBBBBBBBBBBBBBBBBBB .         .         .         .         .         .
   CPU WAIT          52.83    .         .         .         .         .        WWWWWWWWWWWWWWWWWWWWWWWWWWWWWWWWWWWWWWWWWWWWWWWWWWW WWWWWWWWWW W
   CHANNEL 3 BUSY    41.09    .         .         .         .  3333333333333333333333333333333333333333333 .         .         .
   CHANNEL 1 BUSY    21.76    .         .         .         . 11111111.         .         .    1111111111111.         .         .
   CHANNEL 4 BUSY    15.18    .         .         .         .4        4444      .         . 444444 .         4444     .         .
   CHANNEL 2 BUSY     0.00    .         .         .         .         .         .         .         .         .         .         .
                              .         .         .         .         .         .         .         .         .         .         .
                              +---------+---------+---------+---------+---------+---------+---------+---------+---------+---------+

                                                   * * * * *

C. COMBINATIONS OF CONFIGURATION ACTIVITY

         COMBINATIONS                                             PERCENT OF
                                                                  TOTAL TIME

   ANY SELECTOR CHANNEL BUSY                                        53.63
   CPU WAIT AND ANY SELECTOR CHANNEL BUSY                           36.27
   ANY DEVICE ON A SELECTOR CHANNEL BUSY                            69.49
                      .                                               .
                      .                                               .
                      .                                               .
   ANY DEVICE BUSY                                                  82.13
   CPU*(CH3+CH4)                                                     7.33
   CPU*CH3*CH4                                                       4.06
   CPU+CH1+CH2+CH3+CH4+DV0+DVS                                      86.37

                                                   * * * * *
```

Figure 4.15 Example of utilization profile of an MBRS system with four channels and a CPU, measured with a commercial tool [CU77].

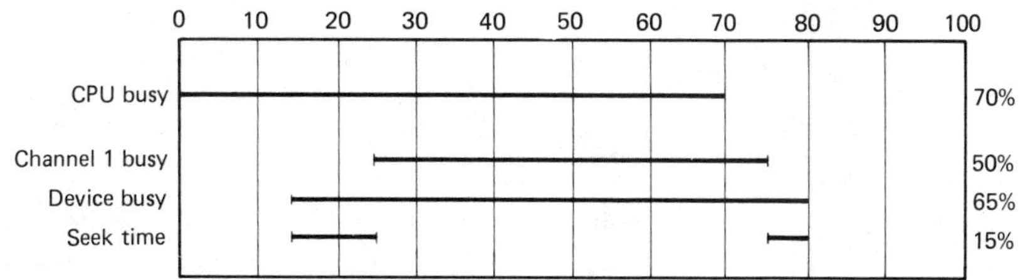

Figure 4.16 Utilization profile showing a disk unit's total seek time.

The first element of the matrix (CPU–CPU) represents the *CPU only* variable, that is, CPU busy and no channel busy. The matrix is symmetric, and the values on the main diagonal should be minimized, while the other values should be maximized. If we construct an overlap matrix periodically, we may observe the variations in time of the variables appearing there and plot diagrams to detect interesting trends in the system's behavior.

4.2.2 Kiviat Graphs

A kind of graph that became immediately popular in performance evaluation studies was introduced in 1973 by Kolence and Kiviat [KO73a]. Kiviat suggested that several variables could be reported on semiaxes irradiating from a point, called a *pole,* and that the points corresponding to their values (according to predetermined scales) could be connected by straight-line segments, thereby obtaining a polygon, called a *Kiviat graph.* A Kiviat graph can be drawn when a circle, whose center is the pole, and three or more semiaxes from the pole are given. The intersection of the circle with a semiaxis corresponds to the maximum value of the variable being displayed on that semiaxis. The number of semiaxes is arbitrary and generally selected according to completeness requirements for the data represented; in practice, the conventions described in the following are very frequently followed.

The system profile in Fig. 4.17a may be represented in Kiviat graph form as in

TABLE 4.7 OVERLAP MATRIX CORRESPONDING TO THE UTILIZATION PROFILE IN FIG. 4.13

%	CPU	CH1	CH2	CH3
CPU	25	7	15	5
CH1	7	33	10	10
CH2	15	10	15	0
CH3	5	10	0	10

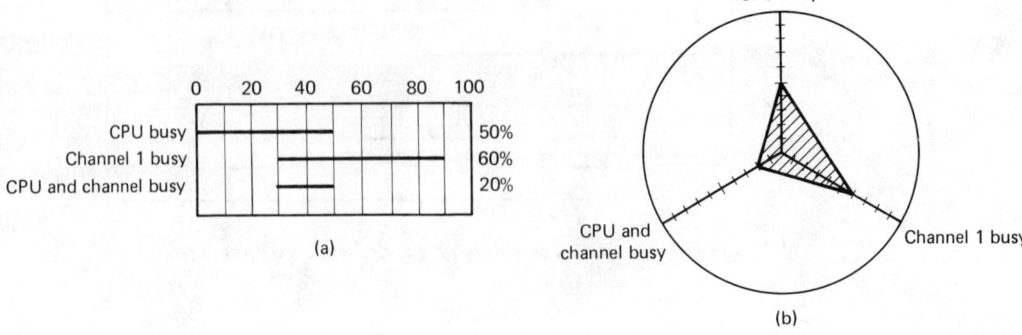

Figure 4.17 Example of a utilization profile and a Kiviat graph for the same workload conditions.

Fig. 4.17b, where the variable *CPU busy* is on the vertical semiaxis and the variables *channel 1 busy* and *CPU and channel 1 busy* are on the other two. The Kiviat graph for the optimum (though purely hypothetical) case corresponding to the CPU and channels always busy (perfect overlap) would be an equilateral triangle (see Fig. 4.18b). This type of graph is more immediately interpretable than Gantt charts since it is based on the human ability to recognize shapes, and therefore permits a faster qualitative evaluation of a system's utilization characteristics. The evolution of a Kiviat graph's shape, due to variations of the workload and other conditions, provides an effective means for detecting and evaluating changes in system utilization.

The initial applications of Kiviat's technique led to the definition of a few simple rules that produce results comparable with some popular system classifications (for example, CPU-bound, I/O-bound, and balanced systems) [MO73], [MO74].

A free interpretation of Kiviat's suggestion favored the implementation of many versions of the original idea. Among these, the most common is the one known as *Kent's version,* which is based on the following conventions [MO74]:

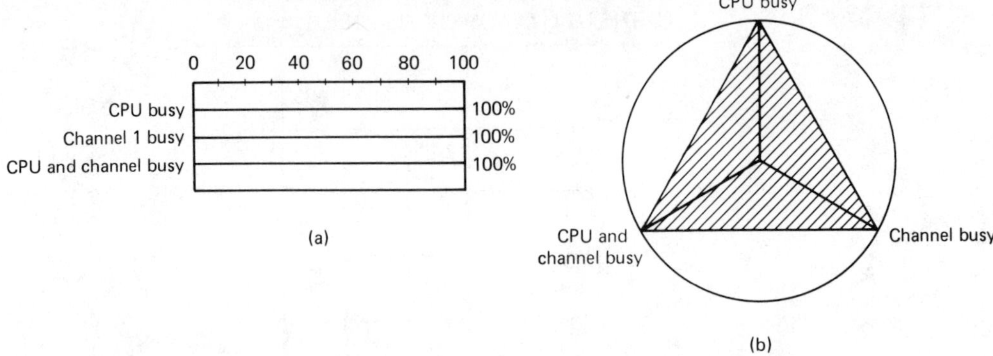

Figure 4.18 Theoretical optimum conditions for the system considered in Fig. 4.17.

1. Select an *even* number of variables to be studied, half of which must be good performance indexes (that is, indexes whose value increases when performance is improved), and half bad performance indexes.
2. Subdivide the circle into as many sectors as there are variables; a side of the first sector should coincide with the upward-going vertical semiaxis.
3. Number sequentially (preferably clockwise) the semiaxes starting with the upward-going vertical semiaxis.
4. Associate good performance indexes to odd semiaxes, and bad indexes to even semiaxes.

With these conventions, a $(n/2)$ -pointed star graph (if n is the number of variables chosen) is obtained for a well-balanced system. A possible distribution of variables on the semiaxes according to Kent's conventions is represented in Fig. 4.19. Figure 4.20 shows the Kiviat graph and the corresponding Gantt chart for a well-utilized system.

The importance of the assignment of performance indexes to semiaxes according to the alternate good variable–bad variable criterion (convention 4 of Kent's version) clearly appears in Figs. 4.21 and 4.22. Figure 4.21 shows two Kiviat graphs drawn according to *Noe's version*. The only rule of this version is that of consistently representing on a Kiviat graph the same performance indexes always in the same order. Thus, an analyst will become familiar with the type of graph always plotted for the system and in a reasonably short time will learn to evaluate, on the basis of changes in shape, the effects of system or workload modifications. To achieve this familiarity, Noe's version requires frequent use, whereas Kent's version is definitely more transportable and does not have to be used so frequently.

In the application of Noe's version described in [SN74], 11 performance indexes were considered, both before and after the addition of some memory modules. Figure 4.21 shows the changes in the geometry of the graph caused by the modification of memory size when the performance indexes are randomly assigned to the axes. Figure 4.22 describes the same phenomenon, but displays only 10 performance indexes assigned to the semiaxes following the alternation criterion.

Axes	Good performance indexes	Abbrev.
1	CPU busy	CPU
3	CPU and channel busy	CPU*CH
5	Any channel busy	CH
7	User programs CPU	PPB

Axes	Bad performance indexes	Abbrev.
2	CPU only busy	$CPU*\overline{CH}$
4	Channel only busy	$\overline{CPU}*CH$
6	CPU idle	$\overline{CPU}$
8	Supervisor CPU	SUP

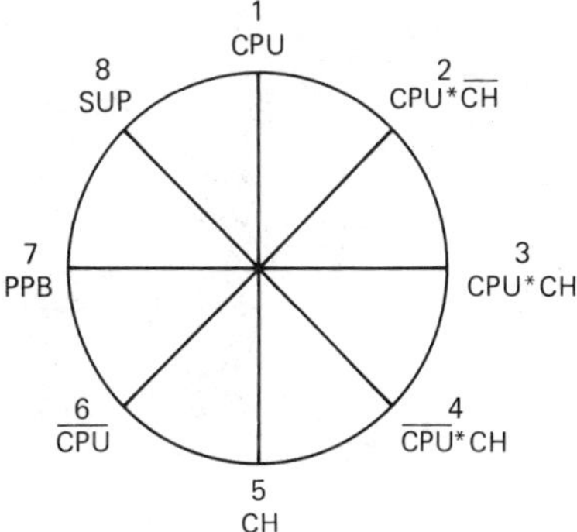

Figure 4.19 Semiaxes and assignment of variables according to Kent's version of a Kiviat graph.

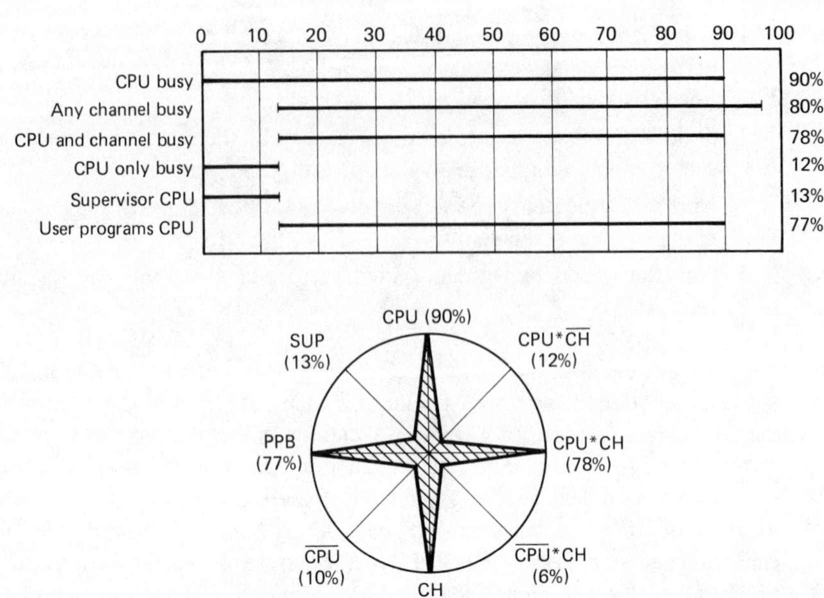

Figure 4.20 Star-shaped Kiviat graph (Kent's version) of a well-utilized system.

While the interpretation of the graphs in Fig. 4.21 is rather difficult, especially for someone unfamiliar with the environment being considered, Fig. 4.22 immediately suggests that the changes have probably improved performance, since the graph's shape has become closer to that of a star.

Clearly, the choice of the variables and their assignment to the semiaxes determine the figures that will result and may make their interpretation easier or harder. Figure 4.23 shows a Kiviat graph obtained with a commercial measurement tool [CU77].

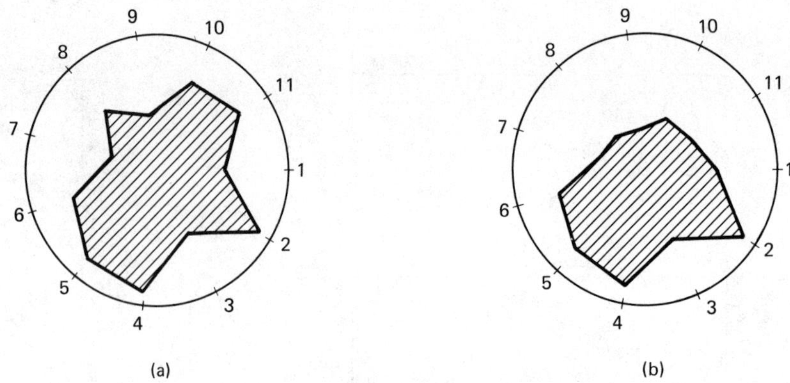

Figure 4.21 Variations of a Kiviat graph (a) before; (b) after an increase of memory size with a random assignment of performance indexes.

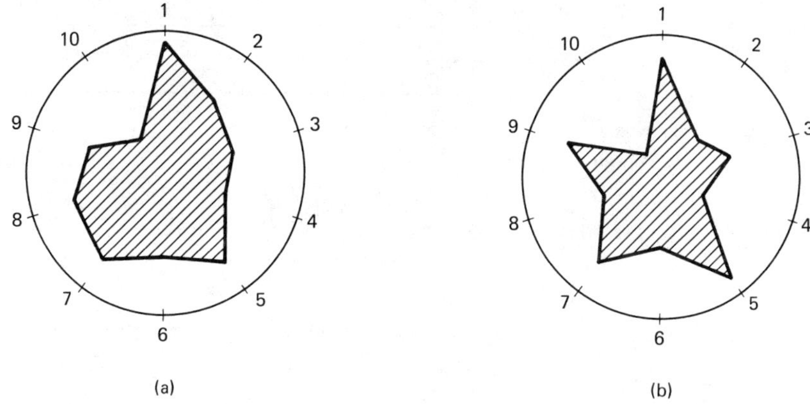

Figure 4.22 Kiviat graph for the example in Fig. 4.21 with alternate assignment of performance indexes to semiaxes.

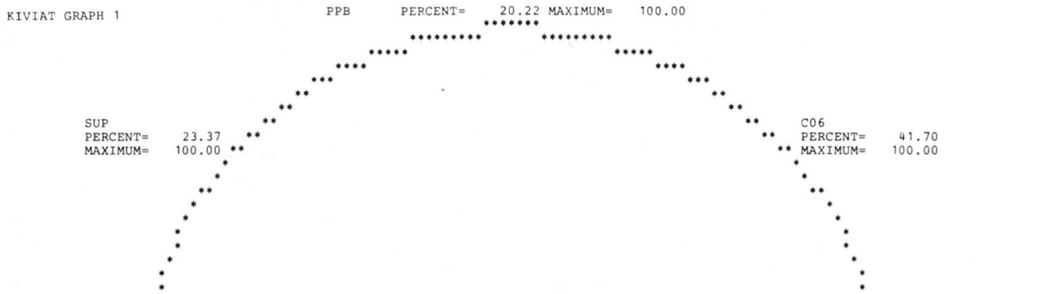

```
KIVIAT GRAPH 1

PPB      PERCENT=    20.22 MAXIMUM=    100.00

SUP
PERCENT=     23.37
MAXIMUM=    100.00

C06
PERCENT=     41.70
MAXIMUM=    100.00

CPU
PERCENT=  46.41
MAXIMUM= 100.00

C02
PERCENT=     83.55
MAXIMUM=    100.00

C04
PERCENT=      4.25
MAXIMUM=    100.00

C03
PERCENT=     41.39
MAXIMUM=    100.00

C01      PERCENT=    42.16 MAXIMUM=    100.00
```

Figure 4.23 Kiviat graph produced by a commercial software monitor [CU77].

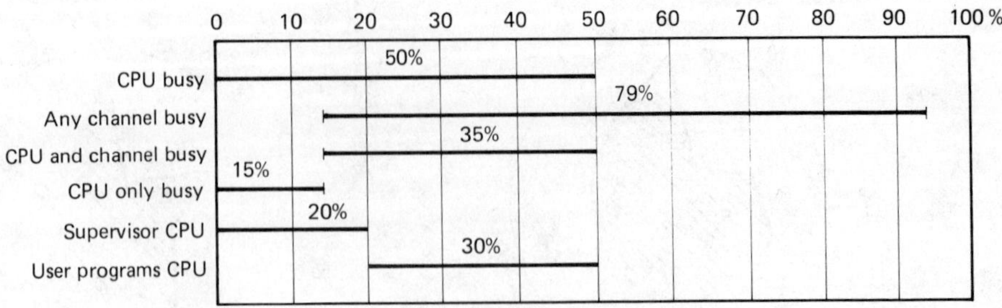

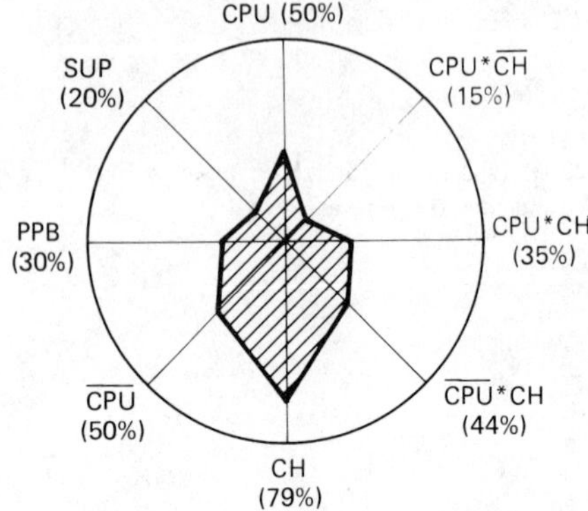

Figure 4.24 Utilization profile and the corresponding Kiviat graph of the *I/O arrow* type.

4.2.3 Standard Shapes of Kiviat Graphs

Using Kent's convention, we have obtained a Kiviat graph with eight semiaxes and a four-pointed star shape for a well-balanced system (see Fig. 4.20). In practice, however, before performing any system improvement actions, the graph's shape is often quite different from that of a star.

Some of these shapes are typical of certain loading situations and have therefore been given special names. The most common shapes are as follows:

1. *I/O arrow:* An I/O arrow is shown in Fig. 4.24. This graph is typical of an I/O-bound system that also uses the CPU fairly heavily. This type of workload, which tends to saturate the I/O resources, requires an intervention that should move the center of gravity of the polygon toward the center of the circle.
2. *CPU sailboat;* A CPU sailboat graph is shown in Fig. 4.25. This graph is characteristic of systems and workloads with high CPU demands and relatively low channel utilizations.
3. *I/O wedge:* An I/O wedge is shown in Fig. 4.26. This is the shape typical of a system with high utilization of the I/O resources and low CPU usage.

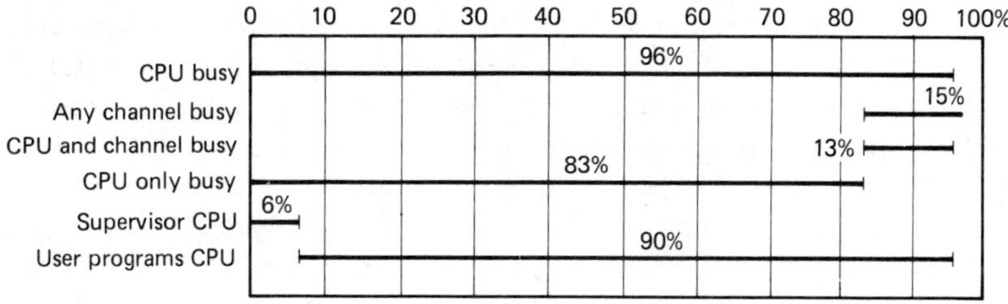

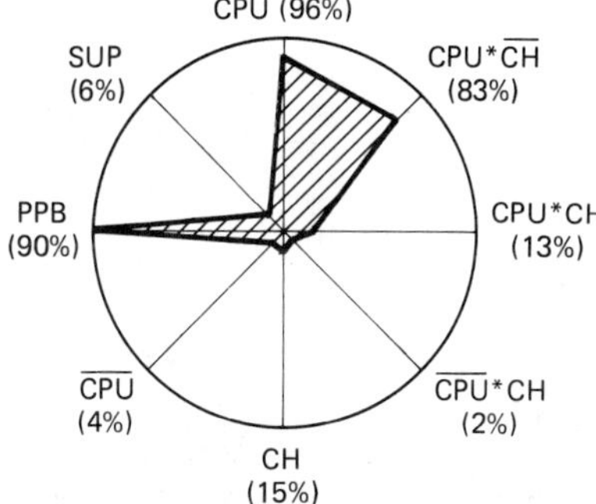

Figure 4.25 Utilization profile and the corresponding Kiviat graph of the *CPU sailboat* type.

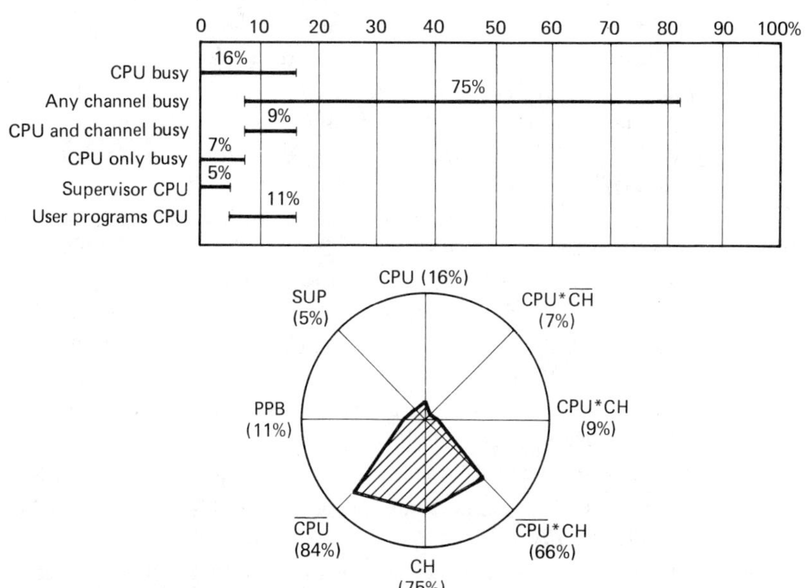

Figure 4.26 Utilization profile and the corresponding Kiviat graph of the *I/O wedge* type.

An interesting extension of the applications of Kiviat graphs can be obtained using the definition of software unit (see [KO76]). For example, the one in Fig. 4.26 can be considered a Kiviat graph typical of a sorting program rather than of a whole workload.

We must point out that to obtain a four-point star shape it is often not sufficient (although always necessary) to make certain improvements to systems software, to the distribution of files and data base on disks and channels, to the I/O subsystems, to the input job mix, and so on. It is therefore convenient to modify the workload so that all system resources be used as uniformly as possible. This concept will be developed further in Chapters 7 and 8.

REFERENCES

Entries marked with an asterisk (*) are referenced in the text.

[BR74] Brotherton, D. E., The computer capacity curve—A prerequisite for computer performance, evaluation and improvement, *Proc. 2nd ACM-SIGME Symposium on Measurement and Evaluation,* pp. 166–179, Sept. 1974.

[CA76] Calcagni, J. M., Shape in ranking Kiviat graphs, *ACM SIGMETRICS Perf. Evaluat. Review,* vol. 5, Jan. 1976.

*[CM77] *CMF-REAL TIME Comprehensive Management Facility—User Guide,* Boole & Babbage, Sunnyvale, Calif., Dec. 1977.

*[CU77] *CUE—User Guide—Version 3.5,* Boole & Babbage, Sunnyvale, Calif., March 1977.

[DR73] Drummond, M. E., Jr., *Evaluation and Measurement Techniques for Digital Computers Systems,* Prentice-Hall, Englewood Cliffs, N.J., 1973.

[DS77] *DSO—Data Sets Optimizer User Guide—Version 4,* Boole & Babbage, Sunnyvale, Calif., Jan. 1977.

[HA74] Harder, M. C., The computer capacity curve, *J. System Manag.,* n. 7, pp. 25–36, Apr. 1974.

[KO72] Kolence, K. W., Software physics and computer performance measurement, *Proc. ACM Nat. Conf.,* pp. 1024–1040, 1972.

*[KO73a] Kolence, K. W., Kiviat, P. J., Software unit profiles and Kiviat figures, *ACM SIGMETRICS Perf. Evaluat. Review,* vol. 2, n. 3, pp. 2–12, Sept. 1973.

[KO73b] Kolence, K. W., The software empiricist, *ACM SIGMETRICS Perf. Evaluat. Review,* vol. 2, n. 2, pp. 31–36, June 1973.

*[KO76] Kolence, K. W., *An Introduction to Software Physics,* Institute for Software Engineering Inc., Palo Alto, Calif., 1976.

[LO77] *LOOK User Handbook,* Applied Data Research Inc., Princeton, N.J., Feb. 1977.

[ME74a] Merrill, H. W., Further comments on comparative evaluation of Kiviat graphs, *ACM SIGMETRICS Perf. Evaluat. Review,* pp. 1–10, 1974.

[ME74b] Merrill, H. W., A technique for comparative analysis of Kiviat graphs, *ACM SIGMETRICS Perf. Evaluat. Review,* vol. 3, n. 1, pp. 34–39, March 1974.

*[MO73] Morris, M., Pomerantz, A., Shapes highlight strains as performance plotted, *Computerworld,* Newton, Mass., p. 13, Oct. 3, 1973.

*[MO74] Morris, M., Kiviat graphs—Conventions and figures of merit, *ACM SIGMETRICS Perf. Evaluat. Review,* vol. 3, n. 3, pp. 2–8, Oct. 1974.

[MO76] Morris, M., Kiviat graphs and single-figure measures evolving, *Computerworld,* Feb. 1976.

[NU75] Nutt, G. J., Computer system monitors, *Computer,* vol. 8, n. 11, pp. 51–61, Nov. 1975.

*[PL77] *PLAN IV—Report Explanations,* Capex Corp., Phoenix, Ariz., 1977.

[PP76] *PPE—Problem Program Evaluator User Guide—Version 4,* Boole & Babbage, Sunnyvale, Calif., June 1976.

[SN67] Snedecor, G. W., Cochran, W. G., *Statistical Methods,* 6th ed., Iowa State University Press, Ames, 1967.

*[SN74] Snyder, R., A quantitative study of the addition of extended core storage, *ACM SIGMETRICS Perf. Evaluat. Review,* vol. 3, n. 1, pp. 10–33, March 1974.

[ST74] Stevens, B. A., A note on figure of merit, *ACM SIGMETRICS Perf. Evaluat. Review,* pp. 11–19, 1974.

*[TE80] *Tesdata MS 109 Data Communication Monitor,* Tesdata Systems Corporation, P.O. Box 1056, McLean, Va., 1980.

[TS76] *TSA—Total System Analyzer—User Guide—Version 1.2,* Boole & Babbage, Sunnyvale, Calif., Aug. 1976.

5

INSTRUMENTATION

5.1 THE CHARACTERISTICS OF A MEASUREMENT TOOL

Usually the purpose of a measurement tool is to quantify the results of an observation. The set of tools used for an investigation is called the *instrumentation* for it. The development of tools for measuring computer systems under a given workload has followed two separate directions, characterized by the different technologies used for their implementation. *Software monitors* are made of programs that detect the states of a system or of sets of instructions, called *software probes,* capable of event detection (see Sec. 3.2). *Hardware monitors* are electronic devices to be connected to specific system points (the connections are made with their probes) where they detect signals (voltage levels or pulses) characterizing the phenomena to be observed.

Like all tools measuring physical phenomena, computer measurement instruments subtract energy from the system being measured. The energy consumed by a tool should be as low as possible so that the overhead caused by the instrument does not in any way alter the result of the measurement. As far as hardware monitors are concerned, this factor hardly exists; the only areas of possible energy loss are the system points connected to the tool. The very high impedance probes used normally make this dispersion negligible.

On the other hand, software monitors increase the system load and therefore alter performance. However, they have many other advantages with respect to hardware monitors, and only they can provide certain data. Also, the effects of their presence can often be reduced to a minimum.

Another fundamental characteristic of a measurement tool is its accuracy, which may be expressed by the error affecting the values obtained for the measured quantity. When a set of tools is used, each element of the set contributes with its inaccuracy to

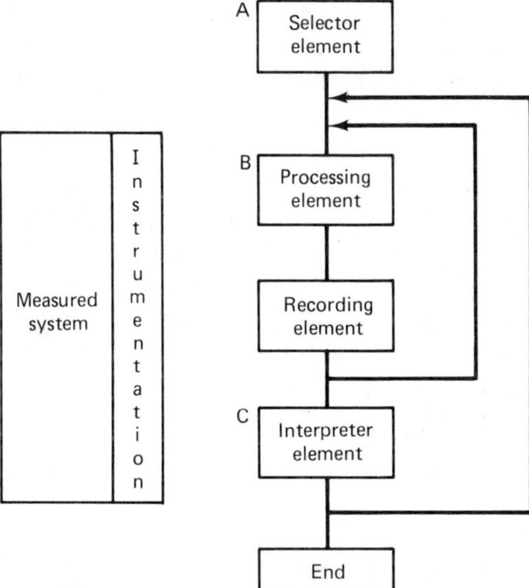

Figure 5.1 Conceptual scheme of a measurement tool [SV76].

the total error. One should be able to account for this error, but usually the indications given by the tool's manufacturer are the only available data. Only in the case of sampling software monitors can the user evaluate, and even influence, the accuracy of the measurements (see Sec. 3.4). The conceptual scheme of a tool for measuring computer system performance is presented in Fig.5.1 [SV76].

The connection between monitor and system is made through the *instrumentation interface*. This interface includes, for example, sections of code inserted into the operating system, existing timers, the available backplane pins, and so on. A filtering element (A) permits a selective observation of the measurable activities. This allows the experimenter to orient the measurements toward specific aspects of the activity of the object being observed. The processing element (B) carries out tests on the state of the components of the system to be measured. The outcomes of the tests are recorded on a storage medium and at a later time operated upon by the analyzing and interpreting element (C), which will provide the results.

Sometimes the interpretation phase is performed in parallel with event detection and data collection. In this case we have *real-time measurements*. Tools that provide this possibility can be used to control dynamically the system's performance [SE70], [BA73], [LO77].

5.2 SOFTWARE MONITORS

In Sec. 3.1 a state transition was called an *event*. An event indicates the start or the end of a period of activity (or inactivity) of any hardware or software component in a computer system. Between an event and the next, the system, or one of its parts, is in a given state. The system remains in a certain state for some time; the start and the end of a state are marked by the occurrence of events, and most states and state transitions can be detected by looking at the contents of given memory locations. Thus, the idea of obtaining data on system components through a program that captures the contents of these memory locations is quite natural. For this, *software monitors* are used.

Software monitors that detect event occurrences are called *event-driven* monitors. They were discussed in Sec. 3.2. Those whose method of data collection consists of detecting the states of individual system components at predetermined time instants are called *samplers*.

The two techniques for data collection are not mutually exclusive. In fact, often they coexist within a single tool. Thus, the term software monitor is generally used to indicate that the tool is based on software technology (as opposed to hardware technology, which is used in hardware monitors). The use of these monitors requires the insertion of extra code in the measured system. This may be done in three ways:

1. Addition of a program.
2. Modification of the software to be measured.
3. Modification of the operating system or of a system program.

Method 1 is generally preferred to the others because it makes it easier to use a tool when required and remove it when no longer needed. Also, in this way the operating system's and, more generally, the measured program's integrity is maintained. Tools of this kind include those adequate for detecting a whole system's activity and those used for measuring the activity of individual programs.

Method 2 is based on the use of *software probes*. These are groups of instructions inserted at critical points into the programs to be observed. Each probe must detect the arrival of the flow of control at the critical point at which it is placed. In this way the number of times certain logical program paths are executed can be known. Also, the contents of given memory areas (for example, tables, data structures, single operands) may be examined when these paths are executed.

Method 3 is used when the data about the variables to be measured are not directly available (for example, are not in a system table) and hence the occurrence of the corresponding events associated with the operating system is to be intercepted. This method is used, for instance, to calculate the response time required to process a transaction in an interactive environment. Instructions can be put into the module that manages the transaction queues; these instructions will read the system's internal clock at the instant a transaction arrives. Other instructions can be put into the program managing the response queues in order to detect the time at which the result of the transaction reaches the output queue. In this way, by calculating the difference between these instants, the response time can be obtained.

Besides occupying some memory space, a software monitor uses the CPU and performs I/O operations. Thus, in general, the following requirements should be satisfied by a software tool [KO71]:

1. It should be able to extract quantitative and descriptive data from the system (descriptive data include information about the identity of the active programs, of the files accessed, and so on).

2. It should require as little modification to the operating system as possible.
3. It should use event-detection and data-collection techniques that do not appreciably alter the workload's characteristics and thus the performance of the measured system.
4. It should require as little memory as possible.

Obtaining descriptive data, which is easy for software tools, eliminates the need to correlate at a later time the values obtained to the software entities that produced them. For example, it is useful to know the names of frequently accessed disk files or the most often used program sections. This knowledge may be exploited in a virtual memory environment to evaluate the convenience of restructuring the program in order to improve its performance. Since a software tool obtains descriptive data by reading the contents of certain memory locations or tables, the amount of data to be collected depends on the operating system's structure and not only on the features of the tool.

In some cases the interference caused by data collection, event detection, and sampling is tolerable; at other times, it may become intolerable. This mostly depends on the tool's design characteristics and, in any case, on the amount of data to be obtained.

We have seen that the *interference* (that is, the *overhead*) caused by event detection and data collection depends on the frequency with which the events occur. However, often the additional load generated in this way is a penalty to be paid in order to obtain certain data, for example, the exact sequence of occurrences of a specific type of event.

A good sampler interferes with the measured system much less than an event-driven tool since it only takes samples of the states of interest. With a sampler it is possible to control the interference by using two of its characteristics: the *selectivity* of the measurements to be performed and the *variability* of the sampling interval. The amount of interference grows with the number of activities measured at each sampling instant and with the sampling frequency (in samples per second).

Whoever plans and conducts the measurement experiments must choose, whenever possible, the variables to be measured at each sampling time in order to avoid undesirable overheads. At first, when preparing to measure a computer system or a program with a software monitor, there is a tendency to collect as much data as possible. It may even be necessary to add a considerable amount of load to the system or to slow down the program's execution. After analyzing the initial results, it will be possible to focus the experiment on specific activities in more detail. In this way the overhead can usually be kept within reasonable limits.

When controlling the interference caused by a tool, the event-detection frequency becomes as important as the selection of the variables to be measured. Its choice cannot be made arbitrarily. From the general theory of sampling we know that, when a sample is obtained from a population by extracting random elements, the accuracy of our statistical inferences increases with the number of elements in the sample. In Sec. 3.4.1 we have seen that, in the case examined there, a representative sample of 20,000 elements provided an estimate of the true values of the variables with a very high degree of accuracy (the error was below 1 percent in 99 percent of the cases).

Let us suppose we are working with a medium-sized third-generation computer and that we want to measure some activities of the system in which the processor is the most important part. Let the processor be capable of executing about 1000 instructions per millisecond. Assume that a sampling software tool is available that executes about 4000 instructions every time it gains control of the CPU (we shall come back to this point later). A tool with these characteristics can detect a considerable amount of data on the activity of system components.

If we define the *sampling overhead* as the percentage of time, with respect to the duration of the whole measurement session, in which the tool controls the CPU, we immediately realize that, once the amount of data to be collected has been decided, the overhead is inversely proportional to the length of the measurement interval.

Under the assumptions made about the tool and the processor, Table 5.1 shows how the sampling overhead varies when the sampling frequency varies and the size of the sample remains the same. Note that the error is kept below 1 percent, at a confidence level above 99 percent, in all cases. When measuring the system for only 2 hours, a time often sufficient to observe its behavior in peak load conditions, the overhead is just over 1 percent.

The minimum extraction interval (83 ms) in Table 5.1 may still be too long when data are required on phenomena whose evolution in time must be known in greater detail. This is, for example, the case when we want to measure the number of times a given event occurs during the session. This number can be precisely determined only if the minimum time interval between occurrences is known and if it is possible to establish the extraction interval so that the sampling frequency will be greater than or equal to the maximum frequency of the event. In this way a sampler can be used as a counter that, unlike one obtained with an event-driven software tool, has the advantage of not requiring any operating system modifications. The following example illustrates this case.

We want to determine the number of *seeks* of a disk unit during a session. As well as the number of arm movements, we must know the addresses of the cylinder pairs between which the movements take place and the names of the libraries or files corresponding to them. The minimum seek time for the unit considered is 10 ms (this represents the time for moving from one cylinder to the next). The available software monitor can take selective measurements, collecting the data on an individual disk unit every 10 ms. Let us suppose that in this case each monitor intervention causes the execution of 200 instructions. Under the assumptions of the previous example, this corresponds to 0.2 ms of CPU time per intervention.

Initially, the monitor reads the volume's table of contents and copies it onto tape or disk, where a data-reduction program will find it after the end of the session. Then the sampler detects the position of the arm every 10 ms, using a counter for the number

TABLE 5.1 SAMPLING OVERHEAD CAUSED BY A SOFTWARE TOOL

Measurement session duration (h)	*Measurement interval duration (ms)*	*Sampling frequency (samples/s)*	*Sampling overhead (%)*	*Sample size*
3	500	2	0.8	21,600
2	333	3	1.2	21,600
1	166	6	2.4	21,600
0.5	83	12	4.8	21,600

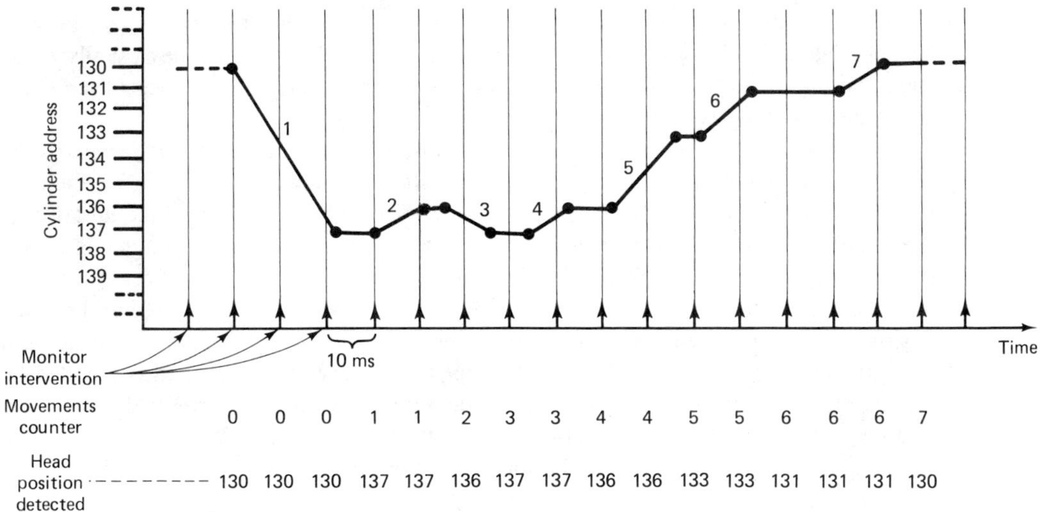

Figure 5.2 Counting the number of disk seeks by a sampling monitor.

of movements, a register where the monitor stores the cylinder address at the time of the last measurement, and a buffer, where the address pairs between which movements occur are collected.

Figure 5.2 shows schematically this particular application of a sampler. The sampling overhead caused by the monitor, in terms of CPU time, will be 2 percent.

5.2.1 Sampling Monitors

There are two types of sampling software monitors: batch and on-line. In theory they are not different, as both collect data and produce results at later times. What makes them different is the delay with which the results are produced. Batch monitors include a program running batch mode, which reduces the collected data off line. On-line monitors, on the other hand, provide results on line, displaying them on a display screen or on the system's console. There are always two programs, the *extractor* and the *analyzer,* but in on-line tools the analyzer is called periodically (and very often) rather than only after the completion of the data-collection phase of the experiment.

The extractor, which is the *sampler* proper, uses a clock, usually an *interval timer,* to interrupt system activity at regular time intervals for the extraction of data concerning the system's state. Using random-length intervals with a predetermined average length, rather than equal-length intervals, would be safer. However, the periodic sampling solution is acceptable in most cases, since the only possible problem could be that of synchronization of sampling operations with an operating system's or a measured program's activity. Indeed, some functions or events of the operating system are periodic with a period multiple of the interval used by the extractor. For example, the EXEC operating system for UNIVAC 1100 systems updates and reorganizes all job queues every 6 s. Then, these activities are not always included in the sampler's observations, but not always excluded either. When the object of measurement is a program, there may be synchronization with the duration of a loop. When these cases occur, they usually cause such distortions in the results that the presence of synchronization between events and sampling can easily be detected.

Figure 5.3 shows the functional scheme of a sampler in an *interrupt-driven system* in which it is possible to access a clock and have timed interrupts. Having verified the validity of the commands for the monitor (the variables to be measured, the duration of the sampling interval, and the length of the session are assumed to be assignable by the experimenter) and having obtained the memory space needed by the extractor's buffers and work areas, the system is asked to set the interval timer (see Sec. 5.2.2) to the value desired by the experimenter for the sampling interval. The extractor remains inactive until the time an interval expires. When this happens, an interrupt occurs and is handled by the appropriate operating system module. Having dealt with the interrupt, the operating system will assign the CPU to the program with the highest priority. To avoid the risk of losing the data for this sampling instant, the program with the highest execution priority must be the extractor itself. Because of its small CPU request, this usually does not noticeably slow down the other jobs.

Before collecting the data, the extractor must make sure it will be able to complete its task without being interrupted (for example, by the completion of an I/O operation). Thus, it must disable all interrupts, except those caused by hardware errors or failures.

The collected data can be divided into two groups:

1. Data about activities suspended when the timer interrupt occurred (for example, the CPU state or the contents of some operating system control areas).
2. Data about activities in progress, detectable by the extractor through the execution of specific instructions (for example, testing the channel status) or by reading the contents of certain memory areas.

Once the collection has been made, the data, adequately encoded to reduce their memory space requirements, are transferred to a buffer area from which they will be copied onto an external storage medium until all the available space has been filled. Generally, two buffer areas are used to overlap the internal transfer time to the recording time. Having completed its activity, the extractor restores the interrupt status of the system that existed prior to the timer-generated interrupt.

The data recorded on the file produced by the extractor are subdivided into temporal groups, sometimes called *logical records* [CU77]. This term does not refer to the set of data within a block (physical record), but to the set of data collected during a time interval whose length can be chosen by the user. The length of this interval is usually a few minutes or even, if the total measurement period is short, a few seconds. Thus, logical records are subsets of the sample taken, and each logical record constitutes the smallest set on which the analyzer will calculate means, percentages, and other statistics.

Figure 5.4 illustrates schematically the process of collection and analysis of system activity data using a batch sampling software monitor. The user asks the monitor to detect the CPU and channel state every 333 ms (extraction interval) from 10:25 A.M. until 12:30 P.M. The length of the measurement session is therefore 2 h, 5 min, while the total number of elements in the sample is 22,800. Since a logical record is to be stored every 5 min,

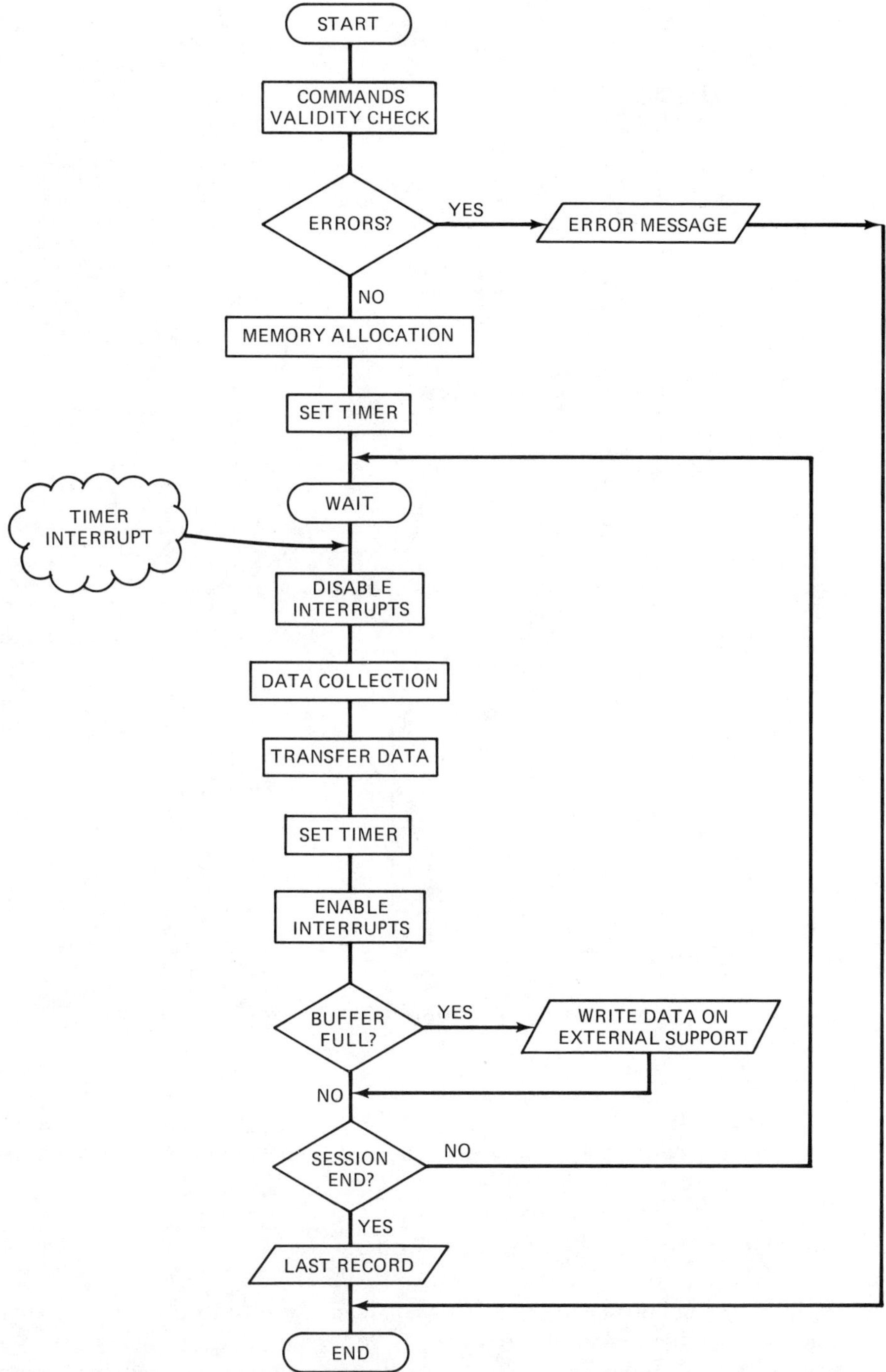

Figure 5.3 Functional scheme for the data-collection phase of a sampling software monitor.

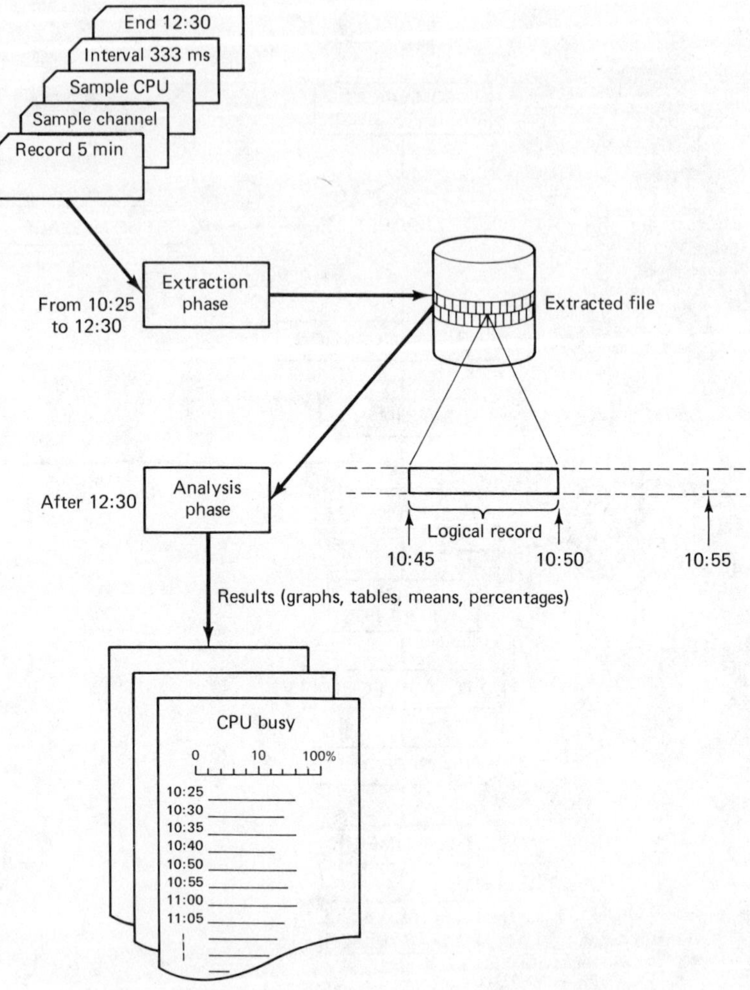

Figure 5.4 Sampling and analysis performed by a software monitor.

each record will contain a set of about 900 sample elements on the average. This will allow, during the analysis, timing diagrams and histograms with a minimum interval of 5 min to be obtained.

5.2.2 Time Measurements, Clocks, and Timers

A software monitor, among other things, should be able to give an indication of the length of the observed phenomena, that is, to perform time measurements. A software tool can do this in two ways: by sampling or by direct measurement. We have seen that a sampling monitor collects data on the states and on the activities of system components at various time instants.

This method of data collection makes it possible to determine the duration of the phenomena of interest (for example, high or low CPU utilization, high paging frequency, high or low utilization of a peripheral, and so on). In this way it is also possible to measure the average duration of other phenomena (for instance, the average time between the issuing of a request for a page not in memory and its arrival in memory, or the average access time of a disk file). On the other hand, direct measurements are obtained from the difference between the time at which a phenomenon ends and that at which it started. In this case both time instants must be detectable. Unfortunately, the direct-measurement method cannot always be used because of temporary interruptions and suspensions of the activity being measured due to higher-priority requests.

In principle, it would be possible to measure directly the durations of all the periods of time in which an activity is performed and to add up these values. In many practical cases, however, this method is less accurate than would be desirable, and sometimes it is difficult to implement.

Both types of time measurements, direct and by sampling, assume the existence of a system clock (if performed by a software monitor). But this is not enough. The clock must be accessible via software with instructions available to programmers. If this is the case, we are allowed to take direct measurements. For sampling to be possible, it is necessary to be able to interrupt system activity at regular intervals. Thus, we need a timer that can generate an interrupt at the end of a predefined time interval. Finally, the operating system must be capable of managing a queue of multiple timing requests from the jobs in memory and of leaving these jobs in a wait state until the intervals they have requested expire [HO71]. A sampler will then be able to use different timings depending on the types of activities to be observed.

A method normally followed to implement a clock accessible to programs is to use a reserved location in main memory (or a CPU register) as a binary counter to be incremented or decremented by a hardware device capable of producing pulses at regular intervals. Usually, this device is a quartz crystal oscillator, having a highly stable frequency in time and within a wide range of temperatures. The frequencies adopted for this oscillator are, for instance, 1 MHz in most IBM/370 computers, and 5 kHz in UNIVAC 1108 and 1110 computers.

The pulses generated by the oscillator constitute the ticks of the clock. The time interval between two consecutive ticks defines its *resolution* (that is, the minimum time period measurable with it). A resolution of 1 μs corresponds to a frequency of 1 MHz, one of 200 μs to 5 kHz. The oscillator's resolution and the size (number of bits) of the memory area reserved for the binary counter define the clock's *cycle time,* that is, the time for the counter to reach its maximum value from zero, or its minimum value in the case of a down counter. With 52 bits and a frequency of 1 million ticks per second, the cycle time is about 143 years.

The counter associated with the oscillator is usually accessible via software, but in read only mode, while its value may only be modified by an external and manual intervention on certain hardware switches. For this reason the oscillator-counter device is often said to be a *physical* or *hardware clock* and the time measured with it *hardware time* [WO76].

The physical clock is used mainly by the operating system for the timing of CPU usage and other resource consumptions. Normally, this is done by keeping a counter, or *software clock,* associated with each program, which is incremented by the hardware clock only when the CPU is processing the corresponding program. This clock is also called a *virtual clock* [SV76] or a *logical clock* [WO76]. It starts counting time when the CPU is first allocated to a user program and stops when CPU control is gained by another program. Its value must be saved as part of the program's status when the program's execution is interrupted. When the CPU is reassigned to the program, the logical clock will continue counting CPU time from the value it contained when the program was last interrupted.

This method for measuring CPU usage may, at least theoretically, be used to measure the usage of any resource. However, it has some drawbacks that may cause nonnegligible inaccuracies. In fact, it introduces an undesirable variability in the measurement of time, in the sense that the values obtained are not repeatable. These drawbacks are:

1. There may be a variable delay between the initiation or the end of an activity and the starting or stopping of the associated logical clock.
2. The operating system may not be totally "honest" in its management of the logical clock; in other words, the time needed for dealing with certain interrupts may be charged to the program that had CPU control when they occurred rather than to the job that caused it.
3. A clock access usually implies a request to the supervisor, and the service time of this request is variable.

Another vitally important element for the definition of the accuracy of direct time measurements is the *resolution* of the clock. If it is too low (that is, if the time between two consecutive ticks is large), the clock may not be suitable for measuring the duration of certain activities or, in any case, it may give results that are far from correct. Let us suppose, for example, that there are s milliseconds between two ticks. Then the situation presented in Fig. 5.5 will lead to the following results:

1. Work W_1, of duration $T_1 = \tau_1 - \tau_0$, will be considered equal to $s(t_1 - t_0)$ in length, that is, smaller than its real value.
2. Work W_2, of duration $T_2 = \tau_2 - \tau_1$, will be considered of zero length $(t_1 - t_1)$.
3. Work W_3, of duration $T_3 = \tau_3 - \tau_2$, will be considered equal to $s(t_3 - t_1)$ in length, that is, longer than in reality.

In general (see Fig. 5.6), the clock is read when an activity starts (instant T_1). Let us suppose that T_a is the value read at that time, and T is the duration of the interval

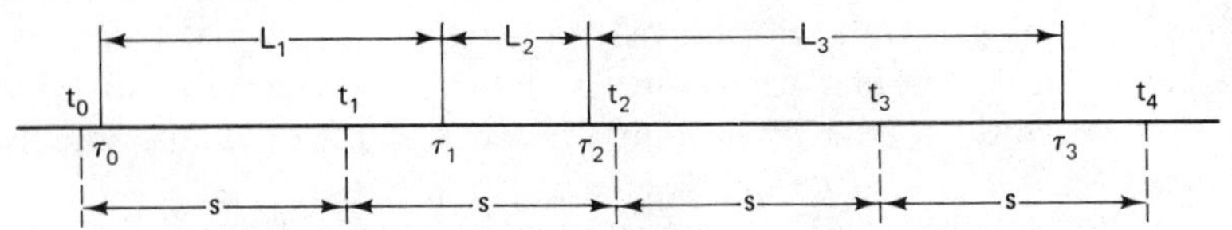

Figure 5.5 Time measurement with a low resolution clock.

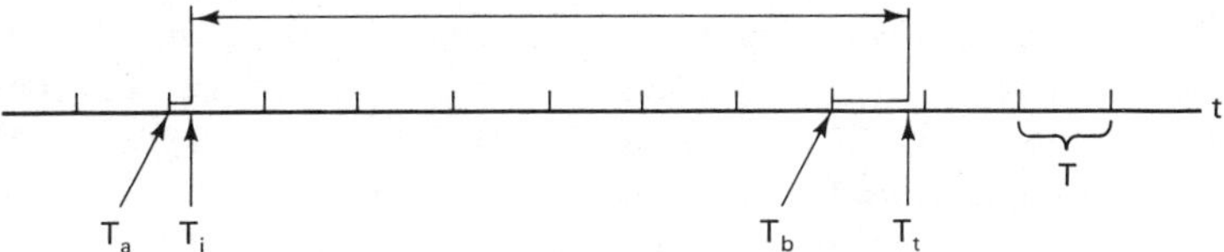

Figure 5.6 Errors made in detecting the duration of a phenomenon with a discrete software clock.

between two clock updates. Then, if the activity ends at T_t and the clock is read at that moment, it will contain value T_b. The real duration of the activity is

$$T_r = T_t - T_i$$

while the measured value is

$$T_m = T_b - T_a$$

The difference between the two is given by

$$t_\Delta = T_r - T_m = (T_t - T_i) - (T_b - T_a)$$

that is,

$$t_\Delta = (T_t - T_b) - (T_i - T_a)$$

is the difference between the errors made in the two readings. Both these errors can vary from 0 to T.

If the start and the end of a phenomenon occur at instants independent of the clock's ticks, T_i and T_t can be considered random variables with a uniform distribution in the interval $(0, T)$.

Thus, the error varies in the interval $(-T, T)$, and a time measurement performed in this way can lead to an incorrect estimate of the true time [MO76]. One must remember that this random error is introduced in the measurement every time the activity is suspended and restarted, and that therefore the global error due to these causes depends also on the number of times the activity is interrupted. This implies a dependence of a measurement tool's accuracy on the system's workload.

We have seen that the data-extraction process carried out by a software monitor through sampling requires that the system provide functions that allow the monitor to be invoked at regular intervals defined by the monitor itself. One of these functions is that of *interval timing*. It may be obtained by a software clock used as a binary counter whose contents are handled as if they were a signed integer. The clock can be read from programs with an instruction or macroinstruction *(test timer)* and can be loaded with another *(set timer)*. The value loaded into the software clock by this instruction expresses, in multiples of the timer's resolution, the length of the interval at the end of which an interrupt will be generated by the clock itself. Loaded as a positive integer in the counter, the value is decremented until it becomes negative. The change of its sign bit causes an interrupt request to the supervisor.

Having dealt with the interrupt and executed the *dispatcher* (the system program that decides which program will gain CPU control on the basis of priorities), the supervisor allocates the CPU to user programs. The program requesting the timing is served first if it has the highest priority; otherwise, it is released from the wait state in which it was put when it made the timing request, and will obtain the CPU later, when its turn will come. A timer is decremented both when the CPU is busy and when it is in the wait state. Usually, it is not decremented when the CPU is halted from the outside.

Sampling (that is, the repetitive use of a timer) is a simple and fairly quick method of measuring the time a program requires for the execution of certain instruction sequences without modifying its code [CA68]. This can be done by collecting the addresses of the instructions being executed at the times when sampling interrupts occur. The sampling must be performed at short intervals (1 ms or even shorter, for greater accuracy), and this causes substantial overhead. However, this method can provide time measurements sufficiently accurate for the evaluation of program performance.

From what we have seen it is obvious that, in the design of a software monitor, the characteristics of the operating system and certain aspects of the architecture of the processor whose performance is to be measured must be considered. For this reason software monitors are oriented toward a given type of computer and operating system. Their use on different types of systems is generally not possible without modifications that are often substantial and sometimes practically impossible.

5.3 HARDWARE MONITORS

Hardware monitors are devices built for measuring computer systems. They are connected to the system being measured with *probes* and are capable of detecting significant events, from which the values of many important performance indexes and system variables can be deduced. The main characteristic of these monitors is that they are external to the system being measured. Thus, they do not need any of its resources and, unlike software monitors, they do not cause any substantial interference with the system, nor do they modify the values of any variables being measured. For these reasons, hardware monitors are in principle more accurate [CA71b], [DR73], [FE78].

The comparison between hardware and software monitors, however, cannot be made as if they had equivalent capabilities and fields of application. While many variables can be measured by both, there are some that are only measurable with hardware monitors, others only with software tools. Even for measurements that can be made with both types of monitor, one type is usually more convenient than the other (economically or technically, or both). This stems from the basic differences between the events the two types of monitor can detect and between the levels of system data that they can access. Since hardware monitors are external to the system to be measured and use electric sensors, they have access to the voltage levels and pulses present at the pins of the machine's circuits. For security reasons, and to simplify the connections, this access is usually limited to those system points electrically connected to the pins on the backplane of the system's hardware components. The probes are circuits of high impedance, capable of detecting at any pin the two voltage levels used to represent the two binary values within the device and the transitions from one level to the other. In this way the monitor can detect voltage pulses, as long as their duration is not less than the minimum detectable by the probes. The high-impedance requirement is necessary to guarantee that the overhead will be minimal. In many computers, especially the faster ones, there are critical points to which the addition of an electrical load, even as small as the load due to a very high impedance probe, is sufficient to cause random errors and other serious system perturbations. These critical points, and those thought to be critical, must be excluded from the list of observable points.

If we compare what has just been said about the data and events a hardware monitor can access and detect with what was said about software monitors in Sec. 5.2, we clearly see the different nature and level of the data they collect. While software monitors work at a logical level and thus hardly know what happens at the physical level, the converse is true for hardware monitors. This difference is also found in the typical frequencies of the phenomena observable with the two types of monitor, which are much higher in the case of hardware tools.

The basic functions of hardware monitors are schematically summarized in Fig. 5.7, which shows the structure of a very simple tool. Besides the probes, which detect the significant signals, there is an *event filter,* which may be used to process the signals logically. The logic elements with which a monitor is equipped may be connected to each other in many ways by inserting jumper cables into the hubs of a patch panel to which the pins of the logic elements are connected.

In this way a flexible monitor can be obtained. The signals produced by the filter are sent to a set of *counters*. When a counter counts pulses representing elementary events or their logical combinations, it is used in *count mode*. When, on the other hand, the clock pulses between two elementary events are counted, the counter is used in *time mode*. We shall see some examples of this type of use in Sec. 5.3.1. At the start of an experiment, all counters are reset. At the end, or periodically, their contents are written onto a mass storage device (usually disk or tape). From there they are later taken and processed to produce easy-to-interpret reports. This process, called *data reduction,* is carried out off line by a monitor like that in Fig. 5.7. Data may be reduced either on the system that has been measured or on another system. An on-line reduction by the system is definitely possible but causes more interference.

A monitor of the type described is controlled by hard-wired logic. The operations

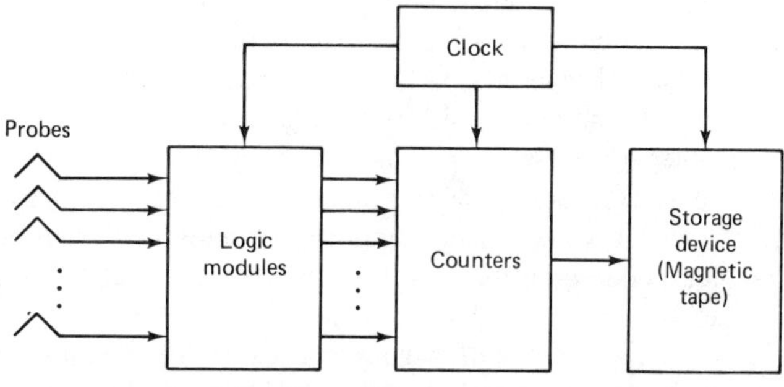

Figure 5.7 Scheme of a wired program hardware monitor.

carried out by the event filter on the signals coming from the system remain fixed throughout the measurement session, once they have been chosen and the connections manually implemented. These monitors, which may be called *wired program tools,* were soon extended, not only with output units for the on-line checking and control of the experiments (numeric displays, display screens), but also with comparators, registers, and random-access memories. With a sufficient number of sensors, registers permit the acquisition and storage of machine register contents (stamped, if desired, with the time of collection, measured by the monitor's clock). The comparators compare these contents with binary patterns assigned by the experimenter or with those of other machine registers. In this way new events, corresponding to the logical conditions "equal," "greater," "less than or equal to," "between limits," and so on, can be defined and observed. These events can then be counted or timed as described previously.

It is important to have registers and comparators in a hardware monitor since they make it possible to collect coded signals. These signals are actually binary vectors whose bits are only meaningful if considered all together. A hardware monitor can thus approach the logical level, which is sometimes reached through the contents of certain machine registers.

The use of random-access memories as buffers and, at times, as an extension of the array of counters with which the monitor is equipped make hardware tools even more powerful. For a memory cell to work as a counter, there must be a mechanism capable of reading its contents, incrementing it by 1, and writing back the result. For equal technologies, an integrated hardware counter is much faster than a memory cell provided with this mechanism. Thus, some very frequent events can only be counted with hardware counters. In this case, memory cells can be used as counter extensions, working at much lower frequencies, that is, at the frequencies of a counter's overflow signal. When the highest event frequency is below 1 or 2 MHz, the memory cells can be used directly for counting, with a cost per bit much lower than that of the counters and thus with larger sizes for the same total cost.

If there is a random-access memory, it is much easier to obtain histograms directly. This only requires a *distribution* device, which determines in what interval of the values of the variable being considered each sample lies, and a number of counting devices equal to the number of these intervals. The presence of a RAM usually allows a much greater number of intervals to be chosen, but imposes a lower frequency constraint on event detection. The frequency cannot be high anyway if the interval in which the sample lies must be determined by comparing the value of the sample with the entries of a table (stored in registers or memory cells). In some cases, however, the correspondence between sample and interval values is particularly simple and easy to determine. Two examples of this type of measurement will be discussed in Sec. 5.3.1.

The other main use for random-access memory in a hardware monitor is *tracing*. This amounts to considering the memory, or a part of it, as a buffer area for the temporary storage of variable values or descriptions of events. An event description may contain, for example, a code indicating its type, the time at which it occurred, and the values of some variables collected at that time.

The time to fill the buffer area depends on its size and on the average frequency of the events being considered. A tracing experiment will be generally quite short, unless the buffer area is regularly written onto tape or disk.

In the development of hardware monitors, the next step could only be the replacement of the control logic, which had become quite complex, with an actual processor. In this way *stored program tools* composed of one or more minicomputers were obtained. These minicomputers are now being replaced by microprocessors or microcomputers. In a stored program tool, the basic functions in Fig. 5.7 are still performed, at least partially, by ad hoc modules, and often there are comparators, sometimes even buffers, that are not implemented as part of the minicomputer's memory. The probes, logic elements, counters, comparators, buffers, and other special devices are required to reduce the frequency of the events to be processed by the minicomputer. Thus, they act as interfaces (performing an initial data reduction) between the measuring machine and the system to be measured. This can be seen in Fig. 5.8, which illustrates the general configuration of the Tesdata MS series monitors [TE76]. In a tool of this type, there are four parts.

1. The probes, totally similar to those of a wired-program tool.
2. The measurement processing unit, containing the concentrators, which collect the signals arriving from various probes, convert them into signals compatible with the tool's internal conventions, and send them to the event filter. The filter combines the signals logically as specified by the user with the connections on the patch panel. The collectors or distributors may count, time, distribute, and trace events. The controller, which also contains a small buffer, is capable of generating a memory address for the minicomputer and of sending measurements to it as a DMA (direct memory access) device.
3. The measurement control unit, composed of a minicomputer, a tape unit, and a system console, which can be used to define the measurements and control their

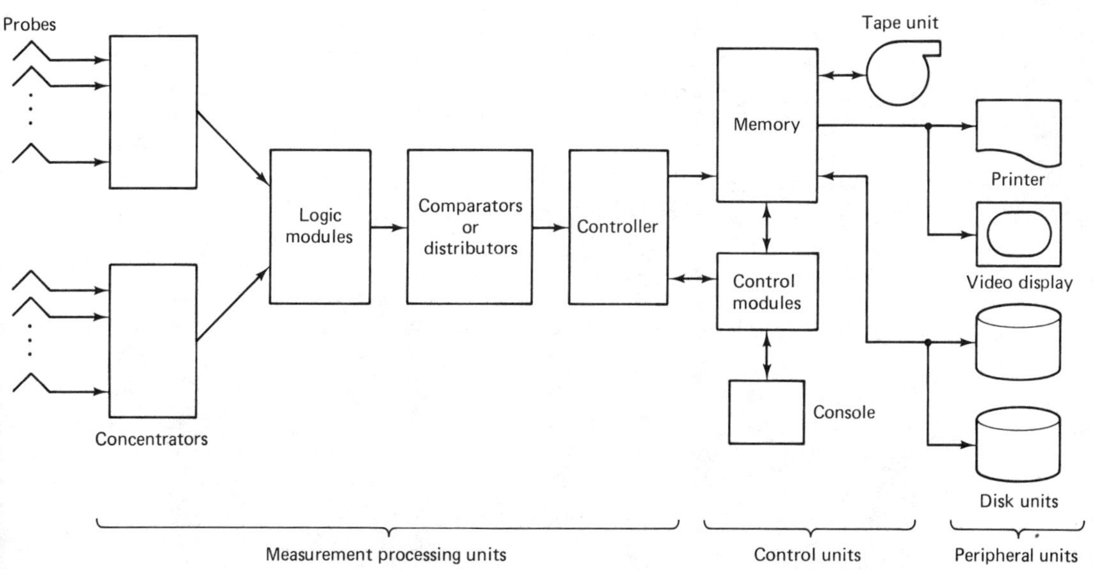

Figure 5.8 Scheme of a stored-program hardware monitor [TE76].

execution. The controller of the processing unit may interrupt the minicomputer with the highest priority to minimize the risk of data losses.

4. The peripheral units, which store the system and user programs and the measurement results, and also present in proper form the results of the data-reduction phase. The system's programs, as well as those for data reduction and for the presentation of the results, are usually delivered together with the hardware tools, especially the stored program ones.

The main technical characteristics of one of the tools in the series just described, the Tesdata MS-58N, are summarized in Table 5.2 [TE79].

During the initial part of an experiment's design phase, the measurements to be performed are defined. The variables and the events to be observed are specified, as well as the length of the sessions and the form in which data are to be collected. With a tool of the type in Fig. 5.8, the requirements may be expressed through commands on the console. Thus, the necessary hardware resources (for example, buffers) are allocated for the experiment. A good tool should also help the user during the verification of the measurement's accuracy, for example, by providing probe simulators and interactive data reduction and presentation programs.

The second phase, that of data collection, starts with the connection of the probes to the pins on the system's backplane. For this to be done correctly, considerable experience with the logical and wiring diagrams of the system is required and great care must be taken, when verifying the connections, to check they are the desired ones. Some

TABLE 5.2 CHARACTERISTICS OF THE TESDATA MS-58 MONITOR [TE79]

Sensors	
Number	72–144
Speed	40 MHz
Sensitivity	10 ns
Concentrators	4–8
Concentrator cables	4–8
Max. cable length (Sensor to monitor)	250 ft
Collectors	
Number	4–8
Min. sampling period	2 μs
Max. count rate	40 MHz
Functional modes	Count, Time, Map, Store, Time-Map/Store, Half Map
Patch panel	Single–double logic
Processor	
Memory	64 Kbytes
Cycle time	1 μs/2 bytes
Peripherals	
Diskette	630KB floppy diskette drive
Console	Keyboard/printer
Real-time displays (Optional)	Graphic display, 16 bars Message display, 32 characters

tool manufacturers provide lists of the significant pins for measuring the most common systems. These lists, even in the most complex systems, do not usually include more than 100 to 200 measurement points.

The reduction and presentation of the data constitutes the third phase of an experiment. Because of both these operations and the previous phases, a programmable tool should be equipped not only with programs that make its ordinary use easier, but also with programs for software development that help in the preparation of special measurement experiments.

Among the most useful summaries are the general reports (counter contents, histograms, utilization profiles, Kiviat graphs, seek activities on each disk, and others) and those related to individual jobs or processes, to single users or applications. The preparation of the latter type of summary requires the knowledge of each event's *logical cause* (that is, the process responsible for its occurrence). This problem is particularly difficult to solve with a wired-program tool, while it is certainly easier with a stored program tool and even more so with a *hybrid hardware-software tool*.

Hybrid tools [SV76] are those whose hardware portion is supported, in data collection, by a software counterpart. This software portion of the tool is executed intermittently by the system being measured and sends out to the hardware portion internal system information. The concept of a hybrid tool, which has not yet been fully exploited commercially, looks very promising since it couples the advantages of both hardware and software tools, with the exception of the portability aspects, while minimizing most of their disadvantages.

5.3.1 Examples of Hardware Monitor Applications

To illustrate in more detail the capabilities of a hardware monitor, we shall now discuss a few simple applications. In the measurement schematically represented in Fig. 5.9a, we assume that the device, whose utilization during a period T is to be measured, has a flip-flop with output voltage Q high when the unit is busy and low when it is idle. The *utilization* is the fraction of the time period T during which the unit is busy. A wired-program tool, with two counters CA and CB and an AND gate that makes CB operate as a counter in time mode, is sufficient to measure it. Note that CA is a counter that counts clock pulses (see Fig. 5.9b).

At the end of the measurement period, the ratio between the contents of CB and CA (which are both reset at the beginning) will provide the value, affected by sampling errors and perhaps other types of errors, of the desired utilization. In the example considered the ratio is $21/34 = 0.617$.

The measurement of the *overlap* between the activities of two units is shown in Fig. 5.10. The overlap is the fraction of the measurement period during which both units are active. Following the procedure used in measuring the utilization, it is easy to see that the setup in Fig. 5.10 will provide the correct result (affected, as usual, by some errors) if the ratio between the contents of CB and CA is calculated at the end of the time interval. The same figure also provides an example of how a counter can be used to count events. In this case, what is counted is the number of words transferred to memory from the peripheral units connected to the channel, and vice versa. If a separate

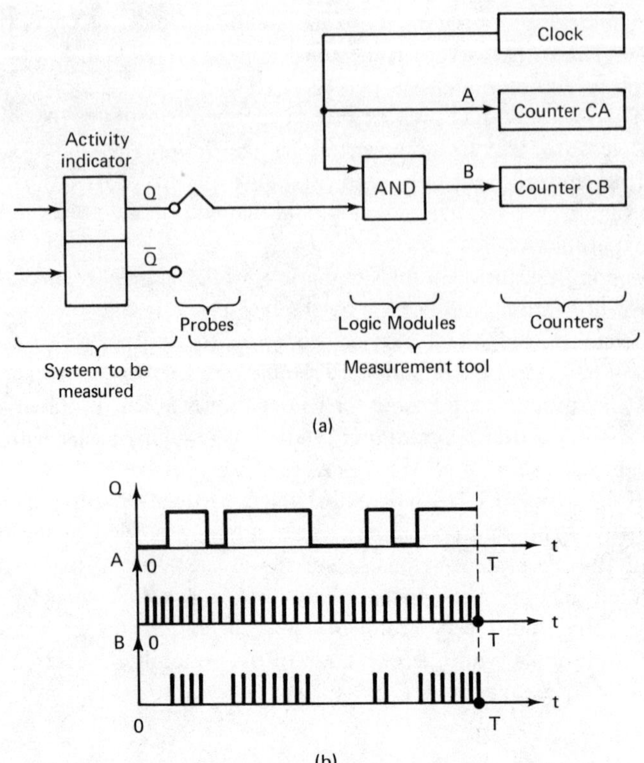

Figure 5.9 Measurement of the utilization of a unit with a wired program tool: (a) diagram of the connections; (b) the main signals involved.

request signal for each direction of transfer of an I/O word is available, it is sufficient to count their logical sum (note that there cannot be pulses on both lines simultaneously).

If a tool with a random-access memory is used, the addresses of the cylinders on which the arm of a disk unit is successively positioned can be traced, as shown in Fig. 5.11. The *arm-moving* signal is high when the arm is moving. When the signal becomes high, the disk address, corresponding to the cylinder number toward which the arm is moving, is loaded in the tool's input register and from there transferred to the monitor's memory.

Before the transfer, which occurs with a delay D with respect to the *arm-moving* signal, the memory address in the tool is incremented so that later measurements will not overlap. In Fig. 5.11 the mechanism for detecting memory overflow is not represented, nor is that for writing the contents of memory into secondary storage. If a stored-program tool is used, these operations can be carried out by the tool's software, given the relatively low frequency of arm movements (this, however, may not be feasible if the tool controls many other measurements at the same time).

An example of a stored-program tool used to collect distributions, or rather histograms, is shown in Fig. 5.12. The measurement is to produce a program profile [KN71],

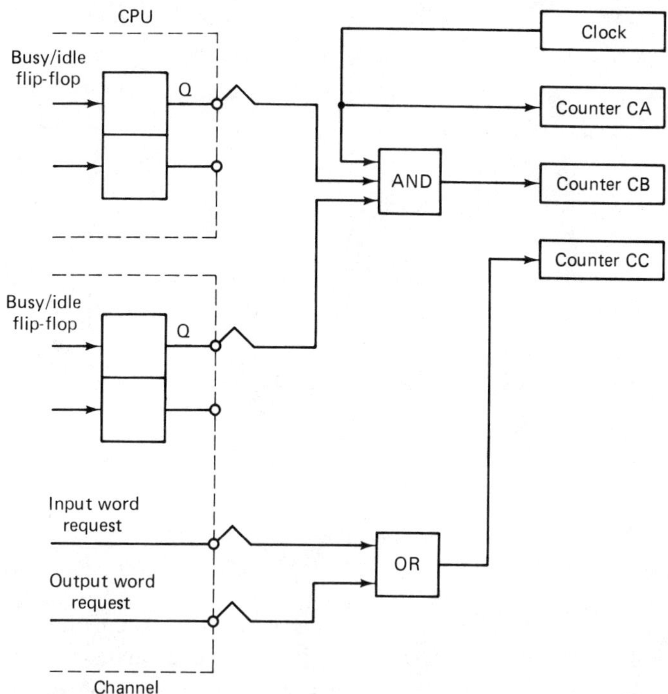

Figure 5.10 Measurement of the overlap between CPU and channel activity and of the number of words transferred by the channel during a given time interval.

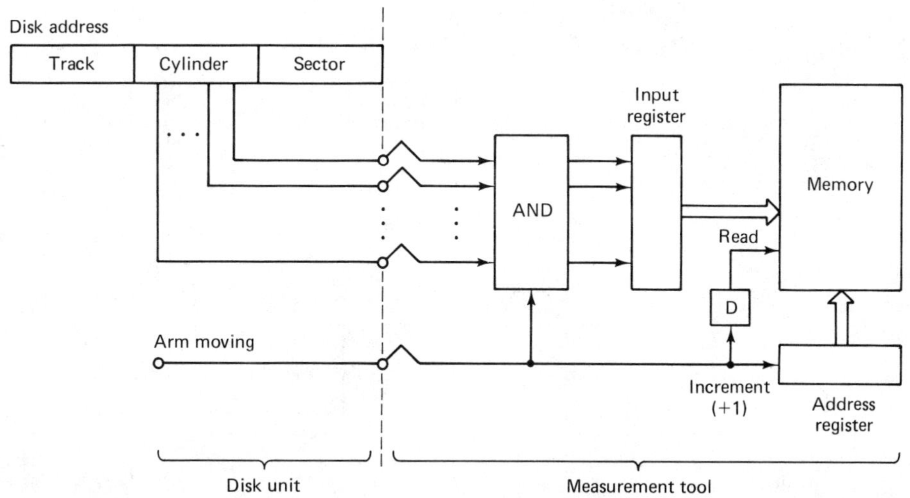

Figure 5.11 Measurement of the seek activity of a disk unit.

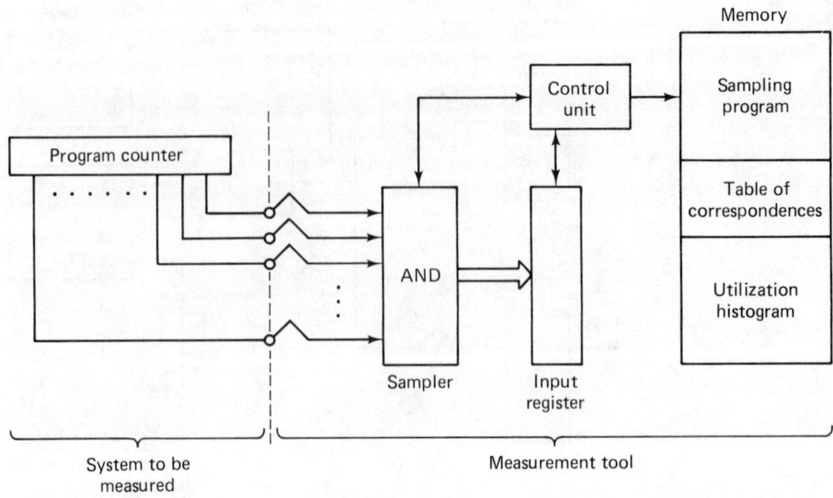

Figure 5.12 Measurement of a program's profile with a stored-program hardware tool

that is, the value of the execution frequency of each statement in the program. To obtain this profile, we should determine the program areas containing consecutive statements characterized by the property that, whenever one of them is executed, the others are also executed. Having found these sets of statements, a memory cell is assigned to each of them to store the number of corresponding samples. The contents of the program counter are periodically sampled during the program's execution.

Using a table of correspondence loaded in the tool's memory, the monitor can determine the area to which the program counter's contents point at each sampling instant and the address of the corresponding monitor memory cell. That cell's contents are then incremented by 1. At the end of the experiment, the memory cells where the histogram

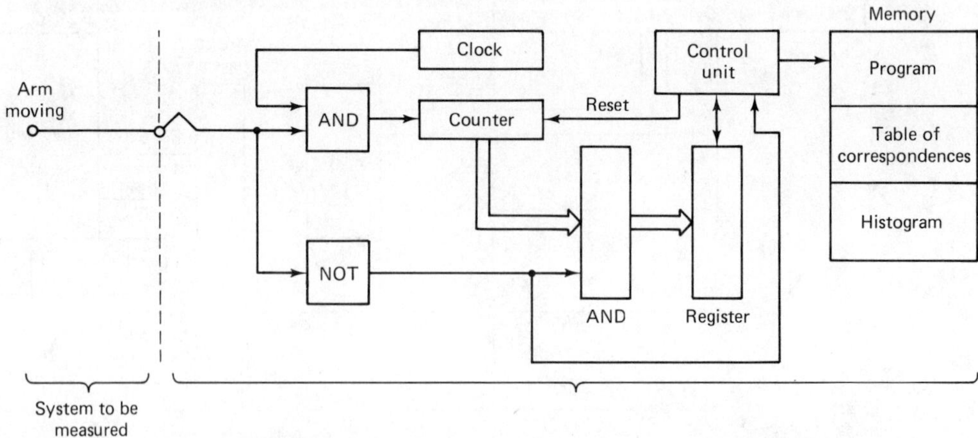

Figure 5.13 Measurement of a disk's seek time with a stored-program hardware tool.

has been collected will contain an approximation of the program's profile. The higher the number of samples taken, the smaller the differences between this histogram and the true profile.

Another distributive use of a stored program monitor, coupled with a counter in time mode, is presented in the measurement setup of Fig. 5.13. The purpose of the experiment is to obtain the histogram of disk *seek time*. A probe connected to the *arm-moving* line, used in Fig. 5.11, is sufficient since the interesting events are the departure and the arrival of the arm, represented by the low-to-high and high-to-low transitions of this signal. The time between this pair of events is measured with the approximate method described in Fig. 5.9. The counter is reset each time its contents are transferred to the register. Having decided the time ranges for the histogram's construction, one proceeds as in the case of Fig. 5.12.

The operations to be performed after the arm's arrival can be greatly simplified (and their maximum frequency increased) if the intervals are adequately chosen. The greatest simplification is obtained when the first bits of the arm's movement time (expressed in number of clock pulses) can be used directly as the address of the cell whose contents are to be incremented.

REFERENCES

Entries marked with an asterisk (*) are referenced in the text.

[AS71] Aschenbrenner, R. A., Natarajan, N. K., The Neurotron monitor system, *AFIPS Conf. Proc., FJCC,* vol. 39, pp. 31–37, 1971.

*[BA73] Baner, M. J., McCredie, J. W., AMS—A software monitor for performance evaluation and system control, *Proc. 1st ACM-SICME Symposium on Measurement and Evaluation,* pp. 147–160, Feb. 1973.

[BE72b] Bell, T. E., Choose your tools to check your computer, *Computer Decisions,* vol. 4, n. 11, pp. 12–15, Nov. 1972.

[BL80] Blake, R., Xray: Instrumentation for multiple computers, *PERFORMANCE 80, Perf. Eval. Review,* vol. 9, n. 2, pp. 11–25, 1980.

*[CA68] Cantrell, H. N., Ellison, A. L., Multiprogramming system performance measurement and analysis, *AFIPS Conf. Proc., SJCC,* vol. 32, 1968.

[CA71a] Carlson, G., Hardware monitoring of a software monitor, *Proc. SUM Users Group 1st Annual Meeting,* Jan. 1971.

*[CA71b] Carlson, G., A user's view of hardware performance monitors, *Proc. IFIP Congress 71,* pp. 128–132, North-Holland, Amsterdam, 1971.

*[CU77] *CUE—User Guide—Version 3.5,* Boole & Babbage Inc., Sunnyvale, Calif., March 1977.

[DE71] Deutsch, P., Grant, C. A., A flexible measurement tool for software systems, *Proc. IFIP Congress 71,* North-Holland, Amsterdam, 1971.

*[DR73] Drummond, M. E., Jr., *Evaluation and Measurement Techniques for Digital Computer Systems,* Prentice-Hall, Englewood Cliffs, N.J., 1973.

[FE75] Ferrari, D., Liu, M., A general-purpose software measurement tool, *Software-Practice and Experience,* vol. 5, n. 2, pp. 181–192, 1975.

*[FE78] Ferrari, D., *Computer Systems Performance Evaluation,* Prentice-Hall, Englewood Cliffs, N.J., 1978.

[FU73] Fuller, S. H., Swan, R. J., Wulf, W. A., The instrumentation of C.mmp, a multi-(mini) processor, *Proc. COMPCON 73,* pp. 173–176, Feb. 1973.

[GE73] Gentleman, W. M., Wichmann, B. A., Timing on computers, *Computers Architecture News,* vol. 2, Oct. 1973.

[GR72] Grochow, J. M., Utility functions for time-sharing system performance evaluation, *Computer,* pp. 16–19, Sept.–Oct. 1972.

*[HO71] Holtwick, G. M., Designing a commercial performance measurement system, *Proc. ACM-SIGOPS Workshop on System Performance Evaluation,* pp. 29–58, Harvard University, Cambridge, Mass., Apr. 1971.

[HO74] Howard, P. C., Update on hardware monitors, *EDP Performance Review,* vol. 2, n. 10, Oct. 1974.

[HO75] Howard, P. C., Third annual survey of performance-related software packages, *EDP Performance Review,* vol. 3, n. 12, Dec. 1975.

[HO76] Howard, P. C., ed., Evaluation and comparison of software monitors, *EDP Performance Review,* vol. 4, n. 2, Feb. 1976.

[HU73] Hughes, J., Cronshaw, D., On using a hardware monitor as an intelligent peripheral, *ACM SIGMETRICS Perf. Evaluat. Review,* vol. 2, n. 4, pp. 3–19, Dec. 1973.

*[KN71] Knuth, D. E., An empirical study of FORTRAN programs, *Software—Practice and Experience,* vol. 1, pp. 105–133, 1971.

*[KO71] Kolence, K. W., A software view of measurement tools, *Datamation,* vol. 17, pp. 32–38, Jan. 1971.

*[LO77] *LOOK User Handbook,* Applied Data Research, Inc., Princeton, N.J., Feb. 1977.

[LU74] Lucas, H. C., Software monitors, *Infotech State of the Art Report, "Computer Systems Measurement,"* 1974.

*[MO76] Mohr, J. M., Agrawala, A. K., An error analysis of the CPU usage measurement in EXEC8 systems, *Proc. CMG-VII, 7th International Conf.,* Atlanta, Nov. 1976.

[MO73] Morris, A., Hardware measurement—past, present and future, *Paper presented to Share,* vol. 2, pp. 308–332, 1973.

[NO74] Noe, J. D., Acquiring and using a hardware monitor, *Datamation,* vol. 20, n. 4, pp. 89–95, 1974.

[NU75] Nutt, G. J., Tutorial: Computer Systems Monitors, *Computer,* vol. 8, n. 11, pp. 51–61, Nov. 1975.

[NU76] Nutt, G. J., Tutorial: Computer Systems Monitors, *Perf. Eval. Review,* pp. 41–51, Jan. 1976.

[PE74] Peterson, T. G., A comparison of software and hardware monitors, *ACM SIGMETRICS Perf. Evaluat. Review,* vol. 3, n. 2, pp. 2–5, June 1974.

[PO72] Pomeroy, J. W., A guide to programming tools and techniques, *IBM Systems J.* vol. 11, n. 3, pp. 234–254, 1972.

[SA70] Saltzer, J. H., Gintell, J. W., The instrumentation of Multics, *CACM,* vol. 13, n. 8, pp. 495–500, Aug. 1970.

[SE74] Sebastian, P. R., Hybrid events monitoring instrument, *Proc. 2nd ACM-SICME Symposium on Measurement and Evaluation,* pp. 127–139, Sept. 1974.

*[SE70] Sedgewick, R., Stone, R., McDonald, J. W., Spy—A program to monitor OS/360, *AFIPS Conf. Proc. FJCC,* vol. 37, pp. 119–128, 1970.

[SV73] Svobodova, L., Online system performance measurements with software and hybrid monitors, *Proc. 4th ACM-SIGOPS Symposium on Operating System Principles,* pp. 45–53, Oct. 1973.

*[SV76] Svobodova, L., *Computer Performance Measurement and Evaluation Methods: Analysis and Applications,* Elsevier, New York, 1976.

*[TE76] *Tesdata MS Series Reference Manual.* Tesdata Systems Corp., McLean, Va., 1976.

*[TE79] Tesdata AMS, MS-58, *Performance Measurement System, General Information Manual,* Publication GIM-058, 1979.

[WA74] Waldron, M., Hardware monitoring and simulation, *INFO Software '74, Infotech,* 1974.

[WA75] Warner, C. D., Measurement tools, *Nat. Bureau of Standards Special Publ. 406,* pp. 99–102, Aug. 1975.

*[WO76] Wortman, D. B., A study of high-resolution timing, *IEEE Trans. Software Engineering,* June 1976.

6

A TUNING METHODOLOGY

6.1 BASIC CONSIDERATIONS

The first step to improve the efficiency of an existing computer system is to analyze its operation. That is, a *performance evaluation study* of the system must be undertaken. A study was presented in Sec. 1.2 as an interactive procedure composed basically of a diagnosis phase and a therapy phase (see Fig. 1.1).

The diagram in Fig. 1.1 can be extended and specified in more detail to show the phases and steps of a performance improvement methodology. One such extended diagram is presented in Fig. 6.1. The operations to be performed have been grouped into the following phases:

1. Definition of the objectives.
2. Workload characterization.
3. Instrumentation.
4. Design of the experiments.
5. Validation.

Phase 2 is not discussed in this chapter, since Chapter 2 was devoted to it.

The need to define objectives becomes obvious as soon as decisions on the method for analyzing the system's performance, on its degree of accuracy, on the amount of resources to be used, and on how to justify the investment have to be made. These questions cannot be adequately answered if the goals of the evaluation study have not been previously identified, even if only approximately.

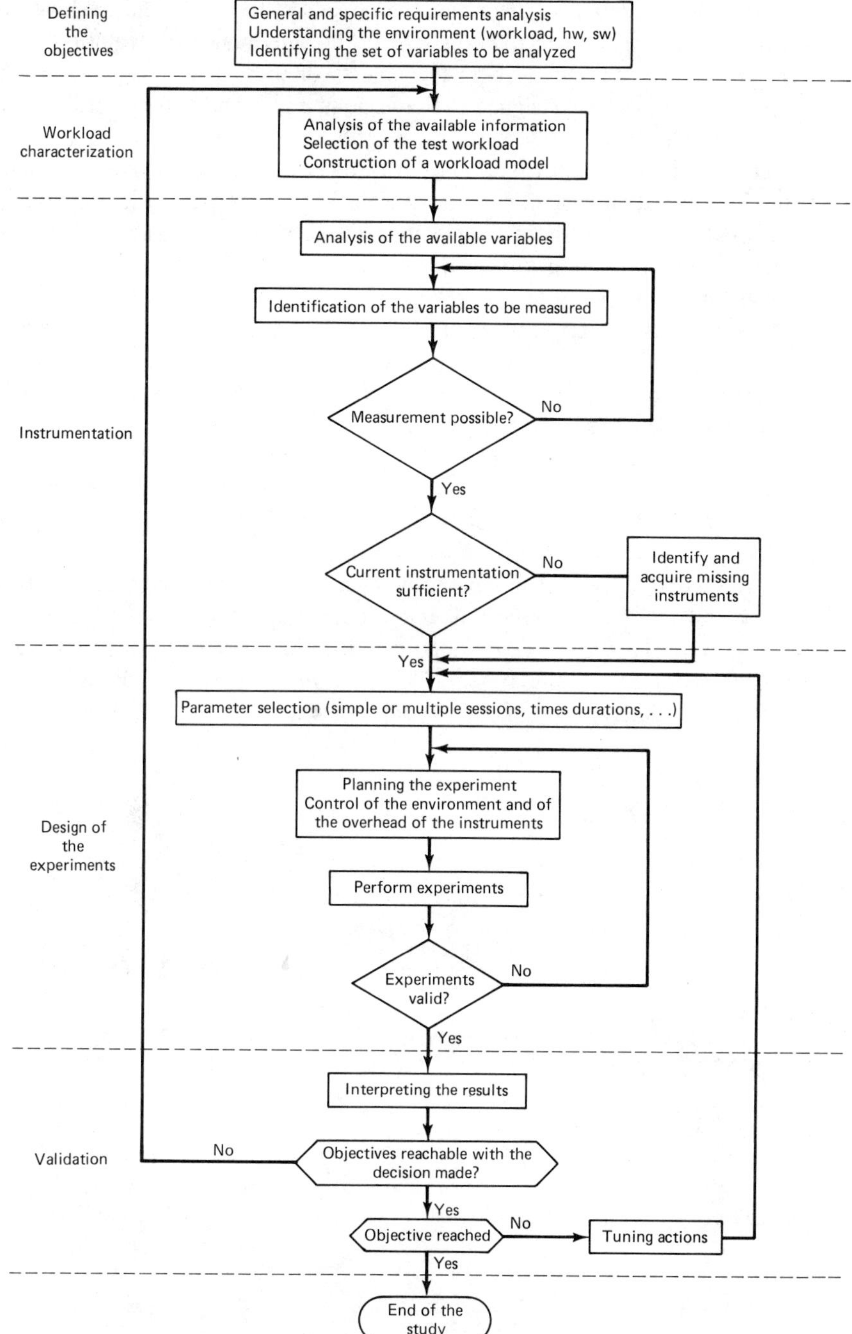

Figure 6.1 Phases of a performance improvement methodology.

Basically, one has to determine the objects of the study and the kind of data to be obtained about these objects. Furthermore, the importance of acquiring information of each type being considered about the objects of the study should be specified so that correct priorities can be assigned to the various aspects and phases of the study, and the methodology and tools to be used can be chosen.

In practice, a performance study is often originated by suspicions of inefficiencies, by the feeling that the system's performance is lower than expected, or by user complaints, rather than by an analysis of the situation. With such vague data, it is unreasonable to expect that just procuring a measurement tool will be sufficient to produce a complete documentation of the system's activity in a few weeks and to provide a satisfactory solution to the problems. It is better to choose more modest objectives, at least initially. For example, an analysis of the data collected by the *logging routines* will often provide starting points by revealing aspects and problems previously unknown. These problems can be subdivided into classes (for example, analysis of hardware utilizations, of program efficiency, and of the workload, and search for bottlenecks). These categories will be the areas that the evaluators will investigate with adequate tools and techniques. It is also convenient to decide at the outset whether the study will be concerned with a specific problem or whether it will have a wider scope.

The workload will then have to be analyzed in detail, for example, by attempting to break down the total elapsed time into the times spent performing the various activities (see Fig. 6.2). This kind of workload classification, although rough, shows the weight each application has on the system. From the initial analysis of the workload, it should be possible to determine some of its major characteristics (for example, its tendency to

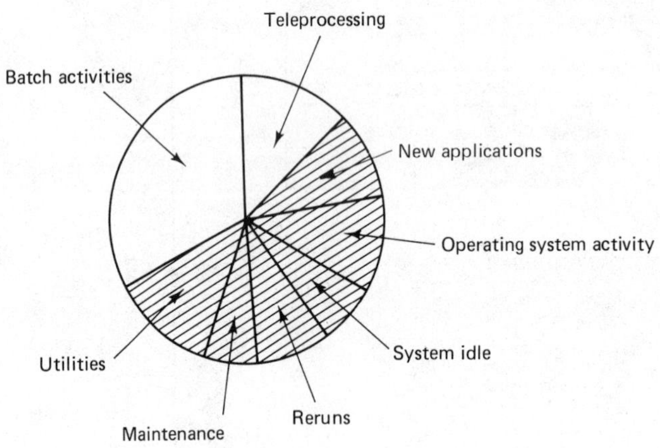

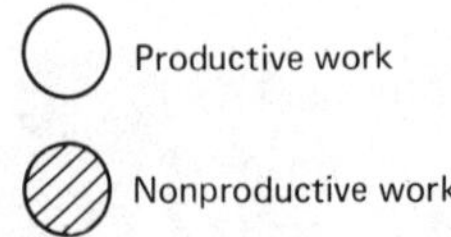

Figure 6.2 Example of workload classification [HO77].

load the I/O subsystem rather than the CPU, the average program length, the main aspects of resource consumption and arrival pattern in each shift, and so on). It is also useful to examine the reasons why given programs are run at certain times rather than at others and to verify that these choices are consistent with the objectives of the installation.

The measurements could not explain about 6 percent of the response time. It was found that only 14 percent of the response time was due to disk activities, whereas 46 percent of it was due to waiting for the completion of uninterruptible supervisor activities. Thus, most of the delay was found to be related to the operating system's characteristics, not to the slowness of the disk units. Even the use of infinitely fast disks would only produce a 14 percent reduction of the mean response time.

1. To verify whether there are conditions for avoiding, or postponing for some time, the acquisition of new hardware (memory, peripherals, another CPU).
2. To reduce the system's overhead and other nonproductive activities.
3. To reduce the existing workload.

The achievement of the second or third objective will increase the system's residual capacity, for example, to make room for new applications without expanding the system's configuration. Even though objectives 2 and 3 appear similar, they require totally different approaches. To reduce the nonproductive activities may entail working on the operating system and on system programs, considering a new hardware configuration, and introducing operational modifications. Reducing the workload, on the other hand, usually means improving the performance of the existing programs. It is in fact possible to analyze and optimize programs in order to reduce their resource consumption (see Chapter 8). This approach to workload reduction is particularly effective when the optimization of application programs has never been done before. In certain cases, a reduction can be obtained by moving part of the workload to another system. Both the first and, especially, the second of the objectives listed usually require that a *search for bottlenecks* be undertaken (see Sec. 6.4).

Examples of objectives that are concerned with specific aspects, and hence are more clearly defined, are:

1. To reduce by a given percentage the average terminal response time.
2. To determine whether the paging rate is so high as to require some intervention (for example, an expansion of primary memory size).
3. To determine the best allocation of volumes and files on the disks connected to the various channels.
4. To determine the demand for the teleprocessing management program, or, more in particular, to find the correlation between memory and CPU usage and the number of logged-on users.
5. To balance and optimize channel activities.

At times, in order to reach a specific objective, other problems must previously be analyzed and solved. For example, to reach objective 5, it is often necessary first to examine the activity of each channel, as well as their overlaps with each other and with the CPU. Then, the utilizations of the devices connected to the channels must be analyzed to evaluate how much each contributes to the total channel load. Finally, the frequencies of file accesses to the volumes mounted on direct-access devices must be considered. Thus, to reach the objective desired, the following actions may have to be carried out:

1. Improvement of file allocation on direct-access devices.
2. Optimal distribution of the volumes over the different devices.
3. Possible reconfiguration of the connections between channels and peripherals.

Note that action 1 reaches a specific objective on its own: it reduces the disk access time.

Clearly, the objectives listed are only some of the many possible ones. When choosing how to attack a problem, it is best not to trust too much to the most obvious solutions, even though sometimes intuition provides immediate results with very little effort. A useful example of the risks of intuitive solutions is provided by objective 1. It is commonly thought that an important cause of high terminal response time is the inadequate disk access speed for real-time applications and for the teleprocessing management program. Consequently, alternative disk units to the ones currently installed are often examined, for example fixed head disks. This choice is based on some apparently well founded reasons: the terminals are connected to very fast controllers, these are connected to a CPU that has cycle times on the order of microseconds or of fractions of a microsecond, and finally the CPU interacts with disks whose access times are on the order of tens of milliseconds. Thus, it is natural to attribute most of the delay to the slowness of the disks.

A study of this problem was performed with the aid of a hardware monitor, without disregarding any possible hypothesis [CA76]. The monitor was used to log the set of events that occurred while each user was waiting for the response at the terminal. An adequate number of measurements were collected and statistically analyzed to determine the variables that most influenced the response time. The results are shown in Table 6.1.

The measurements could not explain about 6 percent of the response time. It was found that only 14 percent of the response time was due to disk activities, whereas 46 percent of it was due to waiting for the completion of uninterruptible supervisor activities.

TABLE 6.1 FACTORS THAT INFLUENCE RESPONSE TIME [CA76]

Activity	*Influence on response time (%)*
Terminal control unit	21
Disk unit busy (access only)	14
Channel activity	5
Teleprocessing management	15
Lack of synchronism between CPU and memory cycles (inhibit pulse)	18
Supervisor not interruptible	46
Any activity	94

Thus, most of the delay was found to be related to the operating system's characteristics, not to the slowness of the disk units. Even the use of infinitely fast disks would only produce a 14 percent reduction of the mean response time.

Sometimes a clear definition of the objectives is not possible even after performing the initial phase, which has been called "understanding the system." This may be due to the existence of contradictory situations that make the problem difficult to define precisely. In these cases, the preliminary investigation should be continued to collect information that may lead the evaluator to the formulation of initial working hypotheses.

6.2 CHOICE OF INSTRUMENTS

Having defined the objectives of the study, everything that could influence them should be measured. To measure, as already stated in the previous chapters, means to collect data on system activities by suitable techniques and tools. But what techniques and tools should be used? This question immediately leads to other questions. First, are all the variables to be analyzed measurable? If yes, where? And finally, how can they be measured with sufficient accuracy? In this section we shall discuss some general aspects of a performance evaluation study, the criteria for choosing the measurement tools, and the measurability of the variables by means of these tools. We shall thus try to provide sufficiently satisfactory replies to the previous questions, capitalizing on what we have learned in the preceding chapters.

The areas to be investigated are:

1. The system's *hardware* components.
2. The system's *software,* which includes the operating system and the system's programs (teleprocessing managers, data-base management systems, spooling routines, time-sharing executives, and so on.).
3. The *workload,* seen as the set of programs the system must process during a given time period.

Hardware and software activities can be measured with hardware monitors (see Sec. 5.3) and software monitors (see Sects. 3.2, 3.3, and 5.2). Either type of tool is better than the other for certain measurements and is sometimes the only one capable of detecting certain events.

When detailed quantitative data on the resource demands of the programs are required, the workload may be analyzed with tools improperly called *accounting tools.* These are tools capable of processing the data collected by the accounting routines that log the resource requirements of each user program. They can also provide data on certain system hardware and software activities.

1. Hardware

It is essential to know the utilizations of each hardware component in order to determine whether it is overloaded, underloaded, or rightly utilized. It is always important to detect both the components causing bottlenecks and those almost inactive or underutilized. The elimination of bottlenecks and the attainment of a more balanced distribution of the loads on the hardware components is necessary to improve performance.

Determining component utilizations is also important to establish whether the system could accept workload increases without too much degradation of performance (that is, whether a portion of its capacity is still unusued).

The following lists provide, for each major hardware component, variables of immediate usefulness and the type of tool with which these variables can be measured is given.

Central processing unit.

1. *CPU busy:* this is the utilization of the CPU.
2. *CPU only:* when compared with variable 1, it allows one to quantify the degree of overlap between the CPU and other activities.
3. *CPU busy in supervisor state:* the magnitude of the system's overhead.
4. *CPU busy in user (or problem) state:* indicates how much of the CPU time is spent in user program execution.
5. *CPU busy for each user:* indicates which users contribute to the utilization in variable 4 and how much each one of them contributes.

Variables 2 through 4 can be measured with both hardware and software tools, like variable 1, which is also measurable by accounting tools. Variable 5 can only be measured with software or accounting tools.

Channels.

1. *Channel busy:* shows the utilization of each channel for data transfers to and from devices.
2. *Channel balance:* indicates the relative demands for channels and whether I/O activities are balanced for all channels; it is easily derived from the utilizations of all channels.
3. *Channel overlaps:* indicate the amounts of overlap among individual channels and between each channel and the CPU; as many overlap factors can be defined as there are combinations of two or more components.
4. *Channel queue:* shows the amount of contention for each channel, that is, whether and to what extent each channel causes a bottleneck; the mean and maximum lengths of a queue, as well as the length of time for which the queue is nonempty, are usually of interest.

Variables 1 through 3 can be measured with both hardware and software tools, while variable 4 can only be measured with software tools.

Control units.

1. *Control unit busy:* always greater than the busy time of the channel accessing it (if there is only one such channel); indeed, a control unit is busy both during the data

transfer (*busy connect* state) and during the transmission of commands to the devices and to the channels (*busy disconnect* state); a high control unit utilization could indicate the existence of an I/O request queue for one of the units connected to it; if a control unit serves channels connected to different CPUs, there may be competing requests for it.

The utilization of a control unit can only be measured with hardware tools, while control unit contention is also measurable with software tools.

Direct access (disk) devices.

1. *Device busy:* indicates how much time the disk unit spends for data read–write operations, for seeks, and in latency waits; a high device busy time is usually accompanied by a large delay in the completion of I/O requests to that device.
2. *Seek time:* indicates the time durations and frequencies of seeks; it also provides information about the adequacy of the relative positions of files on the volume mounted on each disk spindle.
3. *Device queue:* measures the length of time for which a queue is nonempty and the queue's mean length; both indexes describe the amount of contention for the device being examined.

The values of variables 1 and 2 can be measured with hardware and software tools. The measurement of device usage for data transfers only can be obtained simply with accounting tools. The data in variable 3 can only be obtained by software tools.

Sequential access units (magnetic tape units).

1. *Device busy:* measures the read–write and positioning–rewinding times of each tape unit.
2. *Allocation overlap:* refers to the overlap with the activities of other tape units; it gives an indication about whether the number of tape units in the configuration is adequate.

The values of variable 1 can be measured with software or hardware tools, those of variable 2 with software or accounting tools.

Line printer.

1. *Available time:* the printer's availability can noticeably influence the system's throughput; frequent down periods can seriously degrade global system performance, especially in certain types of system organizations.
2. *Device busy:* usually expressed in number of lines printed; in a batch environment, the printing speed of the printers can severely limit the system's throughput.

Variable 1 can be obtained with hardware or software tools, and variable 2 also with accounting tools.

2. Software

Operating system. The system's overhead always influences the performance delivered by a system as well as its capacity. The overhead may vary considerably with the characteristics of the configuration, in particular with the available memory size. Knowledge of the utilizations of system modules can be very useful when choosing the system generation parameters. It is also useful to know how the operating system uses its disk work areas (for example, the *spool* areas and the paging areas in virtual memory systems) in order to better choose the values for these parameters. This information definitely helps in the allocation of those areas and of the most often used files on disk packs. Finally, the existence of bottlenecks in an operating system function may considerably limit the system's performance.

The use of hardware tools yields very accurate measurements of CPU utilization by the operating system. However, software tools are needed to determine the utilization of each individual module and to measure resource queue lengths.

System programs and user programs. Unlike operating system modules, most system and user programs can be modified if proved inefficient. It is useful to know how much each program uses the CPU, both globally and in each of its sections or segments, and how many I/O operations it executes. Sometimes it is necessary to use hardware or software tools, since logging routines do not always measure the CPU and I/O demands of system programs.

With hardware or software monitors, it is, for example, possible to determine the frequency distribution of program instruction execution and the number of supervisor requests that each program generates.

3. Workload

The programs that process the data collected by the logging routines generally work as shown in Fig. 6.3.

Initially (a) the validity of the data is verified, as there may be inconsistencies due to anomalies in the system's behavior, and converted into a format suitable for the programs that will process it. There are then two types of data reduction: a detailed reduction (b), which covers variable time periods (a few hours, a day, or more) chosen by the evaluator to analyze specific workload situations, and a global reduction (d), which, on the basis of the contents of a *performance data base* (c) [CO72] [ME80], produces reports on the whole measured workload and on system activities during periods of fixed length (one month, one quarter, one semester, and so on). The performance data base is updated during the detailed reduction. Sometimes reductions (b) and (d) produce a breakdown, per user or groups of users, of CPU and device utilizations. It is also possible to derive, in doing this, the amounts that might have to be charged for the usage of each resource if a fair cost recovery policy is to be applied. This is what gives these routines the name of accounting tools.

The use of these tools makes it possible to obtain a wealth of data on the system's workload. For example:

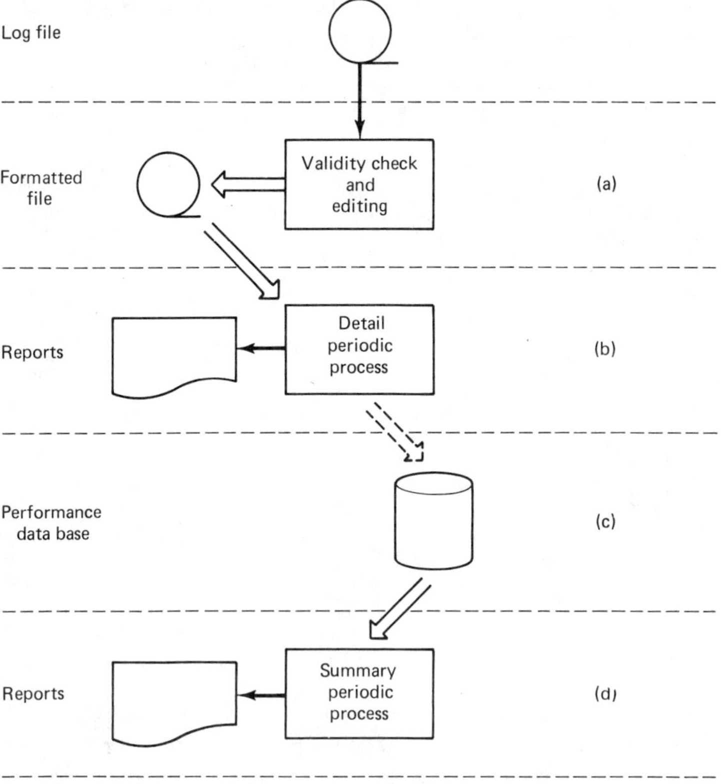

Figure 6.3 Example of logging routine data reduction.

1. Breakdown of system component activities during each shift.
2. Existence of peak loads during one or more days.
3. Behavior of the multiprogramming level in time.
4. Total number of I/O operations performed by each individual program on a given device.
5. Breakdown of CPU and I/O device activities into *on-line* and *batch* contributions.
6. Paging activity per user program (in virtual memory environments).

The precision and reliability of the measurements depends on the tool used for data collection, as well as on the way the tool is used and on the experience of its user (see Sec. 6.3).

Hardware tools have the advantages of system independence and no interference (that is, of not consuming resources during measurement periods). This is particularly true for the CPU, whose utilization can be very accurately measured with a tool of this type since it is unaffected by the uninterruptability of certain operating system activities.

TABLE 6.2 CHARACTERISTICS OF HARDWARE AND SOFTWARE MONITORS

	Sampling software monitor	*Hardware monitor*
Measurements	Quantitative (CPU, channel, disk utilizations) and descriptive (e.g., names of programs waiting for a file)	Quantitative
Operating mode	As a system or user program	Electrically connected to system
CPU overhead	1% to 6% during measurement session	None
Memory overhead	Variable (from 1 to 30 Kbytes)	None
System dependence	Hardware and operating system dependent	System independent
Flexibility	Good	Limited by the characteristics of the tool
Installation	Few minutes of computer time required	Some days and several tests required
Training	2 to 3 days	At least two weeks; user must have good knowledge of system hardware
Program performance measurements	Can measure program activities (user and system modules), control existence of queues, and measure queue lengths	Difficult or impossible, depending on monitor characteristics
Cost	$4,000 to 25,000	2 to 10 times the cost of software monitors

This problem, unfortunately, limits the accuracy of a software tool. On the other hand, hardware tools are not capable of detecting conditions that may cause resource contention. Indeed, they cannot usually inspect the request queues for the various resources. In general, hardware tools are not suitable for the direct measurement of contention.

Another characteristic of hardware monitors is their flexibility, which comes from the possibility of combining in many ways the signals coming from the sensors. In this way they permit the simultaneous observation of a large number of concurrent activities, and hence the measurement of their overlaps.

Software tools, which tend to collect data serially, although lacking a similar degree of flexibility in combining hardware component activities, adapt more easily than hardware monitors to modifications of the system's configuration. They do not require new connections between tool and system (see Secs. 5.3 and 6.3) in order to measure the new configuration, but only some slight change to the commands for data extraction. The analyst thus has a standard set of possible measurements that can be combined. This helps reduce the preparation time for a measurement session. Tables 6.2 and 6.3 summarize the main characteristics of the two types of monitor and indicate their applicability to the measurement of various quantities.

6.3 PLANNING A MEASUREMENT SESSION

Having defined the objectives of the study, detected the specific problems to be solved to reach these objectives, and chosen the tool or tools, the measurement experiments must now be carefully planned before they are actually performed.

TABLE 6.3 APPLICABILITY OF TOOLS TO THE MEASUREMENT OF SYSTEM VARIABLES*

Variables	*Tool*
CPU	
Total utilization	H/S/A
Total supervisor utilization	H/S
Total user program utilization	H/S/A
Single user program utilization	H/S/A
Single system module utilization	S
Queue of requests	S
Channels	
Channel utilization	H/S/A
Channel balance	H/S
CPU–channel overlap	H/S
Operating system	
Allocation activities	S/A
Memory usage	H/S/A
Queue to serial resources	S
Direct access devices	
Availability	H/S
Total utilization	H/S
Seek time	H/S
Error recovery	H/S
Space allocation	S/A
Latency time	H
Overlapped seeks	H
Tape units	
Availability	H/S
Total utilization	H/S
Allocation overlap	H/S
Rewind time	H
Workload	
Peak periods	H/S/A
Multiprogramming level	H/S/A
CPU time per program	S/A
Paging activity per user program	S/A
I/O operations per user program	A

S, software tool, H, hardware tool, A, accounting tool

As it is not possible to discuss in detail the various aspects of this planning activity without referring to a specific workload, configuration, and environment, in what follows we shall only make general considerations that are valid when using any type of tool. We shall also note the operational differences between the two types of measurement and indicate the possible causes of operator errors in both cases.

To plan a measurement session, the workload and its evolution in time must be at least roughly known. The measurement must be made in a "controlled" environment: the workload should be known and no hardware modifications should be carried out during the session, nor should any change be made to the normal operational procedures.

To know the workload means to possess information on its characteristics during the different shifts and on its variations during each day, week, or month. Thus, the occurrence times of its peaks must also be at least approximately known and taken into account in the planning of the experiments, which usually include measurements during peak periods. For instance, if the response time of a real-time system is particularly long in the morning, data useful for improving it will not usually be obtained by afternoon measurements.

When planning measurements with a software monitor, one must remember that such a monitor is a program and therefore must reside, partially or completely, in the system's main memory for execution. A software tool can either be an application program (as is the case of many sampling software tools on the market) or part of the operating system (for example, on-line samplers, event detectors, tracers). Thus, less main memory will be available to users when the tool is active.

Normally, a software monitor's memory demand is moderate (up to a few Kbytes). But if the operating system subdivides the memory into a fixed number n of predefined partitions, one of these will have to be allocated to the measurement tool, unless the tool is in memory as a part of the operating system itself. In the former case, at most $n - 1$ simultaneous program executions can be planned during the measurement session; in the latter, a slight reduction of the memory space available to users should be expected.

In virtual memory environments (see Sec. 7.4), this problem has different aspects and is in practice less important. On the other hand, the interference caused by the tool's CPU overhead when the tool is active is almost always, and for all systems, a more delicate problem.

For tracing tools (see Sec. 3.2), the CPU overhead in time (the fraction of the total time the CPU is used by the tool) increases with the number of events detected. The collection of the data must thus be limited only to the detection of those events whose tracing is considered essential for a complete handling of the problems to be solved. Also, with sampling tools, the CPU overhead grows with the number of different data items collected; in this case, however, it is not the overhead per unit time but the total overhead that is to be considered.

The total CPU time consumed by the tool can be kept roughly constant, independent of the measurement session's duration if the sampling interval (see Sec. 5.2) is properly selected. The accuracy of the results given by a sampler depends, under certain assumptions, on the total number of elements in the sample and not on the sampling frequency (see Sec. 3.3). Because of this, it is important to define the length of the measurement session (hence, the sampling frequency) so as to perturb the system as little as possible while obtaining sufficiently accurate results.

The characteristics of the workload must not be ignored. Indeed, reconsidering the example in Table 5.1, and assuming that bottlenecks arise during the first shift but not during the second, the sample should be extracted only during the first shift, even though this will double the CPU overhead. Clearly, the data collected in this way will provide more useful information.

The statement concerning maintaining the CPU overhead constant must be explained. It is undoubtedly true that this possibility exists if the tool allows only one measurement interval duration to be specified, that is, if this length is the same for all the quantities to be measured. However, the statement may not be valid if the user has the possibility of selecting different sampling intervals for the different activities to be observed (this facility exists in practically all commercial software monitors). Thus, for example, to observe disk file accesses or to measure the frequency of system module loadings from disk, the extraction interval should be relatively short (20 to 30 ms) if detailed and reliable data are required. This interval is, of course, independent of the session's length. Thus, the CPU overhead is in some way related to the measured quantities.

The preparation of a session with a hardware monitor has different and perhaps more complex aspects than that of a session with a software monitor, although the problem of minimizing the interference does not arise. The first requirement is a list of the connection addresses of the sensors to the various hardware devices. The reliability and completeness of this list is fundamental for the correctness of the signals to be monitored. Experience has shown that there is nothing easier than connecting sensors incorrectly. Another common source of errors is given by faulty grounding of system equipment. This may cause distortions in the signals collected, making the measurements incorrect or, at least, questionable.

Other problems to be kept in mind are:

1. The length of the connecting cables: long cables can delay some signals with respect to others, whose cables are shorter.
2. The choice of signals: often more than one signal is available for detecting the same event or measuring the same quantity.
3. The combination of signals by making use of logical circuits.
4. The differences between signals representing a given variable in different models of the same hardware component; errors can easily be made when changing models without verifying signal validity again.

Since hardware monitors normally remain connected to the system being measured for rather long time periods, it is important to verify the results carefully. This verification will allow the evaluator to detect periods during which the measurements may have been affected by exceptional events (short circuits, electromagnetic noise, and so on) or by the interruption of system activity for maintenance purposes (some systems require that the CPU be in supervisor state during maintenance).

6.4 BOTTLENECK DETECTION

As we saw in Sec. 6.1, a considerable part of the activities for system performance improvement are concerned with the detection and elimination of bottlenecks. A *bottleneck* is a limitation of system performance due to the inadequacy of a hardware or software component or of the system's organization. The term bottleneck is sometimes used to indicate the component or part of the system that causes the bottleneck. Thus, people say that a disk, or a compiler, is a bottleneck rather than, more correctly, the cause of a bottleneck.

A bottleneck causes a considerable slowing down of the traffic of processes in a particular area of a system. When the service requests for a given component exceed in frequency and intensity the service capacity of that component, the conditions for the appearance of a bottleneck arise. However, a bottleneck will appear only if the other system components are relatively less requested and thus work at a less intense pace. Because of the nature of the requests each process makes sequentially and not simultaneously for most resources, if a bottleneck arises in a part of the system, the other parts become much more lightly loaded. Indeed, many active processes end up in the wait queues of the overloaded resources and cannot contribute to other queues. In a system in which all or most components are overloaded, specific sources of bottlenecks cannot be found; this kind of system, which is said to be *saturated,* is clearly too small for its workload. To improve performance, a more powerful system should replace it or the workload should be reduced.

The term bottleneck is only appropriate when the responsibility for insufficient or unsatisfactory performance can be attributed to one or two system resources. When a bottleneck occurs, any attempt to eliminate it will be almost useless unless such an attempt is directly concerned with the component (or components) causing the bottleneck. The effect of a faster CPU on a system in which the insufficient speed of a channel causes a bottleneck is easily imagined. Although quite expensive, this change will have practically no effect on the system's throughput and mean weighted turnaround time, but will only contribute to the traffic jam in the channel. Therefore, bottleneck detection is vitally important. Only by acting on components causing bottlenecks can advantages be obtained that justify the costs of system improvement.

This leads to an extension of our definition of bottleneck, which only applies to multiprogramming systems where many processes are simultaneously active and request services from various resources. The wider definition, which could be called *economic* because it is based on the cost–benefit ratio, applies also to uniprogramming systems, and in fact to any type of system. According to this definition, a part of the system causes a bottleneck if the incremental improvement of the system's performance (to be properly defined) is maximum per unit cost invested in it.

The application of this definition to programs will be studied in Chapter 8. Its use in determining the component(s) that limits the throughput and turnaround time of a uniprogramming system is obvious and needs no further comment. More will be said on the cost–benefit ratio in Chapter 10. In the rest of this chapter and in Chapter 7, we shall only discuss multiprogramming systems. Thus, we shall refer to the restricted definition of bottleneck, which is still the one generally adopted in the technical literature. In Sec. 6.4.1 we shall describe an iterative method for bottleneck detection based on the off-line interpretation of measurement results. Examples of the use of that method are given in Chapter 7. There are many other approaches to this type of bottleneck detection, all conceptually similar, but based on different techniques (for example, simulation or analytic modeling). But the one consisting of data collection with standard tools and of off-line interpretation is the most common because the tools are available on the market and thus can be immediately used.

The conceptual procedure common to these methods is shown schematically in Fig. 6.4. Symptoms of inefficiency, or the results of regular verification of system performance, lead the evaluator to wonder about the possible existence of bottlenecks, their locations, and the availability of economically justifiable methods for their elimination. Then a hypothesis on what causes the bottleneck is formulated, and its validity is verified by

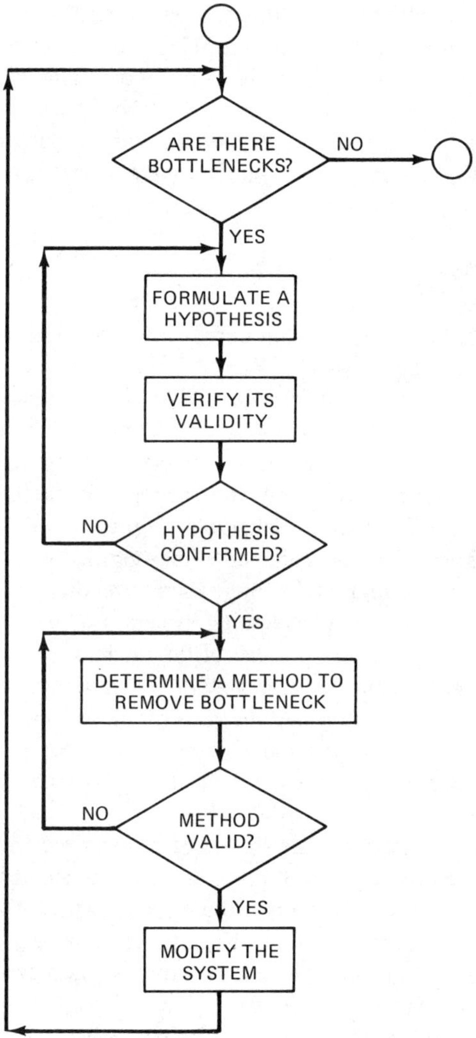

Figure 6.4 Iterative removal of bottlenecks.

analyzing the data collected or by collecting more data and analyzing them in turn. When a hypothesis is confirmed, we face the problem of eliminating the bottleneck or at least of reducing its effects. Sometimes, the removal of a bottleneck causes another to appear. This bottleneck can in turn be studied with the same procedure, which is repeated until the system is *balanced,* that is, bottleneck free.

Bottlenecks are not inherent to a given configuration, but mostly depend on the workload. Given two identical configurations with different workloads, one of them could have a bottleneck in a given resource while the other could have one in another, or none at all. Since the workload of many systems varies, even considerably, in time, transient bottlenecks may appear for a relatively short time with respect to a session's length.

These bottlenecks, which show up as temporary peaks of traffic, may not be easily detected when analyzing the cumulative data collected by the measurement tools during an experiment. Also, it may be very difficult to correlate these phenomena with their causes, so as to understand and cure them efficiently, hours or days after the measurements were taken. These problems vanish or are considerably reduced if the evaluator is capable of controlling the partial results of an on-line experiment during the session itself. An example of bottleneck detection based on an on-line measurement tool will be described in Sec. 6.4.2.

6.4.1 Off-line Bottleneck Detection

The bottlenecks of a system can be detected through experiments during which suitable tools collect data to be analyzed later by the evaluator. As an example, we shall briefly describe a procedure based on the use of the commercial software monitor CUE [CU77]. A flow chart of this procedure is presented in Fig. 6.5. This flow chart refers to three sets of data that the tool can provide: one concerning the operating system calls (SVC's), one giving the arm movements for each disk unit, and one regarding hardware utilization. Each set of data is analyzed according to the scheme in Fig. 6.4.

The hypotheses are suggested by the data, sometimes verified with other data, and, if their validity is confirmed with a high probability, used to modify the relevant part of the system being evaluated. In the case of operating system modules, one of the main changes that can be suggested is to modify the list of the modules permanently resident in main memory. Some of the choices made at system generation time may no longer be valid with the current workload, thereby causing *resident* modules to be used less than *nonresident* modules. When analyzing arm movements, an obvious therapy that could be suggested is that of file reorganization, which consists of moving files from disk to disk, or from a part of a disk to another.

Sometimes, tools may suggest how files should be reorganized. Some instruments are even capable, based on previous results, of providing an estimate of the time savings that can be obtained by implementing the reorganization that they recommend.

The hypotheses that can be formulated on the basis of hardware component utilizations and the possible system modifications that they may suggest are more numerous and more complex. Result interpretation often uses graphical techniques for presenting utilization profiles, continuous diagrams, and Kiviat graphs (see Chapter 4).

When the main objective is to maximize a system's throughput, the actions to be performed on the basis of utilization data must:

- Balance the system by eliminating the major bottlenecks
- Maximize the overlaps of the various activities
- Minimize the time during which the system is idle

These three objectives are, as we shall see, distinct but not disjoint; some system modifications bring the system close to achieving more than one of them.

Considering a utilization profile (see Sec. 4.2.1), it is easy to see how all these objectives derive from the objective of maximizing the throughput. Given a certain workload, the throughput with which it is processed is inversely proportional to the processing time. The latter can be reduced by increasing the overlap, reducing the idle

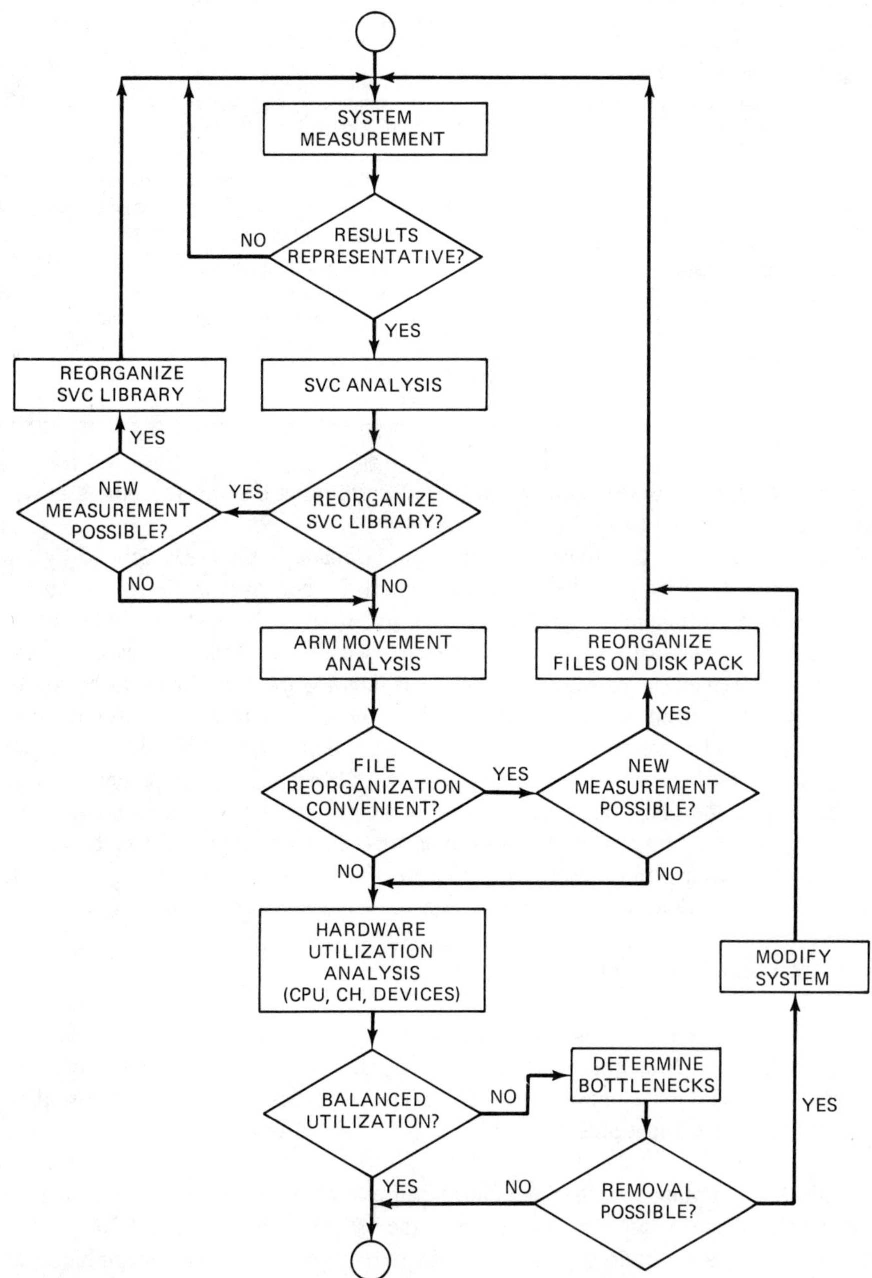

Figure 6.5 Flow chart of a bottleneck detection process.

TABLE 6.4 HYPOTHESES THAT MAY BE SUGGESTED BY UTILIZATION DATA

Symptom	*Hypothesis*
The utilization of a hardware component is much higher than those of all the others.	There is a bottleneck in the component.
The overlaps of some activities are insufficient.	1. The number of programs that can be multiprogrammed is too low. 2. The competition for some resources causes congestion, hence one or more bottlenecks. 3. The scheduling of programs is unable to mix various types of programs effectively.
The system is idle for too long a time.	1. The number of programs is insufficient to make the system busier. 2. Too much time is lost in mounting and dismounting disks or tapes. 3. The amount of seek time nonoverlapped to other activities is excessive.

time, and reducing the workload on the saturated units (thus making the others busier and increasing the possibility of activity overlaps).

Table 6.4 presents a few hypotheses that can be made in the areas defined by the objectives just listed. These hypotheses usually require further investigations. It is sometimes possible to perform such investigations with the existing data, while at other times it is necessary, or better, to remeasure the system (see Fig. 6.5). In any case, for the results of a measurement to be representative, and thus for the experiment to be reproducible, the workload must be *representative*. Thus, the system must be measured either under a test workload representing as accurately as possible the real workload or under the real workload during the periods of interest. The former solution is potentially less representative than the latter but requires shorter measurement sessions to provide the same accuracy. On the other hand, a natural workload does not require the system to be completely dedicated, and thus allows users to access the system during the experiments, while an artificial workload is much more under the experimenter's control.

6.4.2 On-line Bottleneck Detection

To describe briefly the principles and possibilities of on-line bottleneck detection, we shall refer to the commercial software tool LOOK [LO77]. Some hardware tools, not only among the commercial ones, have similar characteristics, in that they allow their user to follow an experiment and the variations of the quantities being measured in real time.

LOOK is a sampling software tool capable of extracting variable-sized samples (at least 100 elements) during an interval chosen by the user (but between 5 and 300 s). The overhead it produces depends on the user's requests, but is usually acceptable. The commands, which can be entered from any authorized console or terminal, are listed and briefly described in Table 6.5. The results are displayed on a display screen or, if high speed is not required, on a console's teleprinter. LOOK also provides the facility of logging all the results and printing them at the end of the measurement.

TABLE 6.5 MAIN COMMANDS OF AN ON-LINE SOFTWARE TOOL [LO77]

Command	*Description*
D CPU	Displays information about the utilization of the CPU by the various programs and by the operating system
D I/O	Displays information about the utilization, the seek times, and the channel wait times of all files requested by the active programs, of all devices and of all channels
D PAGE	Displays the number of pages of each active program, the total paging rate, and other performance information about a virtual memory system
D M	Displays a memory map, distinguishing between allocated memory and utilized memory
D WAIT	Displays a list of waiting programs and messages, with the respective reasons for waiting

A possible application of a real-time software monitor is shown in Fig. 6.6. The flow chart describes the commands, hypotheses, and changes that it would be reasonable to make if the system were exceedingly slow. The first command, D CPU, displays the name of each active program, the step it is at, the percentage of time it has spent in the CPU, the percentage of time it has spent waiting for the CPU or for the various I/O devices, and its priority. It is thus fairly easy, even for an inexperienced evaluator, to reply to the questions following the issuing of the D CPU command in the flow chart in Fig. 6.6.

Depending on the replies given to the questions, different actions are taken, many of which aim at the removal of the transient bottlenecks mentioned in Section 6.4. If the system's situation leads the evaluator along certain paths, other commands must be given. For example, the D I/O or D CPU command may have to be repeated a few times. In the diagram there are commands like D PAGE and D WAIT, which do not appear in the figure.

LOOK responds to the D I/O command by outputing a table containing, for each active file, its device type (channel, disk, tape) and device number, its usage and volume, the program and step using it, and the average arm movement time (in cylinders). Also, the total utilization of each device and the fraction of time spent by it waiting for the channel are given. The flow chart in Fig. 6.6. and the operational charts in Tables 6.6 and 6.7 represent a possible track for the evaluator's actions, to be followed when malfunctionings seem to appear or the system's performance drops. These measures will make it possible to keep the system's performance at a suitable level, to make the execution of routine functions faster and, generally, to manage the available resources better.

The main advantages of the on-line method, which make it interesting and sometimes particularly useful, are the speed with which important symptoms are detected, the ease with which their causes are often found, and the possibility of quickly removing many of the temporary bottlenecks that occur.

6.5 BOTTLENECK REMOVAL

Often in evaluation studies the removal of a bottleneck is attempted as soon as a probable cause is identified. This is the case, for example, when measurement techniques are used, since further bottlenecks cannot be detected until the main one is removed. And, when the detection is carried out on-line, some (often transient) bottlenecks can be removed

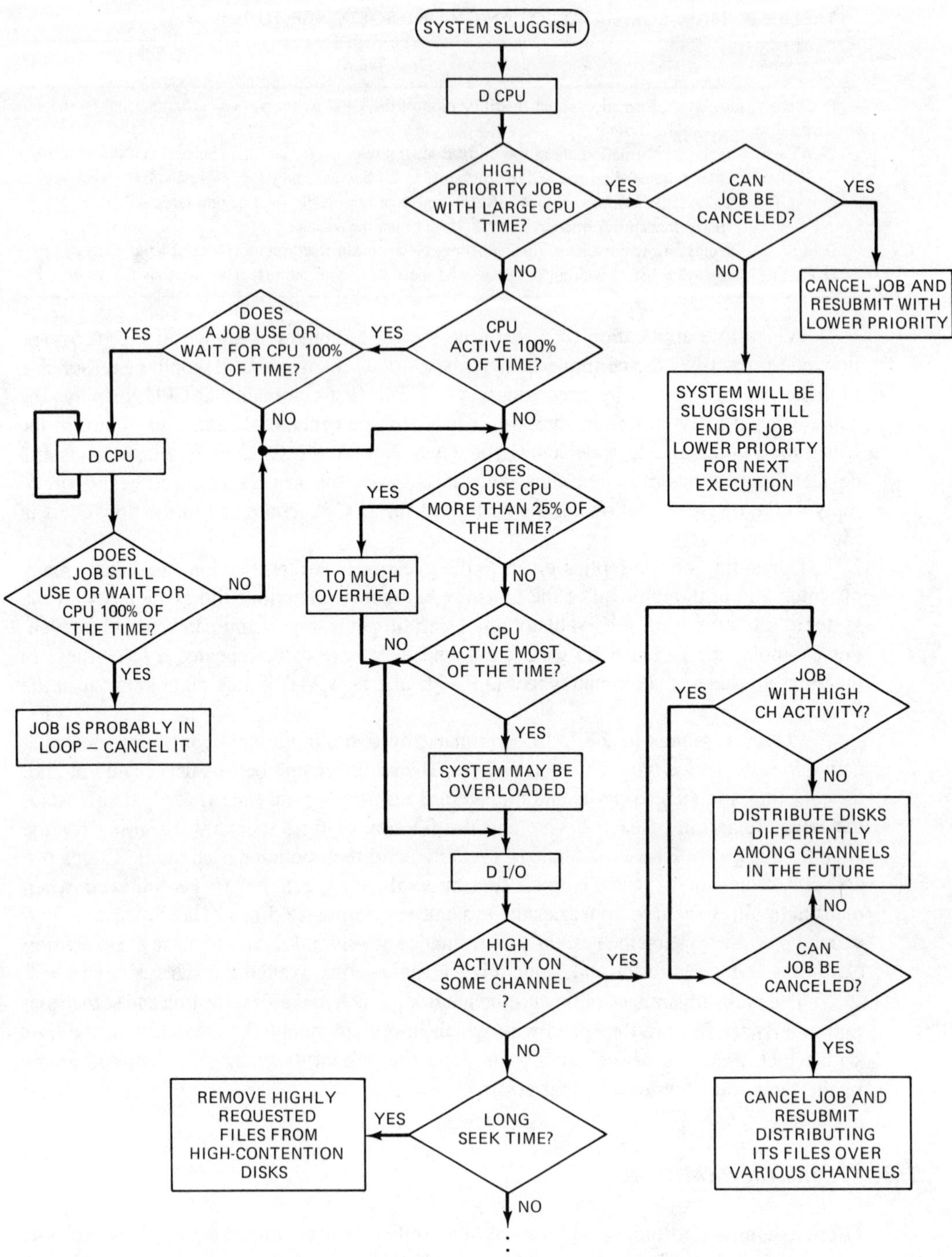

Figure 6.6 Flow chart of an on-line software tool application [LO77].

TABLE 6.6 ON-LINE OPERATIONS WITH AN EXCESSIVELY SLOW JOB

Symptom
- Program is proceeding too sluggishly

Actions
- Check whether the program is inactive (i.e., waiting) or in an infinite loop:
  - If in loop, cancel it
  - If inactive, check whether there are messages pending for the operator
  - If so, answer; otherwise, increase the program's priority
- Check whether there is a situation of contention for I/O devices (either not allocated to the program or monopolized by another program):
  - If so, try to avoid running programs during successive executions that require the exclusive use of those I/O devices
- If the system has virtual memory, check the value of the system's paging rate and that of the program's paging rate:
  - If the system's paging rate is high, the multiprogramming level is probably too high; stop temporarily the initiation of new programs
  - If the program's paging rate is high, it should be restructured to increase its locality

immediately. Thus, it is not realistic to assume that bottlenecks and, more generally, inefficiencies can all be detected first and then, later, all eliminated together. Nevertheless, the types of actions one can take for this removal are conceptually the same, whether measurement tools (on-line and off-line) or modeling techniques are used.

First, the changes to be made must be chosen. Having verified the hypothesis that, say, a system disk causes the main bottleneck does not mean that the actions to be taken are clearly and completely defined. In this case, the system's performance can be improved in many ways, for instance by:

1. Replacing the disk device with a faster one.
2. Moving some of the most frequently used files to disk packs to be mounted on less loaded disk drives.
3. Reallocating disk space to reduce arm movements.
4. Modifying the arm scheduling policy to reduce seeks, or the waits caused by disk's latencies, or both these sources of inefficiency.

TABLE 6.7 ON-LINE ACTIONS WHEN THE CPU IS IDLE

Symptom
- CPU is idle

Actions
- Check whether there are any pending messages
- Check whether there is a deadlock:
  - If so, cancel one of the programs
- Check whether there is any I/O operation that cannot be completed due to the loss of an I/O interrupt:
  - Restore the connection with the appropriate I/O device

These actions are not mutually exclusive. On the contrary, the bottleneck caused by the disk can be cured by the simultaneous application of more than one therapy. The risks and costs of a cure vary with the cure. Thus, the therapies to be adopted should be carefully selected, evaluating the cost–benefit convenience of undertaking each cure for removing the bottleneck. These decisions will be based on the results of further measurements or analyses.

As seen in Sec. 6.4, and in the preceding example, there are two major classes of system modifications for the elimination of a bottleneck:

1. Hardware modifications: the addition, replacement, or even sometimes removal of one or more hardware components.
2. Modifications that do not change the configuration but somehow have effects on the system's organization.

The modifications in these classes can be called *upgrading* (1) and *tuning* (2) therapies, respectively. These terms are normally used more restrictively, but will be employed here in the more general sense of the preceding definitions. The former are usually more radical; the latter can be riskier if they require system software changes not foreseen by the software designers. Usually, tuning therapies are cheaper. The most expensive and risky changes should anyway only be made when the evaluators are quite sure of the convenience of their implementation. In other words, their influence on system performance should be reliably predicted. This is the type of problem that a suitable and sufficiently accurate model is or should be able to solve completely. One can, for example, use a simulator or an analytic model. Alternatively, one could take the risk and modify the system without having studied the effects of the changes. In doing this, performance analysts will usually be helped by their knowledge of the system, the workload, and the main advantages those particular tuning therapies usually provide in similar cases.

REFERENCES

Entries marked with an asterisk (*) are referenced in the text.

[AN72] Anderson, H. A., Jr., Sargent, R. G., Modeling, evaluation and performance measurements of time-sharing computer systems, *Comput. Rev.*, vol. 13, pp. 603–608, 1972.

[BA71] Bard, Y., Performance criteria and measurement for a time-sharing system, *IBM Systems J.*, vol. 10, n. 3, 1971.

[BA76] Bard, Y., An experimental approach to system tuning, *Proc. International Symposium on Computer Performance Modeling, Measurement and Evaluation*, pp. 296–305, March 1976.

[BE73a] Beilner, H., The method of good balance: A tool for improving computing system performance, *Proc. Computer Science and Statistics: 7th Annual Symp. on the Interface*, pp. 110–116, Oct. 1973.

[BE72] Bell, T. E., Boehm, B. W., Watson, R. A., Framework and initial phases for computer performance improvement, *AFIPS Conf. Proc. FJCC*, vol. 41, pp. 1141–1154, 1972.

[BE73b] Bell, T. E., Performance determination—The selection of tools, if any, *AFIPS Conf. Proc. NCC,* pp. 31–38, 1973.

[BE74] Bell, T.E., Computer performance variability, *AFIPS Conf. Proc. NCC,* vol. 43, pp. 761–766, 1974.

[BL72] Blatny, J., Clark, S. R., Rourke, T. A., On the optimization of performance of time-sharing systems by simulation, *CACM,* vol. 15, n. 6, June 1972.

[BO75] Boyse, J. W., Warn, D. R., A straightforward model for computer performance prediction, *ACM Computing Surveys,* vol. 7, n. 2, pp. 73–93, June 1975.

[BR72] Brookman, P. G., Brotman, B. A., Use of measurement engineering for better system performance, *Computer Decisions,* Apr. 1972.

[BU73] Burke, E. L., A computer architecture for system performance monitoring, *Proc. 1st SIGME Symposium on Measurement and Evaluation,* pp. 161–169, Feb. 1973.

[BU71] Buzen, J. P., Analysis of system bottlenecks using a queueing network model, *Proc. ACM-SIGOPS Workshop on System Performance Evaluation,* pp. 82–103, Harvard University, Cambridge, Mass., Apr. 1971.

[CA71a] Callaway, P., Performance considerations for the use of the virtual machine capability, *IBM Research Report RC-3360,* Yorktown Heights, N.Y., May 12, 1971.

[CA71b] Carlson, G., A user's view of hardware performance monitors or how to get more computer for your dollar, *Proc. IFIP Congress 71,* pp. 128–132, Aug. 1971.

*[CA76] Carlson, G., Fallacies of intuition of performance tuning, *EDP Performance Review,* vol. 4, n. 4, Apr. 1976.

[CH78] Chandy, K. M., Yeh, R. T., eds., *Current Trends in Programming Methodology: Vol. III—Software Modeling,* Prentice-Hall, Englewood Cliffs, N.J., 1978.

[CO71] Cockrum, J. S., Crockett, D. E., Interpreting the results of a hardware systems monitor, *AFIPS Conf. Proc. SJCC,* vol. 38, pp. 23–38, 1971.

*[CO72] Cooperman, T. A., Lynch, H. W., Tetzlaff, W. H., SGP. An effective use of performance and usage data, *Computer,* vol. 5, n. 5, pp. 20–23, Sept.–Oct. 1972.

*[CU77] *CUE—User Guide—Version 3.5,* Boole & Babbage Inc., Sunnyvale, Calif., March 1977.

[DE71] DeMeis, W. M., Weizer, N., Measurement and analysis of a demand paging time-sharing system, *Proc. 24th Nat. Conf. on Systems Science,* University of Hawaii, pp. 449–451, Jan. 12–14, 1971.

[DE71] Denning, P. J., Eisentein, B. A., Statistical methods in performance evaluation, *Proc. ACM SIGOPS Workshop on System Performance Evaluation,* pp. 284–307, Harvard University, Cambridge, Mass., Apr. 1971.

[DE73] Denning, P. J., Why our approach to performance evaluation is Sdrawkcab, *ACM SIGMETRICS Perf. Evaluat. Review,* vol. 2, n. 3, pp. 13–16, Sept. 1973.

[DR73] Drummond, M. E., *Evaluation and Measurement Techniques for Digital Computer Systems,* Prentice-Hall, Englewood Cliffs, N.J., 1973.

[FR72] Freiberger, W., ed., *Statistical Computer Performance Evaluation,* Academic Press, New York, 1972.

[GR72] Grenander, U., Tsao, R. F., Quantitative methods for evaluating computers system performance: A review and proposals, in: Freiberger, W., ed., *Statistical Computer Performance Evaluation,* pp. 3–24, Academic Press, New York, 1972.

*[HO77] How to get started in performance evaluation, *EDP Performance Review,* vol. 5, n. 6, June 1977.

[HU73] Hughes, P. H., Moe, G., A structural approach to computer performance analysis, *AFIPS Conf. Proc. NCC,* vol. 42, p. 109, 1973.

[KI72] Kimbleton, S. R., Performance evaluation—A structured approach. *AFIPS Conf. Proc. SJCC,* pp. 411–416, 1972.

[KI75] Kimbleton, S. R., A heuristic approach to computer systems performance improvement. I. A fast performance prediction tool, *AFIPS Conf. Proc. NCC,* Vol. 44, pp. 839–846, 1975.

*[LO77] *LOOK User Handbook,* Applied Data Research Inc., Princeton, N.J., Sept. 1977.

[LU71] Lucas, H. C., Performance evaluation and monitoring. *Computing Surveys,* vol. 3, n. 3, pp. 79–91, Sept. 1971.

*[ME80] Merrill, H. W., *Merrill's Guide to Performance Evaluation,* SAS Institute, Inc., Cary, N.C., 1980.

[NO74] Noe, J. D., Acquiring and using a hardware monitor, *Datamation,* pp. 89–95, Apr. 1974.

[PE74] Peterson, T. G., A comparison of software and hardware monitors, *ACM SIGMETRICS Perf. Evaluat. Review,* vol. 3, n. 3, pp. 2–5, Sept. 1974.

[RO72] Rodriguez-Rosell, J., Dupuy, J., The evaluation of a time-sharing page demand system, *AFIPS Conf. Proc. SJCC,* pp. 759–765, 1972.

[SH74] Shetler, A. C., Controlled testing for computer performance evaluation, *AFIPS Conf. Proc. NCC,* pp. 693–699, 1974.

[SV73] Svobodova, L., Online system performance measurements with software and hybrid monitors, *Operating Systems Review,* vol. 7, n. 4, pp. 45–53, Oct. 1973.

[SV76] Svobodova, L., Computer system measurability, *Computer,* vol. 9, pp. 9–17, June 1976.

[WA73] Waldbaum, G., Evaluating computing system changes by means of regression models, *Proc. 1st ACM-SICME Symposium on Measurement and Evaluation,* pp. 127–135, Feb. 1973.

[WI73] Winder, R. O., A data base for computer performance evaluation, *Computer,* vol. 6, n. 3, pp. 25–29, March 1973.

7

SYSTEM TUNING

7.1 INTRODUCTION

In this chapter the evaluation methodologies and techniques previously described are applied to the study of some practical performance improvement studies. The analysis of the various cases will allow us to follow the strategy adopted each time and to evaluate the effectiveness of the actions undertaken.

The cases described have been chosen to illustrate general problems that are encountered in most studies and by most evaluators. For greater generality, we shall not describe in detail the technical characteristics of the components involved in the studies or those of the measurement tools used; we shall only give indications useful for understanding the choices made to solve the problems encountered in each study. In some cases the objectives of the study are of a general nature, for instance, the reduction of response and turnaround times, while in others they are more specific, like the optimization of file allocation on a disk unit or the balancing of channel loads. Even in the latter type of study, however, the final goal is to improve the performance indexes we are interested in.

The descriptions of the cases are sometimes incomplete; for the sake of brevity we have chosen to describe only the most characteristic aspects of the situations encountered by the evaluators. With the presentation of these cases we want to provide paths that may be followed in tuning projects, both when selecting the necessary measurements and instruments and when deciding which actions are required to reach the desired objectives. Readers will sometimes be able to identify their problems with those dealt with in one or more studies, although perhaps only partially and incompletely, and will find a methodology that can be followed for attacking them.

The descriptions of the cases follow the flow chart shown in Fig. 1.1 and are presented with a common format, which consists of these three steps:

1. *The problem:* the problem being faced is briefly described, the external symptoms of inefficiency that motivated the decision to undertake the study are discussed, and the system's configuration, as well as the objectives to be reached, is presented.
2. *Measurements and interpretation:* the measurement results are given, using some of the graphical techniques described in Chapter 4, and, on the basis of the measured values, improvement hypotheses are formulated.
3. *Actions and verification of their effects:* on the basis of the hypotheses formulated, the changes made for system improvement and their effects are described; if the bottlenecks have been totally or partially removed, and the results satisfy the objectives of the study, the study is considered completed; otherwise, step 2 is repeated, and so on.

The problems have been somewhat artificially subdivided into those concerned with (1) multiprogramming batch systems (MBRS) (for example, load balancing, correct sizing, more efficient scheduling), (2) interactive systems (MIRS) with a mixed load (response time reduction, adequate workload subdivision in twin systems), and (3) virtual memory systems (MIVRS) (correct memory sizing, virtual memory influence on throughput, performance degradation due to excessive paging). Finally, the problems connected with the use of data bases are discussed, and some general criteria for optimizing such use are defined.

Chapter 8 is devoted to the problem of program performance improvement. Case studies illustrating the applications of analytic modeling techniques to system tuning are presented in Chapter 9. The economic advantages that may be obtained from some of the improvement studies discussed will be described in Chapter 10.

7.2 BALANCING A MULTIPROGRAMMING SYSTEM

In this section we shall describe some evaluation studies aimed at improving the performance of a multiprogramming system. The systems considered are both of the MBRS type and of the mixed (batch and interactive, MIRS) type. The problems and solutions discussed apply equally well to all multiprogramming systems, independent of their type. Sections 7.3 and 7.4, on the other hand, illustrate problems that are peculiar to interactive systems, without and with virtual memory, respectively.

To improve a multiprogramming system's performance, the first step is to establish whether there are any bottlenecks and, if so, where. After the diagnosis phase, there must be a therapy phase, in which the bottlenecks are eliminated or reduced. Often, the existence of a bottleneck is revealed, as mentioned in Sec. 6.4, by imbalances in the activities of the system's components. The case described in Sec. 7.2.2, however, shows that this is not always true: a system could be relatively well balanced and yet have bottlenecks. This is not only the case when the main bottleneck is caused by an insufficient main memory size. It has been proved [BU71a] that a perfectly balanced system does not usually produce a maximum performance. Let us consider, for example, a system with two disk units having average service times (sum of the seek, latency, and data transfer times) of 10 and 20 ms, respectively (see Fig. 7.1). If the total request rate for the two disks is 45 requests per second, it would seem reasonable to subdivide it between the disks so that their utilizations are identical. This can be done by sending 30 requests per second to the faster unit and 15 to the slower. If we assume that the interarrival times and the service times are exponentially distributed, the mean response time of each disk is (see Secs. 9.4 and 9.4.2)

$$R_i = \frac{S_i}{1 - S_i\lambda_i} \qquad (i = 1, 2) \tag{7.1}$$

where S_i is the mean service time and λ_i is the arrival frequency of the ith device. This formula gives mean response times of 14.2 ms for the faster disk and of 28.4 ms for the slower. The mean response time R for the disk complex is therefore

$$R = \frac{\lambda_1}{\lambda} R_1 + \frac{\lambda_2}{\lambda} R_2 = 19 \text{ ms} \tag{7.2}$$

This performance, which corresponds to a situation of equal disk utilizations (both are on the average busy 30 percent of the time, since $S_1\lambda_1 = S_2\lambda_2 = 0.3$) and thus of load balance, can be improved. If, for example, 38 requests per second are sent to the

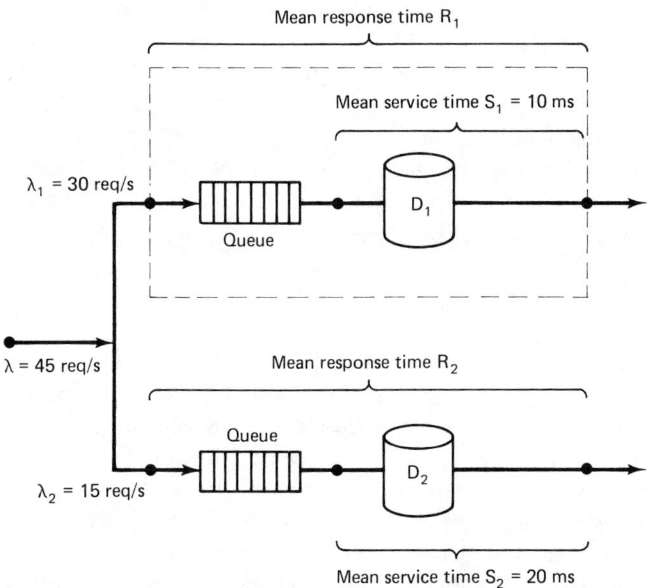

Figure 7.1 Workload subdivision between two disks of different speeds to equalize their utilizations.

faster disk and only 7 to the slower, response times of 16.1 ms and 23.2 ms, respectively, are obtained. The weighted average of these times, from Eq. (7.2), is 17.2 ms, thus noticeably less (by roughly 10 percent) than the average produced by the system with perfectly balanced loads. Thus, a higher performance is obtained when the faster components (except the CPU) are more heavily loaded than the slower. The system's state of balance can give valuable information on the existence of bottlenecks but not on their absence, nor can it be considered a precise indicator of the system's "distance" from its point of maximum performance.

When diagnosis reveals that the system is highly unbalanced, or at least potentially improvable, it is necessary to go on to the therapy phase after having evaluated the convenience of an improvement action. The following cases discuss examples of successful therapies. However, the actions to be described do not exhaust those that can be undertaken to eliminate bottlenecks, balance channels, improve overlaps, and so on. In particular, an important set of improvement actions are those concerning the workload: a system's performance can be improved by acting on the workload rather than on the system itself. Chapter 8 illustrates the major methods that can be used to make the programs in the workload more efficient. Another method of workload improvement, which may be used to balance the resource requests, consists of modifying the loading and execution order of the programs. Thus, for example, it is useful to execute together programs that have high CPU usage and programs that have high I/O activity. If there are great concentrations of similar programs in memory, they can create temporary bottlenecks at the CPU, at the channels, or at the secondary storage devices. The input job mix is prepared by the scheduler, which must base its decisions on the data given to the operating system by the user (through job control language or interactive commands) and, in more sophisticated systems, on measurements collected in previous executions of the same program or during that part of the program's execution that may have preceded the time of the decision. To act on the internal scheduler, when this can be done, is one way to influence the job mix, that is, the composition of the instantaneous workload.

In many installations it is clearly possible to act on external scheduling by properly instructing the machine operator. The less homogeneous the programs in the workload, and the greater the freedom to change their order and time of execution, the more successful these methods are likely to be.

7.2.1 Case 7.1: Bottlenecks in Disks and Channels

The problem. The configuration of the MBRS system being considered is shown in Fig. 7.2. The size of main memory M is 1024K characters; M is subdivided into seven partitions, five of which are dedicated to the execution of the programs being tested, one is used by the system, and one is reserved for urgent, high-priority programs. Administrative programs constitute 80 percent of the workload, and scientific applications account for the remaining 20 percent. The disk units connected to channel C_1 contain work areas, libraries, and user files. Those connected to channel C_2 are dedicated to the operating system and contain, together with the system itself, its libraries and work areas; all volumes are constantly on line. The general objective of the study is to see whether the system generation parameters have been well chosen and to obtain quantitative data on the utilization of each component in order to plan future upgrades.

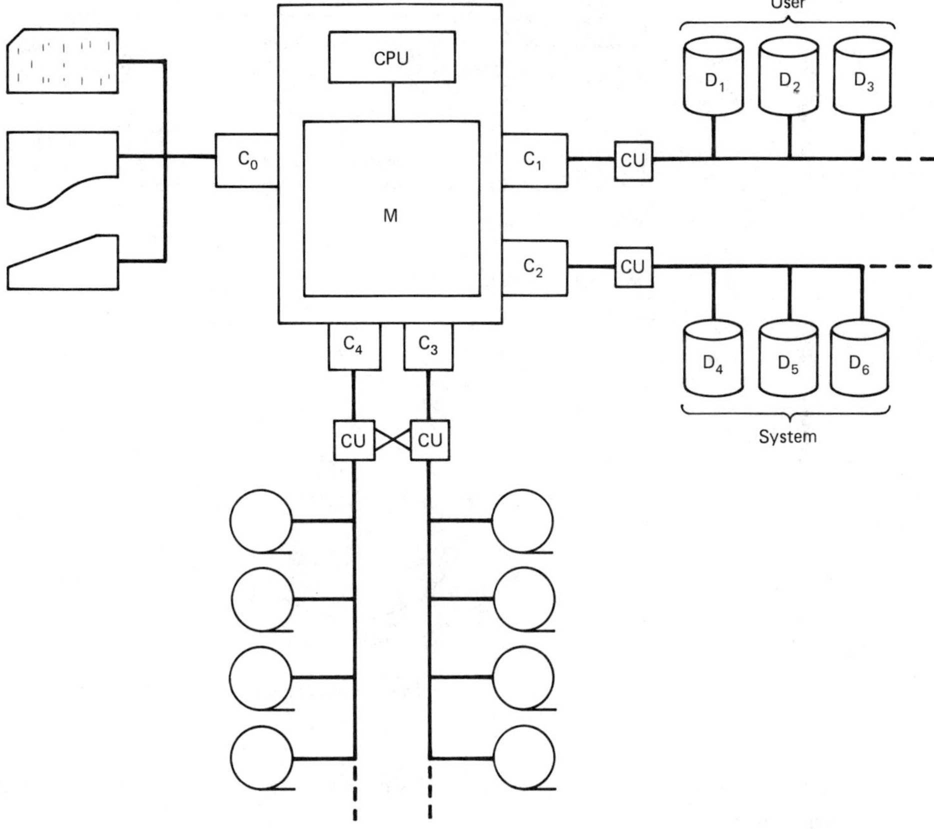

Figure 7.2 Configuration of the MBRS system to be evaluated.

Measurements and interpretation. The measurements are taken with a sampling software monitor. The measurement sessions take place:

1. Following periods during which a noticeable throughput reduction has been observed.
2. During peakload periods, usually on working days between 10 A.M. and 4 P.M.
3. After every modification of the configuration and of the system generation parameters.

The average length of each measurement session is 3 h. The initial measurements yield the utilization profile and Kiviat graph in Fig. 7.3.

The mean CPU utilization is 70 percent, with oscillations during the day between 95 and 60 percent. On the average 30 percent of the CPU busy time is spent performing supervisor functions. The analysis of channel activity shows that, while the load on C_1 and C_2 to which the disk units are connected, is balanced, that on the tape channels C_3

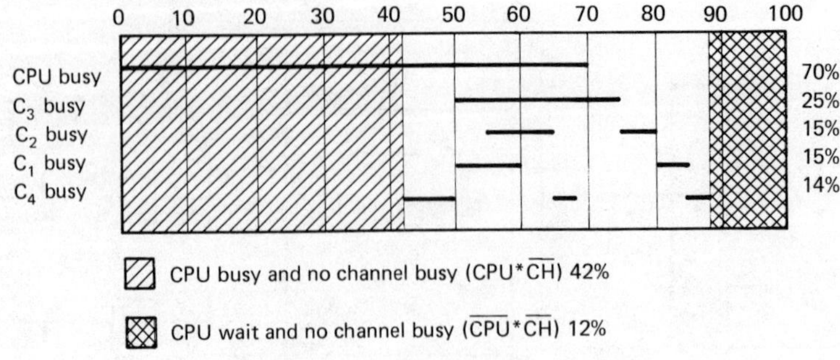

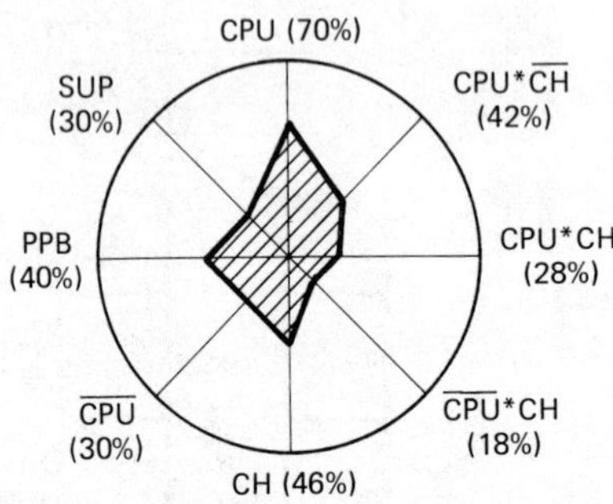

Figure 7.3 Initial utilization profile and Kiviat graph for the system in Fig. 7.2.

and C_4 is rather unbalanced. Figure 7.4 shows the utilizations C_3 and C_4 during a peak load period.

The most heavily used among the disk units connected to C_1 and C_2 is unit D_4, which is served by C_2 and contains the system's libraries. A more detailed study of the utilization of its contents shows that the library of supervisor modules is the most frequently requested.

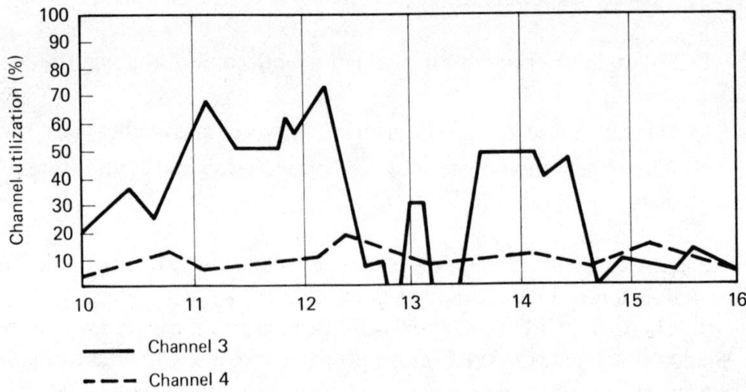

Figure 7.4 Measurement of the utilizations of C_3 and C_4 during a peak load period

Some of the more commonly used supervisor modules are loaded from disk each time they are needed instead of being kept in main memory. Thus the list of the memory resident programs should be revised.

Actions and effects. On the basis of the measurements collected, the possibility of increasing the CPU's availability to user programs (which was 40 percent) is considered through the following actions:

1. Reduction of the load on D_4 (a) by optimizing the list of resident supervisor modules, and (b) by optimizing file allocation.
2. Balancing of the loads on C_3 and C_4.

The revision of the list of resident supervisor modules, made on the basis of their request frequencies, produces a considerable reduction of the disk loads. Consequently, the access rate to the corresponding library is reduced by 70 percent.

In Fig. 7.5 the values of CPU utilization by user programs and by the supervisor, before and after the change to the list of resident modules, are shown. The allocation of files on D_4 is improved by considering the access sequence (which may be inferred from a trace of arm movements) and by trying to minimize the distances between the most frequently used files.

Figure 7.6 shows the arm movement addresses, expressed as cylinder numbers (in groups of 25), before and after the modification of file allocation. A reduction in arm movement time causes a reduction of the CPU's idle time.

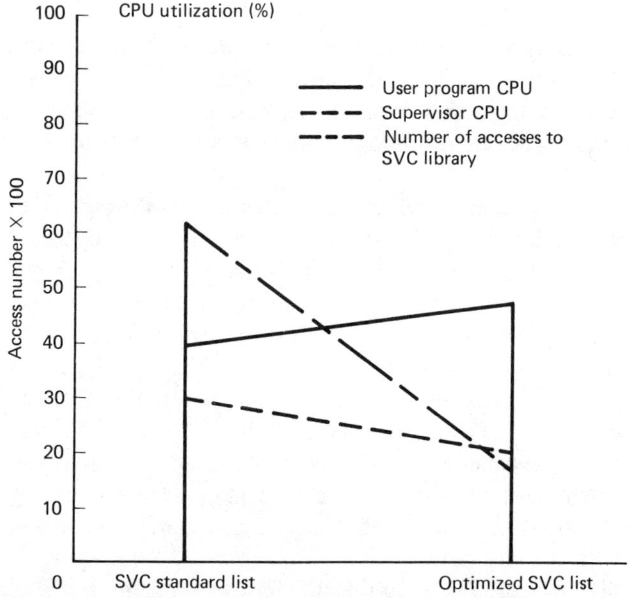

Figure 7.5 CPU utilization by user programs and by the supervisor. The numbers of accesses to the SVC library, before and after therapies, are also shown.

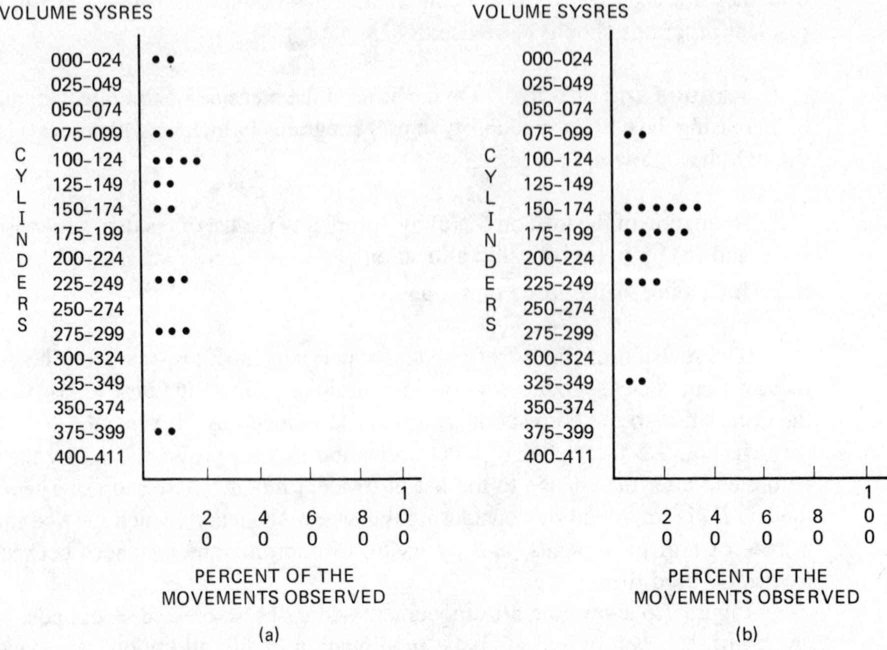

Figure 7.6 Seeks on D_4 (a) before; (b) after the modification of file allocation.

An analysis of the system generation parameters shows that channel C_3 was declared primary with respect to C_4. Because of this, C_3 was frequently used for the transmission of data in I/O operations involving the tape units connected to C_4. This can occur through the switching device that allows both sets of tape units to be accessed from either of the channels.

If the switching device is disconnected and the tape unit connections are changed, channel activities will be substantially more balanced even though C_3 maintains an average utilization (22 percent) slightly higher than that of C_4 (17 percent), since it is still the primary channel. Later measurements, taken during peak load periods similar to those of the initial sessions, produce the Kiviat graph in Fig. 7.7.

As a consequence of the actions taken, the CPU utilization for user programs increases by 17 percent. This increase is due partially (8 percent) to the reduction of the frequency of library accesses and partially (9 percent) to the reduction of wait times for D_4 and to the balancing of the loads on C_3 and C_4. The global CPU utilization (CPU busy) increases by 8 percent (to 78 percent) and the variable *any channel busy* is reduced from 46 to 40 percent. Of this reduction, 5 percent is channel activity nonoverlapped with CPU activity ($\overline{CPU} * CH$).

The increase in CPU utilization for user programs brings about an increase in system throughput that can be estimated to be around 10 percent.

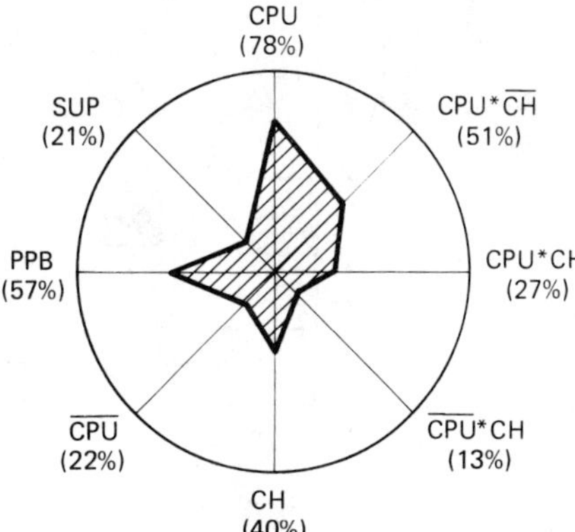

Figure 7.7 Kiviat graph after the system tuning actions

7.2.2 Case 7.2: Insufficient Memory

The problem. The system this study refers to is of the MBRS type. Its configuration, shown in Fig. 7.8, includes a CPU and five channels. Slow peripherals (line printers and card readers–punches) are connected to channel C_0, which is of the *multiplexor* type; its utilization is low, and thus it has not been considered in this study. Storage devices of various speeds are connected to the other channels, which are of the *selector* type; a fixed head disk is connected to C_1, movable-arm disks with higher access times to C_2 and C_3, and a tape unit to C_4. The size of main memory is 512K characters, 256K of which are reserved to the operating system.

The system's throughput is insufficient. There are long queues of programs waiting for the memory space they need. Often the system is not capable of processing its daily workload within the same day, and some larger programs have to be processed the next day or even after several days.

On the other hand, the system's capacity is such that the present workload is very unlikely to be able to saturate it. The purpose of the study is therefore to see whether a bottleneck exists and to determine whether the configuration should be redesigned to be made suitable for the current workload.

Measurements and interpretation. In this study we use the data collected by the logging routines. These routines constitute an event-driven software tool, which costs practically nothing, as it is part of the system. To make the results easier to compare with those that will be obtained after our attempts to remove bottlenecks are made, and to control the environment completely during the measurements, a test workload is used.

A sample of programs is taken from the real workload, according to the method described in Sec. 3.3.1. Our purpose is to obtain a natural synthetic workload with characteristics similar to those of the real workload. From the measurements taken during the test workload's execution, we obtain the utilizations of the CPU and of the channels. It should be noted that the degree of overlap is rarely determinable through tools of the type used in this study (see Sec. 6.2).

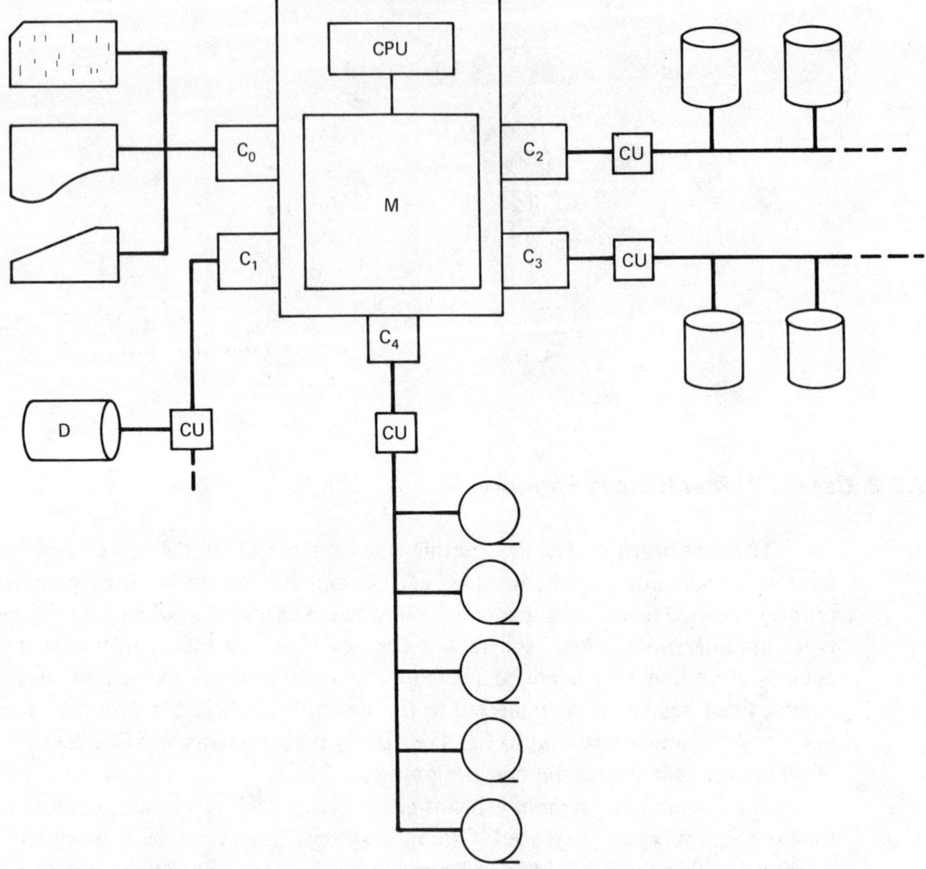

Figure 7.8 Configuration of the MBRS system studied in Case 7.2.

The utilizations measured are shown in the first column of Table 7.1. As can be seen there, the suspicion that one of the components being observed is the cause of a bottleneck is not justified since all the utilizations are very low. On the basis of these considerations, the following hypotheses are formulated:

1. The workload is not big enough to load the system components substantially.
2. The management of all the resources or of the input queues is inefficient (bottleneck caused by the job scheduler).
3. There is an insufficient main memory size (the value of the degree of multiprogramming is too low compared to the power of system components).

Hypothesis 1 is discarded for both the test and the real workload; indeed, in both cases the system works under a full load for most of the time of observation. Hypothesis 2 is discarded, too, because it is known that the same type of system, in very similar instal-

TABLE 7.1 RESULTS OF MEASUREMENTS MADE ON THE SYSTEM OF FIG. 7.8 BEFORE AND AFTER THE INCREASE OF MEMORY SIZE

Components	*Utilization level (% of test workload execution time)*	
CPU	58	76
Channel 1	27	40
Channel 2	25	37
Channel 3	45	62
Channel 4	25	35
Main memory size (Kbytes)	512	768

lations, has a much higher utilization level for each component. Thus, hypothesis 3 is the only one to be investigated further.

Actions and effects. The size of main memory is increased from 512 Kbytes to 768 Kbytes. Since the operating system still uses 256 Kbytes, the amount of memory at the disposal of the user is doubled. The results obtained from a new measurement experiment are reported in the second column of Table 7.1. They show, without doubt, that hypothesis 3 was correct: the bottleneck was indeed caused by insufficient memory.

With a higher mean degree of multiprogramming, the test workload's execution time is reduced to roughly 75 percent of that before the change in memory size. The throughput, which is proportional to the inverse of this time, is 33 percent greater.

7.3 IMPROVING AN INTERACTIVE SYSTEM

The improvement of interactive systems differs from those of other systems because of the different emphases to be attributed to the various performance indexes. Furthermore, the workload of an interactive system is almost always composed of two or three sub-workloads with different characteristics. Besides the workload generated by the on-line, local, or remote users, there usually is a batch-type (or *background*) workload. In other words, an interactive system is often hybrid rather than purely interactive.

On-line users can be divided into two categories: those whose programs are dealt with by the *time-sharing* technique, and those who send commands or transactions to be processed in real time under the control of a *teleprocessing* program.

A common application of the first class of users is the interactive development, debugging, and execution of programs. Interactively, the user can verify, instruction by instruction, the existence of syntax errors in his program, and also analyze on his or her terminal the results of the program's execution, thereby avoiding the production of large amounts of useless printouts and drastically reducing waiting times. The mean turnaround time is therefore considerably reduced and a programmer's productivity is usually higher than in a batch environment.

The commands used by this type of user are mainly of the light types (see Sec. 1.4.2); examples are the deletion and insertion of text, the substitution of characters, and the printing of program listings. Thus, this type of workload is characterized by a considerable amount of I/O activity together with a low CPU time demand.

The users who, on the other hand, interact with the system in order to execute one or more programs or to respond to the requests these programs make during their execution cause a highly variable workload. Real-time applications generally require that users introduce data through local or remote terminals, which are then validated and processed by the applications programs.

The requirement expressed by a minimum response time is typical of teleprocessing applications. This type of workload is characterized by a large number of I/O operations and by a CPU time demand that depends on the complexity of the calculations and data verifications made by the application programs.

In an attempt to satisfy the different requirements of the classes of users described, especially in large installations, twin systems are sometimes used in which each system is dedicated to a processing mode; typically, one system is dedicated to interactive users and the other to running batch jobs.

This solution is in principle capable of satisfying the user requirements in terms of response time and continuity of service, but its cost is generally very high compared to the amount of work done. Indeed, the speed characteristics of the interactive system must provide acceptable response times during peak load periods in order to maintain the mean response time at the minimum levels required. This problem is usually solved by oversizing the system, thereby further increasing the already high global cost of the installation.

The batch system or subsystem may clearly suffer from all the previously discussed problems. These problems must be successfully solved if a good utilization of its resources is to be achieved.

It is also possible to use a single system, with one or more CPU's, to carry out the three types of processing described. In this case, it is more difficult to balance the system since, besides the large number of components, different workloads coexist in a single system.

For example, an increase in the batch workload could degrade the interactive response times beyond acceptable bounds, or if the number of logged-on users grows beyond a certain limit, the batch turnaround times could become unbearably long.

The number of programs in execution at any time is greater in MIRS systems, and it is thus harder to break down the utilizations of the system's components into the contributions of the different components of the workload. Having defined the limits for the response and turnaround times, suitable resource allocation and scheduling policies for each type of load must be chosen. The coexistence of the various workloads makes the selection of adequate management policies more difficult.

Section 7.3.1 describes the actions to improve an interactive system's response time: the approach taken there consists of removing the bottlenecks caused by certain devices and reconfiguring the I/O subsystem.

The case discussed in Sec. 7.3.2 is concerned with an inefficient subdivision of the load in a twin system. The analysis leads to a new subdivision, which, once the disk file allocation is optimized, yields a more productive use of the two systems.

7.3.1 Case 7.3: Overloaded Channels

The problem. The configuration of the MIRS system considered is shown in Fig. 1.4. It is a *multiprocessor* system whose two CPUs share the secondary storage peripherals. The operating system resides on the disks connected to channel C_2. Some of the disk drives connected to C_1 are fixed-head units permanently on line; others are movable-arm units, and are mounted on the basis of user requests. The workload is composed of the programs input by two classes of users: batch programs, and time-sharing processes, which are submitted from about 120 terminals.

At some time in the past, the main performance indexes, that is, response and turnaround times, kept getting worse until they reached unacceptable levels. During peak periods an interactive user could wait up to 1 or 2 min for the response to a light command; a batch user, with a medium-sized program whose execution time was less than 5 min, had to wait 3 or 4 h before getting a printout.

Thus, it was decided to analyze the system in order to establish whether its efficiency could be increased by removing bottlenecks or by increasing its size; in the latter case, the components that should be added were also to be determined.

Measurements and interpretation. The system's activity was observed during a peak load period in which response were particularly long. The measurement interval considered was 1 h, and 11 min, on 4260 s. The overhead caused by the measurement tool (an event-driven software monitor) was only 104 s, or 2.1 percent of the measurement session duration.

While the utilizations of channels C_2 (C_2' and C_2'') appear normal, those of channels C_1' and C_1'' are not. Thus the utilizations of the units connected to C_1' and C_1'' are measured.

Figure 7.9 shows the channels C_1' and C_1'' as well as the units connected to them. The fixed-head disks T_1, T_2, T_3 are constantly on line, and the system allocates their space to temporary files (used by the programs being executed, by the compilers, for spooling, for swapping), the relocatable program libraries, the most commonly used compilers, the utility program files, and other files the system needs to handle interactive users. The movable-arm disks D_1, D_2, D_3, D_4, D_5 are dedicated to the users and are mounted on the basis of individual program requests having a highly variable frequency. They contain large data bases, sequential files, and private work areas.

The system sends its I/O requests to the peripherals primarily through channel C_1' (which has been declared as the primary channel). If C_1' is found busy, that is, if it is either already transferring data, the CPU sends the request to channel C_1'', which has been declared to be the secondary channel.

The diagram in Fig. 7.10 displays the utilizations of channels C_1' and C_1''. As can easily be seen, channel C_1' is very heavily used; its mean utilization is 69 percent (2942s), very close to the 70 percent limit that experience has shown should not be exceeded. On the contrary, channel C_1'' has a low mean utilization (33 percent; 1390 s).

A further study of the I/O operations on the two channels reveals a bottleneck due to the competing requests for access to T_1, T_2, and T_3. Indeed, out of 28 requests/s, 25.9 (92 percent) are addressed to units T_1, T_2, and T_3 and only 2.1 percent are addressed to

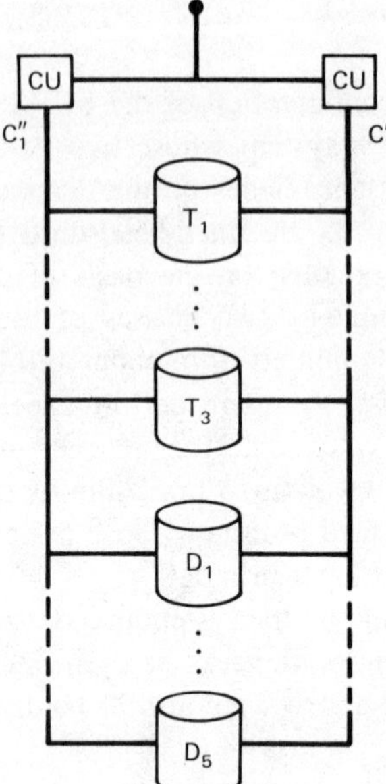

Figure 7.9 Block diagram of the units connected to channels C_1' and C_1''.

units D_1, D_2, D_3, D_4, and D_5. Table 7.2 shows the utilization of each individual unit. In this table one can see that the percentages of requests to units T_1, T_2, T_3 that have to wait are very high, respectively 85, 89, and 90 percent. In particular, 28 percent of the requests to be queued are placed in queues already containing at least three requests. Thus, the lines tend to be rather long.

The queuing of requests occurs for the following reasons:

- Channels busy and units free: 16 percent
- Channels and units busy: 43 percent
- Channels free and units busy: 41 percent.

Thus, 84 percent of the requests are queued because the unit is busy.

The request queues cause an increase in response and turnaround times since they increase the average access times to T_1, T_2, and T_3. Also, the system overhead due to the handling of the queues adds further delays.

An analysis of the causes of such a large amount of I/O activity on C_1' and C_1'' shows that the system has too high a degree of multiprogramming. The average numbers of programs being executed, of programs loaded in memory, and of programs awaiting execution are shown in Table 7.3. Figure 7.11 displays the behavior in time of the quantities considered in Table 7.3 during the measurement session.

We can see that only about half (22.1) of the programs being executed are in memory at the same time. This causes heavy swapping between primary and secondary memory (in this case the secondary memory is disk T_1). The mean number of interactive users having programs in execution, 30, is too big. Since interactive programs have a

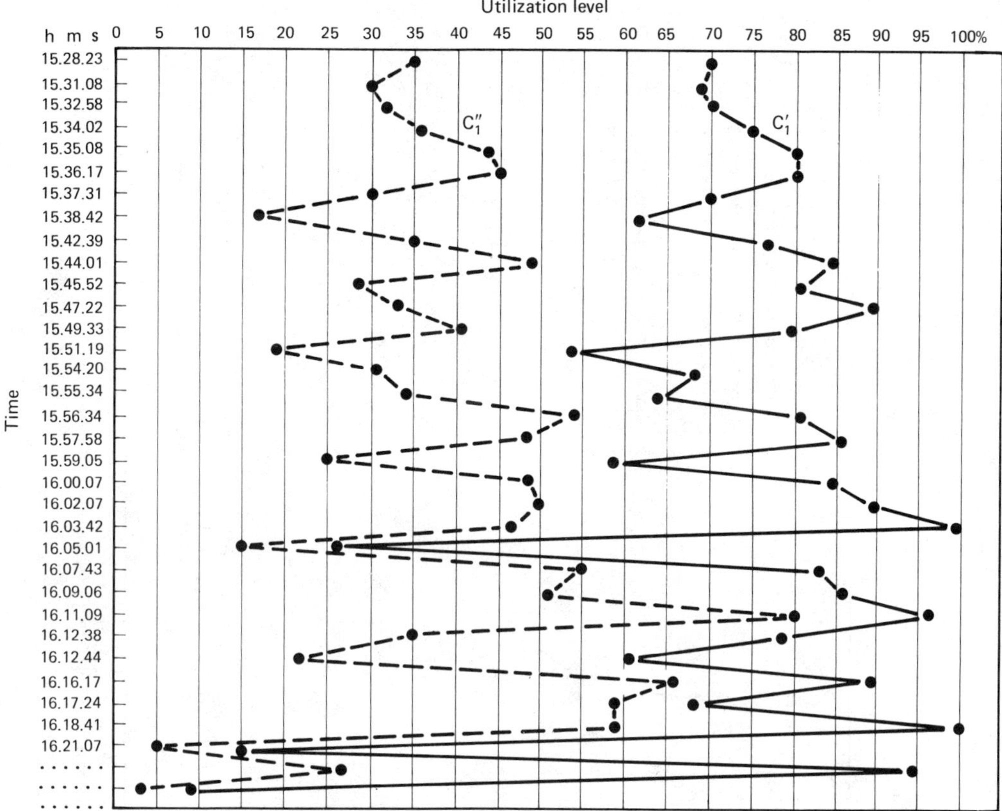

Figure 7.10 Utilizations of channels C_1' and C_1''.

TABLE 7.2 UTILIZATIONS OF THE UNITS CONNECTED TO CHANNELS C_1' AND C_1''

	T_1	T_2	T_3	T_{tot}	D_1	D_2	D_3	D_4	D_5	D_{tot}	Total
Requests/s	15.3	3.4	6.9	25.9	0.5	0.1	0.4	0.7	0.4	2.1	28
Queued requests	85%	89%	90%		—	—	—	—	—		

TABLE 7.3 AVERAGE NUMBERS OF PROGRAMS IN EXECUTION, LOADED IN MEMORY, AND WAITING TO BEGIN EXECUTION

	Batch	*Interactive*	*Total*
Programs in execution	15.1	29.8	44.9
Programs in main memory	6.5	15.6	22.1
Programs waiting to begin execution	48.2	—	48.2

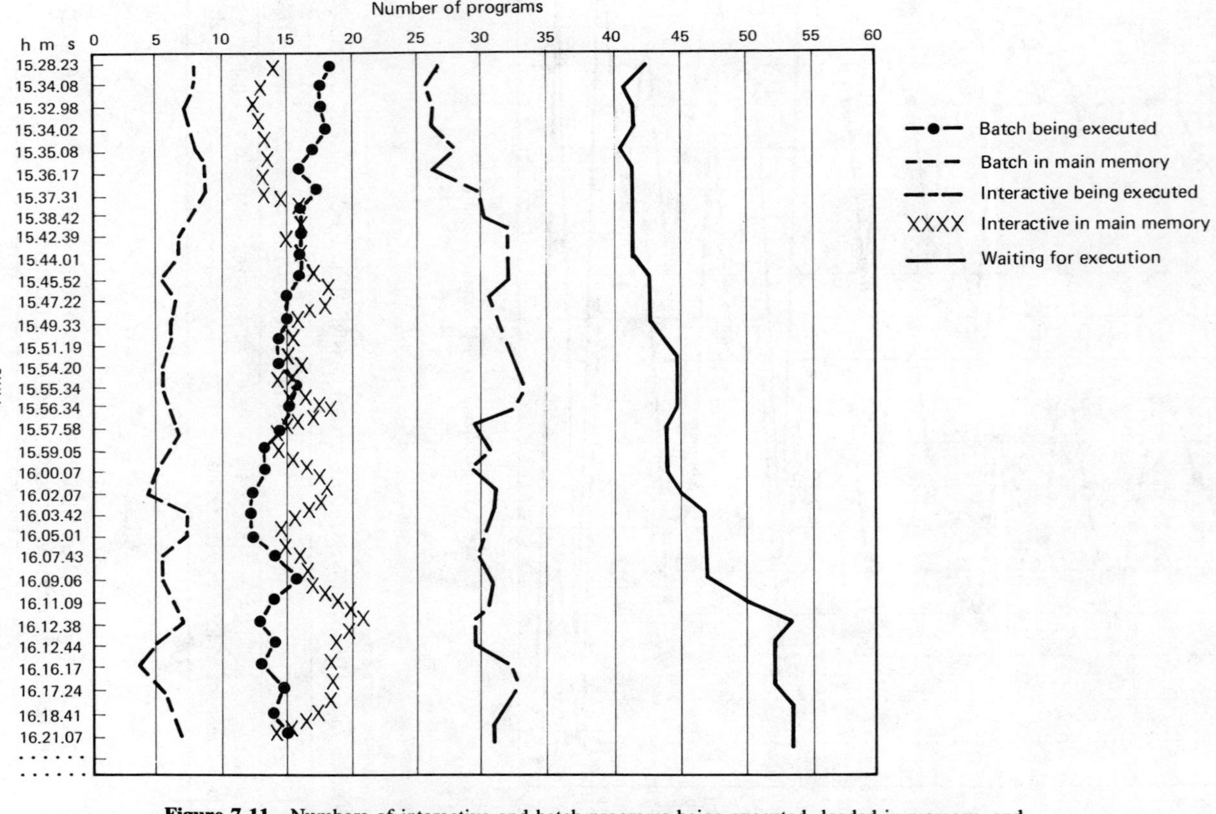

Figure 7.11 Numbers of interactive and batch programs being executed, loaded in memory, and waiting to start execution.

higher execution priority than batch programs, the system's performance for batch programs becomes particularly unsatisfactory, as their execution is frequently interrupted. On the other hand, the sizable length of the queue of programs waiting execution clearly shows that the system is not suitable for the workload it has to process.

Actions and effects. A possible action to reduce the swapping activity is to increase the size of main memory. In this case, as the CPU utilization level could be increased, a larger number of programs could be in memory at any one time, thereby reducing the need for swapping. This solution would reduce the load on disk T_1, but it would not remove the bottleneck due to T_2 and T_3. In fact, it would probably make it worse.

Thus, the possibility of reducing the loads on the units with the longest request queues is examined. After analyzing each file on T_1, T_2, and T_3, the decision is made to expand subsystem C_1 as shown in Fig. 7.12. Now there are four fixed-head disks and eight movable-arm disks available to users.

The reason for the high terminal usage is investigated next. It is established that about 10 percent of the interactive users use this facility simply to run programs with a higher priority than batch users. Thus, the maximum number of terminals connected is reduced by 16.

As a result of these actions, the system's performance improves considerably. The maximum response time for light commands becomes 30 s and the weighted mean turnaround time is reduced to one-quarter of the previous one. Clearly, the degree of user satisfaction cannot improve in the same way for all users, especially for those whose terminals have been disconnected.

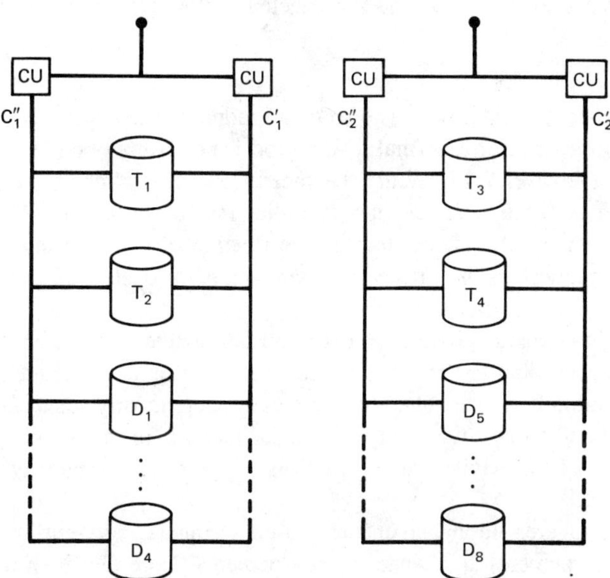

Figure 7.12 Final configuration of the I/O system in Case 7.3

7.3.2 Case 7.4: Ineffective Load Partitioning Between Two Systems

The problem. In 1978 the computer center of a company was drastically modified: the three small, functionally distributed systems which existed at that time were replaced by a single, more powerful centralized system (A). This system performed all functions, that is, administrative applications, scientific programs, and teleprocessing applications. The expansion of the firm caused a considerable increase in its processing needs so that in 1983 its requirements became:

- A more powerful network of terminals managed in teleprocessing mode
- Several data bases, obtained partly by converting old files and partly by designing new data bases for the new requirements
- Interactive processing for scientific and technical users.

Having determined the capacity of the existing system and the computational power needed to process the new workload, the installation of a second system (B) was decided on. The configuration of the twin-system installation is shown in Fig. 7.13.

The workload was distributed in the following way:

System A: scientific applications, interactive debugging of scientific and administrative programs, systems applications

System B: application procedures, data bases, and teleprocessing (DB/DC)

After an initial period of successful operation, the installation's performance started to drop and no longer seemed adequate to the twin system's capacity. Thus, a study was carried out, using a sampling software monitor, to determine whether the workload's distribution between the two systems had been properly selected and how heavily utilized were the system's components.

Measurements and interpretation. The software monitor was kept active 4 h per day during five consecutive days of a normal load period. The results obtained on the two systems are displayed in Fig. 7.14. While the mean CPU utilization for user programs was high in system A (83.6 percent), it was rather low in system B (22.7 percent). The existence time of the CPU queue, that is, the fraction of the time during which there was at least one request in the queue, was very high for system A (82.4 percent) and much lower for system B (9.7 percent).

System A showed workload characteristics typical of an interactive system. There were remote users logging on according to their needs, thus making program scheduling more difficult. The programs submitted or invoked by these users were mostly scientific, with a high CPU time demand and a low I/O activity. This characteristic of the workload can be derived from the shape of the Kiviat graph, which is of the *CPU sailboat* type (see Sec. 4.2.3).

Thus, system A's channels were seldom and unevenly used: channel C_{1A} was utilized almost three times as much (21 percent) as channel C_{2A} (8 percent). Note that both the

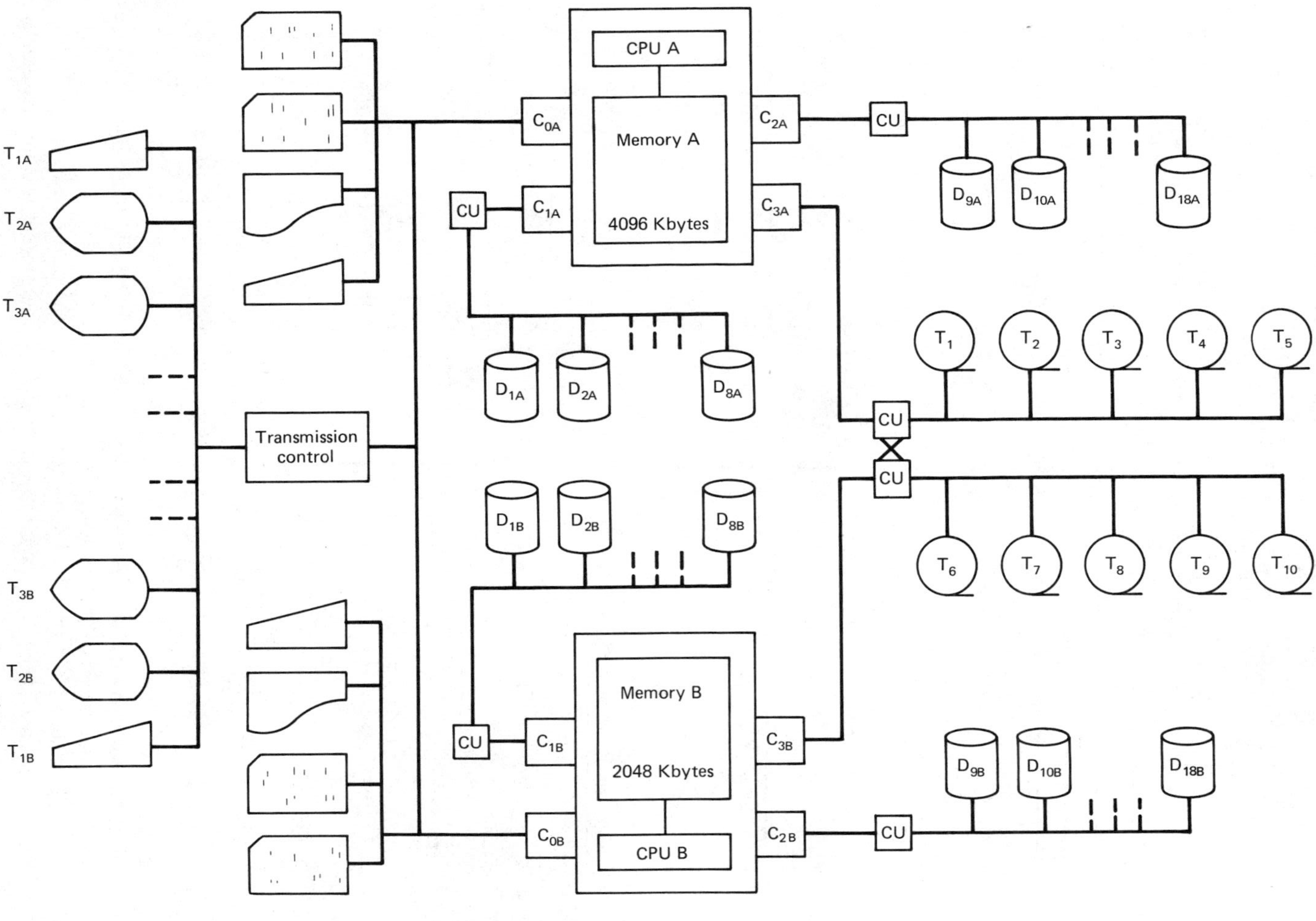

Figure 7.13 Configuration of the installation considered in Case 7.4.

	System A	System B
Total CPU utilization	95%	38.6%
CPU utilization in supervisor state	11.4%	15.9%
CPU utilization for user programs	83.6%	22.7%
Time CPU queue exists	82.4%	9.7%
Average queue length	5	2

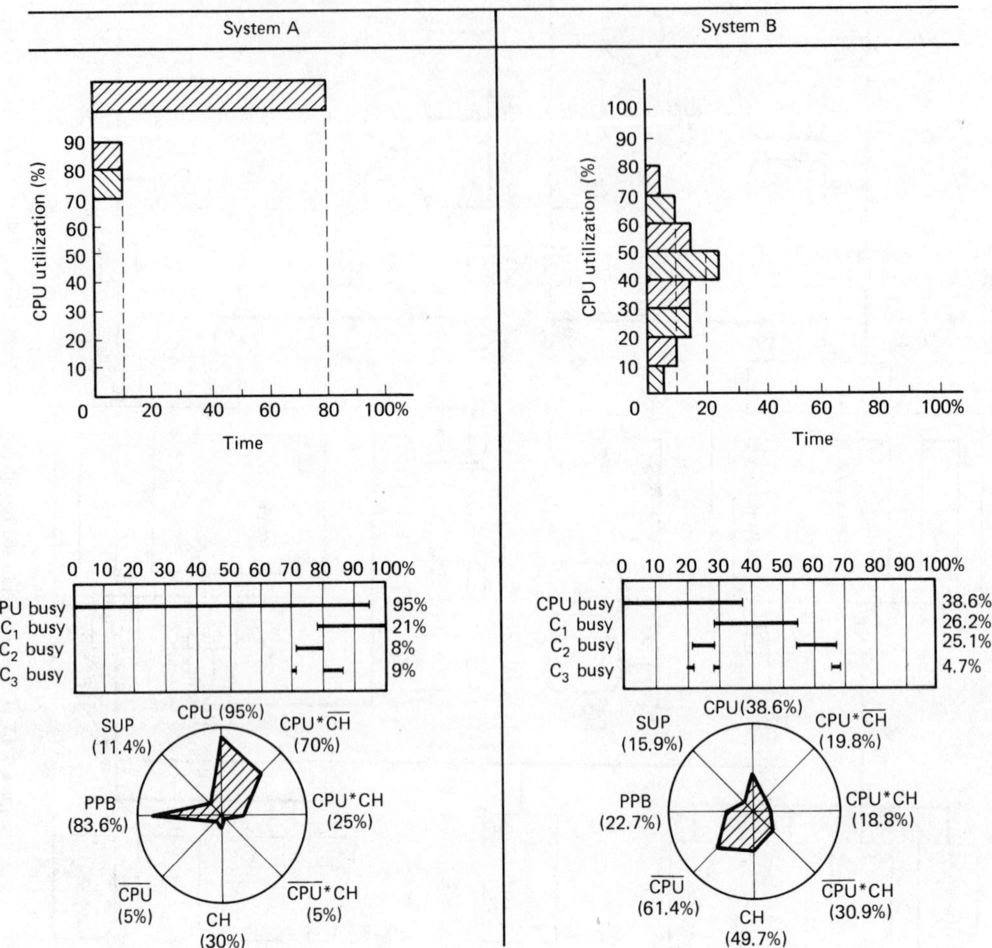

Figure 7.14 Utilizations of systems A and B at the beginning of the study.

disks employed by the system for interactive user handling and those reserved for user work files and test data are connected to channel C_{1A}.

The diagrams in Fig. 7.14 show that system B was hardly used. Its CPU was idle for 61.4 percent of the observation period, and the whole system was idle for almost 30 percent of the time.

The workload used the channels in a balanced way (C_{1B} for 26.2 percent and C_{2B}

for 25.1 percent of the total time), with peaks that rarely went above 60 percent. The substantial amount of I/O activity is characteristic of the administrative applications processed. The corresponding Kiviat graph is close to the *I/O arrow* shape, typical of an I/O-bound workload.

On the basis of these considerations, the decision was made to try to improve the system by changing the distribution of the workload.

Actions and effects. Using the data collected by the accounting routines, as well as those measured by the software monitor, the non-DB/DC application procedures were moved to system A. They did not require data-base accessing and were characterized by a large amount of I/O activity. All debugging activities and system applications, characterized by a high CPU time demand, were moved to system B. Both the amount of memory available to scientific programs in system A and that dedicated to debugging in system B were increased.

Thus, the workload was subdivided as follows:

System A: scientific computation, interactive debugging, application procedures that do not use data bases

System B: data-base management and teleprocessing (DB/DC), systems applications, program testing

The measurements made under about the same workload conditions as the previous ones gave the results presented in Fig. 7.15. As expected, system A's CPU utilization was decreased (75.2 percent), while channel utilization was increased (48.1 percent). Most of the CPU's supervisor activity was due to systems programs handling application procedures. There was still CPU contention, though less than before (48.5 percent as opposed to 82.4 percent), and the length of the request queue was still substantial (about six requests). This was due to interactive programs that, having higher priorities than batch programs, interrupted the execution of the CPU bound scientific programs, which returned to the CPU wait queues.

The channel load was clearly unbalanced toward channel C_1 (39 percent). Indeed, the disks containing time-sharing work areas, the operating system and user and system libraries were connected to C_1. Furthermore, two of its units were dedicated to the files most frequently used by application procedures.

CPU utilization in system B increased (from 38.6 to 69.7 percent) because of the greater number of compilations and executions due to the testing of systems programs and applications. Channel utilization decreased and was substantially balanced.

Stored on the disks connected to C_1 in system B were the operating system, the compiler work areas, and the user libraries containing systems-type applications. The administrative applications that use data bases were on the disks connected to C_2 with the test files used by the programs being debugged.

On the basis of the values in Fig. 7.15, it appears that the new workload distribution used the systems in a more balanced way. However, the loads on channels C_1 and C_2 of system A still remained unbalanced. Having analyzed the utilizations of the units connected to C_1, some files that were probably responsible for the bottleneck were moved

	System A	System B
Total CPU utilization	75.2%	69.7%
CPU utilization in supervisor state	19.7%	17.2%
CPU utilization for user programs	55.5%	52.5%
Time CPU queue exists	48.5%	29.3%
Average queue length	6	2

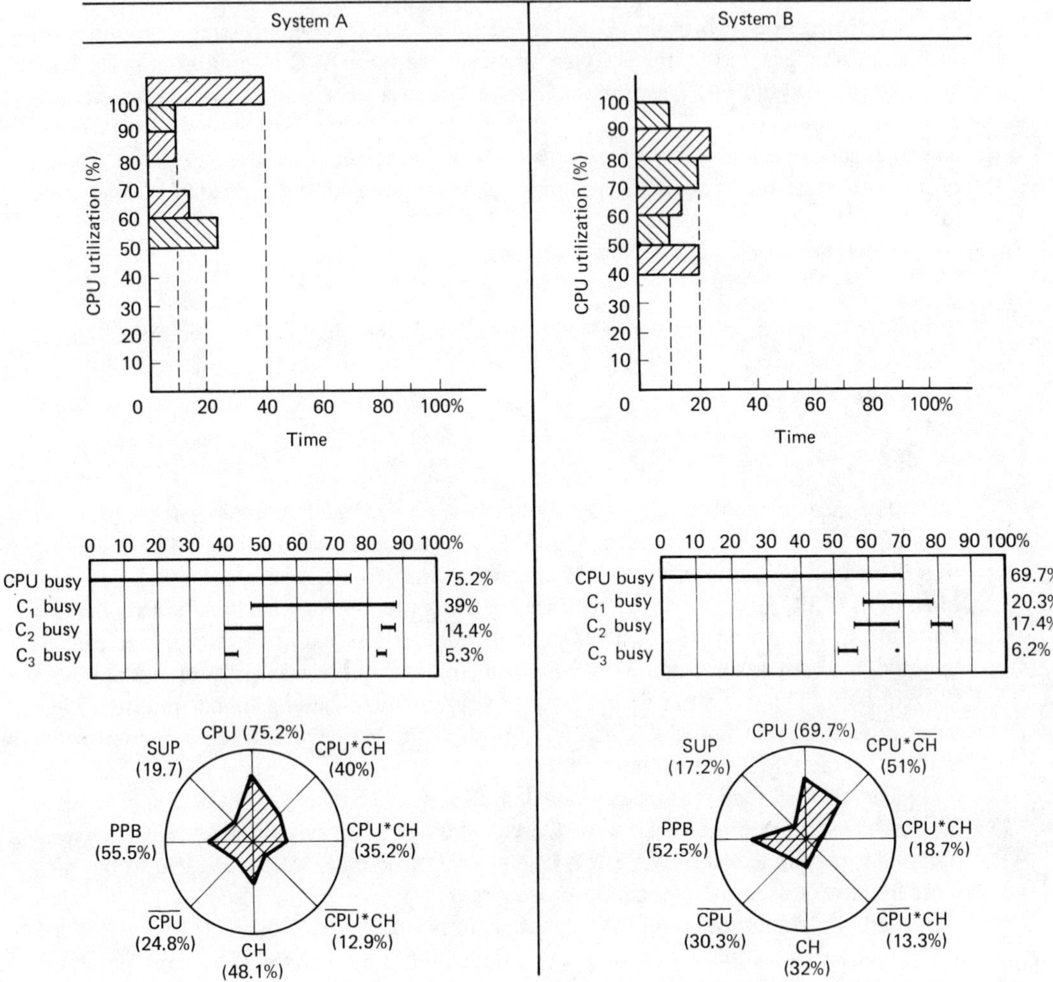

Figure 7.15 Utilizations of systems A and B after balancing their loads.

to the units on C_2. These included, for instance, the time-sharing library file and other data files often used by application procedures.

The results obtained from a new measurement of system A showed a somewhat better utilization of the components. Both the time of existence and the length of the CPU's request queue had been reduced. The CPU utilization for users had been increased

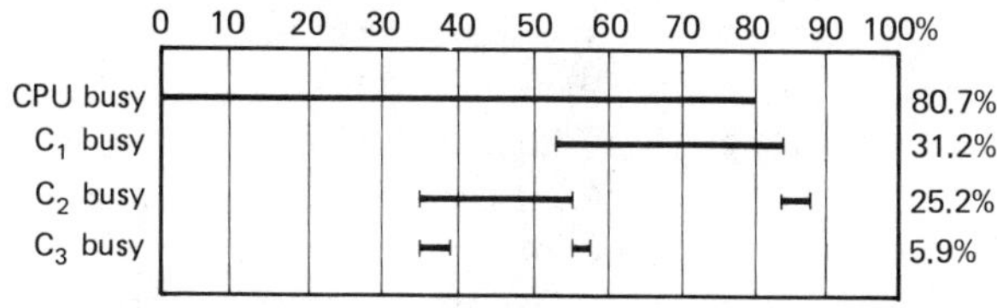

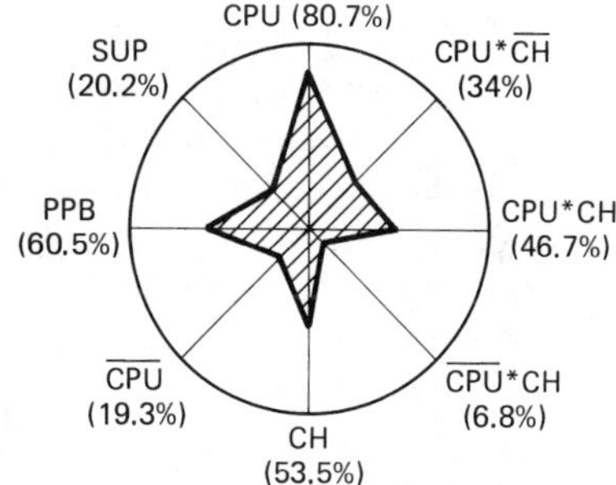

Figure 7.16 Utilization profile and Kiviat graph of system A after the channel balancing actions.

by 5 percent; the channels were more balanced and overlapped better with the CPU (see Fig. 7.16). Furthermore, throughput increased and the weighted turnaround time and response time to light commands decreased. The utilization levels of the twin system's components were far from saturation (in particular those of B), and thus the installation seemed to be able to absorb future workload increases without any upgrades.

7.4 IMPROVING A VIRTUAL MEMORY SYSTEM

This section discusses the principles and the performance aspects of virtual memory systems. The reader who is already familiar with these basic concepts should skip this section and jump to the case study in Sec. 7.4.1.

In a program the instructions, the operands, and the memory areas the program refers to are identified by a set of symbolic names. We can say that the program makes references to a *name space*. When the program is compiled, the compiler associates addresses to the instructions, operands, and areas so that the name space becomes an *address space*. Before execution, the program will be loaded into memory and will occupy a certain number of locations, each of which corresponds to a memory address. The set of memory locations is the *physical address space* or *memory space* of the system.

The loaded portion of a program cannot be greater than the memory space available to each user (note that the operating system occupies part of the memory). If the program's size is greater, the program must be divided into *overlays,* each of which must have an address space smaller than the space available to the program. The individual overlays must be executable in a certain sequence since, normally, only one of them will be in memory at any one time, occupying the space previously or later used by some of the others. The only exception is the main overlay or *root,* which is always in memory and calls the other overlays from mass storage. Thus, with this organization, the programmer has to worry about managing efficiently the memory space assigned to his or her program.

In virtual memory systems a program's address space need no longer be smaller than the memory size, nor is it necessary for program addresses (the *virtual* addresses) to correspond before execution to the addresses of the memory locations it will occupy (the *real* addresses). Furthermore, if this correspondence is only established at runtime, then the memory locations a program uses need no longer be contiguous.

With the distinction between a program's address space and the physical address space (memory space), an address still identifies an information item but no longer provides directly the memory location in which it resides. In systems of this kind the management of memory is left to the operating system.

There are many ways of implementing virtual memory management. A particularly efficient way is by subdividing a program's address space into fixed-length *pages* and the main memory space into *page frames* of the same size. The maximum amount of space usable by a program is called the *virtual space* or *virtual memory V* of the system (see Sec. 8.3.4), whereas the main memory space is called the *real space* or *real memory R* of the system (see Fig. 7.17). To determine the position of any instruction or operand in real memory, a device is needed between CPU and main memory capable of transforming a virtual address v into a real address r in a very short time. This device must also be able to notify the operating system of the absence from main memory of the information item corresponding to v if this is the case (see Fig. 7.18).

Usually, when a program's execution starts, only one or some of the program's pages are loaded in memory. The rest of the program is stored in a purposely reserved space, called the *paging area,* on a direct-access storage device (disk or drum) to which the whole program is transferred when its execution is requested.

If the remaining pages are loaded only when their presence in memory is needed

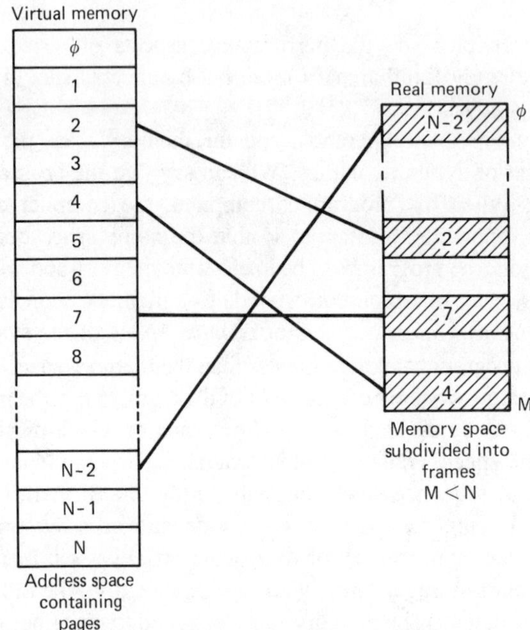

Figure 7.17 Correspondence between virtual (address space) pages and physical (memory) page frames.

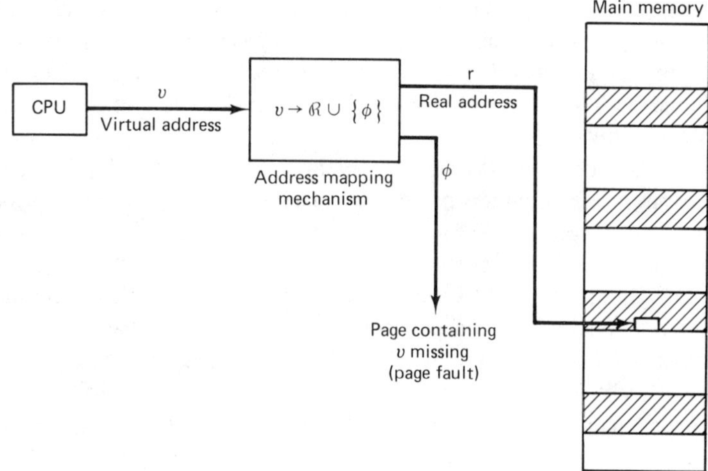

Figure 7.18 Device transforming virtual addresses into real addresses. It implements a correspondence between υ and the union of R with the empty set $\{\phi\}$ (for the missing pages).

to continue the program's execution, the operating system is said to follow the *demand paging* rule. If, on the other hand, a page is loaded in memory before it is required, then the system implements an *anticipatory rule*. As most virtual memory systems use demand paging, we shall always assume paging on demand in the sequel.

When an information item (instruction or operand or result) that is not in any of the loaded pages must be reached (that is, when a *page fault* occurs), the program's execution is suspended and the operating system performs a series of operations aimed at:

1. Establishing whether there is an empty page frame for the required page.
2. Choosing (on the basis of its *replacement rule* [AH70]) which of the loaded pages is to be replaced with the missing one if there is no empty page frame.
3. Managing the page transfer or transfers.

A major justification of the paging technique is its reasonably high efficiency in solving the problem of automatic memory allocation. What allows the system's productivity not to be intolerably degraded, though, is the fact that the sequence of the references made by a program is never completely random. Almost all programs keep their references to addresses within relatively small areas for a relatively long period of time; this property is called *locality of reference* (see Secs. 8.3 and 8.3.4).

An investigation aimed at establishing the average behavior of a large number of programs (see [CO68]) showed that often the memory space needed for a program to work efficiently is about half the size of its address space. Introducing the concept of a program's *working set,* that is, the set of pages to which a program refers during a given time interval, usually chosen on the basis of the relative speeds of the CPU and of the paging device, we can restate that conclusion by saying that the mean size of a program's working set is often about half the memory size necessary to contain the program completely. Intuitively, the working set represents the minimum set of program pages that should be loaded in memory to allow execution without too frequent interruptions due to page faults.

The memory allocation problem arises from the fact that, for purely economic reasons, an information processing system must have more than one type of memory. Main memory (or cache memory), the only one the CPU can access to read and write data, is by far more expensive on a per bit basis than disks or tapes. This strongly limits its maximum size in all systems and raises the need to implement the remaining memory capacity required by cheaper technologies, thereby obtaining a memory hierarchy over whose levels the information must be distributed as effectively as possible.

A virtual memory system has at least two automatically managed levels of memory: a main memory and one or more direct-access storage devices (usually disk units). The two levels constitute a hierarchy since only the data in the first level, that is, in the main memory, can be processed directly by the CPU, while the others will have to be transferred to the main memory before they are accessed by the CPU. The automatic transfer of a program's pages from one level to another influences the system's throughput since the benefits that can be derived from it are limited by the considerable difference between the access times of the two types of memory. Figure 7.19 shows a schematic diagram of three levels of memory and the order of magnitude of the minimum time required by each to make a data item available to the CPU.

While the mean access time t of main memory depends on the memory's cycle time (the inverse of the maximum frequency at which the memory can be accessed), which is usually on the order of 10^{-7} to 10^{-6} s, the transport time S_p of a page from mass storage is at least several milliseconds. S_p is defined as the time between the instant a page fault occurs and the instant a required page becomes available in main memory. Thus, S_p is composed of:

- Wait time in the paging channel and paging device access queues
- Data search time on disk (seek and latency times)
- Transfer time between the memory levels.

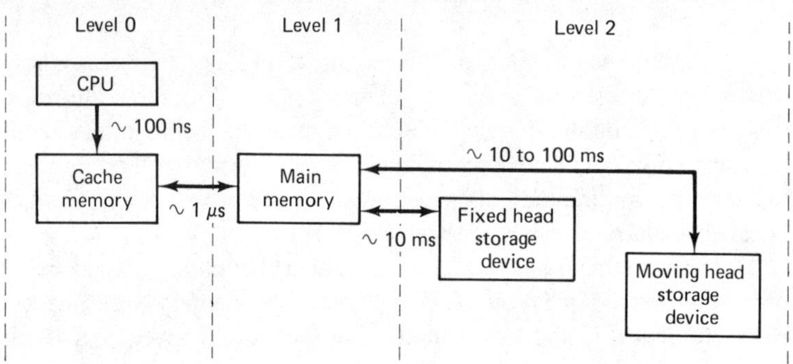

Figure 7.19 Memories in a hierarchy and order of magnitude of their access times.

Because of the usually large value of the S_p/t ratio, the paging activity between memory levels must be kept within limits that allow the CPU satisfactorily to process the programs whose pages are in main memory during the I/O operations due to page faults. If the overlap between these two activities becomes too low because of excessive paging activity (the critical value of the number of pages that may be transferred per second also depends on the speed of the CPU), we have long CPU idle periods, and the system can perform only very little productive work, thereby falling into a *thrashing* condition. This is a situation of performance degradation from which the system must be kept away at all costs.

The thrashing phenomenon, characteristic of virtual memory systems, manifests itself when the degree of multiprogramming is too high with respect to the sizes of the working sets of the programs being executed. This means that a system can get into the thrashing state if the degree of multiprogramming goes beyond a certain level or if, with a given number of programs active at the same time, the locality of their references becomes so low that they cause an excessive number of page faults.

Let us denote the total size of virtual memory at a given time by V (V is the sum of the sizes of all programs being executed and is therefore time variant) and by R the size of real memory. Thrashing can be seen as the condition the system reaches when the ratio V/R grows beyond a certain critical value. Figure 7.20 shows the page fault rate versus the V/R ratio. In the shaded area the system does very little, practically nothing, for its users.

The probability P that, for a given program, a page fault will occur is related to the program's size d, to the number n of programs simultaneously in memory, and to the size R of main memory. For the ith program in execution, we have [DE68]

$$P_i \text{ (page fault)} = P_i(d_i, n, R)$$

If we denote by $l(t, \Delta)$ the size of a program's working set at time t, the probabilities P_i remain low, because of the weak contention for memory between programs, as long as

$$\sum_{i=1}^{n} l_i(t, \Delta) \leq R$$

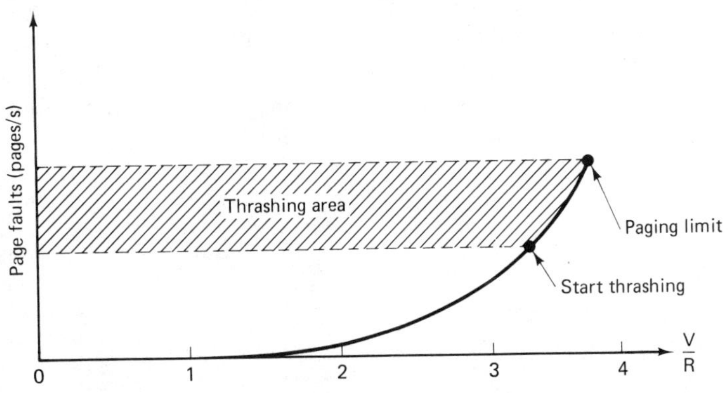

Figure 7.20 Page fault rate versus the V/R ratio and trashing limits.

As n increases, the critical value n_c of the degree of multiprogramming will be reached. Then we shall have

$$\sum_{i=1}^{n_c} l_i(t, \Delta) > R$$

and pages will tend to be stolen from the working sets of one or more of the programs because of the greater memory demand by one or more other programs. From this point on, the probability of page faults increases very rapidly with n, as shown in Fig. 7.21.

We shall define as a program's *processing efficiency E in a virtual environment* the ratio between its *virtual time* t_v (which excludes the periods during which its execution is suspended) and the sum of t_v with the total wait time $t_{w\ \mathrm{page}}$ caused by page faults:

$$E = \frac{t_v}{t_v + t_{w\ \mathrm{page}}}$$

We note that E is a function of the probability P and that, when P is low, the greater the value of page service time S_p, the more sensitive this function is to small variations of P.

Under the simplifying assumption that P will remain constant during the processing of a program, the total wait time $t_{w\ \mathrm{page}}$, which is given by the number N of page faults times the mean service time S_p, can be written as

$$t_{w\ \mathrm{page}} = S_p N = S_p P t_v$$

Thus,

$$E = E(P) = \frac{t_v}{t_v + S_p P t_v} = \frac{1}{1 + S_p P}$$

We can now plot diagrams of $E(P)$ versus the page service time S_p. In Fig. 7.22 one can see how rapidly the processing efficiency of a program drops for small variations of P when the page service time is around 10 ms, a value that is quite low and can only be obtained with fixed-head disks. It is mainly this strong dependence of E on P that makes it so easy for high paging rate situations, and sometimes even thrashing to occur.

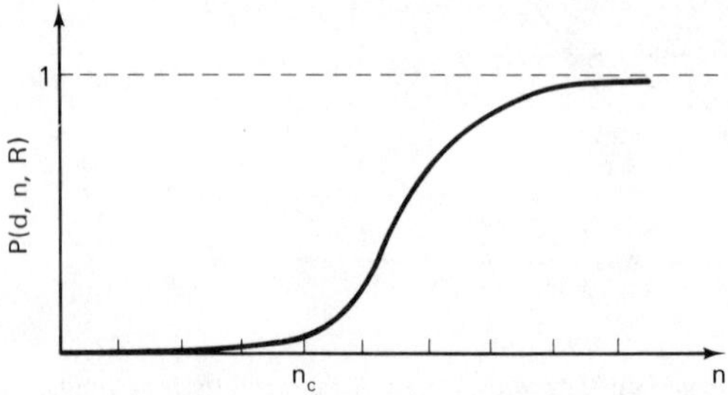

Figure 7.21 Page fault probability P versus multiprogramming level n.

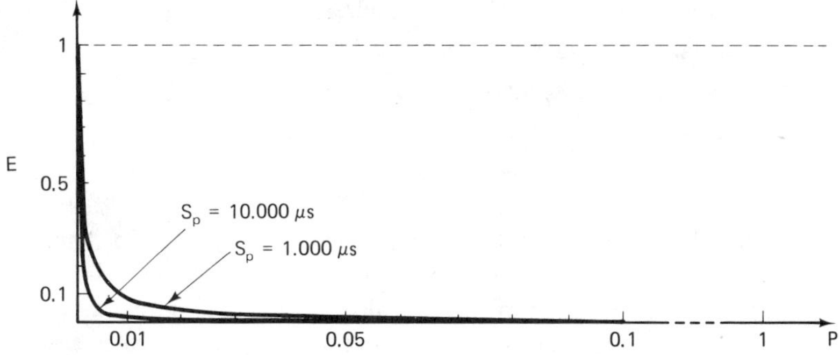

Figure 7.22 Processing efficiency E of a program versus page fault probability P for two values of the page service time.

To obtain a sufficiently high performance from a virtual memory system, it is thus necessary to keep the probability of page faults at a minimum and to reduce the paging service time as much as possible.

A virtual memory system offers many advantages with respect to a system whose memory is manually managed. However, to obtain these advantages certain conditions must be met without which virtual memory may considerably reduce system performance. Some of the positive aspects of virtual memory systems are:

1. It is no longer necessary to divide large programs in order to execute them; from an economic viewpoint, some studies have shown that the cost of developing a software system containing many programs grows quite rapidly as the memory space required by the system for its execution increases beyond a certain threshold [BO73].
2. The fact that most programs do not require all of their code to be continuously present in main memory during their execution can be conveniently exploited to increase the degree of multiprogramming, thereby utilizing the system's components better.
3. Virtual memory results in a higher memory utilization since it reduces fragmentation (on the average at most half a memory page per program being executed is lost); the greater efficiency of memory usage is also due to the greater percentage in it of really useful program sections.
4. The system is generally better prepared to absorb unpredicted increases in its load since, even though the execution time of the other programs will slightly increase, the execution of a high-priority (batch or interactive) program is likely to be started sooner even when the scheduling discipline is nonpreemptive.

Unfortunately, the facilities provided by a virtual memory environment require the execution of several rather complex functions by the operating system. The overhead caused by these functions is directly related to the paging rate. Thus, with respect to a nonvirtual system, a greater amount of CPU time is needed. The most important of the paging functions are:

- Conversion from virtual to real addresses
- Translation of channel program addresses
- Treatment of page faults
- Treatment of interrupts caused by the paging activity
- Management of paging I/O activity.

Besides the additional CPU usage, there is an increase in channel and disk activity for the storage devices that contain paging areas. A larger main memory is generally needed by a virtual memory system also because of the extra space required by the operating system. Among the factors that influence a computer system's performance, the following must be particularly considered in a virtual environment:

- CPU speed
- Main memory size
- Speed of the devices containing the paging areas
- Number of the devices containing the paging areas
- Locality of the programs in the workload.

The importance of CPU speed lies in the fact that the CPU, besides its normal tasks, also has to perform the functions listed.

Main memory size is the factor that has the greatest influence on the paging activity. More precisely, the determining element is the V/R ratio. The value of V/R varies with the fluctuations of the workload, since some workload characteristics, that is, the memory space demands of the programs active during a given time interval, influence the value of V. Furthermore, for equal V/R ratios, the mean working set size of the active programs influences the performance of a paging system substantially through the value of multiprogramming.

The real memory available to paged programs may be relatively small, although a large main memory will generally favor system performance. Incidentally, it should be noted that not all programs are paged; examples of nonpaged programs are certain parts of the operating system, or some special programs that cannot be paged if a given level of performance is to be maintained.

The external paging space is always on direct-access devices. When it is divided in parts, each part should be located on a different device, since this improves the mean access time to the pages and reduces the waiting times in the I/O queues. If the devices containing the paging areas are connected to different channels, the page transport or service time will tend to be even shorter.

In many installations there is only one paging area allocated on a single device. There are, however, operating systems that allow for a given number of distinct areas to reduce the paging service times to a minimum.

As for other types of systems, for virtual memory systems the search for the causes of an unsatisfactory level of performance should also be carried out by analyzing the factors that may be responsible for the observed degradation. The data on most of the variables considered for nonvirtual memory systems must be collected also for virtual memory systems, but they ought to be supplemented with information on the quantities that characterize virtual memory management. Table 7.4 contains a list of some of the most important such quantities. It is generally useful to measure or estimate their minimum, maximum, and mean values.

Virtual memory operating systems often incorporate a *thrashing monitor* that prevents thrashing conditions from arising. When the number of page faults during a relatively short period of time is greater than a given upper bound, one of the programs in execution is suspended, usually a low-priority program. This causes the pages of the suspended program to be transferred to the external paging area, thus freeing the real memory space previously occupied by them. As soon as the page fault rate falls below a given lower bound, a previously interrupted program is restarted. In this way the average number of active programs is determined by the size of the main memory area at the disposal of the programs and by the memory demands of the active programs.

While it is fairly easy to detect when paging becomes excessive, it is rather difficult to determine the cause of this phenomenon, which could be the referencing behavior of one of the active programs or an unreasonably higher degree of multiprogramming than allowed by the working set sizes of the programs in the workload.

We have already noted the impact of program locality on the performance of a virtual memory system. Figure 7.23 shows the results of an experiment [BR68] carried out on a workload consisting of n copies of a sorting procedure that was available in an optimized (high-locality) version and in a nonoptimized (low-locality) version. The same experiment was performed with and without an algorithm for paging control, and the degree of multiprogramming was varied from 1 to 5. The graphs show by how much the execution times of the nonoptimized programs increase with the degree of multiprogramming, and how effective the control algorithm is in maintaining the throughput at acceptable levels.

TABLE 7.4 SOME VARIABLES THAT CHARACTERIZE VIRTUAL MEMORY ENVIRONMENTS

Variables concerning main memory
Size of the nonpageable operating system area
Size of the pageable operating system area
Size of the pageable user program space
Size of the nonpageable user program space
Size of the free page frame pool (time variant)
Size of the set of pages being paged in or paged out
Variables concerning paging activity
Number of page transfers per second (includes the paging activities of user and system programs)
Number of page-ins per second
Number of page-outs per second
Page fault service time (total duration of a paging operation)
Correlation between paging and CPU activities
Variables concerning the I/O operations due to paging
Number of read–write operations on disk paging areas
Length of the queue(s) for the paging disk(s)
Paging device utilizations

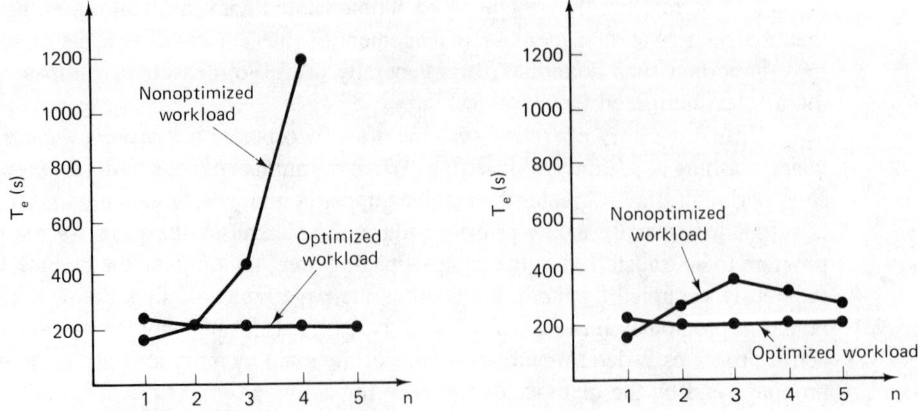

Figure 7.23 Effects of the paging control algorithm on a workload that tends to bring the system to a thrashing condition.

Since page transfers are I/O operations, they compete for channels, control units, and mass storage devices with ordinary I/O operations. If the workload is mainly composed of administrative programs, or if it is mainly I/O-bound for other reasons (for example, an on-line workload), this contention may considerably contribute to degrading system performance. In these cases, the main component of the page service time S_p is given by the waiting time in the I/O request queues. If, on the other hand, the I/O activity is not very high, the dominant component of S_p is given by the time to find the pages on disk.

Let t_r be the disk's revolution time, t_p the mean head positioning time, and v_t the speed at which data are transferred. For a movable-arm disk (user paging areas are allocated on this type of unit) having

$$t_r = 16.7 \text{ ms}, \qquad t_p = 25 \text{ ms}, \qquad v_t = 800 \text{ Kbytes/s}$$

the mean service time S_p of a 4 Kbyte page, with no queuing time, is given by

$$S_p = \frac{t_r}{2} + t_p + \frac{4 \times 1000}{v_t} = 8.35 + 25 + 5$$

$$= 38.35 \text{ ms}.$$

If, for example, a page request has to wait for two previous requests to be served, and if $t_p = 15$ ms, the mean service time of the request will be 85.05 ms, assuming no other types of delay.

Improving the mean page service time (with fixed-head disks, faster units, paging areas distributed on distinct units, separate paging channels) is not usually effective against performance reductions due to high paging activity. This is because such therapies do

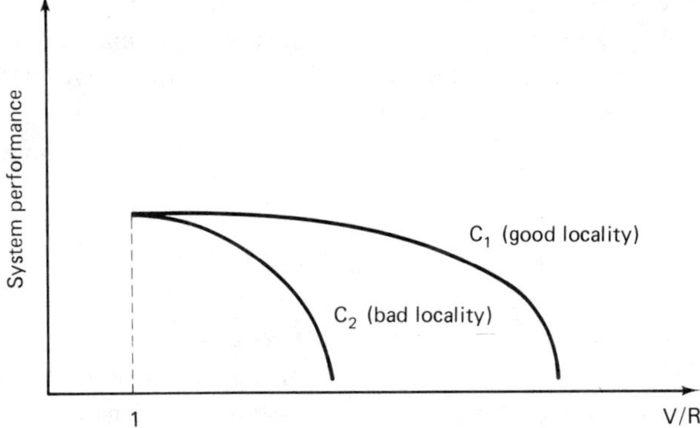

Figure 7.24 Degradation of system performance due only to paging with two different types, C_1 and C_2, of workload.

not remove the causes but simply reduce somewhat the effects. The most important remedies are:

- Reducing the degree of multiprogramming
- Restructuring the programs that page too much to improve their locality (see Sec. 8.3.4)
- Increasing the main memory size.

From what has been said, it appears that a virtual memory system's performance strongly depends on how the programs in the workload use their memory. The paging activity always degrades performance. However, if kept within certain limits (defined by the speed of the CPU and by the characteristics of the I/O load), the CPU overhead deriving from it can be more than compensated for by a better global resource allocation (greater overlap) due to the higher mean degree of multiprogramming. The programs in the workload must nevertheless exhibit a sufficient degree of locality.

Figure 7.24 shows how performance due to paging alone may vary as a function of the *V/R* ratio. Performance is evaluated with two different workloads, one having good

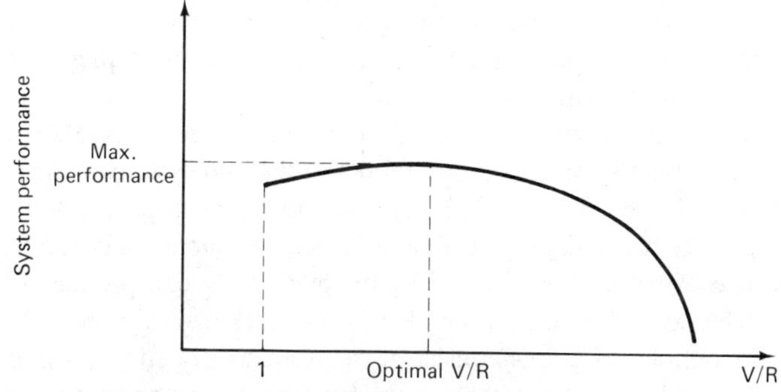

Figure 7.25 Total system performance versus *V/R* ratio.

locality and the other bad locality (see curves C_1 and C_2, respectively). Figure 7.25 shows, on the other hand, a plot of global system performance, which reaches its maximum for an optimal value of V/R. This value is influenced by the characteristics of the workload.

In Sec. 7.4.1, a case presenting problems typical of a virtual environment is described. Several of the therapies introduced so far are applicable, and are indeed applied, also to these problems.

7.4.1 Case 7.5: Paging Rate Reduction in a Two-System Installation

The problem. This case discusses a computer center equipped with two quite powerful processors, each controlled by an operating system that supports virtual memory. Both CPUs have the same computational power and the two operating systems are of the same type. CPU A, which processes a *batch* workload consisting of administrative, systems, and scientific programs, has a real memory of 4096 Kbytes. CPU B, which has a real memory of 2048 Kbytes, processes a mixed *batch* and *on-line* workload. The *batch* workload is mainly composed of programs submitted by remote users via a *remote-job-entry* system, while the *on-line* load consists of processes invoked by users working in an interactive or *time-sharing* mode. The system program that manages time sharing (TS) is on the average running 8 to 9 h/day.

The two processors share some hardware resources, that is, all the tape units and some disk units. Figure 7.26 illustrates the hardware configuration of the twin installation. The shared disk units are those driven by the control unit CU_{AB}. As can be seen in Fig. 7.26, there is a certain symmetry in the configuration of the peripherals. Both systems have four block multiplexor channels, two (C_1 and C_2) serving the disk units and the other two serving the tape units (C_3 and C_4), and a byte multiplexor channel (C_0) for the slow I/O units. In system B this channel is also used for communication with the remote batch users and with those under TS.

The placement of the volumes on the disk units was decided considering the different types of requests usually directed to each volume; in particular, the most commonly used libraries only needed by one of the two systems have been stored on units controlled by CU_A for system A and by CU_B for system B. The other volumes, and all those shared by the two systems, are mounted on the eight units driven by the controller CU_{AB}. Thus, this configuration reflects a compromise between requirements of different types.

The connections between control units and channels have been made so that both machines can access all the peripheral units for backup in case of failure or during preventive maintenance periods.

From the accounting data and from the measurements taken with an on-line software monitor on both systems the throughput of the two systems seems to have decreased with respect to the recent past. This is to be attributed in part to the progressive increase in paging activity, easily detectable with the available tools, and in part to the obvious existence of bottlenecks created by the additional load produced by time-sharing users.

The need to control more closely the workload of system B is increased by the fact that the remote programs consist of many relatively short programs and form an unpredictable workload, since their arrival sequence during normal working hours is quite random.

A study is undertaken to clarify in as much detail as possible the problem, to decide

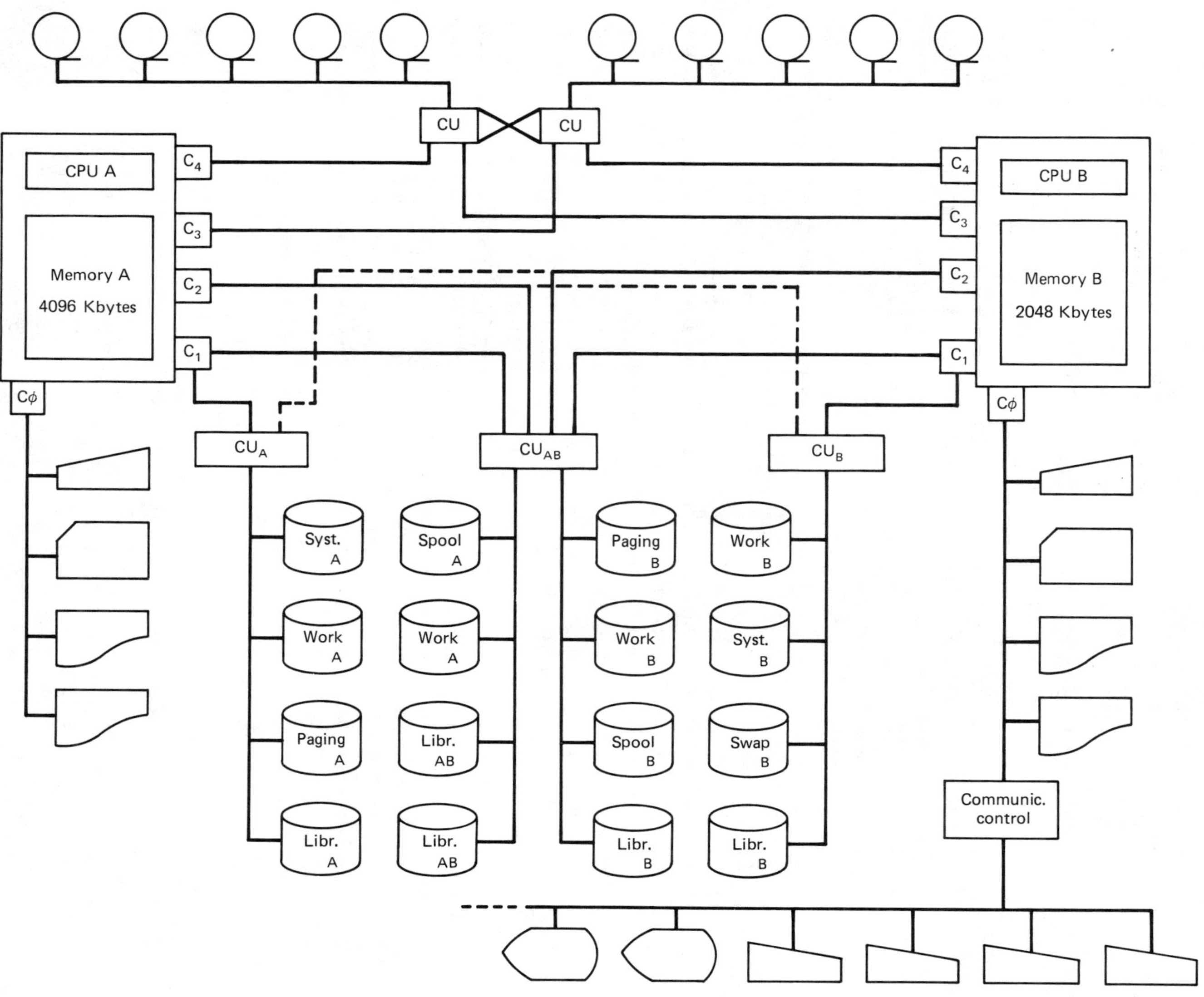

Figure 7.26 Configuration of the MIVRS system examined in Case 7.5.

whether the real memory sizes of the two systems must be increased, and, if so, by how much. A sampling software monitor is added to the existing tools. Data collection is performed continuously for a few weeks, always giving greater importance and higher priority in the data reduction phase to the information collected during peak load periods. These periods coincide with the normal daytime working hours.

Measurements and interpretation. Both systems use the CPU rather intensively. However, while the CPU utilization of system A is rather constant in time, that of system B oscillates slightly because of the on-line workload's fluctuations. Data about the CPU time demand in the two systems is summarized in Table 7.5.

By comparison with the global CPU usage, the CPU-bound nature of the workloads in both machines can be deduced from the high percentage of time during which there is at least one program waiting for the CPU. The mean and maximum values of the CPU request queue indicate that the central processing unit actually does create a bottleneck in both systems. This is partly due to the amount of time the CPU dedicates to the execution of the supervisor. In particular, system B's CPU spends more time for the supervisor than for user programs. The utilization profiles of the two systems can be derived from the plots in Fig. 7.27.

In system A there is a visible imbalance between the loads of channels C_1 and C_2, which control the disk units. Channel C_1, which can control up to eight units, is the *primary* channel. Consequently, C_2 is used only when the I/O requests for the units controlled by CU_{AB} cannot be served by C_1. A similar problem exists in system B, where the phenomenon is not so macroscopic only because C_1, with a mean utilization of 40 percent, is already close to its saturation.

In system A, the average paging rate is 11 pages/s, with peaks reaching 35 pages/s for relatively short periods (1 to 2 min). The mean page service time is 55 ms. This is not a very large value, but it can definitely be reduced by distributing the paging area over two disk units, possibly serviced by two different channels. However, this action does not solve the basic problem, which, for this machine, as well as for the other, is the high paging rate.

System B has two paging areas on mass storage. One, as in system A, for system and batch program paging, the other, called the *swapping area,* for paging the programs running under TS.

The main memory section in which time-sharing user programs run is subdivided into *regions*. Only one program at a time can be loaded in each region. This program

TABLE 7.5 CPU UTILIZATIONS IN THE TWO SYSTEMS

	A	*B*
Global CPU busy (% of total time)	84%	80%
CPU busy (supervisor state)	35%	42%
CPU busy (problem state)	49%	38%
Maximum length of the CPU queue	12	9
Mean length of the CPU queue	3.5	3
Average time of existence of the queue	60%	70%

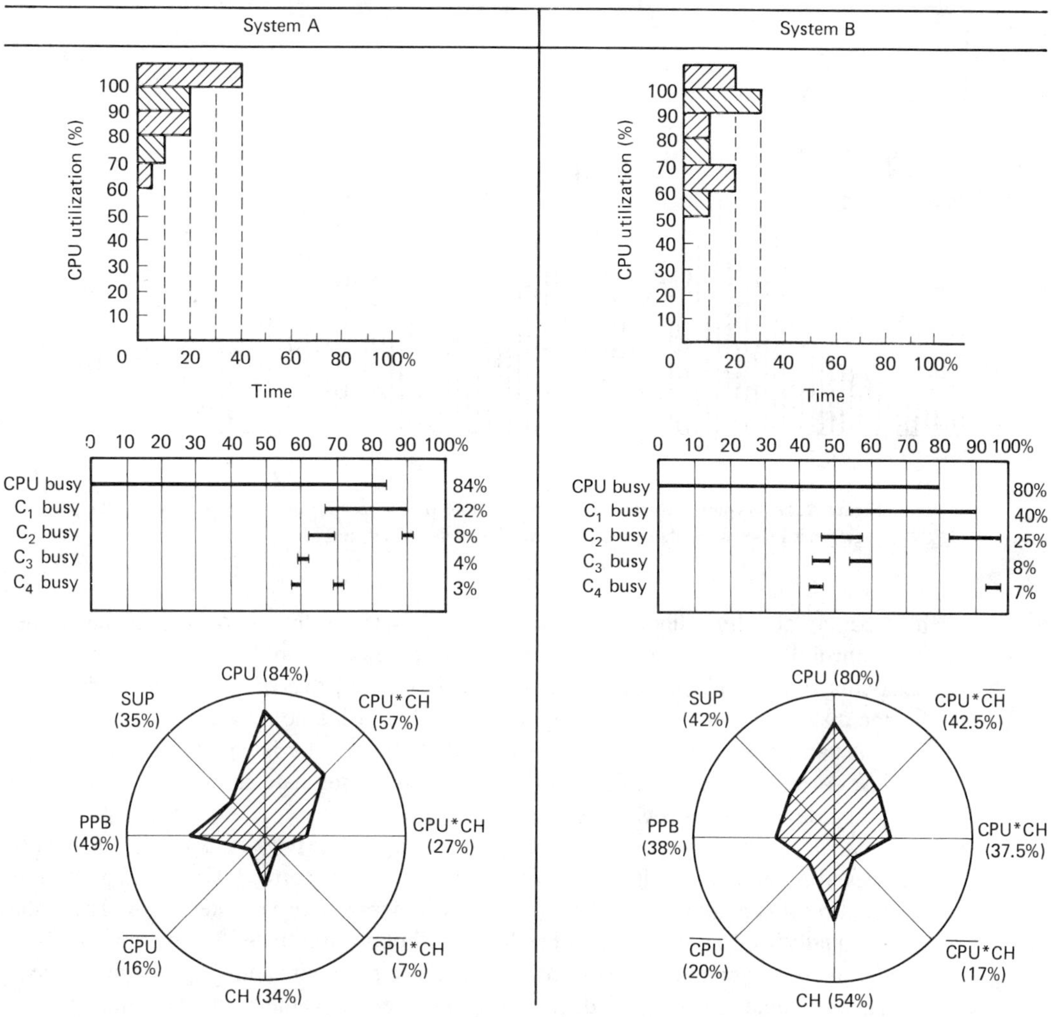

Figure 7.27 CPU and I/O utilizations in the two systems.

remains active for a given *time slice*. Once the time slice is over, the program is transferred page by page to secondary storage *(swap-out)*, where it remains until its priority becomes larger than those of the other programs; at that time it is retransferred to main memory to continue its execution *(swap-in)*. The total paging activity on system B amounts to roughly 820,000 pages transferred per day, 635,000 of which are only for swapping (these data are obtained from the information stored by the logging routines).

The average paging rate, during the 10 h of the TS system's activity, is 22 pages/s, with peaks of 50 pages/s for relatively long periods of time (10 to 15 min). Figure 7.28 shows the variations of the paging rate during a typical day.

The high CPU utilization in supervisor state (42 percent) should be related to the

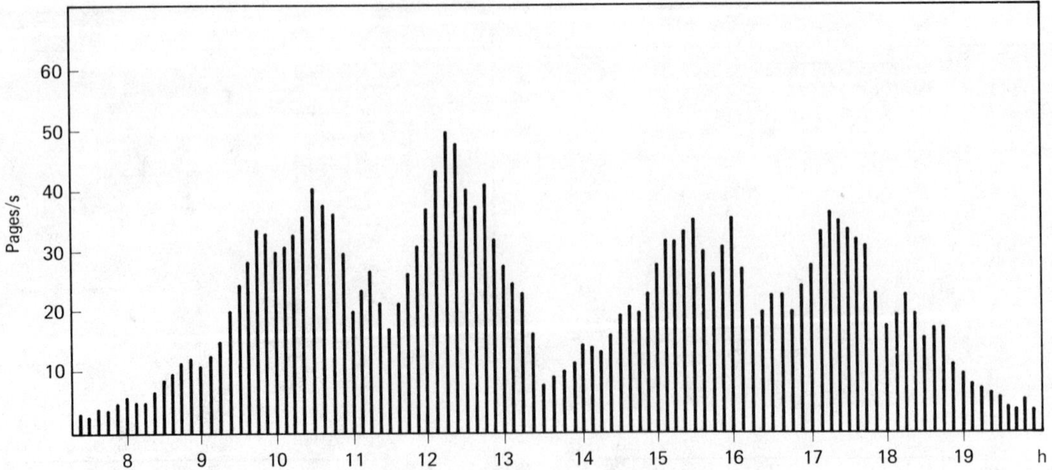

Figure 7.28 Typical behavior of the paging rate (pages/second) during a day (system B). The paging rates shown are those averaged over intervals of 7.5 min.

high paging activity, although the latter obviously is not the only cause of the former. To confirm this, the sampling software monitor is asked to produce a graph showing the behaviors in time of total CPU and supervisor activity, that of the length of the queue for the disk containing the swapping area, and this disk's utilization.

A part of the continuous graph provided by the monitor is represented in Fig. 7.29. A clear correlation between CPU utilization in supervisor state and the utilization of the swapping device can be observed in this diagram.

Since the reason for such great page swapping activity is not clear, a detailed analysis of programs submitted by time sharing users is performed. One of the first things revealed by this analysis is that most of these programs are not interactive. Thus, they could equally well be executed in batch mode, but are run under TS to avoid the batch queue, thereby damaging system performance. The program controlling the time-sharing system determines a program's degree of interactiveness on the basis of the time between two consecutive terminal I/O requests. The time between two such requests is called *interaction time*. A program having long interaction times does not require short response times. Thus, the system will lower the priority of that program, causing its *preemption* (interruption and swap out) as soon as a more interactive program requests CPU control. The fewer the regions available to on-line users, the more macroscopic this phenomenon, whose intensity therefore depends also on the size of physical memory.

Even the analysis of individual operating system module activity reveals a strange fact. The I/O module that deals with the end-of-block condition (see Sec. 8.3.3) on disk files and libraries turns out to be among the modules requiring a particularly high amount of CPU time. This leads to the hypothesis that the block size is on the average too small. And since all the CPU activities connected to the management of I/O operations take place under supervisor control, this could be another reason why the CPU is insufficiently available to user programs.

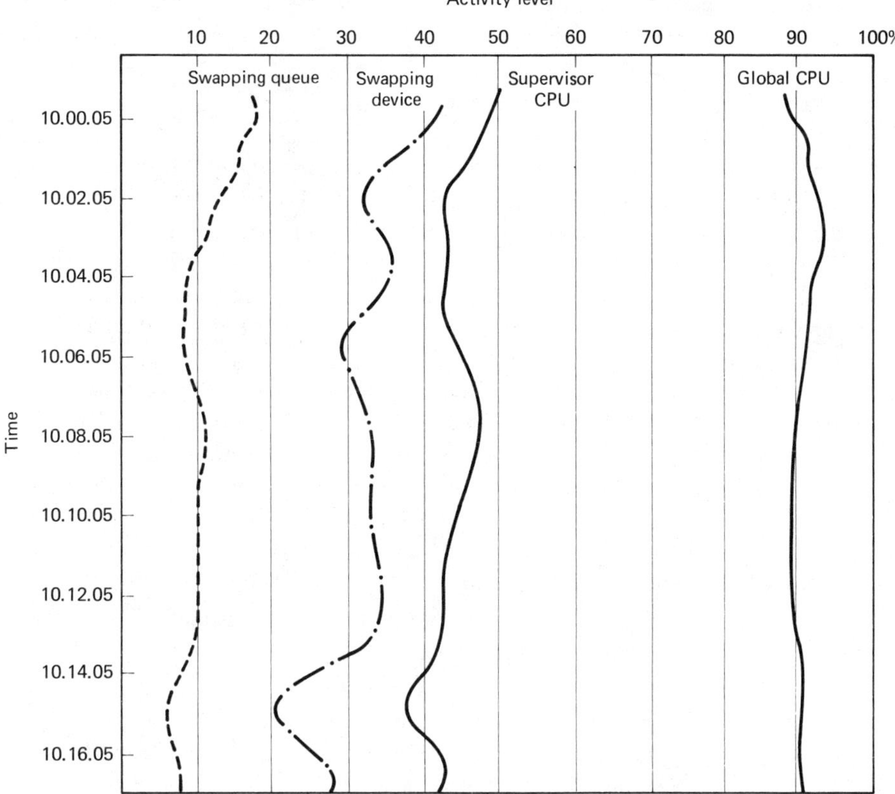

Figure 7.29 CPU utilization (total and supervisor state) and swapping activity on system B.

The average block size of most files and libraries is found to be 1600 bytes. An analysis of compilation procedures shows that data are produced by the compilers in blocks of 80 bytes.

Actions and effects. The main problem with system A is to increase the availability of the CPU to user programs. Indeed, it appears clearly from the measurements that the I/O activity is not sufficient to create serious bottlenecks.

At least for the moment, it is not necessary to increase the memory size of the system to regain part of the productivity lost because of the increased paging activity. Instead of doing this, the following modifications are made:

1. The paging area on disk is divided into two parts, and each is placed on a different volume; these volumes are then mounted onto units belonging to different *strings* (a string is a set of units controlled by the same CU) and connected to distinct channels (C_1 and C_2).

2. To balance the utilization of channels C_1 and C_2 and effectively separate at the channel level the activities of the disk units controlled by CU_A and CU_{AB}, CU_{AB} is disconnected from channel C_1.
3. The maximum degree of multiprogramming is reduced by 1.

The first two actions are intended to reduce the mean service time for page requests, thereby decreasing the waiting time of the CPU for the completion of these I/O operations, and to reduce the I/O activities not overlapped with CPU activity. The goal of the third action is, on the other hand, to reduce paging activity, and hence the amount of CPU time spent in supervisor state. This therapy should cause programs to run faster, since the CPU could become more available to users. The greater availability should also be expected to decrease CPU contention.

For system B, the need for another memory bank of 1024 Kbytes arises mainly from the consideration that, since B must process different workloads (batch and on line), any factor that could damage response times must be reduced to a minimum. However, in this type of system, an increase in memory size may not be sufficient to obtain substantial improvements in throughput. The following additional tuning actions are performed:

4. As in system A, CU_{AB} is disconnected from channel C_1.
5. The page swapping area is divided into two volumes placed so as to be served by the two channels that work on separate groups of units (parallel swap); this is not done for the batch and the system paging area.
6. To discourage on-line users from starting programs that are not really interactive, a control routine, which aborts programs requiring more than 10 s of CPU time during a relatively short time period, is added to the TS system.
7. The increase in memory size is used mainly to make more regions available to on-line users; the number of regions grows from four to eight; the number of users per region becomes 2.5 instead of 5 (the on-line users are 20 on the average); thus, the swapping probability decreases.
8. The use of bigger blocks when creating new files (at least 3200 bytes per block) is recommended; the existing files are reblocked and the compilation procedures are changed to produce object modules with bigger blocks.

TABLE 7.6 CPU AND PAGING ACTIVITIES OF THE TWO SYSTEMS AFTER TUNING

	System A	*System B*
Global CPU busy (% of total time)	94%	89%
CPU busy (supervisor state)	30%	28%
CPU busy (problem state)	64%	61%
Maximum length of the CPU queue	9	10
Mean length of the CPU queue	2	1.8
Average time of existence of the queue	52%	26%
Paging rate (pages/s)	7	6
Mean page-fault service time (ms)	38	43

The effects of the modifications made to the two systems confirm the validity of the therapies described. Observations made on system B, during periods similar to those previously considered, show a nonnegligible productivity improvement. Table 7.6 displays the mean daytime values of CPU utilization for the two systems after the tuning actions were undertaken.

System A, which basically had a paging bottleneck, now clearly shows the inad-

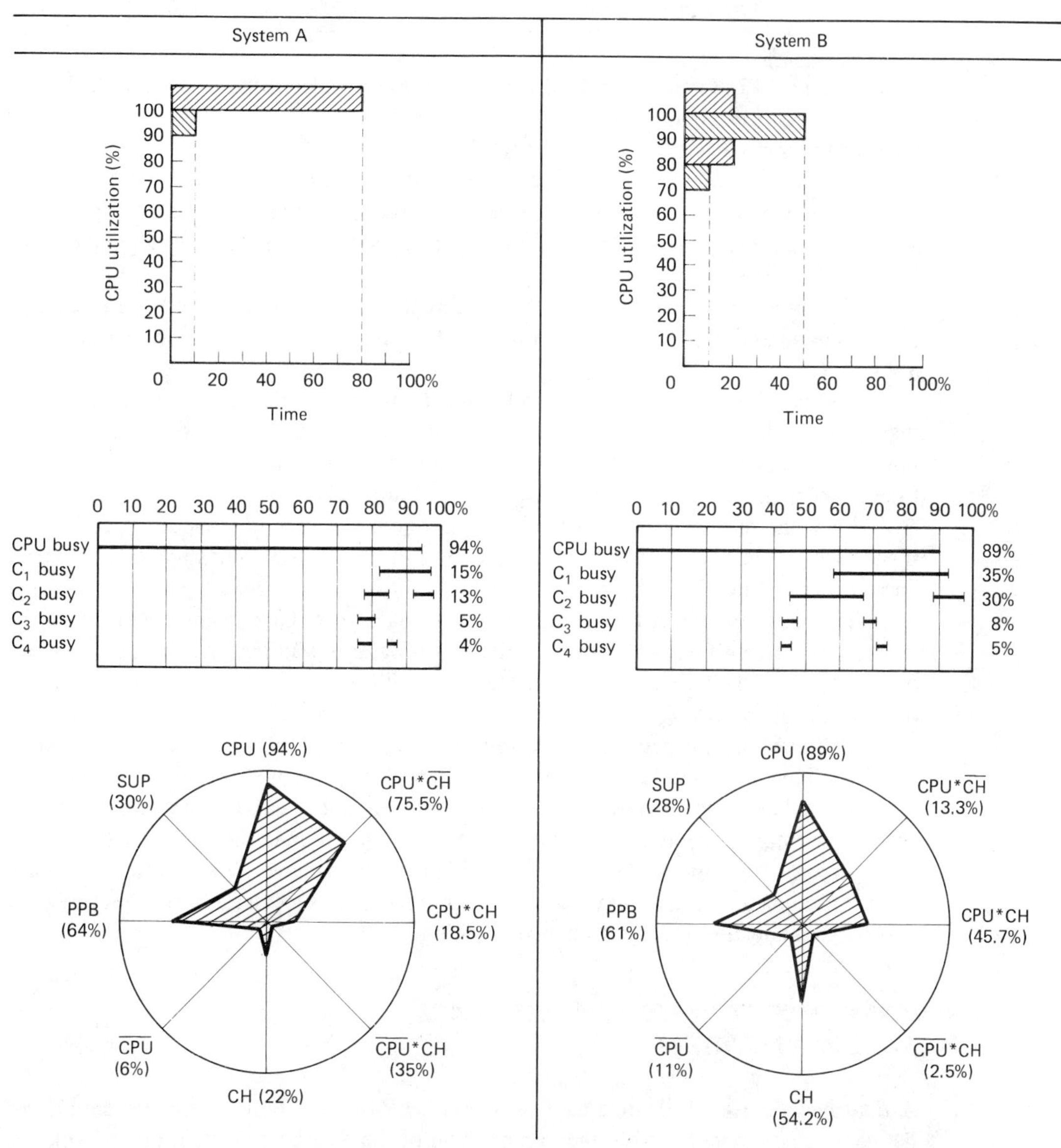

Figure 7.30 CPU and I/O utilizations in the two systems after tuning.

TABLE 7.7 VARIATIONS IN THE MEAN DAILY PAGING ACTIVITY OF SYSTEM B

Paging operations	*Before tuning*	*After tuning*
Paging due to batch programs	65,000	10,000
Paging due to operating system	58,000	25,000
Swapping activity	635,000	200,000
Paging due to time-sharing program	61,000	22,000
Total paging operations	819,000	257,000

equacy of its CPU for the workload it has to process. Indeed, the mean existence time of the CPU queue remains rather high (52 percent), although the utilization of the CPU for user programs has increased by about 30 percent.

The actions on system A have nevertheless caused a considerable increase in the throughput, which probably cannot be easily improved further, and have revealed the system's real limits. The I/O load is now well balanced between channels C_1 and C_2 (see Fig. 7.30).

The situation of system B is quite different. Here, as could have been predicted, the system's paging activity has been drastically reduced, even more than expected (see Table 7.7).

The considerable increase (by 60 percent) of CPU utilization for user programs, visible in Table 7.6, is mainly due to the reduction of the paging rate. The system is now used at its best: there is no contention for the CPU, the mean page-fault service time is acceptable, and channel loads are sufficiently balanced, as shown in Fig. 7.30.

Even the response times provided to on-line users have improved: for light commands they were about 4 to 5 s and are now 1 to 2 s. These values are also less time variant than before.

The mean weighted turnaround times of batch users have been decreased on the average by 35 to 40 percent, and the queue of programs waiting for execution contains on the average 25 to 30 programs. Before the modifications, there was a constant queue of 40 to 50 programs.

On the whole, the actions undertaken have been successful. Had system A's memory size been increased, the fact that its real bottleneck was the CPU would have probably remained hidden. For the other system, the results are not as easy to interpret as it might seem. The improvements are certainly not only due to the increase in memory size, but also to most of the tuning operations, which also tend to have positive effects on each other. Often an action that may cause an improvement is successful only if preceded by another that apparently did not change anything.

7.5 PERFORMANCE CONTROL IN A DATA-BASE MANAGEMENT SYSTEM

A *data base* is usually defined as a structured set of data. The relationships among the data are somehow reflected in the organization of the data base, so that the information required is easy to access while, at the same time, being stored with as little duplication

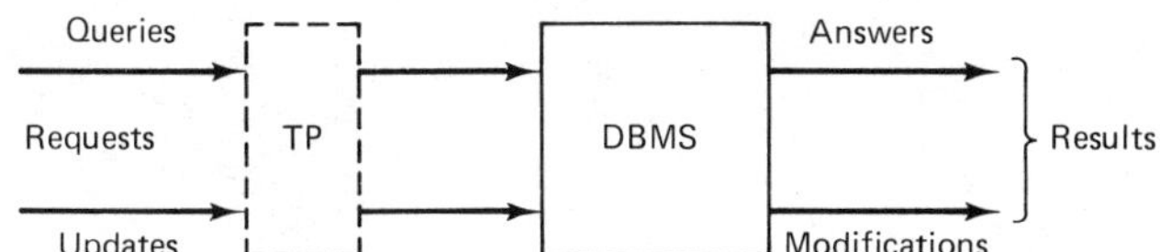

Figure 7.31 Service requests and results provided by a DBMS.

as possible. The elements of a data base are accessed and handled using a set of programs, called a *data base management system* (DBMS). A data base is structured according to the access requirements of the applications and updated by addition, deletion, or substitution of data. Users can access the elements of a data base specifying their requests according to the rules of a language that is a part of the DBMS. This language is usually called a *data language* or *query language*.

The work unit for a DBMS is the *transaction*. This term indicates all the activities that take place as a consequence of a user request made to a DBMS. The requests, which can be queries or updates, may be contained in application programs executed in batch mode *(batch transactions)* or may be sent from local or remote terminals *(on-line transactions)* and handled by a *teleprocessing* program (see Fig. 7.31).

An environment where data bases are accessible to both batch and on-line users is usually called a *data base/data communication* (DB/DC) system, while a system accessible only in batch mode is usually designated as a DB system.

Given the nature of a data base, its contents are normally accessed and possibly updated by more than one user. Thus, a data base is a sharable resource, one which may be requested and used by multiple users simultaneously. This creates competition among user transactions and raises the problem of evaluating the efficiency of a DBMS system.

The most significant *performance indexes* of a DBMS are (1) the response time of individual transactions (measured in seconds) for on-line systems, and (2) the throughput (measured in transactions per hour) for batch and on-line systems.

For DB/DC systems, the response time of a transaction is related to the complexity of the request made and to the workload existing on the system when the transaction is processed. A qualitative diagram of the response time versus the complexity of the request is shown in Fig. 7.32.

Among the many factors influencing the performance of a DB or DB/DC system, some of the most important are:

- Organization of the data base (logical data structure, block size, physical placement of the structure in mass storage)

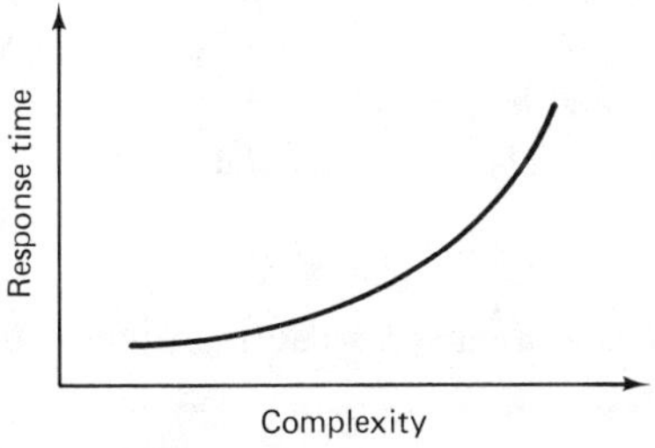

Figure 7.32 Response time of a transaction versus the complexity of the request made to the DB/DC system.

- Complexity of the logical access paths to data
- Characteristics of the mass storage units used (generally disk units)
- Connections of the peripherals to the available channels
- Memory size reserved for the buffer pool
- Arrival rate and the complexity of the queries
- Number of I/O operations on each data base required by each individual transaction
- DBMS generation parameters
- Operating system generation parameters
- Operations needed to maintain the integrity of the data base (checkpointing, consistency checking, transaction logging); while these operations are performed, many activities are suspended
- Algorithms and techniques used by the DBMS for data access control and protection.

It is often difficult to predict, when its structure is designed, how a data base will be used. Considerable performance problems in a data-base system are usually due to the explosion of user requests and their effects on all the other activities managed by the DB/DC system. Even the modifications made to the data base during its lifetime (addition and deletion of data) often cause performance degradations for the transactions accessing it, while the increased volume of transactions sometimes reveals intrinsic structural inefficiencies of the data base and reduces the resources available to each transaction.

The activities of a DB/DC system are among the most important ones in many computer centers and are generally quite expensive for the system to support. It is therefore particularly advisable that these activities be systematically controlled and that the performance of the DB/DC system be monitored on a continuous basis. This will make timely decisions about an expansion or better utilization of the available resources possible. This will guarantee the continuous existence of some spare capacity and help maintain an optimal balance between the level of service provided to the users and the running costs of the DB/DC system. As usual, the main goal of the measurements should be the detection of operational bottlenecks and of an insufficient or inefficient usage of some resource.

The main components of a DB/DC system are displayed in Fig. 7.33. From a functional viewpoint, they can be subdivided into communication and teleprocessing modules, activity control modules, and query language and data-management modules.

The measurement techniques previously described in this book (though not always the specific tools) can be used to control the performance of a DB/DC system. The data on the activity of such a system are usually divided into *static* and *dynamic* data [CO75]. The former describe the physical state or condition of the DBMS, the data bases, and the individual transactions at a given moment; the latter are collected on a continuous basis using event detection or sampling techniques.

For example, the following data are of the static type:

- Physical and logical characteristics of a data base
- Set of modifications made to a data base during a given time period
- Set of transactions waiting to be processed

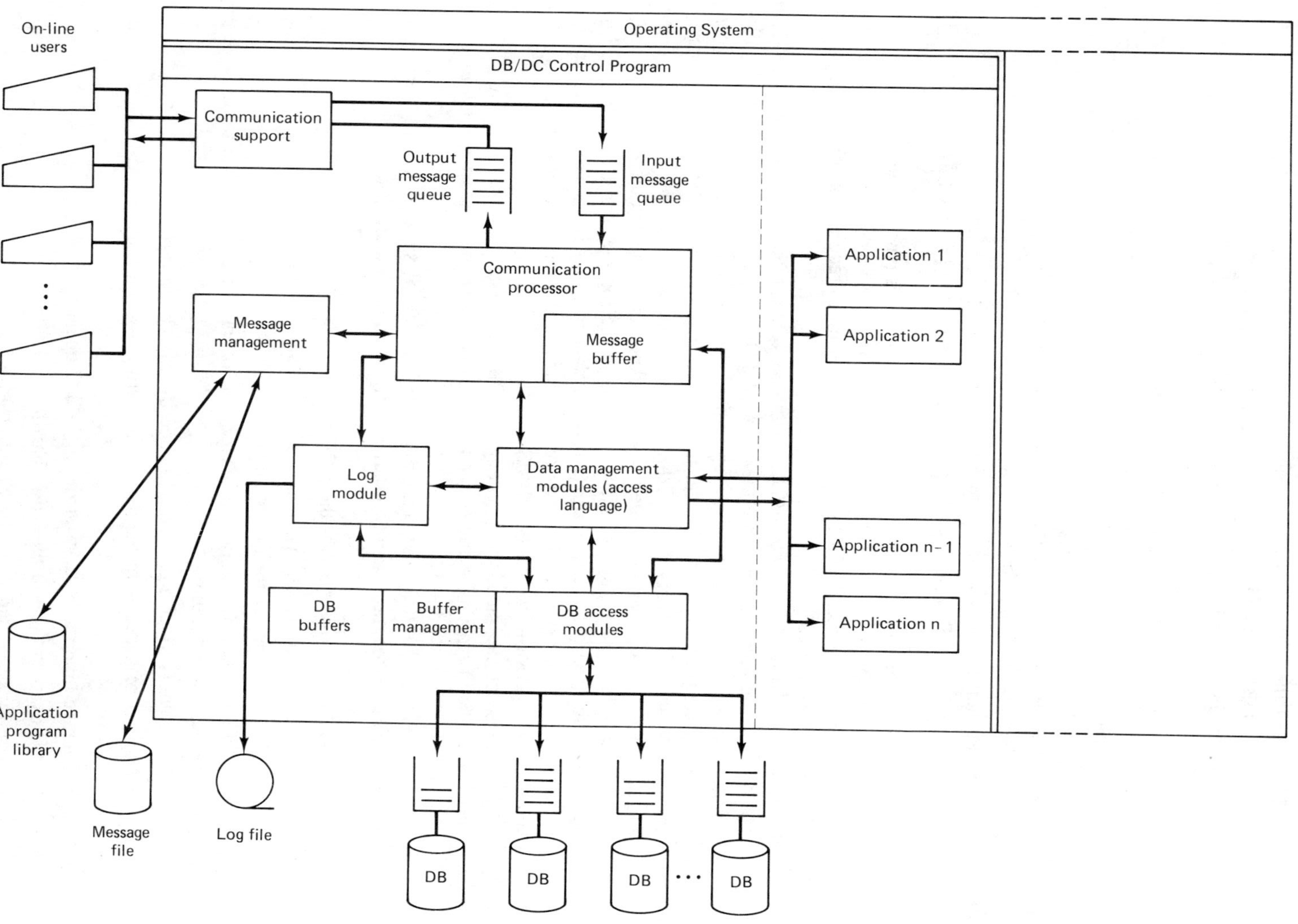

Figure 7.33 Functional scheme of a DB/DC system.

- Sizes of the buffers used
- Set of DBMS modules in main memory
- Set of active application programs

The following are examples of dynamic data:

- Transaction processing time
- Time spent by a transaction in the I/O queues
- Minimum, mean, and maximum lengths of the queues
- Volume of data transferred to and from the terminals
- Frequencies of access and of update to a data base
- Utilizations of direct-access devices and channels due to the DBMS

Normally, the DB/DC system produces data of both types without requiring that any special tool be installed. These tools are only necessary when the data provided by the system are not sufficient for the detailed investigations required or for building a full picture of its activities.

The data collected by the DB/DC system are often stored by a *logging module* on one or more log files from which a great deal of statistics can be obtained. The log files are usually sequential files stored on tape where the events are recorded as they occur. Thus, they constitute a chronological trace of all activities related to the handling of transactions and of the data bases. While dynamic data are continuously written to the log files, static data are only recorded when checkpoints or anomalous conditions occur.

From a functional point of view, the data in the log files can be subdivided into those that are needed to restore a data base, if data integrity is lost, or to recreate the conditions existing before an interruption of system operation, and those useful for determining the performance of the DBMS.

Because of the interactions among the DB/DC system modules (see Fig. 7.33), there could be competing requests for resources, causing the request queues to grow longer and the service level to deteriorate.

Because of the structural complexity of this kind of system, a large number of performance indexes must be measured. Among the most important are:

- Global CPU utilization for the DB/DC system
- CPU utilization for the various control modules
- CPU utilization for the query language
- CPU utilization for individual transactions of on-line users and for those input by application programs
- I/O requests to each data base divided by transaction type
- Number of accesses to the data bases during a given time period (1 day, 1 hour, and so on)
- Average time the requests spend in the I/O queues
- CPU overhead due to the buffer handler
- Memory space demanded by each transaction

The importance of these variables lies in the fact that, to a greater or lesser extent, the response time, which is often the only index on whose basis a DB/DC system is evaluated, depends on them. Figure 7.34 shows schematically how the response time depends on these variables.

The data on the system's activities and performance are obtained by processing the log files. Usually, data summarizing the activities on the system are produced; these data, recorded in a data base, sometimes called the *performance data base,* constitute the basis for medium- and long-term planning of resources (see Fig. 7.35).

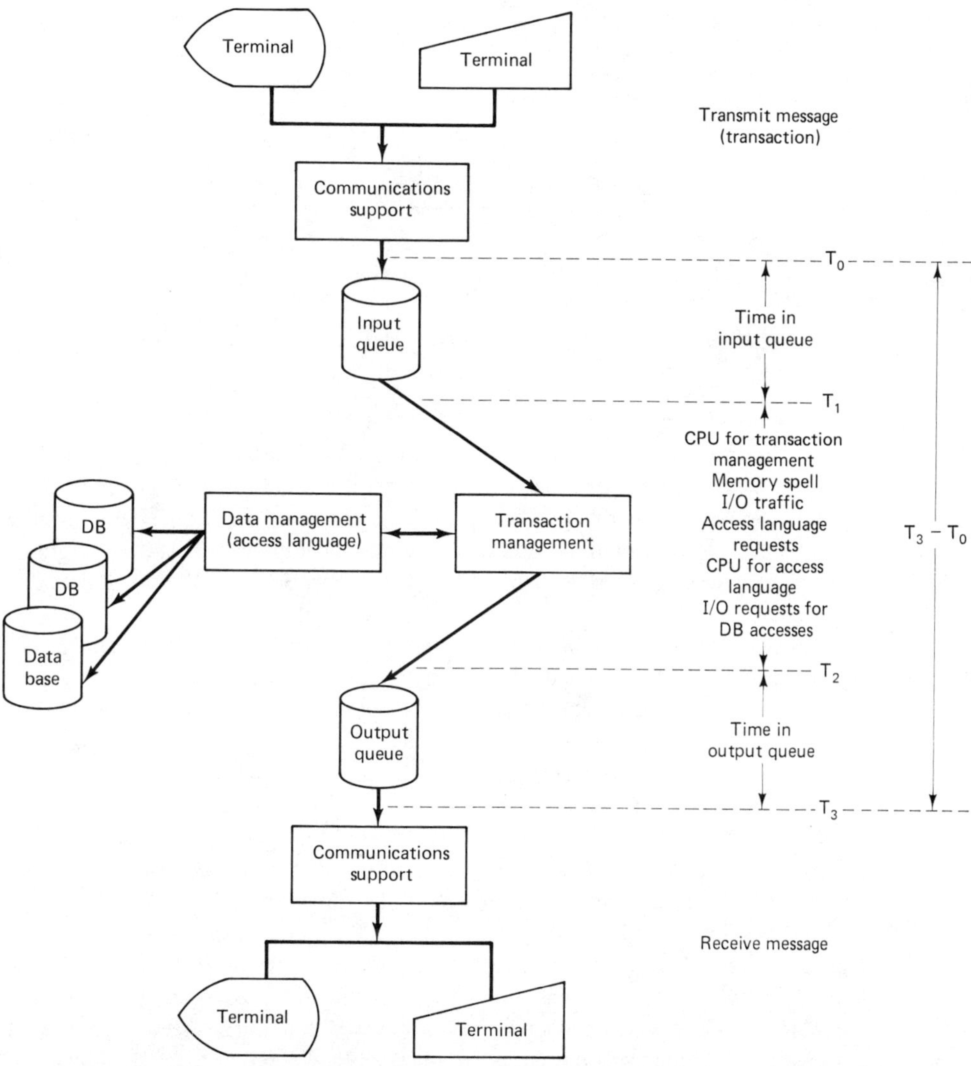

Figure 7.34 Components of the response time of a transaction and the quantities that influence it.

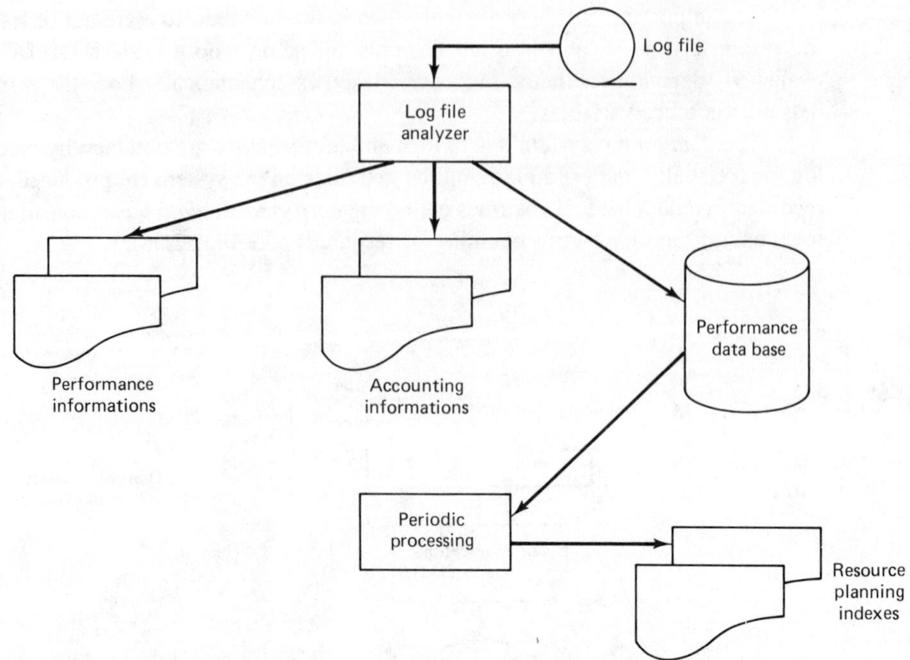

Figure 7.35 Processing scheme of a log file.

A sample graphical analysis is shown in Figs. 7.36 and 7.37, where the sudden and considerable response time increase is due to a sudden increase in the load. This increase, however, has drastically affected the response times only after overcoming a critical value below which they remained quite low. Figure 7.37 shows diagrams of the requests of access to the data base and of the corresponding CPU utilization due to the data-management modules.

Among the possible actions to improve the performance of a data base are the *reorganization* and *restructuring* of its data. Reorganization is intended to reduce the length of pointer chains (chains of physical addresses of logically correlated data), to regain free space, and to make correlated records physically adjacent. Thus, useless data transfers are reduced and transaction processing time decreases.

Restructuring acts both on the physical displacement of data in mass storage and on its logical structure. Since data transfers are made by blocks of records (see Sec. 8.3.3), a real improvement is obtained if, because of restructuring, there is a high probability that some of the other records in the same block of the requested record will be used within a relatively short time. Thus, the basic problem in restructuring is to identify the possible patterns of accesses to data and their probabilities. If there are any, that is, if the accesses are not completely random, the portion of the information in a record that is really used when a reference is made to it should be discovered. Furthermore, the records in a block that are accessed when a block is requested should be established.

On the basis of these data, the information most commonly used in each record

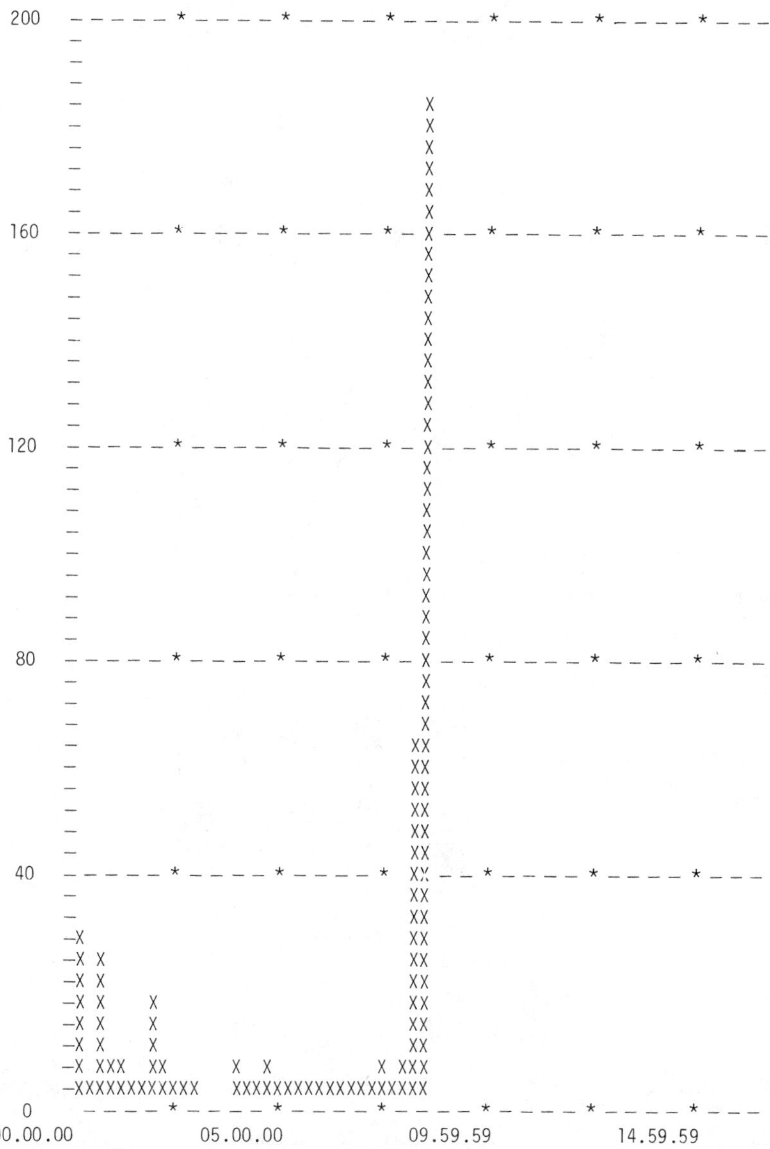

Figure 7.36 Mean response time of transactions versus the load, expressed by the number of programs executed [CO78].

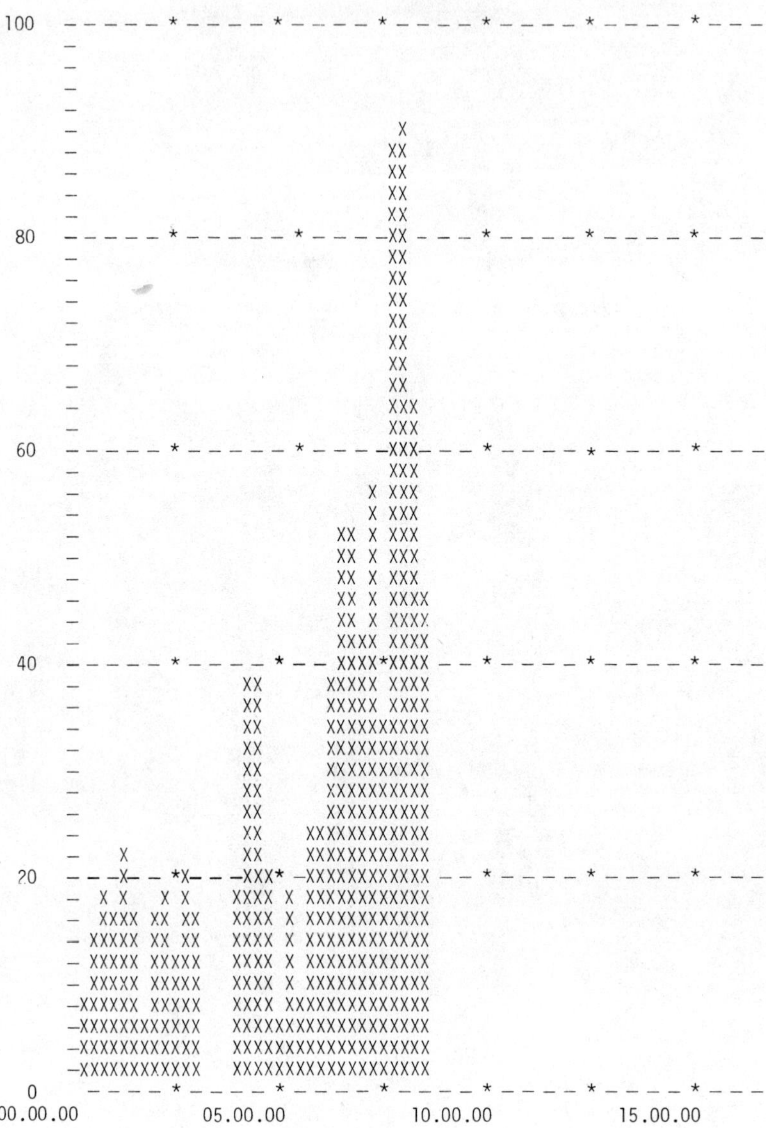

Figure 7.36 (continued).

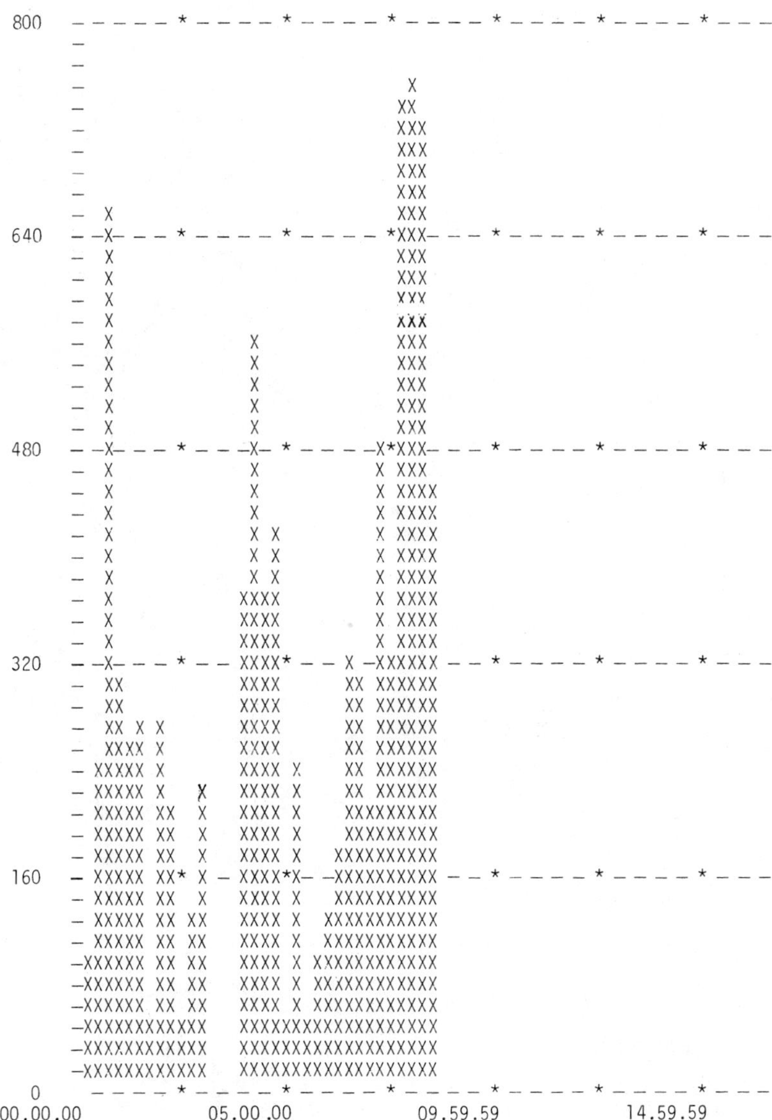

Figure 7.37 Number of calls to the data access language DL1 of the IMS DB/DC system versus CPU utilization [CO78].

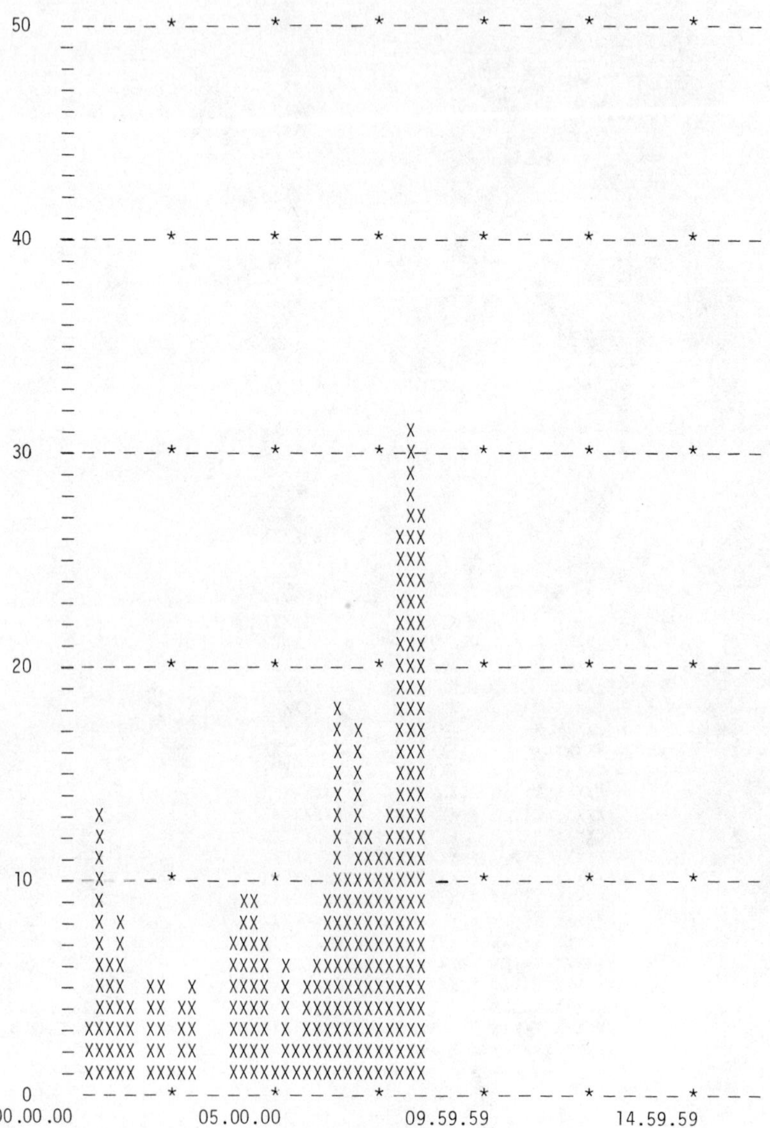

Figure 7.37 (continued).

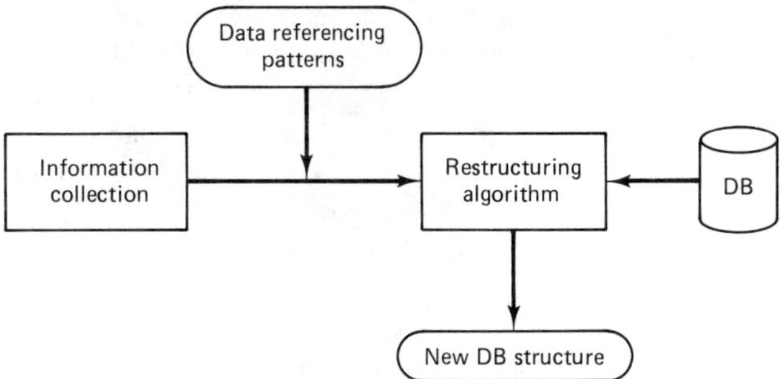

Figure 7.38 Restructuring phases of a data base.

can sometimes be grouped together and within each block, and the records most likely to be requested when one of them is accessed can often be stored in adjacent locations.

A restructuring algorithm can therefore only be used when enough data on access modes and on data referencing patterns (see Fig. 7.38) have been collected.

The possibility of performing a more or less effective reorganization of a data base depends on the availability of supplementary tools (programs for data collection, reorganization, and restructuring) associated with the DBMS.

REFERENCES

Entries marked with an asterisk (*) are referenced in the text.

[AB70] Abell, V. A., Rosen, S., Wagner, R. E., Scheduling in a general purpose operating system, *AFIPS Conf. Proc. FJCC,* vol. 37, pp. 89–96, 1970.

*[AH70] Aho, A. V., Denning, P. J., Ullmann, J. O., Principles of optimal page replacement, *Computer Science Tech. Rep.,* n. 82, Princeton, N.J., Jan. 1970.

[AM72] Amiot, L. W., Aschenbrenner, R. A., Natarajan, M. K., Evaluating a remote batch processing system, *Computer,* pp. 24–29, Sept.–Oct. 1972.

[AN72] Anderson, H. A., Sargent, R. G., A statistical evaluation of the scheduler of an experimental interactive computing system, in: Freiberger, W., ed., *Statistical Computer Performance Evaluation,* Academic Press, New York, 1972.

[AN75] Anderson, H. A., Reiser, M., Galati, G. L., Tuning a virtual storage system, *IBM Systems J.,* n. 3, 1975.

[BA71] Bard, Y., Performance criteria and measurement for a time-sharing system, *IBM Systems J.,* vol. 10, n. 3, pp. 193–214, 1971.

[BE71] Bernstein, A. J., Sharp, J. C., A policy-driven scheduler for a time-sharing system, *CACM,* vol. 14, n. 2, Feb. 1971.

[BO72] Bookman, P. G., et al., Use measurement engineering for better system performance, *Computer Decisions,* vol. 4, n. 4, pp. 28–32, Apr. 1972.

*[BO73] Boehm, B. W., Software and its impact: a quantitative assessment, *Datamation,* pp. 48–59, May 1973.

*[BR68] Brawn, B., Gustavson, S., Program behavior in paging environment, *AFIPS Conf. Proc. FJCC,* vol. 33, pp. 1019–1032, 1968.

*[BU71a] Buzen, J. P., Analysis of system bottlenecks using a queueing network model, *Proc. ACM-SIGOPS Workshop on System Performance Evaluation,* pp. 82–103, Harvard University, Cambridge, Mass., Apr. 1971.

[BU71b] Buzen, J. P., Optimizing the degree of multiprogramming in demand paging systems, *IEEE Computer Society Conference,* Boston, Mass., pp. 141–142, Sept. 22–24, 1971.

[BU73] Buzen, J. P., Optimal balancing of I/O requests to sector scheduled drums, *Proc. 7th ACM-ASA Symposium on the Interface of Computer Science and Statistics,* pp. 130–137, Oct. 1973.

[BU74] Buzen, J. P., Chen, P. P. S., Optimal load balancing in memory hierarchies, *Proc. IFIP Congress 74,* pp. 271–275, North-Holland, Amsterdam, 1974.

[BU77] Buzen, J. P., Load balancing on I/O devices, *Infotech State of the Art Report "System Tuning,"* pp. 241–252, 1977.

[CA75] Cardenas, A. F., Analysis and performance of inverted data base structures, *CACM,* vol. 18, n. 5, pp. 253–263, May 1975.

[CE73] Cerveny, R. P., Knight, K. E., Performance of minicomputers, *Proc. 2nd Texas Conf. on Computer Systems,* 28-1–28-7, Nov. 1973.

[CH73] Chen, P. P. S., Optimal file allocation in multi-level storage systems, *AFIPS Conf. Proc. NCC,* pp. 277–282, 1973.

[CH75] Chiu, W., Dumont, D., Wood, R., Performance analysis of a multiprogrammed computer system, *IBM Research Development,* vol. 19, n. 3, pp. 263–271, March 1975.

[CO71] Cockrum, J. S., Crockett, D. E., Interpreting the results of a hardware systems monitor, *AFIPS Conf. Proc. SJEC,* vol. 38, pp. 23–38, 1971.

*[CO75] *CODASYL-BCS-DDLC, Data base administration working group report,* June 1975.

*[CO68] Coffman, E. G., Varian, L. C., Further experimental data on the behavior of programs in a paging environment, *CACM,* vol. 11, n. 7, July 1968.

[CO73] Coffman, E. G., Denning, P. J., *Operating Systems Theory,* Prentice-Hall, Englewood Cliffs, N.J., 1973.

[CO76] Coffman, E. G., Jr., *Computer and Job/Shop Scheduling Theory,* Wiley-Interscience, New York, 1976.

*[CO78] *Control/IMS—Introductory Guide,* Boole & Babbage, Sunnyvale, Calif., 1978.

[CO81] Coffman, E. G. Jr., Gelembe, E., Plateau, B., Optimization of the number of copies in a distributed data base, *IEEE Trans. on Software Engineering,* vol. SE-7, n. 1, pp. 78–84, Jan. 1981.

[CO74] Cox, S. W., Interpretive analysis of computer system performance, *Proc. 2nd ACM-SICME Symposium on Measurement and Evaluation,* pp. 140–155, Sept. 1974.

[DE69] DeMeis, W. M., Weizer, N., Measurement and analysis of a demand paging time sharing system, *Proc. ACM Nat. Conf.,* pp. 201–216, 1969.

*[DE68] Denning, P. J., Trashing: Its causes and prevention, *AFIPS Conf. Proc. FJCC,* vol. 33, pp. 915–922, 1968.

[DE70] Denning, P. J., Virtual memory, *Computing Surveys,* vol. 2, n. 3, pp. 153–189, Sept. 1970.

[DE75a] Denning, P. J., Kahn, K. C., Some distribution-free properties of throughput and response time, *Purdue Univ. Technical Report n. 159,* Lafayette, Ind., May 1975.

[DE75b] Denning, P. J., Graham, R. S., Multiprogrammed memory management, *Proc. IEEE,* vol. 63, n. 6, pp. 924–939, June 1975.

[DI73] Diethelm, M. A., A method for evaluating mass storage effects on system performance, *AFIPS Conf. Proc. NCC,* pp. 69–74, 1973.

[DS77] *DSO-Data Sets Optimizer—User Guide—Version 4,* Boole & Babbage, Sunnyvale, Calif., Jan. 1977.

[ER74] Erikson, W. J., The value of CPU utilization as a criterion for computer system usage, *Proc. 2nd ACM-SICME Symposium on Measurement and Evaluation,* pp. 180–187, Sept. 1974.

[EW75] Ewing, J. C., Measurement and analysis of an interactive-remote job entry subsystem in a batch oriented system, *Research Report, Purdue Univ. Computing Center,* Lafayette, Ind., 1975.

[FU75] Fuller, S. H., Baskett, F., An analysis of drum storage units, *J. ACM,* vol. 22, n. 1, pp. 83–105, Jan. 1975.

[GO74] Gold, D. E., Kuck, D. J., Implementation considerations for masking rotational latency by dynamic disk allocation, in: *Computer Architecture and Networks,* pp. 207–237, North-Holland, Amsterdam, 1974.

[GO73] Gotlieb, C. C., Metzger, J. K., Trace driven analysis of a batch processing system, *Proc. ACM-SIGSIM Symposium on the Simulation of Computer Systems,* pp. 215–222, June 1973.

[HE70] Hellerman, H., Smith, H. J., Throughput analysis of some idealized input, output and compute overlap configurations, *Computing Surveys,* vol. 3, n. 3, pp. 111–118, June 1970.

[HU73] Hughes, P. H., Moe, G., A structural approach to computer performance analysis, *AFIPS Conf. Proc. NCC,* vol. 42, pp. 109–120, 1973.

[JO74] Jones, R. P. L., A user's experience with software monitors on IBM 360 and 370 computers, *Infotech State of the Art Report "Computer Systems Measurement,"* 1974.

[KI72] Kimbleton, S. R., Core complement policies for memory allocation and analysis, *AFIPS Conf. Proc. FJCC,* pp. 1155–1162, 1972.

[KU78] Kumar, D., Smith, A. D., A query/response system evaluation and enhancements, in: *Performance of Computer Installation, Proc. ICPCI,* pp. 305–321, North-Holland, Amsterdam, June 1978.

[LU73] Lucas, L. W., Improving computer performance—a case study, *Bulletin Op. Res, Soc. of America,* vol. 21, n. 2, p. B-199, 1973.

*[MA74] Madnick, S.E., Donovan, J.J., *Operating Systems,* McGraw-Hill, New York, 1974.

[PI75] Piepmeier, W. F., Optimal balancing of I/O requests to disks, *CACM,* vol. 18, n. 19, pp. 524–527, Sept. 1975.

[PR72] Price, T. G., An analysis of central processor scheduling in multiprogrammed computer systems, *Technical Report n. 57, Digital Systems Laboratory,* Stanford University, Stanford, Calif., Oct. 1972.

[RO72] Rodriguez-Rosell, J., Dupuy, J., The evaluation of a time sharing page demand systems, *AFIPS Conf. Proc. SJCC,* pp. 759–765, 1972.

[RY70] Ryder, K. D., A heuristic approach to task dispatching, *IBM Systems J.,* vol. 9, n. 3, pp. 189–198, 1970.

[SC73] Schneiderman, B., Optimum data base reorganization points, *CACM,* vol. 16, n. 6, pp. 362–365, June 1973.

[SC72] Schwetman, H. D., Browne, J. C., An experimental study of computer system performance, *Proc. ACM Nat. Conf.*, pp. 693–703, 1972.

[SC74] Schwetman, H. D., Analysis of a time-sharing subsystem: A preliminary report, *ACM SIGMETRICS Perf. Evaluat. Review,* vol. 3, n. 4, pp. 65–75, 1974.

[SE81] Sevcik, K. C., Data Base System Performance Prediction using an Analytical Model, *Very Large Data Base Conference,* Cannes, pp. 182–198, 1981.

[SH70] Shope, W. L., and others, System performance study, *Proc. SHARE,* vol. 34, n. 1, pp. 439–530, March 1970.

[SN74] Snyder, R., A quantitative study of the addition of extended core storage, *ACM SIGMETRICS Perf. Evaluat. Review,* vol. 3, n. 1, pp. 10–33, 1974.

[SN78] Snyder, R., An analysis of system requirements, capacity, and resource utilization in a university computer center, in: *Performance of Computer Installations, Proc. ICPCI,* pp. 289–303, North-Holland, Amsterdam, June 1978.

[SR76] Sreenivasan, K., Application of accounting data in evaluating computer system performance, *Software—Practice and Experience,* vol. 6, pp. 239–244, 1976.

[ST71] Strauss, J. C., A simple thruput and response model of EXEC 8 under swapping saturation, *AFIPS Conf. Proc.*, vol. 39, pp. 29–49, 1971.

[TE72a] Teorey, T. J., Pinkerton, T. B., A comparative analysis of disk scheduling policies, *CACM,* vol. 15, n. 3, pp. 177–194, March 1972.

[TE72b] Teorey, T. J., Properties of disk scheduling policies in multi-programmed computer systems, *AFIPS Conf. Proc. FJCC,* pp. 1–11, 1972.

[WA71] Waters, S. J., Blocking sequentially processed magnetic files, *Comput. J.,* vol. 14, n. 2, pp. 109–112, May 1971.

[WR76] Wright, L. S., Brunett, W. A., An approach to evaluating time sharing systems: MH-TSS a case study, *ACM SIGMETRICS Perf. Evaluat. Review,* vol. 5, n. 1, pp. 8–28, Jan. 1976.

8

PROGRAM TUNING

8.1 GENERAL CRITERIA AND PROGRAM SELECTION

The need for ever-decreasing cost–performance ratios has led users to the tuning not only of the systems but also of their workloads and individual programs. Workload optimization may be achieved by (1) optimizing individual programs, in particular those that contribute the most to the workload, and/or (2) optimizing the program mix. The criteria according to which the input job stream is modified to optimize the mix are based on the use of techniques that should guarantee a balanced use of the resources. This objective of the criteria (having general validity) suggests assigning higher priorities of execution to I/O-bound programs than to CPU-bound programs.

The actions performed on the workload to optimize the job stream and those performed on the system to balance the utilizations of the components are clearly complementary. Both contribute to the optimization of the whole installation's performance. Every action to improve the workload should be followed by a verification of system utilizations, since the resource demands are likely to have changed, possibly causing the system to be unbalanced. Scheduling plays an important part in determining system performance since it influences the composition of the job stream. The scheduler usually acts on the basis of user requests and of statistical data produced by accounting routines or by other software tools. The validity of the criteria used by the scheduler can be verified on line with software tools that allow the operator to control dynamically program execution and the queues of the various components.

In Sec. 6.4.2 the use of an on-line software monitor was described for detecting bottlenecks in real time. Figure 8.1 displays a sample output, obtained using an on-line software monitor [LO77], where one can notice a wrong priority assignment. Indeed,

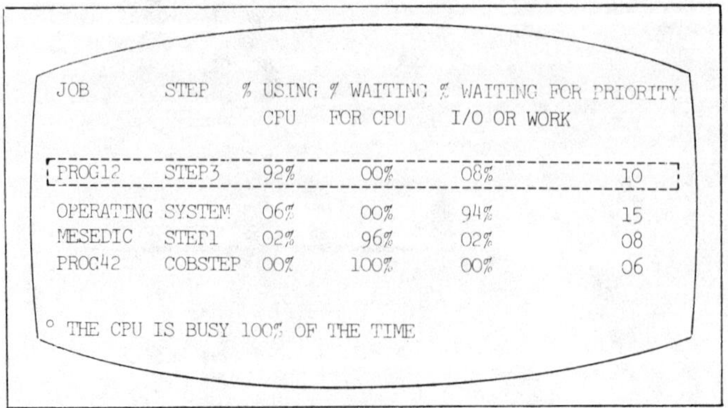

JOB	STEP	% USING CPU	% WAITING FOR CPU	% WAITING FOR I/O OR WORK	PRIORITY
PROG12	STEP3	92%	00%	08%	10
OPERATING SYSTEM		06%	00%	94%	15
MESEDIC	STEP1	02%	96%	02%	08
PROG42	COBSTEP	00%	100%	00%	06

° THE CPU IS BUSY 100% OF THE TIME

Figure 8.1 Example of an incorrect priority assignment detected with an on-line software tool [LO77].

program PROG12, which was given high priority, has used the CPU during most of the observation period (92 percent) and has performed little I/O activity (8 percent). This CPU-bound program has blocked the execution of PROG42 (which has been waiting for the CPU during the entire observation period) and allowed MESEDIC to use the CPU for only 2 percent of the period. Evidently, PROG12's priority (10) is too high with respect to MESEDIC's (8) and PROG42's (6).

Our first approach consists of acting on individual programs to improve their performance. In discussing it, we shall be concerned with programs that have already been coded and tested. Thus, the various programming techniques that can be used to increase program performance will not be discussed.

The optimization of programs is usually carried out with two objectives: (1) memory space reduction, and (2) processing time (CPU and I/O time) reduction. On the basis of the specific needs of each installation, one objective may become more important than the other. There is no universally valid relationship between the two objectives. It is possible to achieve one without the other.

In practice, both reductions are often obtained, but there are cases in which a space–time tradeoff appears; for example, certain searches on list structures, which use a lot of memory space, are faster than similar searches on vectors that require less memory space.

Program optimization is important not only from the individual user's viewpoint, but also in that it directly influences the values of the system's mean throughput rate and turnaround time.

Since the general definition of productivity is (see Sec. 1.4.3.)

$$X = \frac{N_p}{t_m} \tag{8.1}$$

the reduction of the processing time of N_p programs decreases the denominator t_m, whereas the reduction of resource demands increases N_p, the number of programs executed during the interval t_m. These considerations suggest that program optimization may substantially improve system productivity. However, it is extremely difficult to estimate a priori the advantages to be gained.

In many practical cases, the incremental improvement of system performance per unit cost due to the optimization of certain programs turns out to be higher than that due to the improvement actions performed on other system components. However, the analysis of program optimization results shows that often only a few programs influence the improvement of performance appreciably. These programs may be called the *critical programs*. The identification of critical programs must precede any optimization effort, since this will maximize the benefits achieved per unit effort.

The improvement of a program requires a detailed analysis of the source code to determine redundant or inefficiently implemented sections. This type of analysis requires, if performed manually, large amounts of time, and does not allow the quality of the results to be easily predicted. The various types of optimization and of software tools available for this purpose are discussed in the next section. Here we shall only consider the problem of *choosing* which programs will be optimized. Critical programs can only be determined after performing a detailed analysis of the workload (see Chapter 2 and Sec. 3.3.1).

On the basis of the data collected by the system's logging routines, we must look for (1) the most frequently executed programs, and (2) the programs with the greatest resource demands. The programs to be optimized are a subset of those belonging to classes 1 and 2. Indeed, the optimization of a program that is often executed is not necessarily worthwhile. For this to be the case, the resource demands made by its executions must be reasonably high. For example, the optimization of a program executed 300 times a day that uses 6 s of CPU time at each execution may be less advantageous than that of a program only executed once a day, but requiring 45 min of CPU time.

In particular, those programs with the greatest demands on CPU time, I/O time, memory space, error interrupts, and paging activity (for virtual memory systems) are eligible for optimizing actions.

To obtain this kind of data, commercial software tools may be used. It is also possible to implement ad hoc programs that will process the data collected by the system's routines. Figure 8.2 presents a list obtained with a commercial software tool [PL77] of the characteristics of the 30 programs that requested most CPU time during a certain time interval in a particular installation. Similar lists can be obtained for any of the quantities mentioned previously (memory space, I/O activity, and so on). The problem of correlating the various values of these quantities is automatically solved by tools of this type, if they provide a list of the programs whose demands are high for more than one resource. For example, in Fig. 8.3 GENPROC turns out to be the seventh program most often executed, the eighth heaviest user of the CPU, and the one with the highest number of error interrupts.

The evaluator analyzes the workload data, calculating the resource demands of each program by suitable algorithms and producing a list of the programs that should be optimized on the basis of all executions. Among the algorithms that may be used, the simplest determines the *load* L_x caused on the system by a program x as a linear combination of the loads caused by x on individual components; that is,

ANALYSIS OF CRITICAL PROGRAMS

** MOST TOTAL CPU TIME **

```
REPORTING PERIOD
FROM   SUNDAY      02/04/79 0809
TO     SATURDAY    02/10/79 1931
```

NO.	PROGRAM NAME	TOTALS: NO. RUNS	NO. ABENDS	EXECUTION TIME	CPU TIME	PROGRAM AVERAGES: EXECUTION TIME	CPU TIME	STOR USED	EXCPS (100S) DISK	TAPE	PAGING IN/OUT	PAGING (PER CPU SEC)	EXCPS (PER CPU SEC)	SERVICE UNITS(100S)	PERCENTAGE: CPU/ EXEC	CPU TOTAL	CUMUL CPU
1.	SM010	383	11	51.19.34	16.25.42	.08.02	.02.34	392	11	23	96	1	22	1010	32.0	22.7	22.7
2.	DFSRRC00	458	12	146.10.26	12.13.30	.19.09	.01.36	761	31	18	111	1	50	757	8.3	16.9	39.6
3.	RMS2P20	5	0	6.19.35	4.13.24	1.15.55	.50.41	506	148	1840	118	0	65	24683	66.7	5.8	45.4
4.	PCOST	10	0	18.52.37	3.54.08	1.53.16	.23.25	1120	7	0	7595	5	0	10716	20.6	5.3	50.8
5.	SPF	1024	53	273.39.24	1.54.28	.16.02	.00.07	341	2	0	2451	365	32	31	0.6	2.6	53.5
6.	DFSMVRC0	5	0	75.22.41	1.48.23	15.04.32	.21.41	1084	250	401	10998	8	50	8155	2.3	2.4	56.0
7.	IELOAA	759	15	23.56.22	1.44.37	.01.54	.00.08	460	10	0	135	16	123	60	7.2	2.4	58.4
8.	GENPROC	504	158	238.11.41	1.22.42	.28.21	.00.10	435	7	0	2363	240	74	72	0.5	1.9	60.3
9.	SORT	392	3	12.08.20	1.18.46	.01.51	.00.12	550	17	9	24	2	210	83	10.8	1.8	62.1
10.	FDR	61	0	12.11.30	1.15.07	.12.00	.01.14	305	76	65	86	1	190	323	10.2	1.7	63.8
11.	WA99MXXX	3	2	9.17.52	1.01.38	3.05.57	.20.33	490	617	0	3982	3	50	6566	11.0	1.4	65.3
12.	P43500	1	0	6.30.30	.58.14	6.30.30	.58.14	1192	18	412	46167	13	12	43758	14.9	1.3	66.6
13.	TEST2	17	3	7.29.53	.57.31	.26.28	.03.23	1131	1	0	1435	7	1	1566	12.7	1.3	67.9
14.	MAIN	85	8	7.01.11	.53.06	.04.57	.00.37	785	32	3	362	10	92	588	12.6	1.2	69.2
15.	RMS2P02	5	0	1.27.51	.50.49	.17.34	.10.10	344	151	0	27	0	25	3777	57.8	1.1	70.3
16.	PWRF1000	87	0	9.02.21	.43.46	.06.14	.00.30	1121	9	1	773	26	32	313	8.0	1.0	71.3
17.	PGM=*.DD	150	13	6.55.27	.41.08	.02.46	.00.16	497	16	1	73	4	102	77	9.9	0.9	72.3
18.	PWRF1800	21	3	5.32.51	.37.50	.15.51	.01.48	1176	17	0	903	8	16	1071	11.3	0.8	73.2
19.	NTRAN$	4	1	2.39.28	.34.56	.39.52	.08.44	480	0	4	311	1	1	2531	21.9	0.8	74.0
20.	IEBGENER	1497	4	14.59.39	.34.40	.00.36	.00.01	279	2	3	12	9	350	10	3.8	0.7	74.8
21.	RMS2M440	5	0	1.43.48	.33.01	.20.46	.06.36	392	0	1284	18	0	324	2319	31.8	0.7	75.5
22.	PAN#7	5	0	2.35.00	.31.04	.31.00	.06.13	573	644	0	52	0	173	1569	20.0	0.7	76.2
23.	AWBPNCDF	5	0	.55.35	.30.01	.11.07	.06.00	241	81	78	59	0	44	1882	53.9	0.6	76.9
24.	LEX170	137	3	3.15.34	.29.38	.01.26	.00.13	483	15	7	28	2	170	97	15.1	0.6	77.6
25.	SM050	263	0	2.46.18	.28.44	.00.38	.00.07	362	1	5	7	1	79	35	17.2	0.6	78.3
26.	IDCAMS	272	0	8.52.20	.26.42	.01.57	.00.06	531	5	1	78	13	108	43	5.0	0.6	78.9
27.	PR87PXXX	11	0	4.43.32	.24.54	.25.47	.02.16	830	195	122	778	6	233	1234	8.7	0.5	79.5
28.	GRSLOADR	35	0	3.44.25	.23.50	.06.25	.00.41	584	49	24	99	2	178	254	10.6	0.5	80.0
29.	FAULT700	21	0	5.12.10	.22.55	.14.52	.01.05	598	134	2	460	7	207	400	7.3	0.5	80.5
30.	RXXCEM	7	2	2.42.01	.21.37	.23.09	.03.05	588	56	30	882	5	46	1393	13.3	0.4	81.0

*** SUMMARY SHOWING RELATIVE IMPORTANCE ***

36.5 PER CENT OF TOTAL NUMBER OF RUNS
81.0 PER CENT OF TOTAL PROBLEM PROGRAM CPU TIME
57.4 PER CENT OF TOTAL PROBLEM PROGRAM DISK EXCPS
67.3 PER CENT OF TOTAL PROBLEM PROGRAM TAPE EXCPS
85.7 PER CENT OF TOTAL PROBLEM PROGRAM PAGE-INS AND PAGE-OUTS
67.2 PER CENT OF TOTAL PROBLEM PROGRAM EXECUTION TIME
56.8 PER CENT OF TOTAL ABENDS
79.3 PER CENT OF TOTAL PROBLEM PROGRAM SERVICE UNITS

Figure 8.2 Characteristics of the 30 programs that required the greatest amounts of CPU time during the period considered [PL77].

A N A L Y S I S   O F   C R I T I C A L   P R O G R A M S

REPORTING PERIOD
FROM SUNDAY 02/04/79 0809
TO SATURDAY 02/10/79 1931

** CORRELATION REPORT **

PROGRAM NAME	NO. RUNS	TOTAL CPU TIME	AVER. CPU TIME	DISK EXCPS	TAPE EXCPS	PAGING RATE	NO. ABENDS	STOR USED	I/O BOUND	CPU BOUND	SERVICE UNITS
IEBGENER	1	20	-	11	5	-	24	-	-	-	19
PAN#1	2	-	-	-	-	-	15	-	-	-	-
SPF	3	5	-	16	-	-	2	-	-	-	12
IELOAA	4	7	-	2	-	-	4	-	-	-	7
DFSILNK0	6	-	-	27	-	-	13	-	-	-	-
GENPROC	7	8	-	9	-	-	1	-	-	-	10
DFSRRC00	8	2	-	1	3	-	7	-	-	-	2
SORT	10	9	-	3	9	-	-	-	-	-	11
SM010	11	1	-	5	2	-	10	-	-	12	1
IEWL	12	-	-	30	-	-	-	-	-	-	-
IEBCOPY	13	-	-	8	-	-	-	-	-	-	-
IDCAMS	14	26	-	23	27	-	-	-	-	-	23
SM050	16	25	-	-	16	-	-	-	-	-	-
HEWL	18	-	-	28	-	-	9	-	-	-	-
RETRIEVE	19	-	-	-	-	-	-	3	-	-	-
PAN#2	21	-	-	29	7	-	-	-	-	-	-
PGM=*.DD	24	17	-	15	-	-	6	-	-	-	25
LFX170	25	24	-	18	17	-	28	-	-	-	21
LIONSPRE	26	-	-	-	15	-	21	-	-	-	-
SM020	28	-	-	-	12	-	-	-	-	-	-
RMS2P20	-	3	2	-	1	-	-	-	-	3	3
PCOST	-	4	3	-	-	-	-	16	-	26	4
DFSMVRC0	-	6	4	25	11	23	-	18	-	-	9
FDR	-	10	-	4	6	-	-	-	-	-	17
WA99MXXX	-	11	5	20	-	-	-	-	-	-	16
P43500	-	12	1	-	25	12	-	10	-	-	8
TEST2	-	13	25	-	-	28	-	14	-	-	14
MAIN	-	14	-	14	-	16	14	-	-	-	6
RMS2P02	-	15	11	-	-	-	-	-	-	4	18
PWRF1000	-	16	-	-	-	5	-	15	-	-	13
PWRF1800	-	18	-	-	-	25	-	12	-	-	15
NTRAN$	-	19	12	-	-	-	-	-	-	24	26
RMS2M440	-	21	15	-	4	-	-	-	24	13	24
PAN#7	-	22	16	10	-	-	-	-	-	28	-
AWBPNCDE	-	23	19	-	26	-	-	-	-	6	-
PR87PXXX	-	27	-	17	14	-	-	-	-	-	20
CRSLOADR	-	28	-	21	20	-	-	-	-	-	-
FAULT700	-	29	-	12	-	27	-	-	-	-	-
RXXCFM	-	30	27	-	-	-	-	-	-	-	28
PM06PXXX	-	-	6	-	-	-	-	-	-	10	-
MM60P000	-	-	8	26	29	-	-	23	-	19	-
RA28P00	-	-	9	-	19	-	-	-	-	-	-
PM05PXXX	-	-	10	-	-	-	-	-	-	7	-

Figure 8.3 Example of correlations between values of the programs that made the heaviest usage of the resources during the period considered [PL77].

$$L_x = K_1 t_{\text{CPU}} + K_2 B_{ms} t_m + K_3 \sum_{j=1}^{n} \left(t_{\text{ch}_j} + K_4 \sum_{i=1}^{m_j} t_{\text{dev}_{ij}} \right) \tag{8.2}$$

where the K coefficients represent weights that account for the actual importance of each component in the configuration being considered, the t's are the allocation times of the various resources to program x, and B_{ms} is the number of main memory blocks required. By assigning different values to the K's, some possible differences among the programs analyzed can be accounted for (for example, their programming languages, execution priorities, and so on).

The loads caused by each execution of a program must be added together, and, at the end of the observation period, the values of L_x for all programs must be sorted in decreasing order. The list of values obtained in this way allows us to recognize which programs should be improved first because of their low presumable cost–benefit ratio.

We shall now describe an example in which expression (8.2) is used to rank the programs in an installation's workload. In the system being considered, roughly 13,000 programs are run every month. Of these, 40 percent are scientific or technical programs written in FORTRAN or in assembly language, and 60 percent are administrative programs written in COBOL. About 30 percent of the total processing time is spent for scientific and technical programs and 70 percent for administrative programs.

The analysis of the L_x values for the workload considered, which consists of 2600 distinct programs, reveals that only about 100 of these programs make a greater than average use of the resources (see Figs. 8.4 and 8.5). In particular, the first 80 programs

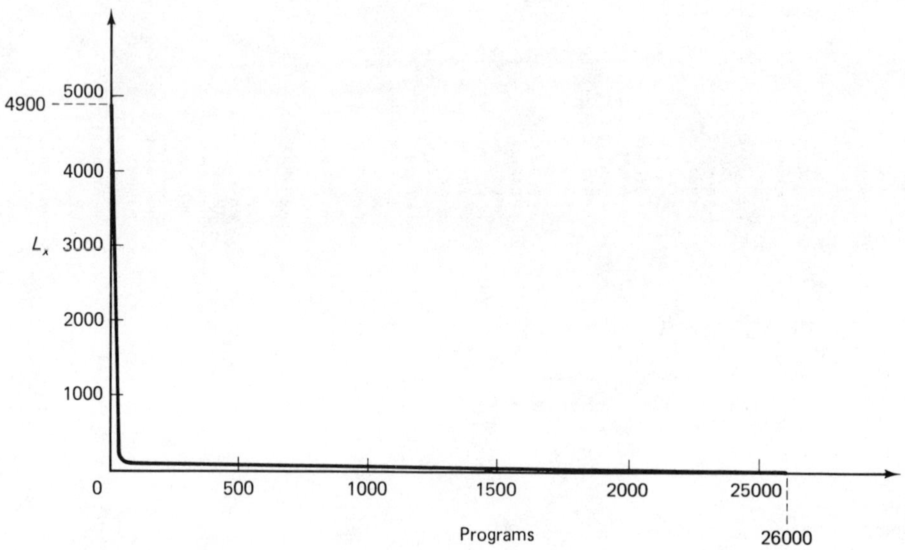

Figure 8.4 Values of function L_x, the global resource demand made by the programs in the workload (linear scale).

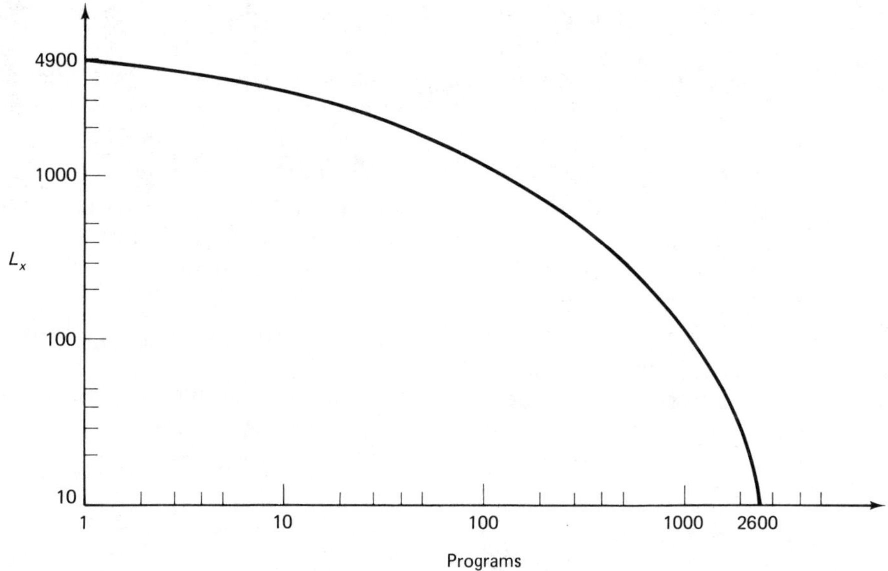

Figure 8.5 Values of function L_x for the workload considered (logarithmic scale).

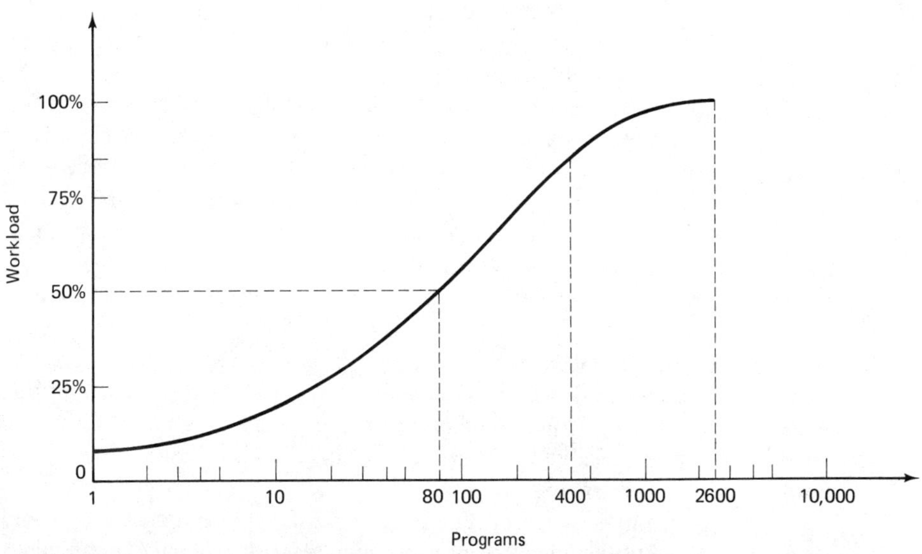

Figure 8.6 Resource usage caused by the programs considered according to the decreasing values of function L_x.

represent 50 percent of the whole workload's resource demand, while the first 400 demand 80 percent of the total (see Fig. 8.6).

On the basis of these data, the first optimization actions are performed on programs that represent a considerable portion of the workload in terms of resource demand, although numerically they constitute a tiny fraction of all the programs examined. The iterative approach to bottleneck removal described in Sec. 6.4 can also be applied here. The initial restriction on the number of programs to be considered guarantees the convenience of the investment if the criteria used for selecting them are valid.

Having improved the programs in the first group, new measurements are made to evaluate the results obtained. If these results are not good enough, new programs can be chosen among those not yet examined, using the criteria described previously, and the necessary improvement actions undertaken.

The procedure stops when the results obtained are sufficiently satisfactory or when all programs have been considered. Thus, the method described for choosing programs defines the order in which programs should be considered so as to obtain the maximum result with the minimum effort.

8.2 TYPES OF PROGRAM OPTIMIZATIONS

There are two approaches to the reduction of a workload's global resource demands:

1. The *generalized approach* tries to reduce the use of all resources.
2. The *selective approach* tries to reduce the total demand for the most requested (or *critical*) resources.

The difference between these two approaches is in the number of programs that they consider (all those in a given group in the first; only the few critical ones in the second) and, therefore, in the methods they apply.

The generalized approach normally employs tools that try to optimize the programs *automatically;* no user intervention is required. The selective approach only operates on critical programs, and thus on critical resources, and uses both automatic tools and tools that "guide" the user's interventions. The latter is called *guided optimization*.

Because of what was said in the previous section, the selective approach is a priori more likely to produce the best results for a given investment. This approach determines the programs to be optimized first, and then chooses the optimization method.

One type of automatic optimization can be found in some optimizing compilers and in some commercial software tools, which may be viewed as postprocessors of the standard compilers. Both work on the object code, and their principles of operation are illustrated in Fig. 8.7. However, this type of optimization is not always possible since the compilers being used may not be optimizing compilers, nor are there postprocessors for all programming languages.

The optimization of *object code* is made possible by the imperfections of high-level language compilers, which often produce redundant or otherwise inefficient code. Examples of redundancies are conversions performed on data each time they are needed in arithmetic operations, and instructions operating on data that are not modified or not used

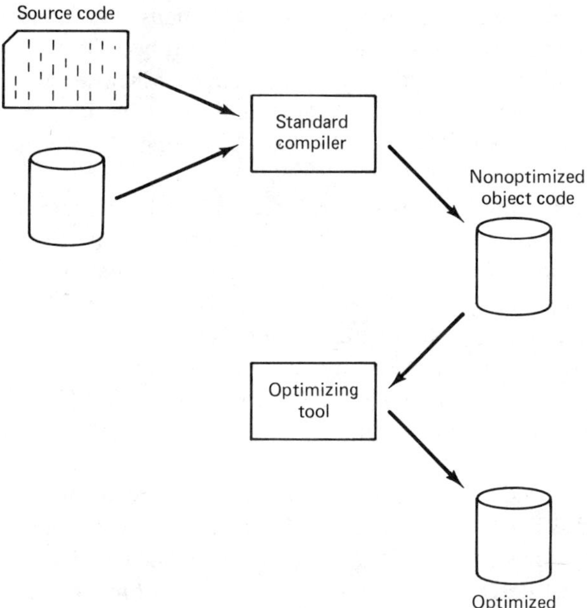

Figure 8.7 Scheme of a possible procedure for the automatic optimization of object code.

elsewhere within a loop (see Sec. 8.3.1). In the latter example, optimization consists of reducing the number of object instructions executed, thereby reducing the CPU time required by the program. In the former, optimizing actions result in a reduction of the number of object instructions generated, and hence in memory space savings. The savings that can be achieved vary from program to program and depend on its size, processing time, and language (that is, on the compiler's efficiency), on the tool used and, partially, on the programmer's experience. For example, with commercial software tools that perform the automatic optimization of COBOL programs, mean savings of about 25 to 30 percent on the number of instructions and of about 15 to 20 percent on the execution time have been obtained [OP78].

There are also automatic optimization procedures oriented toward virtual memory systems. In these systems, a program's paging rate or mean memory occupancy or some function of both indexes can be automatically reduced by modifying the program's placement in virtual memory (see Sec. 8.3.3).

The reliability of an automatic optimization method is strictly related to that of the tool and can be determined a priori by analyzing the characteristics of the available tools. If the choice of tool is made following adequate criteria, the reliability may turn out to be quite high.

Automatic optimization is easy to carry out and its costs can easily be predicted on the basis of the tool's cost and of the machine time needed. On the other hand, its effectiveness is modest when applied to some programs, even though on the average its results are usually positive.

With guided optimization, the user is driven by appropriate tools in his or her actions on the source code; the changes are in this case made manually by the user. If no tool is available, the results of sometimes lengthy manual operations intended to reduce a program's resource demands are likely to be disappointing. This is because of the effort required to optimize a program without having any information on which sections of the program to concentrate on. Certain statistics indicate that, on the average, in commercial programs about 75 percent of the processing time is spent executing 10 percent of the program's object code.

Even though the numerical values of these percentages might be questioned, their orders of magnitude are likely to be found in most similar cases. Thus, the general statement can be made that most of a program's processing time is spent executing a small subset of its instructions. An optimizing intervention on this subset has a much greater potential impact than actions on other parts of the program.

Some software tools permit the detection, during program execution, of each instruction's frequency of execution (that is, construct *the program profile*) [PP76]. The object code of the program is divided into sections of equal length established by the evaluator. At the end of the analysis, reports displaying the frequency of execution of each section of code are produced. In successive steps, the most frequently executed sections are in turn subdivided into subsections of smaller size until the frequencies are known with the desired resolution (which could even be the individual instruction level).

The iterative process just described avoids excessive costs in time and space by concentrating on the most frequently used parts of the program. Data collection is carried out with sampling techniques similar to those described in Chapter 3. Sections 8.3.1 and 8.3.2 contain examples of guided optimizations performed with sampling software tools.

Guided optimization often makes it possible to reduce the processing time of a program appreciably. The amounts of CPU and I/O time saved vary from program to program and depend on how the program was coded, that is, on the programmer's skill and experience. The reliability of a program optimized in this way greatly depends on the experience of the person who performs the optimization; in any case, it is useful to carry out a test execution before the program starts running in production mode. The costs of this method depend substantially on the application and are basically determined by the number of man-hours needed to study the program and carry out the improvement actions, the machine time for the test executions, and the price of the tool.

The machine time required can be considerably reduced by verifying the correctness of the changes during production executions, but in this case the method's reliability decreases. Program processing times are usually reduced by this approach, and sometimes by even more than expected (improvements of 50 to 60 percent have been reported); however, it is difficult to predict the results that will be obtained. This technique is particularly recommended when a program must have optimal performance even if this were to require an (apparently) uneconomical effort.

Other guided optimization techniques are tracing, simulation, and source code analysis. With tracing, the program itself provides data on its most often executed sections by printing out *traces* (*diagnostic messages*) that indicate the path followed by the flow of control. The instructions for printing out these traces must be added by the user; in some languages the compiler will generate them if a particular option is requested.

Source code analysis can be performed by a preprocessor capable of finding inefficient code and of checking the correct use of source statements. For example, the preprocessor should determine whether and where "heavy" statements are used too often,

TABLE 8.1 MAIN CHARACTERISTICS OF THE TWO TYPES OF PROGRAM OPTIMIZATION

	Types of optimization	
Characteristics	*Automatic (object code)*	*Guided (source code)*
Cost (per program):		
Computer time	Lower than compilation time	One run for verification
Programmer time	None	Variable
Results:		
Memory space reduction	Depends on program, usually good (20–30%)	Generally low
CPU time reduction	Depends on program, usually good (45–20%)	Depends on program, may reach high values
I/O time reduction	Low	Good on the average
Reliability	That of the instrument, usually high	Depends on the experience of the human optimizer
Ease of application	High	Good
Opportunities to modify systems programs	No	Yes
Controllability of the program's logic	No	Yes
Preventive evaluation of cost–performance ratio	Indicative	Difficult
Instrumentation costs	Similar	Similar
Dependence on programming language	Yes	No

or whether statements appear in the source that generate a longer object code. The latter is the case of IFs followed by an arithmetic expression in FORTRAN; to make them faster it is often sufficient to calculate the arithmetic expression before executing the IF statement. It is also the case of MOVE statements in COBOL having operands of different lengths or an unsigned destination address (an extra object code instruction is generated in these cases). This kind of optimization can be performed even before entering the testing phase of a program, thereby possibly saving considerable machine time, since test executions will be performed on an optimized program.

Table 8.1 contains the main characteristics of the two types of optimization we have discussed, including information about which can help the user choose the better for the case at hand. Figure 8.8 shows a possible sequence of application of the various techniques described during the implementation of a program. The use of one technique does not necessarily imply that of the others; the users must decide, on the basis of their requirements and of the considerations made here, which techniques should be applied, if any. Although these techniques can be used at any time during a program's life, it is convenient to employ them after the testing phase.

8.2.1 Program Performance Indexes

Program performance indexes are quantities that may be used to express the efficiency with which a program is processed. There is no unique global index that quantifies the

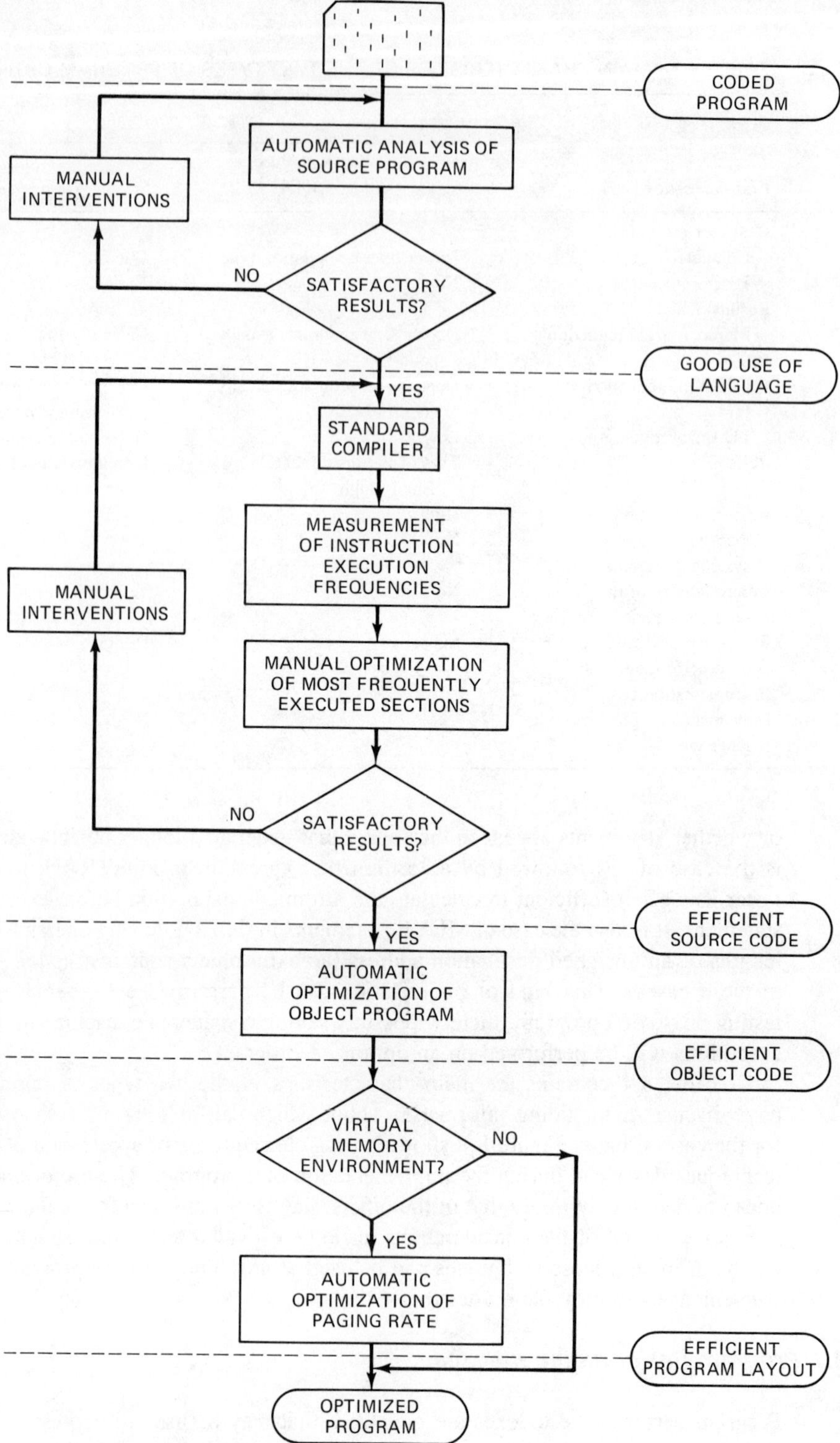

Figure 8.8 Application of the optimization methods described; the use of one technique does not necessarily imply that of the others.

efficiency of execution of a program, but there are several quantities, each of which provides indications on various aspects of such efficiency. Different individuals interpret the notion of *efficient processing* in different ways: for one user it may substantially coincide with the concept of minimum memory usage, for another it may be equivalent to minimum response time, another may be interested in maximum data compression on mass storage, and so on. It is important to consider the connections existing among all the indexes of interest and the influence of the system's workload on them. Indeed, some indexes depend on the workload, whereas others are not influenced by it.

In general, for instance, it is conceptually wrong to compare the indexes of two programs unless all the other conditions existing in the system when they were processed are taken into account. The values of the indexes also depend on the system that processes the program. It is therefore necessary, before making any comparison between programs running on different systems, to analyze the characteristics of the systems in order to establish whether and how much the differences between them may have influenced the performance index values that have been measured.

Since most program performance indexes have been described in Secs. 1.4.1 to 1.4.3, in the sequel greater attention will be paid to the connections between the indexes than to their definitions. The indexes to be considered are only a small subset of those that could be proposed, but are among the most popular because of their easy derivation and interpretation.

Let us consider a batch-processing environment; let P be the instant at which the printing out of the results of a program's execution is completed and R the instant at which the first card of the program's deck is read in. The *turnaround time* of the program is then

$$T = P - R \tag{8.3}$$

If the processing time of the same program is t_p, the program's total wait time (that is, the sum of all the periods during which its execution is suspended since the resources needed by the program are not available) is given by

$$t_{\text{wait}} = (P - R) - t_p \tag{8.4}$$

The various times that characterize the execution of a program are reported in the diagram in Fig. 1.8.

The *weighted turnaround time,* defined in Sec. 1.4.1 as the ratio between the turnaround time and a program's processing time, is given by

$$T_w = \frac{T}{t_p} \tag{8.5}$$

Substituting t_p with the value obtained from Eq. (8.4), we have

$$T_w = \frac{P - R}{(P - R) - t_{\text{wait}}} = \frac{1}{1 - t_{\text{wait}}/(P - R)} \tag{8.6}$$

If t_{wait} tends to zero, we obtain the optimal value of T_w, $T_w = 1$ (in other words, the program's execution is not delayed). The weighted turnaround time, a pure number greater than or equal to 1, may be used to represent a program's processing efficiency and can be directly compared with that of other programs in a workload since it is a normalized quantity.

The weighted turnaround time is also called the *stretch factor* [HE75], since it quantifies the stretching of a program's processing time due to multiprogramming.

Considering a job stream of n programs, their mean turnaround time is given by

$$T_m = \frac{1}{n}\sum_{i=1}^{n} T_i = \frac{1}{n}\sum_{i=1}^{n} (t_{wait\ i} + t_{pi}) \tag{8.7}$$

while their mean weighted turnaround time is

$$T_{wm} = \frac{1}{n}\sum_{i=1}^{n} T_{wi} \tag{8.8}$$

Substituting for the value of T_w obtained from Eq. (8.6), we have

$$T_{wm} = \frac{1}{n}\sum_{i=1}^{n} \frac{1}{1 - t_{wait\ i}/(P_i - R_i)} \tag{8.9}$$

The performance indexes we have just defined provide an indication of the processing efficiency of one or more programs. Their values are, in most cases, very sensitive to the variations of internal system conditions. For example, the mean turnaround time, and thus also the mean weighted turnaround time, is greatly affected by the scheduling algorithm used by the system. If the scheduler employs the SJF (shortest job first) algorithm, described in Sec. 1.4.1, the values of T_m and T_{wm} obtained will be minimum, assuming that all programs are loaded into the system at the same time.

The turnaround times T_i of the shorter programs are minimized, and so is T_m. Since the values of the T_i, $t_{wait\ i}$ and t_{pi} are always nonnegative, and the values of the t_{pi} are assumed not to be modified, from Eq. (8.7) we deduce that also the global wait time of the n programs will be minimal.

Substituting Eq. (8.4) into Eq. (8.5), we have

$$T_w = \frac{T}{t_p} = \frac{t_{wait} + t_p}{t_p} = \frac{t_{wait}}{t_p} + 1 \tag{8.10}$$

which shows that, to obtain the minimum value of T_w, the ratio t_{wait}/t_p must be made as small as possible.

The value of T_{wm} can be expressed as follows:

$$T_{wm} = \frac{1}{n}\sum_{i=1}^{n} \left(\frac{t_{wait\ i}}{t_{pi}} + 1\right) \tag{8.11}$$

The ratio t_{wait}/t_p can easily become quite large with programs having short processing times. Indeed, the smaller t_p, the greater the probability that t_{wait} will be equal to or greater than t_p. Since the SJF algorithm minimizes the $t_{wait\ i}$ especially for the shorter programs, the value of T_{wm} obtained with this algorithm is smaller than those obtained with other algorithms.

Unfortunately, these considerations on the efficiency of the algorithm cannot be extended to the processing of individual programs or to the system's throughput. In particular, the processing efficiency of programs does not coincide with the utilization efficiency of the system.

According to its general definition, the productivity X is given by

$$X = \frac{n}{t}$$

where t is the time needed to process completely the n programs in the workload. The value of t can be calculated as follows:

$$t = \max_{i=1,n} P_i - \min_{i=1,n} R_i \tag{8.12}$$

where $\max_i P_i$ is the largest of the stop printing times of the n programs and $\min_i R_i$ is the smallest of the start reading times. Thus, the value of the throughput does not provide any information on the processing efficiency of individual programs, but gives an indication of the global processing efficiency for the n programs in the workload.

The throughput is affected by the simultaneity of operations; more precisely, the greater the processing overlap, that is, the intersections of the T_i's, the higher the throughput. In Sec. 1.4.3, an example is discussed in which X does not vary as the scheduling algorithm changes from FCFS (first come first served) to RR (round robin), while the values of T, T_w, T_m and T_{wm} are affected by the change. These values are calculated assuming that the time needed by the system to suspend a program's execution and start another's (*setup–setdown* time) is negligible. This assumption favors the RR algorithm, since the number of setups–setdowns it performs (one per quantum) is clearly greater than that produced by FCFS. Therefore, if the setup–setdown time is taken to be greater than zero, the throughput of the system using RR turns out to be lower than that obtained with FCFS, while T_m and T_{wm} have better values under RR. Thus, the system is more efficiently utilized with the FCFS algorithm, but program processing is less efficient (since the values of T_m and T_{wm} are greater).

With a different input job mix, leaving the other conditions unaltered, these conclusions cannot be applied without repeating the preceding considerations. In fact, different conclusions are often reached. The results obtained with the FCFS algorithm are much more sensitive to workload variations than those provided by the RR algorithm.

8.3 REDUCING EXECUTION TIME

Reducing the execution time of a program, or of a group of programs, is one of the possible objectives of a performance improvement study. The objects to be improved may be user programs, chosen with the criteria described in Sec. 8.1, or systems programs such as, for example, spooling routines, teleprocessing monitors, and data-base management systems.

The reasons for modifying programs in order to reduce their execution times are usually the following:

1. To increase the productivity or, more generally, the performance of a system with a given configuration (that is, without adding new hardware).
2. To reach minimum response or turnaround times for certain batch programs.
3. To reduce the cost of running a given program or application.

The objective is the reduction of a program's processing time, which is given by the sum of its CPU time T_{cpu} and I/O time T_{io}. In turn T_{cpu} is the sum of two terms:

$$T_{cpu} = T_{sup} + T_{pr}$$

where T_{sup} is the CPU time consumed by the supervisory functions needed for the program's execution, and T_{pr} is the CPU time required to execute its instructions.

T_{io} may also be viewed as the sum of two terms:

$$T_{io} = T_{io1} + T_{io2}$$

where T_{io1} represents the I/O time overlapping CPU busy periods due to the program's activity, and T_{io2} is the rest of the I/O time. Note that in certain architectures T_{io1} is identically equal to zero, and $T_{io} = T_{io2}$.

The processing time can thus be expressed as (see Fig. 8.9)

$$T_p = T_{sup} + T_{pr} + T_{io2}$$

with $0 \leq T_{io2} \leq T_{io}$.

One can try reducing the processing time by acting on T_{cpu} or on T_{io2} or on both. The instruction execution time T_{pr} can sometimes be decreased by making the execution of some algorithms used by the program more efficient. In some cases, this may be done by replacing an algorithm with another. Often there are various ways of implementing a given function in a program, and sometimes the one chosen by the programmer is not the most efficient. For example, a list or a table can be scanned using different techniques (sequential search, binary search, and so on), each of which presents advantages and

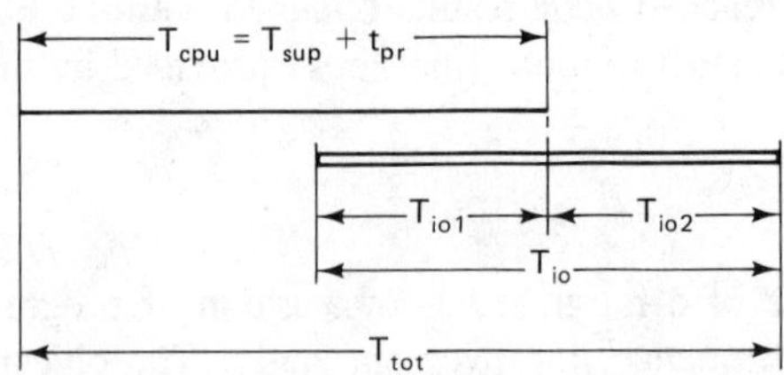

Figure 8.9 Components of a programs processing time T_{tot}.

disadvantages depending on the size of the list or table and on the application. The first problem consists of identifying the most time-consuming algorithms in the program so that they can be attacked first for possible improvement (see Sec. 8.3.1).

The value of T_{sup} is mostly influenced by the I/O activity of the program. Each read or write operation must be initiated and terminated by a supervisor intervention, while data transfers are performed by channels, whose activity can be overlapped with that of the CPU.

Thus, the reduction of the number of I/O operations has a double effect: it reduces the number of supervisor interventions, thereby saving CPU time, and it determines a reduction of the total I/O time T_{io}. For example, as we shall see in Sec. 8.3.3, an accurate choice of the blocking factor for the files handled by the program often reduces the I/O time considerably. Figure 8.9, however, suggests that, besides trying to reduce the total number of I/O operations, it is useful to attempt a reduction of T_{io2}, the time during which the read–write activities do not overlap the program's CPU activity. For an equal number of I/O operations, in order for T_{io2} to be reduced, T_{io1} must be increased. To achieve this goal, double or triple buffering may be used. This makes it possible to transfer a block of records into main memory while the program is processing and updating the records of a previously transferred block. And, at the same time, the data in the last completely processed block may be written back to mass storage. The cost of all this, if the system is equipped with channels that permit this mode of operation, is a larger main memory space for the buffers.

In *virtual memory* environments (see Secs. 7.4 and 8.3.4), it is possible to satisfy additional memory space demands without having to increase the amount of real memory available or to reduce the number of programs partially loaded in memory, as long as these do not cause a high paging activity. Except for special cases, in a virtual memory environment a program, subdivided into pages by the operating system, is never completely in main memory during its execution. When the program references a virtual address that does not correspond to a real memory address, a page fault occurs. Then the operating system has to find on the paging device the page containing the required address and to load it in memory. The page will be loaded after the operating system has chosen the page frame it will occupy in main memory.

One criterion used to choose the page frame is the LRU (least recently used) algorithm (or derivations of it), according to which the new page will occupy the frame of the least recently referenced page, either among those belonging to the program (*local* LRU) or among all pages in memory (*global* LRU).

For efficiency reasons, only those pages in memory whose contents have been modified by a program will be written back to the paging device when necessary. The others will simply be zeroed or overwritten. These activities are all carried out by the memory management functions of the operating system. One consequence is that part of the CPU's time must be devoted to executing these operations, and T_{sup} increases. At the same time, there is an increase in I/O activity due to the need for transferring pages from the paging device to main memory (page-in) and, in the case of a page that has been modified, from main memory to the paging device (page-out). The increase of a program's T_{sup} and T_{io} due to paging can be considerable and seriously affect its execution time. A page-out/page-in operation usually requires a few thousand machine instructions to be executed by the supervisor. The concurrent execution of programs with a high paging rate can dramatically affect the whole system's performance and degrade it considerably (see Secs. 7.4 and 7.4.1). When studying program performance in virtual memory environments, one must consider, besides the CPU time required to execute its instructions and its I/O activity, two additional aspects: its *locality* and its *working set*. These notations were introduced in Sec. 7.4 and will be discussed in more detail in Sec. 8.3.4; some useful considerations will be made here. In a virtual memory system the size of a program can be looked at from two different viewpoints: that of its *virtual size* V_p and that of its *real size* R_p. The former (in spite of the name) is the actual amount of space required to store the program completely. The latter is the real memory size available to the program. If a program is executed many times, with different amounts of available memory, its paging activity will vary. A diagram can be constructed depicting a program's sensitivity to memory restrictions. Figure 8.10 shows a possible shape for this curve. For every program there usually is an optimal amount of real storage [MO73], at which the number of page faults is considered irrelevant if compared to the real memory savings due to virtual memory techniques. It is generally possible for the program to maintain a reasonable performance level as long as a certain *paging threshold* is not overcome.

Clearly, programs do not exhibit the same paging behaviors as the amount of real storage varies, nor does a program usually behave in the same way as its input data varies. Figure 8.11 shows the paging curves of three different programs. Note that the execution of program A in a virtual memory environment does not lead to any appreciable improvement, whereas for program B, and even more for program C, considerable real memory savings (44 and 58 percent, respectively) can be achieved without causing excessive paging activity. However, paging curves should be used with caution, since they usually plot the number of page faults generated by a program within a fixed-size memory partition. Within another type of environment, paging performance cannot be predicted by using paging curves, since the amount of memory allotted to a program varies dynamically during execution. Yet these curves may qualitatively indicate how likely it is that a program will be efficiently executed in a virtual memory system. The number of page faults generated by a program is considerably influenced by its structure. Thus, the problem of adequately structuring it arises.

The behavior of a program in a virtual environment is not affected by the number of pages it references (not all of them are always referenced, as can be seen in Fig. 8.12),

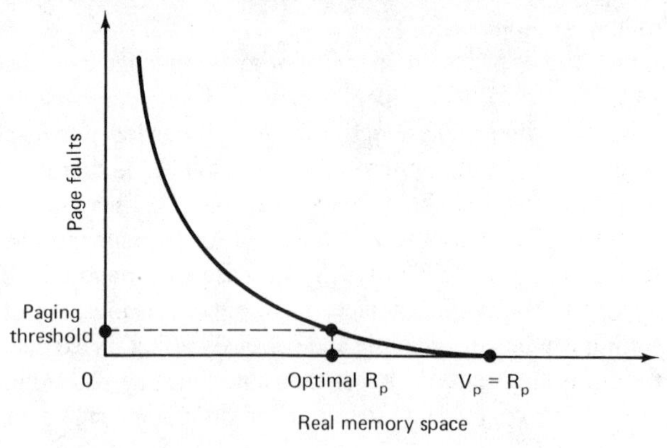

Figure 8.10 Number of page faults versus the real memory space available to a program.

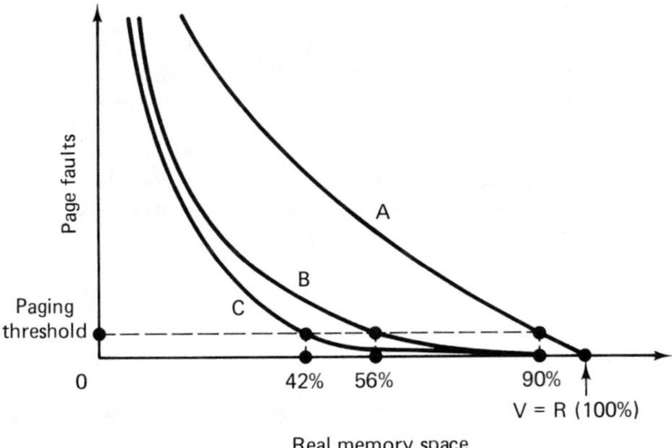

Figure 8.11 Paging curves of three programs.

but by the order in which it references them. For example, if all the 180 elements of a table are to be reset to zero, and each occupies a 4-byte memory word, assuming that the page size is 128 bytes, six pages will be required to contain the table. Using FORTRAN, the program to clear the table can be written in two ways (A and B below):

```
          A                            B
      INTEGER T (60,3)             INTEGER T (60,3)
      DO 100 I = 1,60              DO 100 I = 1,3
      DO 100 J = 1,3               DO 100 J = 1,60
100   T (I,J) = 0           100    T (I,J) = 0
      STOP                         STOP
      END                          END
```

Since T is stored by columns (this is a convention usually adopted by compilers), the contents of the six pages will be as shown in Fig. 8.13.

Besides referencing the page (or pages) containing the program's object code, both when executing A and B, it will be necessary to access the six pages containing T. Program A touches each page 25 times, first in the order 1, 3, 5 (for $I = 1, 25$), then in the order 2, 4, 6 (for $I = 26, 50$). Program B touches each page only once, and the

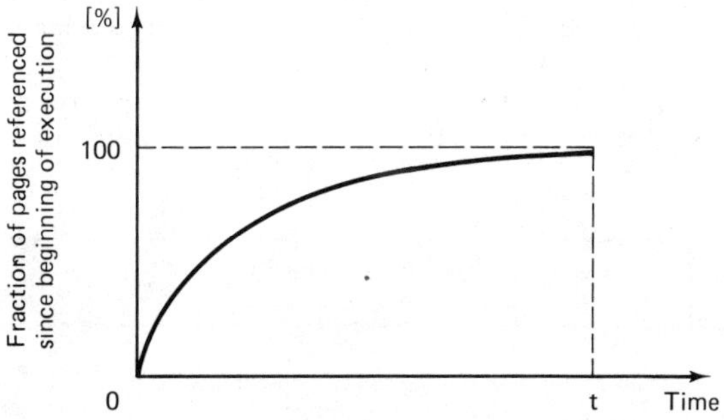

Figure 8.12 Sample curve representing the cumulative percentages of the pages requested by a program during its execution of duration t. The program has never executed the instructions of some of its paths.

T1, 1
T26, 1
T1, 2
T26, 2
T1, 3
T26, 3
T25, 1
T50, 1
T25, 2
T50, 2
T25, 3
T50, 3
Page 1
Page 2
Page 3
Page 4
Page 5
Page 6

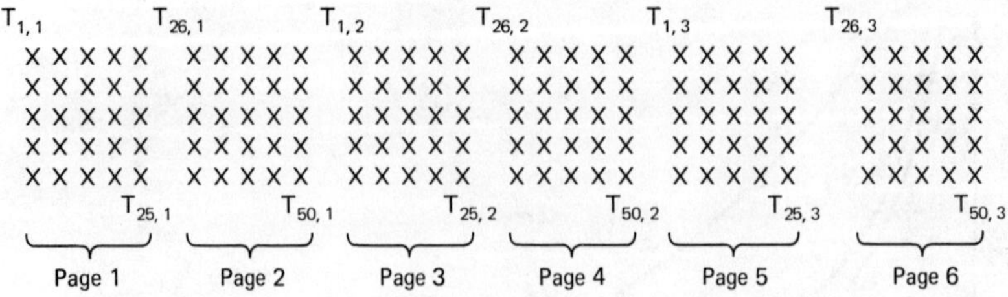

Figure 8.13 Layout of matrix T in virtual memory.

TABLE 8.2 PERFORMANCE OF A TABLE-RESETTING PROGRAM: BY ROWS (A) AND BY COLUMNS (B)

	CPU time (s)	*Execution time (s)*	*Total paging I/O operations (page-ins & page-outs)*
A	51	2410	77,448
B	3	14	233

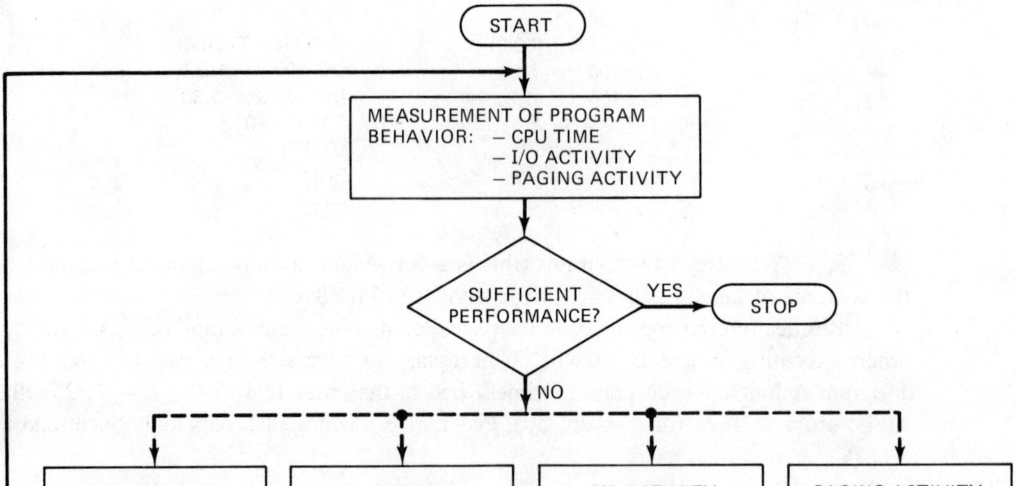

START
MEASUREMENT OF PROGRAM
BEHAVIOR: – CPU TIME
– I/O ACTIVITY
– PAGING ACTIVITY
SUFFICIENT
PERFORMANCE?
YES
STOP
NO
STRUCTURAL
MODIFICATIONS
REVIEW OF
PROGRAM
FUNCTIONS
CODE
OPTIMIZATION
REPLACEMENT
OF SOME
ALGORITHMS
WITH MORE
EFFICIENT ONES
I/O ACTIVITY
REDUCTION
REVISION OF
BLOCKING FACTORS.
BETTER USE OF
FILING DEVICES AND
BUFFERS
PAGING ACTIVITY
REDUCTION
AUTOMATIC
RESTRUCTURING.
REVISION OF
OPTIMALITY
CRITERIA

Figure 8.14 General scheme of the performance improvement process for a program.

pages are accessed in the order 1, 2, 3, 4, 5, 6. An experimental verification of the behaviors of two versions like A and B for a table of 500 columns and 200 rows produced the results in Table 8.2 [WA76]. This was done in a virtual memory environment having pages of 2048 bytes each and making 120,000 real memory locations available to the program (whose virtual size was 400,000 bytes). The conclusion can be drawn from this example that even simple modifications to a program may have enormous effects on its performance in a virtual memory system.

Several methods can be used when writing a program to reduce the probability of high paging rates in a virtual memory system. Some of them are general; others are specific to the programming language used. A comprehensive list of these methods can be found in [MO73] and [HA71]. Although undoubtedly useful, their application is sometimes difficult, especially because some of them would require knowledge of the program's dynamic behavior. Their effectiveness may therefore be limited by the lack of sufficiently accurate data or by the difficulty of analyzing a program's behavior.

Another alternative to this approach to the problem of optimally structuring a program is that of *automatically restructuring* it. This topic will be discussed in detail in Sec. 8.3.4. A general scheme of the process of program tuning is depicted in Fig. 8.14.

8.3.1 Code Improvement

The improvement of code can be carried out efficiently, in terms of costs and benefits, by two approaches: automatically or with a "guide" (see Sec. 8.2). The former approach is not always possible (not every programming language has an optimizer), while at least one of the "guided methods" (sampling, tracing, simulation, and source code analysis) can almost always be used. A common characteristic of all these optimization methods is the need for a tool. This tool can be either *software* or *hardware*. The most popular types of software tools are the automatic object code optimizers, tracers, simulators, source code analyzers, and sampling software monitors used to measure the execution frequencies of the instructions in a program to be optimized. These frequencies, however, can be measured also with a hardware monitor, following the method briefly described in Sec. 5.3.1. Clearly, the purpose of these tools is to facilitate the programmer's task and shift as much of the work as possible to the system.

The only tools that do not require programmer intervention are the automatic object code optimizers, which are used after a program has been compiled (see Fig. 8.7) and are transparent to the programmer. These tools try to produce code less bulky than that generated by the compiler and characterized by a faster execution. In other words, their objective is to obtain a program requiring less memory space and less CPU time for its execution. Since these tools act only on that part of the program containing the instructions to be executed, significant memory and execution time savings can be obtained especially when the program is rather large and also has a rather complex logic. For a COBOL program, for example, this means having many IF, GO, PERFORM, MOVE, COMPARE, and TRANSFORM statements. The technique employed by a commercial COBOL program optimizer, whose use is schematically described in Fig. 8.15 [OP78], is that of subdividing the object program into blocks of sequential code so that all jumps to a block are jumps to its starting address. General registers, used as base registers for addressing,

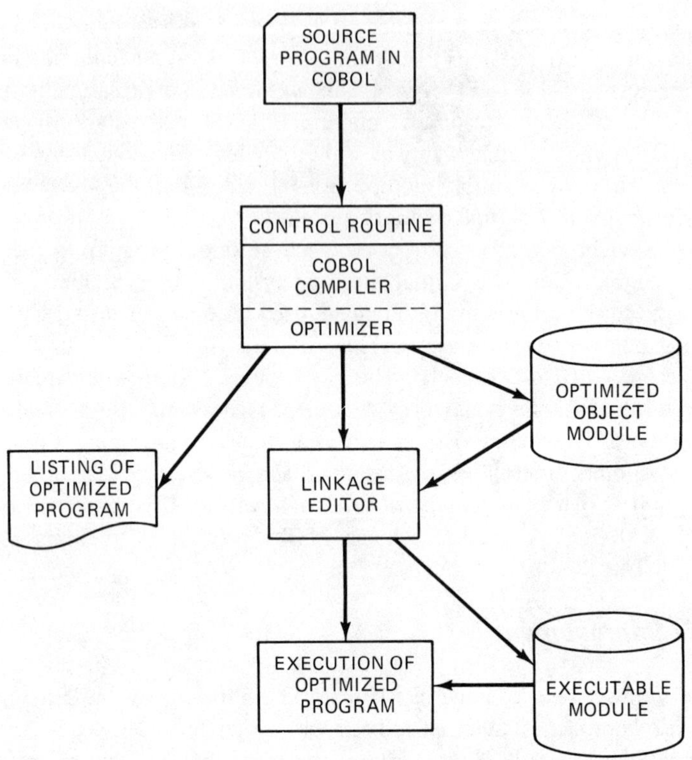

Figure 8.15 Application of an automatic COBOL program optimizer [OP78].

are loaded, when necessary, at the beginning of a block and keep their initial contents for the whole execution of the block. This produces a considerable reduction in the number of instructions and makes it possible to find and remove those program sections that, due to multiple modifications made to the program's logic, would never be executed (the "untouched branches").

Execution time can be reduced in two ways:

1. By removing from loops any code that is invariant with respect to the loop's function.
2. By eliminating the code sections that, having been repeatedly generated by the compiler, turn out to be redundant in the execution of a given operation or function.

Loop optimization. Generally, when optimizing loops, it is not the number of instructions that is reduced, but the number of times some of them are executed. When the code is subdivided into blocks with a single entry point, a loop can be represented as in Fig. 8.16a. Figure 8.16b shows the invariant instructions that are removed from within the loop by the optimization procedure. Let us consider the following loop:

```
IF-TEST
    ADD 1 TO COUNT
```

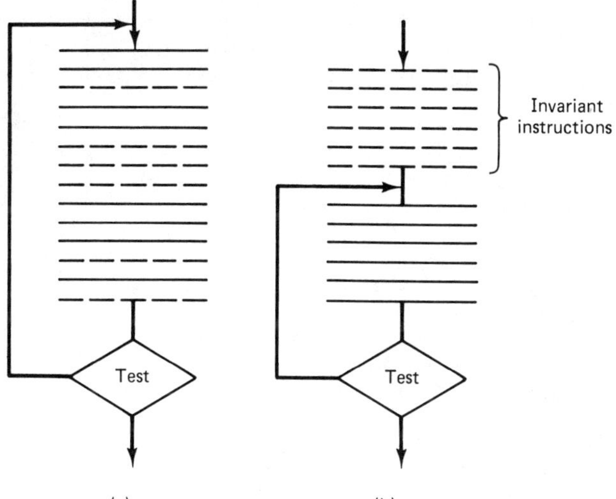

Figure 8.16 Schematic representation of a loop before and after optimization.

```
IF COUNT > 10
  IF NUMBER = TIMES GO TO NORMAL END ELSE
    MOVE ZERO TO SWITCH
    ADD 1 TO NUMBER
    GO TO IF-TEST
NEXT-PAR.
```

The corresponding flow chart is represented in Fig. 8.17. The loop will be executed a number of times equal to the value of TIMES. This value is assumed to have been loaded before the loop was entered. The source code translation made by the compiler, as well as the result of object code optimization, can be seen in Fig. 8.18, where the expansion of each source language statement is shown next to it.

In this example, the savings in terms of execution time derive mainly from the fact that the instructions that convert TIMES from decimal to binary have been removed from the loop. Indeed, these instructions are invariant within the loop since they convert the same value every time, as TIMES is defined outside the loop. After optimization they will only be executed once.

The time saved can be estimated by evaluating (through addition of instruction execution times) the execution time of the optimized loop and that of the nonoptimized loop. If a medium-speed processor is used to execute the loop 10 times, the results in Table 8.3 are obtained. The CPU time is reduced by 44 percent, and 63 percent of this reduction is due to the removal of the conversion instructions from the loop. It is interesting to note that their presence within the loop cannot be avoided by the programmer, but is entirely due to the translation technique used by the compiler.

Redundant Code Optimization. The number of instructions is reduced by eliminating, wherever possible, code duplications. Figure 8.19 illustrates schematically

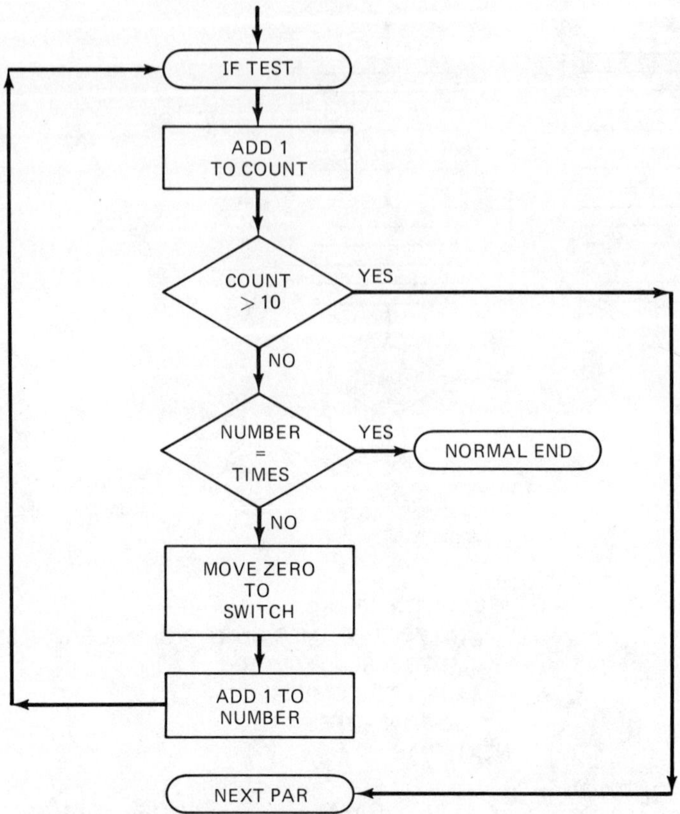

Figure 8.17 Flow chart of the loop considered in Sec. 8.3.1.

how a section of code containing duplicate instructions is transformed and made shorter through this kind of optimization.

Let us consider the following COBOL instructions, which are part of a compiled and optimized program:

```
|
|
00311    ADD VALUE1 VALUE2 VALUE3 GIVING RESULT1.
00312    ADD VALUE1 VALUE2 VALUE3 GIVING RESULT2.
00313    ADD VALUE1 VALUE2 GIVING RESULT3.
00314    SUBTRACT VALUE1 VALUE2 VALUE3 FROM VALUE4 GIVING RESULT4.
|
|
```

We can see in Fig. 8.20 that in the optimized version not only has code duplication in statement 312 been removed, but also three instructions of the third sum and five of the subtraction have been eliminated because previously executed. The 24 machine code instructions produced by the compiler were reduced to 12 by automatic optimization.

Source statements	Assembly language instructions produced by the compiler	Changes made by the optimizer
IF–TEST		LA
		PACK
		CVB
		LH
ADD 1 TO COUNT	LH	LR
	AH	AH
	STH	STH
IF COUNT > 10	LH	
	CH	CH
	L	BC
	BCR	
IF NUMBER = TIMES	L	
	PACK	
	CVB	
	LH	
	CR	CR
	L	BC
	L	
	BCR	
MOVE ZERO TO SWITCH	MVC	MVC
ADD 1 TO NUMBER	LH	LR
	AH	AH
	STH	STH
GO TO IF–TEST	L	BC
	BCR	

Figure 8.18 Sample optimization of the instructions in a loop.

TABLE 8.3 EXAMPLES OF EXECUTION TIME REDUCTION OBTAINABLE WITH AUTOMATIC OPTIMIZATION

Source statements	*Run times before optimization (μs)*	*Run times after optimization (μs)*
IF–TEST	—	16
ADD 1 TO COUNT	48	42
IF COUNT > 10	51	26
IF NUMBER = TIMES	121	14
MOVE ZERO TO SWITCH	35	35
ADD 1 TO NUMBER	49	43
GO TO IF–TEST	25	11
Total (μs)	329	187

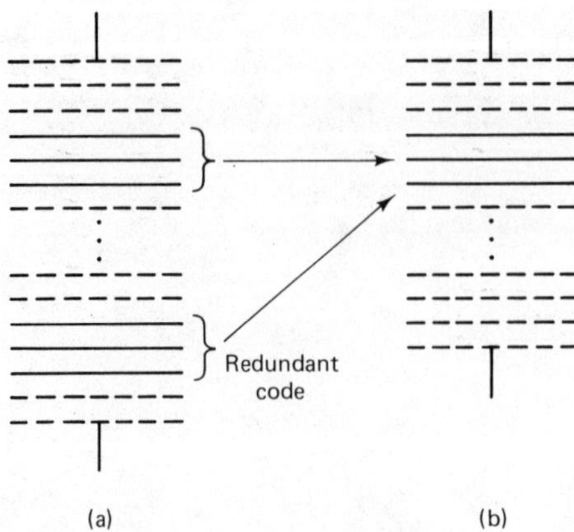

Figure 8.19 Removal of duplicate instructions in the object code produced by a compiler.

To determine the most frequently executed sections of a program, we can use a tool that observes the program's behavior and stores the addresses of the memory areas containing the instructions executed. The subsequent processing of the recorded data will produce frequency distributions or histograms. Their reading will provide an immediate identification of those program sections on which the optimization efforts should concentrate to minimize the expected cost–benefit ratio. Section 5.3.1 (Fig. 5.12) describes how this type of measurement can be carried out with a hardware tool, while Fig. 8.21

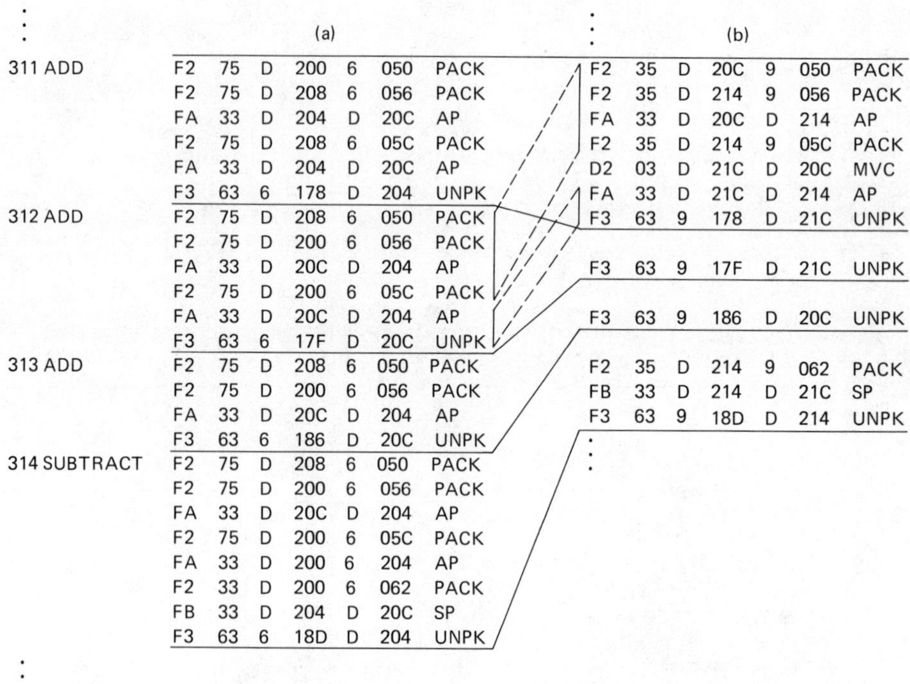

(a)
311 ADD
F2 75 D 200 6 050 PACK
F2 75 D 208 6 056 PACK
FA 33 D 204 D 20C AP
F2 75 D 208 6 05C PACK
FA 33 D 204 D 20C AP
F3 63 6 178 D 204 UNPK
312 ADD
F2 75 D 208 6 050 PACK
F2 75 D 200 6 056 PACK
FA 33 D 20C D 204 AP
F2 75 D 200 6 05C PACK
FA 33 D 20C D 204 AP
F3 63 6 17F D 20C UNPK
313 ADD
F2 75 D 208 6 050 PACK
F2 75 D 200 6 056 PACK
FA 33 D 20C D 204 AP
F3 63 6 186 D 20C UNPK
314 SUBTRACT
F2 75 D 208 6 050 PACK
F2 75 D 200 6 056 PACK
FA 33 D 20C D 204 AP
F2 75 D 200 6 05C PACK
FA 33 D 200 6 204 AP
F2 33 D 200 6 062 PACK
FB 33 D 204 D 20C SP
F3 63 6 18D D 204 UNPK
(b)
F2 35 D 20C 9 050 PACK
F2 35 D 214 9 056 PACK
FA 33 D 20C D 214 AP
F2 35 D 214 9 05C PACK
D2 03 D 21C D 20C MVC
FA 33 D 21C D 214 AP
F3 63 9 178 D 21C UNPK
F3 63 9 17F D 21C UNPK
F3 63 9 186 D 20C UNPK
F2 35 D 214 9 062 PACK
FB 33 D 214 D 21C SP
F3 63 9 18D D 214 UNPK

Figure 8.20 Example of object code reduction through redundant code removal [OP78].

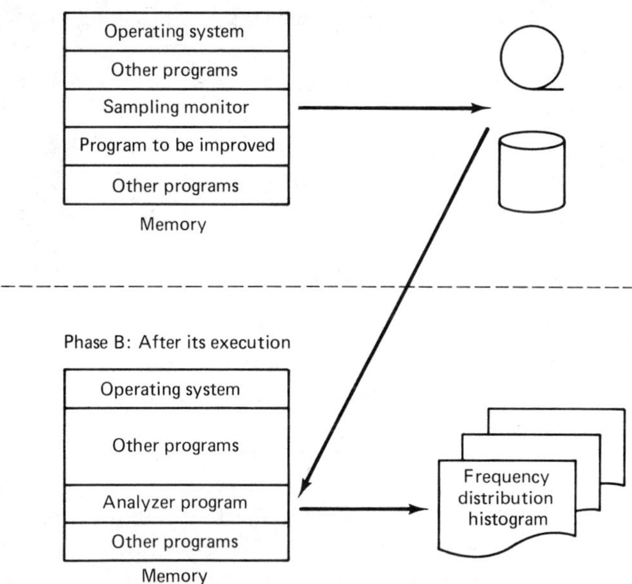

Figure 8.21 Application of a sampling software monitor to the measurement of a program's behavior.

shows how the same measurement can be performed with a sampling software monitor. In this case, the principle of operation of the tool is similar to that of a software monitor, which observes the evolution of a system's activity (see Sec. 5.2.1), but the object of the measurement is an individual program. The sampling monitor resides in memory with the program to be improved and, at preselected regular intervals, interrupts the ongoing execution to check whether the CPU was referencing some of the memory locations occupied by the program. Clearly, this can only be done if, as for the system monitors previously discussed, it is possible to determine the state of the CPU by reading the contents of certain memory locations and, in particular, the address of the last instruction executed (or of the next to be executed). The monitor will thus collect samples of the observed program's activity in which every instruction (or block of instructions) will appear a number of times roughly proportional to the number of its executions. One may wonder whether, observing several program executions with the same input data, the results would be the same. In a multiprogramming environment the results will in most cases not be the same. Indeed, the results of these measurements depend on all those factors that can make execution time or CPU time (T_{cpu}) vary even when a program is executed without being perturbed by a measurement tool. Among these factors are the different amounts of contention for the CPU existing in the programs being run, the different frequencies of execution of error-recovery procedures, and, in general, the different amounts of system overhead.

However, these variations do not always impair the validity of the measurements, but one should try to measure within an environment as close as possible to that the program is normally executed in. If the normal environment changes, one can combine the results of several measurements' sessions into one set of results, which will be closer to the program's average behavior. As in the case of sampling system activity, the accuracy of the results depends on sample size. Each sample element is composed of the set of data collected after every interruption caused by the tool. During its execution, a program may be:

- Running, when its code is being executed
- Running, but indirectly (that is, when some supervisory function is being executed on its behalf)
- Idle, waiting for the completion of an I/O operation it has requested
- Idle, waiting for a needed page to be loaded (in a virtual memory environment)
- Idle, waiting to gain control of the CPU or to be loaded into memory (this state is sometimes called *involuntary wait*)

There are two methods for measuring a program's behavior. The first refers to the program's entire execution time and records both running and idle times. In this case, the purpose is to record, along with the most frequently executed instructions, the reasons for the program's periods of idleness. These data can then be used to check the effectiveness of the I/O techniques used in the program and, possibly, to discover whether its degree of locality is low. The sampling interval I_e (see Sec. 5.2), expressed in ms, should then be determined using the relationship

$$I_e = 1000 \frac{T_e}{N}, \tag{8.13}$$

where T_e is the mean execution time of the program (in seconds) and N is the total number of interruptions (that is, the sample size).

The second method for program activity measurement only observes its CPU bursts in order to achieve a greater accuracy in determining the most frequently executed instructions. In this case, the sampling interval is given by

$$I_{\text{cpu}} = 1000 \frac{T_{\text{cpu}}}{N} \tag{8.14}$$

As usual, N must be established using confidence curves (see Sec. 3.3.1, Fig. 3.10).

When sampling programs, a suggestion that proves valid in most cases is that the value of N be greater than 5000; of these 5000 interruptions, at least 2000 should occur while the program is running *(active interruptions)*. Clearly, whether this condition is satisfied can only be determined at the end of the measurement experiment. If the value of T_{cpu} is known, I_e can be selected so as to obtain a sufficient number of active interruptions. Let us assume that for a program we have

$$T_{\text{cpu}} = 30 \text{ s}, \qquad T_e = 8 \text{ min}$$

```
  .
  .
00619   00617      If LIST-3 (VALUE4) =  5 MOVE 'VALUE  IS 5    ' TO DISPL2      OPT38DH   002BEA
                                                                                   MOVE  002RFC
00620   00618                         GO TO IF-3-END.                            OPT38DH   002C02
00621   00619      IF LIST-3 (VALUE4) =  7 MOVE 'VALUE  IS 7    ' TO DISPL2      OPT38DH   002C0E
                                                                                   MOVE  002C20
00622   00620                         GO TO IF-3-END.                            OPT38DH   002C26
00623   00621      IF LIST-3 (VALUE4) =  9 MOVE 'VALUE  IS 9    ' TO DISPL2      OPT38DH   002C32
                                                                                   MOVE  002C44
00624   00622                         GO TO IF-3-END.                            OPT38DH   002C4A
00625   00623  IF-3-END.
                                       ***EXIT FROM PERFORMED PARAGRAPH(S).                002C56
00626   00624  IF-DEMO-4 SECTION.                                                OPT38DH   002C72
00627   00625  *                                                                 OPT38DH
00628   00626  *   NOTE    DEMO4       MORE COMPLEX RELATIONAL COMBINATIONS.     OPT38DH
00629   00627  *                                                                 OPT38DH
00630   00628      IF VALUE4 LESS THAN 15 GO TO ID4-1.                           OPT38DH   002C84
                                                                                     GO  002C9C
00631   00629      IF VALUE4 GREATER THAN 10 GO TO ID4-2.                        OPT38DH  -UNCOND-
                                                                                     GO  002C80
00632   00630      MOVE 'NN ' TO DISPL3 GO TO ID4-END.                           OPT38DH |-UNEXEC-|
                                                                                     GO |-UNEXEC-|   (A)
00633   00631  ID4-1.                                                            OPT38DH   002C84
00634   00632      IF VALUE4 LESS THAN 20 GO TO ID4-3.                           OPT38DH  -UNCOND-
                                                                                     GO  002CC8
00635   00633      MOVE 'YN ' TO DISPL3 GO TO ID4-END.                           OPT38DH |-UNEXEC-|
                                                                                     GO |-UNEXEC-|   (A)
00636   00634  ID4-2.                                                            OPT38DH   002CCC
00637   00635      IF VALUE4 LESS THAN 14 MOVE 'NYY' TO DISPL3 GO TO ID4-END.    OPT38DH |-UNCOND-|
                                                                                   MOVE |-UNEXEC-|
                                                                                     GO |-UNEXEC-|   (A)
00638   00636      MOVE 'NYN' TO DISPL3 GO TO ID4-END.                           OPT38DH   002CE4
                                                                                     GO  002CEA
00639   00637  ID4-3.                                                            OPT38DH   002CEE
00640   00638      IF VALUE4 NOT LESS THAN 20 MOVE 'YYY' TO DISPL3               OPT38DH |-UNCOND-|
                                                                                   MOVE |-UNEXEC-|   (A)
00641   00639                         GO TO ID4-END.                             OPT38DH |-UNEXEC-|
00642   00640      MOVE 'YYN' TO DISPL3.                                         OPT38DH   002D06
  .
  .
```

Figure 8.22 Report produced by a logical automatic analyzer of source programs [OP78].
A: statements that will never be executed since they are preceded by contradictory IF statements.

and that we wish to extract a sample reflecting its behavior with sufficient accuracy. The preceding two methods would yield, respectively,

$$I_e = \frac{480 \times 10^3}{5 \times 10^3} = 96 \text{ ms}$$

and

$$I_{\text{cpu}} = \frac{30 \times 10^3}{5 \times 10^3} = 6 \text{ ms}$$

For I_e, however, a value of 96 ms would only give, at least as a first approximation, about 300 active interruptions, too few for the results on CPU activity to be valid. If I_e were 15 ms, the active interruptions would be around 2000, and the total number of

```
                          INPUT & DIAGNOSTICS
      :
      001070      OPEN INPUT TRANS-FILE.
      001080      OPEN OUTPUT PRINT-FILE.
      001090      OPEN I-O VENDOR-FILE.
      001100      CALL 'TIMEDATE' USING TIME D-A-T-E.
*** NOTE         N99  EFF15A-MULTIPLE USING OPERANDS <---------- (A)
      001110      MOVE TIME TO HEADING-TIME.
*** NOTE         N99  EFF19A-OPERANDS ARE UNEQUAL IN LENGTH <--- (B)
      001120      MOVE D-A-T-E TO HEADING-DATE.
*** NOTE         N99  EFF19A-OPERANDS ARE UNEQUAL IN LENGTH <--- (B)
      001130      PERFORM UPDATE-HEADING.
      001140      GO TO READ-TRANS.
      001150 COUNT-TRANS.
      001160      ADD 1 TO SUMMARY-COUNTS (SUB1 SUB2).
*** NOTE         N99  EFF01A-UNSIGNED NUMERIC-(SUMMARY-COUNTS)         (C,D)
*** NOTE         N99  EFF21A-(SUMMARY-COUNTS) TABLE=MULTIPLE=USE       (C,D)
      001170 READ-TRANS.
      001180      READ TRANS-FILE
      001190        AT END
      001200        GO TO SUMMARIZE.
      001210      MOVE TRANS-RECORD TO REPORT-IMAGE.
*** NOTE         N99  EFF19A-OPERANDS ARE UNEQUAL IN LENGTH <--- (B)
      001220      MOVE '0' TO FORM-CONTROL.
      001230      PERFORM PRINT-A-LINE THRU PRINT-A-LINE-EXIT.
      001240      MOVE 1 TO SUB1.
*** NOTE         N99  EFF01A-UNSIGNED NUMERIC-(SUB1) <---------- (C)
      001250      MOVE 1 TO SUB2.
      001260      IF TRANS-CODE = 'A'
      001270        GO TO ADD-VENDOR.
      001280      MOVE 2 TO SUB1.
*** NOTE         N99  EFF01A-UNSIGNED NUMERIC-(SUB1) <---------- (C)
      001290      IF TRANS-CODE = 'C'
      001300        GO TO CHANGE-VENDOR.
      001310      MOVE 3 TO SUB1.
*** NOTE         N99  EFF01A-UNSIGNED NUMERIC-(SUB1) <---------- (C)
      001320      IF TRANS-CODE = 'D'
      001330        GO TO DELETE-VENDOR.
      001340      ADD 1 TO SUMMARY-COUNTS (4 2).
*** NOTE         N99  EFF01A-UNSIGNED NUMERIC-(SUMMARY-COUNTS) <--- (C)
      001350      MOVE 'INVALID TRANSACTION CODE' TO REPORT-IMAGE.
      001360      PERFORM PRINT-A-LINE THRU PRINT-A-LINE-EXIT.
      001370      GO TO READ-TRANS.
      001380 ADD-VENDOR.
      001390      MOVE TRANS-RECORD TO WORK-AREA.
*** NOTE         N99  EFF19A-OPERANDS ARE UNEQUAL IN LENGTH <--- (B)
      001400      MOVE SPACE TO WORK-DELETE.
      001410      MOVE WORK-NUMBER TO SYM-KEY.
      001420      PERFORM EDIT-CHECK.
      001430      IF SUB2 = 2
      001440        MOVE 'ADDITION REJECTED' TO REPORT-IMAGE
      001450        PERFORM PRINT-A-LINE THRU PRINT-A-LINE-EXIT
      001460        GO TO COUNT-TRANS.
      001470      WRITE VENDOR-RECORD FROM WORK-AREA
      001480        INVALID KEY
      001490        GO TO ADD-VENDOR-1.
      001500      MOVE 'ADDITION ACCEPTED' TO REPORT-IMAGE.
      001510      PERFORM PRINT-A-LINE THRU PRINT-A-LINE-EXIT.
      :
```

Figure 8.23 Report produced by a syntactic automatic analyzer of source programs [ME73].

interruptions would become about 32,000, a value that would guarantee a high level of accuracy.

The interference caused by the tool grows as the time between interruptions decreases and also depends on the CPU's processing speed. An effect of interference that is sometimes quite important is the increase of the program's execution time. If the critical performance index of the program is its execution time, it is advisable to use values above those of I_e or I_{cpu} given by Eqs. (8.13) and (8.14). One can select interval durations even twice or three times the values of I_e or I_{cpu}, provided that the program is measured more than once. By collecting the results of the various measurement sessions and processing them together, it will still be possible to obtain significant information about the program's behavior. When the experimenter is more interested in obtaining the distribution of instruction executions than in keeping the program's execution time at a minimum, the sampling interval may be made shorter than we have suggested. This will increase the accuracy of the measurement results.

Automatic source code analyzers are tools usually applied before a program is debugged and tested. Their goal is to pinpoint all those instructions that, due to intrinsic inefficiencies of the compiler or to their inappropriate usage by the programmer, can cause inefficient object code to be generated.

A program should be analyzed before being compiled. The analyzer will produce a listing of the instructions in the program and print diagnostics corresponding to instructions that are possibly improvable. This type of analysis can be called *syntactic* since it is independent of the program's logic structure; that is, it does not help one discover the inefficiencies of the algorithms implemented by the program. It is valid, nevertheless, in that it removes some of the effects of bad programming habits, avoiding unnecessarily long execution times. There are also automatic analyzers that point out some inefficiencies in a program's logic.

Figures 8.23 and 8.22 contain, respectively, the table produced by an automatic COBOL source code analyzer of the syntactic type [ME73] and that produced by a similar analyzer of the logic type [OP78].

8.3.2 Case 8.1: Loop Optimization

As an example of how to use a sampling software monitor in a program improvement study, let us consider the following case, where use is made of PPE [PP76]. The program to be analyzed, written in FORTRAN, implements the method of Gaussian elimination for the solution of a system of linear equations. In its original form (see Fig. 8.24), the program, called FORT1, is capable of solving systems of linear equations correctly, but performance-wise it can be considerably improved by reducing its execution time.

With a very fast processor, the CPU time needed to solve a given system is about 30 s. Choosing a sampling interval of 10 ms, the number of active interruptions obtained will suffice to guarantee the measurement's validity. The observation of the program's behavior and the analysis of the data collected are done following the scheme in Fig. 8.20. The sampler and the program are started independently (the sampler first) in two separate memory regions (note that PPE can run even in the region of the program).

The sampler knows the name of the program to be improved; hence it can find its work area in main memory. Then, during the program's execution, the sampler stores

```
C                  *  FORT1  *
C     GAUSSIAN METHOD WITH PARTIAL PIVOTING
C
      DIMENSION A(100,100),B(100),X(100)
      INTEGER ROW(100)
C
C     READ LIMITS
C
      READ(5,30) MAX,MIN
   30 FORMAT(2I2)
      IF(MAX .LE. 0) MAX=2
      IF(MIN .GT. MAX) MIN = MAX
      IF(MIN .LE. 0) MIN =1
      DO 180 M=MIN,MAX
      N=M+1
C
C     MATRIX CREATION
C
      DO 60 I=1,N
      DO 50 J=1,N
      Z=I+J
      A(I,J)=((-1)**(I+J))/Z
   50 CONTINUE
      B(I)=((-1)**I)*I
   60 CONTINUE
      DO 70 I=1,N
      ROW(I)=I
   70 CONTINUE
C
C     MATRIX TRIANGULARIZATION
C
      N1=N-1
      DO 130 J=1,N1
C
C     FIND PIVOT FOR COLUMN J
C
      BIG=ABS(A(ROW(J),J))
      I=J
      J1=J+1
      DO 80 I1=J1,N
      IF(BIG .GE. ABS(A(ROW(I1),J))) GO TO 80
      I=I1
      BIG=ABS(A(ROW(I1),J))
   80 CONTINUE
      IF(BIG .GT. 0) GO TO 100
      WRITE(6,90) M
   90 FORMAT(' CASE  SINGULAR ', I4)
      GO TO 180
C
C     SWITCH ROWS
C
  100 ITEMP=ROW(J)
      ROW(J)=ROW(I)
      ROW(I)=ITEMP
C
C     BASIC CALCULATION
C
      DO 120 K=J1,N
      DO 110 L=J1,N
      A(ROW(K),L)=A(ROW(K),L)-A(ROW(J),L)
     1*A(ROW(K),J)/A(ROW(J),J)
  110 CONTINUE
      B(ROW(K))=B(ROW(K))-B(ROW(J))
     1*A(ROW(K),J)/A(ROW(J),J)
```

Figure 8.24 FORTRAN program to be improved by using a sampling software monitor [PP76].

```
        120  CONTINUE
        130  CONTINUE
C
C            BACKWARD SOLUTION
C
             X(N)=B(ROW(N))/A(ROW(N),N)
             N1=N-1
             DO 150 I1=1,N1
             I=N-I1
             SUM=B(ROW(I))
             J1=I+1
             DO 140 J=J1,N
             SUM=SUM-A(ROW(I),J)*X(J)
        140  CONTINUE
             X(I)=SUM/A(ROW(I),I)
        150  CONTINUE
C
C            OUTPUT SOLUTION
C
             WRITE(6,160) M
        160  FORMAT(' CASE ', I4)
             WRITE(6,170) (I,X(I),I=1,N)
        170  FORMAT(6(I6,E15.6))
        180  CONTINUE
             STOP
             END
```

Figure 8.24 *(continued)*

the collected data on an external memory for later reduction. Once sampling operations have been completed, the data can be used over and over again by the analyzer to produce reports with various degrees of detail.

From an initial analysis of FORT1 (we do not yet know which of its sections deserve a detailed analysis), the table in Fig. 8.25 is obtained. In it, we can see that 92.78 percent of the program's activity is within the section called MAIN. Along with the amounts of activity in FORT1's individual sections, the table displays those detected in the modules present in dynamic memory areas used by the program for I/O operations. The next step is to request from the analyzer the profile of MAIN so as to pinpoint its code sections with the highest CPU activity. Since the program's I/O activity is not particularly interesting, we want the calculations of percentages to be made with respect to the CPU time, that is, to the number of active interruptions.

MODULE	SEG	CSECT	ORIGIN	LENGTH	ACTIVE	DATASET WAIT	PAGE WAIT	OTHER WAIT	TOTALS	STUDY
FORT1			37EE20	E9E0	97.05	.00	.00	.00	97.66	*
		MAIN	0	A8D2	92.78	.00	.00	.00	92.78	*
		IHCFIXPT	A8D8	14F	2.89	.00	.00	.00	2.89	*
		IHCFCOMH	AA28	CF9	.37	.00	.00	.00	.37	*
		IHCFCVTH	BB60	11B5	.74	.00	.00	.00	.74	*
		IHCFIOSH	D0B8	100E	.27	.00	.00	.61	.88	*
@NUCLEUS			0	35000	.00	.35	.00	.16	.50	
IGG019CF			3FCA78	270	.32	.00	.00	.00	.32	
IGG019CC			3FD918	308	.00	.00	.00	.08	.08	
IIGG019BB			3FCE88	178	.00	.00	.00	.05	.05	
IGG019BA			3FD148	1C0	.03	.00	.00	.00	.03	

Figure 8.25 Amounts of activity within the individual sections of FORT 1 and within the modules in dynamic memory areas [PP76].

Figure 8.26 shows the profile of MAIN, subdivided into sections of 16 memory locations whose initial addresses are expressed in hexadecimal form. The CPU time spent within each group is shown at the right of the corresponding addresses. The instructions using most of the program's CPU time (around 85 percent) are those between the addresses A5E2 and A654.

To increase the degree of detail of the study, the analyzer is to be executed again. The instructions between A5E2 and A654 are now divided into groups of four memory locations. In this way one can determine the instructions causing the heaviest use of the CPU.

The new profile is shown in Fig. 8.27. We see that location A636 absorbed a much greater amount of CPU time than any of the others; so we must find the instruction it contains and the statement it corresponds to. Among the printouts provided by the compiler, there is a listing that shows the correspondences between source statements and object code instructions. As this printout is optional, for this type of analysis it must be explicitly requested (see Fig. 8.28). Since the tool always records the address of the instruction following the one being executed when the interruption occurs, in the list in Fig. 8.28 we can see that the instruction responsible for most of the high CPU demand of statement 39 is the division at location A632. This, in turn, is part of a loop (see Fig.

```
        GROUP    CUM    PERCENT OF TIME AT THIS LOCATION:
LOC     PCT      PCT  0.30       3.00        6.00        9.00        12.00

                                 CSECT = MAIN

A3B8    0.33    0.33  .*
A3CA    0.57    0.90  .**
A3DA    0.52    1.42  .**
A3EC    0.44    1.85  .*
A3FC    0.57    2.43  .**
A40C    1.17    3.60  .****
A41E    0.33    3.92  .*
A4D6    0.57    4.50  .**
A540    0.46    4.96  .**
A592    0.57    5.53  .**
A5E2    8.26   13.79  .****************************
A5F2    9.46   23.25  .********************************
A602    6.46   29.71  .**********************
A612    7.33   37.04  .************************
A622   12.18   49.22  .*****************************************
A632   31.15   80.38  .************************************************
A644    8.37   88.74  .***************************
A654    3.71   92.45  .************
A664    0.33   92.78  .*
A684    0.38   93.16  .*
A6A4    0.63   93.79  .**
A6C4    0.52   94.30  .**
A6FA    0.44   94.74  .*
A7DC    0.41   95.15  .*
A81C    0.11   95.26  .
```

Figure 8.26 Histogram of the locations corresponding to the most frequently executed instructions in the MAIN section [PP76].

```
      GROUP    CUM   PERCENT OF TIME AT THIS LOCATION:
LOC   PCT      PCT   0.30      3.00      6.00      9.00      12.00

                                MAIN

A5E2   4.69   4.69  .****************
A5E6   1.17   5.86  .****
A5EA   1.25   7.11  .****
A5EE   1.14   8.26  .****
A5F2   2.70  10.96  .*********
A5F6   1.39  12.35  .*****
A5FA   1.99  14.34  .*******
A5FE   3.38  17.72  .***********
A602   1.09  18.81  .****
A606   1.14  19.95  .****
A60A   1.36  21.31  .*****
A60E   2.86  24.18  .**********
A612   1.09  25.27  .****
A616   2.29  27.56  .********
A61A   1.25  28.81  .****
A61E   2.70  31.51  .*********
A622   3.13  34.64  .**********
A626   2.45  37.09  .********
A62A   4.77  41.86  .****************
A62E   1.83  43.69  .******
A632   2.94  46.63  .**********
A636  16.65  63.29  .********************************************
A63A   2.89  66.18  .**********
A63E   6.30  72.47  .*********************
A640   2.37  74.84  .********
A644   2.37  77.21  .********
A64B   1.20  78.41  .****
A64C   2.73  81.14  .*********
A650   2.07  83.21  .*******
  .
  .
  .
```

Figure 8.27 Profile of the program section that causes the highest CPU time consumption [PP76].

8.24) in which index L varies, but not indexes K and J, which determine the operands of the division contained in statement 39.

Thus, the operands of the division are invariant within the loop. Note also that the same division is repeated in statement 41. Simply by moving the division outside the loop (as shown in Fig. 8.29), the program's execution time can be reduced considerably. The results of the analysis of the data collected by sampling the modified program show (see Fig. 8.30) a substantial reduction of CPU time demand for the group of instructions considered. The division, now at a location preceding address A606 (the box in Fig. 8.30 shows part of a listing produced by the compiler after the program was modified), makes a negligible use of the CPU compared with that in the original version of the program.

Table 8.4 summarizes the data concerning the two executions of FORT1, before and after the modification, and the number of interruptions caused by the sampler. The execution time T_e has become 37.06 s instead of 49.62, a 26 percent reduction. The percent of reduction of CPU time is certainly greater since, while the sampling of the

```
FORTRAN IV G LEVEL 21                    MAIN                          DATE =
76085
LOCATION   STA NUM  LABEL  OP        OPERAND                       BCD OPERAND
   .                       .         .
   .                       .         .
   .                       .         .
00A5C2                     AR        6,1
00A5C4                     L         0,260(o,13)                        J1
00A5C8                L100 ST        0,272(0,13)                        K
00A5CC       38            LA        1,400(0,0)
00A5D0                     M         0,260(0,13)                        J1
00A5D4                     L         11,76(0,13)
00A5D8                     L         7,1300(0,11)
00A5DC                     AR        7,1
00A5DE                     L         0,260(0,13)                        J1
00A5E2                L108 ST        0,276(0,13)                        L
00A5E6      (39)           L         9,168(0,6)                         ROW
00A5EA                     SLA       9,2(0)
00A5EE                     L         12,76(0,13)
00A5F2                     ST        9,1352(0,12)
   .                       .            .
   .                       .            .
   .                       .            .
00A62A                     L         9,172(0,5)                         ROW
00A62E                     SLA       9,2(0)
00A632                     DE        0,328(9,4)                         A
00A636                     L         9,1364(0,12)
00A63A                     SE        0,4024(9,7)                        A
00A63E                     LCER      0,0
00A640                     L         9,1352(0,12)
00A644                     STE       0,4024(9,7)                        A
00A648       40       110  A         7,1356(0,12)
00A64C                     L         0,276(0,13)                        L
00A650                     L         1,152(0,13)                        108
00A654                     LA        2,1(0,0)
00A658                     L         3,236(0,13)                        N
00A65C                     BXLE      0,2,0(1)
00A660       41            L         9,168(0,6)                         ROW
   .                       .            .
   .                       .            .
   .                       .            .
```

Figure 8.28 Compiler printout showing the correspondence between source and object code [PP76].

original version found the program running 97 percent of the times it was interrupted, that of the modified version found it running only 84 percent of the times. This implies longer wait periods and thus a greater difference between T_e and T_{cpu}. The program considered can be improved further, both by optimizing the use of instructions and by modifying its logic.

```
0037          DO 120 K=J1,N
0038          Z=A(ROW(K),J)/A(ROW(J),J)
0039          DO 110 L=J1,N
0040          A(ROW(K),L)=A(ROW(K),L) - A(ROW(J),L)*Z
0041      110 CONTINUE
0042          B(ROW(K))=B(ROW(K)) - B(ROW(J))*Z
0043      120 CONTINUE
```

Figure 8.29 Modified loop.

```
        GROUP        CUM  PERCENT OF TIME AT THIS LOCATION:
LOC     PCT          PCT  0.30      3.00      6.00        9.00      12.00
                          MAIN                        LOCATION   STA NUM     LABEL      OP
A5E8   0.08    8.48   .                                 00A606               L108       ST
A5F0   0.51    8.98   .**                               00A60A     (40)                 L
A5F4   0.04    9.03   .                                 00A60E                          SLA
A5F8   0.04    9.07   .                                 00A612                          L
A5FC   0.13    9.19   .                                 00A616                          ST
A600   0.04    9.24   .                                 00A61A                          L
A602   0.17    9.41   .*                                00A61E                          SLA
A606   7.76   17.17   .*************************        00A622                          ST
A60A   1.39   18.56   .*****                            00A626                          L
A60E   1.86   20.41   .******                           00A62A                          SLA
A612   1.90   22.31   .******                           00A62E                          LE
A616   4.98   27.29   .*****************                00A632                          ME
A61A   1.77   29.06   .******                           00A636                          L
A61E   1.35   30.41   .****                             00A63A                          SE
A622   2.15   32.56   .*******                          00A63E                          LCER
A626   3.71   36.27   .************                     00A640                          L
A62A   1.35   37.62   .****                             00A644                          STE
A62E   4.39   42.01   .***************                  00A648     41        110        A
A632   3.33   45.34   .***********
A636   8.31   53.65   .*****************************
A63A   3.37   57.02   .***********
A63E   9.70   66.72   .*********************************
A640   3.80   70.52   .*************
A644   4.09   74.61   .**************
A648   1.86   76.47   .******
A64C   3.50   79.97   .************
A650   4.01   83.97   .*************
A654   1.77   85.74   .******
A658   1.77   87.52   .******
A65C   1.86   89.37   .******
A660   0.13   89.50   .
```

Figure 8.30 Histogram obtained after modifying the program [PP76].

8.3.3 I/O Activity Improvement

Every program that executes I/O operations to transfer data to or from mass storage is delayed because of them. This is mainly due to the differential between the speed of execution of operations on data in main memory and that of access to mass storage locations. The processing time of a program can often be reduced considerably by improving the program's I/O activity. This may be done by transferring as much data as possible at every access to mass storage, or by increasing the overlap between a program's I/O and CPU activities.

In mass storage, data are grouped in records; each record contains a certain number

TABLE 8.4 RESULTS OF THE MEASUREMENT OF FORT1

	Execution time T_e (s)	*Total number of interruptions*	*Active interruptions*	*% active interruptions*
Original program	49.62	3767	3669	97
Optimized version	37.06	2808	2371	84

of characters. Data transfers between main and mass storage are always performed in blocks. The number of records in a block is called *blocking factor*.

On disk and tape, data blocks are separated by a gap. Since these gaps are fairly large (for example, half an inch on tapes containing 800 characters per inch), a high blocking factor makes the use of mass storage space more efficient. However, this is a totally marginal advantage with respect to the other deriving from an increased blocking factor, that is, the reduction in the number of I/O operations required to read or write a given number of records.

Reducing the number of I/O operations means decreasing, often drastically, the total I/O time of a program. The data transmission rate of a channel is almost 1 million characters per second, sometimes even higher, while a disk unit just preparing for transmission may require 40 or 50 ms because of the seek time, the latency time, and the queuing time for the channel.

A desirable consequence of a program's I/O time reduction is the reduction of the CPU time needed for executing the supervisory functions that initiate an I/O operation. Thus, T_{sup} decreases (see Fig. 8.9), and, generally, the system's throughput increases.

A determining factor for the value of T_{io} is the blocking factor, that is, the size of the blocks to be handled by the program. Note that the blocking factor cannot be made as large as one would like, since block sizes are limited by memory size and performance considerations. Thus, there is for every program an optimal value for the blocking factor of the files to be accessed by it, that value which minimizes the processing time. This time is given by (see Sec. 8.3)

$$t_p = T_{cpu} + T_{io} = T_{sup} + T_{pr} + T_{io}$$

Ignoring T_{sup} for simplicity, it is easy to find an approximate relationship between processing time and block size. If there is no overlap between CPU and I/O time (that is, in the case of purely sequential activities), we have

$$t_p = T_{pr} + T_{io} = T_{pr} + Nt_{io} \tag{8.15}$$

where N is the total number of I/O operations to be executed and t_{io} is the (mean) time required to execute a single I/O operation. If

t_{acc} = mean access time to a block in mass storage

t_{tr} = transfer time of a block between main and mass memory

V_{tr} = nominal transfer rate of the mass storage unit being considered (in characters/second)

C = total number of characters to be transferred

b = block size (in characters)

$$r = \text{record size (in characters)}$$

$$f = \text{blocking factor } (fr = b)$$

we have

$$t_p = T_{pr} + Nt_{io} = T_{pr} + N(t_{acc} + t_{tr})$$

$$= T_{pr} + \left(\frac{C}{b}\right)\left(t_{acc} + \frac{b}{V_{tr}}\right) = T_{pr} + \left(\frac{1}{b}\right) Ct_{acc} + \frac{C}{V_{tr}}$$

Setting $K_1 = Ct_{acc}$ and $K_2 = \dfrac{C}{V_{tr}}$

we obtain

$$t_p = T_{pr} + \left(\frac{1}{b}\right) K_1 + K_2 \tag{8.16}$$

The constant K_2 is generally much smaller than K_1. Indeed, there are I/O subsystems (channel, control unit, disk unit) that can reach a transfer rate greater than 1 million characters per second, while the mean access time to a disk block is on the average (with zero seek time) half the time needed by the unit for a complete rotation, which is about 15 to 20 ms.

A diagram of the function in Eq. (8.16) is shown in Fig. 8.31. Let

$$C = 400{,}000 \text{ characters}$$

$$V_{tr} = 800{,}000 \text{ characters/s}$$

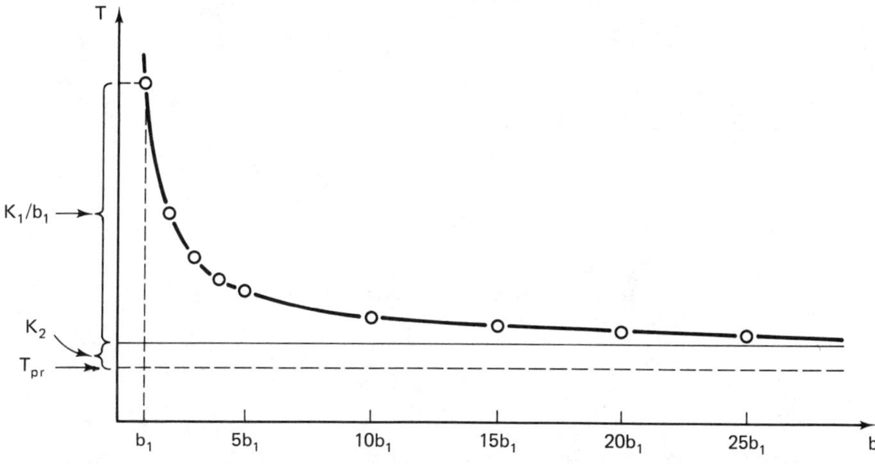

Figure 8.31 Variation of a program's processing time T with the size b of the blocks to be accessed.

$$T_{pr} = 30 \text{ s}$$

$$t_{acc} = 24 \times 10^{-3} \text{ s}$$

Then, for purely sequential activities, we would have

$$K_1 = 9600 \text{ characters/s}, \qquad K_2 = 0.5 \text{ s}$$

and we would obtain, for various values of b, the processing times displayed in Table 8.5. One can see that, if a program uses only one file whose records contain 100 characters ($r = 100$), changing the blocking factor from 1 to 10 reduces the processing time by about two-thirds.

Using two buffers in main memory (see Sec. 8.3), the I/O and CPU activities can partially overlap. The degree of overlap depends on the block size and on program characteristics. For a given block size, the overlap grows with the processing time of a block, or of a record.

Let b be the buffer size and let there be two buffers available. If a program processes the data in the records of a block read from mass memory without writing them back at the end (that is, if there is no updating of the file), and if t_{cpu} is the CPU time per block and t_{io} the I/O time per block, two cases can arise: either $t_{cpu} \geq t_{io}$, or $t_{cpu} < t_{io}$. In the first case (see Fig. 8.32a) we have

$$t_p = Nt_{cpu} + t_{io} = T_{cpu} + t_{io}$$

and, for a sufficiently large N,

$$t_p \cong T_{cpu}$$

In the second case (see Fig. 8.32b),

$$t_p = t_{cpu} + Nt_{io}$$

which for large N can be approximated as

$$t_p \cong Nt_{io} = T_{io}$$

TABLE 8.5 EFFECT ON PROGRAM PROCESSING TIME OF THE BLOCK SIZE b

$b = 100$	$t_p = 30 + 96 + 0.5 = 126.5$ s
$b = 1{,}000$	$t_p = 30 + 9.6 + 0.5 = 40.1$ s
$b = 2{,}000$	$t_p = 30 + 4.8 + 0.5 = 35.3$ s
$b = 4{,}000$	$t_p = 30 + 2.4 + 0.5 = 32.9$ s
$b = 8{,}000$	$t_p = 30 + 1.2 + 0.5 = 31.7$ s

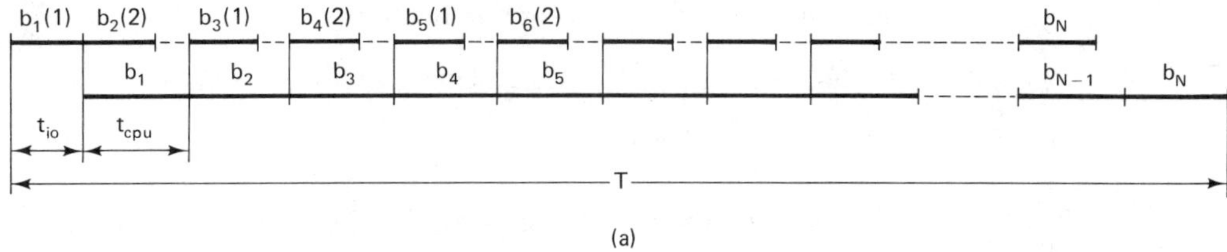

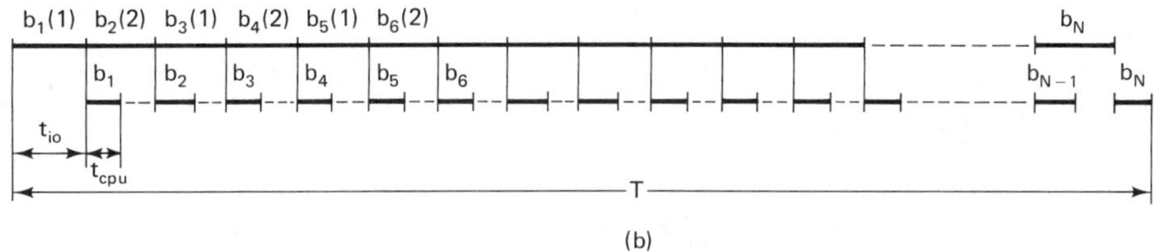

Figure 8.32 Overlap between t_{cpu} and t_{io} for (a) $t_{io} < t_{cpu}$; (b) $t_{io} > t_{cpu}$.

From this simple example we can see immediately that double buffering can considerably influence a program's processing time. The program may be considered CPU-bound when $t_{cpu} > t_{io}$ and I/O bound when $t_{io} > t_{cpu}$.

In general, if a program reads, processes, and writes back the updated blocks to mass storage, we have

$$t_p \cong \max\,(T_{cpu}, T_{io})$$

if all the I/O operations use the same channel, or

$$t_p \cong \max\,(T_{cpu}, \tfrac{1}{2}\,T_{io})$$

if two channels can be used (one for reading, one for writing).

As we have seen, a high blocking factor reduces the number of I/O operations needed to handle the file. On the other hand, it requires larger buffers and thus more main memory space for any program which accesses that file.

If a program uses several files, even simultaneously, we wish to determine the *optimal blocking factor* for each file. In this case, "optimal" means such that the number of blocks transferred from and to all files (that is, the number of I/O operations) is minimal compatibly with a given maximum main memory space for the buffers. Let

F = number of files

R_i = number of records in the ith file

f_i = blocking factor of the ith file

r_i = number of characters per record in the ith file

M_B = size, in characters, of the main memory area for file blocks

N_B = total number of blocks in all files

Then, R_i/f_i is the number of blocks in the ith file, and $r_i f_i$ is the block size in the ith file.

The problem to be solved is thus the following: Find

$$N_B = \min_{f_i} \sum_{i=1}^{F} \frac{R_i}{f_i} \tag{8.17}$$

under the constraint

$$\sum_{i=1}^{F} r_i f_i - M_B \leqslant 0 \tag{8.18}$$

and the conditions

$$R_i > 0, \qquad r_i > 0, \qquad f_i > 0$$

We can see that, for positive values of R_i, r_i, and f_i, the function N_B decreases as the f_i's increase and that, since the r_i's are positive, the maximum possible values for the f_i's will be those that satisfy constraint (8.18) with the equal sign, that is,

$$\sum_{i=1}^{F} r_i f_i = M_B \tag{8.19}$$

Thus, the problem can be solved with the method of Lagrange multipliers. By setting equal to zero the partial derivatives (with respect to the f_i's and to the Lagrange multiplier λ) of the function

$$Z = \sum_{i=1}^{F} \frac{R_i}{f_i} + \lambda \left(\sum_{i=1}^{F} r_i f_i - M_B \right) \tag{8.20}$$

we obtain

$$\frac{\partial Z}{\partial f_i} = \frac{-R_i}{f_i^2} + \lambda r_i = 0 \qquad (\text{for } i = 1, 2, \ldots, F) \tag{8.21}$$

$$\frac{\partial Z}{\partial \lambda} = \sum_{i=1}^{F} r_i f_i - M_B = 0 \tag{8.22}$$

From Eq. (8.21) we have

$$f_i = \frac{1}{\sqrt{\lambda}} \sqrt{\frac{R_i}{r_i}} \tag{8.23}$$

Hence

$$\frac{1}{\sqrt{\lambda}} \sum_{i=1}^{F} r_i \sqrt{\frac{R_i}{r_i}} - M_B = 0$$

and

$$\frac{1}{\sqrt{\lambda}} = \frac{M_B}{\sum_{i=1}^{F} \sqrt{R_i \, r_i}}$$

Substituting $1/\sqrt{\lambda}$ in Eq. (8.23), we find the optimal blocking factor for the ith file:

$$f_i = \frac{M_B}{K_F} \sqrt{\frac{R_i}{r_i}} \tag{8.24}$$

where

$$K_F = \sum_{i=1}^{F} \sqrt{R_i \, r_i} \tag{8.25}$$

can be calculated only once.

Let us assume that a program handles simultaneously three files with the following characteristics:

$$r_1 = 80 \qquad R_1 = 2000$$

$$r_2 = 120 \qquad R_2 = 8000$$

$$r_3 = 200 \qquad R_3 = 6000$$

and that the memory space available for buffers is 6000 characters

$$(M_B = 6000).$$

Then

$$K_F = \sqrt{16 \times 10^4} + \sqrt{96 \times 10^4} + \sqrt{120 \times 10^4} = 2475.23$$

$$\frac{M_B}{K_F} = 2.424$$

and we obtain

$$f_1 = 2.424 \cdot \sqrt{25} = 12.12$$

$$f_2 = 2.424 \cdot \sqrt{66.66} = 19.79$$

$$f_3 = 2.424 \cdot \sqrt{30} = 13.276$$

$$r_1 f_1 + r_2 f_2 + r_3 f_3 = 5999.6 \cong M_B$$

$$N_B = \frac{R_1}{f_1} + \frac{R_2}{f_2} + \frac{R_3}{f_3} = 1021.19$$

In practice, the value to be used for N_B will not coincide with the calculated one but will be an approximation to it due to the obvious necessity of replacing the real values of the f_i's with the nearest integers. If we set the f_i's equal to 12, 20, and 13, respectively, we obtain the following block sizes:

- For file 1: 960 characters
- For file 2: 2400 characters
- For file 3: 2600 characters

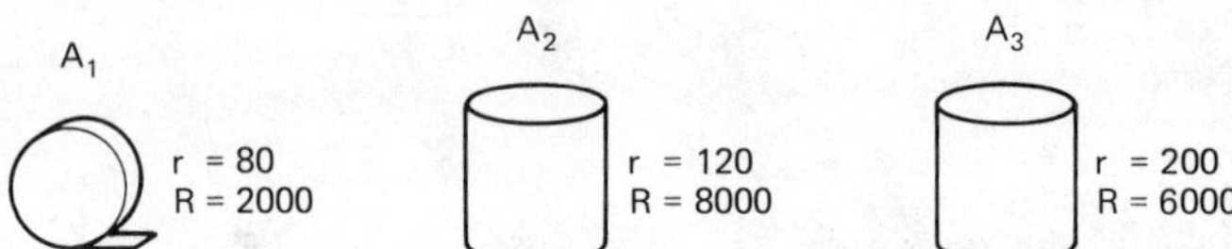

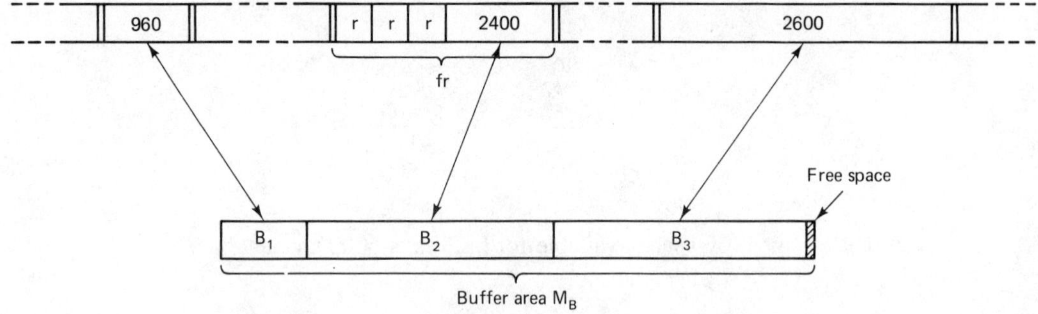

Figure 8.33 Optimal block sizes for the example in Sec. 8.3.2.

The buffer area can contain simultaneously a block of each file since the sum of their sizes is 5960 characters (see Fig. 8.33); the corresponding value of N_B is 1029. If double buffering is used, the value of M_B will have to equal half of the memory available for buffers.

The buffer area M_B could be completely utilized if, instead of the blocking factors selected, the values 12, 22, and 12 were used. In this case, the block sizes would be 960, 2640, and 2400 characters, respectively, which add up to exactly 6000. The number of I/O operations needed to read the three files completely becomes 1031 instead of 1029.

Our discussion is only an example of how to determine the blocking factors that minimize the number of I/O operations for programs that deal with several fixed-length record files [MU74]. For files with variable-sized records, one could choose as a first approximation the average record length and proceed as in the preceding example. The mathematical model which describes this case exactly is quite complicated.

8.3.4 Paging Rate Reduction

In a virtual memory system, a program's execution time (hence, the productivity and the responsiveness of the system) depends on its *dynamic behavior* [DE70]. This term usually indicates the space–time pattern followed by the program's accesses to the information in its *virtual* address space. In virtual memory environments, programs are designed and written as if the main memory size were equal to the maximum addressable memory capacity. For instance, if the machine has 32-bit instructions, with 8-bit operation codes and 24-bit addresses, each program can be written as if the user had a memory of 2^{24} words, even if the real main memory is of only 2^{18} words and only 2^{15} of these can be assigned to a program during its execution.

It is the operating system that makes sure that those parts of the program needed to continue execution be present in the allocated physical space. In nonvirtual memory environments, if a program is larger than the available memory, the programmer must take care of the problem. Clearly, this is easier if the program is well behaved, that is, if its sequence of memory references has a high degree of locality; in other words, if the references, during fairly long time periods, are limited to fairly small areas in virtual memory. Only in this case will it be possible to execute the program while keeping in main memory the necessary blocks of contiguous instructions and data without too many interruptions. Indeed, when a program refers to a word not in main memory, its execution must be suspended until that word is retrieved from mass storage and loaded into main memory. Since mass storage has much longer access times than main memory, data are not transferred by word but in groups of words called pages or segments. A page contains a fixed number (like 512 or 1024) of words, while a segment has a variable size. The principle that justifies paging is the same that allows a virtual memory machine to run with an acceptable performance: the *principle of locality*. It only makes sense to transfer a whole page if there is a high probability that the program will use most of the words in it quite soon. Otherwise, this transfer would be a waste of time and memory space.

Luckily, programs usually obey the principle of locality, although to different extents. This is because the human mind works effectively only by concentrating sequentially on individual subproblems rather than by facing global problems in all their complexity. This characteristic is also reflected in the structures usually present in programming languages: subprograms, vectors and matrixes, iterations, modules, blocks with single-entry and single-exit points in structured programs, and so on. By using these structures adequately and knowing how the system manages its memory, a programmer can strongly influence the performance of his or her programs, since the locality of their references depends on how they are structured and how their various parts are placed in virtual memory space.

However, it is conceptually wrong and practically inefficient to expect that programmers will be able to optimize the dynamic behavior of their programs. To assume that programmers know exactly how the system works and can exploit their knowledge effectively contradicts the main argument in favor of virtual memory systems, that users need not worry about memory management. And experience has shown that a program's dynamic behavior is generally too complex for a human mind to fully understand the changes caused by structural modifications to it. Thus, the programmer's care in trying to make a program local is always necessary but rarely sufficient to achieve a completely satisfactory performance.

A method that has been very successful at improving the locality of programs, thereby reducing their page fault rate, is that of *automatic restructuring* [FE76]. This method consists of collecting data on the behavior of the program to be improved during its execution and of using these data to determine the locations in virtual space of the program's sections. A procedure to obtain this result can be summarized as follows:

Step 1. The program to be restructured is subdivided into *blocks*. The relative positions of words within a block are fixed. However, blocks can be placed anywhere in virtual space. For restructuring to work, the mean size of a block must be substantially smaller than the page size. A convenient criterion for block selection is the one which makes them coincide with relocatable parts of the program (subroutines, functions, procedures, arrays, COMMON areas, and so on).

Step 2. The program is executed with reasonable input data and its dynamic behavior is recorded, for example, in the form of a *block reference string*. This string contains the temporal series of access requests to the program's blocks made by the CPU. Clearly, other equivalent types of characterization can be used instead.

Step 3. A *restructuring algorithm* is applied to the block reference string; this produces a *restructuring graph*. Its nodes represent the blocks of the program and its edges are labeled with a number that quantifies the desirability that the two corresponding blocks be grouped into the same page. An example of a restructuring graph is displayed in Fig. 8.34, which refers to a program containing eight blocks; the behavior of the program is represented by the string in Fig. 8.35.

Step 4. A *clustering algorithm* is applied to the restructuring graph. This algorithm tries to group the nodes so that:
(a) The sum of the intracluster edge labels is maximum.
(b) The sum of the block sizes in each group is less than the size of a page.
The result obtained when all blocks are assumed to be the size of half a page is represented in Fig. 8.34 by the dotted lines.

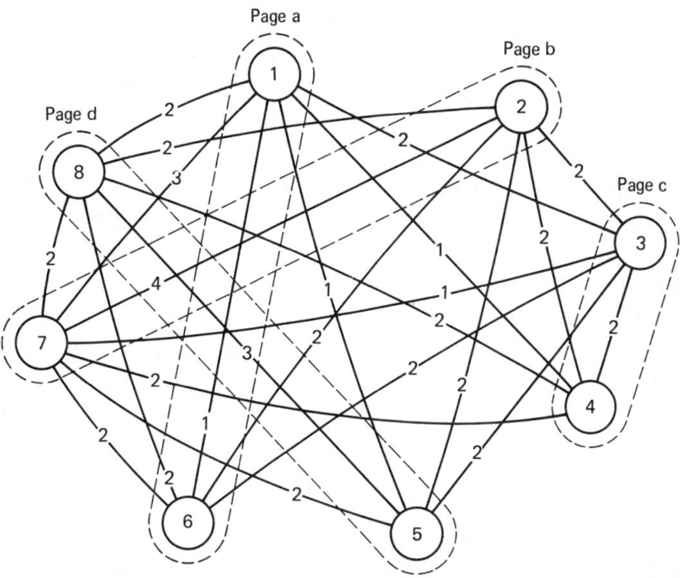

Figure 8.34 Restructuring graph for the string in Fig. 8.35a.

Step 5. The program is rearranged as suggested by step 4, placing the blocks of each cluster in a page. The size of a cluster will not generally equal the size of a page. Therefore, if the empty spaces in the program are to be eliminated, another algorithm may be applied to the graph to determine the best ordering of the pages. If no space compaction is made, the page order is immaterial.

Among the existing restructuring algorithms, the most effective are those that explicitly take into account the memory management technique used by the system the program runs on. As an example, we shall illustrate the CWS *(critical working set)* algorithm, which is the basis of the Automatic Paging Optimizer, a commercial tool for automatic program restructuring [AP77]. The memory management technique assumed by the CWS algorithm is the working set policy [DE68]. A version implemented in several systems can be described as follows. A program's working set at time t is the set of pages W_p (t, Δ) (or of blocks $W_b(t, \Delta)$) that the program has accessed in the interval $(t - \Delta, t)$, where Δ is a parameter called *window size,* the window being the interval of observation. The working set policy considers W_p as an estimate of the current locality, that is, of the set of pages the program will need in the near future, and tries to keep in memory the pages in W_p. In practice, W_p is measured periodically, for instance as follows.

(a) 21218127878345672751218187834567275 6

(b) aaaadaaddddbbccdadcaaadadddbbccdadcc

(c) babadabbdbdccdabbbdabadadbdccdabbbda

Figure 8.35 Block reference string and two corresponding page reference strings.

A bit in the page table of the program is associated to each page and is set to 1 every time the program accesses the corresponding page. Periodically, the operating system reads the page bits, removes from the working set those pages whose bit is 0, and then resets all the bits. When a page not in the working set is requested, real memory space for it must be found. If there is not enough room for a program's working set, one of the programs partially loaded in memory is swapped out; on the other hand, no program can be partially loaded in memory if there is not enough room for its working set. The latter constraint means that, although the memory space used by a program during its execution varies, the size of this space can be determined at each instant of its execution, even though the identities and behaviors of the programs sharing the main memory with it are unknown. The CWS algorithm tries to minimize the page transfers requested by a program and thus also its paging rate, assuming that the program is executed by a system that implements the sampled working set policy for memory management. This policy measures the working set periodically, as described previously, with period Δ often set equal to the window size used to define the working set itself.

The number of transfers can be calculated by applying this strategy to the page reference string. If the same technique is applied to the block reference string, it is possible to determine which blocks will certainly be in main memory during each interval of duration Δ (the time referred to here is the *CPU* or *virtual time,* which does not include those intervals during which program execution is suspended). For instance, after the first interval containing four references, the block working set for the string in Fig. 8.35a consists of blocks 1 and 2. Let us now consider the blocks referenced during the next interval (in the example they are 8, 1, 2, 7). The blocks not included in the current working set (8 and 7) will cause page faults unless they belong to the same pages of the blocks in the working set (1 and 2). Thus, it is desirable to group them together (in the example 8 with 1 or 2, and 7 with 1 or 2). So the CWS algorithm increases by a constant amount (for example, by 1) the weights of the edges 8–1, 8–2, 7–1 and 7–2, and then repeats the procedure for the subsequent intervals.

The initial weight of all the edges in the restructuring graph is 0. Once the string has been processed, the weights are such that an optimal clustering algorithm would reach the absolute minimum number of page transfers if not more than two blocks were grouped into each page. If, as is always the case in practice, there are more than two blocks in each page, the solution obtained by this method (even using an optimal clustering algorithm) is not optimal. However, many experiments made by researchers have shown that the restructured program is almost always considerably better than the original (some of these results are listed in Table 8.6).

In the case of the string in Fig. 8.35a, the weights generated by the CWS algorithm are shown in the graph of Fig. 8.34. The clustering algorithm will thus suggest the grouping of blocks 1 and 6, 2 and 7, 3 and 4, 5 and 8, so that the new structure of the program will be the one illustrated in Fig. 8.36b. The page reference string generated by the program (with the same input data) will thus be the one in Fig. 8.35c instead of that in Fig. 8.35b, which would characterize the original program (Fig. 8.36a). It can easily be seen that, applying the sampled working set policy to both of these strings, the one corresponding to the restructured program requires 5 page transfers instead of 7. Because of what was said above, 5 is in this case the absolute minimum number of page faults.

TABLE 8.6 SOME EXPERIMENTAL RESULTS OBTAINED WITH THE CWS ALGORITHM [FE 76]

Restructured program	*Reduction factors of* *Paging rate*	*Mean memory occupancy*
Interactive editor	1.86	—
File system	3.60	—
FORTRAN compiler	2.1–5.5	1.15–1.42
FORTRAN compiler	3.2–12	1.08–1.34
Application program	1.4–16.2	0.79–0.99
Application program	3.8–20.8	0.85–1.21
Pascal compiler	1.2–2.4	1.18–1.22
Simulator	1.7–3.2	1.06–1.42

The effect of restructuring on a program's dynamic behavior is clearly visible in Fig. 8.37; here time proceeds vertically toward the bottom, while the block numbers are reported on the horizontal axis. A dot indicates one or more references to the corresponding block during the corresponding interval.

Restructuring permutes blocks to make this diagram representing the dynamic behavior much more compact (compare Fig. 8.37b with Fig. 8.37a). Of all the doubts that may arise on these and other similar algorithms, the most serious are perhaps those about the influence of the input data and of the sampling frequency on the results. Does a program restructured with the CWS algorithm behave better than its nonrestructured version even when its input data change and when the frequency and phase with which its working set is measured is modified? The experiments carried out so far on several programs [FE76] have provided a positive reply to this question. Clearly, the amount of improvement and its robustness with respect to the variations mentioned depend on the program itself. Nevertheless, for most of the frequently executed programs, which often constitute the heaviest portion of the workload, restructuring seems to be economically worthwhile.

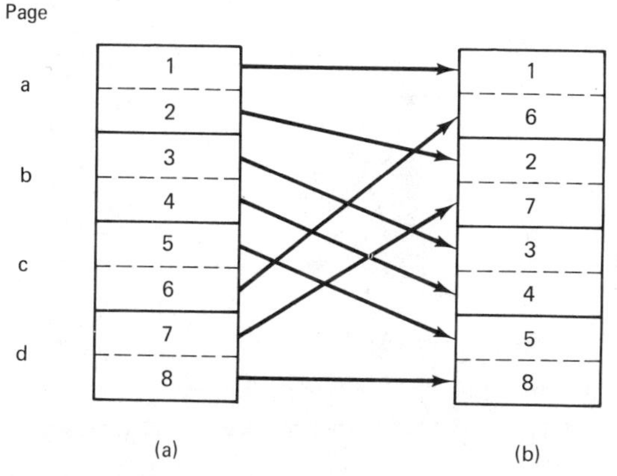

Figure 8.36 Eight-block program (a) before; (b) after being restructured. The two rectangles in the figure represent the virtual address space of the program.

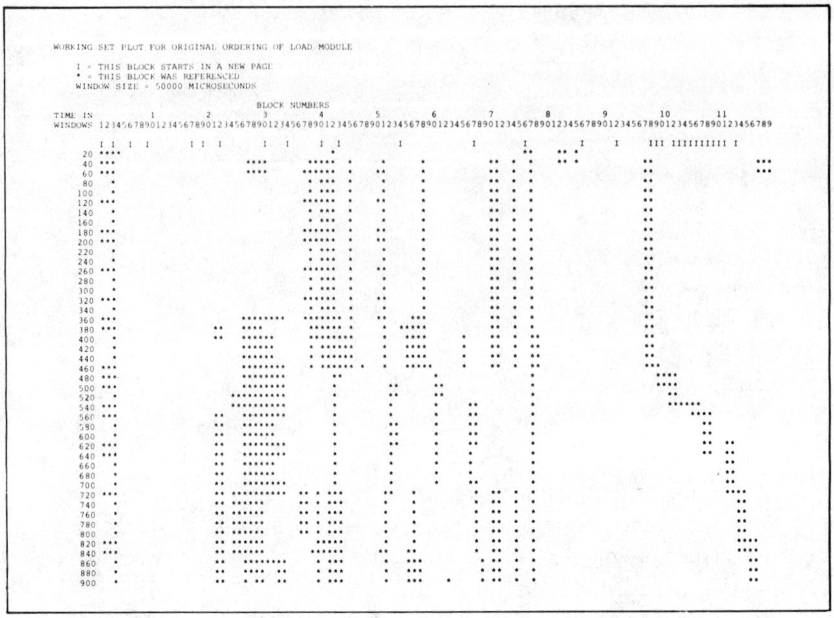

```
WORKING SET PLOT FOR ORIGINAL ORDERING OF LOAD MODULE

     I = THIS BLOCK STARTS IN A NEW PAGE
     * = THIS BLOCK WAS REFERENCED
    WINDOW SIZE = 50000 MICROSECONDS

                                              BLOCK NUMBERS
TIME IN
WINDOWS
```

(a)

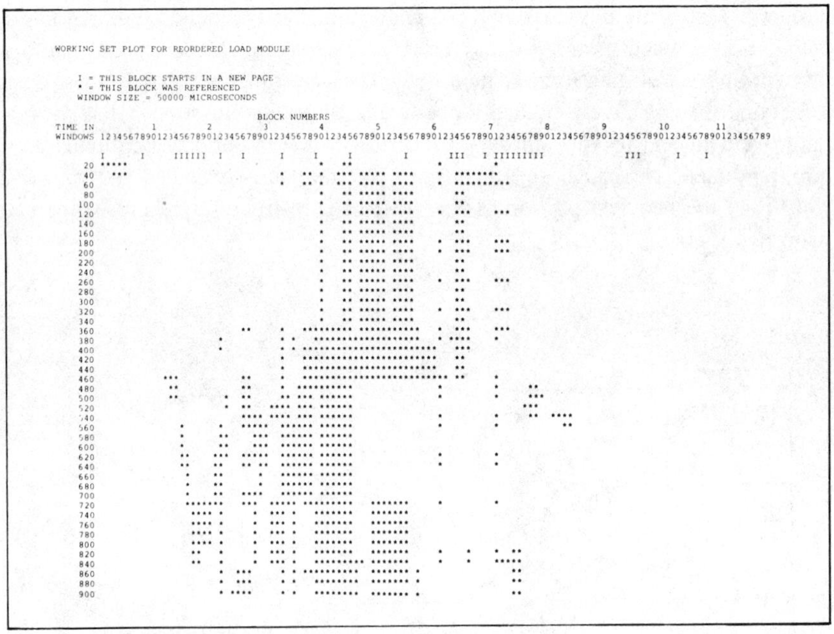

```
WORKING SET PLOT FOR REORDERED LOAD MODULE

     I = THIS BLOCK STARTS IN A NEW PAGE
     * = THIS BLOCK WAS REFERENCED
    WINDOW SIZE = 50000 MICROSECONDS

                                              BLOCK NUMBERS
TIME IN
WINDOWS
```

(b)

Figure 8.37 Dynamic behavior of a program (a) before; (b) after being restructured with the CWS algorithm [AP77].

REFERENCES

Entries marked with an asterisk (*) are referenced in the text.

[AC78] Achard, M., and others, Clustering algorithms in the OPALE restructuring system, in: *Performance of Computer Installations Proc. ICPCI,* D. Ferrari, ed., pp. 137–153, North-Holland, Amsterdam, June 1978.

*[AP77] *APO—Automatic Paging Optimizer—User Guide.* Boole & Babbage Inc., Sunnyvale, Calif., Feb. 1977.

[BA74] Baird, G. N., Johnson, L. A., System for efficient program portability, *AFIPS Conf. Proc., NCC,* vol. 43, pp. 423, 429, 1974.

[BE70] Beizer, B., Analytical techniques for the statistical evaluation of program running time, *AFIPS Conf. Proc., FJCC,* vol. 37, pp. 519–524, 1970.

[BE73] Brandwajn, A., and others, A model of program and system behavior in virtual memory, *IRIA-LABORIA,* Rocquencourt, France, 1973.

[BR74] Brown, G. G., Approaches to program performance measurement, *INFO Software 74,* Infotech, 1974.

[CO73] Coffman, E., Denning, P. J., *Operating System Theory.* Prentice-Hall, Englewood Cliffs, N.J., 1973.

[CO76] Collins, J. P., Performance improvement of the CPV loader through use of the ADAM hardware monitor, *ACM SIGMETRICS Perf. Evaluat. Review,* vol. 5, n. 2, pp. 63–68, Apr. 1976.

[DA72] Dahl, O. J., Djikstra, E. W., Hoare, C. A. R., *Structured Programming,* Academic Press, New York, 1972.

*[DE68] Denning, P. J., The working set model for program behavior, *CACM,* vol. 11, pp. 323–333, 1968.

*[DE70] Denning, P. J., Virtual memory, *Computing Survey,* vol. 2, n. 3, pp. 153–189, 1970.

[DO72] Donovan, J. J., *Systems Programming,* McGraw-Hill, New York, 1972.

[FE74] Ferrari, D., Improving locality by critical working sets, *CACM,* vol. 17, n. 11, pp. 614–620, Nov. 1974.

[FE75] Ferrari, D., Tailoring programs to models of program behavior, *IBM J. Research Development,* vol. 19, n. 3, pp. 244, 251, May 1975.

*[FE76] Ferrari, D., The improvement of program behavior, *Computer,* pp. 39–47, Nov. 1976.

[GE71] Gelenbe, E., Optimum choice of page sizes in a virtual memory with a hardware executive and a rapid-access secondary storage medium, *Proc. ACM-SIGOPS Workshop on System Performance Evaluation,* Harvard University, Cambridge, Mass., pp. 321–336, Apr. 1971.

[GE73] Gelenbe, E., The distribution of a program in primary and fast buffer storage, *CACM,* vol. 16, n. 7, pp. 431–434, July 1973.

[GU72] Guertin, R. L., Programming in a paging environment, *Datamation,* vol. 18, n. 2, pp. 48–55, Feb. 1972.

*[HA71] Hatfield, D. J., Gerald, J., Program restructuring for virtual memory, *IBM Systems J,* vol. 10, n. 3, pp. 168–192, 1971.

*[HE75] Hellerman, H., Conroy, T. F., *Computer System Performance,* McGraw-Hill, New York, 1975.

[IN72] Ingalls, D., The execution-time profile as a programming tool, in: Rustin, R., ed., *Design and Optimization of Compilers,* Prentice-Hall, Englewood Cliffs, N.J., 1972.

[IN73] Inglis, J., Dee, E. G., Flexibility of block length for magnetic files, *Comput. J,* vol. 16, pp. 303–307, Nov. 1973.

[JO69] Jones, R. M., Factors affecting the efficiency of a virtual memory, *IEEE Trans. Computers C-18,* n. 11, pp. 1004–1008, Nov. 1969.

[JO70] Joseph, M., An analysis of paging and program behavior, *Comput. J.,* vol. 13, n. 1, pp. 48–54, Feb. 1970.

[KN71] Knuth, D. E., An empirical study of FORTRAN programs, *Software—Practice and Experience,* vol. 1, n. 1, pp. 105–133, 1971.

[LE71] Lewis, P. A. W., Yue, P. C., Statistical analysis of program reference patterns in a paging environment, *IEEE Computer Society Conference,* Boston, pp. 133–134, Sept. 1971.

*[LO77] *Look User Handbook,* Applied Data Research, Inc., Princeton, N.J., Sept. 1977.

[MA71] Margolin, B. H., Parmelee, R. P., Schatzof, M., Analysis of free-storage algorithms, *IBM Systems J.,* vol. 10, n. 4, 1971.

[MA74] Masuda, T., et al., Optimization of program organization by cluster analysis, *Proc. IFIP Congress 74,* pp. 261–265, North-Holland, Amsterdam, 1974.

*[ME73] *MetaCOBOL—Source Program Optimization Procedure,* Applied Data Research, Inc., Princeton, N.J., Sept. 1973.

[MI74] Millbrandt, W. W., Rodriguez-Rosell, J., An interactive software engineering tool for memory management and user program evaluation, *AFIPS Conf. Proc., NCC,* pp. 153–158, 1974.

[MO74] Morgan, H. L., Optimal space allocation on disk storage devices, *CACM,* vol. 17, n. 3, pp. 139–142, March 1974.

*[MO73] Morrison, E. J., User program performance in virtual storage systems, *IBM Systems J.,* n. 3, pp. 216–237, 1973.

*[MU74] Mulin, J. K., Stuart, G. F., Optimal blocking factors for a mix of sequentially processed jobs, *Comput. J.,* vol. 17, n. 3, pp. 224–228, Aug. 1974.

[NE71] Nemeth, A. G., Rovner, P. D., User program measurement in a time-shared environment, *CACM,* vol. 14, n. 10, pp. 661–666, Oct. 1971.

*[OP78] Optimizer III—User Guide, Capex Corp., Phoenix, Ariz., 1978.

*[PL77] *Plan IV Report Explanations Manual,* n. SPA-575-24, Capex Corp., Phoenix, Ariz., 1977.

*[PP76] *PPE—Problem Program Evaluator—User Guide—Version 4,* Boole & Babbage, Inc., Sunnyvale, Calif., June 1976.

[RA76] Ramage, I., Experience in program and system optimization, *Infotech State of the Art Report "Program Optimization," 1976.*

[RY74] Ryder, K. D., Optimizing program placement in virtual systems, *IBM Systems J.,* vol. 13, n. 4, pp. 292–306, 1974.

[SP72] Spirn, J. R., Denning, P. J., Experiments with program locality, *AFIPS Conf. Proc., FJCC,* vol. 41, pp. 611–621, 1972.

[VE71] Verhoef, E. W., Automatic program segmentation based on boolean connectivity, *AFIPS Conf. Proc., SJCC,* vol. 38, pp. 491–496, 1971.

*[WA76] Walker, J. R., McKittrick, T. E., Performance evaluation of programs in a VS environment, *Proc. CMG-VIII Conf.,* pp. 62–78, Atlanta, Nov. 1976.

[WA71] Waters, S. J., Blocking sequentially processed magnetic files, *Comput. J.,* vol. 14, n. 2, pp. 109–112, May 1971.

9

ANALYTIC MODELS AND THEIR APPLICATIONS

9.1 INTRODUCTION

Evaluation techniques have evolved with the continuous evolution of knowledge and of practical requirements in the field of computer systems performance. Among the first techniques to be used, one can mention *rules of thumb, benchmarking,* and *simulation.*

The rules of thumb, usually extracted from experience or based on information provided by the system's manufacturer, give valuable advice on how the operation of a system may be controlled. Statements like: the utilization of a channel should not be higher than x percent, the utilization of a disk device should not be higher than y percent, the mean block size should be z Kbytes, and so on, are some of the most popular types of rules that are followed in many installations to detect symptoms and suggest actions for tuning a system.

Benchmarking, as seen in Sec. 2.3.2, is a direct measurement approach. A model of the workload is input into the system to be evaluated (for example, a system to be tuned, before and after the tuning actions, or a new system being considered for procurement), and the values of various performance indexes are measured during the run.

A drawback of both these techniques is that the effects of tuning actions can be evaluated only *after* their actual implementation. And it should be noticed that often the actual implementation of system modifications is expensive and disrupts the normal operation of a system. Because of these problems, the benchmarking technique is heavily utilized only in equipment procurement studies.

Thus, these techniques cannot be effectively applied to problems for which performance is to be *predicted.* The class of these problems is large and has grown in importance with the progressive computerization of the various sectors of organizations.

Performance prediction is not only needed in tuning studies, but also in design, upgrading, and capacity planning problems. The concept of prediction is naturally associated to the one of *model*. To predict, it is necessary to have a model whose output must be "similar" to the observations of the phenomenon being considered. Thus, for instance, if the effects of workload changes are to be determined, a model of the workload capable of representing the modifications under consideration will have to be available. The model may then be executed on the system itself, adopting the technique of benchmarking, or on a model of that system.

A *structural model* of a system is a representation of the system capable of reproducing its *states*. A system's evolution in time may be described by the chronological sequence of the states the system operates in. This history of the system's states must be reproduced also by any structural model of the system.

The difficulties one encounters in describing analytically the functions performed by a system's components and in computing the analytic solution of the resulting model have favored the initial diffusion of *simulation modeling* techniques. The design and implementation of a simulator for a computer system can be carried out without explicitly considering the mathematical constraints that characterize analytic models and can exploit the facilities of simulation-oriented programming languages. However, as was pointed out in Sec. 3.4, simulation techniques have such drawbacks as large implementation costs and times, high probabilities of errors, debugging and validation difficulties, and often substantial usage costs.

The deepening of our knowledge of *analytic models,* in particular of those based on classical queuing network theory and on approximate solutions, has allowed us to extend substantially the class of systems that may be modeled with analytic techniques. These techniques have become quite popular because of their relatively low cost, general applicability, and ease and flexibility of use. Obviously, not all the problems that may arise in practice can be solved by analytic modeling. In these cases, simulation still remains the only adequate modeling technique.

This chapter presents and discusses some of the methods for building and solving analytic models. More than to a description of the various solution techniques, which the reader will find in the textbooks concerned with this topic, the chapter is devoted to an illustration of the applications of these models to system tuning and upgrading. Our goal is to provide the basic notions of the various approaches, reducing the mathematical treatment to the essential aspects, and to show, by a discussion of case studies, the types of problems that may be solved by analytic modeling. The symbols of the same quantities dealt with by the various approaches have been unified. A table listing these symbols can be found at the end of the chapter.

9.2 IMPLEMENTATION OF AN ANALYTIC MODEL

A computer system can be viewed as an ensemble of interconnected components. The variables that describe the state of a component at time t are called *state variables*. The state of a system is defined by the values of the state variables of its components. Nonnegligible variations of these values correspond to *state transitions*. A system's dynamic behavior is completely specified by the chronological sequence of its states, i.e., by its *history of the states*. A model of a system can be seen as a system of equations that represents the history of the system's states.

Besides the state variables, a model includes:

1. *Input variables,* also called *parameters;* these variables represent either the world external to the model or those aspects of the model that are to be modified when using it; they usually describe the characteristics of the system's workload and components.
2. *Output variables,* whose values are determined by the solution of the model; they usually represent internal and external performance indexes.

When the functional relationships of a model, which describe the interactions between input and state variables, can be expressed by equations that may be solved by analytic methods, we say that an *analytic solution technique* is used for the analytic model that has been constructed.

Although the running of a system is a typically deterministic phenomenon, in most cases it is modeled probabilistically. A main motivation for this is that systems and workloads are usually too complex to be accurately representable by manageable deterministic models. In Chapter 2, we saw that most of the various techniques for characterizing a workload are statistical in nature. Even though each class of components into which a workload is subdivided is represented in a workload model by some of its members, the workload components in a class have different characteristics, and the distributions of these characteristics are very imperfectly modeled by the class' representatives. Furthermore, the large number of variables needed to describe a system and their interaction levels cause certain events to appear as having random occurrences. Thus, the values of most parameters are assigned as distributions, and the results are also obtained as distributions of values.

Another major reason for the appropriateness of probabilitistic models is their ability to represent the natural uncertainty about future workloads and contexts in predictive applications.

The need to make a model analytically solvable often imposes the introduction of simplifying assumptions that influence both the degree of detail and the configuration of the model. Even in this case, as for workload models, an accurate analysis of the study's objectives and of the intended use of the model is necessary for selecting the proper *level of abstraction* at which the system is to be represented and the aspects to be considered.

To expand the class of analytically solvable problems, the *hierarchical modeling* approach has been introduced. The analysis of a system according to this approach consists of identifying modules, or *subsystems,* hierarchically contained within each other so that the results of analyzing a module can be easily utilized in the analysis of the module that contains it at the immediately higher level in the hierarchy. Starting from the bottom of the hierarchical tree, each subsystem can be studied in isolation. At the level immediately above it, each subsystem is replaced by an equivalent subsystem, that is, by a simpler module that has the same effects on the rest of the system (see Fig. 9.1). For a hierarchical decomposition to work well, the degree of interaction among the components of a sub-

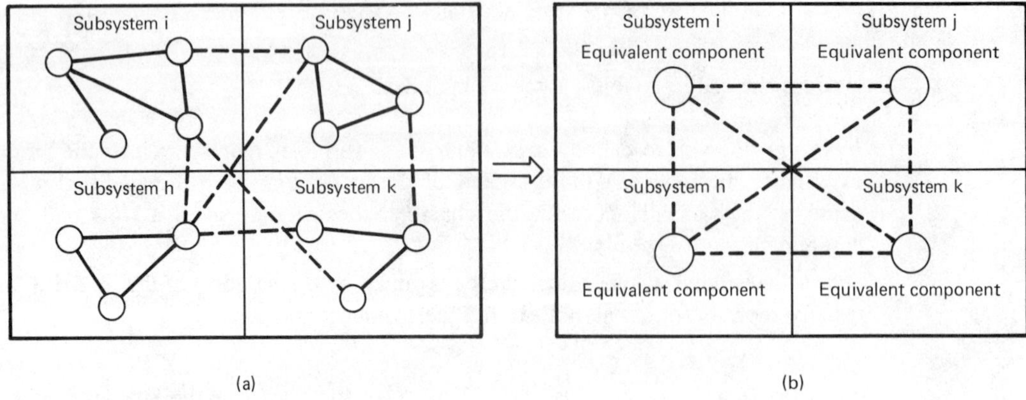

Figure 9.1 Hierarchical modeling of a generic system. Each of the four subsystems identified in (a) is analyzed in isolation and replaced in (b) by an equivalent component, which produces the same effects on the flow of information to be processed by the subsystem.

system should be high with respect to that existing among the components of subsystems at different levels [CO77]. Some applications of this technique will be described in Section 9.6. For instance, in a computer system we can identify, based on the time scales of their activities, three hierarchical levels [KO78a], [KO78b]:

1. A *microlevel,* whose subsystems operate on a nanosecond or microsecond time scale; examples of components that may be studied at this level are CPUs, cache memories, and main memories; this is the level at which the performance of interleaved memories and that of cache or memory replacement algorithms is to be investigated.
2. An *intermediate level,* where the times of the activities are measured in milliseconds; this is, for instance, the time scale typical of I/O devices, and examples of problems to be studied at this level are I/O scheduling, memory allocation, and processor scheduling.
3. A *macrolevel,* whose characteristic times are expressed in seconds; typical quantities defined at this level are the response time and the turnaround time; the system here can be seen as a black box, and the meaningful events are the beginning of a new command being keyed in at a terminal, the submission of a new program in batch mode, the end of a system's response to a command, the completion of the printing out of the results of a batch program, and so on.

The techniques for analyzing each subsystem are the same as those that can be used for the whole system, that is, analytic modeling, simulation, and measurement. Since models cannot always be solved by analytic techniques, sometimes it may be necessary to apply analytic and simulation techniques within the same model for the analysis of different subsystems. This approach is known as *hybrid simulation* [SC78].

Computer systems performance is highly sensitive to contention for systems resources. Probabilistic models based on *queuing theory* are especially suitable for the study of computer systems in which several requests may compete for each resource (for example, multiprogramming systems). From the viewpoint of contention, a system may be seen as a network of queues, one for each resource for which the various processes compete. A process is viewed as a sequence of requests to be satisfied by the system's resources. When a request has been satisfied by a resource, the process immediately migrates to another resource; if this is already servicing another request, the process joins the queue of the requests for that resource.

Evaluating the performance of a system through a model means, in this case, computing the values of the performance indexes of interest for each resource represented in the model. The indexes to be computed usually include the throughput of the resource, the mean length of the queue, the mean waiting time in the queue, the fraction of total time the resource is busy, and the mean number of processes in the resource (either being serviced or waiting for service).

The solution of models based on queuing theory can be obtained by introducing a number of assumptions that often seem to be quite unrealistic. However, in spite of these discrepancies with respect to reality, queuing network models have proved to be capable of representing reasonably complex systems with acceptable accuracy.

On the basis of some observations (for example, that the values of some indexes do not seem to depend on the distributions of the parameters involved but only on their

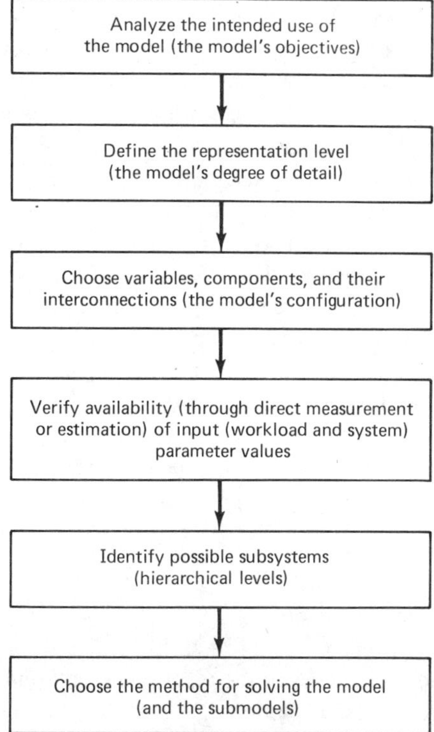

Figure 9.2 Main steps of the formulation phase for a system model.

mean values; also, that the validity of some of the assumptions on which most solution techniques for queuing models are based can never be experimentally verified), in 1976 Buzen introduced *operational analysis* [BU76]. Using only assumptions normally valid in practice and easy to verify experimentally, operational analysis has derived most of the results of queuing network theory in a more natural way, closer to the mental attitudes of most performance analysts. Just because of this greater understandability, our treatment of operational analysis and its applications precedes that of queuing network models.

As we already saw in Chapter 2, the modeling process consists of three fundamental phases: *formulation, solution,* and *calibration* and *validation*. The most important operations of the formulation phase for a system model are summarized in Fig. 9.2.

9.3 OPERATIONAL ANALYSIS

Among the principal reasons for the introduction of operational analysis are:

1. The need for providing performance analysts with mathematical relationships involving experimentally measurable quantities and characterizing a system's performance during a given time interval.
2. The possibility of interpreting the results of queuing network models in a concrete way, deriving them by using only measurable quantities under assumptions that can be experimentally verified.

The variables measured over an *observation interval* are called *operational variables*. Operational analysis tries to provide a framework in which system performance can be studied using only operational variables and mathematical relationships among them (called *operational laws*) and applying *operationally testable hypotheses*.

In this section, we shall only outline the general concepts of operational analysis and provide some examples of its application. A more complete treatment can be found in [DE78] and in the articles referenced in that tutorial.

There are two main assumptions on which operational analysis is based. First, the system, during the measurement period, is in *operational equilibrium,* that is, *flow-balanced;* in the interval [0, T] being considered, the number A of processing requests that the system or one of its resources receives must be equal (or at least very close) to the number C of requests processed by the system or by the resource; if the observation interval is reasonably long, then the probability that $A \cong C$ is high; in any event, it is easy to verify the validity of this assumption by seeing whether

$$\left| \frac{A - C}{C} \right| < \varepsilon \tag{9.1}$$

where ε is the maximum acceptable error.

Second, the arrival rate λ of processing requests at one of the system's resources is independent of the length of the queues of the other resources *(homogeneous arrivals);* similarly, the mean time between completions S of one of the system's resources is independent of the system's queue length or of the length of the queues for the other resources *(homogeneous services)*. Essentially, the homogeneity assumptions state that there must not be interactions between the behavior of a resource and that of the rest of the system except for those occurring through the local queue of the resource. These assumptions are approximately satisfied by real systems if they are observed for sufficiently long periods.

Let us consider a system with A arrivals and C departures of programs during the observation interval. If we denote by B the amount of time spent by the system processing programs ($0 \leqslant B \leqslant T$), we can easily derive the following operational variable:

$$\lambda = \frac{A}{T} \quad \text{(programs/s)}, \qquad X = \frac{C}{T} \quad \text{(programs/s)},$$
$$U = \frac{B}{T} \qquad\qquad S = \frac{B}{C} \quad \text{(s/program)} \tag{9.2}$$

which represent the *arrival rate*, the *completion rate* (or *output rate*), the system's *utilization*, and the *mean service time* per program, respectively.

For any duration T of the observation interval, the following relationship (the *utilization law*) always holds:

$$U = XS \tag{9.3}$$

which, because of the flow balance assumption $A \cong C$, can also be written as

$$U = \lambda S \tag{9.4}$$

Example 9.1

The mean arrival rate λ of a system is 1.5 programs/min. The service times of the programs are independent of their arrival times and have a mean value of 0.5 min. What is the mean utilization of the system?

From Eq. (9.4), we have $U = 1.5 \times 0.5 = 0.75$; thus, the system is busy 75 percent of the observation interval. This system will be considered again in the examples of this section and will be modeled by a queuing theoretical approach in Sec. 9.4.1 (Case 9.3).

When $U = 1$, the system is busy throughout the observation interval and is said to be *saturated*. The corresponding value of X is $1/S$ and cannot be increased by increasing the arrival rate λ. In this case, an increase in λ will only increase the length of the queue. If a system is saturated, we may have $A \gg C$; hence the balanced flow assumption may not hold. For this assumption to be satisfied, one must have $U < 1$; hence

$$X = \lambda < \frac{1}{S} \tag{9.5}$$

By R we denote the *mean response time* of a program, that is, the mean time a program spends within the system either being processed or waiting for the various resources. To derive R, consider the diagram in Fig. 9.3, which shows the number $N(t)$ of programs in the system during an interval T. Denoting by W the area between the curve and the horizontal axis, the mean value N of $N(t)$, that is, the mean number of programs in the system, is

$$N = \frac{W}{T} \tag{9.6}$$

Observing that W is the sum of the times spent by all the programs in the system, we have

$$R = \frac{W}{C} \tag{9.7}$$

Substituting Eq. (9.6) into Eq. (9.7) yields

$$R = \frac{NT}{C}$$

Hence, since $C/T = X$,

$$R = \frac{N}{X} \tag{9.8}$$

Equation (9.8) states that the mean response time equals the ratio between the mean number of programs in the system and the system's output rate. If the system is in operational equilibrium, it will be $X = \lambda$; then from Eq. (9.8) we have $N = R\lambda$. This equation, or its equivalent (9.8), is called *Little's law*.

Example 9.2

(See also Sec. 9.4.1, Case 9.3.) Assume that Fig. 9.3 represents $N(t)$ for the system considered in Example 9.1 and that the operational assumptions are valid within interval T. We wish to calculate R.

From the diagram, we have $A = C = 15$ programs, $B = 7.5$ min. From Eq. (9.2),

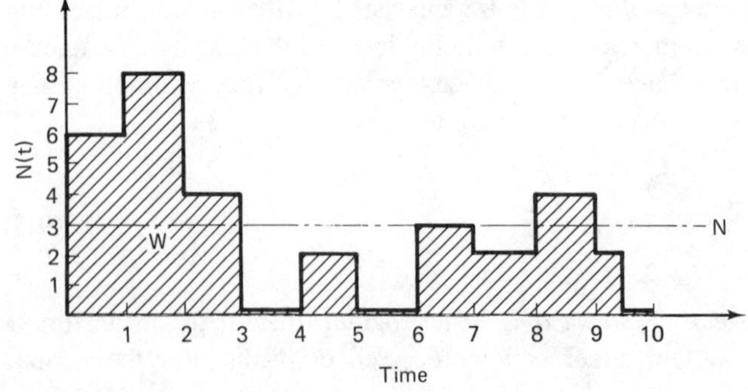

Figure 9.3 Number of programs in the system (being processed or waiting) versus time.

we derive $\lambda = X = 1.5$ programs/min, $U = 0.75$, $S = 0.5$ min. The value of W is given by $W = 6 + 8 + 4 + 2 + 3 + 2 + 4 + 1 = 30$ program $\times$ min. The mean number of programs in the system is, from Eq. (9.6), $N = 3$ programs. The mean response time is given by Eq. (9.7): $R = 2$ min.

If we shift downward by 1 unit the nonzero portions of the curve in Fig. 9.3, we obtain the curve of $N_q(t,)$ the number of programs in the system's queue. The procedure applied to $N(t)$ yields, when applied to $N_q(t)$, the mean number N_q of programs in the queue and the mean waiting time t_q:

$$W_q = 22.5 \text{ program} \times \text{min}, \qquad N_q = 2.25 \text{ programs}, \qquad t_q = 1.5 \text{ min}$$

Up to this point, the system has been viewed as a black box containing a number N of programs (either waiting or being processed) that can arbitrarily vary in time. When the system is not saturated, that is, when $U < 1$, its output rate X, or *throughput*, is known since it coincides with the arrival rate. The study of the performance of such a system through a model, which is called an *open model*, usually assumes X to be known and is concerned with determining the values of N, of the queue length, and of the response time.

Another class of models whose use in multiprogramming studies is widespread is that of *closed models*, in which the number of programs is constantly equal to N. In a closed model, N is usually assumed to be known, and the values of X, R, and the other performance indexes are to be determined. Note that X and R can be defined also in a closed model, as will be shown later.

A simple closed model, the *central server model*, is presented in Fig. 9.4. In a central server model, which is often used in the study of multiprogramming batch systems, a program's execution is seen as a sequence of CPU–I/O cycles that the program goes through until it terminates and exits. Since the system to be modeled is assumed to be heavily loaded, another program is always ready to enter the model at the instant one program departs. Thus, the total number of programs in the model remains constant, and the model's scheme can be drawn, as in Fig. 9.4, with a direct connection between the output and the input, as long as we assume that all programs have the same properties.

Closed models are also used to represent interactive systems. In this case, however, two interacting submodels can be identified, representing the terminals and the system's resources proper, respectively (see Fig. 9.5). The commands issued by the M independent terminals are processed by the central subsystem, which, at the end of their execution, returns the results to the terminal subsystem. A terminal then waits some time before issuing the next command; this time, denoted by Z, represents the user's think and keying-in times, and is called *think time* for the sake of brevity. Note that in this model the number of programs coincides with the number of active terminals; if this number is M, then $N = M$.

The system's response time R is in this case the mean time taken by the central subsystem to process a command. In the model in Fig. 9.5, the total lifetime of a command is $Z + R$. By Little's law, assuming balanced flows, we have for the whole model in Fig. 9.5

$$Z + R = \frac{M}{X}$$

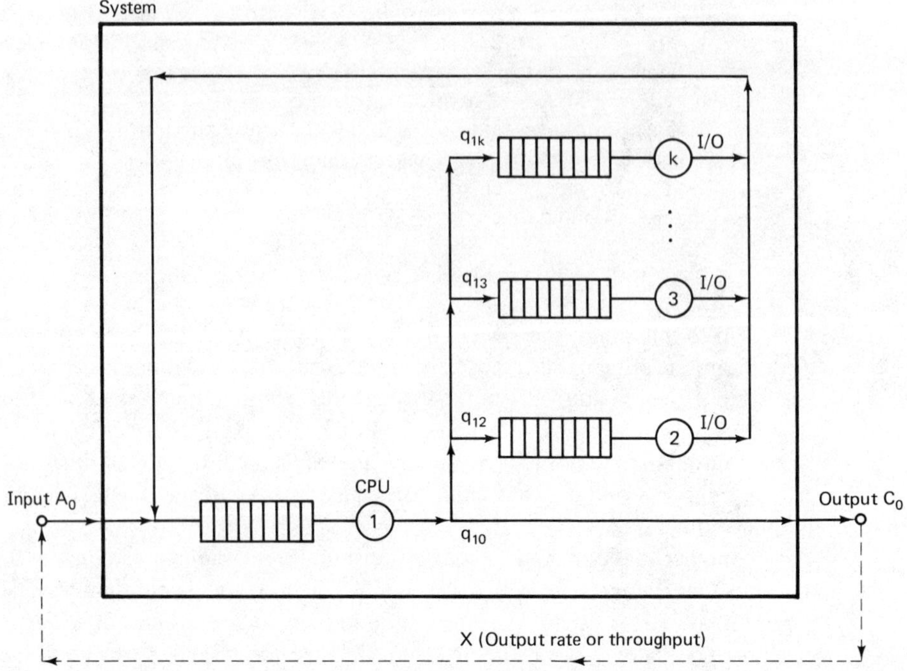

Figure 9.4 Closed model of the central server type.

Hence,

$$R = \frac{M}{X} - Z \tag{9.9}$$

which is called the *interactive response time formula*.

It should be observed that in the simple models introduced so far an I/O subsystem, consisting for instance of a block multiplexer channel with several disk drives, is represented by a single station (see for example Fig. 9.4).

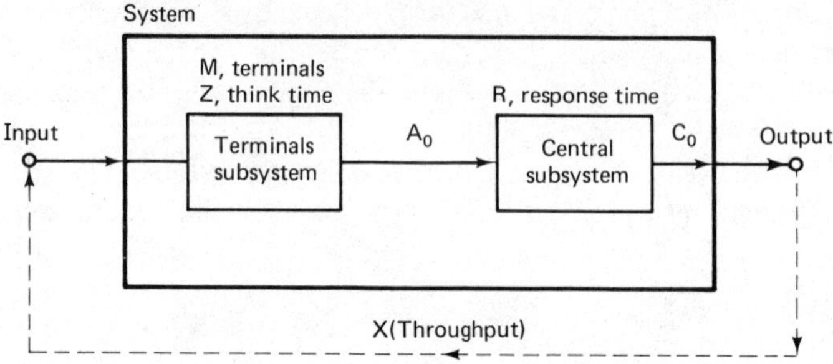

Figure 9.5 Closed model representing an interactive system.

We now wish to derive relationships that will allow the influence of the system's topology on its performance to be evaluated. Consider the model in Fig. 9.4. In it, index 0 has been adopted to designate the "outside world", whereas the other indexes refer to the system's resources. A_o and C_o represent the number of input and output requests, respectively. For simplicity, the system's throughput X_o will continue to be denoted by X in the sequel. C_{ij} is the number of requests that, after having been processed by resource i, are to be processed by resource j, whereas C_i represents the total number of requests processed by resource i. Denoting by K the maximum number of resources, we will have for each resource i

$$C_i = C_o + C_{i1} + \cdots + C_{ik},$$

and the rate of transitions from resource i to resource j is given by

$$q_{ij} = \frac{C_{ij}}{C_i} \tag{9.10}$$

The q_{ij}'s are also called *routing frequencies*.

When the flow balance assumption is satisfied for each resource, we have $A_i \cong C_i$. Thus,

$$A_j = C_{oj} + C_{1j} + \cdots + C_{kj} = C_j$$

and, from Eq. (9.10),

$$C_j = q_{oj}\, C_o + q_{1j}C_1 + \cdots + q_{kj}\, C_k$$

Dividing both sides by T and recalling that $X_i = C_i/T$, we obtain the *flow balance equations*

$$X_j = \sum_{i=o}^{K} q_{ij}\, X_i \tag{9.11}$$

That is, during the observation interval the number of requests processed by resource j equals the total number of requests processed by the other resources and shipped to resource j.

We denote by V_i the mean number of requests sent to resource i by each program; that is, $V_i = C_i/C_o$ or $V_i = X_i/X$ or

$$X_i = V_i\, X \tag{9.12}$$

Equation (9.12), called the *forced flow law*, relates the global system's behavior to the behavior of a single resource, and states that the throughput of a generic resource determines the throughputs of all other resources and that of the whole system.

Example 9.3

(See Sec. 9.4.5, Case 9.7.) Consider a central server model like that shown in Fig. 9.4. Assume that resource 2 represents a disk whose mean service time is $S_2 = 55$ ms and whose mean utilization is $U_2 = 0.097$. If each program sends $V_2 = 7$ requests to it, what is the system's throughput?

Applying the utilization law (9.3), the throughput X_2 of the disk is calculated as

$$X_2 = \frac{U_2}{S_2} = \frac{0.097}{0.055} = 1.7636 \text{ requests/s}$$

The system's throughput is then obtained from the forced flow law (9.12):

$$X = \frac{X_2}{V_2} = \frac{1.7636}{7} = 0.252 \text{ programs/s}$$

By using the data reported in Case 9.7 for the other resources, one may verify that the same value of X is obtained from the application of the forced flow law to those resources.

We wish now to investigate how a closed system's performance varies when N changes. The mean service times S_i and the numbers of visits V_i are assumed not to vary with N. From Eq. (9.12) we have

$$\frac{X_i}{X_j} = \frac{V_i}{V_j} \tag{9.13}$$

and, since $U_i = X_i S_i$,

$$\frac{U_i}{U_j} = \frac{V_i S_i}{V_j S_j} \tag{9.14}$$

Note that $V_i S_i$ is the total time spent by resource i to process all the requests of a program. Because of our assumptions, Eqs. (9.14) are valid for all values of N.

We already saw that resource i is *saturated* when $U_i = 1$, and that in this case X_i takes its maximum value $1/S_i$. In general, as N grows, only one resource tends to become saturated, that is, to become the *bottleneck* of the system, while for the others U remains less than 1. From Eq. (9.14) we conclude that the bottleneck is that resource b for which the product VS has the maximum value $V_b S_b$.

In saturation conditions, we have $U_b = 1$ and $X_b = 1/S_b$; thus, from Eq. (9.12), the system's throughput is

$$X = \frac{1}{V_b S_b} \tag{9.15}$$

This is the maximum throughput the system can produce when resource b is the bottleneck.

Recalling the meaning of V_iS_i, the minimum time required by the system to process all the requests of a program is

$$R_{\min} = V_1S_1 + V_2S_2 + \cdots + V_KS_K \tag{9.16}$$

$R_{\min}$ would be the mean response time if the requests did not have to wait for the resources in the various queues, that is, if there were a single program in the whole system. In this case, no resource would be saturated, and the system's throughput would be $X = 1/R_{\min}$. Note that, if the system were interactive, the throughput would be $1/(R_{\min} + Z)$. If no queues formed when N increases, X would grow linearly up to its maximum value $1/V_bS_b$ (see Fig. 9.6).

Since, on the other hand, queues are present in real systems because of contention for certain resources, the throughput cannot grow linearly with slope $1/R_{\min}$. The value of N at the intersection of the straight line $X = N/R_{\min}$ with the asymptote $X = 1/V_bS_b$ is the maximum theoretical number of programs that can be processed without queues. When N goes beyond this value N^*, which is also called the *saturation point,* queues are certainly present, at least on resource b.

In an interactive system with M active terminals, the mean response time (see Eq. (9.9)) is $R = (M/X) - Z$. Since the throughput X of the central subsystem (see Fig. 9.5) can never be greater than $1/V_bS_b$, Eq. (9.9) yields

$$R \geqslant MV_bS_b - Z \tag{9.17}$$

Hence, as the number M of terminals increases, the mean response time R tends to the asymptote $MV_bS_b - Z$. Figure 9.7 shows a plot of R versus M. It should be recalled that V_i, S_i, and Z are assumed not to be affected by changes in M.

For $R = 0$ we have $M_b = Z/V_bS_b = ZX$. That is, M_b is the product of the mean response time of the terminal subsystem (the think time) and the throughput of the central subsystem in saturation conditions. Note that this throughput is also the input rate of the terminal subsystem.

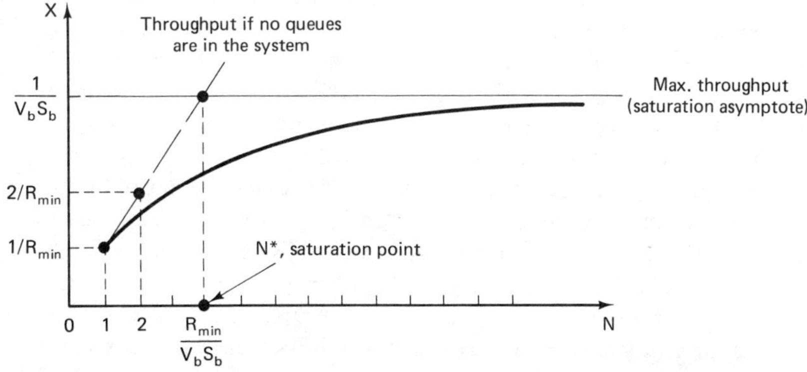

Figure 9.6 System throughput versus the number of programs being processed.

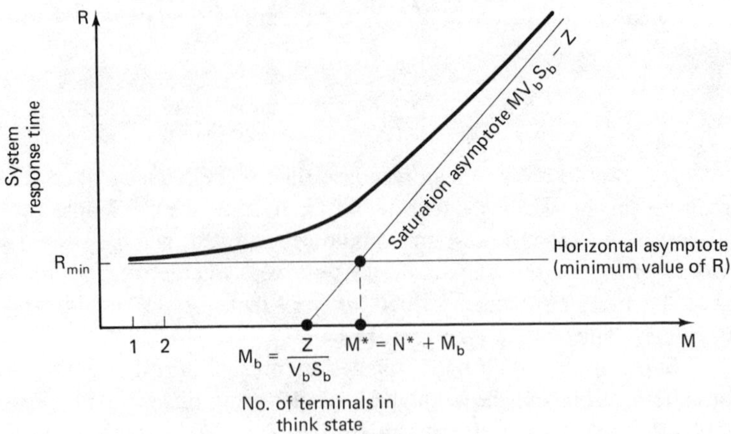

Figure 9.7 Mean response time R of an interactive system versus the number M of active terminals.

The lower bound of response time is R_{min} [see Eq. (9.16)], which corresponds to $M = 1$. In these conditions, if in the central subsystem there were no queues, the response time would remain at R_{min} when M grows, up to the value denoted by M^* in Fig. 9.7, beyond which queues will certainly exist and the value of R will have to increase. The intersection of the two asymptotes determines M^*:

$$R_{\text{min}} = M^*V_bS_b - Z$$

from which we have

$$M^* = \frac{R_{\text{min}}}{V_bS_b} + \frac{Z}{V_bS_b} = N^* + M_b$$

M^* is therefore the number of terminals beyond which in the interactive system at least one resource is saturated; M^* is said to be the *saturation point* of the system.

We have briefly introduced the basic concepts of operational analysis and described some of its simplest applications. Clearly, some of the assumptions, for example, the invariance of service times and of the number of departures when the number of programs in the system varies, may not be satisfied in practical cases. Furthermore, by applying only the laws that have been introduced, the values of some of the important performance indexes cannot be obtained, for instance, the distributions of queue lengths.

Operational analysis has been extended so as to be successfully applicable to many of the problems that are encountered when analyzing models of real systems. The case in which resources have a *load-dependent behavior,* an assumption less restrictive than that of invariant behavior, can be treated by operational analysis techniques. This means that the mean service times S_i and the transition rates q_{ij} may be functions of N. Furthermore, the notion of queue length distribution for resource i has been introduced as the fraction of the observation interval during which $N_i = n$, denoted by $p_i(n)$.

The analysis of the workload has been extended to include workload models consisting of programs representing various homogeneous classes into which the real workload has been partitioned. The whole field of operational analysis is still under development. Some of the most recent results can be found in [RO79], [BU80], and [BR82].

The notions and the operational laws we have introduced, although elementary, allow one to solve some interesting practical problems. Two of these problems are discussed in the next two sections.

9.3.1 *Case 9.1: Optimal Multiprogramming Level of a Virtual Memory System*

The virtual memory system to be analyzed, whose configuration is shown in Fig. 9.8, includes one CPU and three disk drives, two of which have fixed heads and are therefore designated as *drums*. One of the two drums is used as a paging device. The following data are known, either from the manufacturer or from direct measurement:

1. The service rates μ_2, μ_3, μ_4 of the drums and of the file disk; these rates, reciprocals of the mean service times of the devices, are $\mu_2 = 1/S_2 = 80.455\ s^{-1}$, $\mu_3 = 1/S_3 = 80.455\ s^{-1}$, $\mu_4 = 1/S_4 = 33.734\ s^{-1}$.
2. The *lifetime curve* of a typical program in the system's workload; this curve, reported in Fig. 9.9, represents the mean length *L(N)* of virtual time between two consecutive page faults as a function of the number N of programs in memory; note that, in a virtual memory system, the service rate μ_1 of the CPU depends on the multiprogramming level N, since this level influences the number of page frames available to each program and therefore also the mean duration of a CPU burst; the lifetime curve is used just to calculate $\mu_1(N)$.
3. The mean utilization U_1 of the CPU during the observation interval, the numbers of visits made by a program to the various resources, and the total CPU time consumed by a program, which equals 3 s; note that the numbers of visits to the file drum, $V_3 = 150$, and to the file disk, $V_4 = 250$, are constant, whereas the numbers of visits to the CPU, V_1, and to the paging drum, V_2, are functions of N, and their values can be derived from the lifetime curve.

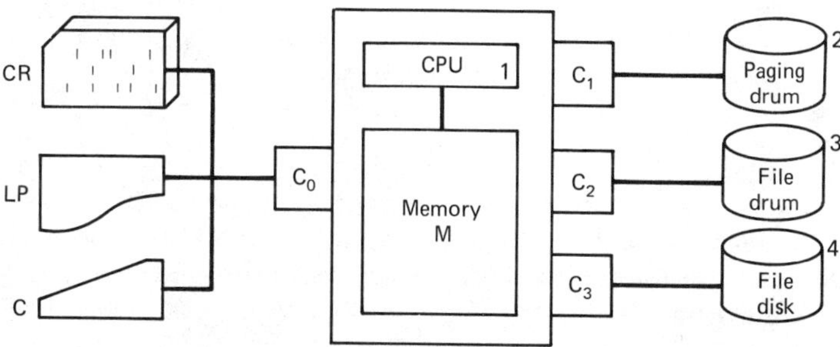

Figure 9.8 Configuration of the system analyzed in Case 9.1.

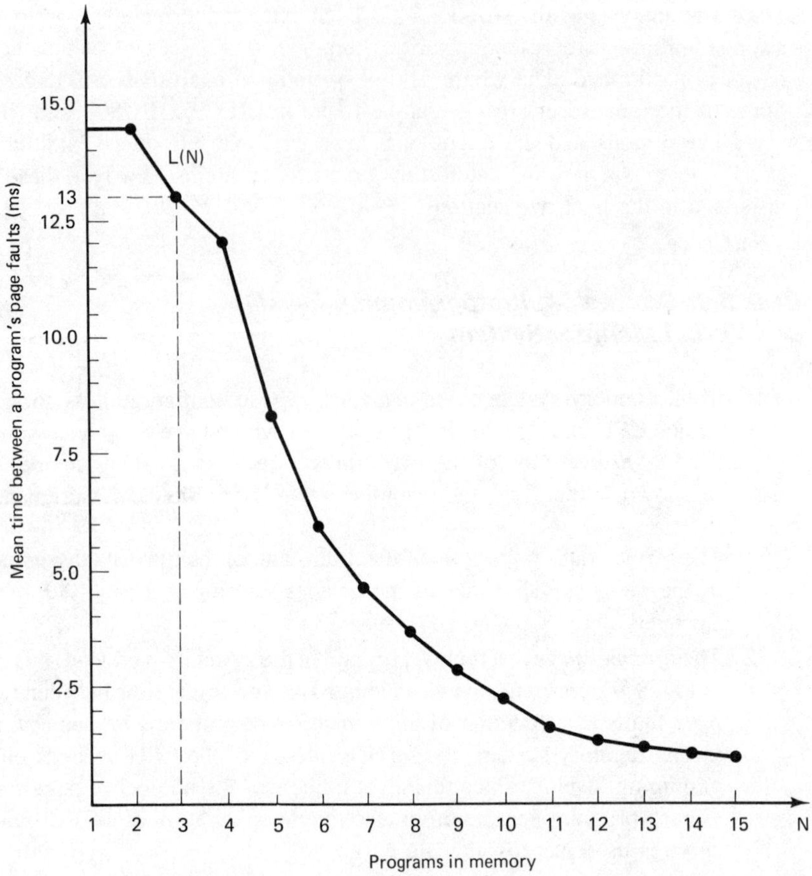

Figure 9.9 Lifetime curve of a representative program in the workload of the system considered in Case 9.1.

The following problems are to be dealt with:

9.1. Based on the characteristics of the programs to be processed and of the system's resources, determine the *optimum multiprogramming level,* that is, the one corresponding to the maximum throughput.

9.2. Determine the *tuning actions* that can have the greatest influence on the system's throughput, and predict their effects.

The study of these problems is performed by applying operational analysis techniques to a central server model of the system like that in Fig. 9.4. In this case, server 1 represents the CPU, server 2 the paging drum, server 3 the file drum, and server 4 the file disk.

Problem 9.1

First, we must compute V_1 and V_2, the numbers of visits to the CPU and to the paging drum, respectively. Let $N = 3$. The lifetime curve in Fig. 9.9 yields a mean interfault time of 13 ms. Since the mean total CPU time is 3 s, the mean number of visits to the paging drum is

$$V_2(3) = \frac{3}{13 \times 10^{-3}} = 230 \text{ visits}$$

Substituting V_iX to X_i in the flow-balance equations (9.11) for a central server model, we obtain

$$V_1(N) = 1 + V_2(N) + V_3 + V_4 \tag{9.18}$$

$$q_{10} = \frac{1}{V_1(N)} \tag{9.19}$$

$$q_{1i} = \frac{V_i}{V_1(N)} \tag{9.20}$$

In our case we have $V_1(3) = 1 + 230 + 150 + 250 = 631$ visits, $q_{10} = 0.0016$, $q_{12} = 0.3645$, $q_{13} = 0.2377$, and $q_{14} = 0.3961$. The mean duration of a visit to the CPU is $S_1 = 3/V_1$; hence $\mu_1 = V_1/3 = 210.33 \text{ s}^{-1}$. We denote by $1/a_i$ the mean CPU interval between two consecutive requests for resource i. The a_i's represent the rates at which programs depart from the CPU to reach the various resources: $a_i = \mu_1 q_{1i}$. Clearly, it is $1/a_2 = L(N)$, $1/a_1$ is the mean execution time of a program, and a_1 is the departure rate from the system.

The mean number of requests sent by the CPU to resource i per unit of time is U_1a_i; because of the flow balance assumption, we have

$$U_1a_i = U_i\mu_i \tag{9.21}$$

That is, the flow of input requests equals the output flow for every resource i. Hence

$$U_1 = U_i\frac{\mu_i}{a_i} \qquad (i = 2, 3, 4)$$

Recalling that $U_i \leqslant 1$ and $U_1 \leqslant 1$, we can write

$$U_1 \leqslant \min\left\{1, \frac{\mu_2}{a_2}, \frac{\mu_3}{a_3}, \frac{\mu_4}{a_4}\right\} \tag{9.22}$$

The utilization of the CPU will at most equal μ_i/a_i if resource i is saturated, that is, when $U_i = 1$. Flow-balance also yields

$$X = U_1a_1 = U_1\mu_1q_{10} \tag{9.23}$$

Thus, the system's throughput is proportional to the utilization of the CPU. By Eq. (9.15), we know that

$$X \leqslant 1/\max \{V_1S_1,\ V_2S_2,\ V_3S_3,\ V_4S_4\} \tag{9.24}$$

and that the resource whose V_iS_i product is maximum corresponds to the system's bottleneck. Note that inequalities (9.22) and (9.24) express the concept of system saturation.

Denoting by I that part of Eq. (9.22) that does not depend on N (also called the *I/O constant*), that is,

$$I = \min\left\{1,\ \frac{\mu_3}{a_3},\ \frac{\mu_4}{a_4}\right\}$$

inequality (9.22) can be written as

$$U_1 \leqslant \min\left\{I,\ \frac{L(N)}{S_2}\right\} \tag{9.25}$$

and, by Eq. (9.23),

$$X \leqslant a_1 \min\left\{I,\ \frac{L(N)}{S_2}\right\}$$

I and $L(N)/S_2$ are two upper bounds for U_1. The former is tighter when the bottleneck is an I/O resource different from the paging device, whereas the latter acts when the bottleneck is the paging device. The case $I = 1$ is that of a non-I/O-bound system, one having so much I/O capacity that no I/O resource is saturated.

We now apply the preceding relationships to our system. For $N = 3$ we have

$$a_2 = 76.665, \qquad a_3 = 49.995, \qquad a_4 = 83.311$$

hence

$$I = \min\left\{1,\ \frac{80.455}{49.995},\ \frac{33.734}{83.311}\right\} = \min \{1,\ 1.609,\ 0.404\} = 0.404$$

$$\frac{L(3)}{S_2} = \frac{\mu_2}{a_2} = 1.049$$

$$U_1 \leqslant \min \{0.404,\ 1.049\}$$

Thus, the bottleneck is resource 4, the file disk. Since from direct measurement we have $U_1(3) = 0.35$, we can compute by Eq. (9.21) the utilization of the file disk:

$$U_4 = \frac{a_4}{\mu_4} U_1 = 0.865$$

TABLE 9.1 MODEL VARIABLES CORRESPONDING TO THE ORIGINAL SYSTEM'S CONFIGURATION

Number of programs in execution	*Measured CPU utilization,* U_1	*CPU service rate,* μ_1	$L(n)/S_2$, μ_2/a_2	*Throughput X (prog/s)*	*Paging drum utilization* U_2	*File drum utilization* U_3	*File disk utilization* U_4	*Resource where bottleneck is*
1	0.202	202.6	1.166	0.067	0.173	0.125	0.499	4
2	0.302	202.6	1.166	0.100	0.259	0.188	0.747	4
3	0.350	210.3	1.045	0.117	0.334	0.217	0.865	4
4	0.375	217.0	0.965	0.125	0.388	0.233	0.927	4
5	0.376	252.7	0.675	0.126	0.557	0.234	0.930	4
6	0.361	300.3	0.482	0.120	0.749	0.224	0.893	4
7	0.329	352.9	0.366	0.109	0.898	0.204	0.814	2
8	0.286	406.8	0.294	0.095	0.972	0.177	0.707	2
9	0.235	473.8	0.236	0.078	0.995	0.146	0.581	2
10	0.193	550.3	0.193	0.064	0.999	0.119	0.477	2

From Eq. (9.23) we obtain the throughput as

$$X(3) = 0.35 \times 210.33 \times 0.0016 = 0.1179 \text{ program/s}$$

Table 9.1 shows the values of some of the variables, computed as described, for all N from 1 to 10. The ratios μ_3/a_3 and μ_4/a_4 always coincide with 1.609 and 0.404, respectively. Figures 9.10 and 9.11 exhibit the plots of U_1 and X with their asymptotes. They show that the bottleneck is the file disk for N between 1 and 6, and the paging drum for $N \geq 7$. In the latter case, the high paging activity decreases the system's throughput considerably. The system is in *thrashing* conditions. The figures also show that the optimum multiprogramming level is between 4 and 6. The control policy known as the $L = S$ *criterion* [DE76] seeks to keep the value of N as close as possible to the one such that $L(N)/S_2 \geq Id$, where d is a small constant > 1. This value is therefore slightly lower than that corresponding to the intersection of the two asymptotes $L(N)/S_2$ and I.

Problem 9.2

To improve the system's performance, the saturation asymptotes in Figs. 9.10 and 9.11 are to be modified by tuning. Since we assume we cannot modify the programs in the workload,

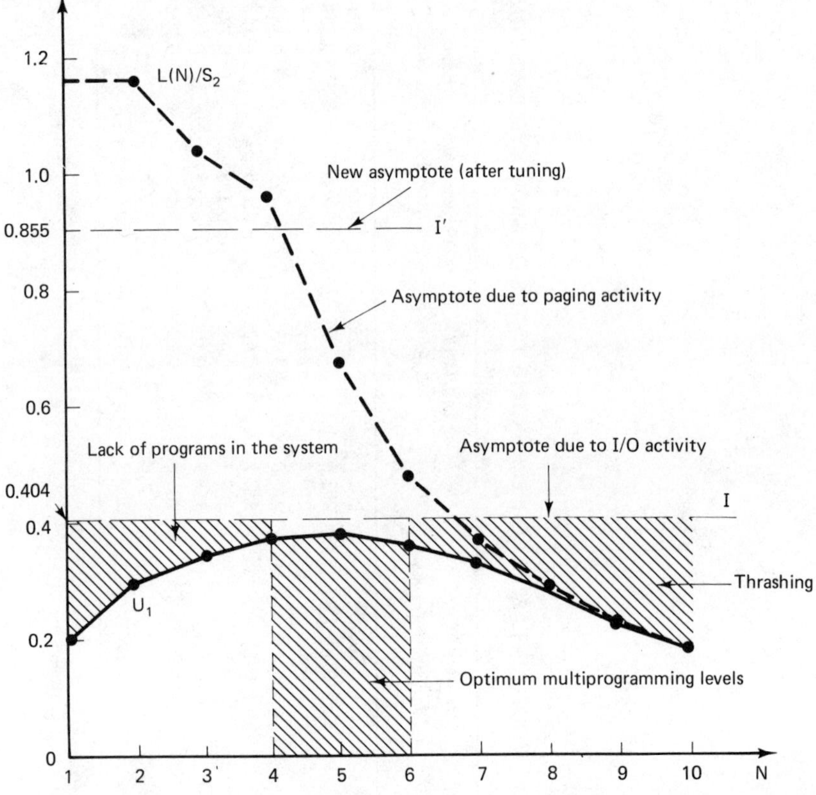

Figure 9.10 CPU utilization (U_1) and asymptotes due to I/O activity (I) and paging activity, $L(N)/S_2$.

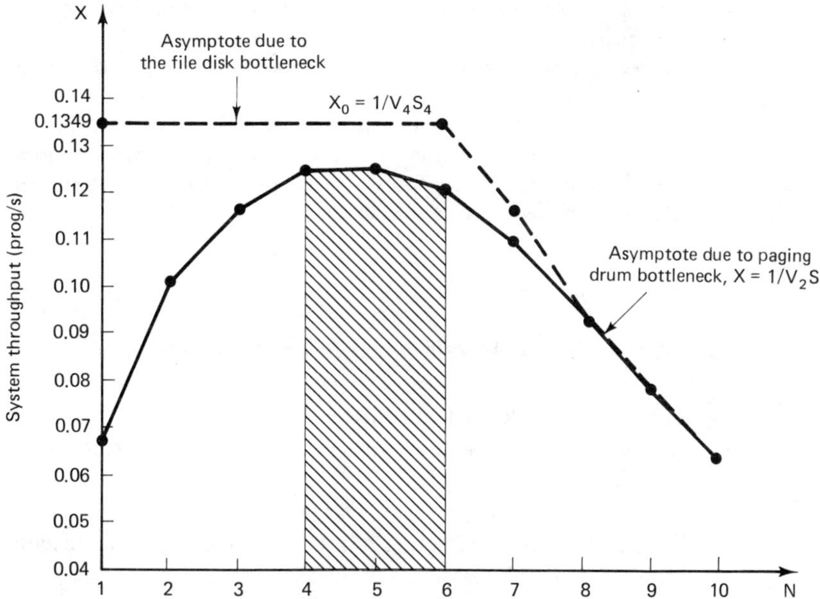

Figure 9.11 Throughput X and its asymptotes due to the bottlenecks at the file disk and paging drum.

the asymptote corresponding to the paging activity cannot be modified. However, the horizontal asymptote can be moved upward, thereby making the system less I/O-bound. In Table 9.1, we see that the utilizations U_3 and U_4 are unbalanced. By tuning actions of the file migration type, we then try to reach a situation of equal utilizations. An analysis of file sizes and activities shows that files can be moved so as to transfer for each program 132 visits from the file disk to the file drum. Thus, the new values of V_3 and V_4 will be 282 and 118, respectively. The times required by these two resources to process the requests from a program become:

$$\text{For the file drum:}\quad \text{from } V_3S_3 = \frac{150}{\mu_3} = 1.864 \text{ s} \quad \text{to} \quad V_3S_3 = \frac{282}{\mu_3} = 3.505 \text{ s}$$

$$\text{For the file disk:}\quad \text{from } V_4S_4 = \frac{250}{\mu_4} = 7.411 \text{ s} \quad \text{to} \quad V_4S_4 = \frac{118}{\mu_4} = 3.497 \text{ s}$$

The new value of I is

$$I' = \min\left\{1, \frac{\mu_3}{a_3}, \frac{\mu_4}{a_4}\right\} = \min\{1, 0.855, 0.858\} = 0.855$$

Thus, the bottleneck is practically equidistributed over the two file storage devices. Figure 9.10 shows that the file drum is the bottleneck for $1 \leqslant N \leqslant 4$ (note that μ_3/a_3 is slightly smaller than μ_4/a_4). The new optimum multiprogramming level is thus 4. Since the new asymptote has a value about twice that of the previous one, the utilization of the CPU could in principle be twice the one of the original system. However, in practice, resource contention phenomena limit the increment to substantially smaller factors. The new horizontal asymptote of the system's throughput is about twice the previous one, that is, $1/V_3S_3 = 0.285$.

In summary, these tuning actions should be considered as highly beneficial for the system's throughput, which can potentially be doubled by them. A more complete analysis of the effects on performance indexes of these tuning actions is presented in Case 9.6, Sec. 9.4.4, where the same problem is attacked by queuing theory techniques.

9.3.2 Case 9.2: Saturation Analysis of an Interactive System

The system to be considered is an MIRS system (see Fig. 1.4); that is, it is multiprogrammed, interactive, and with no virtual memory. The characteristics of its hardware components are as follows:

1. CPU speed (for the instruction mix being processed at the installation): $v_{CPU} = 1$ MIPS (10^6 instructions/s).
2. Fixed-head disks ("drums") for the nonresident systems programs, system files, swapping areas: three drives, revolution speed $R_{dr} = 3000$ rpm, word transfer time $t_{wdr} = 3\ \mu s$.
3. Movable-arm disks ("disks") for user files: two drives, revolution speed $R_{ds} = 1500$ rpm, mean seek time $t_{seek} = 70$ ms, word transfer time $t_{wds} = 15\ \mu s$.

Only one drum or disk drive may be transferring information through the corresponding channel at any given time. The size of main memory is assumed to be sufficient to allow M processes (or sets of processes) to be in execution, where M is the number of active terminals. The case of an interactive system whose memory size limits the maximum degree of multiprogramming to a value smaller than M will be dealt with in Sec. 9.6.

The system is to be evaluated while processing the following interactive workload:

1. Mean number of CPU instructions to be executed per command: $L = 240{,}000$ instructions.
2. Mean number of CPU time intervals per command: $V_1 = 20$.
3. Mean number of words transferred per drum access: $r_{dr} = 2000$ words.
4. Mean number of drum accesses per command: $V_2 = 15$.
5. Mean number of words transferred per disk access, $r_{ds} = 2000$ words.
6. Mean number of disk accesses per command: $V_3 = 4$.
7. Mean think time: $Z = 5$ s.

The system is modeled at an intermediate level by the closed model shown in Fig. 9.12. The following problems are to be investigated.

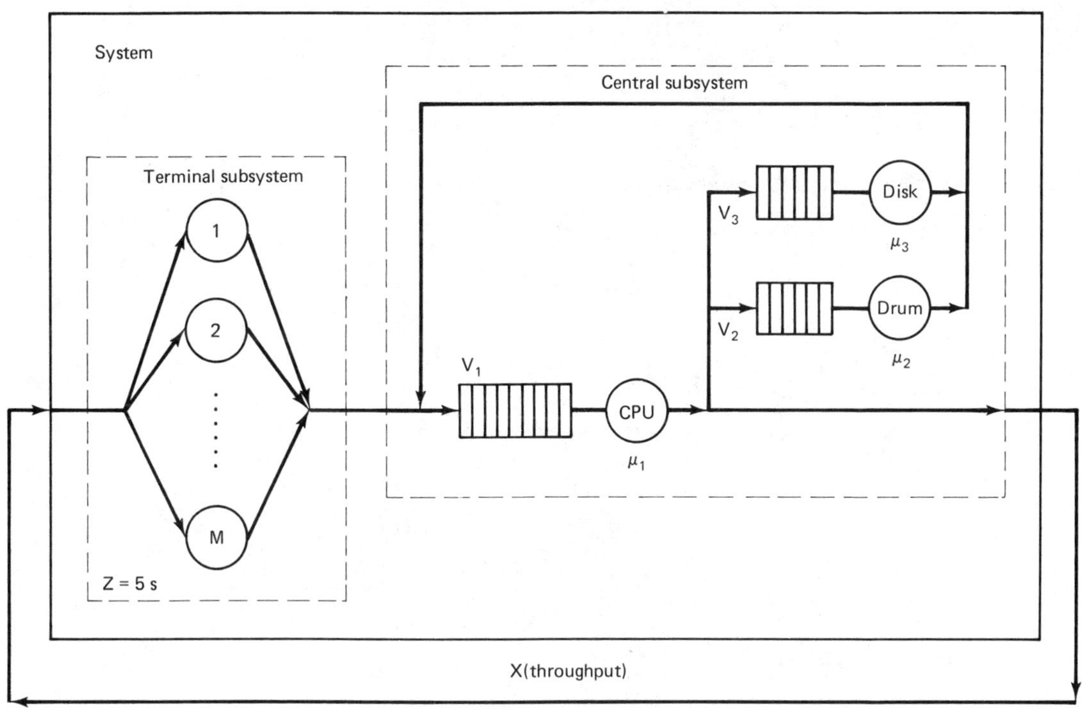

Figure 9.12 Closed model used to study the interactive system considered in Case 9.2.

9.3. Locate the system's bottleneck and determine the asymptotes of the mean response time R and of the mean throughput rate X versus the number of terminals (which in reality varies between 1 and 30).

9.4. Determine how the saturation asymptotes change when disks are replaced by new disks whose mean service time is half that of the previous ones.

9.5. Evaluate the effects of file relocations from disks to drums on the saturation asymptotes, and compare them to those obtained in Problem 9.4.

9.6. Determine whether the mean response time of the original configuration with 25 terminals is less than 5 s, and, if it is not, whether the tuning actions studied in Problems 9.4 and 9.5 allow this objective to be reached.

9.7. Determine the system's mean response time when 20 terminals are connected during the observation period and the measured utilization of the drums is 95 percent.

First, we derive the model parameters from the given system and workload parameters. The mean CPU service rate is

$$\mu_1 = \frac{1}{S_1} = \frac{v_{CPU} V_1}{L} = 83.33 \text{ s}^{-1}$$

The mean drum service rate is

$$\mu_2 = \frac{1}{S_2} = \frac{1}{(1/2R_{dr})\,60 + t_{wdr}r_{dr}} = 62.5\ \text{s}^{-1}$$

The mean disk service rate is

$$\mu_3 = \frac{1}{S_3} = \frac{1}{(1/2R_{ds})\,60 + t_{seek} + t_{wds}r_{ds}} = 8.33\ \ \text{s}^{-1}$$

Problem 9.3

The total times required by each resource to process all the requests from a command are given by

$$V_1S_1 = 20\,\frac{1}{83.33} = 0.24\ \text{s}$$

$$V_2S_2 = 15\,\frac{1}{62.5} = 0.24\ \text{s}$$

$$V_3S_3 = 4\,\frac{1}{8.33} = 0.48\ \text{s}$$

Thus, the disks are the bottleneck in this system. The minimum response time is $R_{min} = V_1S_1 + V_2S_2 + V_3S_3 = 0.96$ s. The horizontal asymptote, to which R tends as the number of terminals M tends to 0, is given by $R = 0.96$ s. The asymptote to which R tends as M tends to infinity is given by $R = MV_3S_3 - Z = 0.48M - 5$.

Figure 9.13 shows the asymptotes of the response time curve. The corresponding values of M, N^*, and M^*, that is, the mean number of thinking terminals in saturation conditions, the saturation point of the central subsystem, and the saturation point of the system, denoted by M_1, N_1^*, and M_1^*, respectively, are

$$M_1 = \frac{Z}{V_3S_3} = 10.4\ \text{terminals}$$

$$N_1^* = \frac{R_{min}}{V_3S_3} = 2\ \text{processes}$$

$$M_1^* = \frac{Z + R_{min}}{V_3S_3} = M_1 + N_1^* = 12.4\ \text{terminals}$$

The maximum throughput rate is given by

$$X_{max} = \frac{1}{V_3S_3} = 2.08\ \text{commands/s}$$

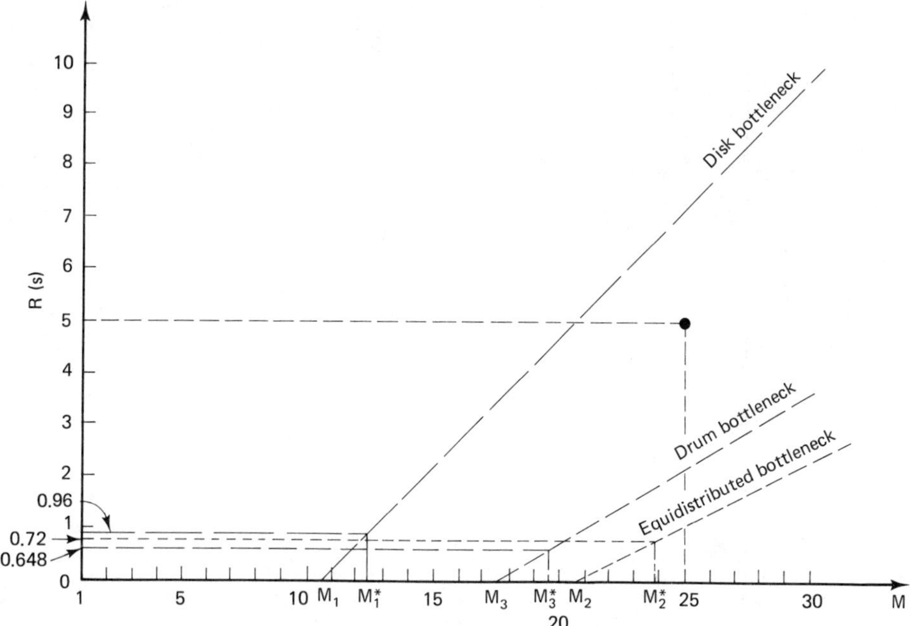

Figure 9.13 Response time asymptotes for the original system (the disks are the bottleneck), for the system with the faster disks (equidistributed bottleneck), and after tuning (the drums are the bottleneck).

The throughput asymptote is a straight line going through the origin, as represented by the equation

$$X = \frac{M}{Z + R_{\min}} = 0.167M$$

Problem 9.4

The new value of μ_3, denoted by μ_3', is 16.66 s^{-1}. The new total times spent by each resource are

$$V_1S_1 = 0.24 \text{ s}, \qquad V_2S_2 = 0.24 \text{ s}, \qquad V_3S_3 = 0.24 \text{ s}$$

Thus, the resources are equally utilized and the bottleneck is distributed over them. The value of $R_{\min}$ is 0.72 s, and the asymptote of R has the equation

$$R = 0.24M - 5$$

The corresponding values of M, N^*, and M^*, denoted by M_2, N_2^*, and M_2^*, are

$$M_2 = 20.83 \text{ terminals}, \qquad N_2^* = 3 \text{ processes}, \qquad M_2^* = 23.83 \text{ terminals}$$

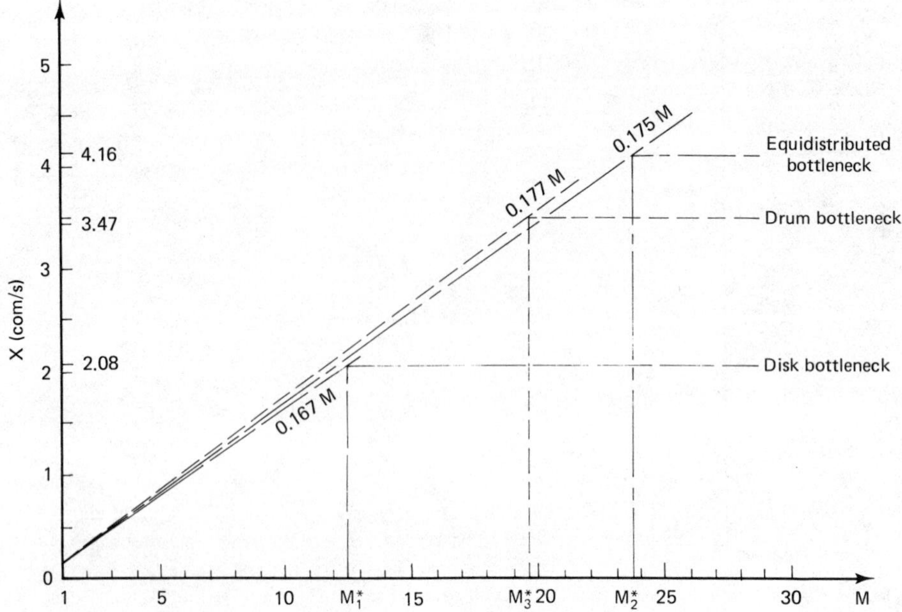

Figure 9.14 Throughput asymptotes for the original system, the upgraded system, and the tuned system.

The maximum throughput rate is

$$X_{max} = 4.16 \text{ commands/s}$$

and the equation of its asymptote is

$$X = 0.175M$$

The asymptotes of R and X are reported in Figs. 9.13 and 9.14.

Problem 9.5

By appropriate tuning actions, the numbers of visits each command makes to the drums and to the disks are modified as follows: $V_1 = 20$, $V_2 = 18$, $V_3 = 1$. The new values of the V_iS_i products then become

$$V_1S_1 = \frac{20}{83.33} = 0.24 \text{ s}$$

$$V_2S_2 = \frac{18}{62.5} = 0.288 \text{ s}$$

$$V_3S_3 = \frac{1}{8.33} = 0.12 \text{ s}$$

The drums are in this case the bottleneck. The minimum response time is R_{min} = 0.648 s, and the equation of the asymptote

$$R = 0.288M - 5$$

The values of M, N^*, and M^*, denoted by M_3, N_3^*, and M_3^*, are

$$M_3 = 17.36 \text{ terminals}, \qquad N_3^* = 2.25 \text{ processes}, \qquad M_3^* = 19.61 \text{ terminals}$$

The maximum throughput rate becomes

$$X_{max} = 3.47 \text{ commands/s}$$

and the equation of its asymptote

$$X = 0.177M$$

The asymptotes of R and X are shown in Figs. 9.13 and 9.14. While the asymptotes of X with positive slope are almost the same in both the upgrading and the tuning case, the horizontal asymptote of R after tuning is below the one obtained by upgrading the system. Thus, when the number of active terminals is lower than the saturation point, it seems that tuning (whose cost is certainly lower) is more effective than the type of upgrading that has been considered. Note that the maximum throughputs reachable in the two cases do not differ much from each other.

It should also be observed that the best results, in nonsaturated conditions, are obtained when the system has a bottleneck coinciding with the fastest resource (excluding the CPU), not when all resources are equally utilized. This conclusion was first reached by Buzen in 1971 [BU71].

Problem 9.6

The response times that can be obtained from the original system satisfy the inequality

$$R \geqslant 0.48M - 5$$

When there are 25 terminals, we have

$$R(25) \geqslant 0.48 \times 25 - 5 = 7 \text{ s}$$

which does not satisfy the condition $R \leqslant 5$ s. After doubling the speed of the disks, R satisfies the inequality

$$R \geqslant 0.24M - 5$$

Hence

$$R(25) \geqslant 0.24 \times 25 - 5 = 1 \text{ s}$$

Tuning actions will result in the following inequality for R:

$$R \geqslant 0.288M - 5$$

Hence

$$R(25) \geqslant 0.288 \times 25 - 5 = 2.2 \text{ s}$$

Thus, both upgrading and tuning are capable of reducing the mean response time below the desired threshold (see Fig. 9.13).

Problem 9.7

From the utilization law (9.3), we derive the drums' throughput:

$$X_3 = \frac{U_3}{S_3} = \frac{0.95}{1/8.33} = 7.91 \text{ transfers/s},$$

and from the forced flow law (9.12) we have

$$X = \frac{X_3}{V_3} = \frac{7.91}{4} = 1.978 \text{ commands/s}.$$

Thus, from the interactive response time formula,

$$R = \frac{M}{X} - Z = \frac{20}{1.978} - 5 = 5.1 \text{ s}$$

9.4 QUEUING MODELS

Queuing models of computer systems are constructed by considering each relevant resource as a *server,* which receives requests for service from the programs processed by the system; when a request finds the server busy, it joins a *queue* where it waits its turn to be served. Depending on the model's degree of detail, a request may represent an entire program, a program step, an interactive command, an I/O instruction, and so on.

A *service center,* or *station,* may contain more than one server and is therefore capable of serving more than one request simultaneously. Furthermore, a station may have more than one queue. In the sequel, however, only single-server, single-queue stations will be considered. A generic request i arrives at a station at time t_i, which is said to be its *arrival time* at the station, and requires S_i time units to be processed by the station; S_i is said to be the request's *service time* at the station.

In Fig. 9.15, the components of a station are shown together with some of the variables that are used to describe the phenomena occurring when the station is working. Other variables that describe the behavior or the state of a station are N_q, the mean number of requests in the queue, and N, the mean number of requests in the station.

Denoting by U the *utilization* of the station, that is, the limit of the ratio between the server's busy time and the total duration of the observation interval as this duration tends to infinity, we always have $N = N_q + U$. Note that this relationship holds also among the corresponding operational quantities, that is, over any finite observation interval.

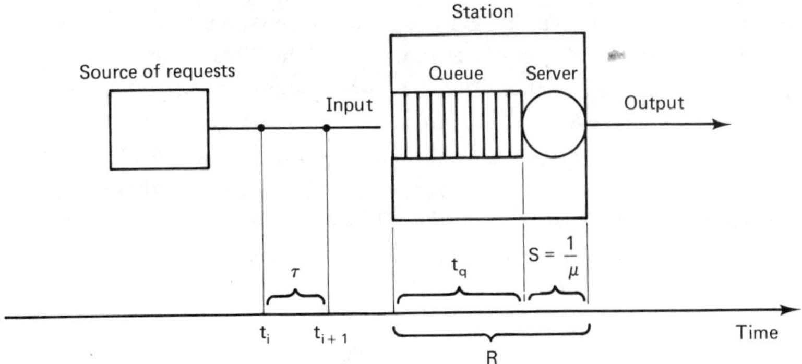

Figure 9.15 Components of a single-server station and some of the variables used to describe its behavior: τ (interarrival time), t_q (mean queueing time), S (mean service time), R (mean residence time in the station).

Queuing systems are usually studied in *steady-state* conditions. In other words, the assumption is made that the system has been working for a long period of time so that the distribution descriptors of the random variables we use to represent it are no longer influenced by the system's initial conditions, and are therefore independent of time. A prerequisite assumption that is always at least implicitly made is that the system is *stationary;* that is, in the long term the distributions of all random variables are time invariant.

A *source* of requests may be *finite* or *infinite,* depending on whether the number of requests it can generate is limited or unlimited. A source is completely characterized by its request generation process, that is, the random variable τ, and by the *resource demands* of the requests it generates. A *station* is characterized by its number of servers and of queues, by the maximum admissible length of its queues (*queue capacity*), by the speeds of its servers, and by its *service discipline,* that is, by the rules used to select the next request to be processed among those waiting in each queue.

To analyze the behavior of a station, detailed descriptions of its arrival process, service process, and service discipline must be provided. Let us discuss the arrival and service processes first.

The complexity of arrival and departure phenomena is such that describing them deterministically is either very difficult or impossible. Because of this, they are represented by stochastic models, that is, by random variables. A random variable is characterized by its *probability distribution function.* This function, for random variable x and for each real x_0, is given by

$$F_x(x_0) = P[x \leq x_0]$$

that is, by the probability that the value of x is not greater than x_0. The derivative of this function with respect to x is the *probability density function* $f_x(x_0)$.

Consider now the arrival process for an on-line seat reservation system. A customer walks to a window to reserve a seat at a time that, from the viewpoint of somebody who ignores the customer's plans, cannot be predicted with any certainty and is therefore to be regarded as random. In general, we may assume that all arrivals (or all interactive reservation commands) occur at random instants. The probability that a command related to a particular customer is issued within a short time interval, for example of a 1-min duration, is very low, but that of receiving a command from any customer is normally very high. The arrival process is usually assumed to be a Poisson process, an assumption that is supported by the results of several experimental studies of interactive systems (see for instance [AN72], [LE72]). In a *Poisson arrival process,* the probability of having k arrivals within a given time interval of length t is

$$P_k(t) = \frac{(\lambda t)^k}{k!} e^{-\lambda t} \qquad (k \geq 0, t \geq 0) \tag{9.26}$$

where λ is the *mean arrival rate*. The average number of arrivals occurring during each time interval of length t is λt. The probability that no arrivals will take place in t is $P_0(t) = e^{-\lambda t}$; thus, the probability of at least one arrival is $1 - e^{-\lambda t}$; note that this probability may be interpreted as the chance that a new arrival will occur τ time units after the most recent arrival, with $\tau \leq t$:

$$F_\tau(t) = P[\tau \leq t] = 1 - e^{-\lambda t} \qquad (t \geq 0) \tag{9.27}$$

The distribution function (9.27), which is the one of interarrival times τ, is a *negative exponential distribution* with parameter λ.

Thus, there are various equivalent descriptions for a random arrival process. One can state that the probability of a particular arrival within a short time interval is very low and equal for all intervals having the same duration, in other words, that each arrival is uniformly distributed over the period being considered. Alternatively, one can say that the probability of k arrivals within a given interval has Poisson distribution [see Eq. (9.26) and Fig. 9.16a]. Also, one can state that the interarrival times are exponentially distributed (see Fig. 9.16b).

The standard deviation of an exponentially distributed random variable is equal to its mean, that is, to $1/\lambda$. Thus, the *coefficient of variation c,* which is the ratio of the standard deviation to the mean, is equal to 1. This parameter describes in a compact way some very important characteristics of a probability distribution. A crucial property of the exponential distribution is the *Markov* or *memoryless property,* whose importance in simplifying the solution of probabilistic models, and in particular of queuing models, is fundamental. In an arrival process having this property, the probability that a new request will arrive during the next t units of time is independent of the amount of time already elapsed since the last arrival.

The service process has characterizations similar to those that are used to model the arrival process. Service times are always assumed to be statistically independent of (that is, neither functionally dependent on nor correlated to) interarrival times. Often, especially to simplify the mathematical treatment of the model, service times are assumed to be exponentially distributed. If we denote by μ the *mean service rate,* that is, the

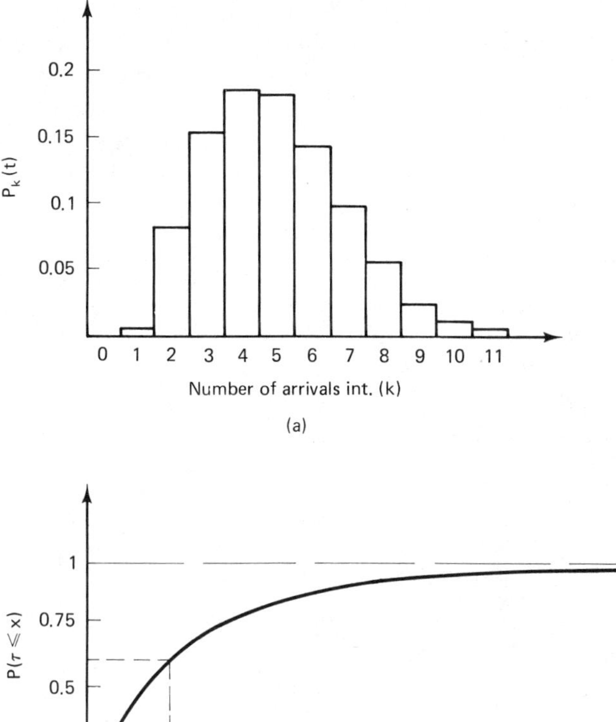

Figure 9.16 Characterization of a random arrival process by means of (a) a Poisson distribution or (b) an exponential distribution.

reciprocal of the mean service time S, the probability that a generic request will not need more than t time units of service is given by

$$F_S(t) = P[S \leq t] = 1 - e^{-\mu t} \tag{9.28}$$

In this case, the standard deviation of service times equals $1/\mu$. In practice, however, the measured distributions of service times for the various resources tend to differ quite substantially from the exponential distribution shown in Fig. 9.16b. For example, in many experiments CPU service times have been found to have coefficients of variation considerably greater than 1, and I/O service times to have coefficients of variation lower than 1. In general, distribution functions having a shape similar to that of a negative exponential but with greater variability are called *hyperexponential,* and those with less variability are called *hypoexponential*. Figure 9.17 shows density and distribution functions with different coefficients of variation and equal means. Suppose the probability that the service time is less than 0.8 time units is to be calculated. This probability is equal to the area under the curve $f_S(t)$ between $t = 0$ and $t = 0.8$, and to the difference between $F_S(0.8)$ and $F_S(0)$ [note that $F_S(0) = 0$].

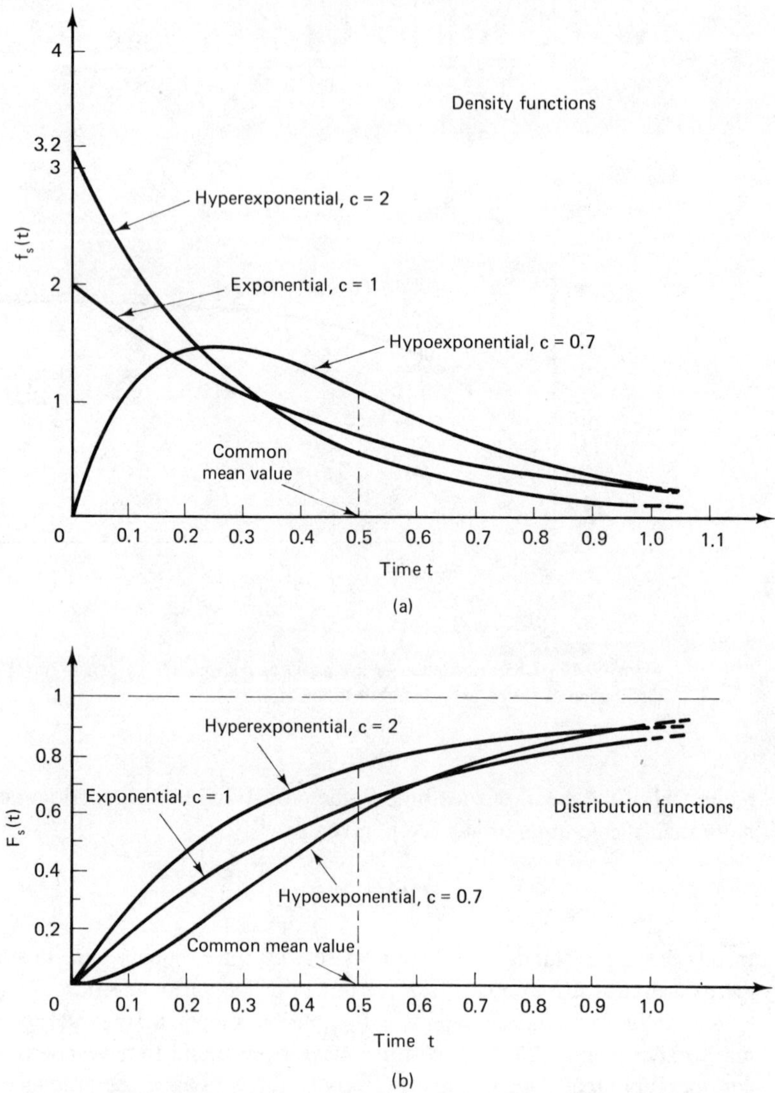

Figure 9.17 Examples of distributions having the same means (0.5) and different coefficients of variations.

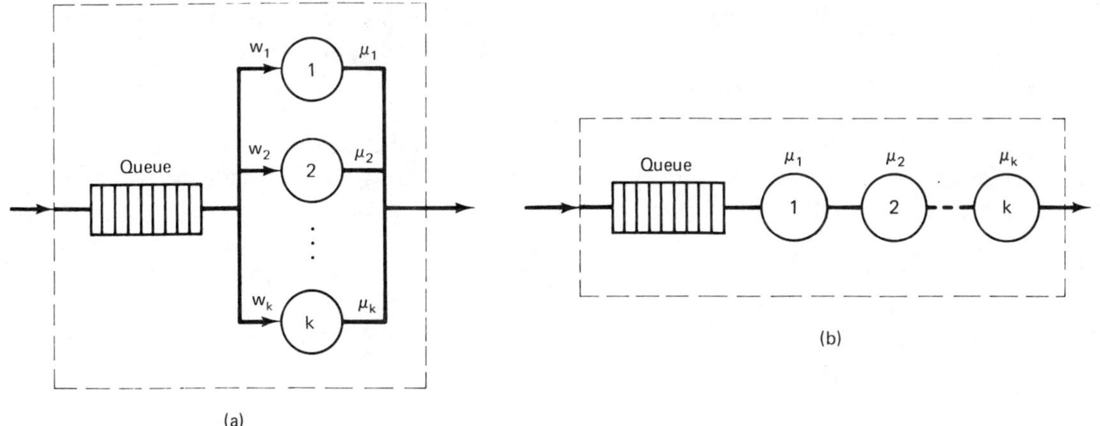

Figure 9.18 Exponential service equivalents of (a) a hyperexponential-service station and of (b) a hypoexponential-service station with Poisson arrivals.

A hyperexponential distribution can be approximated in a queuing model by a weighted sum of exponentials:

$$F_S(t) = \sum_{i=1}^{k} w_i(1 - e^{-\mu_i t}) \qquad \left(\mu_i > 0,\ w_i > 0,\ \sum_{i=1}^{k} w_i = 1\right) \tag{9.29}$$

and can be represented in the model as a set of k exponential servers connected in parallel (see Fig. 9.18a). The equations of the hyperexponential functions in Fig. 9.17 are

$$f_S(t) = 0.05e^{-0.45t} + 3.14e^{-3.54t}, \qquad F_S(t) = 1 - 0.113e^{-0.45t} - 0.887e^{-3.54t}$$

A hypoexponential distribution can be approximated with a function like

$$F_S(t) = 1 - e^{-k\mu t} \sum_{i=0}^{k-1} \frac{(k\mu t)^i}{i!} \tag{9.30}$$

which is also called *Erlang-k distribution,* and which can be obtained by connecting k exponential servers in series (see Fig. 9.18b). The equations of the hypoexponential functions in Fig. 9.17 are

$$f_S(t) = 16te^{-4t}, \qquad F_S(t) = 1 - e^{-4t}(1 + 4t)$$

whereas those of the exponential functions are

$$f_S(t) = 2e^{-2t}, \qquad F_S(t) = 1 - e^{-2t}$$

In Sec. 9.4.1, Case 9.3, we describe a procedure that may be used to approximate with functions of the types described in Eqs. (9.28) through (9.30), the measured distributions of service times.

A fundamental performance index for a single-server station is the server's *utilization* U, which may be defined as the steady-state probability that the server is busy, and which equals the ratio λ/μ, that is, the product of the mean arrival rate λ and the mean service time $1/\mu$. The utilization of a server must always be less than or equal to 1, since otherwise the length of the queue would indefinitely grow in time, and the queuing system would never reach a steady state. A very important result for queuing systems in statistical equilibrium (that is, in steady state) is *Little's formula,* which can be applied under very general conditions and may be written both for the whole system and for its queue (or queues) as follows:

$$N = \lambda R, \qquad N_q = \lambda t_q \tag{9.31}$$

where N is the mean number of requests in the system, R is the mean response time (that is, the mean system residence time of a request), N_q is the mean number of queued requests, and t_q the mean waiting time of a request. Little's formula holds for any service discipline, any interarrival time and service time distributions, and any number of queues in the station.

For a single-server station with Poisson arrivals and exponential service times, in which the arrival rate does not depend on the number of requests in the station (the source is infinite), classical results of queuing theory state that at the equilibrium we have

$$N = \frac{U}{1 - U}, \qquad \mathrm{Var}(N) = \frac{U}{(1 - U)^2} \tag{9.32}$$

In steady state, the throughput rate of this station is equal to λ, since at the equilibrium the mean output rate must equal the mean input rate. From Little's formula we obtain, substituting Eq. (9.32) into Eq. (9.31), the station's mean response time:

$$R = \frac{1}{\mu(1 - U)} \tag{9.33}$$

If the service discipline is FCFS (first come first served), the mean waiting time of a request may be easily seen to equal

$$t_q = \frac{1}{\mu}\frac{U}{1 - U} \tag{9.34}$$

According to the standard notation for classifying single-station queuing systems, the station just described is an M/M/1 system, where the first M indicates that the interarrival time distribution is exponential (M designates a distribution having the Markov memoryless property), the second M that the service time distribution is also exponential, and 1 is the number of servers. The absence of any information about the maximum queue length indicates that this length is unlimited; that is, the source is infinite.

When the service times are not exponentially distributed, the second M is replaced by other symbols, for example, by the letter G if the distribution is *general.*

In an M/G/1 station the mean number of requests is

$$N = U + \frac{U^2(1 + c^2)}{2(1 - U)} \tag{9.35}$$

where c is the coefficient of variation of the general distribution of service times, whose mean is $1/\mu$. The mean response time is easily obtained by substituting Eq. (9.35) into Little's formula (9.31):

$$R = \frac{1}{\mu}\left[1 + \frac{U(1 + c^2)}{2(1 - U)}\right] \tag{9.36}$$

If the service discipline is FCFS, the mean waiting time is

$$t_q = \frac{1}{\mu}\frac{U(1 + c^2)}{2(1 - U)} \tag{9.37}$$

Results (9.35) and (9.36) are also called the *Pollaczek–Kintchine formulas*. They show that R and t_q only depend on the mean and the standard deviation of service times, no matter what the shape of their distribution is. Thus, in this case, the study of an analytic function such as those in Eqs. (9.29) and (9.30) is not required to approximate the real service time distribution.

Figures 9.23 and 9.24 show diagrams of R and N versus U and X for M/M/1 and M/G/1 stations, respectively. It is worth noticing that R tends to infinity as U tends to 1, that is, as the station saturates. If μ is constant, the derivative of R with respect to U is, by Eq. (9.33),

$$\frac{dR}{dU} = \frac{1}{\mu(1 - U)^2}$$

and the variation of R due to a variation ΔU of U, corresponding to $\Delta\lambda/\mu$, is

$$\Delta R = \left(\frac{dR}{dU}\right)\Delta U = \frac{1}{\mu^2}\frac{1}{(1 - U)^2}\Delta\lambda$$

Thus, an increment $\Delta\lambda$ of λ causes R to increase by $4\Delta\lambda(1/\mu)^2$ if $U = 0.5$, by $25\Delta\lambda(1/\mu)^2$ if $U = 0.8$, and by $100\Delta\lambda(1/\mu)^2$ if $U = 0.9$.

Considering now the various existing service disciplines, a first classification of them distinguishes the *nonpreemptive* from the *preemptive* ones. When the discipline is nonpreemptive, a request leaves a station only when its service demand has been satisfied completely; on the contrary, under a preemptive discipline, the processing of a request may be interrupted before its completion. Examples of nonpreemptive disciplines are *first come first served* (FCFS), under which the requests are served according to the order of their arrivals, and *shortest processing time first* (SPTF), which always selects for processing the request whose service demand is the smallest. A common preemptive discipline is *round robin* (RR), which sets an upper bound to the time that may be spent by a request in the server. This bound q is called a *time quantum* or *time slice*. When the quantum of a request expires, the request is sent back to the end of the queue, which is served according to the FCFS policy (see Fig. 9.19a).

A discipline obtained from RR by letting q tend to 0 is the *processor sharing* (PS) discipline. A PS server works as if it processed simultaneously all requests in the station, but devotes to each a fraction of its total capacity inversely proportional to the number of requests. The PS discipline is often used to model the scheduling policy of the CPU of an interactive system in an approximate way (see Case 9.5 in Section 9.4.3). The mean response time R of a PS station coincides with that derived for an M/M/1 model [see Eq. (9.33)]; this result holds for all service time distributions, whose mean value $1/\mu$ is therefore the only distribution descriptor that, through U, influences the value of R. Thus, the use of PS stations simplifies the mathematical analysis of a model considerably.

In some preemptive disciplines, privileged treatment is reserved for some requests, whose arrival causes the servicing of the request being processed to be suspended (unless also the latter is a privileged request). The criteria used to establish the priorities may be

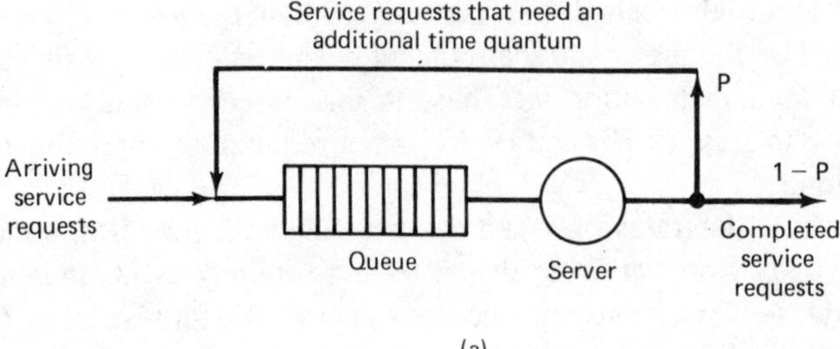

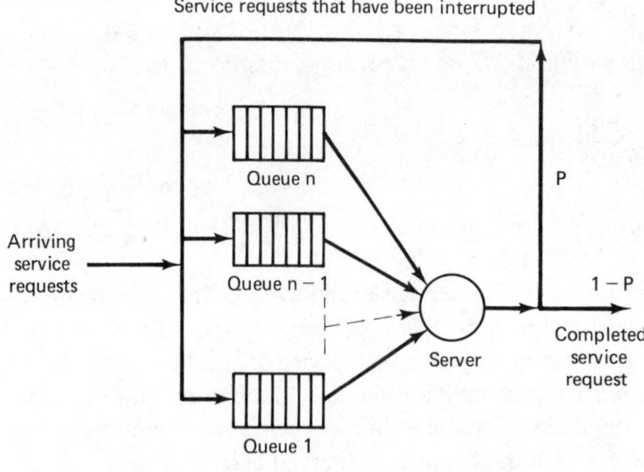

Figure 9.19 Preemptive single-server stations: (a) round robin discipline; (b) n-level foreground-background discipline.

external, as in the *preemptive external priorities* (PEP) discipline, or related to the characteristics of each request, as in the *preemptive shortest processing time first* (PSPTF) policy, or dictated by the *class* to which each request belongs. The latter is the case of a server having several queues, each of which has a different priority and usually a different quantum; the request to be served is taken from the highest-priority nonempty queue, and, if its processing is not completed, joins the next lower-priority, longer-quantum queue. Disciplines of this type are often called *n-level foreground–background* (FB_n), and may be viewed as generalizations of the RR policy (see Fig. 9.19b).

Stations with nonpreemptive priority disciplines are also called *head-of-the-line* (HOL) stations, since the request being served is processed completely in all cases, and the arriving higher-priority requests are put at the head of the queue. A *preemptive-resume* priority discipline is one in which service to a suspended request is resumed, when the request's turn comes, at the point of interruption, whereas under a *preemptive-repeat* discipline, service is to restart from the beginning. As will be seen in the sequel, the difficulty of the mathematical treatment of a queuing model is substantially influenced by the service disciplines of its stations.

The types and complexities of the real systems that can be modeled with a single station are obviously quite limited. In most cases, they allow us to implement macrolevel models only (see Secs. 9.4.1 through 9.4.3). The natural evolution of analytic modeling techniques has been toward the study of *networks of queues*. Queuing networks are much better suited to the construction of intermediate-level and microlevel models of computer systems.

In Sec. 9.3, we saw that queuing networks can be subdivided into *open* and *closed* networks. An open network such as the one presented in Fig. 9.20 has at least one source of requests external to the network (as well as at least one exit that requests can use to leave the network). Networks having no external sources are closed. The *state* of a network consisting of m stations is defined if the state of each station is known; thus, the state is represented by vector $\mathbf{N} = \{N_1, N_2, \ldots, N_m\}$, where N_{1i} is the number of requests in the ith station.

A network of m stations is said to have a *product form solution* if the equilibrium distribution of network state probabilities exists and can be written as

$$p(\underset{\sim}{\mathbf{N}}) = \frac{p_1(N_1)\, p_2(N_2) \ldots p_m(N_m)}{G} \tag{9.38}$$

where $p_i(N_i)$ is the probability that the ith station is in state N_i (that is, with N_i requests in it), and G is a *normalizing constant* that forces the sum of all state probabilities to be equal to 1. Not all queuing networks have an equilibrium state probability distribution that may be expressed in the product form (9.38). Some nonproduct form networks will be discussed in Sec. 9.5. In this section, we shall only consider networks having a product form solution.

In the case of an open network of M/M/1 stations, *Jackson's theorem* states that the network has a product form solution, which is the product of the state probabilities of each station considered as an independent M/M/1 station [thus, G in Eq. (9.38) is in this case equal to 1]. Note that, to obtain the values of such fundamental performance

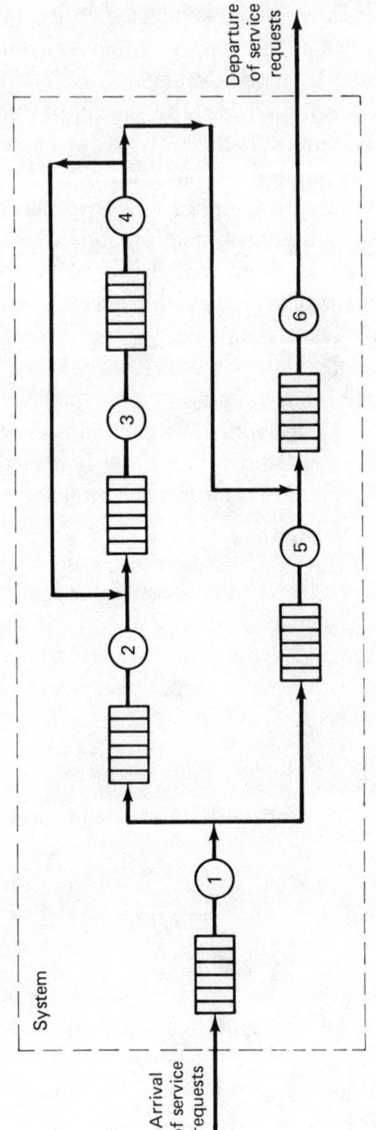

Figure 9.20 Sample open queuing network.

indexes for the whole network as the mean response time R, the throughput rate X, or the mean number of requests in the network, it is not necessary to compute the state probability distribution according to Eq. (9.38). We shall return to this point in the sequel. Note also that Jackson's results [JA63] hold also when the mean arrival rate λ is a function of the total number N of requests in the network and when the service rate μ_i of the ith station is a function of the station's state, that is, of N_i. These are situations that arise in practical modeling problems. In a fast-turnaround batch system, for example, the mean arrival rate is a function of the system's state, since some users are likely to postpone submitting their programs when the system's turnaround time becomes too long. Resources that may have to be modeled by stations with state-dependent service rates include storage devices like disks and drums, whose access times on the average get shorter as N_i increases.

In many practical problems, the assumption of an unlimited number of requests in the system is certainly unrealistic. To model more accurately multiprogramming systems, where the maximum number of active programs is limited by the size of the main memory, or interactive systems, where the number of commands in execution is limited by the number of active terminals, one can make use of *closed queuing networks,* in which the number N of requests (or programs or commands) in the model is kept constant.

Figure 9.21 presents the diagram of a closed network used to implement macrolevel models of interactive systems (see also Fig. 9.5). Each terminal issues a command, which at any given time may be in one of three states: *waiting* to be processed by the central subsystem, *running* in the central subsystem, or *resting* at the terminal. The resting state corresponds to the time between the end of a command's processing by the central

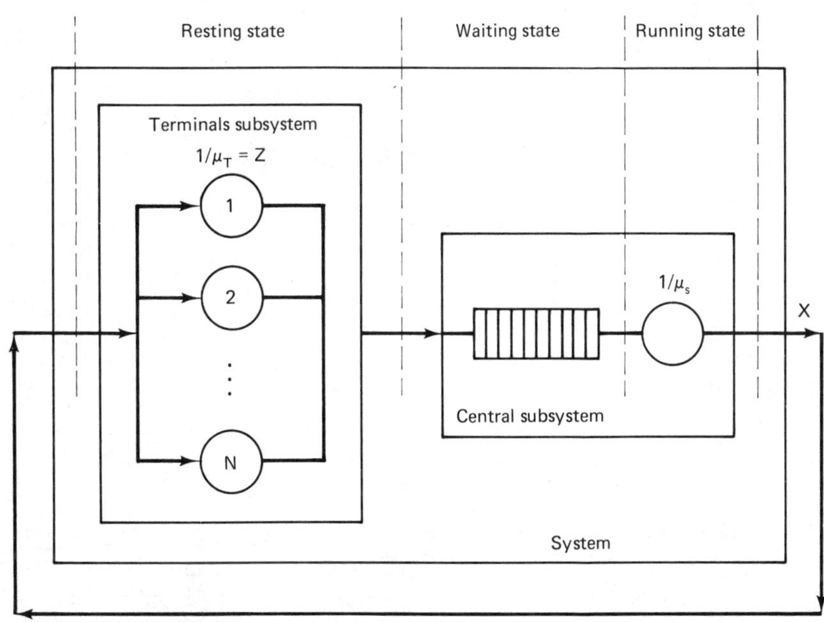

Figure 9.21 Closed-network macrolevel model of an interactive system and command states.

subsystem and the end of the inputting of the next command by the user. Thus, this time encompasses the output time, the user's think time, and the input time, although it is often called the *think time*.

If we assume that the system is time shared and that the quantum is small with respect to the mean service time $1/\mu_s$ of the central subsystem, we may approximate the system's service discipline by the PS policy. To simplify the analysis, we also assume that all interactive commands are statistically identical; that is, that each of their parameters is a sample from the same distribution. Here this means that all service times will be equidistributed, and that all think times will also be equidistributed, although they will be statistically independent of the service times. In other terms, the model has only one *class* of commands.

A simple analysis of the model in Fig. 9.21, based on Little's formula, yields the following results, which are valid under very general conditions [KL76]:

$$R = \frac{M}{\mu_s (1 - p_0)} - Z \tag{9.39}$$

$$X = \frac{M}{R + Z} \tag{9.40}$$

where R is the mean response time of the central subsystem, Z is the mean think time, p_0 is the probability that the central subsystem is idle, X is the throughput rate of the central subsystem expressed in commands processed per unit time, and M is the number of active terminals.

The utilization of the central subsystem, U_s, is equal to $1 - p_0$. The value of p_0 depends on the distributions of service and think times and on the service discipline.

If the service discipline is PS, and both the service time and think time distributions are exponential, p_0 is given by

$$p_0 = \frac{1}{\displaystyle\sum_{k=0}^{M} \frac{M!}{(M - k)!} \left(\frac{1}{\mu_s Z}\right)^k} \tag{9.41}$$

R may thus be calculated from Eq. (9.39) and the throughput rate X from Eq. (9.40) or from the equivalent relationship

$$X = U_s \mu_s \tag{9.42}$$

which states that X coincides with the output rate of the central subsystem.

The saturation analysis performed in Sec. 9.3 applies also to this model. When $M = 1$, the queue is always empty, and $R = 1/\mu_s$. As M grows, the queue is no longer empty at all times and R increases. When M becomes larger and larger, p_0 tends to 0, U_S tends to 1, and, by Eq. (9.39), R tends to the asymptote

$$R \cong \frac{M}{\mu_s} - Z \tag{9.43}$$

This asymptote meets the other asymptote $R = 1/\mu_s$ at

$$M^* = 1 + Z\mu_s \tag{9.44}$$

which is called the system's *saturation point* [KL76]. An analysis of an interactive system based on this model is reported in Sec. 9.4.3, Case 9.5.

If one wants to represent the central sybsystem with a greater level of detail, one must replace the single station in Fig. 9.21 with a network of stations representing the various resources (CPU and I/O devices) and their interconnections. A closed network model often used to represent multiprogramming systems at the intermediate level is the *central server model,* whose diagram was shown in Fig. 9.4. This model has been studied by Buzen [BU71] using the approach to the solution of exponential closed networks proposed by Gordon and Newell [GO67].

Each program goes through a series of CPU–I/O cycles until all its service demands have been completely satisfied. At the end of its execution, the program leaves the system. To keep the number of programs in the system constant, each departing program is immediately replaced by an arriving program. To simplify the treatment of the model, we shall make some restrictive assumptions, which can be somewhat relaxed without impairing the solvability of the model.

All programs are assumed to be statistically identical, all service times to be exponentially distributed, with constant mean service rates, and the probabilities q_{1j} of visiting device j after having visited the CPU (which is represented by the central server, always denoted by index 1) to be constant. The service disciplines of all stations are assumed to be FCFS.

This model would still be solvable (that is, its equilibrium state probability distribution would be computable) even if it contained more than one class of programs, the service disciplines were processor sharing (PS) or preemptive-resume last come first served (LCFS), the number of servers in a station were greater than or equal to the maximum number of programs in the station, and the service time distributions were general, with the only restriction of having rational Laplace transforms.

These results are much more general, since they apply to all open and closed queuing networks [BA75]. Note that, for a network to be solvable, the restrictions assumed must hold whenever the service discipline is FCFS; in other words, an FCFS station must group all programs in a single class (that is, all classes are to have equidistributed service times), and the service time distribution must be a negative exponential. The only possible relaxation of our assumptions is the introduction of the mean service rate's dependence on the station's state.

Because of the topology of the central server model, if k is the number of servers and N the number of programs, balancing the input and output rates of station i yields

$$\mu_i U_i = q_{1i}\mu_1 U_1 \qquad (i = 2, \ldots, k) \tag{9.45}$$

and if we define

$$y_1 = 1, \qquad y_i = \frac{\mu_1}{\mu_i} q_{1i} \qquad (i = 2, \ldots, k) \tag{9.46}$$

the (9.45) become

$$U_i = y_i U_1 \qquad (i = 1, \ldots, k) \tag{9.47}$$

The (9.45) are $k - 1$ homogeneous equations in k unknowns (the U_i's), and their solution can be determined except for a constant, which can be assumed to be equal to U_1. To derive the value of this constant, the balance equations for all the states of the model must be written. These yield a product form solution of the type

$$p(\mathbf{N}) = \frac{1}{G(N)} y_1^{N_1} y_2^{N_2} \ldots y_k^{N_k} \tag{9.48}$$

where $G(N)$ is the normalizing constant that makes the sum of the $p(\mathbf{N})$'s over all the model's states equal to 1. Hence, $G(N)$ is given by

$$G(N) = \sum_{\text{all } \mathbf{N}} y_1^{N_1} y_2^{N_2} \ldots y_k^{N_k} \tag{9.49}$$

With some algebra one can derive

$$U_1 = \frac{G(N - 1)}{G(N)} \tag{9.50}$$

that is, the value of the unknown constant. Note that the most important performance indexes can be computed from $G(N)$, thereby avoiding the calculation of all state probabilities $p(\mathbf{N})$. First, we obtain the utilizations of all other stations from Eq. (9.47):

$$U_i = y_i U_1 = \frac{\mu_1}{\mu_i} q_{1i} U_1 \tag{9.51}$$

The model's mean throughput rate X at the equilibrium is defined as the mean number of programs that go through the loop around the central server. This number may be obtained by multiplying the CPU's output rate times the probability of departure:

$$X = \mu_1 U_1 q_{10} \tag{9.52}$$

The mean response time R of the model follows directly from Little's formula (9.31), since at the equilibrium we have $\lambda = X$:

$$R = \frac{N}{X} \tag{9.53}$$

The probability of finding exactly N_i programs in station i, that is, the *marginal queue length distribution,* is given by

$$p_i(N_i) = \frac{y_i^{N_i}}{G(N)} [G(N - N_i) - y_i G(N - 1 - N_i)] \tag{9.54}$$

where $G(n)$ is defined to be 0 when $n < 0$. The mean queue length at station i, that is, the mean number of programs in the same station, is

$$N_i = \sum_{n=1}^{N} np_i (N_i = n) = \sum_{n=1}^{N} y_i^n \frac{G(N - n)}{G(N)} \tag{9.55}$$

Because of the results reported in Eqs. (9.50) [which makes the formulas (9.51) through (9.53) applicable], (9.54), and (9.55), it is important to compute the values of function G. However, the very large number of operations required by expression (9.49) makes it uninteresting. A computationally efficient algorithm, both in time and in space, for calculating $G(N)$ has been proposed by Buzen [BU73a]. The algorithm, which requires kN additions and kN multiplications, requires the auxiliary function $Y_i(n)$ to be recursively defined as follows:

$$\begin{cases} Y_i(0) = 1 \\ Y_1(n) = y_1^n = 1 \\ Y_i(n) = Y_{i-1}(n) + y_i Y_i(n - 1) \qquad (n = 1, \ldots, N; i = 2, \ldots, k) \end{cases} \tag{9.56}$$

It is easily seen that

$$Y_k(n) = G(n) \qquad (n = 1, \ldots, N)$$

Table 9.2 illustrates Buzen's algorithm for models whose stations have constant mean service times, that is, in which μ_i is independent of N_i for all i. In Secs. 9.4.4 and 9.4.5, we discuss examples of applications of the central server model to the study of multiprogrammed batch systems, with and without virtual memory, and resources having *load independent* characteristics. For the solution of the models, we apply the algorithm and the formulas that have just been described. Other examples of applications of this algorithm can be found in Secs. 9.5.1 and 9.6.1.

For systems with resources having load-dependent service times, the calculation of $G(N)$ is more complex than the one performed by the algorithm we have just presented.

TABLE 9.2 EXAMPLE OF APPLICATION OF BUZEN'S ALGORITHM FOR THE COMPUTATION OF $G(N)$ IN A CENTRAL SERVER MODEL WITH LOAD-INDEPENDENT MEAN SERVICE TIMES

	Servers			
	y_1 Y_1	y_i Y_i	y_k $Y_k = G(N)$	$U_1(n)$
Number of programs in the system: 0	1	⊗	1	
1	y_1^1	⊕	$G(1)$	$1/G(1)$
2	y_1^2		$G(2)$	$G(2)/G(1)$
⋮	⋮	$Y_i(n-1)$ $Y_{i-1}(n) =$ $Y_i(n)$	⋮	
N	y_1^N		$G(N)$	$G(N-1)/G(N)$

In Sec. 9.5, we shall give both the formulas to be used to compute the performance indexes of systems with load-dependent resources and the algorithm for the computation of $G(N)$.

The algorithm in Table 9.2 can be applied also to closed queuing networks with topologies different from that of the central server model, provided they have a product form solution. Obviously, the different topology will require Eqs. (9.45) and definitions (9.46) to be modified.

For example, in the case of a simple closed network consisting of two parallel servers, denoted by indexes 1 and 2, if we define $y_1 = 1$ and $y_2 = (q_2/\mu_2)/(q_1/\mu_1)$, the product form solution is

$$p(N_1, N_2) = p(N_1, N - N_1) = \frac{1}{G(N)} y_1^{N_1} y_2^{N - N_1} = \frac{1}{G(N)} \left[\frac{(q_2/\mu_2)}{(q_1/\mu_1)} \right]^{N - N_1} \tag{9.57}$$

where

$$G(N) = \sum_{N_1=0}^{N} \left[\frac{(q_2/\mu_2)}{(q_1/\mu_1)} \right]^{N - N_1} \tag{9.58}$$

and q_1 and q_2 are the probabilities of branching to station 1 and 2, respectively.

In the case of a closed network consisting of two stations in series, observing that $q_1 = q_2 = 1$, we have $y_1 = 1$, $y_2 = \mu_1/\mu_2$, and the product form solution

$$p(N_1, N - N_1) = \frac{1}{G(N)} \left(\frac{\mu_1}{\mu_2}\right)^{N - N_1} \tag{9.59}$$

where

$$G(N) = \sum_{N_1=0}^{N} \left(\frac{\mu_1}{\mu_2}\right)^{N - N_1} \tag{9.60}$$

In Sec. 9.6, we shall describe some simple applications of these formulas. When a model is not solvable with the exact methods based on queuing theory, its analysis can often be performed by approximate solution techniques. Section 9.6 presents one such technique, flow-equivalent aggregation.

The copious literature on queuing theory and queuing models has been recently enriched by the appearance of several books dealing in particular with the applications of the theory to computer systems modeling for performance evaluation purposes [KL76], [AC78], [AL78], [CH78], [KO78b], [BR80], [GE80], [SA81]. The interested reader will find a deeper and much more extensive treatment of queuing models in any of these books.

9.4.1 Case 9.3: Performance Analysis by a Macrolevel Model

In an MBRS system, the programs to be processed arrive randomly with a mean arrival rate λ of 1.5 programs/min. We assume that all programs are statistically identical and independent, and that their arrival process may be modeled as a Poisson process. Their service times are independent of their arrival times and have the distribution shown in Table 9.3, which has been derived from empirical observations. The system's scheduling policy is FCFS.

The objectives of the analysis of this system are to determine:

9.8. The values of the most important performance indexes.

9.9. The effects on the values of the indexes computed in Problem 9.8 of service time distributions such as those in Tables 9.4 and 9.5.

9.10. The increment in the system's workload that will make the mean waiting time of a program equal to 20 min, and the corresponding increase in the mean number of programs waiting to be processed.

9.11. The capacity of a new system, which, in the loading conditions described in Problem 9.11, will cause the turnaround time of 90 percent of the programs to be lower than or equal to 10 min.

9.12. The variations of the values computed in Problem 9.8 resulting from a 10 percent decrease of the service times due to program performance improvements, assuming the same arrival rate as in Problem 9.8.

TABLE 9.3 SERVICE TIME FREQUENCY DISTRIBUTION TO BE USED IN PROBLEMS 9.8 AND 9.10 THROUGH 9.12

Service time intervals, $1/\mu$ (min)	*0–0.2*	*0.2–0.4*	*0.4–0.6*	*0.6–0.8*	*0.8–1.*	*1.–1.5*	*1.5–2*	*2–3*	*3–7*
Fraction of programs with service time in the corresponding interval, f_i	0.348	0.230	0.125	0.100	0.060	0.090	0.035	0.010	0.002

TABLE 9.4 FREQUENCY DISTRIBUTION OF SERVICE TIMES TO BE USED IN PROBLEM 9.9

Service time intervals $1/\mu_1$ *(min)*	*0–0.2*	*0.2–0.4*	*0.4–0.6*	*0.6–1*	*1–1.5*	*1.5–2*	*2–4*
Fraction of programs with service time in the corresponding interval, f_{i1}	0.200	0.300	0.200	0.250	0.030	0.018	0.002

Problem 9.8

We begin by analyzing the given service time distribution to approximate it by a tractable analytic function, if possible. We first estimate the mean and variance of the distribution in Table 9.3:

$$\frac{1}{\mu} \cong \sum_{i=1}^{9} \frac{1}{\mu_i} f_i = 0.1 \times 0.348 + 0.3 \times 0.23 + 0.5 \times 0.125 + 0.7 \times 0.1$$
$$+ 0.9 \times 0.06 + 1.25 \times 0.09 + 1.75 \times 0.035 + 2.5 \times 0.01 + 5$$
$$\times 0.002 = 0.499 \text{ min} \cong 0.5 \text{ min}$$

$$\text{Var}\left[\frac{1}{\mu_i}\right] \cong \sum_{i=1}^{9}\left(\frac{1}{\mu_i} - \frac{1}{\mu}\right)^2 \cdot f_i = (0.1 - 0.5)^2 \times 0.348 + (0.3 - 0.5)^2 \times 0.23$$
$$+ (0.5 - 0.5)^2 \times 0.125 + (0.7 - 0.5)^2 \times 0.1 + (0.9 - 0.5)^2 \times 0.06$$
$$+ (1.25 - 0.5)^2 \times 0.09 + (1.75 - 0.5)^2 \times 0.035 + (2.5 - 0.5)^2 \times 0.01$$
$$+ (5 - 0.5)^2 \times 0.002 = 0.26 \text{ min}^2$$

To estimate the mean and the variance, we have used the mean value of each service time interval. This is the simplest method, which is obviously affected by errors greater than those of more sophisticated approaches. The resulting coefficient of variation is

$$c = \frac{\sigma_{1/\mu}}{1/\mu} = \frac{\sqrt{0.26}}{0.5} = \frac{0.509}{0.5} \cong 1$$

TABLE 9.5 FREQUENCY DISTRIBUTION OF SERVICE TIMES TO BE USED IN PROBLEM 9.9

Service time intervals $1/\mu_2$ *(min)*	*0–0.2*	*0.2–0.4*	*0.4–0.6*	*0.6–1*	*1–2*	*2–10*
Fraction of programs with service time in the corresponding interval, f_{i2}	0.46	0.23	0.12	0.11	0.05	0.03

Thus, because of the shape of the histogram in Table 9.3, which is similar to that of the curve in Fig. 9.17, and since $c = 1$, an exponential function is a possible candidate for approximating the given distribution, and we can use an M/M/1 station as a macro-level model of the system.

The utilization of the server is given by

$$U = \frac{\lambda}{\mu} = 1.5 \times 0.5 = 0.75$$

The mean number of programs in the system and its variance are

$$N = \frac{U}{1 - U} = 3, \qquad \text{Var}\,[N] = \frac{U}{(1 - U)^2} = 12$$

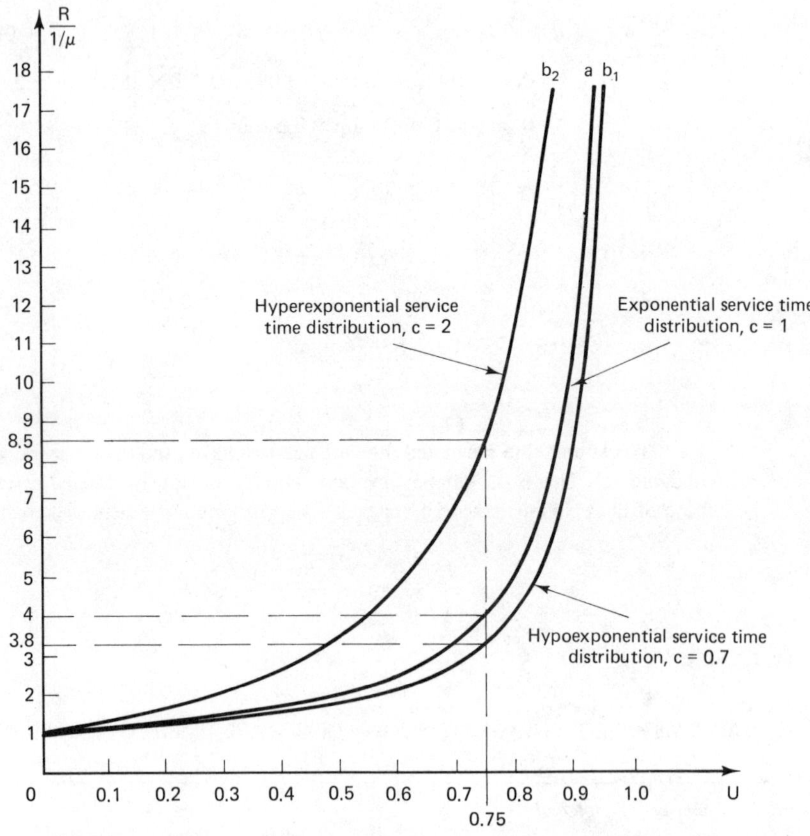

Figure 9.22 Normalized mean turnaround time of single-station models versus U (constant μ): (a) M/M/1 model, service time distribution in Table 9.3, $c = 1$; (b_1) M/G/1 model, service time distribution in Table 9.4, $c = 0.7$; (b_2) M/G/1 model, service time distribution in Table 9.5, $c = 2$.

The mean turnaround time is obtained from Little's formula:

$$R = \frac{N}{\lambda} = \frac{1}{\mu(1 - U)} = 2 \text{ min}$$

and its variance is

$$\text{Var } [R] = \frac{1}{\mu^2(1 - U)^2} = 4 \text{ min}^2$$

The mean waiting time of a program in the input queue is

$$t_q = R - \frac{1}{\mu} = UR = 0.75 \times 2 = 1.5 \text{ min}$$

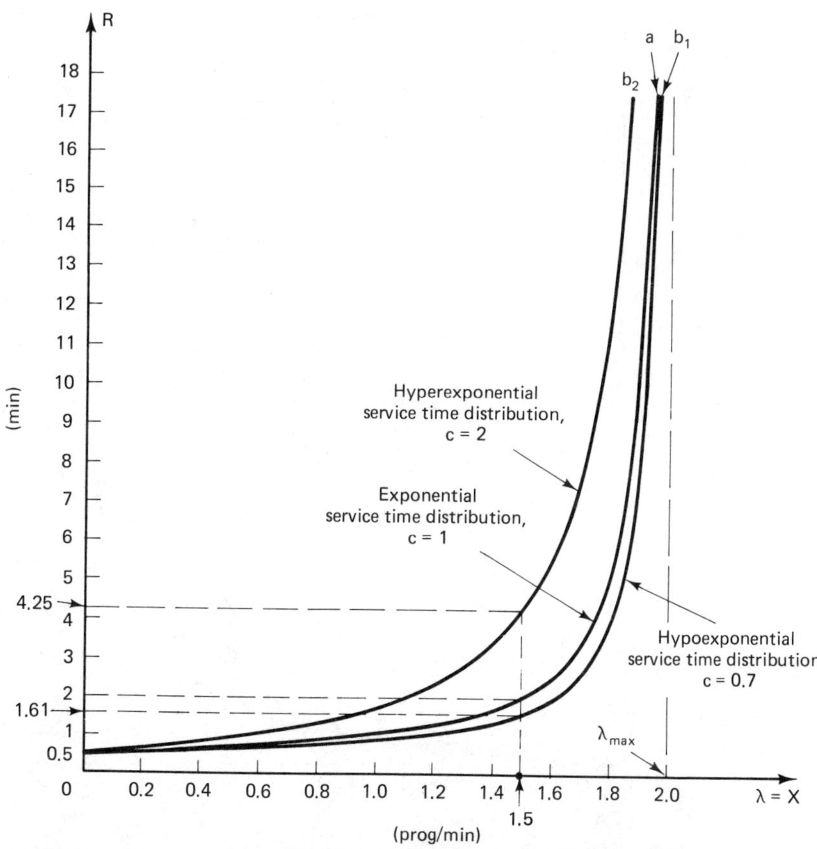

Figure 9.23 Mean turnaround time versus mean throughput rate of single-station models: (a) M/M/1, service time distribution in Table 9.3; (b_1) M/G/1 model, service time distribution in Table 9.4; (b_2) M/G/1, service time distribution in Table 9.5.

and the mean queue length, computed taking into account also the intervals during which the queue is empty, is

$$N_q = \frac{U^2}{1 - U} = 2.25$$

Curve a in Fig. 9.22 represents the normalized mean turnaround time $R/(1/\mu)$ of this model as a function of U, assuming that λ varies from 0 to μ, and that μ remains constant. As mentioned in Sec. 9.4, this curve becomes increasingly steep as U approaches 1 and tends to infinity. Curve a in Fig. 9.23 shows the relationship between the mean response time and the mean arrival rate, which for $\lambda \leq \lambda_{max} = \mu = 2$ coincides with the mean throughput rate X. Thus, the maximum throughput rate of this system will be 2 programs/min. Curve a in Fig. 9.24 represents the mean number N of programs in the system, including the one receiving service, as a function of U.

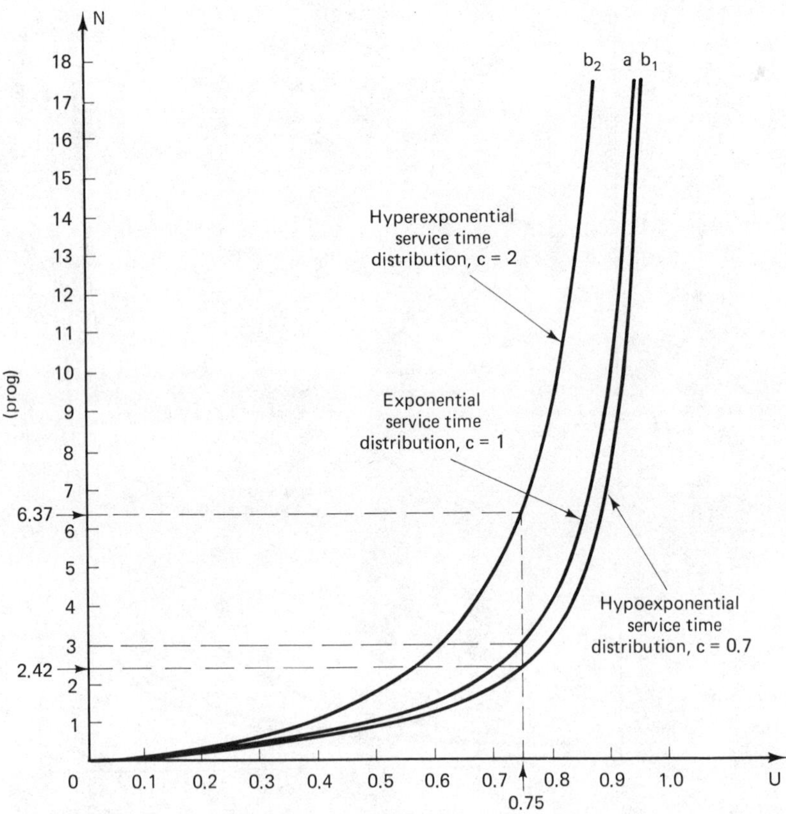

Figure 9.24 Mean number of programs in the system versus U: (a) M/M/1, service time distribution in Table 9.3; (b_1) M/G/1, service time distribution in Table 9.4; (b_2) M/G/1, service time distribution in Table 9.5.

Problem 9.9

As was done in Problem 9.8, we estimate the means and variances of the distributions in Tables 9.4 and 9.5. The one in Table 9.4 yields

$$\frac{1}{\mu_1} \cong \sum_{i=1}^{7} \frac{1}{\mu_{i1}} f_{i1} \cong 0.5 \text{ min}$$

$$\text{Var}\left[\frac{1}{\mu_{i_1}}\right] \cong \sum_{i=1}^{7} \left(\frac{1}{\mu_{i_1}} - \frac{1}{\mu_1}\right)^2 f_{i_1} \cong 0.12 \text{ min}^2$$

$$c_1 \cong \frac{\sigma_{1/\mu_1}}{1/\mu_1} = \frac{\sqrt{0.12}}{0.5} = 0.7$$

Since $c_1 < 1$, we could try to approximate the distribution in Table 9.4 by a hypoexponential Erlang-k distribution (see Fig. 9.17). To determine the value of k, we would compute the inverse of the squared coefficient of variation:

$$k = \frac{1}{c_1^2} \cong 2$$

However, if we are only interested in the values of the most common performance indexes, we can just apply the results of the analysis of the M/G/1 model [see Eqs. (9.35), (9.36), (9.37)] noting that, since λ and $1/\mu$ are the same as in Problem 9.8, we still have $U = 0.75$. The mean number of programs in the system is

$$N_1 = U + \frac{U^2\,(1 + c_1^2)}{2(1 - U)} = 2.42$$

the mean turnaround time is

$$R_1 = \frac{1}{\mu_1}\left[1 + \frac{U(1 + c_1^2)}{2(1 - U)}\right] = 1.61 \text{ min}$$

and the mean waiting time of a program in the input queue is

$$t_{q1} = R_1 - \frac{1}{\mu_1} = \frac{U(1 + c_1^2)}{2\mu_1\,(1 - U)} = 1.11 \text{ min}$$

The mean queue length will be

$$N_{q1} = \lambda t_{q1} = 1.67$$

Thus, with respect to the original M/M/1 model, N decreases by 19 percent, R by about the same percentage, t_q decreases by 26 percent, and N_q by about the same percentage. The (b_1) curves in Figs. 9.22 through 9.24 represent $R_1\mu(U)$, $R_1(X)$, and $N_1(U)$, respectively.

Considering now the service time distribution in Table 9.5, we have

$$\frac{1}{\mu_2} \cong \sum_{i=1}^{6} \frac{1}{\mu_{i2}} f_{i2} \cong 0.5 \text{ min}$$

$$\text{Var}\left[\frac{1}{\mu_{i2}}\right] \cong \sum_{i=1}^{6} \left(\frac{1}{\mu_{i2}} - \frac{1}{\mu_2}\right)^2 f_{i2} \cong 1 \text{ min}^2$$

$$c_2 = \frac{\sigma_{1/\mu_2}}{1/\mu_2} \cong 2$$

Since $c_2 > 1$, the variability of service times is greater than in the exponential case, and, because of the shape of the histogram in Table 9.5, we could try to approximate it by a hyperexponential distribution (see Fig. 9.17). However, we shall apply the M/G/1 results in Eqs. (9.35) through (9.37), with U still equal to 0.75, since λ and $1/\mu$ have not changed with respect to those in Problem 9.8:

$$N_2 = U + \frac{U^2(1 + c_2^2)}{2(1 - U)} = 6.37$$

$$R_2 = \frac{1}{\mu_2}\left[1 + \frac{U(1 + c_2^2)}{2(1 - U)}\right] = 4.25 \text{ min}$$

$$t_{q2} = R_2 - \frac{1}{\mu_2} = 3.75 \text{ min}$$

$$N_{q2} = \lambda t_{q2} = 5.62$$

Thus, the greater variability of service times represented by the increase of c from 1 to 2 causes a 112 percent increase in N, an increase by about the same percentage in R, a 150 percent increase in t_q, and an increase by about the same percentage in N_q.

The (b_2) curves in Figs. 9.22 through 9.24 refer to this case. In general, for equal mean service times, the values of the performance indexes get worse as the variability of service times increases.

Problem 9.10

The mean waiting time of a program in the input queue is given by

$$t_q = R - \frac{1}{\mu} = \frac{\lambda}{\mu(\mu - \lambda)}$$

Thus, if the maximum value of t_q, to be denoted by t_{q3}, is known, the corresponding value of λ can be computed as

$$\lambda_3 = \frac{t_{q3}\mu^2}{t_{q3}\mu + 1} = \frac{20 \times 4}{20 \times 2 + 1} = 1.95 \text{ programs/min}$$

The percent of increase in the arrival rate with respect to the original one is

$$\Delta\lambda = 100\,\frac{\lambda_3 - \lambda}{\lambda} = 100\,\frac{1.95 - 1.5}{1.5} = 30\%$$

With the new load λ_3, the mean number of programs waiting in the input queue becomes

$$N_{q3} = \lambda_3 t_{q3} = 1.95 \times 20 = 39$$

and its percent of increase with respect to the original value of N_q is given by

$$\Delta N_q = 100 \frac{N_{q3} - N_q}{N_q} = 1633.3\%$$

These results show the asymptotic trend of the various indexes computed here as U approaches 1.

Problem 9.11

To determine the capacity needed for the new system, we impose the requirement that the 90th *percentile* $\pi_R(90)$ of the turnaround time be equal to 10 min. $\pi_R(90)$ is the value of R such that 90 percent of the programs have a lower turnaround time. Since the distribution of turnaround times in an M/M/1 model is exponential (see for example [KL75]), and the 90th percentile of an exponential distribution is about 2.3 times the mean,

$$\pi_R(90) \cong 2.3R = 2.3 \frac{1}{\mu - \lambda}$$

we can derive the required value of μ, to be denoted by μ_4, as follows:

$$\mu_4 = \frac{2.3 + \pi_R(90)\lambda_3}{\pi_R(90)} = \frac{2.3 + 10 \times 1.95}{10} = 2.18 \text{ min}^{-1}$$

If we assume that the capacity of the system is directly related to the processing time of a program, that is, to its service time, the increase in capacity needed to guarantee that $\pi_R(90) = 10$ min is

$$\Delta\mu = 100 \frac{2.18 - 2}{2} = +9\%$$

It should be noted that the 90th percentile of turnaround times before the upgrading of the system's capacity equals, under load λ_3, 46 min.

Problem 9.12

If program improvements reduce the mean service time by 10 percent, we have

$$\frac{1}{\mu_5} = 0.9 \frac{1}{\mu} = 0.45 \text{ min}$$

and the utilization of the station becomes

$$U_5 = \frac{\lambda}{\mu_5} = 1.5 \times 0.45 = 0.675$$

The corresponding values of the performance indexes can be easily found to be

$$N_5 = 2, \qquad R_5 \cong 1.43 \text{ min}, \qquad t_{q5} \cong 0.97 \text{ min}, \qquad N_{q5} \cong 1.4$$

Thus, the effects of 10 percent reduction in the mean service time are

$$\Delta N = -33\%$$

$$\Delta R = -28.5\%$$

$$\Delta t_q = -35\%$$

$$\Delta N_q = -37\%$$

9.4.2 Case 9.4: I/O Load Balancing

Some of the most widely applied tuning actions are those intended to balance the use of I/O channels and devices. The expected effect of these actions is the elimination, or at least the reduction, of device or channel contention, thereby decreasing their mean response time and increasing the system's productivity. In practice, there are often disk devices that contain frequently accessed files or areas, for example, paging areas, heavily requested portions of data bases, sets of data common to many procedures, system routines, utility programs, and so on, whereas other devices are only seldom utilized. Another situation often found in computer installations is that of a channel connected to devices with widely differing service times.

In this section we shall study the problem of determining the *optimum loading* of each device in an I/O subsystem, that is, in a subsystem consisting of an I/O channel with all the I/O devices connected to it. The *optimum loadings* are defined as the loadings, one for each resource, that maximize the throughput or, equivalently, minimize the mean response time of the I/O subsystem for a given global load. The response time of the I/O subsystem is the sum of the time spent by a request in the queue for the resource to be accessed and the time needed by the resource to satisfy it.

We already observed in Sec. 7.2 that, in an I/O subsystem with two disk devices having different service times, a subdivision of the load that makes the utilizations of the two disks equal does not correspond to a situation of optimal subsystem performance. In particular, we have seen that, starting from this condition of even utilization and gradually increasing the load of the faster device, the throughput increases up to a maximum value beyond which any load increase causes it to decrease. A rather intuitive explanation of this result can be based on the greater intrinsic efficiency of faster devices: the greater the load they handle, the greater the global processing efficiency. Consequently, the queue of requests for the faster device will on the average be longer than those for the slower ones and, according to what was said in Chapter 6, there will be a bottleneck corresponding to the faster device. Since the maximum productivity is obtained when the faster resources are more loaded, these mild bottlenecks should not be removed [BU77].

A study aimed at increasing an I/O subsystem's throughput can lead to a modification of file allocation in order to move the bottlenecks from the slower to the faster devices.

Since empirical subdivisions of the load rarely lead to good results, it may be convenient to use analytic models that provide, under some simplifying assumptions, the approximate optimum value of each device's load.

Analytic results can be used in a tuning study to obtain a rough indication of the optimum load for each device, as well as after such a study, to determine whether the effects of the balancing actions undertaken are near optimal or can still be improved.

Let us consider the problem of determining the allocation of a large data base on several I/O devices having different speeds. For example, let there be two disk devices, D_1 and D_2, having mean service times $1/\mu_1 = 1/\mu_2 = 8$ ms, and four units, D_3, D_4, D_5, D_6, having mean service times $1/\mu_3 = 1/\mu_4 = 1/\mu_5 = 1/\mu_6 = 12$ ms. We wish to compute the load of each device that minimizes the mean response time R of the I/O subsystem (see Fig. 9.25) containing the data base.

By λ we shall denote the arrival rate of requests, which represents the load on the data base (in our example, $\lambda = 88$ requests/s), and by λ_i and $1/\mu_i$, respectively, the mean arrival rate and the mean service time of the ith device. We assume that the interarrival times of the λ requests to the I/O subsystem and the device service times are exponentially distributed.

In Sec. 9.4, we saw that, under these assumptions, in an open model even the interarrival times of requests to the individual devices D_i are exponentially distributed.

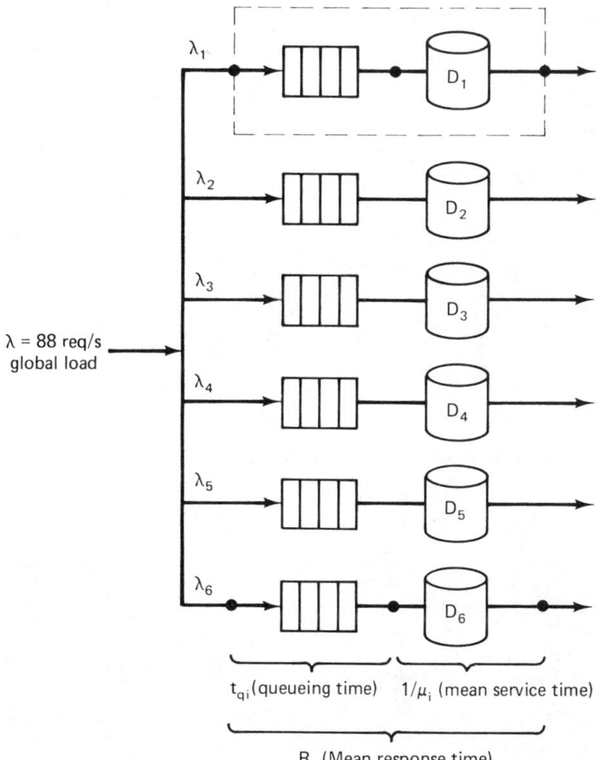

Figure 9.25 Configuration of the I/O subsystem studied in Case 9.4. The model is an open network. Disks 1 and 2 have a mean service time of 8 ms, disks 3, 4, 5, and 6, of 12 ms.

Thus each device D_i with its queue q_i of requests can be studied as an independent M/M/1 model. The scheduling algorithm of all stations is assumed to be FCFS, and no restriction is imposed on the number of entering requests; in other words, the model is an infinite source model.

The mean number N_i of requests in the ith station is

$$N_i = \frac{U_i}{1 - U_i}$$

where $U_i = \lambda_i/\mu_i$ is the utilization of the same station. Then, from Little's formula (9.31), we obtain for the ith station

$$R_i = \frac{1}{\mu_i - \lambda_i}$$

The mean response time R of the entire I/O subsystem is given by the weighted sum of the R_i's. The weights are the ratios λ_i/λ. Thus,

$$R = \sum_{i=1}^{6} \frac{\lambda_i}{\lambda} R_i = \sum_{i=1}^{6} \frac{\lambda_i}{\lambda(\mu_i - \lambda_i)} \tag{9.61}$$

The optimum subdivision of the load λ is the one that minimizes R as the λ_i's vary. To calculate the optimal load of device i, denoted by λ_i^*, the following algorithm proposed by Chen [CH73] can be used. The six devices are ordered by increasing service times (so that $\mu_1 \geqslant \mu_2 \geqslant \ldots \geqslant \mu_6$).

Step 1: Compute the quantities $L(k)$ given by

$$L(k) = \left(\sum_{j=1}^{k} \mu_j\right) - \mu_k^{1/2} \sum_{j=1}^{k} \mu_j^{1/2} \qquad (k = 1, \ldots, 6)$$

$$L(7) = \sum_{j=1}^{6} \mu_j$$

Step 2: Compute the value of $\bar{k}$ such that

$$L(\bar{k} + 1) > \lambda \geqslant L(\bar{k})$$

Step 3: Compute the *optimal values* λ_i^* that are given by

$$\lambda_i^* = \mu_i - \mu_i^{1/2} \left\{\left(\sum_{p=1}^{\bar{k}} \mu_p\right) - \lambda\right\} \Big/ \sum_{p=1}^{\bar{k}} \mu_p^{1/2} \quad (i = 1, \ldots, \bar{k})$$

$$\lambda_i^* = 0 \qquad (i = \bar{k} + 1, \ldots, 6) \tag{9.62}$$

By simple algebraic transformations, Eq. (9.62) can be expressed in the following form:

$$1 - U_i = \text{constant} \times \sqrt{\frac{1}{\mu_i}}$$

which allows us to define the optimum utilization of a device as that value of U_i that makes the fraction of time during which the device is idle proportional to the square root of its mean service time [CH73].

In our example, if the value of $\bar{k}$ found in step 2 is less than 6, the devices between $\bar{k} + 1$ and 6 will have an optimum load λ_i^* equal to zero. If this happens, the subsystem is not correctly sized for the load it has to process. In this case, if the slower units with zero λ_i^* are disconnected or no longer used, the global mean response time R will improve.

Performing *step 1* with our data, we obtain the following values:

$$\begin{aligned} L(1) &= L(2) = 0 \\ L(3) &= L(4) = L(5) = L(6) = 45.87 \\ L(7) &= 583.33 \end{aligned} \tag{9.63}$$

Since $\lambda = 88$ requests, $\bar{k}$ is given by *step 2:*

$$L(7) > \lambda > L(6) \Longrightarrow \bar{k} = 6$$

This value shows that the I/O subsystem has an adequate capacity for the load $\lambda = 88$ requests/s, and that all devices are therefore to be utilized (that is, all λ_i^* are nonzero).

Step 3 provides us with the values of the optimum loads λ_i^*:

$$\begin{aligned} \lambda_1^* &= \lambda_2^* = 30.9 \text{ requests/s} \\ \lambda_3^* &= \lambda_4^* = \lambda_5^* = \lambda_6^* = 6.54 \text{ requests/s} \end{aligned} \tag{9.64}$$

Considering the physical meaning of the λ_i^*'s, that D_1 and D_2 have equal service times and that the same is true for D_3, D_4, D_5, and D_6, the optimal loads calculated in Eq. (9.64) can be approximated as follows: $\lambda_1 = \lambda_2 = 30$ requests/s, $\lambda_3 = \lambda_4 = \lambda_5 = \lambda_6 = 7$ requests/s, or $\lambda_1 = \lambda_2 = 32$ requests/s, $\lambda_3 = \lambda_4 = \lambda_5 = \lambda_6 = 6$ requests/s.

The mean response time R of the I/O subsystem can be found by introducing into Eq. (9.61) the values of λ_i just determined; for instance, with the first distribution of the load, we have

$$R = 2 \times \frac{30}{88} \times \frac{0.008}{(1 - 0.008 \times 30)} + 4 \times \frac{7}{88} \times \frac{0.012}{(1 - 0.012 \times 7)} = 11.34 \text{ ms}$$

The files of the subsystem will have to be allocated on the six devices so as to produce a load on each device as close to the optimum [see Eq. (9.64)] as possible.

The closer the real loads will be to the computed loads, the greater the subsystem's throughput or, equivalently, the shorter its mean response time.

From the values of $L(i)$ computed in Eq. (9.63), which do not depend on λ and can thus be determined once on each I/O subsystem, we can see that, if the subsystem's load decreases below 45.87 requests/s, the four devices with $1/\mu_1 = 12$ ms become useless. To minimize the global response time, they have to be disconnected. Indeed, in this case, $\bar{k}$ becomes 2.

From Eqs. (9.63), we can also deduce that the six devices in the subsystem are capable of processing, with maximum productivity, an average load variable from 45.87 to 583.33 requests/s. Thus, when the total load λ varies, Eqs. (9.63) provide the number of devices required for the subsystem's maximum throughput and Eqs. (9.62) yield their optimum loads.

The utilizations of the devices under the optimum loads λ_i^* are

$$U_i = \frac{\lambda_i}{\mu_i} = 24.72\% \qquad (i = 1, 2)$$

$$U_i = \frac{\lambda_i}{\mu_i} = 7.84\% \qquad (i = 3, 4, 5, 6)$$

This confirms what was seen in Problem 9.5; that is, to obtain the maximum throughput from a system, the faster units (except the CPU) must have higher utilizations than the slower ones.

This load-balancing algorithm may be usefully applied to systems whose workload is reasonably stable, that is, to systems dedicated to some particular processes; also, it can be used to determine the optimal placement of *permanent files* during a reorganization of mass storage. In this context, a permanent file is one whose physical location changes with a very low frequency (daily or even more rarely).

More sophisticated models for optimal balancing of requests for permanent files in heterogeneous memory hierarchies have been described in several papers (see [BU73b], [BU74], [PI75], [FO76], [DO82]). An application of the algorithm presented in this section to the more dynamic case of *temporary file placement* is described in [SE81].

9.4.3 Case 9.5: Performance Analysis of an Interactive System

An interactive multiprogrammed system has 10 active terminals, all being used for the same application. Because of this characteristic, all interactive commands are assumed to be statistically identical. The mean service time $1/\mu_s$ of the central subsystem is 0.5 s. Swapping times can be ignored. Thus, $1/\mu_s$ may be considered as the mean uniprogramming execution time of each interactive command. Since the time quantum is very short with respect to the mean service time, we approximately model the central subsystem as a single server station with a processor-sharing discipline. The mean think time Z is

10 s. The think times are assumed to be exponentially distributed. The closed model adopted for the system is shown in Fig. 9.21.

These are the problems to be investigated and solved:

9.13. Compute the values of the following performance indexes: the mean utilization of the central subsystem, the mean throughput rate in commands processed per second, and the mean response time R.

9.14. Determine the changes in the values of the mean throughput rate and of the mean response time due to a 20 percent reduction of the mean service time $1/\mu_s$, which is the estimated effect of various tuning actions being considered.

9.15. Predict the effects on the values of the performance indexes computed in Problem 9.13 of the addition of five terminals to the system.

9.16. Analyze for capacity planning purposes the asymptotic performance of the system in saturation, considering its initial configuration.

9.17. Determine whether the throughput rate and the response time would improve more by undertaking the tuning actions referred to in Problem 9.14 or by decreasing the mean think time by 10 percent, assuming that this is a feasible change in the application being considered.

Problem 9.13

The probability that the central subsystem is idle is given by Eq. (9.41) with $M = 10$:

$$p_0 = \frac{1}{\sum_{k=0}^{10} [10!/(10 - k)!]\,(0.5/10)^k} = 0.538$$

Thus, the mean utilization of the central subsystem is

$$U_s = 1 - p_0 = 0.462$$

the mean throughput rate is

$$X = U_s\mu_s = 0.462 \times 2 = 0.924 \text{ commands/s}$$

and the mean response time is

$$R = \frac{M}{\mu_s U_s} - Z = \frac{10}{2 \times 0.462} - 10 = 0.822 \text{ s}$$

Problem 9.14

Tuning actions performed on the system and on the programs have reduced the mean service time of the central subsystem by 20 percent:

$$\frac{1}{\mu'_s} = \frac{1}{\mu_s} - 0.2\frac{1}{\mu_s} = 0.4 \text{ s}$$

The new value of p_0 is

$$p_0' = \frac{1}{\sum_{k=0}^{10} [10!/(10 - k)!] (0.4/10)^k} = 0.622$$

and the corresponding mean utilization of the central subsystem is

$$U_s' = 1 - p_0' = 0.378$$

The new values of the mean throughput rate and of the mean response time are

$$X' = U_s'\mu_s' = 0.944 \text{ commands/s}$$

$$R' = \frac{10}{2.5 \times 0.378} - 10 = 0.592 \text{ s}$$

With respect to those of the original system, the mean throughput rate has increased by 2.1 percent and the mean response time has decreased by 28 percent.

Problem 9.15

This is one of the most frequently asked questions when the performance of an interactive system is being evaluated. A more complete answer to this question is given in Problem 9.16.

With $M'' = 15$ active terminals, the values of the performance indexes become

$$p_0'' = \frac{1}{\sum_{k=0}^{15} [15!/(15 - k!)] (0.5/10)^k} = 0.330$$

$$U_s'' = 1 - p_0'' = 0.670$$

$$X'' = U_s''\mu_s = 1.340 \text{ commands/s}$$

$$R'' = \frac{M''}{\mu_s U_s''} - Z = 1.194 \text{ s}$$

Thus, with respect to the configuration with 10 terminals, the mean utilization of the central subsystem, the mean throughput rate, and the mean response time all increase by about 45 percent. The almost equal percentage increases in the last two indexes is to be attributed to their not being saturated or close to saturation (see Figs. 9.26 and 9.27).

Problem 9.16

In Fig. 9.26 we show R versus the number of active terminals as well as the horizontal asymptote corresponding to the minimum value of R, given by $1/\mu_s = 0.5$ s, and the oblique asymptote, whose equation is

$$R = 0.5M - 10$$

The system's saturation point is given by Eq. (9.44):

$$M^* = 1 + Z\mu_s = 1 + 2 \times 10 = 21 \text{ terminals}$$

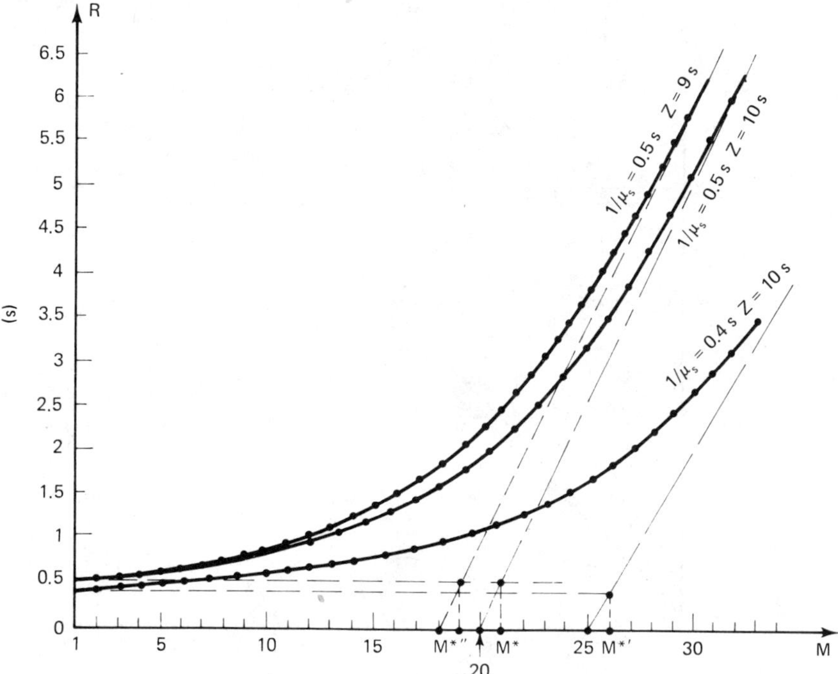

Figure 9.26 Mean response time R versus the number M of active terminals for various values of $1/M_s$ and Z. The asymptotes of each curve are also shown.

and the corresponding value of R,

$$R^* = \frac{21}{2 \cdot (1 - p_0(21))} - Z = 2.08 \text{ s}$$

The value of R_{max} for this application is 3 s. Thus, the system can satisfy this requirement with both 10 and 15 terminals. Figure 9.27 displays the mean throughput rate X versus the number of active terminals for the original system with $1/\mu_s = 0.5$ s and $Z = 10$ s. It can be easily seen that X grows almost linearly with M up to M^* and with smaller and smaller increments beyond M^*, since the system saturates.

Problem 9.17

First, we compute the system's performance with a think time $Z'' = 9$ s. The corresponding values of R and X can be read from the curves in Figs. 9.26 and 9.27 for $1/\mu_s = 0.5$ s and $Z = 9$ s. Similar curves are reported in the same figures for $1/\mu_s = 0.4$ s and $Z = 10$ s (see Problem 9.14).

As can be seen in Figs. 9.26 and 9.27, the lower mean think time of 9 s lowers the saturation point to $M^{*''} = 19$ terminals, whereas the lower mean service time of 0.4 s increases the saturation point to $M^{*'} = 26$ terminals. If the primary objective of modifying the system is to reduce the mean response time as much as possible, then the actions considered in Problem 9.14 are the most effective (see Fig. 9.26). If, on the other hand, the

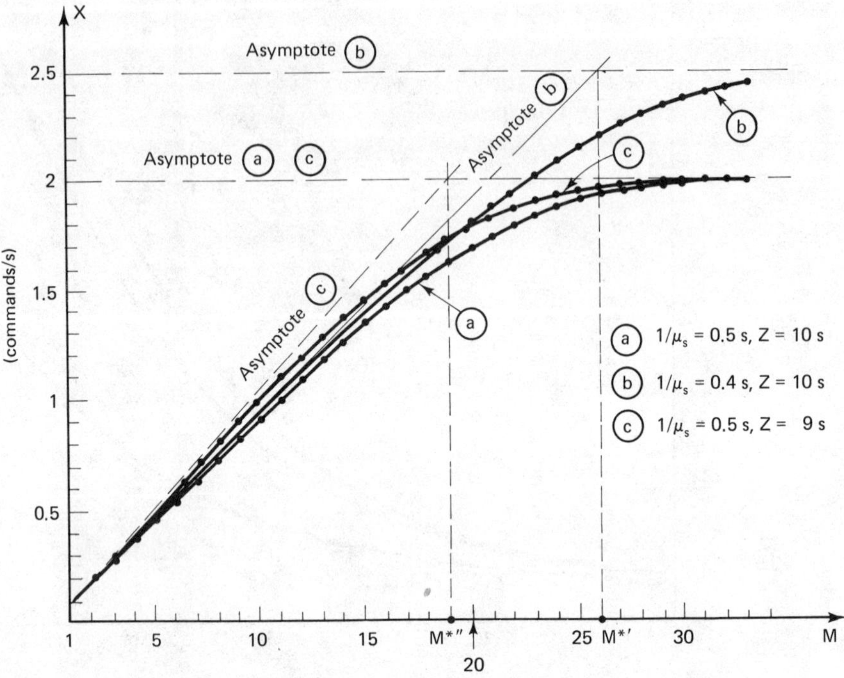

Figure 9.27 Mean throughput rate X versus the number M of active terminals for various values of $1/\mu_s$ and Z. The asymptotes of each curve are also shown.

main goal is to maximize the throughput rate, then the number of active terminals becomes relevant. If this number is less than 19, the actions considered in this problem are more convenient, but, beyond 19 active terminals, those considered in Problem 9.14 are to be preferred (see Fig. 9.27).

The asymptotes in Fig. 9.27 confirm these conclusions: the horizontal one has equation $X = \mu_s$ [see Eqs. (9.15) and (9.42)]; the oblique asymptote, which represents the mean throughput rate in the absence of queues, is given by

$$X = \frac{M}{\dfrac{1}{\mu_s} + Z}$$

whose denominator is the minimum response time, corresponding to the case of a single command in the system. This time is also called the *physical cycle time* of the system.

The angular coefficient of the oblique asymptote given by the modifications in Problem 9.14 is 0.096, whereas that of the oblique asymptote obtained in this problem is 0.105. Thus, for low values of M, when there are no large queuing delays, the mean throughput rate resulting from the changes considered here is greater than that resulting from the changes in Problem 9.14. Note that the intersection of each pair of asymptotes yields the value of M^* already determined with the response time approach.

9.4.4 Case 9.6: Improving a Virtual Memory System's Configuration

The goal of this study is to evaluate the effects of several equipment configuration and software strategy modifications on the throughput of a medium-scale, multiprogrammed virtual memory system supporting a batch workload. Figure 9.8 presents the system's configuration. It consists of a CPU and three secondary storage devices: a paging drum, a file drum, and a file disk. The main memory has a capacity of 400 page frames, 300 of which are available to user programs. The memory management policy currently in use approximates a fixed equipartition; in other words, the available page frames are divided evenly among the programs in the multiprogramming mix. The file disk has a mean seek time of 11 ms, a revolution speed of 2400 rpm, and a transfer time of 6 μs/word; each of the drums has a speed of 3600 rpm and a transfer time of 4 μs/word. A typical program consists of 2.1 million instructions and performs 250 file disk and 150 file drum operations. With the instruction mix that characterizes the workload, the speed of the CPU is about 0.7 MIPS. The number of paging drum operations performed by a program varies with the number of page frames allocated to that program, which is, in turn, determined by the multiprogramming level. At present, the typical program exhibits, under the system's memory policy, the *lifetime curve* shown in Fig. 9.28; this curve expresses the expected CPU time between a single program's page faults as a function

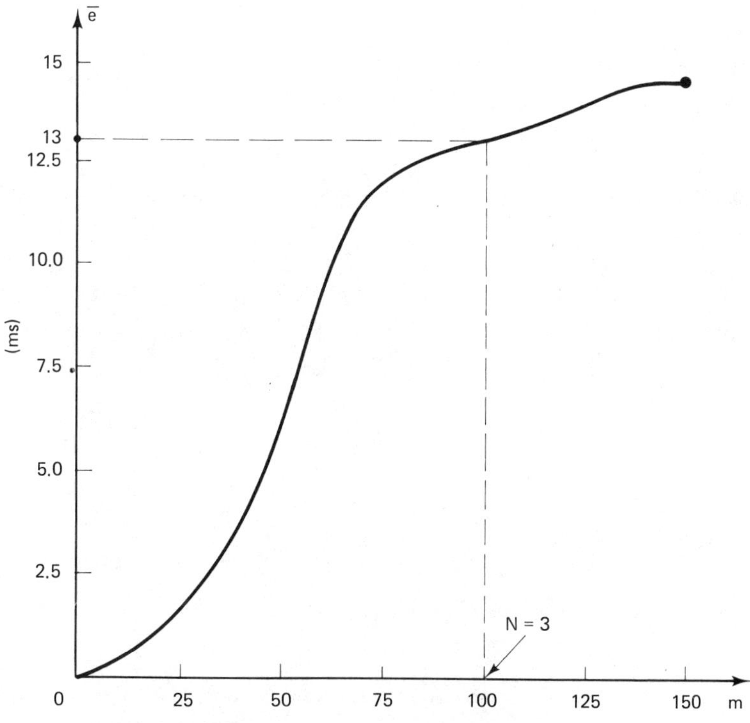

Figure 9.28 Lifetime curve of a typical program.

of its resident set size. The multiprogramming level of the system varies between 1 and 10, but is generally between 5 and 8. The page size and the sizes of file disk and file drum blocks are all 1024 words.

We begin by modeling the current system and analyzing its behavior. For this purpose, we use the central server model shown in Fig. 9.29. The multiplexor channel to which the card reader, the printer, and the console of the system are connected has not been taken into consideration since it is very little utilized and does not therefore limit, or appreciably influence, the system's performance.

The listing of a program for the solution of the model is reported in the Appendix; it applies the algorithm described by Eq. (9.56). The effects on the throughput rate of the following modifications, both individually and comparatively, have to be investigated:

1. Replace the CPU with one from the same family which is 25 percent faster.
2. Replace the file drum with one having a speed of 4500 rpm and the same bit density and data organization.
3. Replace the paging drum with a faster one as described in part 2.
4. Replace both drums with their faster counterparts.
5. Redistribute files between the file drum and the file disk in order to balance the activities of these devices.
6. Increase the size of the memory available to user programs from 300 to 400 page frames.

The input data of the problem are reported in Table 9.6, while the model parameters and the equations used are shown in Table 9.7.

Having established the multiprogramming level N at which the system is assumed to operate, the number of main memory frames available to each program is computed, and the corresponding expected interfault time is derived from Fig. 9.28. Then, from the total CPU time (given by L/v_{CPU}), we obtain the mean number V_2 of accesses to the paging drum made by a program, that is, the mean number of page faults per program. The mean number of CPU intervals, or visits, per program is

$$V_1 = V_2 + V_3 + V_4 + 1 \tag{9.65}$$

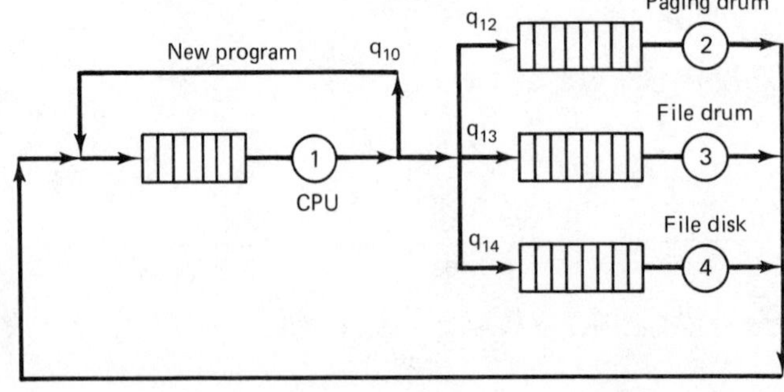

Figure 9.29 Central server model used to represent the system in Fig. 9.8.

TABLE 9.6 INITIAL INPUT DATA

	Workload parameters	
L	Mean number of instructions to be executed per program	2.1×10^6 instructions
V_1	Mean number of CPU intervals per program	depends on V_2
V_2	Mean number of paging drum accesses per program	depends on N
V_3	Mean number of file drum accesses per program	150
V_4	Mean number of file disk accesses per program	250
r	Block size, per drum or disk access, in words	1024 words
m_p	Mean program size	150 pages
	System parameters	
v_{CPU}	Mean CPU instruction execution rate	0.7×10^6 instructions/s
m	Main memory size for user programs	300 pages
R_{pdr}	Paging drum revolution speed	3600 rpm
R_{fdr}	File drum revolution speed	3600 rpm
R_{fds}	File disk revolution speed	2400 rpm
t_{seek}	Mean file disk seek time	11 ms
t_{wdr}	Paging and file drum word transfer time	4 μs/word
t_{wds}	File disk word transfer time	6 μs/word

since a program always visits the CPU after visiting another resource. The last term on the right-hand side, 1, accounts for the last visit to the CPU, which is made just before exiting.

By using the equations displayed in Table 9.7, one can compute all the parameter values needed to solve the model. We shall now describe the operations to be performed in order to solve the model for $N = 3$. The program in the Appendix allows us to analyze the model for N in the desired range (for example, from 1 to 10) in a single run.

Since the size of main memory for user programs is 300 page frames, each program is allotted 100 frames fcr $N = 3$. From Fig. 9.28, we obtain an expected interfault time of 13 ms. The total CPU time per program is $2.1/0.7 = 3$ s. Hence, the mean number of page faults per program is $V_2 = 3/(13 \times 10^{-3}) = 230$, and [see Eq. (9.65)] the mean number of CPU intervals is $V_1 = 230 + 150 + 250 + 1 = 631$.

TABLE 9.7 INITIAL VALUES OF MODEL PARAMETERS AND EQUATIONS USED TO CALCULATE THEM

	Model parameters
$\mu_1 =$	$v_{CPU}V_1/L = 0.3333\ V_1$, mean uninterrupted CPU rate
$\mu_2 =$	$1/[(60/2R_{pdr}) + t_{wdr}\ r \cdot 10^{-6}] = 80.455\ s^{-1}$, mean paging drum service rate
$\mu_3 =$	$1/[(60/2R_{fdr}) + t_{wdr}\ r \cdot 10^{-6}] = 80.455\ s^{-1}$, mean file drum service rate
$\mu_4 =$	$1/[(60/2R_{fds}) + t_{seek} \times 10^{-3} + t_{wds} \cdot r \times 10^{-6}] = 33.734\ s^{-1}$, mean file disk service rate
$q_{10} =$	$1/V_1$, new program probability
$q_{12} =$	V_2/V_1, paging drum request probability
$q_{13} =$	V_3/V_1, file drum request probability
$q_{14} =$	V_4/V_1, file disk request probability

We now compute the branching probabilities from the equations in Table 9.7:

$$q_{10} = \frac{1}{631} = 0.0016, \qquad q_{12} = \frac{230}{631} = 0.3645$$

$$q_{13} = \frac{150}{631} = 0.2377, \qquad q_{14} = \frac{250}{631} = 0.3961$$

The y_k's are then calculated for $k = 2, 3, 4$:

$$y_2 = \frac{\mu_1}{\mu_2} q_{12} = 0.9529$$

$$y_3 = \frac{\mu_1}{\mu_3} q_{13} = 0.6214$$

$$y_4 = \frac{\mu_1}{\mu_4} q_{14} = 2.4696$$

Applying Buzen's algorithm described in Table 9.2, we construct Table 9.8. The last column yields the utilizations of the CPU for $N = 1, 2, 3$, obtained as

$$U_1(N) = \frac{G(N-1)}{G(N)}$$

The utilizations of the other resources for $N = 3$ can be obtained from Eq. (9.51):

$$U_2 = y_2 U_1 = 0.3338$$

$$U_3 = y_3 U_1 = 0.2177$$

$$U_4 = y_4 U_1 = 0.8653$$

TABLE 9.8 COMPUTING $U_1(N)$ BY BUZEN'S ALGORITHM (see Table 9.2)

N	$y_1 = 1$ Y_1	$y_2 = 0.9529$ Y_2	$y_3 = 0.6214$ Y_3	$y_4 = 2.4696$ $Y_4 = G(N)$	$U_1(N)$
0	1	1	1	1	0
1	1	1.9529	2.5743	5.0439	0.1982
2	1	2.8609	4.4605	16.9169	0.2981
3	1	3.7261	6.4979	48.2759	0.3504

The mean throughput rate is given by

$$X = q_{10}\mu_1 U_1 = 0.1179 \text{ programs/s}$$

and the mean turnaround time, by Little's formula,

$$R = \frac{N}{X} = 25.445 \text{ s}$$

In Fig. 9.30, we show the values of the input parameters for the program in the Appendix; the results of the analysis for N from 1 to 10 are reported in Fig. 9.31. The number of visits to the paging drum introduced as an input parameter in Fig. 9.30 is irrelevant, since the program calculates this number for each value of N according to the method described earlier. Note that, because of roundoff errors, the results of the program for $N = 3$ are slightly different from those just derived. Only the outputs for the initial input values are shown in Fig. 9.31; those for the other cases are reported in graphical form. Figure 9.32 shows U_i, X, and R for N from 1 through 10.

It is evident in Fig. 9.32a that the CPU and the file drum are always underutilized; the file disk is overutilized and is the major bottleneck for N from 1 through 6. For $N \geqslant 7$, the paging activity becomes heavier, and the bottleneck migrates from the file disk to the paging drum.

Figure 9.32b shows that, for $N = 10$, the throughput rate is lower than that which may be obtained for $N = 1$ (uniprogramming system). This major deterioration of the system's productivity is due to excessive paging; in other words, the system is in the *thrashing* region.

Modification 1 requires the replacement of the CPU with one 25 percent faster. The program in the Appendix is run again with a new value (0.875 MIPS) for parameter v_{CPU}. Figure 9.33 shows the values of the mean throughput rate corresponding to this case. Since the CPU was always underutilized before (see curve U_1 in Fig. 9.32a), an increase in its speed does not produce impressive results. As may be seen in Fig. 9.33, the most pronounced improvements are those in the thrashing region.

To evaluate the effects of modifications 2, 3, and 4, the model is to be solved again three times, modifying the values of R_{fdr} from 3600 to 4500 rpm, the value of R_{pdr} by the same amount, and the values of both R_{fdr} and R_{pdr}, respectively. The results are plotted in Fig. 9.34. As the file drum is always underutilized, change 2 will not cause any significant improvement. On the contrary, a faster paging drum improves the throughput rate for $N \geqslant 6$, since this drum is the bottleneck in the thrashing region. The effect of both changes simultaneously is practically the same as that due to change 3.

The tuning actions in modification 5 are intended to balance the utilizations of the file drum and of the file disk. The migration of some of the files from one device to the other causes 132 accesses per program to be transferred on the average from the file disk to the file drum. The model is solved again with new values of V_4 (from 250 to 118) and V_3 (from 150 to 282). The results are highly positive, especially in the $1 \leqslant N \leqslant 7$ range (see Fig. 9.35), as could have been predicted, since the file disk is the main bottleneck in that range. For $N \geqslant 8$, the throughput rate does not change, since the paging drum is the bottleneck there.

```
   CENTRAL SERVER MODEL

  FAST MODE?

NO
 TOTAL NUMBER OF SERVERS      0

4
 CPU SPEED(MIPS),MEAN PROG LENGTH(MI),DEPARTURES 0.0000 0.0000      0

0.7,2.1,1
 SERVER  2
 MEAN SEEK TIME(MS),REV SPEED(RMP)           0           0

0,3600
TRANSFER TIME(MICS/WD),BLOCK SIZE(WDS),VISITS          0           0           0

4,1024,150
 SERVER  3
 MEAN SEEK TIME(MS),REV SPEED(RMP)           0           0

0,3600
TRANSFER TIME(MICS/WD),BLOCK SIZE(WDS),VISITS          0           0           0

4,1024,150
 SERVER  4
 MEAN SEEK TIME(MS),REV SPEED(RMP)           0           0

11,2400
TRANSFER TIME(MICS/WD),BLOCK SIZE(WDS),VISITS          0           0           0

6,1024,250
 VIRTUAL MEMORY?

YES
 MAX DEGREE OF MULTIPROGRAMMING

10
 MEMORY SIZE(PAGE FRAMES)     0

300
 ANALYTIC(1) OR EMPIRICAL(2) LIFETIME CURVE?     0

2
 PROGRAM SIZE(PAGES), STEP     0     0

150,25
 MEAN INTERFAULT INTERVALS(MS)

1.5


6.0


12.0


13.0


14.0


14.5
```

Figure 9.30 Input parameters for the model in the initial configuration.

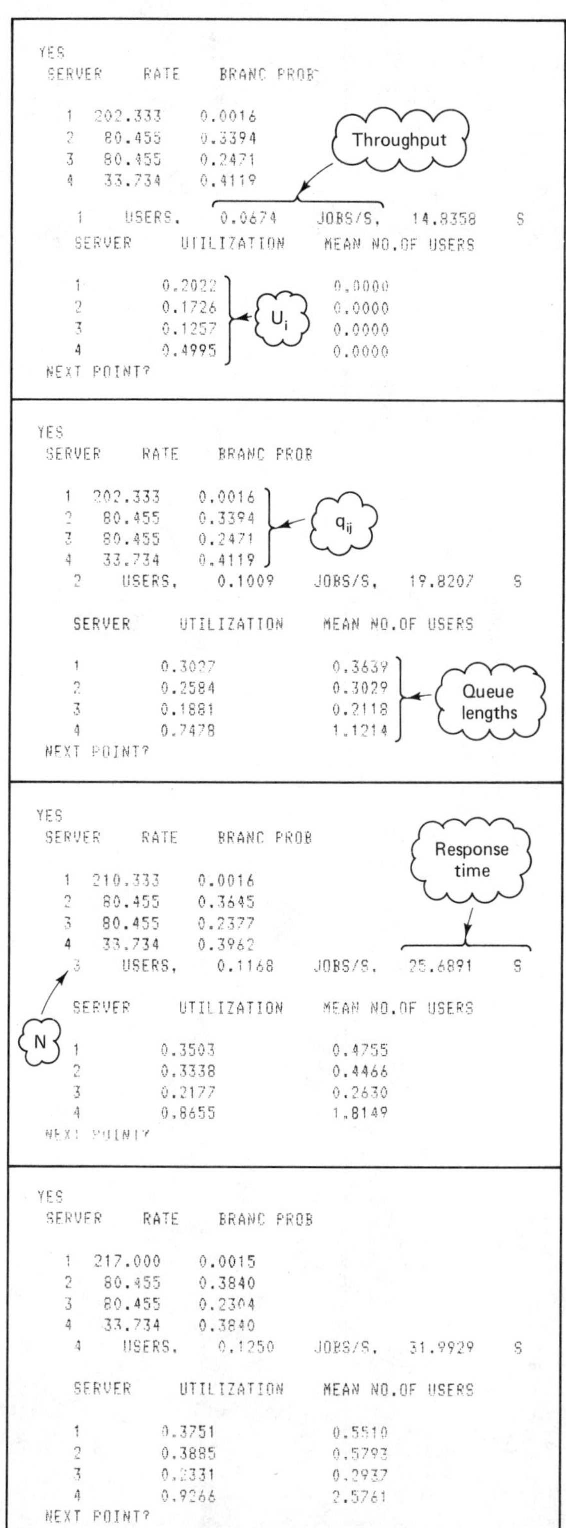

```
YES
SERVER     RATE     BRANC PROB

  1  202.333    0.0016
  2   80.455    0.3394
  3   80.455    0.2471
  4   33.734    0.4119

   1    USERS,     0.0674     JOBS/S,    14.8358     S
   SERVER      UTILIZATION     MEAN NO.OF USERS

   1           0.2022            0.0000
   2           0.1726            0.0000
   3           0.1257            0.0000
   4           0.4995            0.0000
NEXT POINT?

YES
SERVER     RATE     BRANC PROB

  1  202.333    0.0016
  2   80.455    0.3394
  3   80.455    0.2471
  4   33.734    0.4119
   2    USERS,     0.1009     JOBS/S,    19.8207     S

   SERVER      UTILIZATION     MEAN NO.OF USERS

   1           0.3027            0.3639
   2           0.2584            0.3029
   3           0.1881            0.2118
   4           0.7478            1.1214
NEXT POINT?

YES
SERVER     RATE     BRANC PROB

  1  210.333    0.0016
  2   80.455    0.3645
  3   80.455    0.2377
  4   33.734    0.3962
   3    USERS,     0.1168     JOBS/S,    25.6891     S

   SERVER      UTILIZATION     MEAN NO.OF USERS

   1           0.3503            0.4755
   2           0.3338            0.4466
   3           0.2177            0.2630
   4           0.8655            1.8149
NEXT POINT?

YES
SERVER     RATE     BRANC PROB

  1  217.000    0.0015
  2   80.455    0.3840
  3   80.455    0.2304
  4   33.734    0.3840
   4    USERS,     0.1250     JOBS/S,    31.9929     S

   SERVER      UTILIZATION     MEAN NO.OF USERS

   1           0.3751            0.5510
   2           0.3885            0.5793
   3           0.2331            0.2937
   4           0.9266            2.5761
NEXT POINT?
```


Figure 9.31 Output of the program in the Appendix for N from 1 to 10 (initial configuration).

```
YES
 SERVER    RATE    BRANC PROB

   1  252.667    0.0013
   2   80.455    0.4710
   3   80.455    0.1979
   4   33.734    0.3298
    5    USERS,    0.1255    JOBS/S.   39.8383    S

    SERVER     UTILIZATION    MEAN NO.OF USERS

    1          0.3765           0.5696
    2          0.5569           1.0673
    3          0.2340           0.2986
    4          0.9301           3.0645
 NEXT POINT?
```

```
YES
 SERVER    RATE    BRANC PROB

   1  300.333    0.0011
   2   80.455    0.5549
   3   80.455    0.1665
   4   33.734    0.2775
    6    USERS,    0.1206    JOBS/S,   49.7610    S

    SERVER     UTILIZATION    MEAN NO.OF USERS

    1          0.3617           0.5447
    2          0.7493           2.0373
    3          0.2248           0.2855
    4          0.8936           3.1325
 NEXT POINT?
```

```
YES
 SERVER    RATE    BRANC PROB

   1  352.667    0.0009
   2   80.455    0.6210
   3   80.455    0.1418
   4   33.734    0.2363
    7    USERS,    0.1098    JOBS/S,   63.7617    S

    SERVER     UTILIZATION    MEAN NO.OF USERS

    1          0.3294           0.4803
    2          0.8965           3.5550
    3          0.2047           0.2550
    4          0.8136           2.7097
 NEXT POINT?
```

```
YES
 SERVER    RATE    BRANC PROB

   1  406.667    0.0008
   2   80.455    0.6713
   3   80.455    0.1230
   4   33.734    0.2049
    8    USERS,    0.0953    JOBS/S.   83.9530    S

    SERVER     UTILIZATION    MEAN NO.OF USERS

    1          0.2859           0.3969
    2          0.9700           5.3520
    3          0.1777           0.2152
    4          0.7062           2.0359
 NEXT POINT?
```

Figure 9.31 *(continued)*

```
YES
 SERVER     RATE     BRANC PROB

   1  473.667    0.0007
   2   80.455    0.7178
   3   80.455    0.1056
   4   33.734    0.1759
    9     USERS,     0.0785    JOBS/S,  114.6599    S

    SERVER      UTILIZATION    MEAN NO.OF USERS

    1          0.2355           0.3074
    2          0.9951           7.1756
    3          0.1463           0.1713
    4          0.5817           1.3455
 NEXT POINT?
```

```
YES
 SERVER     RATE     BRANC PROB

   1  550.333    0.0006
   2   80.455    0.7571
   3   80.455    0.0909
   4   33.734    0.1514
   10     USERS,     0.0643    JOBS/S,  155.4457    S

    SERVER      UTILIZATION    MEAN NO.OF USERS

    1          0.1930           0.2391
    2          0.9995           8.7172
    3          0.1199           0.1363
    4          0.4768           0.9074
 MORE ANALYSIS?
```

Figure 9.31 *(continued)*

The effects of an increase in memory space for user programs from 300 to 400 frames can be evaluated by running the model again with a different value of m. The new throughput curve is plotted in Fig. 9.36. As could have been predicted, a memory space increase reduces the paging activity, thereby increasing the throughput rate when the paging drum is the bottleneck. For the same reason, this modification has no effect for $N \leqslant 5$, since the bottleneck there is the file disk.

In conclusion, the throughput rate of the system being evaluated is mainly limited by (1) the bottleneck in the file disk for $1 \leqslant N \leqslant 6$, and (2) the excessive increase of the paging activity for $N > 6$. All system modifications not directly connected to these two causes do not produce appreciable effects.

Suppose that the size of the main memory and the speeds of the CPU and of the file drum are increased so much that the influence of servers 1, 2, and 3 on the system's performance is negligible. Then the throughput rate will only be limited by the 250 file disk requests made by each program. In this case, the throughput of the system may be considered equal to that of the file disk; that is,

$$X = \frac{1}{250 \times 1/\mu_4} = 0.135 \text{ programs/s}$$

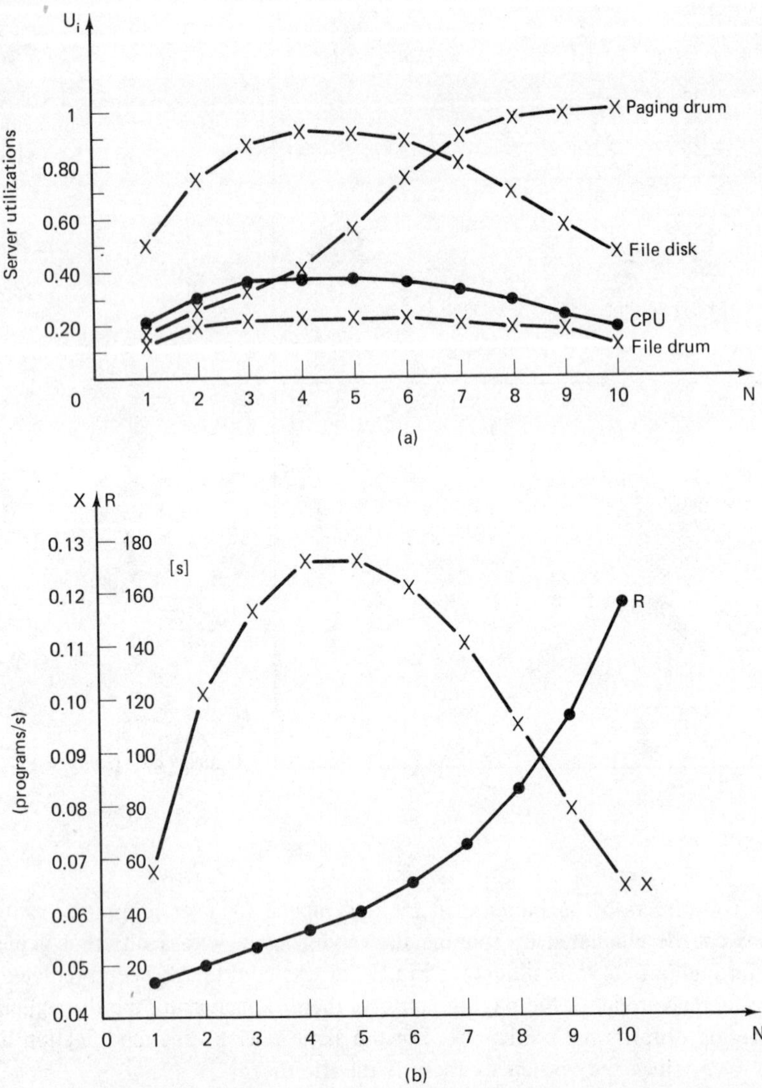

Figure 9.32 (a) Utilizations and (b) mean throughput rate and mean response time of the system in its initial configuration.

which is quite close to the maximum throughput rate for the given configuration ($X_{max} = 0.1255$ programs/s for $N = 5$; see Fig. 9.31). Hence, the first and most important step toward the improvement of system performance is to eliminate or reduce the bottleneck due to the file disk. Indeed, the tuning actions in modification 5 gave the best results among all the actions we have considered. Depending on the characteristics of the applications (file sizes, request patterns to the various disk drives, and so on), other tuning actions, for example, the reorganization of files on each disk to reduce seek times, or the addition of a new drive, may also be considered.

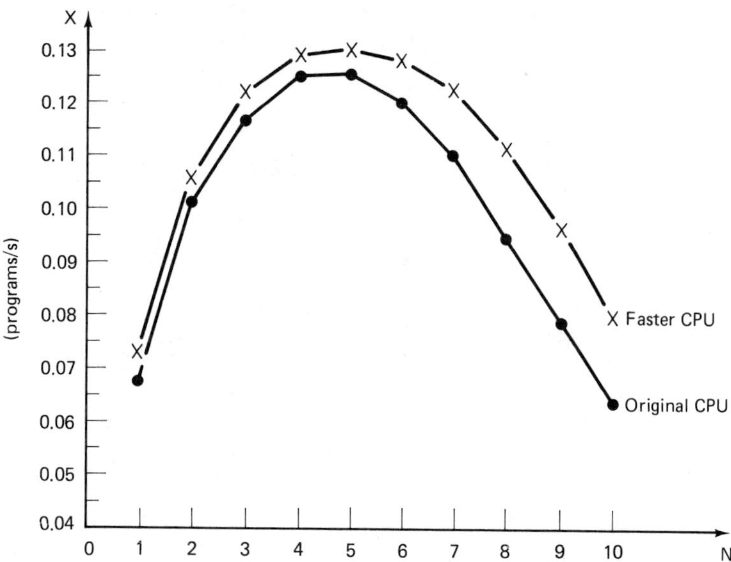

Figure 9.33 Effects on the throughput rate of replacing the CPU with a faster one.

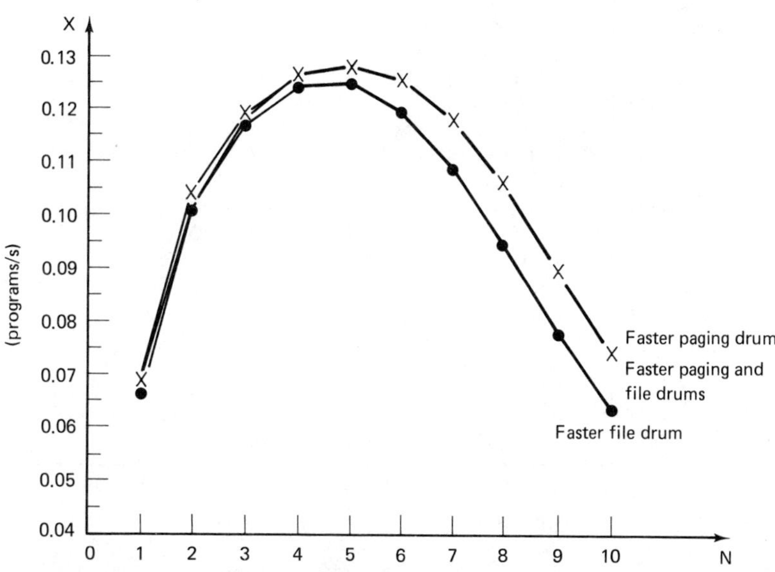

Figure 9.34 Effects on the throughput rate of the replacement of the file drum with a faster one; the paging drum with a faster one; both drums with faster ones. The revolution speed of the faster drums is 4500 rpm in all cases.

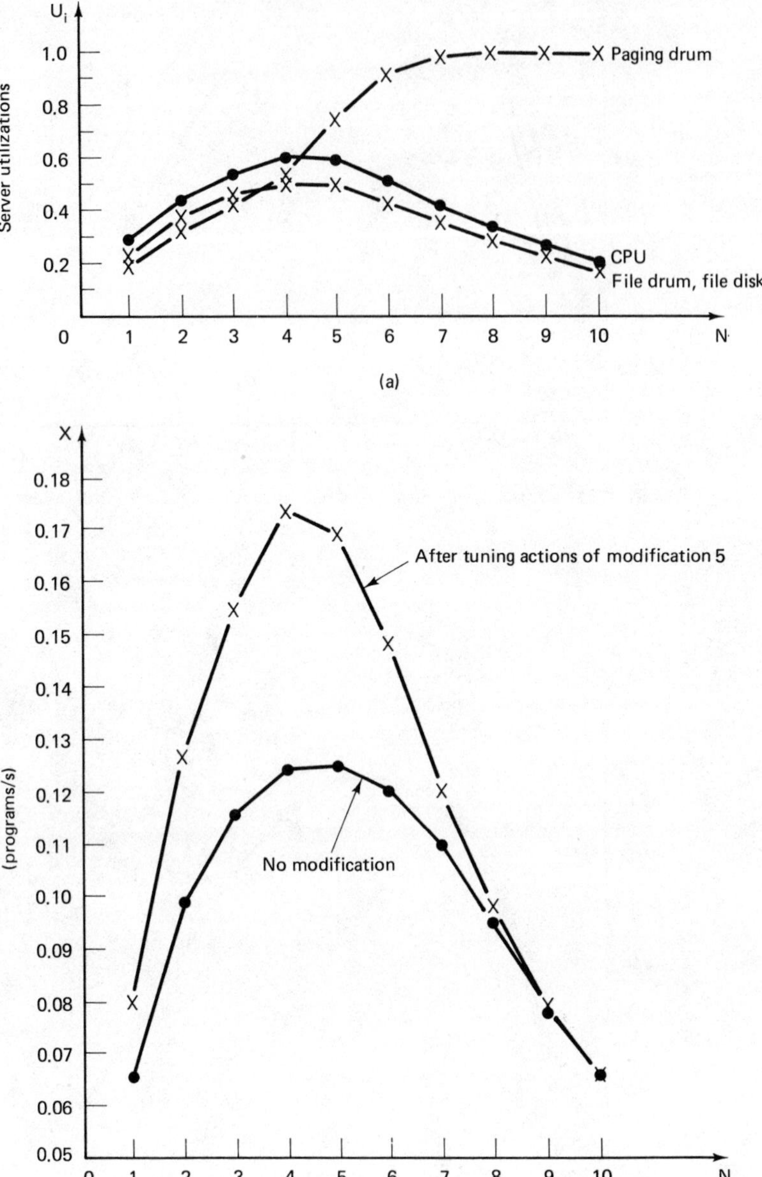

Figure 9.35 (a) Utilizations of resources and (b) throughput rate versus N after the tuning actions considered in modification 5.

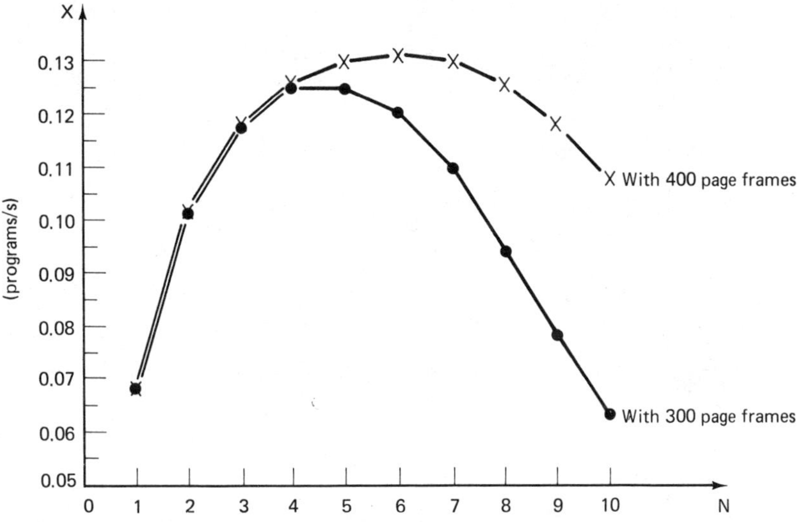

Figure 9.36 Effects of memory expansion from 300 to 400 page frames for user programs.

The deterioration of system performance for $N \geq 6$ is evidently due to the increasing paging activity. To improve performance in this situation, two therapies have been evaluated: (1) the speed of the paging drum has been increased (modification 3), and (2) the main memory space available to each program has been expanded (modification 6). Both have been found to be effective, but greater advantages have resulted from the expansion of main memory.

In summary, taking cost–benefit considerations into proper account, the following modifications, in decreasing order of priority, should be recommended:

1. Tuning actions (modification 5) intended to balance the loads of the file disk and of the file drum.
2. Main memory size expansion (modification 6).
3. Increase of paging drum performance (modification 3).

To predict the effects of all these changes together, the model has been run with the following parameter modifications: V_4 from 250 to 118, V_3 from 150 to 282, m from 300 to 400, and R_{pdr} from 3600 to 4500 rpm. The main results are plotted in Fig. 9.37. Comparing Fig. 9.37a with Fig. 9.32a, we see that, for $1 \leq N \leq 6$, the file disk is still the system's bottleneck, but U_4 has decreased. In the same range, the CPU is more utilized; hence the throughput rate is greater. For $N > 6$, the paging drum is still the bottleneck, but the utilizations of the other servers are higher, and the throughput rate is greater. The shaded area in Fig. 9.37b represents the throughput increase due to the

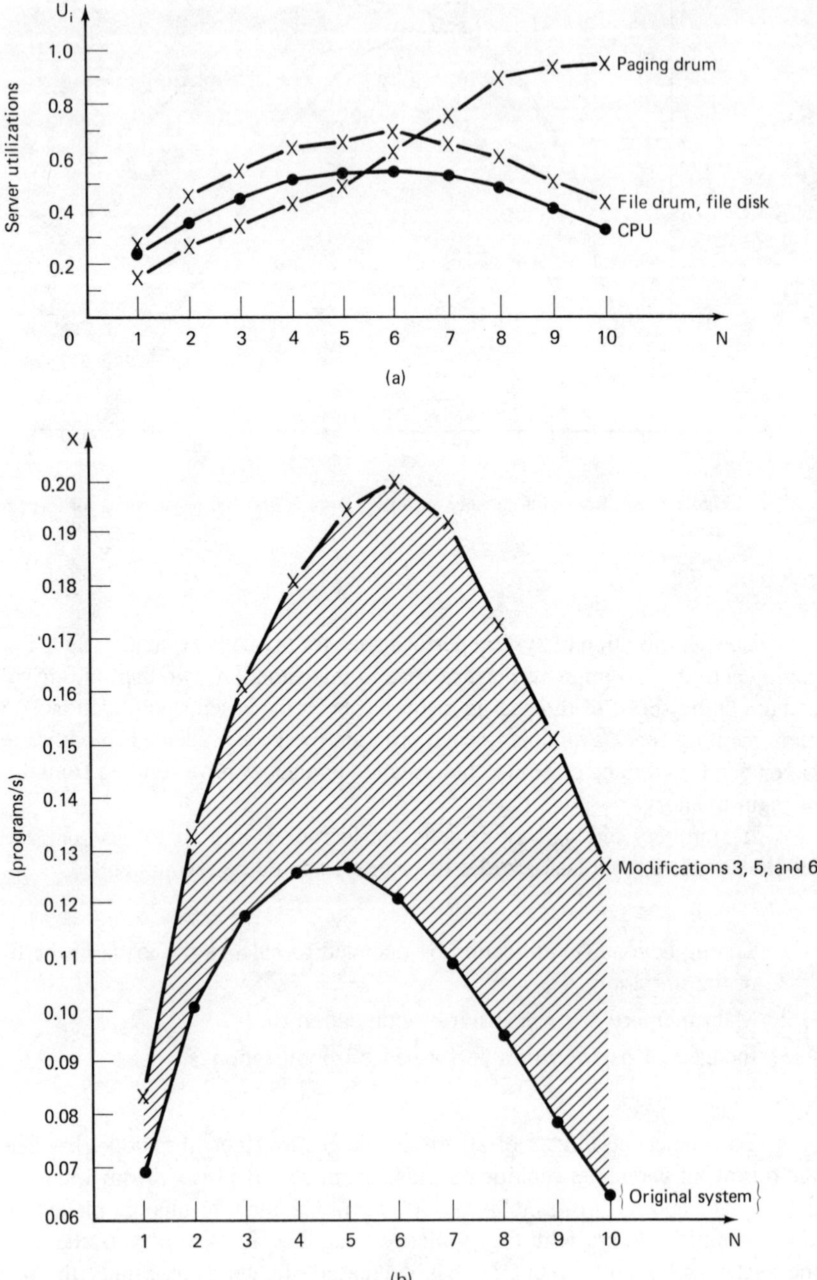

Figure 9.37 (a) Utilizations and (b) throughput rate versus N for the system with modifications 3, 5, and 6.

changes made to the system. The difference between the two maximum values, obtained for $N = 5$ and $N = 6$, respectively, is

$$\Delta X_{max} = \frac{0.2 - 0.1255}{0.1255} = 59.36\%$$

9.4.5 Case 9.7: Bottleneck Forecasting for a Real-time Application

In Case 2.3, we analyzed a real-time application and predicted the load it would cause when running on a system. In this case study, we predict the performance effects of its execution on the minicomputer system whose configuration is shown in Fig. 2.40. In particular, we want to obtain information on resource utilizations, bottlenecks, the mean response time for each command, and the system's residual capacity when all three video terminals are connected to the minicomputer. To determine whether the sizing of the system is adequate with respect to the performance requirements of the application, the most important performance indexes (mean program execution time, mean command response time, mean throughput rate) are to be computed.

We shall adopt the central server model shown in Fig. 9.38. Because of the characteristics of the real-time application and of its performance requirements, the *star* topology has to be adopted for the connection of the three terminals to the system; in other words, a separate line has to be dedicated to each terminal. The dedicated nature of each line and of each terminal control unit (TCU) has been approximately modeled in the central server model adopted by assigning a server to each of the three connected users (see Fig.9.38). More appropriate techniques to model these aspects will be described in Secs. 9.5 and 9.6.1. CPU requests may arrive at the CPU queue via one of two paths:

1. The "new program" exit.
2. The broken line in Fig. 9.38, that may be seen as representing a station with an infinite service rate, which may be requested by programs leaving the CPU station; this is the method we have chosen to model the scheduling requests mentioned in Section 2.6.2.

The data related to the load produced by each application program (see Fig. 2.48c) and to the system are displayed in Table 9.9. The system's memory size has not been considered in the model since it is assumed to be able to hold a large number of application programs, definitely larger than the number of terminals connected to the system in this study.

From the mean number of CPU intervals per program, that is, the mean number of CPU scheduling requests, we can derive the number V_7 of visits to station 7 (whose service rate is infinite):

$$V_7 = V_1 - V_2 - V_3 - V_{TCU} - 1 = 16.1 - 7 - 0.3 - 3.4 - 1 = 4.4$$

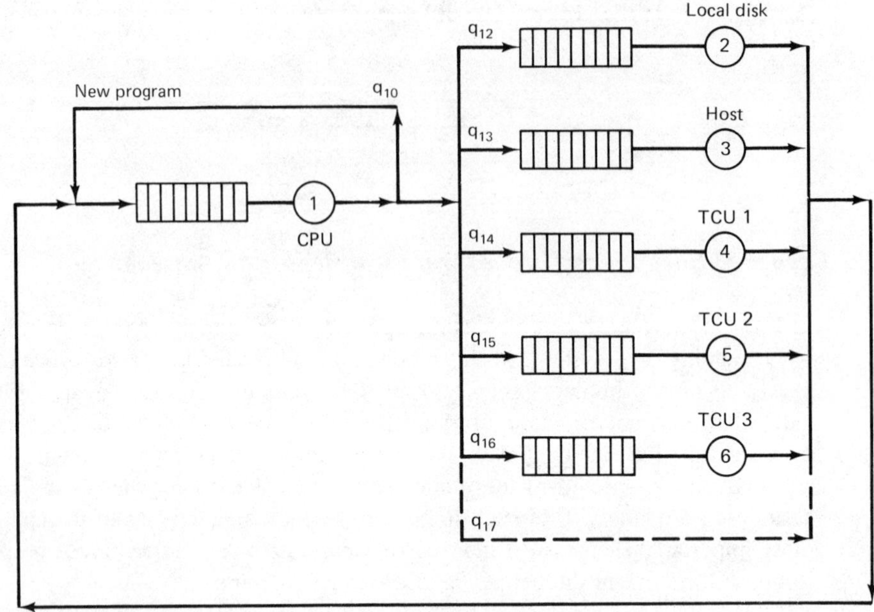

Figure 9.38 Central server model used for the system in Fig. 2.40.

Because of the approximations introduced, we consider $V_{TCU}/3$ as the mean number of requests made by each program to each of the three TCU's:

$$V_4 = V_5 = V_6 = 1.13$$

The relationships to be used to derive the model's parameters are reported in Table 9.10. The table is then constructed for the computation of $G(N)$ according to Buzen's algorithm (see Table 9.2). The y_k's ($k = 2, \ldots, 7$) are given by

TABLE 9.9 WORKLOAD AND SYSTEM DATA FOR THE MODEL IN FIG. 9.38

	Workload parameters (per application program)	
t_{CPU}	Mean global CPU time required	278.5ms
V_{TCU}	Mean number of terminal control unit requests	3.4
V_2	Mean number of disk accesses	7
V_3	Mean number of remote computer (Host) requests	0.3
V_1	Mean number of CPU intervals	16.1
	System parameters	
$1/\mu_2$	Mean disk service time	55ms
$1/\mu_3$	Mean Host service time	1s
$1/\mu_4 = 1/\mu_5 = 1/\mu_6$	Mean TCU service time	2s
$1/\mu_7$	Mean rescheduling service time	0s
N	Number of terminals (or of application programs)	3

TABLE 9.10 MODEL PARAMETER VALUES OBTAINED FROM THE DATA IN TABLE 9.9

Model parameters	
$\mu_1 = V_1/t_{CPU} = 57.8096\ s^{-1}$	Mean CPU rate
$\mu_2 = 1/(55 \times 10^{-3}) = 18.18\ s^{-1}$	Mean disk service rate
$\mu_3 = 1/1 = 1\ s^{-1}$	Mean Host service rate
$\mu_4 = \mu_5 = \mu_6 = 1/2 = 0.5\ s^{-1}$	Mean TCU service rate
$\mu_7 = 1/0 = \infty\ s^{-1}$	Mean "rescheduling" service rate
$q_{10} = 1/V_1 = 1/16.1 = 0.0621$	New program probability
$q_{12} = V_2/V_1 = 7/16.1 = 0.4348$	Disk request probability
$q_{13} = V_3/V_1 = 0.3/16.1 = 0.0186$	Host request probability
$q_{14} = q_{15} = q_{16} = V_{TCU}/(3 \times V_1) = 3.4/(3 \times 16.1) = 0.0704$	TCU request probability
$q_{17} = V_7/V_1 = 4.4/16.1 = 0.2733$	Rescheduling request probability
$N = 3$	Degree of multiprogramming

$$y_2 = \frac{\mu_1}{\mu_2} q_{12} = 1.382, \qquad y_3 = \frac{\mu_1}{\mu_3} q_{13} = 1.075$$

$$y_4 = \frac{\mu_1}{\mu_4} q_{14} = 8.139, \qquad y_5 = \frac{\mu_1}{\mu_5} q_{15} = 8.139$$

$$y_6 = \frac{\mu_1}{\mu_6} q_{16} = 8.139, \qquad y_7 = \frac{\mu_1}{\mu_7} q_{17} = 0$$

Table 9.11 shows the values of the Y functions. The column corresponding to station 7 has been omitted since it coincides with the preceding column, as $y_7 = 0$. The values of $U_1(N)$ are given by Eq. (9.50). The utilizations of the other stations for $N = 3$ are

TABLE 9.11 COMPUTATION OF $G(N)$ BY BUZEN'S ALGORITHM FOR LOAD-INDEPENDENT STATIONS

N	$y_1 = 1$ Y_1	$y_2 = 1.382$ Y_2	$y_3 = 1.075$ Y_3	$y_4 = 8.139$ Y_4	$y_5 = 8.139$ Y_5	$y_6 = 8.139$ Y_6	$U_1(N)$
0	1	1	1	1	1	1	0
1	1	2.3826	3.4578	11.5974	19.7370	27.8766	0.0358
2	1	4.2941	8.0122	102.4102	263.0612	489.9653	0.0569
3	1	6.9371	15.5523	849.1297	2990.3408	6978.4580	0.0702

$$U_2 = y_2U_1 = 0.097$$

$$U_3 = y_3U_1 = 0.075$$

$$U_4 = U_5 = U_6 = y_4U_1 = 0.571$$

The terminal control units, whose utilizations are 57.1 percent, are the most heavily loaded resources. They may therefore be considered as the system's bottlenecks. Each program makes on the average 3.4 terminal requests during its execution, and the mean service time (usually called *think time*), that is, the time for displaying the results, thinking, and typing in the input data, is equal to 2 s.

These resource utilization characteristics are typical of highly interactive real-time applications, where computational activities are limited (in our case the CPU is 7 percent utilized, the host 7.5 percent), and the terminal dialogue is intensive.

The mean throughput rate is given by Eq. (9.52):

$$X = q_{10}\mu_1U_1 = 0.252 \text{ programs/s}$$

and the mean program turnaround time is

$$R = \frac{N}{X} = 11.9 \text{ s}$$

The mean response time R_c to each interactive command is computed as

$$R_c = \frac{R - V_{\text{TCU}} \cdot 1/\mu_4}{V_{\text{TCU}}} = \frac{11.9 - 3.4 \times 2}{3.4} = 1.5 \text{ s}$$

All resources are far from saturation, and there is therefore a substantial residual capacity. Tuning actions like the transfer of the most often accessed parts of the host data base to the local disk or the increase in the number of disks are bound to yield only modest improvements because of the low utilizations of the local disk and of the host.

9.5 RESOURCES WITH LOAD-DEPENDENT BEHAVIOR

So far, we have introduced and analyzed queuing models with load-independent stations, that is, with stations whose mean service time does not depend on the number of requests present in the station. This assumption allows the algorithm for computing the normalizing constant G to be quite simple [see Eqs. (9.56) and Table 9.2], so that obtaining the mean values of all the most important indexes costs relatively few operations.

However, in many practical situations, the assumption of load independence is not very realistic. A typical example is that of the mean seek time of a disk: in high traffic conditions, this time may be smaller than when the traffic is low because of the arm scheduling algorithm, which tries to minimize arm movements. Another example is the arrival rate of processes at an interactive system, which decreases when the number of processes in the system grows beyond a certain threshold.

In stations with load-dependent behavior, the mean service time S_i cannot be expressed by a single value, but is to be assigned as a function of the number of requests in the station. The service time of a request, when in station i there are N_i requests, is often assumed to be an exponentially distributed random variable with mean

$$S_i(N_i) = \frac{1}{a_i(N_i)\mu_i} \tag{9.66}$$

where $a_i(N_i)$ is a function that can take any positive value and is called *capacity function*. Clearly, if station i has a load-independent behavior, $a_i(N_i) = 1$ for all N_i.

To simplify our exposition in this section, as was done in Sec. 9.4, only queuing networks with exponential service times, FCFS scheduling disciplines, and a single class of programs to be processed are considered. The *equilibrium state probability* distribution of a network with k stations has in this case the form

$$p(\mathbf{N}) = \frac{1}{G(N)} \frac{y_1^{N_1}}{A_1(N_1)} \frac{y_2^{N_2}}{A_2(N_2)} \cdots \frac{y_k^{N_k}}{A_k(N_k)} \tag{9.67}$$

where the y_i's are the quantities defined in Sec. 9.4, which are functions of the network's topology and parameters (for example, in a central server model, $y_1 = 1$, $y_i = \mu_1 q_{1i}/\mu_i$) and the $A_i(N_i)$'s are auxiliary functions that may be obtained from the $a_i(N_i)$'s as follows:

$$A_i(N_i) = a_i(1)a_i(2) \cdots a_i(N_i) \tag{9.68}$$

Note that $A_i(0) = 1$. The normalizing constant $G(N)$ is given by

$$G(N) = \sum_{\text{all } \mathbf{N}} \frac{y_1^{N_1}}{A_1(N_1)} \frac{y_2^{N_2}}{A_2(N_2)} \cdots \frac{y_k^{N_k}}{A_k(N_k)} \tag{9.69}$$

Even when the network includes load-dependent stations, the main performance indexes can be derived from the knowledge of $G(N)$ only. The computation of $G(N)$ through Eq. (9.69) is often impossible because of the large number of operations it requires and of the related numerical instability problems. An effective algorithm for the computation of $G(N)$ even in this case has been proposed by Buzen [BU73a]. The auxiliary function $Y_i(n)$ [see Eq. (9.56)] can be recursively computed as follows:

$$\begin{aligned} Y_i(0) &= 1 \\ Y_1(n) &= \frac{y_1^n}{A_1(n)} \\ Y_i(n) &= \sum_{j=0}^{n} \frac{y_i^j}{A_i(j)} Y_{i-1}(n-j) \qquad (n = 1, \ldots, N;\ i = 2, \ldots, k) \end{aligned} \tag{9.70}$$

One can easily see that

$$Y_k(n) = G(n) \qquad (n = 1, \ldots, N)$$

This algorithm can be implemented with only one $(N + 1)$-element vector, since the matrix in Table 9.12 may be constructed column by column, and each column may replace the previous one.

Having computed the $G(N)$, we can then obtain the values of the performance indexes of interest. If the network is a central server model with N programs in execution, the throughput rate of station i is

$$X_i(N) = \mu_1 U_1 q_{1i} = \mu_1 \frac{G(N - 1)}{G(N)} q_{1i} \tag{9.71}$$

TABLE 9.12 SCHEMATIC REPRESENTATION OF BUZEN'S ALGORITHM FOR COMPUTING $G(N)$ WHEN STATIONS HAVE LOAD-DEPENDENT BEHAVIOR

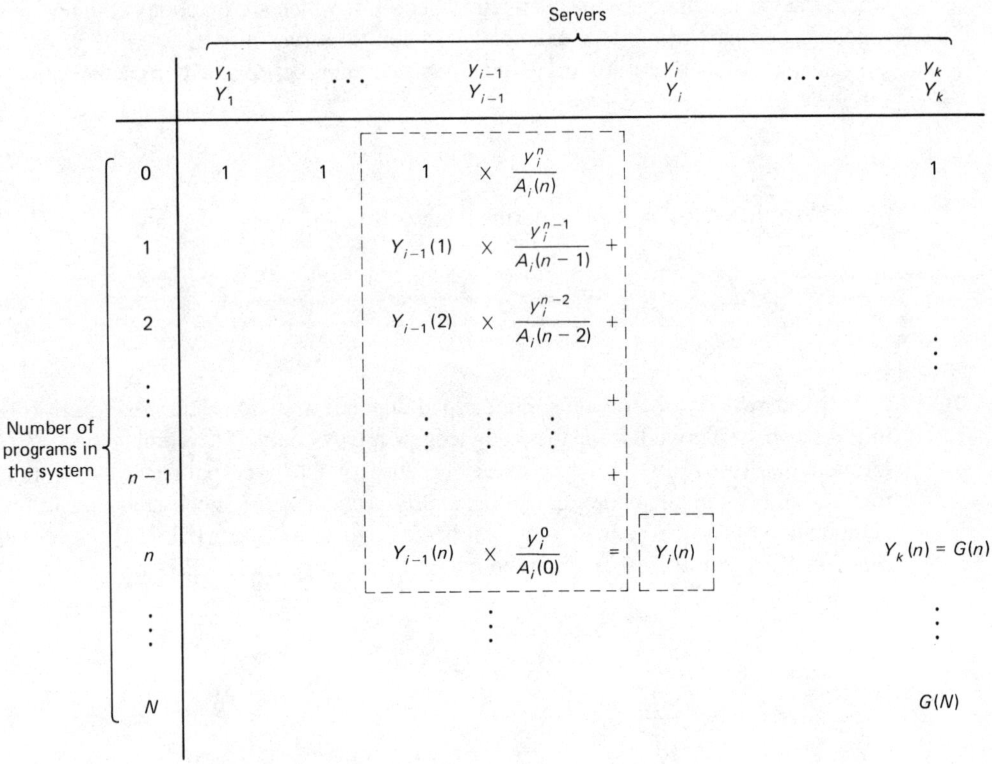

Number of programs in the system	Servers: y_1 Y_1	. . .	y_{i-1} Y_{i-1}				y_i Y_i	. . .	y_k Y_k
0	1	1	1	×	$\frac{y_i^n}{A_i(n)}$				1
1			$Y_{i-1}(1)$	×	$\frac{y_i^{n-1}}{A_i(n-1)}$	+			
2			$Y_{i-1}(2)$	×	$\frac{y_i^{n-2}}{A_i(n-2)}$	+			⋮
⋮			⋮	⋮	⋮	+			
$n - 1$						+			
n			$Y_{i-1}(n)$	×	$\frac{y_i^0}{A_i(0)}$	=	$Y_i(n)$		$Y_k(n) = G(n)$
⋮			⋮						⋮
N									$G(N)$

Note that Eq. (9.71) is valid also for load-independent stations. With simple algebraic transformations, since $q_{1i} = V_i/V_1$ and $q_{10} = 1/V_1$, from Eqs. (9.71) and (9.52) we obtain the forced flow law again [see Eq. (9.12)]:

$$X_i(N) = X(N)V_i$$

The utilization of a load-dependent server is easily computable when it is the kth server in Table 9.12, since we have

$$U_k(N) = 1 - \frac{Y_{k-1}(N)}{G(N)} \tag{9.72}$$

Thus, one way to obtain the utilization of a server is to renumber the stations so that it will appear as the server in the kth station, and then construct the matrix in Table 9.12. An algorithm that avoids these permutations is described in [BR80].

The probability that in the kth station there are h requests, that is, the *marginal distribution of requests,* is

$$p\,(N_k = h) = \frac{y_k^h}{A_k(h)} \frac{Y_{k-1}(N-h)}{G(N)} \tag{9.73}$$

If the station whose marginal distribution of requests is to be determined is not the last (the kth), one can apply the same approach described for utilizations. The mean number of requests in the kth station is then obtained from Eq. (9.73):

$$N_k = \sum_{n=1}^{N} np(N_k = n) = \frac{1}{G(N)} \sum_{n=1}^{N} n \frac{y_k^n}{A_k(n)} Y_{k-1}(N-n) \tag{9.74}$$

The mean response time of the kth station is given by Little's formula (9.31):

$$R_k(N) = \frac{N_k(N)}{X_k(N)} \tag{9.75}$$

Algorithms applicable to models similar to that dealt with here, even with multiple classes of programs, can be found in [BR80] and [SA81]. Usually, the models to be analyzed contain both load-dependent and load-independent stations, and the algorithms for computing the normalizing constant studied in Sec. 9.4 and in this section are to be applied simultaneously. Depending on the type of the ith station, the corresponding column Y_i will be calculated using either Eq. (9.56) or (9.70). Since the values of utilizations and marginal probabilities are easy to compute for a load-dependent station if that station is the last one, it is convenient to assign the first numbers to load-independent stations and the last ones to load-dependent stations.

Besides allowing more realistic models to be constructed, load-dependent servers are essential in the application of the flow-equivalent approximation technique, as will be seen in Sec. 9.6.

9.5.1 Case 9.8: System with a Load-dependent Resource

The system being considered here is of type MBRS. Its main components are:

1. A CPU, characterized by a mean uninterrupted CPU time $1/\mu_1 = 10$ ms.
2. A fixed-head disk, with mean service time $1/\mu_2 = 25$ ms.
3. A movable-arm disk, whose service time is load dependent; when $N \leqslant 2$, $1/\mu_3$ is 150 ms; when $N \geqslant 3$, $1/\mu_3$ is 100 ms.

A central server model is used (see Fig. 9.39). The queues at all stations are managed according to the FCFS discipline, and service times are assumed to be exponentially distributed. The mean numbers of visits of each program to the three stations are $V_1 = 10$, $V_2 = 8$, and $V_3 = 1$.

The following two problems are to be solved for this system:

9.18. Compute the values of the most common performance indexes for N from 1 through 4.

9.19. Determine the influence on the system's throughput rate and response time of replacing the load-dependent disk with a load-independent one having a mean service time of 100 ms.

Problem 9.18

The values of the branching probabilities are

$$q_{10} = \frac{1}{V_1} = 0.1$$

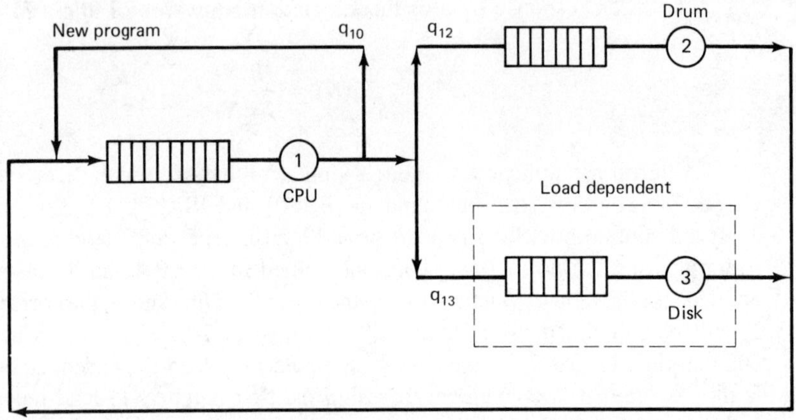

Figure 9.39 Central server model with mixed (load-independent and load-dependent) stations.

$$q_{12} = \frac{V_2}{V_1} = 0.8$$

$$q_{13} = \frac{V_3}{V_1} = 0.1$$

For station 3, which has load-dependent behavior, we have

$$S_3(N) = \frac{1}{\mu_3 a_3(N)} = \begin{cases} 150 \text{ ms}, & \text{for } N \leqslant 2 \\ 100 \text{ ms}, & \text{for } N \geqslant 3 \end{cases}$$

Taking $a_3(1) = 1$ as the reference value, $a_3(N)$ is obtained from Eq. (9.66):

$$a_3(N) = \begin{cases} 1, & \text{for } N \leqslant 2 \\ 1.5, & \text{for } N \geqslant 3 \end{cases}$$

The values of $A_3(N)$ resulting from Eq. (9.68) for N from 1 through 4 are $A_3(1) = 1$, $A_3(2) = 1$, $A_3(3) = 1.5$, and $A_3(4) = 2.25$. Thus, the y_i's turn out to be

$$y_1 = 1$$

$$y_2 = \frac{\mu_1}{\mu_2} q_{12} = \frac{25}{10} \times 0.8 = 2$$

$$y_3 = \frac{\mu_1}{\mu_3} q_{13} = \frac{150}{10} \times 0.1 = 1.5$$

We can now compute the values of the auxiliary functions $Y_i(N)$ by applying to stations 1 and 2 the algorithm described in Table 9.2, and to station 3 the algorithm illustrated in Table 9.12. The computation of $G(N)$ is shown in Table 9.13.

The utilization of the CPU for $N = 1, \ldots, 4$ is given by Eq. (9.50):

$$U_1(1) = \frac{1}{4.5} = 0.222, \qquad U_1(2) = \frac{4.5}{13.75} = 0.327$$

$$U_1(3) = 0.398, \qquad U_1(4) = 0.441$$

and the utilization of the drum is

$$U_2(1) = y_2 U_1(1) = 0.444, \qquad U_2(2) = 0.654$$

$$U_2(3) = 0.797, \qquad U_2(4) = 0.882$$

Since the disk is load-dependent and is the last station considered by the algorithm in Table 9.13, its utilization is given by Eq. (9.72):

$$U_3(1) = 1 - \frac{3}{4.5} = 0.333, \qquad U_3(2) = 1 - \frac{7}{13.75} = 0.49$$

$$U_3(3) = 0.565, \qquad U_3(4) = 0.604$$

TABLE 9.13 COMPUTATION OF THE NORMALIZING CONSTANT G (N) FOR CASE 9.8

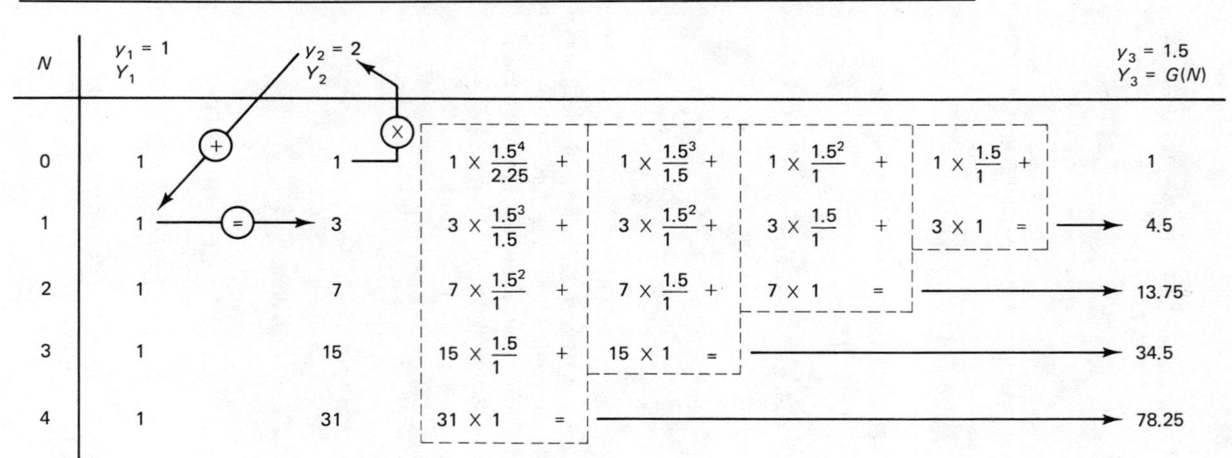

N	$y_1 = 1$ Y_1	$y_2 = 2$ Y_2					$y_3 = 1.5$ $Y_3 = G(N)$
0	1	1	$1 \times \frac{1.5^4}{2.25}$ +	$1 \times \frac{1.5^3}{1.5}$ +	$1 \times \frac{1.5^2}{1}$ +	$1 \times \frac{1.5}{1}$ +	1
1	1	3	$3 \times \frac{1.5^3}{1.5}$ +	$3 \times \frac{1.5^2}{1}$ +	$3 \times \frac{1.5}{1}$ +	3×1 =	4.5
2	1	7	$7 \times \frac{1.5^2}{1}$ +	$7 \times \frac{1.5}{1}$ +	7×1 =		13.75
3	1	15	$15 \times \frac{1.5}{1}$ +	15×1 =			34.5
4	1	31	31×1 =				78.25

The throughput rate X is obtained from Eq. (9.71):

$$X(N) = \mu_1 q_{10} U_1(N)$$

Hence $X(1) = 2.22$ programs/s, $X(2) = 3.27$ programs/s, $X(3) = 3.98$ programs/s, and $X(4) = 4.41$ programs/s.

The mean queue lengths at servers 1 and 2, which are load independent, are computed from the equation

$$N_i(N) = \sum_{n=1}^{N} y_i^n \frac{G(N - n)}{G(N)}$$

which for the CPU yields $N_1(1) = 0.222$, $N_1(2) = 0.4$, $N_1(3) = 0.558$, and $N_1(4) = 0.687$, and for the drum $N_2(1) = 0.444$, $N_2(2) = 0.945$, $N_2(3) = 1.55$, and $N_2(4) = 2.25$.

To calculate the mean queue lengths at server 3, we apply Eq. (9.74), which yields $N_3(1) = 0.333$, $N_3(2) = 0.654$, $N_3(3) = 0.891$, and $N_3(4) = 1.063$.

Note that the correctness of these calculations may be verified by seeing whether the sum of the mean lengths at the three servers for each value of N equals N; that is,

$$\sum_{i=1}^{3} N_i(N) = N$$

The results reported here satisfy this equality for all N from 1 to 4.

The mean response time of the system may be obtained by Little's formula:

$$R(1) = \frac{N}{X(1)} = \frac{1}{2.22} = 0.45 \text{ s}, \qquad R(2) = \frac{N}{X(2)} = 0.611 \text{ s}$$

$$R(3) = \frac{N}{X(3)} = 0.753 \text{ s}, \qquad R(4) = \frac{N}{X(4)} = 0.907 \text{ s}$$

Problem 9.19

In this case, computing $G(N)$ is easier, since all stations are load independent, and the only algorithm to be used is the one in Table 9.2. The matrix and the resulting values of U_1 are shown in Table 9.14. Note that the values of y_1 and y_2 are those of Problem 9.18, whereas y_3 has a new value:

$$y_3 = \frac{\mu_1}{\mu_3} q_{13} = 1$$

The utilizations of servers 2 and 3 are the following:

$$U_2(1) = y_2 U_1(1) = 0.5, \qquad U_2(2) = 0.726,$$

$$U_2(3) = 0.846, \qquad U_2(4) = 0.912$$

$$U_3(1) = y_3 U_1(1) = 0.25, \qquad U_3(2) = 0.363,$$

$$U_3(3) = 0.423, \qquad U_3(4) = 0.456$$

TABLE 9.14 COMPUTATION OF $G(N)$ AND $U_1(N)$ FOR LOAD-INDEPENDENT STATIONS (ALGORITHM IN TABLE 9.2)

N	$y_1 = 1$ Y_1	$y_2 = 2$ Y_2	$y_3 = 1$ $Y_3 = G(N)$	U_1
0	1	1	1	0
1	1	3	4	0.25
2	1	7	11	0.363
3	1	15	26	0.423
4	1	31	57	0.456

Thus, the utilization of the load-independent disk introduced in this problem is lower than that of the previous disk, which was load dependent; conversely, drum utilization is higher, and the drum remains the system's bottleneck. This is not only shown by the value of U_2, which is the highest of all U's, but also by the mean queue lengths $N_2(N)$, which are the greatest.

The system's throughput rate is $X(1) = \mu_1 q_{10} U_1 = 2.5$ programs/s, $X(2) = 3.63$ programs/s, $X(3) = 4.23$ programs/s, $X(4) = 4.56$ programs/s, and the mean response time is

$$R(1) = \frac{N}{X(1)} = 0.4 \text{ s}, \qquad R(2) = 0.55 \text{ s}, \qquad R(3) = 0.709 \text{ s}, \qquad R(4) = 0.877 \text{ s}$$

The maximum increase in the system's throughput rate is 12.5 percent, corresponding to $N = 1$. For the same value of N we obtain the maximum decrease (-11.1 percent) of response time. Figure 9.40 shows the throughput rate and response time curves corresponding to the two cases considered here and in Problem 9.18.

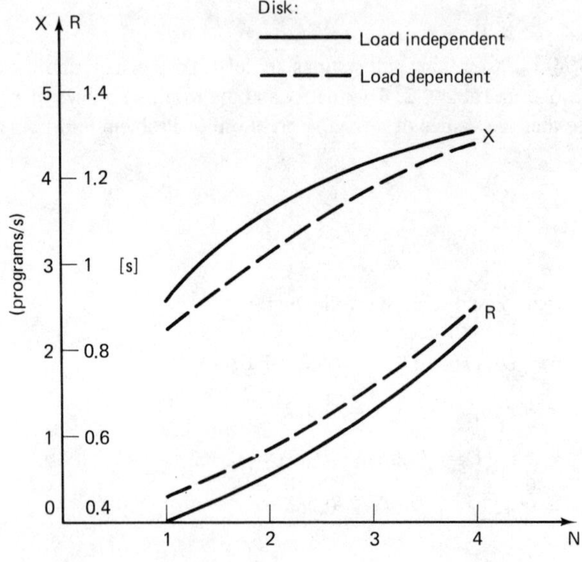

Figure 9.40 Throughput rate X and mean response time R versus N with the two types of disk considered in Case 9.8.

9.6 APPROXIMATE SOLUTIONS BY FLOW-EQUIVALENT AGGREGATION

In Sec. 9.2, we introduced the concept of hierarchical structure for models. The application of the hierarchical approach to performance analysis consists of identifying, according to suitable criteria, submodels that can be studied in isolation and replaced by simpler "equivalent" components; these components produce, exactly or approximately, the same effect as the submodels they replace on the flow of information to be processed. In a queuing network model, this amounts to identifying subnetworks that can be replaced by a *flow-equivalent station,* that is, a station whose mean throughput rate equals that of the replaced subnetwork. This aggregation procedure can then be repeated on the simpler model, until a model whose solution is known, or easy to compute, is obtained.

If the queuing network being considered has a product form solution, then this hierarchical procedure yields an exact solution for the whole network. Otherwise, an approximate solution is obtained, affected by errors that depend on the amount of interaction existing among the subnetworks being considered. The need for approximation techniques is due to the fact that often the more accurate system models do not have a product form solution, and, even when this exists, to their being computationally less expensive than the exact algorithms which compute that solution [BA79], [BA80], [RE80].

Examples of models that require an approximate solution technique are those in which one or more servers do not have an exponential distribution of service times and an FCFS service discipline, or those in which a program during its execution may simultaneously need more than one resource, or those in which the length of a queue is limited (thereby causing requests occasionally to be blocked in other stations).

The case of simultaneous resource possession is particularly interesting since it occurs whenever one wants to consider resources that do not have service times, but nevertheless have queues associated to them. A typical example of these resources, which are called *passive resources,* is the main memory. The time one of its partitions is occupied by a program depends on the speed and congestion of the other resources that are to process the program, and not on its own characteristics. However, when all partitions are occupied, the memory blocks the execution of new programs, which therefore queue up at its input. The memory is thus capable of limiting the number of programs in execution. Other examples of passive resources are buffer pools, busses, and switches. The subnetwork to be replaced is studied in isolation by connecting its output to its input (we are obviously assuming that it is a single-input, single-output subnetwork). We then calculate the mean throughput rate through this connection for all values of N to be considered. The load-dependent mean service rate of the single flow-equivalent server is set equal to the mean throughput rate computed as just described.

Example 9.4

Consider the central server model shown in Fig. 9.41a. The servers are load independent, and the values of the parameters are $q_{12} = 0.8$, $q_{13} = 0.2$, $S_1 = 1/\mu_1 = 10$ ms, $S_2 = 1/\mu_2 = 25$ ms, and $S_3 = 1/\mu_3 = 100$ ms. For this network, we want to determine how the utilization of the CPU varies with N, for N from 1 to 4. The queues at all servers are FCFS, and the service times are exponentially distributed. The subnetwork composed of stations 2 and 3 connected in parallel is isolated from the rest of the network; connecting its output to its input as shown in Fig. 9.41b, we can compute the program flow rate through this

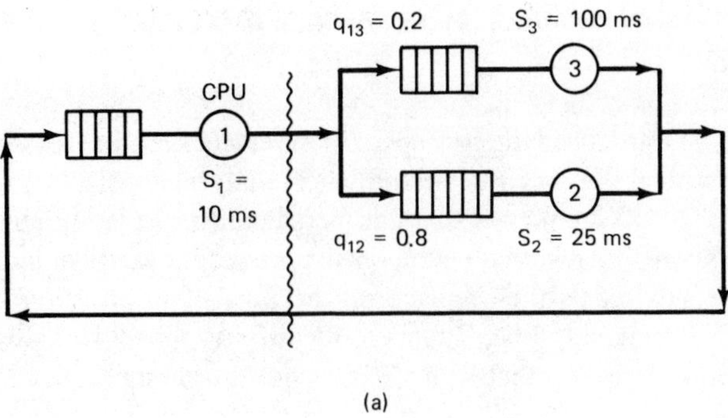

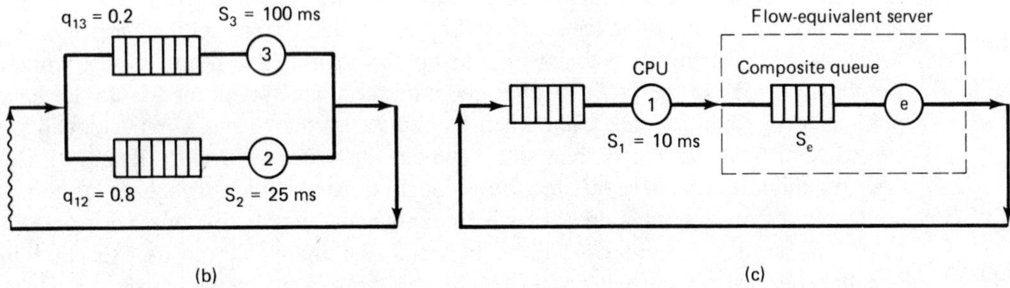

Figure 9.41 (a) Application of the flow-equivalent approximation to a central server model: the subnetwork in (b) is replaced by a flow-equivalent station shown in (c).

connection. Since the network's topology is very simple, the performance indexes can be calculated by the general expressions of the product form solution and of the normalizing constant or by the algorithm described in Table 9.2. We shall apply both methods to explain how they work.

The expressions (9.57) and (9.58) for calculating the product form solution and the normalizing constant for a network like that in Fig. 9.41b are

$$p(j, N-j) = \frac{1}{G(N)} \left(\frac{q_{13}}{\mu_3} \frac{\mu_2}{q_{12}} \right)^{N-j}$$

and

$$G(N) = \sum_{j=0}^{N} \left(\frac{q_{13}}{\mu_3} \frac{\mu_2}{q_{12}} \right)^{N-j}$$

Substituting the values in our example, we have

$$G'(1) = \left(\frac{0.2 \times 0.1}{0.8 \times 0.025} \right)^1 + \left(\frac{0.2 \times 0.1}{0.8 \times 0.025} \right)^0 = 1 + 1 = 2$$

$G'(2) = 1^2 + G'(1) = 3, \quad G'(3) = 1^3 + G'(2) = 4, \quad G'(4) = 1^4 + G'(3) = 5$

The probabilities that server 2 is idle are

$$p'(0, 1) = \frac{1}{G'(1)} 1 = 0.5$$

$$p'(0, 2) = \frac{1}{G'(2)} 1^2 = 0.333$$

$$p'(0, 3) = \frac{1}{G'(3)} 1^3 = 0.25$$

$$p'(0, 4) = \frac{1}{G'(4)} 1^4 = 0.2$$

Thus the utilizations of server 2 are given by

$$U_2'(1) = 1 - p'(0, 1) = 0.5$$

$$U_2'(2) = 1 - p'(0, 2) = 0.666$$

$$U_2'(3) = 1 - p'(0, 3) = 0.75$$

$$U_2'(4) = 1 - p'(0, 4) = 0.8$$

The throughput rate of the subnetwork is obtained from the flow-balance equation:

$$X_e'(N) = \frac{\mu_2 U_2'(N)}{q_{12}}$$

and in our case we have

$$X_e'(1) = \frac{0.5}{0.025 \times 0.8} = 25 \text{ requests/s}, \qquad X_e'(2) = 33.33 \text{ requests/s}$$

$$X_e'(3) = 37.5 \text{ requests/s}, \qquad X_e'(4) = 40 \text{ requests/s}$$

If, on the other hand, we apply the algorithm described in Table 9.2, we must compute the y_i's, which for the network in Fig. 9.41b are

$$y_2' = 1, \qquad y_3' = \frac{q_{13}/\mu_3}{q_{12}/\mu_2} = 1$$

Table 9.15 shows the matrix generated by this algorithm and the values of $U_2'(N)$, $U_3'(N)$, and $p'(0, N)$. As can be easily seen, these values coincide with those computed here.

The throughput rate $X_e'(N)$ of the subnetwork is then considered as the mean service rate of the equivalent station, which is therefore load dependent. As the reference value μ_e we take $X_e'(1)$. Thus, $\mu_e = 25$ requests/s. The values of the capacity function $a_e(N)$ are computed from Eq. (9.66):

$$a_e(1) = \frac{X_e'(1)}{\mu_e} = 1, \qquad a_e(2) = \frac{X_e'(2)}{\mu_e} = 1.333,$$

$$a_e(3) = \frac{X_e'(3)}{\mu_e} = 1.5, \qquad a_e(4) = \frac{X_e'(4)}{\mu_e} = 1.6$$

TABLE 9.15 APPLICATION OF BUZEN'S ALGORITHM FOR LOAD-INDEPENDENT STATIONS TO THE NETWORK SHOWN IN FIG. 9.41(b)

N	$y_2' = 1$ Y_2	$y_3' = 1$ Y_3	$U_2'(N) = G(N-1)/G(N)$	$U_3'(N) = y_3'U_2'(N)$	$p'(0, N)$ [Eq.(9.54)]
0	1	1	0	0	0
1	1	2	0.5	0.5	0.5
2	1	3	0.6	0.6	0.3
3	1	4	0.75	0.75	0.25
4	1	5	0.8	0.8	0.2

The auxiliary function $A_e(N)$ is given by

$$A_e(1) = 1, \qquad A_e(2) = 1.333, \qquad A_e(3) = 1.999, \qquad A_e(4) = 3.199$$

and, by definition, we have $A_e(0) = 1$. The resulting network is shown in Fig. 9.41c; it consists of the station representing the CPU, which has load-independent behavior, and of the flow-equivalent station in series, which has load-dependent mean service times.

The equilibrium distribution of the requests can be easily obtained from Eqs. (9.59) and (9.67):

$$P(j, N - j) = \frac{1}{G(N)} \left(\frac{\mu_1}{\mu_e}\right)^{N-j} \frac{1}{A_e(N - j)}$$

with

$$G(N) = \sum_{j=0}^{N} \left(\frac{\mu_1}{\mu_e}\right)^{N-j} \frac{1}{A_e(N - j)}$$

With our values, we have

$$G(1) = \left(\frac{1}{0.01 \times 25}\right)^1 \frac{1}{A_e(1)} + 1 = 5$$

$$G(2) = \frac{4^2}{1.333} + G(1) = 17$$

$$G(3) = \frac{4^3}{1.999} + G(2) = 49.002$$

$$G(4) = \frac{4^4}{3.199} + G(3) = 129.004$$

and the utilizations of the CPU are

$$U_1(1) = 1 - p(0, 1) = 1 - \frac{1}{G(1)} \left(\frac{\mu_1}{\mu_e}\right) \frac{1}{A_e(1)} = 0.2$$

$$U_1(2) = 1 - p(0, 2) = 0.2941$$

$$U_1(3) = 1 - p(0, 3) = 0.3469$$

$$U_1(4) = 1 - p(0, 4) = 0.3799$$

If we apply to the network in Fig. 9.41c Buzen's algorithm for load-independent and load-dependent servers, we obtain the values reported in Table 9.16, which coincide with those computed here.

We now check the correctness of the flow-equivalent decomposition and aggregation approach by comparing its results with those obtained by solving the whole network in Fig. 9.41a directly. The y_i's required for Buzen's algorithm are

$$y_1 = 1, \qquad y_2 = \frac{\mu_1 q_{12}}{\mu_2} = 2, \qquad y_3 = \frac{\mu_1 q_{13}}{\mu_3} = 2$$

The matrix and the results produced by the algorithm are reported in Table 9.17. The last column in this table shows that the decomposition and aggregation approach is exact in this case.

We must now attack the problem of *reattribution,* that is, of deriving performance indexes for each of the stations in a subnetwork that has been replaced by a flow-equivalent station. Without loss of generality, we may assume that the original network (no matter how complex) has been reduced to an aggregated network like the one in Fig. 9.41c, that is, consisting of the series connection of a station of the original network and of a flow-equivalent station. For these two stations, we have already computed such indexes as the mean throughput rate and the mean queue length versus N. We also know the performance indexes of the stations in the subnetwork when this has been isolated from the rest of the network.

The mean throughput rate of station 2, which belongs to the aggregated subnetwork, is given by

$$X_2(N) = \frac{X_2'(N)}{X_e'(N)} X_1(N) \tag{9.76}$$

That is, the mean throughput rate of station 1 is divided among the stations in the subnetwork proportionally to their contributions to the mean throughput rate $X_e'(N)$ of the equivalent station.

Knowing the mean throughput rate, we can compute the server's utilization from the relationship $U_2 = X_2 S_2$, if the station is load independent, or from Eq. (9.72) if it is load dependent. More generally, one can obtain the queue length distribution of station 2 from

$$p(N_2 = n) = \sum_{i=n}^{N} p(N_e = i)\, p'(N_2 = n \mid i) \tag{9.77}$$

where $p(N_e = i)$ is the marginal distribution of requests in the equivalent station, and $p'(N_2 = n \mid i)$ is the probability that station 2 contains n requests when the isolated subnetwork contains i requests.

TABLE 9.16 RESOLUTION OF THE NETWORK IN FIG. 9.41(c) BY BUZEN'S ALGORITHM

N	$y_1 = 1$ Y_1	$y_e = \mu_1/\mu_e = 100/25 = 4$ Y_e						$U_1(N) = G(N-1)/G(N)$	$p(0, N)$ [eg. (9.54)]
0	1	$1 \times \frac{4^4}{3.19}$ +	$1 \times \frac{4^3}{1.9}$ +	$1 \times \frac{4^2}{1.3}$ +	$1 \times \frac{4^1}{1}$ +	1×1	→ 1	0	
1	1	$1 \times \frac{4^3}{1.9}$ +	$1 \times \frac{4^2}{1.3}$ +	$1 \times \frac{4^1}{1}$ +	1×1 =		→ 5	0.2	0.8
2	1	$1 \times \frac{4^2}{1.3}$ +	$1 \times \frac{4^1}{1}$ +	1×1 =			→ 17	0.2941	0.7058
3	1	$1 \times \frac{4^1}{1}$ +	1×1 =				→ 49	0.3469	0.6530
4	1	1×1 =					→ 129	0.3798	0.6201

TABLE 9.17 COMPUTATION OF $G(N)$ AND $U_1(N)$ FOR THE NETWORK IN FIG. 9.41(a) BY BUZEN'S ALGORITHM FOR LOAD-INDEPENDENT STATIONS

N	$y_1 = 1$ Y_1	$y_2 = 2$ Y_2	$y_3 = 2$ $Y_3 = G(N)$	$U_1(N) = G(N-1)/G(N)$
0	1	1	1	0
1	1	3	5	0.2
2	1	7	17	0.2941
3	1	15	49	0.3469
4	1	31	129	0.3798

Having computed $p(N_2 = n)$, one can derive all the performance indexes of interest by using the formulas of Secs. 9.4 and 9.5.

Example 9.5

For the network in Fig. 9.41a, we want to compute the utilization of server 2, after having solved the aggregated model in Fig. 9.41c. Since we know the values of $X_2'(N)$, $X_e'(N)$, and $X_1(N)$ from Example 9.4, we can apply Eq. (9.76) directly:

$$X_2(1) = \frac{\mu_2 U_2'(1)}{X_e'(1)} \mu_1 U_1(1) = \frac{0.5}{0.025 \times 25} \frac{0.2}{0.01} = 16 \text{ requests/s}$$

and similarly

$$X_2(2) = 23.525 \text{ requests/s}, \qquad X_2(3) = 27.752 \text{ requests/s}$$

$$X_2(4) = 30.392 \text{ requests/s}$$

The actual utilization of server 2 is therefore given by

$$U_2(1) = X_2(1)\, S_2 = 16 \times 0.025 = 0.4$$

$$U_2(2) = 0.5881$$

$$U_2(3) = 0.6938$$

$$U_2(4) = 0.7598$$

To verify the correctness of these results, we compute $U_2(N)$ by solving the whole network directly. From Table 9.17, we have

$$U_2(1) = y_2 U_1(1) = 2 \times 0.2 = 0.4$$

$$U_2(2) = 2 \times 0.2941 = 0.5881$$

$$U_2(3) = 2 \times 0.3469 = 0.6938$$

$$U_2(4) = 2 \times 0.3798 = 0.7596$$

These results practically coincide with those produced by the reattribution method.

Assuming $N = 3$, we now want to calculate $p(N_2 = 2)$, the probability that station

2 contains 2 requests. We first compute the marginal distribution of requests for station 2 when the subnetwork is isolated from the rest of the model. From the results of Example 9.4, we obtain

$$p'(0, 3) = p(N_2 = 0|3) = \frac{1}{G(3)} \times 1^3 = \frac{1}{4}$$

and similarly $p'(1, 2) = \frac{1}{4}$, $p'(2, 1) = \frac{1}{4}$, and $p'(3, 0) = \frac{1}{4}$.

Considering now the network in Fig. 9.41c, the probabilities that the equivalent station contains n requests, $0 \leq n \leq 3$, are

$$p(3, 0) = p(N_e = 0) = \frac{1}{G(3)} \times 4^0 \times 1 = 0.0204$$

$$p(2, 1) = p(N_e = 1) = \frac{1}{G(3)} \times 4^1 \times 1 = 0.0816$$

$$p(1, 2) = p(N_e = 2) = 0.2448$$

$$p(0, 3) = p(N_e = 3) = 0.653$$

Thus, the probability we want to compute is given by Eq. (9.77):

$$p(N_2 = 2) = \sum_{i=2}^{3} p(N_e = i)\, p'(N_2 = 2|i) = 0.2448$$

The correctness of this result may be verified by applying the formula that gives the marginal probability of finding exactly 2 requests in load-independent station 2 when $N = 3$ requests are in execution within the central server model of Fig. 9.41a (see also Table 9.17):

$$p(N_2 = 2) = \frac{y_2^{N_2}}{G(N)} [G(N - N_2) - y_2 G(N - 1 - N_2)] = \frac{2^2}{49}(5 - 2 \times 1) = 0.2448$$

If the model to be analyzed contains a *passive resource,* the values of capacity function $a_e(N)$ for the station equivalent to the subnetwork "encompassed" by this resource are to be suitably modified. The meaning of the term "encompassed" and the reason for the modification of $a_e(N)$ will be understood by looking at Fig. 9.42, where the passive resource represents the main memory of the modeled system. The memory is divided into a number m of partitions, with $m \leq N$. The operation of the passive resource is represented by a queue and by a set of m tokens. Each program entering subnetwork B (the subnetwork "encompassed" by the passive resource) receives a partition (a token), which will be returned to the pool when the program leaves B. When no token is available, the program willing to enter B will wait in the queue until a token is released by another program departing from B.

The capacity function $a_e(N)$ for the station equivalent to subnetwork B for all N is reported in Fig. 9.43; note that the limitation imposed by the maximum number m of available partitions is not taken into account by the curve labeled "subnetwork B." To account for this limitation, $a_e(N)$ must equal $a_e(m)$ for all $N > m$, as shown in Fig. 9.43

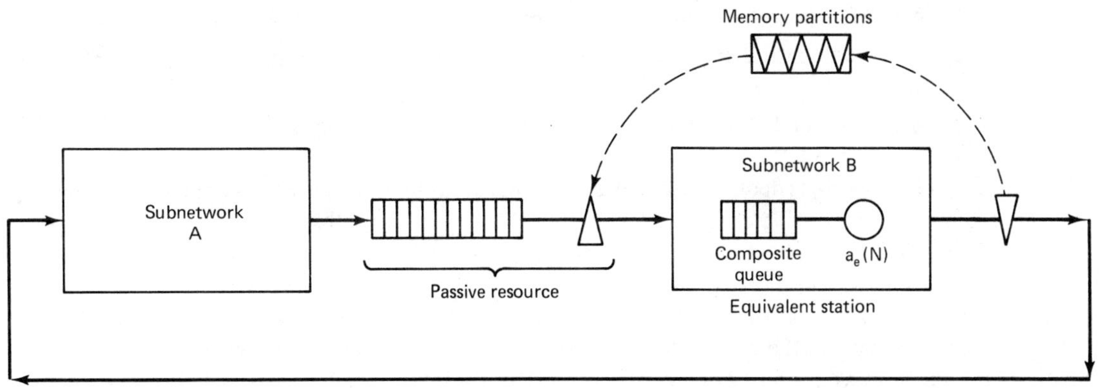

Figure 9.42 Network with a passive resource.

by the curve labeled "subnetwork B and passive resource" for $m = 5$. The straight line in the same figure represents the capacity function that would be obtained for subnetwork B if there were no resource contention (see also Fig. 9.6).

Using the formulas introduced for elementary closed networks consisting of two stations in parallel [Eqs. (9.57) and (9.58)], two stations in series [Eqs. (9.59) and (9.60)], and several stations connected in central-server fashion, it is possible to analyze networks with very complex topologies. The approach to be applied consists of hierarchically decomposing the network into elementary subnetworks to be replaced by flow-equivalent stations, until the whole network is aggregated into a readily solvable one.

9.6.1 Case 9.9: Estimating the Impact of Configuration Changes in an Interactive System

The system to be evaluated in this case study is a minicomputer of the MIRS type (see Fig. 1.4); its main components are:

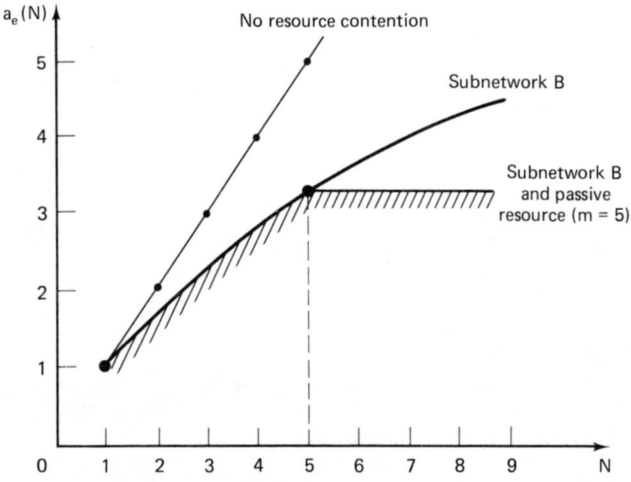

Figure 9.43 Capacity function (normalized throughput or service rate) of subnetwork B in isolation, with and without the passive resource, which acts for $N > 5$. Note that $a_e(N)$ has been calculated as $X_e(N)/X_e(1)$.

1. A CPU, whose mean uninterrupted service time is $S_1 = 1/\mu_1 = 6$ ms.
2. A movable-arm disk ("the disk"), whose mean service time is $S_2 = 1/\mu_2 = 36.3$ ms.
3. A fixed-head disk ("the drum"), whose mean service time is $S_3 = 1/\mu_3 = 16$ ms.

The system is dedicated to real-time applications that, from the viewpoint of resource consumptions, can be considered as homogeneous. Initially, the system's configuration, shown in Fig. 9.44, includes four terminals. The primary memory has sufficient space for three application programs ($m = 3$).

The execution of an interactive program requires, for each visit to the terminals, $V_2 = 23$ visits to the disk, $V_3 = 40$ visits to the drum, and $V_1 = 64$ visits to the CPU; the mean think time is $Z = 4$ s. The service discipline at all queues is FCFS, and all stations are load independent with exponentially distributed service times.

The following problems are to be dealt with:

9.20. Evaluate the performance of the initial configuration.

9.21. Evaluate the system's performance when the number of terminals is increased up to 20, and the size of the primary memory is not modified ($m = 3$), or doubled ($m = 6$), or tripled ($m = 9$), or increased so that it can hold more programs than there are terminals ($m = \infty$); determine the correct sizing of the primary memory for 20 terminals and indicate some possible tuning actions to improve the system's performance.

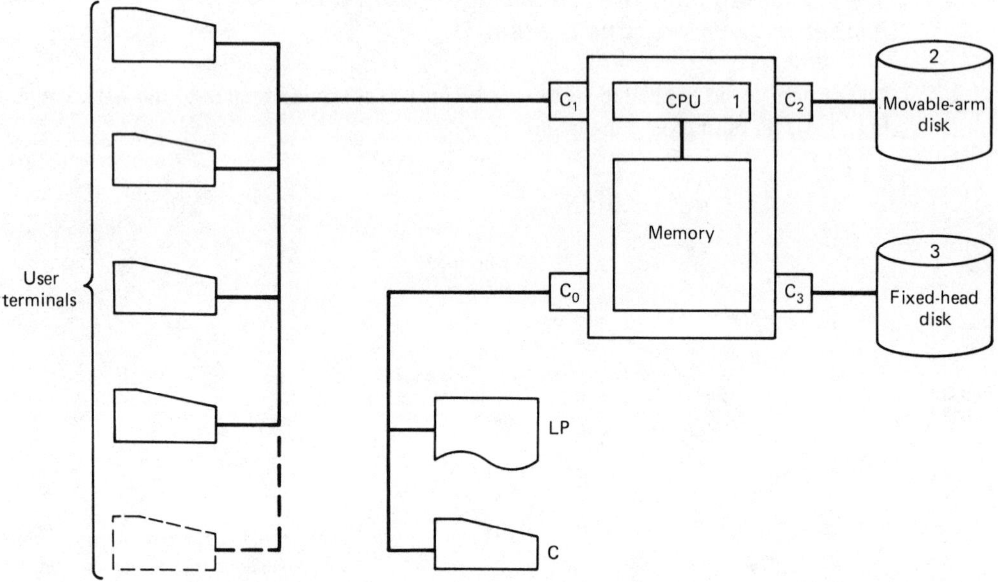

Figure 9.44 Configuration of the system analyzed in Case 9.9.

Problem 9.20

This is a typical case in which the primary memory is to be considered a passive resource. The model we adopt is represented in Fig. 9.45. We analyze it by the decomposition and aggregation approach. Subnetwork A, when studied in isolation (see Fig. 9.46a), is a central-server model with load-independent stations. Table 9.18 shows the values of some of its performance indexes and of the capacity function $a_e'(N)$ of the equivalent station for N from 1 to 4. The branching probabilities and the y_i's have been computed in the usual way; for example,

$$q_{12} = \frac{V_2}{V_1} = \frac{23}{64} = 0.359 \text{ and}$$

$$y_2 = \frac{\mu_1 q_{12}}{\mu_2} = \frac{36.3 \times 0.359}{6} = 2.174.$$

To account for the limitation imposed by memory size, the capacity function $a_e'(N)$ of subnetwork A is easily modified into $a_e(N)$ by setting $a_e(4) = a_e(3)$. Table 9.18 displays the values of $a_e(N)$ and $A_e(N)$ for the server equivalent to subnetwork A and to the memory. The resulting network is represented in Fig. 9.47.

The terminals may be considered as a load-dependent station, whose service rate is a function of the number of terminals in think state. The last columns of Table 9.18 show the values of S_T, a_T, and A_T for this station. If $\mu_T = 1/Z$ is the service rate of one thinking-terminal station, $2\mu_T$ will be the service rate of a two thinking-terminal station, $3\mu_T$ that of a three thinking-terminal station, and so on.

As already discussed, the resulting network in Fig. 9.47 has a product form solution

$$p(j, N - j) = \frac{1}{G(N)} \left(\frac{\mu_T}{\mu_e}\right)^{N-j} \frac{1}{A_T(j)A_e(N - j)}$$

with

$$G(N) = \sum_{j=0}^{N} \left(\frac{\mu_T}{\mu_e}\right)^{N-j} \frac{1}{A_T(j)A_e(N - j)}$$

Thus, with the values reported in Table 9.18, and for $N = 4$, we have

$$G(4) = \frac{(\mu_T/\mu_e)^4}{A_T(0)A_e(4)} + \frac{(\mu_T/\mu_e)^3}{A_T(1)A_e(3)} + \frac{(\mu_T/\mu_e)^2}{A_T(2)A_e(2)} + \frac{(\mu_T/\mu_e)^1}{A_T(3)A_e(1)} + \frac{(\mu_T/\mu_e)^0}{A_T(4)A_e(0)}$$

$$= \frac{0.0466}{1 \times 4.3704} + \frac{0.1003}{1 \times 2.5324} + \frac{0.2159}{2 \times 1.4674} + \frac{0.4647}{6 \times 1} + \frac{1}{24} = 0.243$$

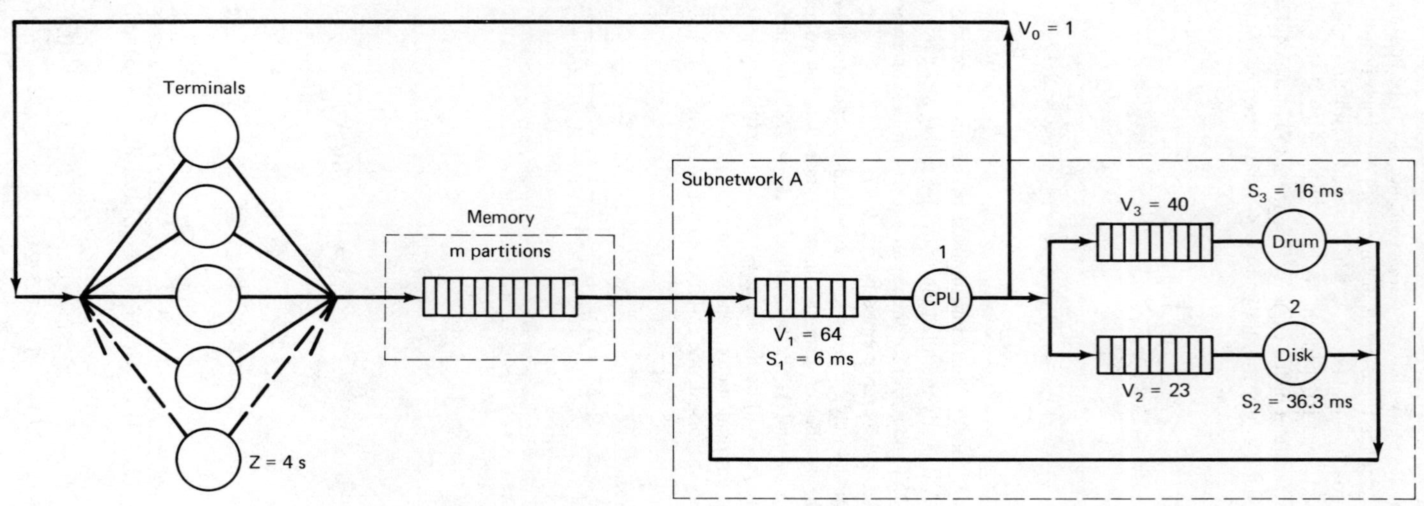

Figure 9.45 Model used to analyze the system in Fig. 9.44.

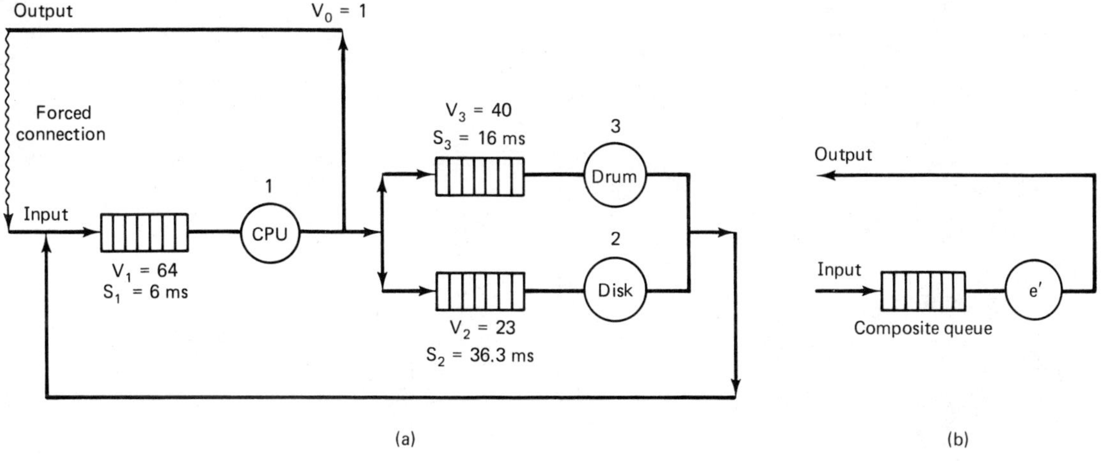

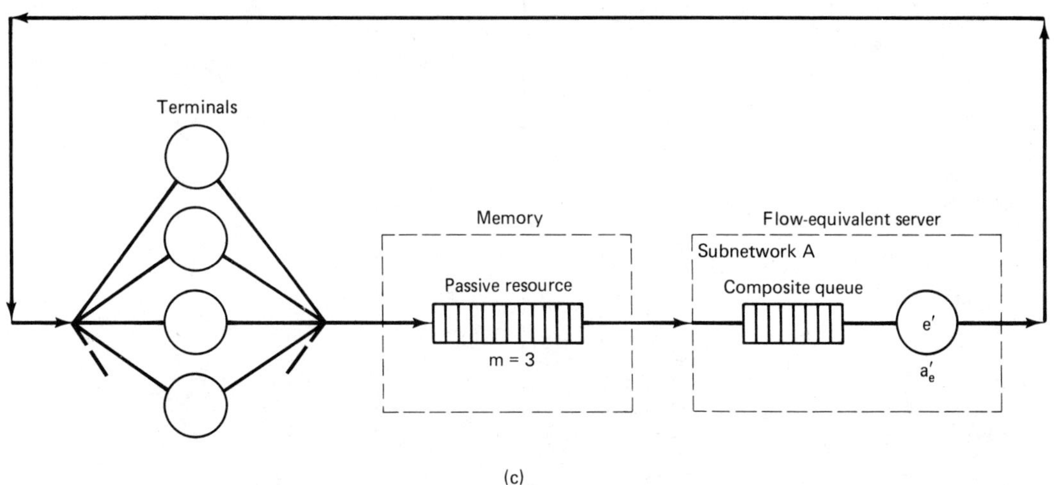

Figure 9.46 Decomposition of the model in Fig. 9.45: (a) subnetwork *A* in isolation; (b) its equivalent server; (c) the resulting aggregated network.

The marginal distribution of requests for the two stations is given by

$$p(0,\,4) = \frac{1}{G(4)} \times \frac{(\mu_T/\mu_e)^4}{A_T(0)A_e(4)} = \frac{1}{0.243} \times \frac{0.0466}{1 \times 4.3704} = 0.0439$$

$$p(1,\,3) = \frac{1}{G(4)} \times \frac{(\mu_T/\mu_e)^3}{A_T(1)A_e(3)} = \frac{1}{0.243} \times \frac{0.1003}{1 \times 2.5324} = 0.1630$$

$$p(2,\,2) = \frac{1}{G(4)} \times \frac{(\mu_T/\mu_e)^2}{A_T(2)A_e(2)} = \frac{1}{0.243} \times \frac{0.2159}{2 \times 1.4674} = 0.3028$$

TABLE 9.18 PERFORMANCE INDEXES OF SUBNETWORK A AND CAPACITY FUNCTIONS a'_e (NO MEMORY LIMITATION) AND a_e (LIMITED MEMORY) OF ITS EQUIVALENT SERVER. SUBSCRIPT T REFERS TO THE TERMINALS.

N	$y_1 = 1$ Y_1	$y_2 = 2.174$ Y_2	$y_3 = 1.6$ $Y_3 = G$	$U'_1 = \frac{G(N-1)}{G(N)}$	$U'_2 = y_2 U'_1$	$U'_3 = y_3 U'_1$	$X'_e = \mu_1 q_{10} U'_1$	a'_e	X_e	a_e	A_e	S_T	a_T	A_T
0	1	1	1											
1	1	3.174	4.840	0.2065	0.4491	0.3442	0.5379	1	0.5379	1	1	4.00	1	1
2	1	7.901	15.969	0.3031	0.6590	0.5052	0.7894	1.4674	0.7894	1.4674	1.4674	2.00	2	2
3	1	18.179	44.795	0.3565	0.7751	0.5941	0.9283	1.7257	0.9283	1.7257	2.5324	1.3	3	6
4	1	40.526	115.185	0.3888	0.8455	0.6481	1.0127	1.8826	0.9283	1.7257	4.3704	1.00	4	24

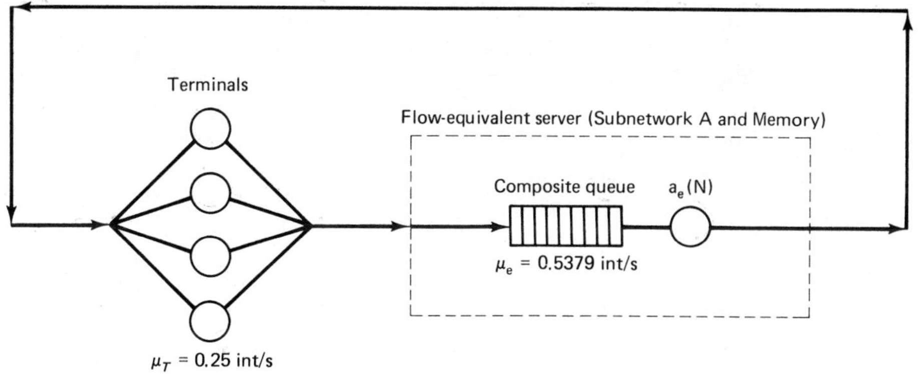

Figure 9.47 Aggregated form of the network in Fig. 9.45

$$p(3, 1) = \frac{1}{G(4)} \times \frac{(\mu_T/\mu_e)^1}{A_T(3)A_e(1)} = \frac{1}{0.243} \times \frac{0.4647}{6 \times 1} = 0.3187$$

$$p(4, 0) = \frac{1}{G(4)} \times \frac{(\mu_T/\mu_e)^0}{A_T(4)A_e(0)} = \frac{1}{0.243} \times \frac{1}{24} = 0.1714$$

The mean utilizations of the terminals and equivalent station are

$$U_T(4) = 1 - p(0, 4) = 0.9560$$

$$U_e(4) = 1 - p(4, 0) = 0.8285$$

The mean throughput rate of the terminals, which coincides with that of the equivalent station when the two stations are connected in series (see Fig. 9.47), is

$$X_T(4) = \sum_{n=1}^{4} p(n, N - n)\, \mu_T a_T(n) = 0.6026 \text{ interactions/s}$$

The mean throughput rate of the components of subnetwork A is obtained from the reattribution equation (9.76):

$$X_1(4) = X_1'(4)\frac{X_T(4)}{X_e'(4)} = \frac{0.3888}{0.006} \times \frac{0.6026}{1.0127} = 38.571 \text{ interactions/s}$$

$$X_2(4) = X_2'(4)\frac{X_T(4)}{X_e'(4)} = \frac{0.8455}{0.0363} \times \frac{0.6026}{1.0127} = 13.861 \text{ interactions/s}$$

$$X_3(4) = X_3'(4)\frac{X_T(4)}{X_e'(4)} = \frac{0.6481}{0.016} \times \frac{0.6026}{1.0127} = 24.107 \text{ interactions/s}$$

The mean throughput rate of subnetwork A is finally given by the product $X_1(4)q_{10}$, whose value is identical to the one of $X_T(4)$ computed here. The utilizations of the CPU and of the two I/O stations are

$$U_1(4) = X_1(4)S_1 = 0.2314$$

$$U_2(4) = X_2(4)S_2 = 0.5031$$

$$U_3(4) = X_3(4)S_3 = 0.3857$$

The mean queue length in the equivalent station is

$$N_e(4) = \sum_{n=1}^{4} np(4 - n, n) = 1.5892$$

Using Little's formula, we can compute the mean time in the equivalent station as the ratio between the mean queue length and the mean throughput rate for the network in Fig. 9.47:

$$t_{qe}(4) = R(4) = \frac{1.5892}{0.6026} = 2.637\text{s}$$

The number of requests at the terminals is

$$N_T(4) = 4 - N_e(4) = 2.4107$$

and the mean utilization of *each* terminal is

$$u_T(4) = \frac{N_T(4)}{4} = 0.6026 \qquad (9.78)$$

The mean queue length at the passive resource, that is, the mean memory queue length, may be computed as follows

$$N_m(4) = \sum_{n=m+1}^{N} (n - m)p(N - n, n) = \sum_{n=4}^{4} (4 - 3)p(0, 4) = 0.0439$$

The value of N_m provides useful indications about the correct sizing of the *terminal buffer pool.*

Note that the analysis of the aggregated model in Fig. 9.47 could have been performed by applying the algorithm in Table 9.12 rather than using the explicit expressions of the product form solution and of the performance indexes. Examining the utilizations, we see that the disk is the most highly utilized server [$U_2(4) = 0.5489$]. With 4 terminals, however, the disk does not yet seriously limit the system's performance. The mean utilization of each *memory partition* can be obtained by dividing the mean number of requests in subnetwork A by m:

$$u_m(4) = \frac{N_e(4) - N_m(4)}{m} = \frac{1.5453}{3} = 0.5151$$

We shall see in Problem 9.21 that this utilization will tend to 100 percent when the number of terminals is increased.

Problem 9.21

The analysis of the variations in the system's performance corresponding to an increase in the number of terminals from 4 to 20 and in the size of primary memory can be carried out by applying the algorithms described in Tables 9.2 and 9.12. The formulas to be used for the computations of performance indexes are the same as those employed in Problem 9.20 for $N = 4$ and $m = 3$, as well as in Sec. 9.5. To obtain the results for this problem, we have used the PNET queuing network solution package (see [BR80]), which applies algorithms derived from those described previously.

Figure 9.48 shows the mean throughput rate X versus the number N of terminals for the various memory sizes of interest. When $m = 3$, X remains practically constant ($X =$

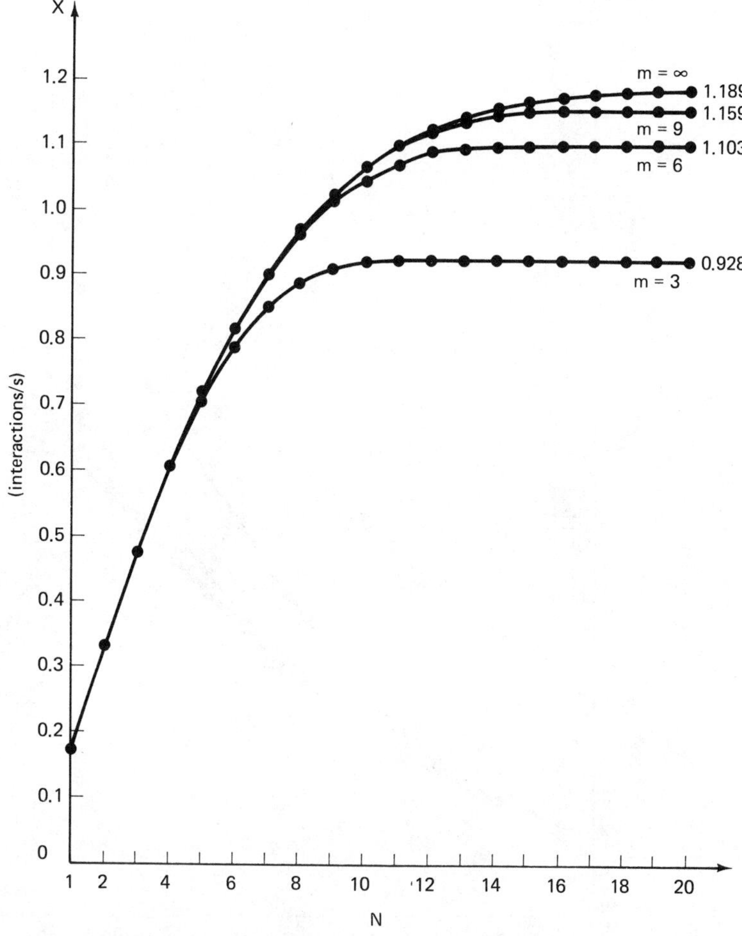

Figure 9.48 Mean throughput rate versus N for various memory sizes.

0.92 interactions/s) beyond $N = 10$. The saturation is caused by the memory size limitation, and this is confirmed by the linear increase of the memory queue length with N in the same range of values of N (see Fig. 9.51). As the memory size increases, this phenomenon occurs for larger and larger values of N. For $m = 6$, the throughput rate in saturation is 1.10 interactions/s, which is reached with 14 terminals; for $m = 9$, X remains at 1.15 interactions/s beyond 15 terminals.

The fact that X does not increase for m from 6 to 9 in the same proportion as for m from 3 to 6 is a symptom that the bottleneck is migrating from the memory to the disk. Thus, it is not convenient to make memory larger than 9 partitions, since the advantages in terms of both throughput rate and response time are minimal (see the $m = \infty$ curves in Figs. 9.48 and 9.49). Similar considerations can be made for the mean response times, whose curves are presented in Fig. 9.49.

The utilizations plotted in Fig. 9.50 confirm that the disk becomes the bottleneck for $m > 9$; the $m = 9$ curve for the disk is almost coincident with the $m = \infty$ curve; the performance for $m = 9$ is close to the maximum, since it is already limited by the disk.

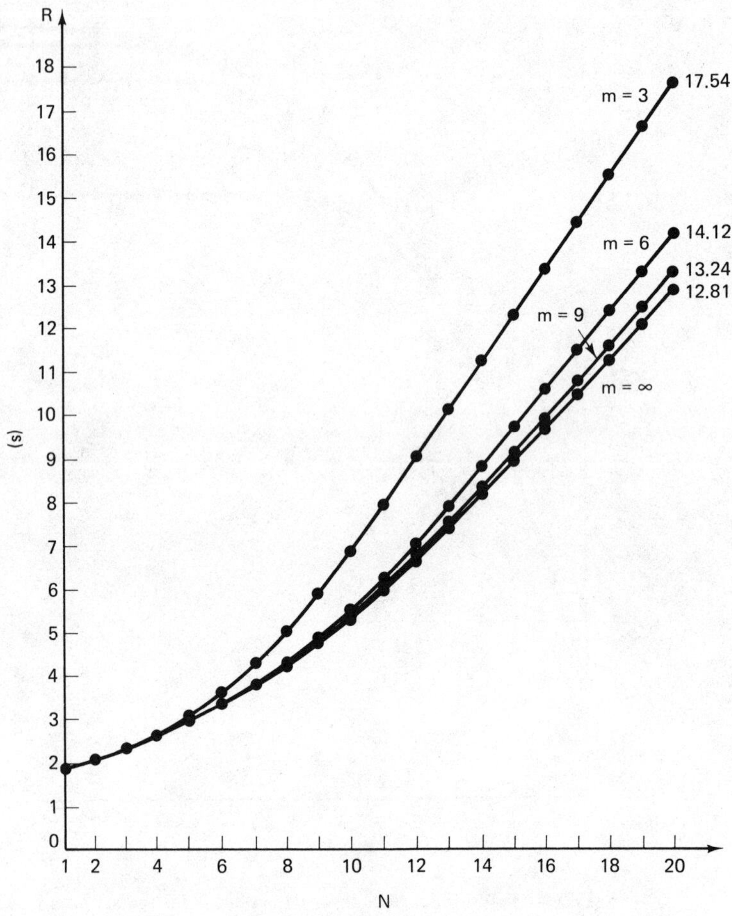

Figure 9.49 Mean response time versus N for various memory sizes.

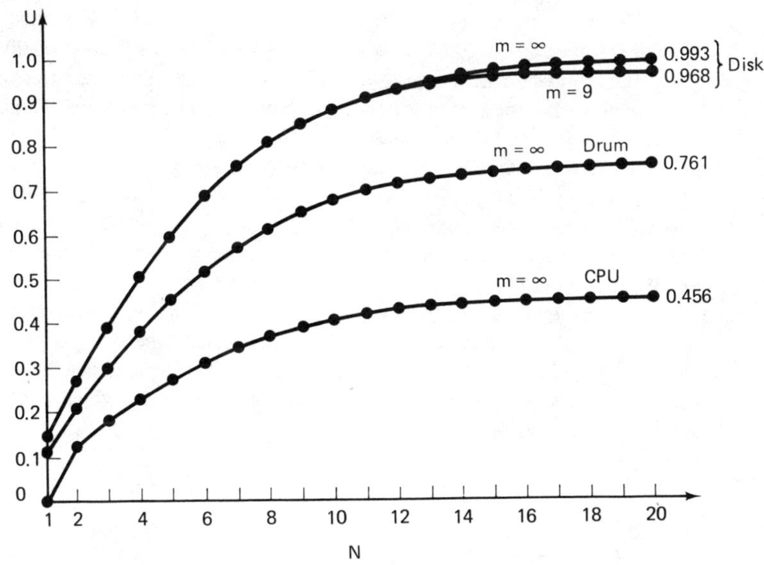

Figure 9.50 Server utilizations versus N.

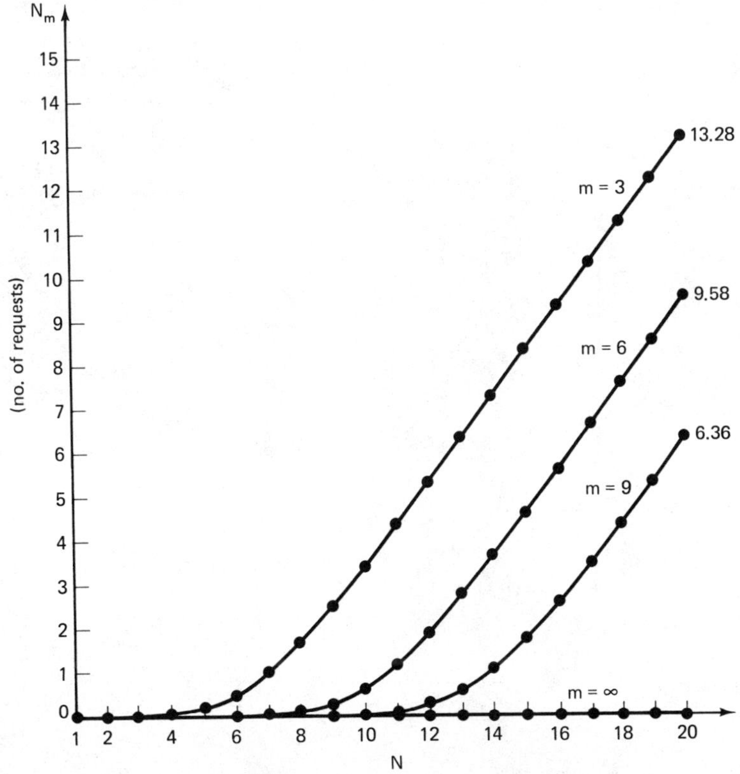

Figure 9.51 Mean memory queue length versus N for various memory sizes.

The mean memory queue length is plotted versus N in Fig. 9.51. When the flow-equivalent station in Fig. 9.47 is saturated, this length grows proportionally to N. The curves in Fig. 9.52 represent the mean number of terminals in the think state versus the total number of terminals. Saturation manifests itself in these curves by limiting the number of thinking terminals. By Eq. (9.78), this mean number divided by N expresses the fraction of time each terminal is busy. This fraction decreases as the number of terminals increases; when N = 20, it equals 18.56 percent for $m = 3$, 22.07 percent for $m = 6$, 23.19 percent for $m = 9$, and 23.79 percent for $m = \infty$.

If the system's performance for $m = 9$ does not satisfy the requirements of the users, tuning actions will have to be undertaken to improve it. The first goal of these actions should be to transfer the bottleneck from the disk to the drum, as this, if accompanied by an increase of memory size, would certainly increase performance. The new performance limits can be obtained by applying the algorithm again with $m = \infty$. The results will allow us to determine whether the desired performance can be achieved with the given configuration or faster components will be needed.

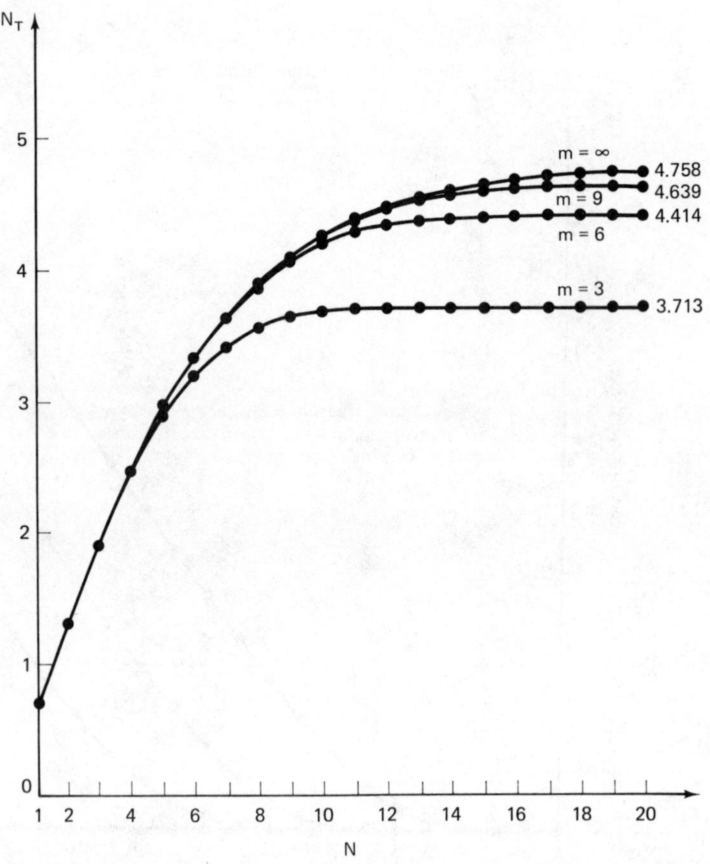

Figure 9.52 Mean number of busy terminals versus total number of active terminals.

9.7 MEAN VALUE ANALYSIS

A new approach to the solution of product form networks, called *mean value analysis,* has been recently introduced by Reiser and Lavenberg [RE80]. Instead of calculating G and deriving from it the values of the performance indexes, this approach computes the indexes by the recursive relationships that exist among them. The validity of mean value analysis extends to all cases in which the normalizing constant approach can be applied [SE79] [LA79]. Its derivation principles naturally lead to approximate solution methods for some non-product-form queuing networks.

Let us consider a closed network with load-independent stations and a single class of programs. We have seen [Eq. (9.55)] that the mean queue length at server i is given by

$$N_i(N) = \sum_{n=1}^{N} y_i^n \frac{G(N - n)}{G(N)}$$

where N is the constant number of programs in the network. By some simple algebra, this expression can be transformed into the recursive form

$$N_i(N) = U_i(N)\,[1 + N_i\,(N - 1)]$$

obviously with $N_i(0) = 0$. By Little's formula, the mean response time can be derived as

$$R_i(N) = \frac{N_i(N)}{X_i(N)}$$

Substituting for $N_i\,(N)$ the preceding recursive expression, and recalling that $U_i(N) = X_i(N)S_i$, we obtain the following recursive expression for the mean response time:

$$R_i(N) = S_i[1 + N_i(N - 1)] \tag{9.79}$$

whose meaning is quite intuitive: the mean time taken by station i to process a request equals the sum of the mean time required to process the requests already queued up and of the request's mean service time.

An expression of the mean throughput rate in which the normalizing constant G is not used can be obtained by applying Little's formula to the whole network. Since the system's mean response time R is the sum of the mean times spent by a program in each of the k stations, that is,

$$R(N) = \sum_{i=1}^{k} V_i R_i(N)$$

the system's mean throughput rate is

$$X(N) = \frac{N}{\sum_{i=1}^{k} V_i R_i(N)} \tag{9.80}$$

The mean throughput rate of station i is given by [see Eqs. (9.71) and (9.12)]

$$X_i(N) = X(N)V_i$$

Applying again Little's formula to station i, we have

$$N_i(N) = X_i(N)R_i(N) \tag{9.81}$$

Equations (9.79), (9.80), and (9.81) are the three basic equations of mean value analysis. Starting from initial condition $N_i(0) = 0$, it is possible to calculate $R_i(N)$, $R(N)$, $X(N)$, $X_i(N)$, $U_i(N)$, and $N_i(N)$ iteratively.

A recursive technique for the computation of the marginal queue length distribution is reported in [RE80]. The technique is based on the observation that a program, when joining the queue of the ith station, finds a queue distribution that equals the distribution that would be seen from the outside if the model contained one less program. That is,

$$p^a(N_i = n|N) = p(N_i = n|N - 1)$$

This result has been proved to hold for all networks with a product form solution (the *arrival theorem* [SE79], [LA79]). In the case of load-independent resources, this queue length distribution formula can be transformed into the following:

$$p(N_i = n|N) = X_i(N)\, S_i\, p(N_i = n - 1|N - 1) \tag{9.82}$$

with $0 \leq n \leq N$. If station i is load dependent, some of the relationships derived here must be modified as follows:

$$U_i(N) = 1 - p(N_i = 0|N)$$

$$R_i(N) = \sum_{n=1}^{N} n\, S_i(n)\, p(N_i = n - 1|N - 1) \qquad 0 \leq n \leq N \tag{9.83}$$

$$p(N_i = n|N) = X_i(N)\, S_i(n) p(N_i = n - 1|N - 1)$$

When there are load-dependent stations, the marginal queue length distribution must always be calculated, since it is needed for the computation of $R_i(N)$.

The iterative algorithm in this case computes the performance indexes in the following order: $R_i(N)$, $X(N)$, $X_i(N)$, $p(N_i = n|N)$, $U_i(N)$, $N_i(N)$, with initial condition $p(N_i = 0|0) = 1$.

9.7.1 Case 9.10: Application of Mean Value Analysis to Case 9.8

We now apply mean value analysis to the model solved in Case 9.8 with the normalizing-constant method. The model is reported in Fig. 9.39. The parameters needed by the mean value analysis equations in Sec. 9.7 are $V_1 = 10$ requests, $V_2 = 8$ requests, $V_3 = 1$ request, $S_1 = 0.01$ s, $S_2 = 0.025$ s, $S_3 = 0.15$ s for $N \leq 2$, and $S_3 = 0.10$ s for $N > 2$.

Table 9.19 displays the performance indexes in the sequence in which they are to be calculated for the solution, as for Problem 9.18. The following is the list of the computations to be performed during the first iteration ($N = 1$):

$$R_1(1) = S_1[1 + N_1(0)] = 0.01[1 + 0] = 0.01 \text{ s}$$

$$R_2(1) = S_2[1 + N_2(0)] = 0.025[1 + 0] = 0.025 \text{ s}$$

$$R_3(1) = \sum_{n=1}^{1} nS_3(n)p(N_3 = n - 1|0) = S_3(1)p(N_3 = 0|0) = 0.15 \text{ s}$$

$$R(1) = \sum_{i=1}^{3} V_iR_i(1) = 10 \times 0.01 + 8 \times 0.025 + 1 \times 0.15 = 0.45 \text{ s}$$

$$X(1) = \frac{1}{R(1)} = 2.2 \text{ programs/s}$$

$$X_1(1) = X(1)V_1 = 2.2 \times 10 = 22.2 \text{ programs/s}$$

$$X_2(1) = X(1)V_2 = 2.2 \times 8 = 17.7 \text{ programs/s}$$

$$X_3(1) = X(1)V_3 = 2.2 \times 1 = 2.2 \text{ programs/s,}$$

$$p(N_3 = 1|1) = X_3(1)S_3(1)p(N_3 = 0|0) = 2.2 \times 0.15 \times 1 = 0.33$$

TABLE 9.19 PERFORMANCE INDEXES COMPUTED BY THE MEAN VALUE ANALYSIS TECHNIQUE FOR THE MODEL IN FIG. 9.39 WITH A LOAD-DEPENDENT STATION (STATION 3)

N	R_1	R_2	R_3	R	X	X_1	X_2	X_3	$p(N_3 = 1\|N)$	$p(N_3 = 2\|N)$
1	0.010	0.025	0.15	0.45	2.2	22.2	17.7	2.2	0.3	—
2	0.012	0.036	0.2	0.611	3.27	32.727	26.18	3.27	0.327	0.163
3	0.014	0.048	0.223	0.752	3.985	39.85	31.88	3.985	0.304	0.195
4	0.015	0.064	0.241	0.907	4.409	44.09	35.27	4.409	0.287	0.201

$p(N_3 = 3\|N)$	$p(N_3 = 4\|N)$	$p(N_3 = 0\|N)$	U_1	U_2	U_3	N_1	N_2	N_3
—	—	0.6	0.2	0.4	0.3	0.2	0.4	0.3
—	—	0.509	0.327	0.654	0.49	0.39	0.945	0.654
0.065	—	0.434	0.398	0.797	0.565	0.558	1.55	0.891
0.086	0.028	0.396	0.441	0.882	0.604	0.687	2.25	1.063

$$p(N_3 = 0|1) = 1 - p\,(N_3 = 1|1) = 1 - 0.33 = 0.66$$

$$U_1(1) = X_1(1)S_1 = 22.22 \times 0.01 = 0.22$$

$$U_2(1) = X_2(1)S_2 = 17.7 \times 0.025 = 0.4$$

$$U_3(1) = 1 - p(N_3 = 0|1) = 1 - 0.66 = 0.34$$

$$N_1(1) = X_1(1)R_1(1) = 22.2 \times 0.01 = 0.22$$

$$N_2(1) = X_2(1)R_2(1) = 17.7 \times 0.025 = 0.44$$

$$N_3(1) = X_3(1)R_3(1) = 2.22 \times 0.15 = 0.33$$

The marginal queue length distributions and the mean response times for station 3, which is load dependent, are computed as follows [see Eqs. (9.83)]:

$$\left.\begin{aligned}
R_3(2) &= 1 \times 0.15\,p(N_3 = 0|1) + 2 \times 0.15p(N_3 = 1|1) = 0.2 \text{ s} \\
p(N_3 = 1|2) &= 3.27 \times 0.15p(N_3 = 0|1) = 0.327 \\
p(N_3 = 2|2) &= 3.27 \times 0.15p(N_3 = 1|1) = 0.163 \\
p(N_3 = 0|2) &= 1 - [p(N_3 = 1|2) + p(N_3 = 2|2)] = 0.51
\end{aligned}\right\} N = 2$$

$$\left.\begin{aligned}
R_3(3) &= 1 \times 0.15p(N_3 = 0|2) + 2 \times 0.15p(N_3 = 1|2) + 3 \\
&\quad \times 0.1\text{p}(\text{N}_3 = 2|2) = 0.2236 \text{ s} \\
p(N_3 = 1|3) &= 3.985 \times 0.15p(N_3 = 0|2) = 0.30435 \\
p(N_3 = 2|3) &= 3.985 \times 0.15p(N_3 = 1|2) = 0.1956 \\
p(N_3 = 3|3) &= 3.985 \times 0.1p(N_3 = 2|2) = 0.06522 \\
p(N_3 = 0|3) &= 1 - [p(N_3 = 1|3) + p(N_3 = 2|3) \\
&\quad + p(N_3 = 3|3)] = 0.435
\end{aligned}\right\} N = 3$$

$$\left.\begin{aligned}
R_3(4) &= 1 \times 0.15p(N_3 = 0|3) + 2 \times 0.15p(N_3 = 1|2) + 3 \\
&\quad \times 0.1p(N_3 = 2|3) + 4 \times 0.1\,p(N_3 = 3|3) = 0.241 \text{ s} \\
p(N_3 = 1|4) &= 4.409 \times 0.15p(N_3 = 0|3) = 0.2875 \\
p(N_3 = 2|4) &= 4.409 \times 0.15p(N_3 = 1|3) = 0.2012 \\
p(N_3 = 3|4) &= 4.409 \times 0.1p(N_3 = 2|3) = 0.08626 \\
p(N_3 = 4|4) &= 4.409 \times 0.1p(N_3 = 3|3) = 0.02875 \\
p(N_3 = 0|4) &= 1 - [p(N_3 = 1|4) + p(N_3 = 2|4) \\
&\quad + p(N_3 = 3|4) + p(N_3 = 4|4)] = 0.3961
\end{aligned}\right\} N = 4$$

The values reported in Table 9.19 coincide with those obtained by the method of the normalizing-constant in Sec. 9.5.1.

When the disk (station 3) is considered load independent with $S_3 = 0.1$ s, the model's performance indexes are computed by Eqs. (9.79) through (9.81). The resulting index values are listed in Table 9.20; they clearly coincide with those obtained in Sec. 9.5.1 for Problem 9.19.

TABLE 9.20 PERFORMANCE INDEXES COMPUTED BY THE MEAN VALUE ANALYSIS TECHNIQUE FOR THE MODEL IN FIG. 9.39 WITH LOAD-INDEPENDENT STATIONS

N	R_1	R_2	R_3	R	X	X_1	X_2	X_3	U_1	U_2	U_3	N_1	N_2	N_3
1	0.010	0.025	0.1	0.4	2.5	25	20	2.5	0.25	0.5	0.25	0.25	0.5	0.25
2	0.012	0.037	0.125	0.55	3.63	36.36	29.09	3.63	0.36	0.72	0.36	0.45	1.09	0.45
3	0.014	0.052	0.145	0.709	4.231	42.31	33.847	4.231	0.423	0.846	0.423	0.615	1.769	0.615
4	0.016	0.069	0.161	0.877	4.561	45.61	36.493	4.561	0.456	0.912	0.456	0.736	2.526	0.736

SUMMARY OF CHAPTER NOTATION

A	number of arrivals during the observation interval
C	number of completions during the observation interval
B	amount of time the system is busy during the observation interval
S	mean service time of a service center
μ	mean service rate of a service center
X	mean thoughput rate or mean output rate
R	mean response time
N	mean number of users in a closed network
N_i	mean number of users in the ith service center
N_q	mean number of users in a queue
t_q	mean queuing (waiting) time
λ	arrival rate of new requests at a service center
U	service center utilization
T	duration of the observation interval
Z	mean user think time at the terminals
M	number of active terminals
N^*	saturation point for a batch-processing system
M^*	saturation point for an interactive system
$a_i(N)$	capacity function for the ith server with load-dependent service times
$F_x(x_0)$	probability distribution function of a random variable x_0
$f_x(x_0)$	probability density function of a random variable x_0
$P_k(t)$	probability of k arrivals during time interval t
c	coefficient of variation
$p(\mathbf{N})$	equilibrium state probability distribution
$G(N)$	normalizing constant
$A_i(N)$, $Y_i(N)$	auxiliary functions used for the computation of $G(N)$

REFERENCES

Entries marked with an asterisk (*) are referenced in the text.

*[AC78] ACM Computing Surveys, *Queueing Network Models of Computer System Performance,* vol. 10, n. 3, Sept. 1978.

*[AL78] Allen, A. O., *Probability, Statistics, and Queueing Theory with Computer Science Applications,* Academic Press, New York, 1978.

*[AN72] Anderson, H. A., Sargent, R. G., A statistical evaluation of the scheduler of an experimental interactive computing system, in: Freiberger, W. (ed.), *Statistical Computer Performance Evaluation.* Academic Press, New York, pp. 73–98, 1972.

[AN75] Anderson, H. A., Reiser, M., Galati, G. L., Tuning virtual storage system, *IBM Systems J.*, n. 3, 1975.

[AR71] Arora, S. R., Gallo, A., The optimal organization of multiprogrammed multi-level memory. *Proc. ACM-SIGOPS Workshop on System Performance Evaluation,* pp. 104–141, Harvard University, Cambridge, Mass., Apr. 1971.

[BA71a] Bard, Y., Performance criteria and measurement for a time-sharing system, *IBM Systems J.,* vol. 10, n. 3, pp. 193–214, 1971.

*[BA79] Bard, Y., Some extensions to multiclass queueing network analysis, *Proc. 4th Int. Symp. on Modeling and Performance Evaluation of Computer Systems,* Vienna, Feb. 1979.

*[BA80] Bard, Y., A model of shared DASD and multipathing, *CACM,* vol. 23, n. 10, pp. 564–572, Oct. 1980.

[BA71b] Baskett, F., The dependence of computer system queues upon processing time distribution and central processor scheduling, *Proc. ACM-SIGOPS 3rd Symp. on Operating System Principles,* pp. 109–113, Oct. 1971.

*[BA75] Baskett, F., and others, Open, closed and mixed networks of queues with different classes of customers, *J. ACM,* vol. 22, n. 2, pp. 248–260, April 1975.

[BE80] Best/1 *User's guide,* BGS Systems, Box 128, Lincoln, MA, 1980.

*[BR80] Bruell, S. C., Balbo, G., *Computational Algorithms for Closed Queueing Networks,* Elsevier North-Nolland, New York, 1980.

*[BR82] Brumfield, J. A., Denning, P. J., Error analysis of homogeneous mean queue and response time estimators, *ACM SIGMETRICS, Perf. Evaluat. Review,* vol. 11, n. 4, pp. 215–221, 1981.

*[BU71] Buzen, J. P., Analysis of system bottlenecks using a queueing network model, *Proc. ACM-SIGOPS Workshop on System Performance Evaluation,* Harvard University, Cambridge, Mass., pp 82–103, April 1971.

*[BU73a] Buzen, J. P., Computational algorithms for closed queueing networks with exponential servers, *CACM,* vol. 16, n. 9, pp. 527–531, Sept. 1973.

*[BU73b] Buzen, J. P., Optimal balancing of I/O requests to sector scheduled drums, *Proc. 7th ACM–ASA Symposium on the Interface of Computer Science and Statistics,* pp. 130–137, Oct. 1973.

*[BU74a] Buzen, J. P., Chen, P. P. S., Optimal load balancing in memory hierarchies, *Proc. IFIP Congress 74,* pp. 271–275, North-Holland, Amsterdam, 1974.

[BU74b] Buzen, J. P., Goldberg, P. S., Guidelines for the use of infinite source queueing models in the analysis of computer system performance, *AFIPS Conf. Proc. NCC,* pp. 371–374, 1974.

*[BU76] Buzen, J. P., Fundamental operational laws of computer system performance, *Acta Informatica,* vol. 7, n. 2, pp. 167–182, 1976.

*[BU77] Buzen, J. P., Load balancing on I/O devices, *Infotech State of the Art Report "System Tuning,"* pp. 241–252, 1977.

*[BU80] Buzen, J. P., Denning, P. J., Measuring and calculating queue length distributions, *Computer,* pp. 33–44, April 1980.

[CA75] Cardenas, A. F., Analysis and performance of inverted data base structures, *CACM,* vol. 18, n. 5, pp. 253–263, May 1975.

*[CH78] Chandy, K. M., Yeh, R. T. eds., *Current Trends in Programming Methodology,* Prentice-Hall, Englewood Cliffs, N. J., 1978.

*[CH73] Chen, P. P. S., Optimal file allocation in multi-level storage systems, *AFIPS Conf. Proc. NCC,* pp. 277–282, 1973.

[CO72] Coffman, E. G., Ryan, T. A., A study of storage partitioning using a mathematical model of locality, *CACM,* vol. 15, n. 3, pp. 185–190, March 1972.

[CO73] Coffman, E. G., Denning, P. J., *Operating Systems Theory,* Prentice-Hall, Englewood Cliffs, N.J., 1973.

[CO76] Coffman, E. G., Jr., *Computer and Job/Shop Scheduling Theory,* Wiley-Interscience, New York, 1976.

*[CO77] Courtois, P. J., *Decomposability: Queueing and Computer System Applications,* Academic Press, New York, 1977.

[DE75] Denning, P. J., Graham, R. S., Multiprogrammed memory management, *Proc. IEEE,* vol. 63, n. 6, pp. 924–939, June 1975.

*[DE76] Denning, P. J., and others, Optimal multiprogramming, *Acta Informatica,* vol. 7, pp. 197–216, 1976.

*[DE78] Denning, P. J., Buzen, J. P., The operational analysis of queueing network models, *ACM Computing Surveys,* vol. 10, n. 3, pp. 225–261, Sept. 1978.

*[DO82] Dowdy, L. W., Foster, D. V., Comparative models of the file assignment problem, *ACM Computing Surveys,* vol. 14, n. 2, pp. 287–313, 1982.

*[FO76] Foster, D., Browne, J. C., File assignment in memory hierarchies, in: Beilner, H., Gelenbe, E. eds., *Modeling and Performance Evaluation of Computer Systems,* North-Holland, Amsterdam, pp. 119–127, 1976.

[FU75] Fuller, S. H., Baskett, F., An analysis of drum storage units, *J. ACM,* vol. 22. n. 1, pp. 83–105, Jan. 1975.

[GA71] Gaver, D. P., Lewis, P. A. W., Probability models for buffer storage allocation problems, *J. ACM,* vol. 18, n. 2, pp. 186–198, Apr. 1971.

*[GE80] Gelenbe, E., Mitrani, I., *Analysis and Synthesis of Computer Systems,* Academic Press, New York, 1980.

*[GO67] Gordon, W. J., Newell, G. F., Closed queueing systems with exponential servers, *Operations Research,* vol. 15, n. 2, pp. 254–265, April 1967.

[GO73] Gotlieb, C. C., Metzger, J. K., Trace driven analysis of a batch processing system. *Proc. ACM-SIGSIM Symposium on the the Simulation of Computer Systems,* pp. 215–222, June 1973.

[HE75] Herzog, U., Woo, L., Chandy, K. M., Solution of queueing problems by a recursive technique, *IBM J. Research and Development,* vol. 19, n. 3, pp. 295–300, May 1975.

[HU73] Hughes, P. H., Moe, G., A structural approach to computer performance analysis, *AFIPS Conf. Proc. NCC,* vol. 42, pp. 109–120, 1973.

*[JA63] Jackson, J. R., Job shop-like queueing systems, *Management Sci.,* vol. 10, n. 1, pp. 131–142, 1963.

[KL70] Kleinrock, L., Analytic and simulation methods in computer network design, *AFIPS Conf. Proc. SJCC,* pp. 569–579, 1970.

*[KL75] Kleinrock, L., *Queueing Systems, Volume I: Theory,* Wiley, New York, 1975.

*[KL76] Kleinrock, L., *Queueing Systems, Volume II: Computer Applications,* Wiley, New York, 1976.

[KL77] Kleinrock, L., Performance of distributed multi-access computer communication systems, *Proc. IFIP Congress 77,* pp. 547–552, North-Holland, Amsterdam, 1977.

*[KO78a] Kobayashi, H., System design and performance analysis using analytic models, in: Chandy, K. M., Yeh, R. T., eds., *Current Trends in Programming Methodology, Vol. III: Software Modelling,* Prentice-Hall, Englewood Cliffs, N.J., pp. 72–114, 1978.

*[KO78b] Kobayashi, H., *Modeling and Analysis: An Introduction to System Performance Evaluation Methodology,* Addison-Wesley, Reading, Mass., 1978.

*[LA79] Lavenberg, S. S., Reiser, M., Stationary states probabilities at arrival instants for closed queueing networks with multiple types of customers, *IBM Research Report RC 7592,* April 1979.

[LA82] Lazowska, E. D., Zahorjan, J., Multiple class memory constrained queueing networks, *ACM SIGMETRICS, Perf. Evaluat. Review,* vol. 11, n. 4, pp. 130–140, 1982.

*[LE72] Lewis, P. A. W., Yue, P. C., Statistical analysis of series of events in computer systems, in: Freiberger, W., ed. *Statistical Computer Performance Evaluation,* Academic Press, New York, pp. 265–280, 1972.

[MU75] Muntz, R. R., Analytic modeling of interactive systems, *Proc. IEEE,* vol. 63, n. 6, pp. 946–953, June 1975.

*[PI75] Piepmeier, W. F., Optimal balancing of I/O requests to disks, *CACM,* vol. 18, n. 19, pp. 524–527, Sept. 1975.

[RE75] Reiser, M., Kobayashi, H., Queueing networks with multiple closed chains: theory and computational algorithms, *IBM J. of Research and Development,* vol. 19, n. 3, pp. 283–294, May 1975.

*[RE80] Reiser, M., Lavenberg, S. S., Mean value analysis of closed multichain queueing networks, *J. ACM,* vol. 27, n. 2, pp. 313–322, April 1980.

[RE81] Reiser, M., Mean-value analysis and convolution method for queue-dependent servers in closed queueing networks, *Performance Evaluation,* vol. 1, n. 1, pp. 7–18, Jan. 1981.

*[RO79] Roode, J. D., Multiclass operational analysis of queueing networks, *Proc. 4th Int. Symp. on Modelling and Performance Evaluation of Computer Systems,* Vienna, Feb. 1979.

[SA79] Sauer, C. H., Chandy, K. M., The impact of distributions and disciplines on multiple processor systems, *CACM,* vol. 22, n. 1, pp. 25–34, Jan. 1979.

*[SA81] Sauer, C. H., Chandy, K. M., *Computer Systems Performance Modeling,* Prentice-Hall, Englewood Cliffs, N.J., 1981.

[SC73] Schneiderman, B., Optimum data base reorganization points, *CACM,* vol. 16, n. 6, pp. 362–365, June 1973.

*[SC78] Schwetman, H. C., Hybrid simulation models of computer systems, *CACM,* vol. 21, n. 9, pp. 718–723, Sept. 1978.

*[SE81] Serazzi, G., The dynamic behavior of computer systems, in: Ferrari D., Spadoni, M., eds., *Experimental Computer Performance Evaluation,* North-Holland, Amsterdam, pp. 127–163, 1981.

[SE77] Sevcik, K. C., Priority scheduling disciplines in queueing network models of computer systems, *Proc. IFIP Congress 77,* pp. 565–570, North-Holland, Amsterdam, 1977.

*[SE79] Sevcik, K., Mitrani, I., The distribution of queueing network states at input and output instants, *Proc. 4th Int. Symp. on Modeling and Performance Evaluation of Computer Systems,* Vienna, Feb. 1979.

[SH71] Shedler, G. S., Yang, S. C., Simulation of a model of paging system performance, *IBM Systems J.,* vol. 10, n. 2, pp. 113–128, 1971.

10

ECONOMIC CONSIDERATIONS

10.1 GENERALITIES

Performance evaluation studies are often undertaken when a workload larger than the current one is to be processed without increasing the system's configuration, or when the current workload's processing costs are to be reduced without worsening the level of the service provided to the users; in other words, when one wishes to decrease the installation's cost–performance ratio.

This objective, more or less explicitly stated, is common to most evaluation studies. Indeed, detecting the system's bottlenecks, predicting the effects of future changes, delaying the purchase of new hardware, improving the utilization of certain units, and other common objectives can all be reduced to the same goal: improving the cost–performance ratio.

Converting performance indexes from technical to economic terms is a delicate and often difficult operation. Moreover, tuning interventions must be prompt and fast if performance is to be kept close to the optimum in the presence of a dynamically changing workload. These continuous variations make the initial and final evaluations of the costs and results of a study even more difficult.

How can one determine in quantitative terms the performance that could be produced by a system that has not yet been tuned? How can one know which decisions would have been made if no measurements collected with adequate tools had been available? These and many more questions must be answered in order to evaluate the risks of an investment in performance improvement studies. To evaluate the risks of an investment, it is necessary to quantify all factors involved as precisely as possible, considering their importance and the times of their appearance and disappearance.

The techniques normally used for economic analyses can be applied. In Sec. 10.2 we shall discuss in more detail the concepts of cost and benefit, and their use in investment evaluation studies.

The analysis of past experiences has made it possible to define some criteria that are valid in general, not only for computer systems. Among the most important such criteria we should mention:

1. The criterion of the maximum result–effort ratio: the major causes of inefficiency can usually be removed with relatively little effort; to obtain further improvements, which will generally be smaller than the ones previously obtained, requires much greater efforts (the informal saying goes that 80 percent of results are obtained with 20 percent of the effort).
2. The criterion of the identification of the main cause: while most performance indexes confirm the assumptions made for bottleneck detection, some seem to indicate other causes; it is important not to be distracted by secondary details when trying to identify the primary cause of inefficiencies.
3. The criterion of the limitation: the variables that can be measured are many; it is necessary to measure only those strictly required to verify the hypotheses formulated when studying the symptoms.

That performance evaluation is very popular, in spite of the several technical and economic difficulties, is proved by the increasing number of applications to all types of medium and large systems. The growing management costs and the structural complexity of systems leads users to consider improvement actions as necessary functions for the correct management of an installation.

An investigation [SU74] whose results were published in 1974 on 147 installations, with 252 systems on which performance evaluation studies were carried out, produced particularly interesting results. In Fig. 10.1 we can see that most of the systems had less than 512 Kbytes of memory, that is, were medium to small systems. They were used in three daily shifts, most of them for over 500 h a month. An analysis of the answers to the questionnaire showed that only in 65 percent of the installations was the CPU utilization known, and even there only approximately. Seven evaluation techniques were listed (hardware monitors, software monitors, accounting products, program optimizers, scheduling, simulation, and benchmarks), and respondents were asked to indicate which techniques they had used and what kinds of results had been obtained. The following options were given for the classification of results:

Excellent:	results were above expectations
Good:	results satisfied expectations and the cost–performance ratio had been favorably influenced
Fair:	results satisfied expectations but the cost–performance picture appeared uncertain
Poor:	results were below expectations and the cost–performance ratio was unfavorably impacted

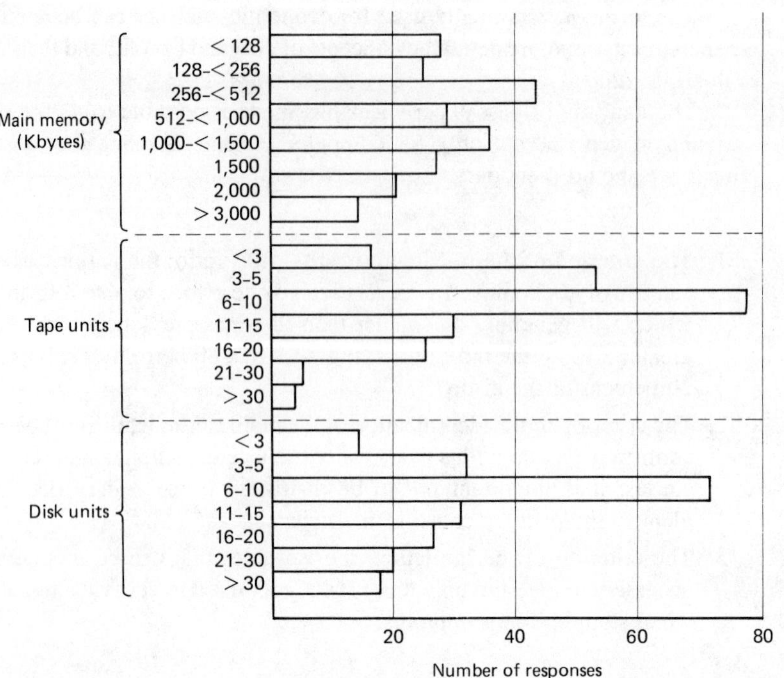

Figure 10.1 Distribution of main memory sizes and of the numbers of tape and disk units in the systems considered by the survey in [SU74].

The frequency of usage for each technique and an estimate of the improvements obtained were also requested. Figure 10.2 summarizes the answers of those users who applied hardware monitors (39 percent), software monitors (46 percent), and program optimizers (37 percent). A large fraction of the users were unable to quantify the improvements obtained and some of them declared they had none. To the question about which technique provided the best cost–performance ratio, the users indicated that software monitors came first, followed by hardware monitors, accounting tools and program optimizers.

The data-processing center within a company is now often considered as an autonomous unit providing services to the company departments that require its resources. Thus, the need for more modern management of a data center arises. Objectives to be verified and updated periodically should be determined. These objectives will be concerned with the quality and quantity of the service, the security of the data, the utilization of the various system components, the cost, and so on. Short-, medium-, and long-term plans must be formulated to make sure that the center will be able to keep up to the company's evolution.

The measurements performed on the system provide the data needed for correct management. For instance, workload analysis can help predict when changes to the system will be required and to establish which components will have to be upgraded or how the charging algorithms can be improved. Table 10.1 shows how some measurement activities can contribute to such management activities as resource planning, machine time charging, cost allocation, and short- and medium-term requirements forecasting. In this table, derived from [CP76], the activities related to performance evaluation and resource usage optimization do not appear since measurement activities are an integral part of them, and their role in performance improvement has been previously discussed. Since it is difficult to translate the costs and advantages deriving from an evaluation study into economic terms, obtaining approval for it is not straightforward. In most environments every request of investment must be supported by a documentation showing the costs to be incurred and the profits to be obtained as well as the risks involved. A description of the existing needs and of how a performance improvement could satisfy them should always be included in a proposal, and the most appropriate techniques should be suggested. The most important parts of a proposal are the *description of the implementation plan* and its *economic justification*. The description of the plan must contain the general objectives (see Sec. 6.1) and indicate the actions necessary to reach them.

The deadlines for the major phases of the study must allow for an appropriate economic evaluation of each phase and for the tests needed to verify that the deadlines are completely satisfied. The existence of *progress verification* mechanisms provides the possibility of checking that the implementation deadlines are not violated and of detecting the causes of any delay, on which a *recovery plan* is to be based.

A detailed description of the human resources necessary for the study, including their experience and the length of their commitment (man-months, weeks, or days), allows their availability to be determined and is vital for the economic analysis of the

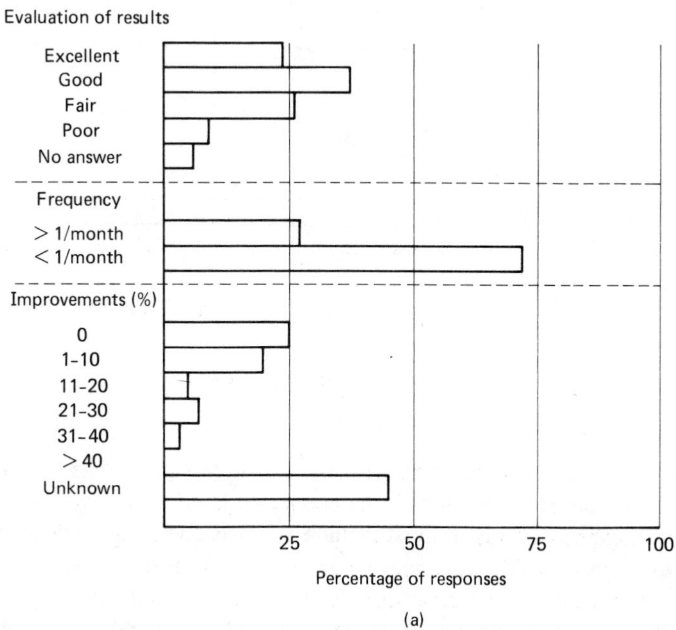

Figure 10.2 Distributions of the answers related to the use of (a) hardware monitors, (b) software monitors, and (c) program optimizers. The percentages are calculated with respect to the number of responses given for each technique.

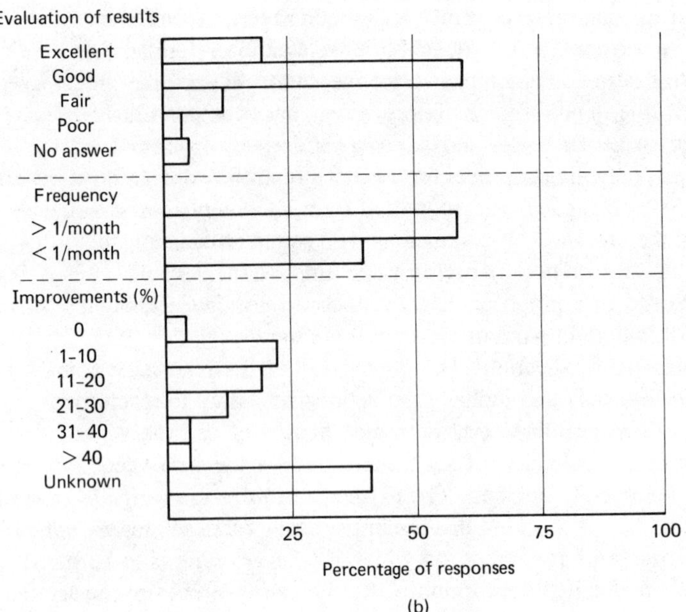

(b)

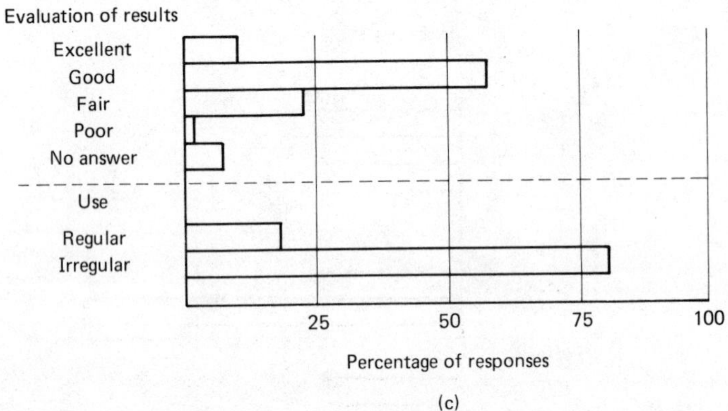

(c)

Figure 10.2 *(continued)*

proposed study. This description must also state which other sectors of the firm, if any, will be involved in the study. The economic justification will be carefully examined by the management. Thus, it must include all costs and tangible benefits. Intangible benefits are to be mentioned but cannot be accounted for in the analysis.

The next section describes in detail the various costs (personnel, purchase and maintenance of equipment, machine time, and so on) and the possible benefits (reduction of rental expenditures, removal of insufficiently used components, postponement of the procurement of a new system, and so on).

The technique used for financial analysis normally coincides with the one that the

TABLE 10.1 POSSIBLE SUPPORT THAT MEASUREMENT CAN GIVE DATA-PROCESSING MANAGEMENT [CP76]

Measurement activity	*Management Activity*: *Forecasting*	*Resource planning, pricing*	*Operational analysis and improvement*	*Cost allocation*	*Performance reporting*
Datacenter service levels	• Estimate service levels at forecasted loading • Identify high-performance services	• Analyze and interpret utilization data • Help set prices on high-performance services	• Help identify and provide guidance to specific improvement projects	• Identify high-performance services	• Report to organization to demonstrate performance versus objectives
Workload, workflow characteristics	• Estimate use of nonmachine services • Project capacity use	• Help set prices on nonmachine services • Characterize workload to project resource requirements • Help compute capacity	• Identify large users of resource • Guide tuning efforts • Identify applications for redesign • Identify bottlenecks	• Aid in accurate determination of true processing costs	• Report troublesome situations
Equipment utilization	• Project capacity use • Help project service levels	• Help compute capacity • Identify equipment requirements, help assess alternatives	• Identify bottlenecks • Identify large users of resource • Guide tuning efforts	• Measure use to compute true cost	• DP internal use reports
Personnel utilization	• Project staffing needs	• Help set prices on nonmachine services • Compute current staff use	• Identify bottlenecks • Identify large users of resource • Aid personnel performance evaluation and productivity analysis	• Measure use to compute true cost	• DP internal use reports

Continued

TABLE 10.1 *Continued*

	Management Activity				
Measurement activity	*Forecasting*	*Resource planning, pricing*	*Operational analysis and improvement*	*Cost allocation*	*Performance reporting*
Processing costs	• Identify services to be avoided	• Help determine resource prices • Aid in selection of alternatives	• Identify high-cost users applications • Guide tuning efforts	• Track actual versus recovered expense	• DP internal use reports • Report to organization on adherence to plan
Hardware characteristics	• Determine accurate time–cost data for pricing	• Aid in evaluation of alternatives	• Aid in tuning	• Determine accurate time–cost data for use charges	• DP internal use reports
Operating system activity	• Determine overhead use of resources	• Analyze and plan for overhead use	• Aid in tuning	• Identify nonuser activities, resource use	• DP internal use reports

other divisions of the company apply in investment evaluation. It is important adequately to select the planning horizon, which is usually 3 to 5 years, since the economic results can be strongly affected by this decision. The *discounted cash flow* technique reduces the risks of choosing an excessively long period of analysis since after 3 or 4 years the contributions to the result of the cost and benefits involved are relatively much smaller than the ones in the nearer future because of the cost of money, which is explicitly considered by this technique.

In this chapter, as was done in the previous chapters, the practical application of economic evaluation methods is shown by discussing a few cases. These are not meant to provide complete examples of the use of financial techniques for evaluation studies, but should provide the reader with indications about how cases at least partially similar to those described can be dealt with.

Since each financial analyst has his or her own preferred method and every company has its standard procedures for cost and revenue calculations, we shall not discuss the financial aspects in detail. However, we shall quantify with different techniques the aspects that are most closely related to the computer system. Thus, the values reported in Sec. 10.2 are only indicative.

The problems of economic evaluation are introduced gradually, starting with a discussion of a profitable case of system optimization, in which the procurement of a new system for the installation is postponed. This is followed by two cases of program optimization, one in which tuning actions are performed on a teleprocessing manager and the other one on user programs; in both cases, the load on the CPU was substantially reduced by the actions undertaken. Finally, the choice of a tool for measuring data-base accessing performance is discussed, comparing the solution of implementing an ad hoc program with that of buying a commercial software tool.

10.2 COST AND BENEFITS OF A TUNING STUDY

The benefits produced by a performance evaluation study for a computer installation and for the organization that is served by it are not usually free. The costs of planning and performing a study should be estimated and compared to the expected benefits before undertaking the study itself. This comparison should also consider the costs of any system modifications the study will suggest. While some of these modifications are relatively cheap (for example, the reorganization of disk files, the regeneration of the operating system with different parameters, and so on), others can be quite costly (for instance, doubling the main memory capacity, replacing the CPU by a faster one, adding channels, control units, and so on). It is very difficult to estimate these costs beforehand and even more difficult to predict the effects that the actions recommended by a study will have on the system. Thus, when estimating the benefits that will derive from a study, one cannot usually go beyond conjectures.

However, the inevitable difficulties of a preventive cost–benefit analysis cannot and should not justify the decision of not performing such an analysis. An evaluation study is an investment and must be considered as such. The methods for estimating and controlling the convenience of an investment are among the fundamental techniques of modern management. Since every investment entails a risk, it is always preferable to calculate it, even though approximately, rather than to face a totally unknown outcome.

The main components of the cost of an evaluation study, as shown in Table 10.2, can be classified as follows:

1. Personnel costs for the study and the recommended modifications.
2. Purchase and maintenance costs for the measurement tools to be used.
3. Instrumentation usage costs for data collection and reduction.
4. Costs of the modifications required to improve the system's performance (or rather the system's cost–benefit ratio).

Table 10.2 also contains some of the most important items in each of these categories.

The cost in categories (2) and (3) are the easiest to estimate, while those in category (4) are the most difficult to predict precisely. Some of the methods most commonly used to estimate these costs are described in the examples of the following sections.

The benefits deriving from an evaluation study are, as we have said, even harder to estimate than the costs. Some of these benefits are intangible or at least very difficult to translate into economic advantages for the organization (for instance, the greater "user satisfaction" that is usually associated with lower turnaround or response times). It is true that greater user satisfaction often makes programmers more productive, but this too is difficult to measure and even harder to predict. In some cases, however, as we shall see, the benefits are at least partially quantifiable in a straightforward way, for instance, when

TABLE 10.2 MAIN COMPONENTS OF THE COST OF AN EVALUATION STUDY

Cost classes	*Examples*
Personnel	Evaluators Systems programmers Application programmers Consultants
Instrument acquisition and maintenance	Purchase or lease of • Hardware monitors • Software monitors • Accounting packages • Simulators • Analytic modeling packages Installation Maintenance contracts
Data collection and reductions	CPU time consumptions Memory space consumptions I/O consumptions Secondary storage space consumptions
System modifications	Upgrades (CPU, channels) Expansions (memory, secondary storage) System generations Reconfigurations File or data-base relocations Verifications of the correctness of the modified programs Program restructurings

a study shows that one or more hardware components are redundant and can be eliminated without substantially affecting the performance of the system.

The extent to which an improvement in the *efficiency* of a computer system becomes an improvement of its *effectiveness* (that is, of the benefits produced by the data-processing function within the organization) depends on the context. For instance, the time for the preparation of the invoices for certain goods or services can have a considerable influence on the profits of a company that distributes them, especially when the cost of money is high. Also, the readiness with which the amount of cash available may become known to the company's management may have important effects on the financial welfare of the company itself. Since the benefits are so different, time variant, and difficult to classify, in the sequel we shall only discuss the major advantages a computer installation can expect from an evaluation study.

Some of these advantages are listed in Table 10.3. It should be noted, however, that in general there is no guarantee of achieving appreciable advantages of these or other types. When the performance of a system is nearly optimal for its workload, the only possible improvements are those that may possibly be obtained by modifying its workload. When even the workload has been optimized, any evaluation study is useless or, more precisely, harmful, since it consumes resources but does not produce any results. This, however, is not a frequent situation, since:

TABLE 10.3 SOME OF THE POSSIBLE BENEFITS OF EVALUATION STUDIES

Reduction of personnel and operations costs due to a reduction of the system's scheduled uptime
Postponement of an upgrade or expansion of the system
Reduction of the rental costs due to the elimination of seldom utilized components
Reduction of the processing activities performed in other installations to eliminate the backlogs
Increase in the productivity of programmers due to the improvements in the system's responsiveness
Possibility to increase the load on the system, hence to increase the profits and/or to reduce the charges for the users
Possibility to absorb higher peaks of load for a given degradation of service quality

1. The performance of most computer installations is often far from optimum.
2. A tuned installation remains in nearly optimal conditions only if its workload remains constant; most workloads change, and often grow larger, in time, so even a system that has been tuned drifts away from this condition and must be periodically re-subjected to an improvement study.

All the techniques known for evaluating investments can be applied to establish whether a performance evaluation study is convenient. These techniques allow one to compare the benefits expected from evaluation activities with those that could be obtained by investing the resources in other activities. In this way the investments that appear most profitable can be chosen. The simplest of these methods are based on the *payback period* and on the *internal rate of return*. The payback period is defined as the time needed to reach the *breakeven point*. Once this point has been reached, all the revenues (with only the subtractions of the running and maintenance costs) will become profits. The curve that represents the profit (or loss) in time due to an investment in a performance evaluation study often takes a shape similar to that of the continuous line diagram in Fig. 10.3 [GI76]. The broken line shows the behavior of a typical computing application project, which is quite different.

If we ignore the cost of money, which can affect the result since most of the costs

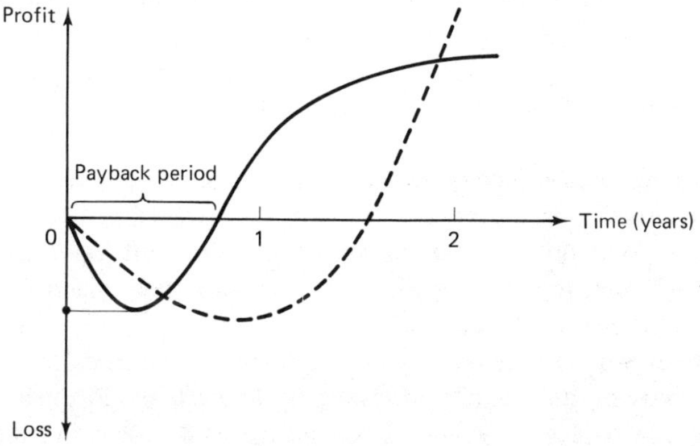

Figure 10.3 Net profit of an evaluation study (continuous curve) and of an application project (broken curve).

TABLE 10.4 COST INCREASES FOR SOLUTIONS 1 AND 2 (10^3 $)

			Solution 1			
Time (years)	Required capacity	Maximum available capacity	Number of monthly shifts	Additional extra shifts per month with respect to the initial value	Monthly cost increase for extra shifts with respect to initial value	Increase in rental costs per month
					1	2
0.0	90.0	100	56.7	0	0	0
0.5	97.2	100	61.23	4.53	0.5889	0
1.0	104.4	140	46.98	−9.72	−0.2244	4
1.5	112.7	140	50.71	−5.98	0.4097	4
2.0	121.1	140	54.49	−2.20	1.0523	4
2.5	130.7	140	58.81	2.11	1.7867	4
3.0	140.4	140	63.18	6.48	2.5296	4

are to be incurred early and rapidly while benefits appear more slowly and later, the payback period t_{Pb} in years, can be calculated using the formula:

$$t_{pb} = \frac{i}{r_a}$$

where i is the total investment and r_a the annual revenue.

There are many ways of calculating the internal rate of return. A simple definition identifies it with the revenue due to an investment per unit time. According to this definition, which ignores the financial effects of the different times at which costs are incurred and revenues accrue (unless they are accounted for explicitly), the internal rate of return is the derivative of the curve in Fig. 10.3. This derivative is usually a function of time. Another very popular method, the *discounted cash flow* technique, will be described in Sec. 10.2.3.

10.2.1 Case 10.1: Postponing the Acquisition of a New System

The amount of processing required by a company increases by 16 percent each year. The system installed is rented and currently used at about 90 percent of its capacity. The data-processing center works almost continuously since the need for a third shift has already arisen. The company is about to rent, for an extra $4000 per month, a new system with a capacity 40 percent greater than that of the current system.

An initial investigation, based on previous similar experiences, indicates that an evaluation study aimed at improving both the performance of the system and those of the most important programs can reduce by about 15 percent the total processing time of the workload, thereby increasing the system's capacity by approximately the same

TABLE 10.4 *Continued*

		Solution 2						
Maximum available capacity	*Number of monthly shifts*	*Additional extra shifts per month with respect to the initial value*	*Monthly cost increase for extra shifts with respect to initial value*	*Increase in rental costs per month*	*Instrument acquisition and maintenance, costs of the study*	*Increases of the extra shift and system rental costs — Solution 1*	*Increases of the extra shift and system rental costs — Solution 2*	*Difference between the costs of the two solutions (6 − 7)*
			3	4	5	6	7	8
100	56.7	0	0	0	0	0	0	0
115	53.24	−3.45	−0.4498	0	15.2	1.767	−1.349	3.116
115	57.19	0.49	0.0638	0	0	13.094	−1.158	14.252
115	61.74	5.04	0.6552	0	0.9	24.556	2.157	22.399
154	49.54	−7.16	0.2108	4	0	28.386	14.598	13.788
154	53.46	−3.23	0.8778	4	0.9	32.517	27.266	5.251
154	57.43	0.73	1.5521	4	0	36.949	31.288	5.661

amount. The convenience of investing resources in this type of study must be estimated, assuming that the expected benefits will be obtained. In this case a way of evaluating such convenience is to compare the temporal behaviors of the total costs in the following two alternative situations:

1. Installation of the new system as soon as needed (that is, within one year).
2. Improvement of the current system's performance and thus postponement of the installation of the new system.

The following assumptions were made when calculating the costs:

1. The current system's maximum capacity, conventionally set to 100, corresponds to a full-time use of the machine during three daily shifts (one regular and two extra), 21 working days per month.
2. The cost of each extra shift is $130 for the current system and $170 for the future system.
3. The improved performance of the programs will imply a reduced workload also for the new system; the reduction is estimated to be around 10 percent.
4. To simplify the calculations, the economic disadvantages deriving from the initial capital outlay and the similar advantages, which in situation 2 lead to a reduction of the installation's running costs, will be ignored.
5. The study's cost has been estimated to be around $4000 for the personnel and $11,200 for the purchase of the measurement tool, whose maintenance costs $900 per year.

The costs calculated for the two alternatives are given in Table 10.4. The last column in this table shows the difference between the cost increase in solution 1 (computed on the basis of the values in columns 1 and 2) and that in solution 2 (computed on the basis of the values in columns 3 and 4). A negative difference means that solution 1 was more advantageous than 2 during the previous semester; a positive difference indicates that the converse was true. The cost increases for extra shifts and rental are averaged over the last 6 months. They are calculated multiplying by 6 the arithmetic mean of the cost increases during the first and last months of each semester.

To calculate the current values (those at time zero) of the costs and benefits in Table 10.9, the classic formula

$$S = \Delta C_R \frac{63}{C_{tot}}$$

where ΔC_R is the increase in required capacity during that semester, 63 is the maximum number of monthly shifts (21 days times 3 shifts per day), and C_{tot} is the total system capacity. Notice that, when going from the current system to the new one, S should be calculated on the basis of the new number of extra shifts, which may be lower than the initial value (this explains the negative numbers in the corresponding columns of Table 10.4).

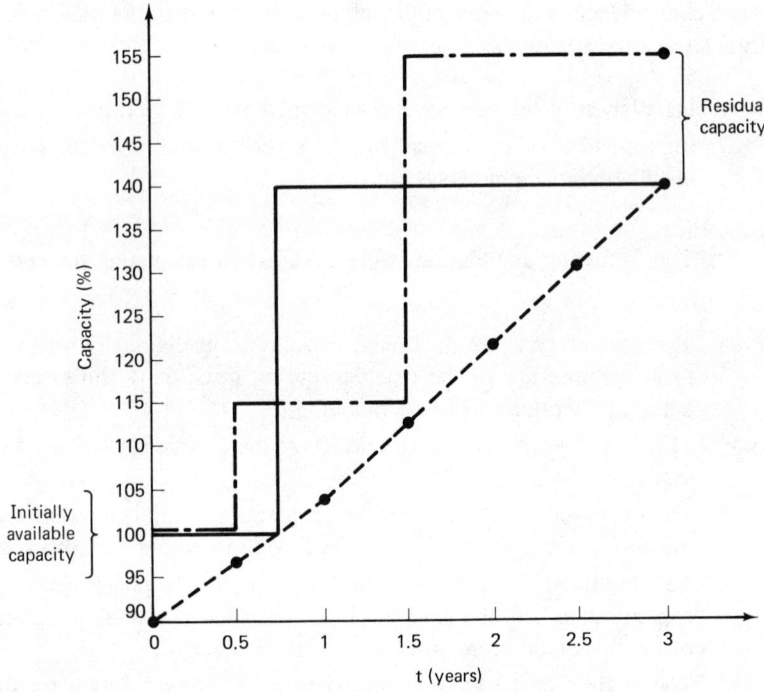

Figure 10.4 Temporal behaviors of the required capacity (----), of the capacity available with solution 1(———), and of the capacity available with solution 2 (— · — · —).

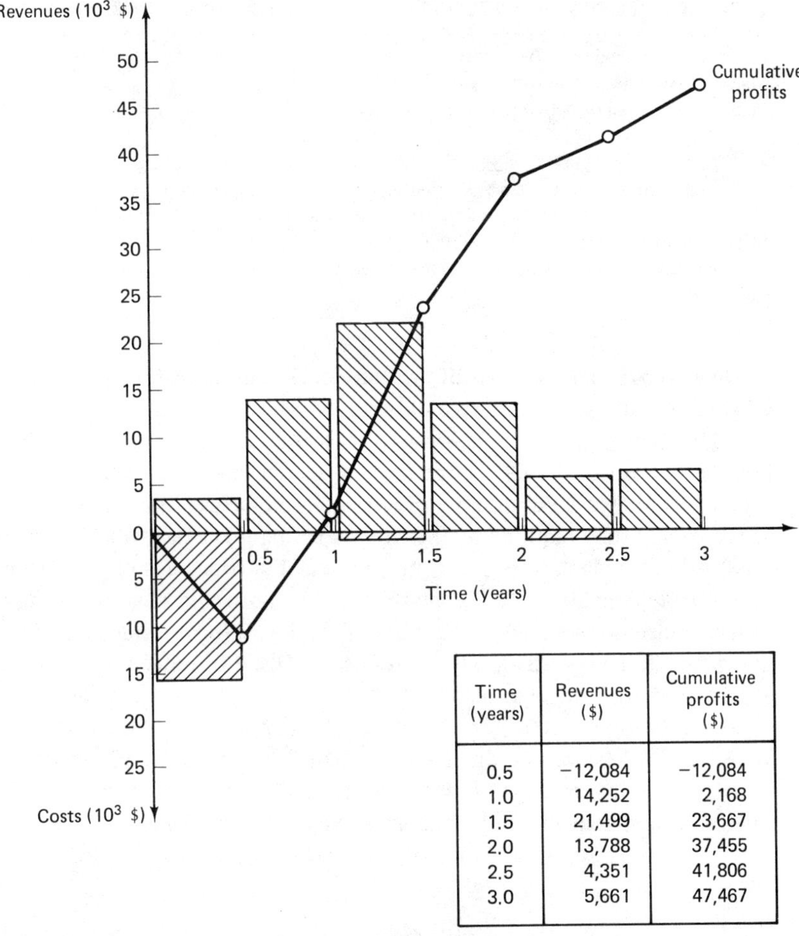

Time (years)	Revenues ($)	Cumulative profits ($)
0.5	−12,084	−12,084
1.0	14,252	2,168
1.5	21,499	23,667
2.0	13,788	37,455
2.5	4,351	41,806
3.0	5,661	47,467

Figure 10.5 Costs, revenues, and profits of solution 2 with respect to solution 1.

Figure 10.4 shows the behaviors of the required capacity and of the available capacity corresponding to the two solutions; only solution 2 has some residual capacity (about 10 percent of the required amount) available at the end of the period considered. The curve in Fig. 10.5, which represents the relative gains of solution 2 versus time, shows that under the assumptions made the payback period of solution 2, with respect to solution 1, is roughly 11 months.

10.2.2 Case 10.2: Optimizing a System Program

The data-processing center of the XYZ Corporation contains a rented system whose performance is limited by the CPU both during the first shift, when about 75 percent of the load consists of teleprocessing jobs, and during the third shift, when the load is almost only of the batch type. We have to determine whether an attempt at optimizing the

TABLE 10.5 COSTS OF A TELEPROCESSING MANAGER OPTIMIZATION STUDY

Purchase of a sampling software monitor	$11,000
Maintanance of the monitor (per year)	$ 1,350
Purchase of a monitor option that makes the activities of nonresident system modules measurable	$ 1,200
Maintenance of the option (per year)	$ 200
CPU time consumption for data collection (4% of total CPU time during 2 h/day, 40 days)	$ 1,094
CPU time consumption for data reduction (5 reports/session, 24 CPU seconds/report)	$ 456
Installation of the monitor (0.5 man-months)	$ 600
Personnel for program modification (2 man-months)	$ 2,400
Total cost	$18,300

workload to reduce the effects of the bottleneck caused by the CPU would be convenient. We shall initially try to improve only the on-line workload.

The main program to be optimized is the teleprocessing manager, which absorbs about 60 percent of the CPU time needed for real time applications. The system spends around 520 min of CPU time per day for on-line processing. A 10 percent reduction in the processing time required by the teleprocessing manager, which is about 312 min/day, would mean a reduction of 31.2 min, or, 1872 s. Since 1 s of CPU time costs, for the system being considered, 9.5 cents, this reduction would mean a savings of about $178 per day. Since on the average there are 48 × 5 = 240 working days per year, the yearly savings would be over $42,700, for a cost of $18,300. Indeed the savings, which would be increased by using the same tools (see Chapter 8) to improve the batch programs processed during the third shift, are to be compared to the costs of the study detailed in Table 10.5. By examining this table, we can conclude that a 10 percent improvement of the teleprocessing manager's performance would be more than enough to justify the expected investment in an evaluation activity (see Fig. 10.6).

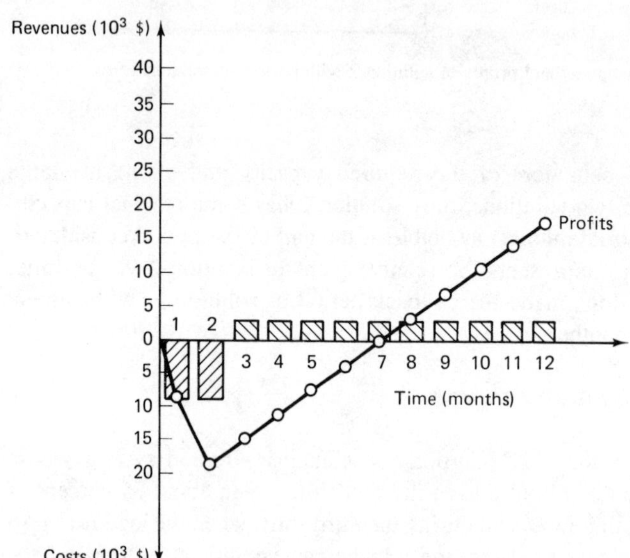

Figure 10.6 Costs, revenues, and profits due to the optimization of a teleprocessing manager.

10.2.3 Case 10.3: Improving User Programs

A company is renting its computer system for a maximum of 168 hours of machine time per month, at the monthly charge of $50,400. If the installation is used more than 168 hours, the company must pay the additional (extra shift) hours at the rate of $35 per hour. The statistics for the last semester show that the additional hours, which initially were not required, have steadily increased, especially during the last two months, and reached the number of 42 per month. An analysis of the likely causes of this increase has established that during that period two new particularly important data-base applications were installed: one for personnel management (obtained by converting part of the old personnel files, which were organized in a traditional way), and the other for spare-part inventory management. Thus, the system's load is likely to keep increasing, although at a lower rate than during the last few months. The data on system component utilization have shown that the CPU is the most critical resource.

Since the workload is composed of many different programs written in COBOL, FORTRAN, and Assembly language, a software tool independent of the programming language used was chosen. A guided optimization approach (Sec. 8.2) for the programs selected according to the criteria described in Sec. 8.1 was chosen.

Two months after the beginning of the study, the 10 programs that turned out from a preliminary analysis to account for about 35 percent of the workload were subjected to the optimization procedure. Table 10.6 contains the results obtained; they will be used in the economic evaluation of the first phase of the study.

Given that the study's objective is a reduction of the number of extra hours of machine time, the time saved has been evaluated on the basis of $35/h, plus $25 for direct and indirect expenses (electricity, overtime, wages, and so on).

Table 10.7 displays some estimates of the costs of the first phase. Just two months after the beginning of the study, savings of about $778/month start accruing. Twelve

TABLE 10.6 PROGRAMS CONSIDERED IN THE FIRST PHASE OF THE STUDY

Program	*Execution time before the study (minutes)*	*Monthly frequency (no. of runs/ month)*	*Monthly load (minutes)*	*Savings (%)*	*Execution time reduction (min/month)*
A	31	21	651	18	117.18
B	135	4.5	607.5	24	145.8
C	9	42	378	8	30.24
D	22	9	198	6	11.88
E	75	4.5	337.5	11	37.12
F	18	42	756	10	75.6
G	38	8	304	14	42.56
H	85	4	340	26	88.4
I	24	21	504	31	156.24
L	45	9	405	18	72.9
Totals			4,481		777.92

TABLE 10.7 COSTS OF THE FIRST PHASE OF THE STUDY (WHICH LASTED TWO MONTHS)

Purchase of the software monitor (includes installation and one year of maintenance)	\$11,200
Computer time for the measurement of execution frequencies (4% of the average daily 1.5 h of measurement gathering)	\$ 151
Computer time for data reduction (0.75 h)	\$ 45
Computer time for recompilations (3 h)	\$ 180
Personnel (one half-time person for 2 months)	\$ 1,200
Total costs	\$12,776

months after the purchase of the tool, its maintenance costs for the following year must be paid. The yearly maintenance fee is \$1200.

The costs of processing time for further measurements and for the necessary recompilations, estimated to be around 2 h, and those of the personnel, expected to amount to 1 man-month, should be added to this fee in order to compute the total cost of the first phase for each subsequent year. Since in these subsequent years only the programs that were heavily modified during the first phase will be acted upon, the costs considered in Table 10.8 have been overestimated. Table 10.8 lists the costs and the benefits of the first phase of the study, calculated for a period of 3 years. Beyond this limit, it is difficult to trust the validity of the programs, of the changes made, and of the tools used. The solid line (a) in Fig. 10.7 represents the time behavior of the net profit. On the whole, not considering the cost of money but making the conservative assumptions mentioned above previously, the payback period is around 21 months. If we wish to take the financial aspects into account, we can apply to the preceding estimates the *discounted cash flow* technique, with the following simplifying assumptions:

1. All investments are made at the beginning of the year.
2. Benefits accrue in the middle of the year instead of every month.
3. The compound interest rate is 15 percent per year; this value is practically the minimum rate of profit the investment may have.

Assumption 1 introduces a safety margin in the evaluation because costs are incurred in various chunks and at different moments, all of which usually occur later than at the very beginning of the year (the tool and its maintenance fees are generally paid 1 or 2 months after the invoice is received, staff members are paid monthly, machine time is used throughout the whole period).

TABLE 10.8 COSTS VERSUS REVENUES FOR THE FIRST PHASE OF THE STUDY

Period	*Costs*	*Revenues*	*Annual balance*	*Cumulative balance*
1st year	12,776	7,780	−4,996	−4,996
2nd year	2,520	9,336	+6,816	+1,820
3rd year	2,520	9,336	+6,816	+8,636

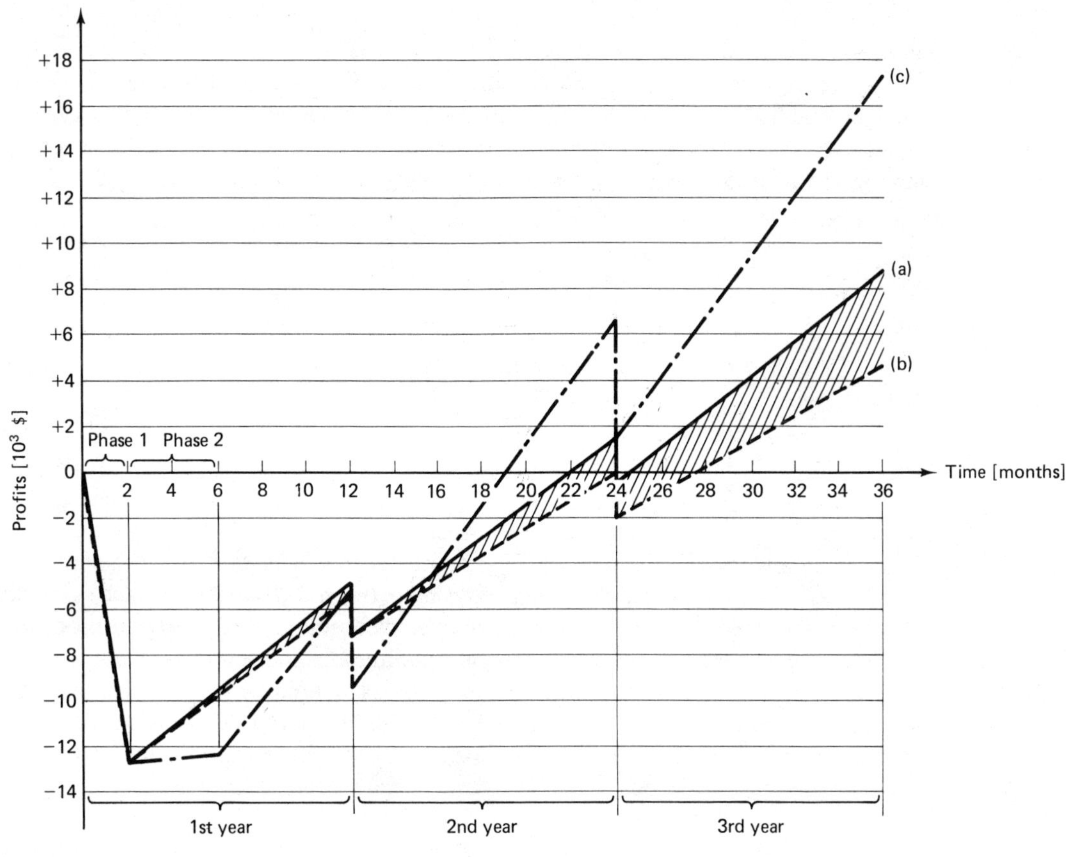

Figure 10.7 Profits for the first phase of the study (a) not considering and (b) considering the cost of money; (c) for the whole study, not considering the cost of money.

TABLE 10.9 DISCOUNTED CASH FLOWS OF THE FIRST PHASE WITH A 15 PERCENT INTEREST RATE

		Costs		*Revenues*		*Profits (present values)*	
Time t		*At time t*	*At the present time*	*At time t*	*At the present time*	*Annual*	*Cumulative*
Year 1	0 months	12,776	12,776				
	6 months			7,780	7,237		
	12 months					−5,539	−5,539
Year 2	0 months	2,520	2,191				
	6 months			9,336	7,551		
	12 months					+5,360	− 179
Year 3	0 months	2,520	1,905				
	6 months			9,336	6,566		
	12 months					+4,661	+4,482
Totals			16,872		21,354		

Table 10.9 shows the discounted cash flow analysis of the study's first phase. We can see that, even though a fairly brief period is considered (3 years), the study ends with a positive balance of about $4482, thus with a profit of roughly 20 percent of the capital invested. The line b in Fig. 10.7 represents the discounted net profits and is derived from Table 10.9. The darkened area represents the error introduced in the analysis by ignoring the financial effects of the different times at which costs were incurred and benefits accrued.

To calculate the current values (those at time zero) of the costs and benefits in Table 10.9, the classic formula

$$V_{t_0} = V_t \cdot \left[\frac{1}{(1 + i)^n}\right]$$

was used, where V_t is the value at time t, V_{t_0} the value at time zero, i the interest rate, and n the number of time units (years) considered.

Having analyzed the first phase, it is necessary to establish the convenience of a second phase, in which other programs could be optimized. If we select, according to the criteria discussed in Sec. 8.1, a set of programs constituting, say, 40 percent of the total workload (on the remaining 25 percent optimizations are felt to be definitely not convenient) and if, on the average, a 10 percent processing time reduction can be obtained for them, the monthly savings would be $512 (512 min saved per month). The time required for their optimization should be expected to be longer than in the first phase since they are more numerous. Thus, the costs of the second phase will be:

Personnel (1 half-time person for 4 months)	$2400
Processing time (for data collection, recompilations, reports)	$ 500

Considering this phase as a separate study, its payback period is given by

$$t_{pb} = \frac{2900}{6144} = 0.47 \text{ years}$$

This value is very low, as could easily have been predicted, since the purchase price of the tool was considered in the first phase. This second phase therefore presents considerable advantages.

If the two phases are taken as a single study in which 75 percent of the workload is optimized, the results in Table 10.10 are obtained. The balance is definitely favorable. Already at the end of the second year the total profit is $6156, and becomes $17,136 at the end of the third year.

In the evaluation of the global study the following hypotheses were introduced:

TABLE 10.10 COSTS, REVENUES, AND PROFITS FOR THE COMPLETE STUDY*

Period		*Costs*	*Revenues*	*Profits*	
				Annual	*Cumulative*
Year 1	Phase 1	12,776	7,780	−4,824	−4,824
	Phase 2	2,900	3,072		
Year 2	Phase 1	2,520	9,336	+10,980	+6,156
	Phase 2	1,980	6,144		
Year 3	Phase 1	2,520	9,336	+10,980	+17,136
	Phase 2	1,980	6,144		

*Optimization of the programs that constitute 75 percent of the load.

1. The two studies are carried out consecutively by the same person, who will be working half-time on them for 6 months.
2. The 512 min saved per month as a result of the second phase are assumed to start only at the end of the second phase, that is, 6 months after the first phase started.
3. The period of validity of the results is 3 years.
4. The costs of the second phase for the years following the first are evaluated on the basis of one half-time person for 3 months ($1800) and of three machine hours ($180); all the maintenance costs of the tool were included in the first phase.

These assumptions provide our evaluation with a safety margin. In Fig. 10.7, line c represents the profits deriving from the whole study calculated without considering the cost of money.

TABLE 10.11 COMPARISON BETWEEN THE COSTS OF DEVELOPING AND THOSE OF BUYING A PERFORMANCE MEASUREMENT TOOL FOR THE DB/DC SYSTEM*

Time (years)	*Costs (10^3\$)*			
	In-house tool design and development		*Acquisition of a commercial tool*	
0	Project starts (3 persons)		Acquisition, installation	20
1	Project completed	60	First-year maintenance	
2	Maintenance (1 person)	22	Maintenance (12.5% of current price)	2.75
3	Maintenance (1 person)	24.2	Maintenance (12.5% of current price)	3.025
4	Maintenance (1 person)	26.6	Maintenance (12.5% of current price)	3.327
5	Maintenance (1 person)	29.3	Maintenance (12.5% of current price)	3.660
	Total	162.1	Total	32.762

*Yearly increase of personnel and commercial tool costs is assumed to be about 10 percent.

As was done for the first phase, a more accurate evaluation of the whole study can be made by applying the discounted cash flow technique to the data in Table 10.10. In this case the balance will be less attractive than the one we just computed but will still be so favorable as to justify the investment. For a more complete evaluation, one should also consider the economic advantages deriving from the postponement of a system upgrade, since the processing time will be reduced by the optimization of the workload (see Case 10.1).

10.2.4 Case 10.4: Selection of a Tool for Data-Base Activity Control

Most of the workload of a powerful two-system installation of a large chemical corporation is due to data-base activities. The installation includes a data-base management system and a communication network between the different sites and the company's headquarters.

The performance of the data-base/data-communication (DB/DC) system is crucially important to the whole organization. Each processor has a 4-Mbyte main memory. The *production* DB/DC system is active roughly 10 h/day on one of them. This system deals with the normal on-line and batch workloads containing access requests to the various data bases of the corporation. The other processor runs a *test* DB/DC system, identical to the other one and used mainly for testing the batch and on-line programs that handle the data bases. Other types of programs are run on both systems; among them, a time-sharing manager, which runs on the test DB/DC processor.

The configuration of the two systems includes 24 tape units, 16 medium-sized disk units, 32 large-sized disk units, and over 100 local and remote terminals. The production DB/DC system handles on the average 20,000 transactions during its daily hours of activity. This figure is the result of an almost constant-rate growth in the volume of daily transactions; this growth rate is about 1000 transactions per month (see Fig. 10.8).

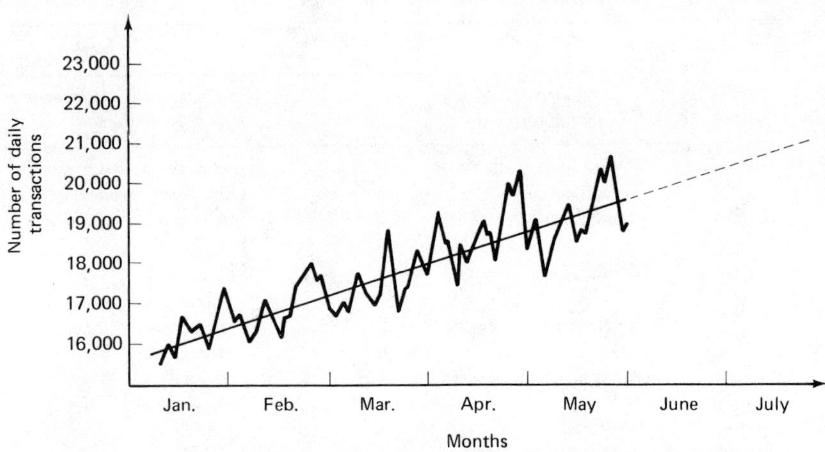

Figure 10.8 Number of transactions executed daily by the production DB/DC system versus time (the solid line indicates the trend of volume growth).

Together with this increase goes a slow but constant increase in the response time to single transactions (see Fig. 10.9).

Thus, the configuration's capacity will shortly become insufficient to satisfy the increasing user demands. Another worrisome factor is the decreasing responsiveness of a fundamental application, which constitutes 20 percent of all the transaction load and should have the shortest possible response time: its mean response times oscillate between a few seconds and half a minute.

The system is equipped with an accounting program that charges batch users for their resource demands, and a software monitor, which measures the total usage of resources. However, an increasing need is felt for a tool capable of controlling the performance of the DB/DC system and of supplementing the data already provided by the logging functions of the DB/DC system with additional data on the individual activities of this system. The tool should also collect sufficiently accurate data on the real costs associated with the two DB/DC systems, on the growth rate of on-line applications, and on the level of service provided to individual users. In other words, the tool should give indications about which areas in the DB/DC systems could be improved so that the purchase of new equipment to maintain the level of on-line services required by the company can be postponed as much as possible.

The possibility of developing such a tool in-house is examined first. In the system programs development group there are experienced people with a sound knowledge of the DB/DC system. The implementation of the tool is estimated to require at least 3 man-years. Given the high level of qualification needed, a minimum investment of $60,000 would be needed. To this figure, we must add the cost of the machine time for compilations and program testing. The estimation of this cost, which is quite difficult, need not be exact since the CPUs are leased. In any case, the cost of machine time is expected to be not less than $20,000 to $25,000. And, once the project is finished, one of the participants will probably have to be employed full time for the maintenance of the tool because of the modifications and improvements to be made to the DB/DC system.

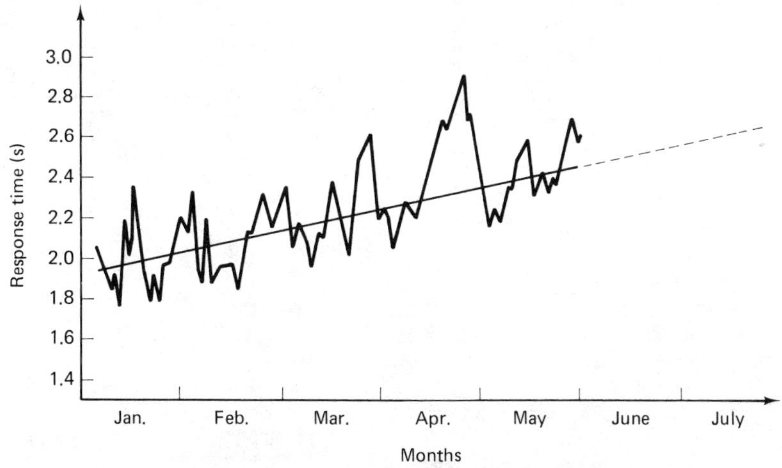

Figure 10.9 Mean response time to single transactions versus time.

Therefore, another $20,000 per year for at least the 4-year period during which the tool will be active will have to be added to the cost previously computed. Of course, salary increases should also be accounted for (see Table 10.11). Optimistically, assuming that the finished product will be available 10 to 12 months after the beginning of the project, an investment of over $160,000 will be required for the 4 years of use expected for the tool.

An analysis of the commercial software tools having characteristics that more or less satisfy the requirements leads to a small group of products. One of these, the most expensive, is capable of integrating the logging data produced by the DB/DC system with data that would otherwise not be available. Its price is about $20,000 and its yearly maintenance fee is 12.5 percent of the purchase price. Clearly, the cost of installation and training should also be included in this analysis.

The data collection and data reduction costs, the salaries of the evaluators, and the costs of the modifications to be made to the DB/DC system (see Sec. 10.2) were not included in Table 10.11 since they are about the same in both cases (purchase and in-house development).

Besides the remarkable difference between the investments required by the two solutions, some considerations on the possible disadvantages deriving from the direct implementation of such a tool suggest that buying the commercial tool would be preferable. The implementation would not only require a rather lengthy commitment of resources, and a greater delay in installing an urgently needed tool, but would not provide sufficient guarantees about the quality and efficiency of the final product. Thus, it seems that the company would not be sufficiently protected against the risks of the investment. On the other hand, the installation of a commercial tool would be immediately possible and is usually a solution open to improvements with relatively small risks for the user since, in most cases, the manufacturer guarantees that the tool will be updated for any new release of the systems software and that any bugs that will be discovered will be corrected.

TABLE 10.12 MEASUREMENTS TAKEN BEFORE AND AFTER THE STRUCTURAL MODIFICATIONS MADE TO THE MOST FREQUENTLY ACCESSED DATA BASE

	Before modifications	*After modifications*	*Savings*
Number of transactions per day	2,638	2,016	—
Mean response time (s)	9.3	2.8	6.5
Mean I/O queuing time (s)	4.1	0.7	3.4
Mean transaction execution time (s)	5.2	2.1	3.1
Mean number of access method requests per transaction	12	13	−1
Mean number of I/O operations per transaction	48	14	34
Mean number of I/O pseudooperations (data already in the buffer) per transaction	706	48	658
Mean CPU time for message processing (per transaction) (s)	0.067	0.071	−0.004
Mean CPU time for the analysis of data base queries (s)	0.3789	0.069	0.3099

TABLE 10.13 MONTHLY REDUCTION IN CPU TIME AND NUMBER OF I/O OPERATIONS CAUSED BY THE MODIFICATIONS MADE TO THE DATA BASE

	Reduction per transaction	*Daily reduction*	*Monthly reduction*
CPU time (s)	0.3099	619.8	13,635.6
No. of I/O operations	34	68,000	1,496,000

After a test period in which the correctness of the results is verified, the tool is installed permanently in the production DB/DC system. Having determined the areas to be investigated and the initial goals, systematic measurements are taken to detect the causes of the long response times mentioned. The data collected by the tool point to the existence of an I/O problem: an excessive number of I/O requests is made to a particular data base. This not only leads to inordinately large transaction execution times, but also produces a long queue of requests and slows down the rest of the on-line workload.

A study of the structure of that data base shows some inherent causes of inefficiency. Thus, the structure is modified by subdividing the original data base into two separate data bases, and changing the techniques for adding new entries and for key-based searches. The results of these operations, which were carried out in 6 days, are represented in Table 10.12.

The most important aspect of the results obtained is the 70 percent reduction of the mean transaction response time. This result is mainly due to the reduction in the CPU time needed to analyze data-base access requests and in the number of I/O operations to be performed on the data base.

The importance of the result in terms of CPU seconds and number of I/O operations saved, considering an average of 2000 transactions per day for 22 days per month, can be derived from the values in Table 10.13. Every month, 3 h, 47 min of CPU time are saved, as well as about 1.5 million I/O operations. This is a remarkable result in the general economics of the computer system being considered and especially in that of the DB/DC system. In monetary terms, only the savings in CPU time, whose charge is 5 cents/s, leads to a savings of over $8000/year. The reduction in the number of I/O operations has the secondary effect of further reducing CPU time because of the reduced demand for supervisory functions.

The tangible benefits obtained by exploiting the information provided by the purchased tool are certainly not as important as those, not immediately convertible into figures, due to the improvement in the level of service provided to on-line users and to the associated increase in productivity.

REFERENCES

Entries marked with an asterisk (*) are referenced in the text.

[AR74] Aris, J. B. B., Quantifying the cost and benefits of computer projects, *IBI Congr. "Economics of Informatics,"* Magonza, Sept. 1974.

[CA72] Carlson, G., How to save money with computer monitoring, *Proc. ACM Nat. Conf.*, pp. 1018–1023, Aug. 1972.

[CO75] Cost justifying performance evaluation projects, *EDP Performance Review,* vol. 3, n. 7, July 1975.

*[CP76] CPE measurement activities for data processing, *EDP Performance Review,* vol. 4, n. 5, May 1976.

[CU73] Cushing, B.E., Dial, D. H., Cost-performance tradeoffs in real-time systems design, *Management Advis.,* vol. 10, n. 6, p. 29, 1973.

[EM74] Emery, J. C., Cost and benefits of information systems, *Proc. IFIP Congress 74,* pp. 967–971, North-Holland, Amsterdam, 1974.

[ER72] Erikson, W. J., Comparative economics of computer systems, *Bulletin Op. Res. Socy. of America,* vol. 20 (suppl. 1), B99, 1972.

[FI74] Finney, J. E., Costing in data processing department, *Management Accounting,* pp. 29–35, Oct. 1974.

[FR75] Frielink, A. B., ed., Economics of informatics, *IBI-ICC Conf. Proc.,* North-Holland, Amsterdam, 1975.

[GE75] Gellman, H. S., Evaluation of the effectiveness of EDP facilities, *RIA Cost and Management,* vol. 49, pp. 16–19, Nov.–Dec. 1975.

*[GI76] Gierach, S. A., Estimating the value of CPE projects, *Proc. CMG-VII, 7th International Conf.,* pp. 18–25, Atlanta, Nov. 1976.

[HE76a] Heath, F. R., Guidelines for identifying high payoff applications, *Data Base,* n. 1, 1976.

[HE76b] Heller, P., Benchmarking the price of computing, *Computer Networks,* June 1976.

[HO74] Holt, G. A., Stern, H. C., Cost-benefit evaluation of interactive transaction processing systems, *AFIPS Conf. Proc.,* vol. 44, pp. 687–694, 1974.

[HO69] Hootman, J. T., The pricing dilemma, *Datamation,* vol. 15, n. 8, pp. 61–66, Aug. 1969.

[LA74] Land, F. F., Criteria for the evaluation and design of effective systems, *IBI Congr. "Economics of Informatics,"* Magonza, Sept. 1974.

[LI73] Liebert, A., Price/performance evaluation of 360 and 370 systems, *Software World,* vol. 4, n. 8, p. 2, 1973.

[LI75] Lietz, B. P., Cost tradeoffs between local and remote computing, *National Technical Information Service, U.S. Dept. of Commerce,* Springfield, Mass., June 1975.

[ME75] Menkus, B., What data cost to process, *Administrative Management,* vol. 36, pp. 22–24, June 1975.

[NI70] Nielsen, N. R., The allocation of computer resources: Is pricing the answer?, *CACM,* vol. 13, n. 8, pp. 467–474, Aug. 1970.

[NO78] Norton, D. P., Rau, K. G., *A guide to EDP performance management,* Q.E.D. Information Sciences Inc., Wellesley, Mass., 1978.

[PA75] Parenteau, R. E., Price/performance ratio cited as motive in buying used 360, *Computerworld,* March 26, 1975.

[SH69] Sharpe, W. F., *The Economics of Computers,* Columbia University Press, New York, 1969.

[SI76] Sigmetrics technical meeting on pricing computer services, *ACM SIGMETRICS Perf. Evaluat. Review,* vol. 5C, n. 1, March 1976.

[ST71] Stimler, S., A methodology for evaluating real time system performance, *Infotech State of the Art Report "Real Time,"* pp. 487–496, 1971.

[ST72] Streeter, D. N., Cost-benefit evaluation of scientific computing services, *IBM Systems J,* vol. 11, n. 3, p. 219, 1972.

*[SU74] Survey of user performance experiences, *EDP Performance Review,* vol. 2, March 1974.

[VE74] Verhelst, M., On possible approaches and techniques for determining financial benefits of organizational information, *IBI Congr. "Economics of Informatics,"* Magonza, Sept. 1974.

[WA71] Warner, C. D., Monitoring: A key to cost efficiency, *Datamation,* vol. 17, pp. 40–49, 1971.

APPENDIX

A SIMPLE QUEUING MODEL ANALYZER

The Fortran program whose listing is reported here solves single-class central server models of computer systems using Buzen's convolution algorithm (see Sec. 9.4). The parameters, which are input interactively, as shown for example in Fig. 9.30, are system oriented or workload oriented rather than model parameters. The program itself derives the model's parameter values from the values of the system and workload parameters. After the model has been specified and solved, its parameter values and even its configuration can be modified interactively by answering 'y' (followed by a carriage return) to any 'change?' question, and then typing in the new values (some of which may of course coincide with the old ones). The previous values are displayed for easy reference by the program just before asking each 'change?' question. If none of the values displayed by the program needs to be changed, the user will simply press the carriage return key. The performance indexes the program can compute are those shown in Fig. 9.31. If not needed, the user may instruct the program not to output the mean numbers of processes in the stations and the utilizations of the servers.

The program can also be used to solve central server models representing paging virtual memory systems. Only one paging device can be modeled, and the corresponding server must by convention be assigned the number 2. The mean number of visits made to that device by the processes in the system is calculated by the program, ignoring the value input by the user. The referencing behavior of programs is represented by their lifetime curve (see for example Fig. 9.28); users may specify this curve by assigning either the values of the two parameters a and k for the analytic approximation $\bar{e} = am^k$ (where $\bar{e}$ is the mean virtual time between successive page faults, and m the amount of memory allotted on the average to each program) or, as shown in Fig. 9.30, some of its points, which will be linearly interpolated by the program.

```
C CESER      *CENTRAL SERVER MODEL*
      DATA SI/1HY/
      INTEGER SEEK,TRAN,REV,BLOK,BR
      COMMON /INTV/IB,ISTEP,KA,LFT,M,MP,MS,NS
      COMMON /REALV/A,AK,P1,RESP,THRU,VCPU,AY
      COMMON /REALAR/B(20),BLOK(20),BR(20),E(40),G(100),Q1(20),REV(20)
      COMMON /RAY/RHO(20),S(20),SEEK(20),TRAN(20),Y(20)
      DOUBLE PRECISION G
      WRITE(6,2)
    2 FORMAT(1H ,'     CENTRAL SERVER MODEL    ',/)
      AY=SI
      KA=0
    5 WRITE(6,7)
    7 FORMAT(1H ,'  FAST MODE?',/)
      READ(5,20)AF
      CALL INP
      WRITE(6,10)
   10 FORMAT(1H ,' VIRTUAL MEMORY?',/)
      READ(5,20)AV
   20 FORMAT(A1)
      WRITE(6,25)
   25 FORMAT(1H ,' MAX DEGREE OF MULTIPROGRAMMING',/)
      READ(5,30)NU
   30 FORMAT(I5)
      IF(AV.NE.AY) GO TO 50
      M=NU
      NU=1
      CALL INV
   45 CALL MOD(NU)
   50 CALL PRE
      KA=1
      IF(AF.EQ.AY) GO TO 80
      IF(AV.NE.AY) GO TO 55
      IF(NU.GT.1) GO TO 80
   55 WRITE(6,60)
   60 FORMAT(1H ,' PRINT MODEL PARAMETERS?',/)
      READ(5,20)AP
   80 IF(AP.EQ.AY) CALL PMP
      CALL COY
   83 CALL SOL(NU)
   85 CALL IND(NU)
      IF(AF.EQ.AY) GO TO 95
      IF(AV.NE.AY) GO TO 87
      IF(NU.GT.1) GO TO 95
   87 WRITE(6,90)
   90 FORMAT(1H ,' PRINT MEAN NUMBERS IN SERVERS?',/)
```

```
      READ(5,20) AQ
   95 IF(AQ.EQ.AY) GO TO 110
      IF(AF.EQ.AY) GO TO 120
      IF(AV.NE.AY) GO TO 97
      IF(NU.GT.1) GO TO 120
   97 WRITE(6,100)
  100 FORMAT(1H ,' PRINT SERVER UTILIZATIONS?',/)
      READ(5,20) AR
      GO TO 120
  110 AR=AY
      CALL QUE(NU)
  120 CALL OUT(NU,AR,AQ)
      IF(AV.EQ.AY) GO TO 170
  125 WRITE(6,130)
  130 FORMAT(1H ,' MORE ANALYSIS?',/)
      READ(5,20)AE
      IF(AE.NE.AY) STOP
      WRITE(6,140)
  140 FORMAT(1H ,' NEW CONFIGURATION?',/)
      READ(5,20) AC
      IF(AC.EQ.AY) GO TO 5
      WRITE(6,150)
  150 FORMAT(1H ,' DEGREE OF MULTIPROGRAMMING',/)
      READ(5,30) M
      IF(M.GT.NU) GO TO 160
      NU=M
      IF(AV.NE.AY) GO TO 85
      NU=1
      GO TO 45
  160 NU=M
      IF(AV.NE.AY) GO TO 83
      NU=1
      GO TO 45
  170 NU=NU+1
      IF(NU.GT.M) GO TO 125
      IF(AF.EQ.AY) GO TO 45
      WRITE(6,180)
  180 FORMAT (1H ,' NEXT POINT?',/)
      READ(5,20) AN
      IF(AN.NE.AY)GO TO 125
      GO TO 45
      END
C INP
      SUBROUTINE INP
      INTEGER SEEK,TRAN,REV,BLOK,BR
      COMMON /INTV/IB,ISTEP,KA,LFT,M,MP,MS,NS
```

```
      COMMON /REALV/A,AK,P1,RESP,THRU,VCPU,AY
      COMMON /REALAR/B(20),BLOK(20),BR(20),E(40),G(100),Q1(20),REV(20)
      COMMON /RAY/RHO(20),S(20),SEEK(20),TRAN(20),Y(20)
      DOUBLE PRECISION G
      WRITE(6,10) NS
   10 FORMAT(1H ,' TOTAL NUMBER OF SERVERS',I5,/)
      IF(KA.EQ.0) GO TO 15
      CALL CHA(AX)
      IF(AX.NE.AY) GO TO 25
   15 READ(5,20) NS
   20 FORMAT(I5)
   25 WRITE(6,30) VCPU,P1,IB
   30 FORMAT(1H ,' CPU SPEED(MIPS),MEAN PROG LENGTH(MI),DEPARTURES',
     & 2F7.4,I5,/)
      IF(KA.EQ.0) GO TO 35
      CALL CHA(AX)
      IF(AX.NE.AY) GO TO 45
   35 READ(5,40) VCPU,P1,IB
   40 FORMAT(2F7.4,I5)
      BR(1)=IB
   45 DO 100 I=2,NS
      WRITE(6,50) I
   50 FORMAT(1H ,' SERVER',I3)
      WRITE(6,60) SEEK(I),REV(I)
   60 FORMAT(1H ,' MEAN SEEK TIME(MS),REV SPEED(RMP)',2I10,/)
      IF(KA.EQ.0) GO TO 65
      CALL CHA(AX)
      IF(AX.NE.AY) GO TO 75
   65 READ(5,70) ISEEK,IREV
   70 FORMAT(2I10)
      SEEK(I)=ISEEK
      REV(I)=IREV
   75 WRITE(6,80) TRAN(I),BLOK(I),BR(I)
   80 FORMAT(1H ,'TRANSFER TIME(MICS/WD),BLOCK SIZE(WDS),VISITS',3I10
     & ,/)
      IF(KA.EQ.0) GO TO 85
      CALL CHA(AX)
      IF(AX.NE.AY) GO TO 100
   85 READ(5,90) ITRAN,IBLOK,IBX
   90 FORMAT(3I10)
      TRAN(I)=ITRAN
      BLOK(I)=IBLOK
      BR(I)=IBX
  100 CONTINUE
      RETURN
      END
```

```
C INV
      SUBROUTINE INV
      INTEGER SEEK,TRAN,REV,BLOK,BR
      COMMON /INTV/IB,ISTEP,KA,LFT,M,MP,MS,NS
      COMMON /REALV/A,AK,P1,RESP,THRU,VCPU,AY
      COMMON /REALAR/B(20),BLOK(20),BR(20),E(40),G(100),Q1(20),REV(20)
      COMMON /RAY/RHO(20),S(20),SEEK(20),TRAN(20),Y(20)
      DOUBLE PRECISION G
      WRITE(6,30) MS
   30 FORMAT(1H ,' MEMORY SIZE(PAGE FRAMES)',I5,/)
      IF(KA.EQ.0) GO TO 35
      CALL CHA(AX)
      IF(AX.NE.AY) GO TO 45
   35 READ(5,40) MS
   40 FORMAT(I10)
   45 WRITE(6,50) LFT
   50 FORMAT(1H ,' ANALYTIC(1) OR EMPIRICAL(2) LIFETIME CURVE?',I5,/)
      IF(KA.EQ.0) GO TO 55
      CALL CHA(AX)
      IF(AX.NE.AY) GO TO 65
   55 READ(5,60) LFT
   60 FORMAT(I5)
   65 IF(LFT.EQ.2) GO TO 90
      WRITE(6,70) A,AK
   70 FORMAT(1H ,' PARAMETERS A,K',/,2F10.6)
      IF(KA.EQ.0) GO TO 75
      CALL CHA(AX)
      IF(AX.NE.AY) GO TO 85
   75 READ(5,80) A,AK
   80 FORMAT(2F10.6)
   85 RETURN
   90 WRITE(6,100) MP,ISTEP
  100 FORMAT(1H ,' PROGRAM SIZE(PAGES), STEP',2I5,/)
      IF(KA.EQ.0) GO TO 105
      CALL CHA(AX)
      IF(AX.NE.AY) GO TO 115
  105 READ(5,110) MP,ISTEP
  110 FORMAT(2I10)
      MQ=MP/ISTEP
  115 WRITE(6,120)
  120 FORMAT(1H ,' MEAN INTERFAULT INTERVALS(MS)',/)
      IF(KA.EQ.0) GO TO 125
      WRITE(6,130) (E(IP), IP=1,MQ)
      CALL CHA(AX)
      IF(AX.NE.AY) GO TO 135
  125 READ(5,130) (E(IP), IP=1,MQ)
```

```
  130  FORMAT(F10.4)
       G(100)=VCPU
  135  RETURN
       END
C PRE
       SUBROUTINE PRE
       INTEGER SEEK,TRAN,REV,BLOK,BR
       COMMON /INTV/IB,ISTEP,KA,LFT,M,MP,MS,NS
       COMMON /REALV/A,AK,P1,RESP,THRU,VCPU,AY
       COMMON /REALAR/B(20),BLOK(20),BR(20),E(40),G(100),Q1(20),REV(20)
       COMMON /RAY/RHO(20),S(20),SEEK(20),TRAN(20),Y(20)
       DOUBLE PRECISION G
       SUM=0.0
       DO 10 I=1,NS
       SUM=SUM+BR(I)
   10  CONTINUE
       DO 20 I=1,NS
       B(I)=BR(I)/SUM
   20  CONTINUE
       IF(IB.EQ.0) B(1)=1.0
       ACPU=1.0/B(1)
       IF(IB.EQ.0) ACPU=SUM
       S(1)=VCPU*ACPU/P1
       DO 30 I=2,NS
       ST=SEEK(I)+BLOK(I)*TRAN(I)/1000.0
       IF(REV(I)) 29,29,28
   28  ST=ST+30000.0/REV(I)
   29  S(I)=1000.0/ST
   30  CONTINUE
       RETURN
       END
C PMP
       SUBROUTINE PMP
       INTEGER SEEK,TRAN,REV,BLOK,BR
       COMMON /INTV/IB,ISTEP,KA,LFT,M,MP,MS,NS
       COMMON /REALV/A,AK,P1,RESP,THRU,VCPU,AY
       COMMON /REALAR/B(20),BLOK(20),BR(20),E(40),G(100),Q1(20),REV(20)
       COMMON /RAY/RHO(20),S(20),SEEK(20),TRAN(20),Y(20)
       DOUBLE PRECISION G
       WRITE(6,10)
   10  FORMAT(1H ,' SERVER    RATE    BRANC PROB',/)
       WRITE(6,20) (I,S(I),B(I), I=1,NS)
   20  FORMAT(I5,F9.3,F10.4)
       RETURN
       END
C COY
```

```
      SUBROUTINE COY
      INTEGER SEEK,TRAN,REV,BLOK,BR
      COMMON /INTV/IB,ISTEP,KA,LFT,M,MP,MS,NS
      COMMON /REALV/A,AK,P1,RESP,THRU,VCPU,AY
      COMMON /REALAR/B(20),BLOK(20),BR(20),E(40),G(100),Q1(20),REV(20)
      COMMON /RAY/RHO(20),S(20),SEEK(20),TRAN(20),Y(20)
      DOUBLE PRECISION G
      Y(1)=1.0
      DO 10 I=2,NS
      Y(I)=S(1)*B(I)/S(I)
   10 CONTINUE
      RETURN
      END
C SOL
      SUBROUTINE SOL(MU)
      COMMON /INTV/IB,ISTEP,KA,LFT,M,MP,MS,NS
      COMMON /REALV/A,AK,P1,RESP,THRU,VCPU,AY
      COMMON /REALAR/B(20),BLOK(20),BR(20),E(40),G(100),Q1(20),REV(20)
      COMMON /RAY/RHO(20),S(20),SEEK(20),TRAN(20),Y(20)
      DOUBLE PRECISION G
      DO 10 J=1,MU
      G(J)=1.0
   10 CONTINUE
      DO 30 I=2,NS
      YY=Y(I)
      G(1)=YY+G(1)
      DO 20 J=2,MU
      G(J)=(G(J-1)*YY) + G(J)
   20 CONTINUE
   30 CONTINUE
      RETURN
      END
C IND
      SUBROUTINE IND(MU)
      INTEGER SEEK,TRAN,REV,BLOK,BR
      COMMON /INTV/IB,ISTEP,KA,LFT,M,MP,MS,NS
      COMMON /REALV/A,AK,P1,RESP,THRU,VCPU,AY
      COMMON /REALAR/B(20),BLOK(20),BR(20),E(40),G(100),Q1(20),REV(20)
      COMMON /RAY/RHO(20),S(20),SEEK(20),TRAN(20),Y(20)
      DOUBLE PRECISION G
      MU1=MU-1
      IF(MU1.EQ.0) GO TO 20
      RHO(1)=G(MU1)/G(MU)
    5 DO 10 I=2,NS
      RHO(I)=Y(I)*RHO(1)
   10 CONTINUE
```

```
      THRU=B(1)*S(1)*RHO(1)
      RESP=MU/THRU
      RETURN
   20 RHO(1)=1.0/G(1)
      GO TO 5
      END
C OUT
      SUBROUTINE OUT(MU,AR,AQ)
      INTEGER SEEK,TRAN,REV,BLOK,BR
      COMMON /INTV/IB,ISTEP,KA,LFT,M,MP,MS,NS
      COMMON /REALV/A,AK,P1,RESP,THRU,VCPU,AY
      COMMON /REALAR/B(20),BLOK(20),BR(20),E(40),G(100),Q1(20),REV(20)
      COMMON /RAY/RHO(20),S(20),SEEK(20),TRAN(20),Y(20)
      DOUBLE PRECISION G
      WRITE(6,20) MU,THRU,RESP
   20 FORMAT(I6,'    USERS,',F10.4,'     JOBS/S,',F10.4,'    S',/)
      IF(AR.NE.AY) RETURN
      IF(AQ.EQ.AY) GO TO 60
      WRITE(6,40)
   40 FORMAT(1H ,'    SERVER     UTILIZATION',/)
      WRITE(6,50) (I,RHO(I), I=1,NS)
   50 FORMAT(I6,F14.4)
      RETURN
   60 WRITE(6,70)
   70 FORMAT(1H ,'    SERVER     UTILIZATION    MEAN NO.OF USERS',/)
      WRITE(6,80) (I,RHO(I),Q1(I), I=1,NS)
   80 FORMAT(I6,F14.4,F18.4)
      RETURN
      END
C QUE
      SUBROUTINE QUE(MU)
      INTEGER SEEK,TRAN,REV,BLOK,BR
      COMMON /INTV/IB,ISTEP,KA,LFT,M,MP,MS,NS
      COMMON /REALV/A,AK,P1,RESP,THRU,VCPU,AY
      COMMON /REALAR/B(20),BLOK(20),BR(20),E(40),G(100),Q1(20),REV(20)
      COMMON /RAY/RHO(20),S(20),SEEK(20),TRAN(20),Y(20)
      DOUBLE PRECISION G
      DOUBLE PRECISION Q
      IF(MU.EQ.1) RETURN
      MU1=MU-1
      DO 20 I=1,NS
      YY=Y(I)
      Q=YY**MU
      DO 10 J=1,MU1
      MUJ=MU-J
      Q=Q+(YY**J)*G(MUJ)
```

```
   10 CONTINUE
      Q1(I)=Q/G(MU)
   20 CONTINUE
      RETURN
      END
C CHA
      SUBROUTINE CHA(AX)
      INTEGER SEEK,TRAN,REV,BLOK,BR
      COMMON /INTV/IB,ISTEP,KA,LFT,M,MP,MS,NS
      COMMON /REALV/A,AK,P1,RESP,THRU,VCPU,AY
      COMMON /REALAR/B(20),BLOK(20),BR(20),E(40),G(100),Q1(20),REV(20)
      COMMON /RAY/RHO(20),S(20),SEEK(20),TRAN(20),Y(20)
      DOUBLE PRECISION G
      WRITE(6,10)
   10 FORMAT(1H ,' CHANGE?',/)
      READ(5,20) AX
   20 FORMAT(A1)
      RETURN
      END
C MOD
      SUBROUTINE MOD(MU)
      INTEGER SEEK,TRAN,REV,BLOK,BR
      COMMON /INTV/IB,ISTEP,KA,LFT,M,MP,MS,NS
      COMMON /REALV/A,AK,P1,RESP,THRU,VCPU,AY
      COMMON /REALAR/B(20),BLOK(20),BR(20),E(40),G(100),Q1(20),REV(20)
      COMMON /RAY/RHO(20),S(20),SEEK(20),TRAN(20),Y(20)
      DOUBLE PRECISION G
      IP=MS/MU
      IF(LFT.EQ.2) GO TO 10
      AIP=IP
      ET=A*(AIP**AK)
      GO TO 20
   10 IF(MP.LE.IP) GO TO 30
      IS=IP/ISTEP
      IR=IP-IS*ISTEP
      AIST=ISTEP
      AIR=IR
      ET=G(100)*(E(IS)+AIR*(E(IS+1)-E(IS))/AIST)
   20 BR(2)=1000.0*P1/ET
      RETURN
   30 MQ=MP/ISTEP
      ET=E(MQ)*G(100)
      GO TO 20
      END
$
```

INDEX

C

D

E

F

G

H

I

J

K

L

M

N

O

P

Q

R

S

T

U

V

W